DATE DUE			
DEC 8 '95			

MT. HOOD COMMUNITY COLLEGE LIBRARY
Gresham, Oregon

The Middle East
from the
Iran-Contra Affair
to the Intifada

Contemporary Issues in the Middle East

The Middle East
from the
Iran-Contra Affair
to the Intifada

Edited by Robert O. Freedman

Syracuse University Press

First Edition 1991
91 92 93 94 95 96 97 98 99   6 5 4 3 2 1

The paper used in this publication meets the minimum
requirements of American National Standard for
Information Sciences—Permanence of Paper for Printed
Library Materials, ANSI Z39.48-1984. ∞™

LIBRARY OF CONGRESS CATALOGING-IN-PUBLICATION DATA
The Middle East from the Iran-Contra affair to the Intifada / edited
by Robert O. Freedman.—1st ed.
    p. cm.—(Contemporary issues in the Middle East)
    Includes bibliographical references and index.
    ISBN 0-8156-2501-4.—ISBN 0-8156-2502-2 (pbk.)
    1. Middle East—Politics and government—1979– I. Freedman,
Robert Owen. II. Series.
DS63.1.M4842 1990
956.05—dc20   90-9977

Manufactured in the United States of America

This book is dedicated to Russ,
Merzy, Julie, Joey, Becky, Zelda, and Evie,
whose friendship I will always cherish.

Contemporary Issues in the Middle East

This well-established series continues to focus primarily on twentieth-century developments that have current impact and significance throughout the entire region, from North Africa to the borders of Central Asia.

Recent titles in the series include:

Contents

Part Three: National Perspectives

Preface

The Middle East has long been one of the most volatile regions on the globe. Wars, coups d'état, rapid shifts in alliances and alignments, numerous intra-Arab, intrastate, and regional conflicts, and constant intervention by the superpowers have wracked the region since the first Arab-Israeli war in 1948. In an effort to increase public understanding of this complex region, the Center for the Study of Israel and the Contemporary Middle East of the Baltimore Hebrew University held a series of conferences bringing together Middle Eastern specialists from various perspectives to analyze and discuss the region.

The first conference, held in 1978, examined the impact of the Arab-Israeli conflict on the Middle East, and the papers were later published as *World Politics and the Arab-Israeli Conflict,* ed. Robert O. Freedman (New York: Pergamon, 1979). The second conference, held in 1979 (two years into the administration of Israeli Prime Minister Menahem Begin), made a preliminary analysis of the dynamics of the Begin regime. Following the Israeli election of 1981, the conference papers were updated and published as *Israel in the Begin Era,* ed. Robert O. Freedman (New York: Praeger, 1982). The third conference, which took place in 1982, dealt with Middle Eastern developments in the period between the Camp David agreements of 1978 and the Israeli invasion of Lebanon in 1982. The conference papers were published as *The Middle East Since Camp David,* ed. Robert O. Freedman (Boulder, Colo.: Westview Press, 1984). Just as the Camp David agreements marked a major turning point in the Middle East, so too did the Israeli invasion of Lebanon. For this reason, three years after the invasion, a fourth conference was held at the Baltimore Hebrew University to analyze the impact of the invasion on the Middle East. The conference papers were published as *The Middle East After the Israeli Invasion of Lebanon,* ed. Robert O. Freedman (Syracuse: Syracuse Univ. Press, 1986). The Iran-Contra affair was yet another key event in Middle East politics with major ramifications throughout the region, and a fifth conference was held at the Baltimore Hebrew University in 1988 to assess its impact on the course of Middle Eastern history. This book is an outgrowth of that conference.

This book was made possible through the help of many individuals and institutions. The conference was cosponsored by the Baltimore Jewish Council and the Peggy Meyerhoff Pearlstone School of Graduate Studies of the Baltimore Hebrew University. Dr. Leivy Smolar, president of the Baltimore Hebrew University, has provided strong support for the Institute for the Study of Israel and the Contemporary Middle East since its founding in 1977. The Baltimore Hebrew University Library staff, its director, Arthur Lesley, and its periodical specialist, Jeanette Katkoff, provided invaluable research services, and my secretary, Elise Baron, did a masterful job of typing the manuscript and preparing it for the computer while also helping manage the college's graduate program. Special thanks also go to my research assistant, Elaine Eckstein, who helped keep the clipping files of the center up-to-date. I would also like to express my deep appreciation to the Pearlstone Family Fund for the financial support that enabled the Baltimore Hebrew University to hold the conference that served as the basis for this book.

Finally, a word about the transliteration system used in this book. Every editor dealing with a Middle East topic must decide between using the exact transliteration of Arabic names, including the initial *hamza,* or using a system that reflects the more common Western transliteration. To aid those readers who do not know Arabic, we have chosen the latter system, which renders the names of Arab leaders and places in a form that English-speaking audiences will recognize. Thus, for example, the reader will find Gamal Nasser (instead of Abd-al-Nasir), Haifiz Assad for Hafiz al-Asad, Muammar Kaddafi for al-Qadhafi, King Hussein for Husayn, and such place names as Dhofar and Oman (for Dhufar and 'Uman, respectively). In addition, because of the often bitter controversy over the name of the body of water lying between Iran and Saudi Arabia—known to the Iranians as the Persian Gulf and to the Arabs as the Arab Gulf—most of the authors have chosen to employ the neutral term *Gulf.*

Baltimore, Maryland   **ROBERT O. FREEDMAN**
April 1990

The Middle East
from the
Iran-Contra Affair
to the Intifada

Introduction

The Iran-Contra scandal had a major impact on the Middle East. The disclosure that the United States, occasionally using Israel as a conduit, had sent arms to Iran undermined the U.S. diplomatic position in the Arab world and helped promote the massive U.S. naval buildup in the Persian Gulf aimed at reassuring the Gulf Arabs of U.S. support against Iran. The Soviet Union, seeking to exploit U.S. discomfiture over the scandal, tried to promote an international peace conference and, in the process, carried on a diplomatic flirtation with Israel. The USSR also allowed Kuwait to charter three Soviet ships but then tilted to the Iranian side as Moscow sought to exploit the rising U.S.-Iranian hostility.

The Iran-Contra affair had an effect on other nations of the Middle East as well as on the superpowers and the protagonists in the Iran-Iraq war. Thus Israel, whose leadership had its own goals in strengthening Iran against Iraq, played an important role in the affair. Egypt and, to a lesser extent, Jordan sought to exploit it to pressure the United States into accepting an international conference on the Arab-Israeli conflict. By contrast, for Syria, Turkey, Lebanon (where the story was first revealed), and the Sudan, the issue was of less significance although all four countries faced more than their share of challenges during the 1985–89 period.

In the Arab world, preoccupation with the threat from Iran diverted attention from the Palestinian-Israeli conflict, helped reintegrate Egypt into the Arab fold, and increasingly isolated Syria. King Hussein and Yasser Arafat signed an agreement in 1985 to form a joint Jordanian-Palestinian negotiating team for talks with Israel, but the agreement collapsed one year later amid mutual recriminations. Israel's divided National Unity government also proved incapable of promoting the peace process, and the Palestinian Intifada, which began in December 1987, underlined the Palestinians' desire to control their own destiny.

This book is an analysis of these developments as case studies in the foreign policies of each of the main actors involved. Domestic forces that have played a major role in the foreign policies of the main actors will be examined as well. Yet it is hoped that the book is more than merely the sum of its parts, however excellent the analysis in each of the chapters may be. Because the book examines Middle East dynamics from three different levels—extraregional forces (the United States, the Soviet Union, Western Europe); regional politics (intra-Arab relations and the Iran-Iraq war); and local politics (Jordan, Israel, the Palestinians, Syria, Egypt, Lebanon, Turkey, and the Sudan)—the reader will come away with a multidimensional view of Middle Eastern political dynamics. Indeed, if there is one lesson to be learned from the Iran-Contra affair, it is that in the Middle East there is a constant interaction of local, national, regional, and extraregional forces and that it is impossible to understand the politics of the region without examining developments at each of these levels.

Finally, because the book presents case studies that encompass the period from 1985 to 1989, each author has provided a background analysis giving the main thrust of forces affecting his or her subject's policies before 1985. It is hoped that the multidimensional nature of the presentation and the background analyses to the various case studies will give the book a dimension beyond the confines of the 1985–89 period.

In the opening chapter, Robert O. Freedman analyzes the policy of the Soviet Union's new leader, Mikhail Gorbachev, since he took office in March 1985. Along with a detailed analysis of the main events in Middle Eastern politics in the 1985–89 period, Freedman traces the Soviets' diplomatic efforts both to reinvolve themselves in the Arab-Israeli peace process and to manage the Iran-Iraq war in such a way that if Moscow could not achieve an end to the Gulf war itself, it would be able to prevent a U.S.-Iranian rapprochement. Freedman demonstrates how Gorbachev sought to exploit the Iran-Contra crisis both to accelerate efforts to bring about an international peace conference, tacitly working with Israeli Foreign Minister Shimon Peres, and to drive a wedge between the United States and the Arab world. Freedman concludes that despite the new rhetoric from Moscow and the USSR's greater flexibility in its relations with Israel, there has been more continuity than change in Soviet policy toward the Middle East under Gorbachev.

In his essay on American policy in the Middle East during the 1985–89 period, Barry Rubin concentrates on the causes, development, and consequences of the Iran-Contra scandal, which he deems a major blunder, and on the on-again, off-again U.S. efforts to promote the Arab-Israeli peace process. He concludes that, despite Iran-Contra, the overall strategic and political situation in the Middle East was not unfavorable to U.S. interests and cites as the reason for this conclusion the failure of Islamic fundamentalism seriously to challenge regimes friendly to the United States; the containment of the Iran-Iraq war;

the continuation of oil exports from the Gulf; the limitation of Soviet influence in the region; the reflagging of Kuwaiti tankers, which reassured the Gulf Arabs after the affair; and the reinforcing of ties between the United States and Israel, which remained the strongest military power in the region.

Although the Soviet Union and the United States were the main external actors affecting the Middle East during the 1985–89 period, the nations of Western Europe, occasionally acting collectively, also had an impact. Robert Hunter, in his study of Western European policies toward the Middle East, notes that in four central questions affecting the Middle East—the Iran-Iraq war, the Arab-Israeli conflict, the response to Middle Eastern terrorism; and the inclusion of the Gorbachev-led Soviet Union in the Middle East peace process—West European countries often took different positions from those of the United States. Although there was some evidence of transatlantic cooperation during this period—the convoy operation to protect Persian Gulf shipping in the 1987–88 period—Hunter contends that this was done more to show solidarity in the NATO alliance than because of agreement with U.S. policy toward Iran. Hunter concludes by suggesting a nine-point program for improving transatlantic cooperation on Middle Eastern issues in the 1990s.

Regional politics during the 1985–89 period centered around the Arab-Israeli conflict and the Iran-Iraq war. In his study of intra-Arab politics, Jerrold Green analyzes these two issues and their interaction. He contends that the issue of the Palestinians became progressively less important to the Arab world as the threat from Iran increased, culminating in the Amman Summit of November 1987, when Egypt, despite its peace treaty with Israel, was de facto readmitted to the Arab world. Green also examines the Iran-Contra affair, castigating it as a major blunder in U.S. policy and noting that it further undermined the already low credibility of the United States in the Arab world.

Within the Arab world there is one major regional organization, the Gulf Cooperation Council (GCC), made up of Saudi Arabia, Kuwait, Bahrein, Qatar, Oman, and the United Arab Emirates. In her study of the GCC, Shireen Hunter notes that despite a strong facade of unity, there have been significant differences within the GCC on such issues as relations with Iran, support for the U.S. reflagging of Kuwaiti ships, and support for Iraq in the Iran-Iraq war. She also contends that although the GCC states considered the Iran-Contra episode a major mistake for U.S. policy, the U.S. reflagging somewhat reassured the Gulf Arabs that the United States placed a high priority on their security.

While the Arab world has sought to meet the challenge from Iran,

Iran itself has had the dual challenges of fighting a war with Iraq and institutionalizing the Islamic revolution that swept the Ayatollah Khomeini into power in 1979. One of the major problems faced by Iran during this period has been its relationship with the United States, and in his analysis of the impact of the Iran-Contra affair on Iranian-American relations, R. K. Ramazani emphasizes that beneath the veneer of Islamic ideology there is a very strong current in Iranian foreign policy which he terms "Islamic realism." He notes that despite a series of military clashes in the Gulf between the two countries, Iran was ready to improve relations with the United States, and he cites the Khomeini regime's willingness to accept a cease-fire in its war with Iraq as proof that realism prevails in Tehran. Ramazani also contends that it is in the interest of the United States to improve relations with Iran and suggests that the way to begin the process would be to employ private or citizen diplomacy to overcome the enormous psychological obstacles on both sides.

The Iran-Iraq war clearly dominated Iraqi life in the 1985–88 period, and its impact on Iraq's domestic politics and foreign policy is described in detail by Fred Axelgard. He notes that although the Iraqi Shia proved loyal to the Saddam Hussein regime, relations between the regime and its Kurdish minority sharply deteriorated, reaching a nadir in an Iraqi poison gas attack against the Kurdish city of Halabjeh in 1988. In foreign policy, Axelgard contends that Iraqi escalation of attacks on Iranian shipping was successful in motivating the superpowers to take a more active role in ending the war. He also notes that although the Iran-Contra affair was a blow to U.S.-Iraqi relations, as were the Iraqi attack on the USS *Stark* and Iraq's use of poison gas against Iran and its own Kurds, nonetheless, Saddam Hussein was able to improve Iraq's ties with the United States during the war while maintaining a steady flow of arms from the Soviet Union.

Jordan, Syria, Israel, the Palestinians, Egypt, Lebanon, the Sudan, and Turkey share a number of commonalities. The first relates to the role of religion in society. In Lebanon and the Sudan the issue has led to civil war; in Egypt, Turkey, and Syria religious opposition movements threaten or have threatened the ruling governments; in Israel religious issues have caused major divisions in society, and for the Palestinians, the basically secular PLO leadership has been challenged by Islamic fundamentalists. In addition to the religious factor—and, of course, the Arab-Israeli conflict among Israel, Jordan, the Palestinians, Egypt, and Syria—economic problems have preoccupied the leaders of all of the countries during the 1985–89 period and in some of the countries that are examined have threatened regime stability.

The internal politics and foreign policy of Israel, a country heavily involved in the Iran-Contra affair, are discussed by David Pollock. After noting the success of Israel's National Unity government in overcoming the two major problems besetting it in early 1985—a runaway inflation and Israel's quagmirelike involvement in Lebanon— Pollock analyzes the problems facing the deeply divided country in moving ahead to solve the Palestinian problem, a problem made more serious by the Intifada, or Palestinian uprising. He also analyzes in considerable detail the U.S.-Israeli relationship and contends that despite Iran-Contra, the Intifada, and the Pollard affair, U.S.-Israeli relations are likely to remain strong.

The Intifada on the Israeli-occupied West Bank and Gaza Strip caught the Israelis and many others in the Middle East by surprise. Helena Cobban, in her analysis of the Palestinians in the 1985–88 period, describes the causes of the Intifada, seeing its roots in both the rising level of Palestinian opposition to Israeli rule and the failure of PLO diplomacy to secure effective gains for the Palestinians in the occupied territories. Cobban also analyzes the collapse of the Hussein-Arafat agreement of 1985, the continued conflict between Arafat and Syrian President Hafiz Assad, the failure of the unofficial Israeli-Jordanian "condominium" on the West Bank, and Arafat's efforts to reunify the PLO in the face of opposition from Israel, Jordan, and Syria.

Jordan is a resource-poor Arab state, with a population of only 3 million, which faces much more powerful states to its west (Israel), north (Syria), and east (Iraq). In addition to serious economic problems, it has a major internal problem—more than half of its population is Palestinian, of questionable political loyalty to the regime of King Hussein. Hussein thus has had to follow a very circumspect foreign policy, which Adam Garfinkle analyzes in great detail, placing considerable emphasis on the interplay between Hussein and PLO Leader Yasser Arafat. Garfinkle contends that each has repeatedly tried to use the other and that despite his speech of July 31, 1988, severing Jordan's ties to the West Bank, King Hussein has every intention of both maintaining contact with the West Bank and playing a major role in the peace process.

John Devlin, in his analysis of Syrian policy, stresses Syrian President Assad's desire to dominate his regional environment (Lebanon, the Palestinians, Israel, and Jordan) and relates the failure of efforts to reconcile Syria and Iraq and Assad and Arafat to this fundamental point. He also analyzes the rapprochement between Jordan and Syria and the continuing alliance between Syria and Iran, seeing in the latter alignment benefits for Syria in religious legitimization for the Alawite regime, economic aid, and political support against Iraqi efforts at hegemony in the Eastern Arab world.

Since the 1975–76 civil war, Lebanon has been a central arena of conflict among both the sectarian forces within the country and the regional powers, particularly Syria and Israel, Lebanon's neighbors. Marius Deeb analyzes the interaction of the numerous Christian and Muslim sectarian groups in the aftermath of the abrogation of the Israeli-Lebanese agreement in March 1984 and concludes that although virtually all the Muslim and Christian communities in Lebanon—with the notable exception of Iranian-backed Hezbollah—are now ready for a settlement, peace is unlikely to come to Lebanon because Syrian President Hafiz Assad has a major interest in maintaining conflict in that country. Deeb, who takes a very different view of the Syrian role in Lebanon than Devlin, demonstrates how, since the Israeli withdrawal from all but the southernmost section of Lebanon in 1985, Assad has shown the ability both to instigate and to manipulate conflict throughout Lebanon.

In his study of Egyptian policy under Hosni Mubarak, Louis Cantori argues that Egypt has scored an important diplomatic success by rejoining the Arab state system as a result both of its efforts to bring about a Palestinian-Israeli settlement and of the need of the Arab world to reincorporate Egypt as a counterbalance to Iran. Cantori notes that Egypt's reentry into the Arab world has helped shore up the domestic position of Hosni Mubarak, whose popularity has been slipping in recent years. Cantori adds that despite Egypt's indebtedness and other economic problems, there is no apparent alternative leader in Egypt and the Islamic forces, many of which have been co-opted by the government, do not appear to have the power to overthrow Mubarak.

The Sudan is one of the most complex countries in the world, with 597 tribes and 400 languages. Even without foreign problems and entanglements, such a country would be difficult to rule, and Peter Bechtold in his study of the Sudan analyzes the domestic and foreign problems facing the regimes that succeeded the dictator Ja'far Numayri, who was overthrown in April 1985. Bechtold describes in detail the country's economic problems and the challenge facing its new leadership from Joseph Garang's Sudanese Peoples Liberation Army (SPLA) rebellion in the south. Bechtold also examines the Sudan's shift from a pro-American alignment to a more neutral position between the two superpowers and the reasons for the limited rapprochement between the Sudan and Libya.

In his study of Turkish foreign policy and domestic politics, George

Gruen notes that Turkey has been gradually moving toward a more democratic system of government following the military coup in 1980 and that extremists from the right and the left have, at least so far, been successfully curbed. Gruen also highlights Turkey's unique position as the only Muslim state with membership in NATO and the tightrope Turkish leaders have had to tread as they have sought to maintain good ties with both Israel and the Arab world. Gruen also analyzes Turkey's role in the Iran-Iraq war and notes that despite some problems, Turkey has succeeded in maintaining good relations with both combatants while profiting economically from the pipelines Iraq has built across Turkey. Despite Turkey's overall successes both domestically and in foreign policy, growing economic problems face the country. Gruen also discusses the threat of Islamic fundamentalists, who have been using the Arab-Israeli conflict, and particularly the Intifada, to advance their own cause.

In sum, the authors of this book have examined the impact of the Iran-Contra scandal and other key Middle East events in the 1985–89 period from a local, national, regional, and extraregional perspective. It is hoped that this volume will aid in understanding this complex period.

Part One

The Role of External Powers

Continuity and Change
in Soviet Policy Toward the Middle East
under Gorbachev

Robert O. Freedman

Mikhail Gorbachev would appear to be the most significant innovator in Soviet politics and foreign policy since the days of Nikita Khrushchev. His proposal for elections to Soviet party offices, the increased *glasnost* (openness) in reporting problems in the USSR, his release of well-known dissidents such as Anatoly Sharansky, Ida Nudel, and Yuri Orlov, the rehabilitation of Boris Pasternak, and his efforts to improve Moscow's image in the West have all indicated that a new approach has replaced the *immobilism* so apparent in Kremlin policy in recent years.

In the Middle East, however, the USSR under Gorbachev's leadership has not distinguished itself by any new breakthroughs. Indeed, when one compares Gorbachev with his three predecessors Konstantin Chernenko, Yuri Andropov, and Leonid Brezhnev, there has been more continuity than change in Soviet policy toward the Middle East, despite the "new thinking" on foreign policy proclaimed in the Kremlin. This essay will explore the main areas of continuity and will also suggest some of the areas in which change has occurred, with particular emphasis on Soviet policy toward the Arab-Israeli conflict and the Iran-Iraq war. First, however, it is necessary to take a look at Soviet goals in the region because any analysis of Gorbachev's policy must be examined against that background. On this question, Western analysts are divided into three different schools of thought, which are of more than academic interest because they lead to very different policy prescriptions, including different opinions as to whether the USSR should be invited to participate in efforts to settle the Arab-Israeli and Iran-Iraq conflicts. The first of these schools of thought may be characterized as "offensive-successful." It looks primarily at Soviet military power in the region and argues not only that Moscow is offensively inclined and seeks to oust the West from the oil resources and strategic communication routes of the Middle East but also that it has been successful in exercising influence, primarily by intimidating the states of the region. Not only should the USSR, according to this school of thought, not be invited to participate in peacemaking efforts in the region, but it must be confronted wherever possible to prevent the Middle East from falling into Soviet hands.[1] On the opposite end of the spectrum is what may be termed the "defensive-unsuccessful school," which argues that Moscow is basically defensively oriented in the Middle East because it has higher priorities elsewhere in the world and has regional problems that are unmanageable and severely curtail Soviet influence. Thus, it is argued, Moscow can be invited to participate in peacemaking efforts because it wants a stable situation along its southern periphery.[2] The final school of thought, to which I belong, may be termed the "offensive-unsuccessful school." It argues that though Moscow is essentially offensively oriented in the Middle East and will seize upon virtually any opportunity to weaken Western, and particularly American, influence there, the USSR has been basically unsuccessful in extending its influence in the region because of the independence of the local actors and their resistance to Soviet control. This school of thought is wary of inviting Moscow to participate in any peace-making efforts, arguing that although the Soviet Union might make tactical compromises in certain situations, it cannot yet be trusted to fulfill its part of any agreement in the long term.[3]

Under Gorbachev, as under his predecessors, Moscow has employed a number of tactics in its efforts to weaken Western influence in the Middle East (and particularly in the Arab world) while promoting its own influence. First and foremost has been the supply of military aid to its regional clients. Next in importance comes economic aid: the Aswan dam in Egypt and the Euphrates dam in Syria are prominent examples of Soviet economic assistance, although each project has had serious problems. In recent years Moscow has also sought to solidify its influence through the conclusion of long-term friendship and cooperation treaties such as the ones concluded with Egypt (1971), Iraq (1972), Somalia (1974), Ethiopia (1978), Afghanistan (1978), South Yemen (1979), Syria (1980), and North Yemen (1984)—although the repudiation of the treaties by Egypt (1976) and Somalia (1977) indicates that this has not always been a successful tactic. Moscow has also attempted to exploit both the lingering memories of Western colonialism and Western threats against Arab oil producers and has—as in the case of the assassination of Indira Gandhi—deliberately used "disinformation" to discredit American policy. The USSR has also sought influence through the establishment of ties between the Communist Party of the Soviet Union (CPSU) and such Arab ruling political parties as the Syrian Ba'ath and the Algerian Front for National Liberation (FLN). Still another tactic aimed at gaining influence has been the provision of security infrastructure assistance to countries like South Yemen and Ethiopia, often with the help of East Germany. Finally, Moscow has offered the Arabs both military and diplomatic aid against Israel, although that aid has been limited in scope because Moscow continues to support Israel's right to exist—both for fear of unduly alienating the United States (with which the Russians desire additional strategic arms agreements and improved trade relations) and because Israel serves as a conventient rallying point for potentially anti-Western forces in the Arab world.

The USSR has used all these tactics, with a greater or lesser degree of success, over the last two decades, but it has also run into serious problems in its quest for influence in the Middle East. First, vis-à-vis the numerous inter-Arab and regional conflicts (Syria-Iraq; North Yemen–South Yemen; Ethiopia-Somalia; Algeria-Morocco; Iran-Iraq; and so on) in that period, usually when the USSR has favored one party it has alienated the other—often to the point of driving it over to the West. Second, the existence of Middle Eastern Communist parties has proven to be a handicap for the USSR because internal Communist activities have on occasion caused a sharp deterioration in relations between Moscow and the country in which the Communist party has operated. (The Communist-supported coup d'état in the Sudan in 1971, Communist efforts to organize cells in the Iraqi army in the mid- and late 1970s, and the activities of the Tudeh party in Khomeini's Iran are recent examples of this problem). Third, the wealth that flowed to the Arab world (or at least to its major oil producers) when oil prices quadrupled in late 1973 has enabled the Arabs to buy high-quality technology from the West and Japan and thereby has weakened the economic bond between the USSR and such Arab states as Iraq. Fourth, since 1967 and particularly since the 1973 Arab-Israeli war, Islam has been resurgent throughout the Arab world, and the USSR—identified in the Arab world with atheism— has been hampered, particularly since the Soviet invasion of Afghanistan in 1979, where Moscow has been fighting against an essentially Islamic resistance force. Fifth, in the diplomacy surrounding the Arab-Israeli conflict, Moscow is hampered by its lack of formal diplomatic ties with Israel, which enables the United States alone to talk to both sides in the conflict. Finally, the United States (and to a lesser extent China and France) has actively opposed Soviet efforts to achieve a predominant influence in the region, and this has frequently enabled

Middle Eastern states to play the extraregional powers off against each other, thereby preventing any one of them from securing predominance.

To overcome these difficulties, Moscow has evolved one overall strategy: the development of a bloc of "anti-imperialist" states within the Arab world. In Moscow's view, these states should bury their potentially internecine rivalries and join together, along with such political organizations as the Arab Communist parties and the Palestine Liberation Organization (PLO), in a united front against what the USSR has called the "linchpin" of Western imperialism in the Middle East—Israel. It is the Soviet hope that under such circumstances the Arab states would use their collective pressure against Israel's supporters, especially the United States. The ideal scenario for Moscow—and one frequently mentioned by Soviet commentators—was the controlled conflict during the 1973 Arab-Israeli war, when virtually all the Arab states supported the war effort against Israel while at the same time imposing an oil embargo against the United States. As is well known, not only did the oil embargo create domestic difficulties for the United States, it caused serious problems within the North Atlantic Treaty Organization (NATO) alliance—a development that was warmly welcomed in Moscow. Unfortunately for the USSR, however, this anti-imperialist Arab unity was created not by Soviet efforts but by the diplomacy of Egyptian President Anwar Sadat; and when Sadat changed his policies and turned toward the United States, the anti-imperialist Arab unity sought by the USSR fell apart. Nonetheless, so long as Soviet leaders continue to think in such Leninist categories as "united fronts" (anti-imperialist Arab unity, in Soviet parlance, is merely another way of describing a united front of Arab government and nongovernment forces), and so long as there is a deep underlying psychological drive for unity in the Arab world, Moscow can be expected to continue to pursue this overall strategy as a long-term goal.

Nonetheless, on the eve of Gorbachev's accession to power in March 1985, the Arab world was badly divided and diplomatic trends were moving against Soviet interests. There were, at the time, three main Arab camps. First was what might be called the Egyptian camp consisting of Egypt, Sudan, Somalia, and Oman. All four states had either openly, as in the case of Egypt, or tacitly supported the Camp David agreements; all had denounced the Soviet invasion and occupation of Afghanistan; and all had major military relationships with the United States, which included joint military exercises. On the other end of the spectrum was the so-called Front of Steadfastness and Confrontation, which bitterly opposed Camp David and was generally supportive of Soviet foreign policy. Syria, Libya, and South Yemen were the main countries in this alignment, although elements of the PLO and Algeria shared some of its policy perspectives and received arms from Moscow. Nonetheless, there were serious divisions within the Steadfastness Front, with both Algeria and most of the PLO opposing Libyan and Syrian aid to Iran in the Iran-Iraq war; Algeria clearly unhappy when Libya signed an alliance with its enemy Morocco in 1984; and Yasser Arafat and Hafiz Assad bitter enemies. In the middle of the Arab spectrum were Saudi Arabia, Jordan, Kuwait, Tunisia, Morocco, Iraq, the United Arab Emirates, and the Yemen Arab Republic (North Yemen). Receiving weapons from both East and West, they had in common with the Egyptian-led camp an aversion to the Soviet invasion of Afghanistan, but they shared with the Steadfastness Front an opposition to Camp David, although they seemed more willing ultimately to sign a peace agreement with Israel than were Steadfastness Front members Syria, Libya, and South Yemen. Moscow worried that this centrist grouping was moving toward Egypt, and Jordan's decision in September 1984 to resume diplomatic relations with Egypt and the frequent meetings between Hosni Mubarak and Saddam Hussein, as well as between Arafat and Mubarak, seemed to indicate that such a movement had begun. Egypt's readmission to the Islamic Conference in 1984 and to the Islamic Development Bank in early February 1985 (and later to the Arab Sports Union in August 1985) were further indications of such a trend.[4]

Consequently, the Soviets reacted negatively to the mid-February announcement in Amman of the Hussein-Arafat agreement on a joint negotiating strategy for the Middle East peace process and its rapid endorsement by Mubarak. Though not immediately attacking Jordan or Egypt directly—Moscow still had hopes of ultimately weaning both away from the United States, and a Soviet-Jordanian arms agreement had just been signed—the Soviet displeasure was clear.[5]

Pravda on March 8 complained that the Amman agreement failed to deal with two critical issues: the creation of an independent Palestinian state and the PLO's participation in the settlement process as the sole legitimate representative of the Palestinian people. The *Pravda* article also asserted that the agreement contradicted the decision of the Arab Summit at Fez, Morocco, in 1982.

This, then, was the rather negative Middle East situation that greeted the new Soviet leader, Mikhail Gorbachev, when he took power. Fortunately for Gorbachev, however, an event occurred in early April which weakened both the American and the Egyptian Middle Eastern positions—the overthrow of the regime of Ja'far Numayri in the Sudan. Numayri had long had close ties with both Egypt and the United States, and the regime that replaced him quickly moved to distance itself from both countries.[6] Thus one week after the coup, the new Sudanese leader, General Abdelrahman Siwar al-Dhahab, noted that he had moved to improve relations with the USSR and its two major African allies, Ethiopia and Libya, and a week later, Libya and the Sudan restored diplomatic relations. These moves seemed aimed at ending Libyan support for Sudanese rebel leader Joseph Garang, and the United States became concerned when the renewal of diplomatic relations was followed by a visit to Khartoum by Libyan leader Muammar Kaddafi in May and then by a military logistic agreement between Libya and the Sudan in July. Sudan further discomfitted the United States by refusing to participate during the summer in joint military maneuvers as it had done under Numayri. As a further demonstration of the Sudan's neutrality in East-West affairs (despite a heavy dependence on U.S. food aid), General Siwar al-Dhahab announced his intention to send high-level delegations to both the United States and the Soviet Union.[7]

Gorbachev could only be pleased by the events in the Sudan. Although it would have been premature for Moscow to hope the Sudan would shift back to its pre-1971 pro-Soviet stance, it had moved far enough from both the United States and Egypt for Moscow to consider the overthrow of Numayri a clear gain in a "zero-sum game" competition for influence with the United States in the Middle East.

Although the new Soviet leadership could only have been pleased with developments in the Sudan, events in Lebanon posed continuing problems for Moscow. To be sure, the withdrawal of Israeli forces from that country, announced in January and completed in early June, was viewed favorably by Moscow, which saw it as a victory for "Lebanese patriotic forces," as well as for its major Arab ally, Syria, which would, Moscow perhaps hoped, now finally dominate Lebanon.[8] In addition, the withdrawal of Israeli troops seemed to lessen the possibility of a serious clash between Israel and Syria—especially since Syria was careful not to move troops south as Israel was withdrawing—thereby, in turn, decreasing the possibility that Syria would call on Moscow to aid it in a war against Israel that could erupt into a superpower confrontation. Yet far from bringing calm to Lebanon, the Israeli withdrawal seemed to exacerbate the internecine conflict there, which Syria either could not or would not suppress. In March came an intra-Christian conflict when Samir Ja'ja openly opposed Amin Gemayel, but for the USSR a much more serious conflict erupted in late May when the Shiite militia Amal, acting almost certainly with Syrian support, attacked the Palestinian refugee camps in Beirut into which Arafat's forces were reinfiltrating. The fighting got so bad that Arafat was later to refer to it as "the second massacres of Sabra and

Shatilla."[9] For Moscow, the dilemma of two of its allies fighting each other must have seemed like the rerun of a bad dream. In 1976, during the civil war in Lebanon, and again in 1983, Moscow had been confronted with fighting between Syria and the Arafat-led PLO, and both times the Soviet leadership (under Brezhnev in 1976 and Andropov in 1983) faced a difficult problem of choice. In both cases, as Syria suffered increased Arab isolation because of its actions, Moscow essentially chose to be neutral while calling for an immediate end to the fighting, which "only benefited the imperialists."[10] The new Soviet leader, Mikhail Gorbachev, was to react in an identical way.

In 1985, as in the previous times, Syria was badly isolated in the Arab world because of its actions, even though in this case it did not attack the PLO with its own troops. Both Libya and Iran were critical of their ally's support of Amal, and even the anti-Arafat Abu Musa Palestinians supported by Syria switched sides and aided their fellow Palestinians against the Amal. Moscow was increasingly critical of Arafat, but the PLO leader still had considerable support among Palestinians and in the Arab world among the centrist and Egyptian-camp states. For this reason, as well as because the Amman agreement at this stage was far from becoming the American-brokered peace settlement Moscow feared, the USSR again took a neutral position in the fighting while publicly calling for its immediate end. The Afro-Asian Peoples Solidarity Organization issued a plea to end the fighting.[11]

Fortunately for Moscow and Syria, however, the fighting between Amal and the Palestinians was temporarily stopped by a cease-fire and was replaced in the headlines by the hijacking of an American Trans-World Airlines (TWA) plane to Beirut.[12] The hijacking provided both an opportunity and a dilemma for Moscow. On one hand, the crisis held the potential of another Lebanese humiliation for the United States that would weaken the American Middle East position. On the other hand, however, Moscow could not rule out the possibility of U.S. military action to free the hostages that would pit the United States against the Syrian-backed Amal militia, which had taken control of the plane and the majority of the hostages after it had landed in Beirut. This would mean a repetition of the Soviet dilemma of December 1983, when it faced the problem of aiding Syria in its confrontation with the United States in Lebanon or doing nothing; when it chose the latter option it lost credibility in the Arab world.[13] As the hijacking drama unfolded, Soviet propaganda blamed Israel and warned of a possible U.S. military attack on Lebanon. Gorbachev also took the opportunity to invite Syrian President Hafiz Assad to Moscow for the first official visit between the two leaders. Tass described the talks as having taken place in a "friendly atmosphere"—a Soviet term that indicates that the two sides took different positions on several issues. These areas of disagreement are evident in the Tass statements that "a thorough exchange of opinions was held on issues concerning the situation in the Middle East, Soviet-Syrian relations, and the international situation" and that, "during an exchange of opinions on questions pertaining to the situation in the Palestine Resistance Movement, the Soviet side especially accentuated the importance of preserving the unity of the Palestine Liberation Organization and overcoming the disagreements between Palestinians as soon as possible on a principled anti-imperialist platform." The Syrian version of the talks portrayed a much warmer meeting, stating that they had taken place in an atmosphere of warm cordiality and mutual trust, making no mention of an "exchange of opinions," and indicating that "regarding the situation in the Middle East and Lebanon, the Syrian and Soviet views were identical." It seems clear that the Syrian propaganda move was aimed at demonstrating Soviet support for Syrian positions in the Middle East—above all, on the Palestinian question. Nonetheless, Moscow was not above using the positive Syrian portrayal of its ties to Moscow as a tool to enhance its own Middle Eastern position by showing the importance Syria placed on the role of the USSR in the Middle East and the world.[14]

In the hijacking incident it is not known whether Gorbachev used his influence with Assad to arrange the release of the hostages (or whether Assad sought Iranian assistance in the process), although there were rumors that this in fact took place.[15] In any case, Syria's intervention was a key factor in their release and Moscow could only have been pleased with the outcome. Not only had a military confrontation between Syria and the United States been avoided but Moscow's ally Syria had emerged from the crisis with increased prestige. This was a clear reversal of the situation of only two weeks earlier when Syria had been severely criticized in the Arab world and abroad for aiding Amal attacks against Palestinian refugee camps.

Nonetheless, despite the sudden improvement in its ally's position, Moscow still faced the dilemma that the Amman agreement was on course despite the hijacking and that American diplomats continued to work to arrange a Palestinian-Jordanian negotiating team acceptable to Israel. Gorbachev evidently decided that if Moscow were not once again to be on the sidelines when a major Middle East peace effort was under way, he had to make some gestures to Israel to be included in the negotiations. To be sure, the USSR and the United States had met in February for high-level talks on the Middle East (the first such superpower meeting on the Middle East in seven years), but President Ronald Reagan gave no indication of wanting to include the USSR in the peace process. Indeed, the most a U.S. official would concede was that the talks were "merely an exchange of thoughts in the hope of reducing misunderstandings. Even to call them explorations would be an exaggeration." Not unexpectedly, therefore, no agreement was achieved in the talks, and the U.S. representative, Assistant Secretary of State Richard Murphy, noted that the USSR lacked credibility as a mediator because of its refusal to resume diplomatic relations with Israel and because its treatment of Soviet Jews had alienated the Israelis. He also stated that while the USSR was pressing for an international conference involving Security Council members and interested parties in the Middle East, including the PLO, the United States felt that such large meetings would be counterproductive and called instead for direct talks between Israel and its neighbors.[16]

Following a late May visit to Washington by King Hussein, who, perhaps both as a sop to Moscow and as a means of diplomatically protecting his flank, continued to call for an international conference with Moscow's participation, State Department spokesman Edward Djerejian listed a number of specific actions Moscow would take to show that it was ready to play a "constructive role" in the Middle East peace process. These included resuming full diplomatic relations with Israel, ending Soviet anti-Semitic propaganda, improving the treatment of Soviet Jews, and ending arms aid to militias in Lebanon. Soviet Middle East specialist Yevgeny Primakov, then director of the Soviet Institute of Oriental Studies, predicted in an interview in Moscow that the USSR would not accept "one side setting preconditions for the other to meet" and stated that it was premature to ask the USSR to recognize Israel as a condition for holding an international conference on the Middle East, but Gorbachev soon moved in just such a direction.[17]

Signals about the possibility of the resumption of the diplomatic relations had been sent from Moscow to Israel almost from the time relations were broken off during the 1967 war, but they increased in intensity soon after Gorbachev took power.[18] The Soviets were to make gestures to Israel despite a series of Israeli actions that bound the Jewish state even more tightly to the United States, including its signing of strategic cooperation and free trade agreements with the United States and its professed willingness to allow the United States to build a Voice of America transmitter on Israeli territory and to enter into the American Strategic Defense Initiative (SDI, known as Star Wars) defense scheme. Indeed, Soviet gestures to Israel may have been aimed not only at gaining entry to the Middle East peace process but also at winning favor in the United States with which a summit was on the horizon. Given Moscow's tendency to overestimate the influence of

American Jews on American policy-making vis-à-vis the USSR, its gestures to Israel, which virtually all American Jews hold dear, could thus also be seen as part of Moscow's presummit maneuvering.[19]

The major Soviet signal was to come in mid-July. With Arafat and Hussein calling for an Arab summit and a review session commemorating the tenth anniversary of the signing of the Helsinki agreements due to open at the beginning of August—a session at which the issue of Soviet Jewry would likely be raised—Gorbachev apparently decided that a major discussion between Soviet and Israeli diplomats about renewing diplomatic relations and increasing the flow of Soviet Jewish emigration to Israel was in order. The meeting took place in Paris at the home of Israeli-born pianist Daniel Barenboim between the Israeli ambassador to France, Ovadia Sofer, and his Soviet counterpart, Yuli Vorontsov. Sofer's description of the meeting was leaked to Israeli radio, which promptly broadcast it. Given the importance of the Israeli radio broadcast—even though Moscow publicly denied that any deal was made—major excerpts are reprinted:

> When will relations between the two countries be renewed, Sofer asked? The Soviet ambassador said the relations had been severed following the Israeli conquest of the territories, and so Israel would have to do something about this. I quote: There must be some sort of movement on the matter of the Golan Heights; negotiations with Syria would supply the Soviet Union with a pretext for the renewal of relations. We will not oppose a section of the Golan Heights remaining in Israeli possession, if this is achieved through negotiations with Syria. Ambassador Sofer asked if it was a coincidence that the Soviet speaker was not mentioning Judea and Samaria. No, it is no coincidence, the Soviet ambassador said. In any event, he added, the severance of relations with Israel was a grave error and a sensitive, ill-considered move that harmed the Soviet Union.
>
> It seemed that the clearest and most amazing things were said on the issue of Soviet Jewry. The problem of Jewish emigration from the Soviet Union can be solved within the framework of a package deal, in return for an end to the anti-Soviet propaganda Israel is conducting in the United States and Europe, the Soviet speaker said. We would be prepared for the Jews to leave if we are promised that they will emigrate to Israel, not the United States. The Soviet Union fears a brain drain to the West. The Soviet ambassador admitted that mistakes had been made by the authorities in their attitude toward refuseniks. Those errors, he said, originated in the behavior of Soviet Jewry and the pressures applied to the Soviet Union. As for the continuation of the political process, the Soviet ambassador again raised the proposal regarding the convening of an international conference with the participation of the Soviet Union. My country, he said, cannot agree to negotiations under the sole aegis of the Americans. On the Palestinian issue, the Soviet ambassador said it was hard to see how it would be possible to find a solution to the Palestinian problem while also satisfying Israel's security demands. Vorontsov

repeated his emphasis on the Soviet Union's commitment to Israel's existence, while expressing concern at the continued freeze in the peace process. Ovadya Sofer asked the Soviet ambassador to organize an urgent meeting between Vice Prime Minister Yitzhak Shamir and his new Soviet counter-part, as early as the U.N. General Assembly session in New York in September.[20]

The Israeli ambassador's description of the meeting must be treated with some skepticism because of the normal tendency of ambassadors to portray themselves and their countries in the best light in such dispatches. Nonetheless, Vorontsov's repetition of several Soviet Middle East positions, including the call for an international conference with Moscow's participation, does lend some credence to the report. In any case, the most interesting aspect of Vorontsov's discussion is that he seemed to indicate that diplomatic relations could be restored if there was at least a partial Israeli withdrawal on the Golan Heights and that Soviet Jews would be allowed to emigrate on a large scale if they went to Israel and not the United States and if Israel ended its "anti-Soviet" propaganda in the United States and Europe.

The Soviet hint of renewed relations, though welcome in Israel, met a highly negative reception by Moscow's Arab allies, especially Syria. Syria, the USSR's main bastion in the Arab world, was incensed that the USSR would consider renewing ties with Israel while even part of the Golan Heights seized during the 1967 war remained in Israeli hands. As a result, in both official visits and radio broadcasts to the Arab world, the USSR repeated the old Soviet position that diplomatic relations would not be restored until Israel gave up all the land conquered in 1967.[21] At the same time, however, Moscow continued to hint to Israel that relations could be restored if Israel agreed to Moscow's inclusion in a Middle East peace conference.[22] Israeli Prime Minister Shimon Peres expressed a keen interest in improving ties with the USSR.[23]

Moscow's primary concern at the time of the Sofer-Vorontsov meeting was that the Arafat-Hussein agreement might be accepted by the centrist Arab states, and this concern was heightened in late July when an Arab summit was scheduled for Casablanca in early August. Although Syria and its Steadfastness Front allies (the People's Democratic Republic of Yemen [PDRY], Algeria, and Libya) and its protectorate, Lebanon, boycotted the session, both Hussein and Arafat actively sought support for their agreement at the conference and Egypt hoped that the summit would restore it to full membership in the Arab League.[24] Meanwhile, the United States continued to play an active role in the Arab world, attempting to form a Jordanian-

Palestinian negotiating team acceptable to Israel and seeking to reinforce its ties to Egypt, Jordan, Oman, and Somalia by carrying out
joint military exercises with them.

The summit, however, did not meet the needs of Hussein and Arafat
or the United States. It neither denounced nor endorsed the Amman
accord. Its final communique merely took note of the Amman
agreement by stating that it "viewed with understanding the explanations it has been given by King Hussein and Yasser Arafat who consider
that the Jordanian-Palestinian initiative is in conformity with the resolution of the 1982 Arab Summit of Fez."[25] Moscow may also have been
pleased that the summit established a committee to seek reconciliations
between Iraq and Syria and between Syria and Jordan,[26] thus indicating not only that the centrist Arabs attending the summit did not want
to alienate Syria by endorsing the Amman accord but also that the
Arabs were again trying to restore a semblance of what Moscow hoped
would be the anti-imperialist unity it had long sought. Finally, Moscow
was pleased that Egypt was not readmitted to the Arab League.[27]

Nonetheless, the Soviet media continued to express concern that
U.S. efforts to obtain an accord between Israel and a Jordanian-Palestinian negotiating team might succeed. It was perhaps for this reason
that Moscow made yet another gesture to Israel, this time in the form
of an agreement between its close Eastern European ally Poland,
and Israel, whereby the two countries agreed in principle to establish
"interest sections" in foreign embassies in each other's capitals—the
first stage in the process of reestablishing diplomatic relations.[28] Although Moscow was not yet resuming diplomatic ties itself, this was a
clear gesture that it was prepared to do so and Gorbachev, during his
visit to Paris in early October, noted "as far as re-establishing relations
[with Israel] is concerned, I think the faster the situation is normalized
in the Middle East, the faster it will be possible to look at this question."
The announced resumption of low-level diplomatic relations with Poland, World Jewish Congress President Edgar Bronfman's visit to Moscow carrying a message from Peres, Peres's meeting with Soviet Foreign
Minister Eduard Shevardnadze at the United Nations in October, and
Gorbachev's visit to Paris reinforced the rumors circulating in Israel
that Moscow was about to release twenty thousand Soviet Jews and
allow them to be flown directly to Israel on French planes.[29]

The momentum toward even a partial Soviet-Israeli rapprochement—if that indeed was Gorbachev's goal—was slowed and then
stopped, however, as the peace process fell by the wayside in the face
of an escalation of Middle East terrorism. Moscow was to suffer both
embarrassment and physical loss as a result of the Middle East terrorism, but the end result was that the peace process, centered around

negotiations between Israel and a Jordanian-Palestinian delegation, was halted, a development from which Moscow was to profit diplomatically.

The root of the problem was that Arafat, in an effort to maintain credibility with the hard-liners in his organization, stressed the escalation of "armed struggle" (terrorism) soon after concluding the Amman agreement with King Hussein.[30] Peres was vulnerable politically even for considering negotiations with Palestinians close to the PLO, and he was frequently attacked by the opposition Likud party for being "soft on terrorism" and "soft on the PLO." As a result, when a wave of terrorist murders struck Israel during the spring and summer of 1985, Peres not only found it increasingly difficult to negotiate with any Palestinian closely linked to the PLO, he also came under increasing pressure to respond. Thus when three Israelis were murdered in Cyprus at the end of September by terrorists who proclaimed they were fighting for the Palestinian cause, Peres authorized an attack on PLO headquarters in Tunis on October 1, 1985, perhaps signaling to Arafat that if the PLO leader wished to fight while he was negotiating, Israel could play the same game.

Moscow lost little time in exploiting the Israeli attack to try to undermine the U.S. position in the Middle East and once again appealed for Arab unity against Israel and the United States. The lack of Arab unity was a particular problem for Moscow at this time because Libya had become even more isolated in the Arab world at the end of September when Tunisia had broken relations with it (Iraq had broken relations with Libya in June) and turned to the United States and Algeria for support. Further complicating the North African situation for Moscow in the period before the Israeli raid was the warming of relations between the United States and Steadfastness Front member Algeria, whose president, Chadli Ben Jedid, had made a very successful visit to the United States in April which had resulted in the Reagan administration's decision to agree to sell arms to Algeria. Indeed, the Algerian ambassador to the United States, Mohamed Sahnoun, was quoted as saying that Algeria was interested in purchasing U.S. weapons to reduce its dependence on its main arms supplier, the USSR.[31]

Thus the raid came at a propitious time for Moscow. Even more propitious was Reagan's initial endorsement of the raid, which was bitterly attacked even in Arab countries friendly to the United States. As the Arab reaction to the bombing intensified, Moscow did what it could to link the Israeli action to the United States. Thus in a radio broadcast in Arabic on October 2, the day after the attack, the Soviet commentator alleged not only that the United States had used its radar posts in the Mediterranean to direct Israeli planes to PLO headquarters in Tunis but also that the Israeli bombers took off from a U.S. aircraft carrier—a classic case of Soviet disinformation.[32]

Even before the uproar over the Israeli attack had died down, another terrorist event from which Moscow was to profit diplomatically took place. This was the hijacking of the cruise ship *Achille Lauro* and the murder of a Jewish passenger, Leon Klinghoffer, by a PLO faction headed by Mohammed Abbas, a hard-line PLO leader, who was linked to Arafat because of their mutual opposition to Syrian leader Hafiz Assad.[33] The hijacking had two major mutual diplomatic benefits for Moscow. First, the action of the United States in forcing down an Egyptian plane carrying the hijackers and Abbas inflamed U.S. relations not only with Egypt but also with Italy, where the plane was forced to land, when Italian Premier Bettino Craxi allowed Abbas to leave his country. Subsequent U.S. aid to Egypt when one of its aircraft was hijacked to Malta somewhat smoothed over the strain in U.S.-Egyptian relations, but there was no question that serious diplomatic damage had been done, which Moscow evidently hoped would lead to a weakening of U.S.-Egyptian relations.

In addition to profiting from the strain in U.S.-Egyptian relations, Moscow also obtained diplomatic benefit from Shimon Peres's policy change on the Middle East peace process. Apparently concluding that Arafat and the PLO had discredited themselves so badly in the United States by the *Achille Lauro* episode as well as by Arafat's failure to go ahead with a previously arranged agreement with British Prime Minister Margaret Thatcher, under which British Foreign Secretary Sir Geoffrey Howe would meet in London with a joint Palestinian-Jordanian delegation that contained PLO members if it agreed to recognize Israel, Peres sought to sidestep the PLO and make a direct deal with Jordan. Realizing that Hussein had become displeased with Arafat because of the diplomatic debacle in London, but also that the king needed a diplomatic cover for his dealings with Israel, Peres proposed at the United Nations on October 21 that Israel and Jordan commence talks under "international auspices."[34] Unfortunately for Peres, however, King Hussein was not to opt for the Israeli offer and moved instead to improve relations with Syria.

Though the spiral of Middle Eastern violence paid some diplomatic dividends for the USSR, it was not without costs. On September 30, three Soviet diplomats stationed in Beirut and the embassy doctor were kidnapped, and two days later one of them, consular official Arkady Katkov, was killed. This incident was particularly embarrassing for Moscow because it occurred on the eve of a much-heralded visit by Gorbachev to France. On his arrival in Paris, the Soviet leader was clearly embarrassed by the kidnapping. The kidnappers, apparently from a shadowy group called the Islamic Liberation Organization, demanded that the USSR pressure Syria to stop an offensive against Tripoli, Lebanon, by its leftist Lebanese allies, which included the Lebanese Communist party.[36] The Syrian-backed forces were attacking the Sunni Muslim fundamentalist group known as the Unification movement, which had ties to Arafat's wing of the PLO and had clashed with Alawites—the ruling Shiite Muslim sect in Syria—who lived in Tripoli. The incident could only have embarrassed the USSR because photographs were published in Beirut and in Western newspapers of the Russians with guns at their heads, demonstrating the impotence even of the USSR in the face of Middle East terrorism. Indeed, Moscow ordered a partial evacuation of its embassy, and the evacuees proceeded overland to Damascus just as did the victims of the TWA hijacking in July. The USSR also suspended operations at its Norodny Bank branch and barricaded its embassy in the face of threats to destroy it. The hostages were released one month after their abduction (reportedly with Syrian and Iranian help), but the experience was clearly a negative one for Moscow and may have been a factor in Soviet willingness to support a U.N. General Assembly resolution on December 9 that condemned all acts of terrorism as "criminal," as well as a unanimous U.N. Security Council resolution on December 18, which for the first time in the organization's history condemned "unequivocally all acts of hostage-taking and abduction" and called for "the immediate release of all kidnap victims wherever and by whomever they were held."[37]

In sum, the abduction of four of its embassy staffers and the murder of one of them was clearly a bitter experience for Moscow. Nonetheless, on balance, the escalation of Middle East terrorism benefited the USSR because it led to the sidetracking of the American-brokered peace process, a cooling of ties between Arafat and Hussein, and a sharp dispute between the United States and Egypt.

The chances for a Middle East peace settlement brokered by the United States receded, and Moscow took a much harder line with Israel as the mid-November summit between Reagan and Gorbachev in Geneva approached, despite reported calls by Egypt and Jordan for Moscow to restore diplomatic relations with Israel as a way to advance prospects for Middle East peace talks.[38] Indeed, on the eve of the summit, a Soviet government spokesman, Albert Vlasov, demanded as the price of renewed relations that Israel agree not only to allow the USSR to participate in the international peace conference but also to allow the PLO to participate—a concession Peres was unwilling to accept.[39] Perhaps because of this condition, Peres again shifted his position and stated that the resumption of Soviet Jewish emigration from the USSR was much more important than the restoration of diplomatic ties. "If they agree to renew Aliya," he stated, "we shall waive our objections to their taking part in an international conference on the Middle East."[40]

Peres thus presented Moscow with an interesting choice. To protect its position in the Arab world, it is far less costly to release Soviet Jews than to reestablish ties with Israel, and Moscow has long wanted to participate in an international conference on an Arab-Israeli settlement. It was doubtful, however, whether the USSR would settle for taking a symbolic role in an international conference—the most Israel seemed ready to concede—in return for sharply increasing the number of Jews allowed to leave the Soviet Union. Nonetheless, Israel clearly did not give up on the possibility, and the attendance of Israel's President Chaim Herzog at the national convention of Israel's Communist party in early December, the first time an Israeli president had ever attended such a function, was a clear gesture to Moscow that Jerusalem was interested in continuing a dialogue with the USSR.[41]

Yet there may have been other reasons for Moscow's harder-line policy toward Israel. Arab leaders, perhaps remembering the 1972 Nixon-Brezhnev summit, seemed concerned that a superpower deal might be worked out at their expense, and Reagan's presummit demand for linkage between an arms control agreement and Soviet behavior in the Third World may have heightened Soviet determination to prove that no such deal had taken place.[42] Indeed, in a spate of articles appearing in the Soviet media at the time of the summit, including Arabic-language radio broadcasts and Novosti statements distributed in Beirut, the USSR dismissed as "fabrications and lies" claims that Arab interests would be compromised at Geneva.[43] An Arabic-language broadcast by a senior Soviet commentator, Alexander Bovin, sought to put an end to Arab concerns about any such deal. "Themes are put forward on the possibility of a new Yalta for the sharing of influence in the Middle and Near East during the Geneva summit meeting. These fabrications and accusations are aimed at giving rise to the idea of a possible Soviet-U.S. collusion at the expense of the Arabs' interests. Despite the fact that the Soviet Union has firmly refuted all this, more unfounded rumors are being spread on the possibility of a Soviet-Israeli resumption of relations even if Israel does not relinquish its expansionist and aggressive line."[44]

Moscow, however, was not to limit to mere words its campaign to demonstrate to the Arabs that there was no U.S.-Soviet deal at Geneva. Less than a month after the Geneva summit, it was revealed that the USSR had sent SAM-5 antiaircraft missiles to Libya, a clear escalation of the Soviet military commitment to that country because heretofore only Syria, of all of Moscow's Third World allies, had received such a weapon.[45] Given the very tense relations between the United States and Libya, as well as Libya's troubled relations with virtually all of its neighbors, the decision to send SAM-5 missiles to Libya was clearly a commitment of support to the Kaddafi regime, but it was one that would ultimately prove costly to Moscow.

The origin of the decision to send the SAM-5s to Libya may have been Kaddafi's visit to Moscow in early October. The Libyan leader, threatened by Egypt, Algeria, and the United States, was clearly looking for increased military assistance and, most probably, a formal treaty of friendship and cooperation with the Soviet Union. If that indeed was Kaddafi's goal, he was not to achieve it during the visit although agreements were signed on political consultation, a consular convention, and a long-term program for the development of economic, scientific-technical, and trade cooperation. Libya was a useful economic partner for Moscow (although the drop in oil prices was making it more difficult for Libya to purchase arms), but Kaddafi's frequent conflicts with his Arab neighbors had often troubled the Kremlin, and it was probably not accidental that in Gorbachev's dinner speech the Soviet leader emphasized the need for unity of action by the Arab countries. Nonetheless, the joint communique issued after the meeting was considerably warmer in tone than previous communiques following meetings between leaders of Libya and the Soviet Union had been, and it took the strongest stand yet demonstrating Soviet support for Libya against the United States. "The two sides condemned the increasing military and economic pressure by the United States on the Libyan Jamahiriyah and its slanderous propaganda campaign against Libya. They opposed the increasing U.S. military presence in the region and also condemned the provocative military maneuvers, which the United States carries out in the Mediterranean, including in the Gulf of Sirte [Sidra] and near the eastern borders of the Mediterranean and North African regions. In this regard they stated that the use of or threat to use force in international relations is inadmissible."[46]

Another factor that might have prompted the USSR to send SAM-5s to Libya was the disclosure in early November that President Reagan had authorized a covert Central Intelligence Agency (CIA) operation to undermine the Libyan government.[47] Moscow denounced the U.S. plan, and Kaddafi may well have asked the USSR to back up its rhetoric with words and the SAM-5s may have been the result. Still, Moscow was taking a major risk by escalating its aid to Kaddafi. In April Kaddafi had formed a pan-Arab command to carry out acts of violence against the United States, other Western nations, and moderate Arab regimes, and a Libyan radio station calling itself "Radio of Vengeance and Sacred Hate" called on North African Arabs in Tunisia, Algeria, and Morocco to kill the Jews living in their countries.[48] Under the circumstances, and particularly after Israel, which considers itself the protector of endangered Jews, had demonstrated its ability to strike at Arab targets far from its borders, Kaddafi may well have felt that an attack by the United States, Israel, Egypt, or Algeria was a major possibility. By sending the missiles to Libya, however, and deepening its commitment to the Kaddafi regime, Moscow ran the risk of either a superpower confrontation or a loss of face if an attack were made against Libya without a Soviet response. Nonetheless, Gorbachev may have felt that the United States, which in the past had rhetorically denounced both terrorism and Kaddafi but had never taken any substantive military action (other than shooting down two Libyan planes over the Gulf of Sidra in 1981) to deal with either, would confine its opposition to Kaddafi to rhetoric such as the statement by the State Department spokesman Charles Redman, who said, "This is a significant and dangerous escalation in the Soviet-Libyan arms relationship. We have made clear our concern about this escalation and Soviet support for an irresponsible and erratic regime."[49] If so, this was a major miscalculation, as was to be seen by the lack of any substantive Soviet response to American military attacks on Libya in 1986.

Yet a possible Libyan-American conflict was not the only military confrontation Moscow had to be concerned about at the close of 1985. Another missile crisis had erupted between Israel and Syria, when Assad, perhaps responding to Israel's shooting down of two Syrian planes over Syrian territory on November 19 after a confrontation over Lebanon, moved SA-2 surface-to-air missile batteries close to its Lebanese border and then moved other SAM missiles into Lebanon, thereby impairing the ability of Israeli jets to fly reconnaissance missions over that country. Although in discussing this incident, Moscow emphasized that the Syrian moves were defensive in nature, the Soviet leadership nonetheless had to be concerned that the missile development raised the possibility of a Syrian-Israeli war. Moscow had reportedly withdrawn its troops manning the SAM-5 missile sites in Syria because Syrians had been trained to replace them, but another Syrian-Israeli clash held the possibility of a rapid escalation, something Moscow appeared to wish to avoid.[50]

Although military confrontations between Israel and Syria and between the United States and Libya were still only potential problems for Moscow in late 1985, the ongoing war between Iran and Iraq continued to plague Soviet policy makers. Not only did Moscow have no success in its efforts to end the war, but it had little to show for its attempts to improve its relations with either combatant. In addition, the war badly split the Arab world and reinforced ties between the United States and the conservative shiekdoms of the Gulf. Moscow did, however, obtain one benefit from the conflict. Both Oman and the United Arab Emirates established diplomatic relations with the Soviet Union as possible insurance against an Iranian victory that would threaten their territories. The war escalated in 1985 with an unsuccessful Iranian offensive in the early part of the year, missile and bombing attacks against the two capitals, Iraq's attacks on the Iranian oil terminal at Kharg Island in August, and Iranian interception of neutral ships in the Gulf beginning in September.

Yet despite the ongoing conflicts in the Middle East, the region could not have been high on Mikhail Gorbachev's priority list at the turn of the year. Gorbachev's primary interest at this time was preparing for the Twenty-seventh Congress of the Communist party of the Soviet Union—his first as party leader. Unfortunately for Gorbachev, however, who might have wished to put the Middle East on the diplomatic back burner, and consolidate his position in the USSR, the Middle East was quickly to force its attention on him, and it was to remain a problematic region throughout 1986.

The first major Middle East problem to thrust itself on Gorbachev in 1986 was a crisis in the People's Democratic Republic of Yemen (South Yemen) in January. For many years Moscow had endeavored to create a set of Marxist institutions for this backward Arabian Peninsula state, which it hoped would become a model of Soviet-style socialism.[51] The crisis, however, was to reveal the thinness of the Marxist patina Moscow had created. Essentially, it involved a struggle for power between PDRY President Ali Nassar Mohammed and the man he had deposed in February 1980, Abdul Fatah Ismail.[52] For reasons that are not fully clear, someone in the Soviet leadership permitted Ismail, then in exile in the USSR, to return to Aden in March 1985, just as Gorbachev was taking power. Following some major disagreements at the PDRY Party Congress in October 1985, where Mohammed saw his position weakened, the PDRY president evidently decided to eliminate Ismail by a preemptive move in which he tried to murder Ismail and his supporters at a cabinet meeting in January 1986. Ismail was killed, and the fighting between factions loyal to Ismail and to Mohammed spread throughout the PDRY. Soviet advisers and dependents were hastily evacuated. Ultimately, a pro-Soviet official, the prime minister, Haidar al-Attas, who was touring India at the time of the crisis, was installed by the USSR as president and Soviet intervention in the fighting tipped the balance against Mohammed, who was forced into exile. Although Moscow was able to regain control of the situation, the crisis had several negative consequences for the USSR. First, with at least four thousand members of the Yemeni Communist party killed and a very pronounced degree of tribalism evident in the Ali Nasser Mohammed–Abdul Fatah Ismail conflict, the Marxist structure of the PDRY, which Moscow was seeking to establish as a model for other Arab states, suffered a major blow.[53] Second, the vaunted security infrastructure Moscow had been providing to the PDRY proved faulty when both the USSR and East Germany seemed taken by surprise by the January events. Finally, the ouster of Ali Nasser Mohammed, who had sought to improve the PDRY's relations with its conservative Arab neighbors, and his replacement by more hard-line elements served to slow Soviet efforts to improve relations with the conservative Arab states of the Gulf. Whether the passage of time and the continuation of the relatively moderate foreign policies of Mohammed's successors (they are, in any case, preoccupied with reconstruction) will change this situation remains to be seen. It is significant, however, that during the visit of the new PDRY party secretary, Ali Salim al-Bayd, to Moscow in February 1987, he was urged by Gorbachev to follow a "realistic policy" taking into consideration the "international position" of South Yemen.[54]

If January 1986 was a difficult month for Gorbachev in the Middle East, February was better. In the middle of the month King Hussein of Jordan broke off his year-long peace initiative with Yasser Arafat, complaining that the PLO leadership had not kept its word. This development could only have been welcomed by Moscow as a major blow to U.S. efforts to promote a separate Israeli-Palestinian-Jordanian peace settlement. Nonetheless, the Middle East received very limited attention from Gorbachev at the Twenty-seventh Party Congress. If one takes Gorbachev's speech as a programmatic listing of his priorities, the Third World was low on his list and the Arab-Israeli conflict barely mentioned. This was in clear contrast with Brezhnev's speeches at previous party congresses at which the Middle East received a great deal of attention and certain Arab countries, such as Syria, were singled out for praise. Gorbachev did, however, refer to the Middle East as one of the world's "hotbeds of the danger of war."[55]

If Gorbachev was seeking to downplay the importance of the Middle East, the region, and particularly the Arab-Israeli conflict, refused to let him do so. Syrian-Israeli relations heated up again in 1986, and there were an increasing number of press reports that war would break out between the two countries. Contributing to the heightened tension were the Syrian decision to construct a series of artillery and tank emplacements near Israel's security zone in South Lebanon, Israel's forcing down of a Libyan plane that contained high-ranking Syrian

Ba'ath party officials (instead of the PLO terrorists Israel was seeking), and perhaps most important, the direct Syrian linkage to terrorist attempts to blow up Israeli civilian airplanes in London and Madrid.

But Gorbachev faced even more problems. After a mini-crisis in January 1986, when the United States blamed Libya for terrorist attacks in Rome and Vienna in late December 1985, two military confrontations between the United States and Libya took place (in March and April 1986). During the U.S.-Libyan crisis of January 1986, the then Soviet Foreign Ministry spokesman Vladimir Lomeiko, in refusing to answer a press conference question on what stand the USSR would take if the United States attacked Libya, noted only that Soviet actions were aimed at "preventing conflicts," not at "constructing scenarios for their escalation."[56] At a Moscow press briefing on March 25 after the first U.S. attack on Libya, Lomeiko noted only that the USSR had provided "moral and political support" to the Libyan people and would take "all measures appropriate within the framework of existing treaties."[57] The absence of any promised military support in Lomeiko's statement and the lack of any formal treaty pledging Moscow to come to Kaddafi's aid demonstrated, however, that the USSR was not willing to back up Kaddafi with more than words, and this was again evident during and after the more extensive American raid on April 15. Indeed, the most Moscow would do at that time was postpone (and only temporarily) a scheduled Shultz-Shevardnadze meeting—a minimal action that could not have impressed many Arab states.

In the aftermath of the U.S. bombing of Libya for its alleged terrorist activities, Moscow could not be certain the United States would refrain from taking action against Syria, another sponsor of terrorism. An American—or an American-backed Israeli—punitive strike against Syria would again raise serious questions of Soviet credibility if Moscow did not aid its Middle Eastern ally in such a situation (especially after its failure to aid Libya). But if Moscow went to Syria's aid, there would be a very real possibility of a superpower confrontation. Given these unpalatable alternatives, Gorbachev seems to have decided to move diplomatically to avert the possibility of such a clash both by publicly cautioning Libya and Syria against terrorism so as not to give "the imperialists" any pretexts for attacks and by negotiating seriously with Israel to arrange consular-level talks in Helsinki, Finland, and also acceding to Israel's demand that the talks be public.[58] Moscow may have felt that the latter diplomatic ploy would deter an Israeli attack on Syria, lest it harm a possible improvement in Soviet-Israeli relations, which in turn held out the possibility of an increase in the number of Soviet Jews being allowed to leave the USSR.

A second Middle East development that may have contributed to

Moscow's decision to initiate public contacts with Israel was the USSR's efforts to play a role in the Middle East peace process. Following Jordanian King Hussein's split with Arafat in February 1986, Moscow sought to exploit the new diplomatic situation by calling for a preparatory committee made up of the U.N. Security Council's five permanent members to prepare for an international conference on the Middle East.[59] When in late July, however, Israeli Prime Minister Shimon Peres and Moroccan King Hassan had a surprise meeting in Morocco, Moscow may have become concerned that it would once again be left on the diplomatic sidelines while a major peace initiative unfolded. (The last surprise summit was Sadat's visit to Jerusalem in November 1977, which led to the Camp David agreements less than a year later.) Moscow may also have agreed to public diplomatic talks with Israel to avert this possibility.

A third contributing factor behind Moscow's request for consular talks may have been the Soviet desire to improve ties with the United States. It would not appear accidental that the Soviet announcement of consular talks with Israel on August 4 coincided with the announcement of the scheduling of the September 19 and 20 meeting between U.S. Secretary of State George Shultz and Soviet Foreign Minister Edward Shevardnadze to prepare for a U.S.-Soviet summit. (The earlier meeting had been postponed by Moscow because of the American bombing of Libya in April.) The nuclear disaster in Chernobyl, the precipitous drop in world oil prices (more than 50 percent of Soviet hard currency earnings come from oil and natural gas sales), Gorbachev's efforts to restructure the Soviet economy, and the major economic difficulties facing the USSR were all factors moving the Soviet leadership toward an arms control agreement that would prevent another expensive spiraling of the arms race. For this reason Gorbachev sought a second summit with the United States, and, given Moscow's tendency to overestimate Jewish influence in the United States, the new Soviet leader may well have felt that the gesture to Israel would help pave the way for the summit.

Nonetheless, the Soviet-Israeli talks in Helsinki, the first such official diplomatic negotiations between the two countries since the 1967 war, did not immediately produce the results either side said it wanted, although the symbolic significance of the talks was probably much more important than their content. The Soviets wished to send a team of officials to inventory Soviet property (primarily owned by the Russian Orthodox church) in Israel, but Israel raised the issue of Soviet Jewry at the talks, and the meeting ended after ninety minutes.[60] Nonetheless, the very facts that the talks were held and that one month later Israeli Prime Minister Peres and Soviet Foreign Minister

Shevardnadze held detailed (and apparently cordial) negotiations at the United Nations.[61] as well as subsequent meetings between the Soviet and Israeli ambassadors to the United States, all indicated that the Soviet Union was keeping alive its contacts with Israel.

Although an opening to Israel was one of the few new Middle Eastern policies undertaken by Gorbachev, the Soviet leader also endeavored to improve ties with Iran. Just as the Khomeini regime was later shown to have exploited U.S. efforts to improve ties during the Iran-Contra debacle, however, so too did it appear to manipulate similar efforts by Moscow.[62] Thus in early February 1986, the USSR First Deputy Foreign Minister Georgii Kornienko visited Tehran—the highest-ranking Soviet official to visit the Iranian capital since the ouster of the shah. When Kornienko obtained an agreement in principle from Tehran to resume Aeroflot flights to Iran, and Iran's foreign minister accepted an invitation to visit Moscow, Gorbachev may well have felt he was making headway in improving the Soviet position in Iran.[63] Less than a week after Kornienko's visit, however, Iran embarked on a major offensive in its war against Iraq and seized valuable terrain around the city of Fao. It might well have occurred to Moscow that Tehran had exploited the Kornienko visit and the impression of an improvement in Soviet-Iranian relations to deter the USSR from increasing its aid to Iraq during the Iranian offensive lest Moscow lose the increased influence in Iran it had apparently just obtained. If Moscow did not see the significance of the Iran ploy in February Iran was to repeat the maneuver again later in the year. Thus in June, Iran announced its agreement to the first meeting in six years of the standing commission on Iranian-Soviet joint economic cooperation; in August there were visits to Moscow by the Iranian Deputy foreign minister for economic and international affairs and the Iranian petroleum minister (the latter promised that Iran would resume natural gas sales to Moscow, which Moscow had long sought); and in December Moscow agreed to return the technicians it had pulled out of Iran in 1985.[64]

Yet once again Iran appeared to exploit the improved ties with Moscow to go on a major offensive against Iraq, this one in early January 1987, less than a month later. Moscow, now perhaps understanding the Iranian ploy, reacted angrily and on January 9 issued its most detailed condemnation of the war to date, clearly timed as a reaction to the Iranian offensive and in its proposed solution to the war far closer to the Iraqi than the Iranian position in that it called for a return to the prewar borders, "non-interference in each other's internal affairs," and the right of every people "to independence and freedom" and "to choose its own way of life"—a clear rejection of the

Iranian goal of deposing Saddam Hussein and setting up an Islamic republic in Iraq.[65] Moscow followed this up with a bitter article in *Pravda* criticizing the mistreatment of jailed Iranian communists, and the new chill in Soviet-Iranian relations was also reflected in Soviet coverage of the February 1987 visit to Moscow of Iranian Foreign Minister Ali Akbar Velayati.[66]

Moscow's unhappiness with Iran was reinforced by the Iran-Contra crisis, which posed both opportunities and dangers for the USSR. On one hand, the loss of confidence of the Gulf Arabs in the United States and the unhappiness of Egypt and Jordan, two of the Arab countries most closely tied to Washington, could only have been welcomed by Moscow. On the other hand, however, the United States was again shipping arms to Iran, which meant the possibility of a reconciliation between Iran and the United States, something Moscow had long feared and had sought to prevent by improving its own position in Tehran.[67] The deterioration of Soviet-Iranian relations was to continue until June 1987, when the major U.S. reflagging effort of Kuwaiti tankers once again prompted Moscow to try to court Iran. Until June, however, Moscow sought to exploit the furor in the Arab world caused by the Iran-Contra crisis by taking an increasingly public anti-Iranian stance. The scandal had put the United States on the diplomatic defensive in the Middle East, and many of the Arab states that had looked to it for protection against Iran became bewildered at the U.S. "arms for hostages" diplomacy with Iran. This created somewhat of a vacuum in Middle East diplomacy, which Moscow sought to exploit in two ways. First, by agreeing to a Kuwaiti request to charter three of its ships, Moscow sought to demonstrate that, as in the case of the Arab-Israeli conflict, while the United States was arming the enemy of the Arabs, the USSR was aiding the Arabs themselves. In a related move, Moscow welcomed a visit by Saudi Arabia's oil minister, Hisham Nazir, who had come to the USSR to get Soviet support for the Organization of Petroleum-Exporting Countries (OPEC) efforts to increase oil prices. Such an outcome also suited Soviet interests so it is not surprising that Nazir was warmly received, and Soviet Prime Minister Nikolai Ryzhkov stated that "the USSR approves of OPEC's constructive efforts and takes them into consideration." Ryzhkov also used the opportunity to call for "mutually advantageous ties with Saudi Arabia" in another effort to convince the Saudi leaders to resume diplomatic relations. Moscow also moved to improve ties with another American Arab ally, Egypt, by rescheduling Egypt's military debt. The Egyptians, perhaps reciprocating the Soviet gesture, agreed not only to reestablish the Egyptian-Soviet Friendship Society but also to appoint Butrus Ghali,

Egypt's minister of state for foreign affairs, as its chairman, and Soviet-Egyptian relations began to warm rapidly.[68]

In what appears to be a second major effort to exploit the Iran-Contra scandal, Moscow stepped up its efforts to achieve an international conference on the Middle East, to be arranged by a preparatory conference of the five permanent members of the U.N. Security Council. By early 1987, the USSR had received support for its position from such diverse groups as the Nonaligned movement and the U.N. General Assembly; and at the end of January 1987, the Islamic Conference had endorsed the proposals.

The idea of an international conference was also increasingly welcome to Shimon Peres, who, after stepping down as prime minister from Israel's National Unity government in October, had become foreign minister and vice prime minister and who saw an international conference as a device to precipitate new elections in Israel. In addition, the United States, its administration weakened by the Iran-Contra affair, came under increased pressure from Arab states such as Egypt and Jordan to agree to an international conference. It was in part to deflect such pressure that Israeli Prime Minister Yitzhak Shamir traveled to the United States in mid-February and branded the idea of an international conference "a Soviet-inspired notion supported by radical Arabs."[69] At the same time, however, Peres went to Cairo, where he and Egyptian President Hosni Mubarak called for an international conference in which Israel would have the right to approve the participants. Their call for an international conference was reinforced by the European Economic Community (EEC), which also called for such a conference.[70]

Shamir stepped up his criticism of the international conference when on March 11 his office published a formal statement repudiating the idea of such a conference. In this document he criticized Soviet efforts to achieve the conference, claiming that rumors that the USSR was trying to improve relations with Israel were essentially "disinformation" and noting that Moscow's goal all along had been a total Israeli withdrawal from territories captured in the 1967 war.[71]

As the internal Israeli debate on an international conference heated up, Moscow began to step up its signals to Israel to demonstrate its desire for improved ties. Thus although a more restrictive emigration decree went into effect on January 1, limiting emigration to first-degree relatives (mother, father, sister, brother, child) of people abroad, statements by a number of Soviet officials indicated that Jewish emigration would rise, and indeed after averaging less than 100 per month in 1986, emigration shot up to 470 in March 1987 and 717 in

April, with a *Novosti* official, Sergei Ivanko, predicting an exodus of 10,000 to 12,000 by the end of the year.[72] It was in this context that two major non-Israeli Jewish leaders, Morris Abram, president of both the National Conference on Soviet Jewry and the Conference of Presidents of Major Jewish Organizations, and Edgar Bronfman, president of the World Jewish Congress, journeyed to Moscow in late March and met with Soviet officials including Anatoly Dobrynin, the former Soviet ambassador to the United States, who was now the director of the International Department of the CPSU Central Committee. According to Abram, they received "assurances" from the USSR in several areas pertaining to Soviet Jewry in return for their willingness to consider changes to the Jackson-Vanik and Stevenson amendments. The "assurances" were as follows:

1. Soviet Jews with exit visas for Israel will travel via Rumania on flights to be established.
2. All Refuseniks and their families will be allowed to emigrate to Israel within a one-year period, except for legitimate national security cases. A procedure will be established, however, to review previous visa denials on national security grounds. This procedure may involve officials on a level as high as the Supreme Soviet.
3. First-degree relatives may emigrate for family reunification within an established time frame. There may be flexibility within the framework of the current narrow interpretation of "first-degree relation."
4. Cases of those Refuseniks recently placed in a "never allowed to emigrate" category will be reviewed.
5. All Jewish religious books may be imported into the USSR, and a recommended list of books will be submitted.
6. Synagogues will be opened in all sites where there is a demonstrated need.
7. Soviet Jews will be allowed greater access to rabbinical training. Some may even be allowed to study in the United States.
8. The teaching of Hebrew in school or synagogue settings will be considered together with similar restrictions applied to other religious groups.
9. A kosher restaurant will be opened in Moscow, and liberal provisions will be made for ritual slaughter.[73]

The Bronfman-Abram mission got a mixed reaction in Israel. Peres warmly endorsed it, but Shamir deprecated its value and Soviet Jewry activists such as Anatoly Sharansky, Lev Elbert, and Yuri Stern, fearing that once the 10,000 Refuseniks were allowed to leave, the gates would close permanently, denounced it, with Elbert claiming it was a "trade of 3,500 families for 2 million people waiting to leave."[74]

In arranging the meeting with Abram and Bronfman (although subsequently denying that any "deal" had been made), Moscow apparently had two goals.[75] With a new summit on the horizon because

Gorbachev had "decoupled" SDI from other arms agreements, and with the Soviet leader now energetically pushing his plan for an intermediate range nuclear arms agreement, the sharp increase in the number of Soviet Jews allowed to leave the USSR, the promise of a still greater exodus inherent in the Bronfman-Abram visit, and the Soviet decision to free almost all of the jailed prisoners of Zion (those imprisoned for wanting to go to Israel), all clearly had major public relations value in the United States. In addition, however, it gave political ammunition to Peres, who saw in the increased emigration the price Moscow was paying to qualify for attendance at an international conference, a price which Peres had cited back at the time of the first Reagan-Gorbachev summit in 1985.

Meanwhile, however, Peres pursued his efforts for an international conference. Meeting for the first time publicly with pro-PLO Palestinians, Peres claimed that the Palestinians expressed the desire for Palestinian representatives acceptable to Israel.[76] At the same time, China, also evidently interested in an international conference, began formal diplomatic talks with Israel at the United Nations.[77] As the momentum for the conference built, the Soviets announced that they again wanted to send a consular delegation to Israel (albeit without any reciprocal visit by an Israel delegation), and Peres stated that Moscow had already requested visas for the delegation.[78]

Thus in early April, as Peres set out for visits to Spain and to the Socialist International meeting in Rome, he was actively pushing for an international conference, and Shamir, who was just as actively opposing the conference, publicly stated that he hoped Peres's efforts to arrange the conference would fail.[79] It was thus in an atmosphere of the beginning of a domestic political crisis in Israel that Peres met with two high-ranking Soviet officials in Rome, Karen Brutents, deputy director of the International Department of the CPSU, and his Middle East adviser Alexander Zotov, in what Peres was later to describe as "the first serious direct dialogue between the two nations."[80] The meeting created a major political stir in Israel, with Peres, although agreeing to keep the details of the six hours of discussions secret, giving the impression that major progress was being made in the negotiations both with regard to the exodus of Soviet Jews and the improvement of Soviet-Israeli relations and asserting that "if there is no international peace conference within the next few months, the chance for peace could slip away."[81] He also leaked the information that the USSR had spoken against any "coercion" by the superpowers in the context of an international peace conference or by the conference itself, that Moscow had agreed to the idea of bilateral talks as part of the conference, and that the Soviets had spoken of Palestinian representation at the conference in more general terms than just the PLO.[82]

The Likud political counterattack was not long in coming. Even as Peres was meeting with the Soviet officials in Rome, the Likud chairperson of the Knesset subcommittee on immigration, Uzi Landau, accused Peres of creating the impression that moves toward an international conference were a condition for Jewish emigration from the USSR.[83] Shamir was even sharper in his criticism on April 10, denouncing the idea of an international conference as "national suicide." Seeking to rally the Soviet Jewish activists in Israel in his political battle to torpedo Peres's plan for an international conference, Shamir also deprecated Peres's efforts to show that there had been a real change in Soviet policy, asserting that "there are only rumors and piecemeal reports about a few hundred Jews who have been allowed out, but this does not represent a change. If the Soviet Union wants to improve its image and attain a different attitude from the West by changing its policy on Jewish emigration, it must open its gates and allow hundreds of thousands of Jews out without imposing any restrictions and qualifications. We must not sell the Jewish cause cheaply."[84]

While the internal Israeli debate raged during April, Moscow was not idle. It was active in helping the PLO achieve a semblance of unity as both Popular Front for the Liberation of Palestine (PFLP) leader George Habash and Democratic Front for the Liberation of Palestine (DFLP) leader Naef Hawatmeh agreed once again to cooperate with Arafat at the Algiers meeting of the Palestine National Council (PNC), albeit on condition that the PLO break with Jordan (Moscow, which hailed the agreement as a "noteable milestone in strengthening the unity of the Palestinian movement"[85] and praised the PNC decision to support an international conference, was apparently rewarded for its efforts with a seat on the PLO executive committee for the pro-Soviet Palestine Communist party). At the same time Gorbachev sought to reemphasize Moscow's interest in improved ties with Israel and to reinforce the idea of a Middle East conference during his talks with visiting Syrian leader Hafiz Assad in late April, when the Soviet leader implicitly warned Assad against going to war because of the danger of nuclear escalation and asserted that the absence of relations between the USSR and Israel "cannot be considered normal."[86] He went on to say, however, that the reason Soviet-Israeli relations were broken was Israel's "aggression against the Arabs." After repeating Moscow's recognition of Israel's right to a "secure and peaceful existence," Gorbachev noted that changes in Soviet relations with Israel were possible only if there were a Middle East settlement. Reportedly, Gorbachev also used his meeting with Assad to press for a Syrian-PLO reconciliation.[87]

A full-fledged political crisis had erupted in Israel with Peres using the issue of an international conference to try to bring down the National Unity government. Indeed, Peres went so far as to claim that Israel had "an opportunity that we have not had since the creation of the State of Israel."[88] In using such hyperbole, he left open some very basic questions about the international conference such as (1) who would represent the Palestinians (Peres claimed Jordan had agreed to abandon the PLO, which had broken with it at the PNC conference in Algiers, which Jordan denied);[89] (2) the role of the USSR at the conference (in none of its public statements had Moscow agreed to the basically ceremonial role that Peres had stated for it); and (3) whether the conference as a whole would have to confirm the decision of the bilateral committees (the USSR had continued to indicate it wanted the conference as a whole to approve all bilateral agreements). In any case, the debate, at least in the short run, became academic because Peres found he did not have sufficient Knesset votes to bring down the government on the issue of an international conference, and by mid-May he announced that he was not going to submit the plan for the international conference to the Israeli cabinet.[90]

Even though Peres was unable to force new elections over the issue of an international conference, Moscow continued to demonstrate its interest in maintaining contacts with Israel, although Israel's development of the Jericho II missile, which Moscow claimed could strike the USSR, was an irritant in the Soviet-Israeli relationship.[91] There were numerous conversations between Soviet and Israeli officials (the longest—ten hours—between a Peres adviser, Nimrod Novik, and Vladimir Tarasov of the Soviet Foreign Ministry in mid-August). The Soviets did not bother to deny the Soviet-Israeli contacts to the Arabs—Yuli Vorontsov openly spoke about them in a *Rose al-Yusuf* interview, as did Radio Moscow in an Arabic-language broadcast in late August.[92]

In addition to the rhetoric, Moscow demonstrated its interest in improved ties with Israel by sending a consular team to Israel in July and by allowing a second East European ally, Hungary to establish low-level diplomatic interest-section relations with Israel in September. Then, after a meeting between Peres and Shevardnadze at the United Nations at the end of September, Peres claimed that Shevardnadze had offered Israel a similar interest-section arrangement (which Peres rejected) and that the USSR did not insist that the PLO represent the Palestinians at an international peace conference.[93] Given Peres's habit of exaggerating Soviet offers, it is not surprising that Moscow publicly denied them, as an Israeli journalist, in commenting on Peres's U.N. performance, noted critically.[94] Nonetheless, it was clear that Moscow was continuing to speak different things to different audiences. It sought to reassure the Arabs by voting to exclude Israel from the General Assembly and hinting that Arafat would soon be coming to Moscow, while at the same time, it moved to reassure Israel by extending the stay of its consular team there for an additional three months.[95] With both the U.S. and Israeli elections now little more than one year away, Moscow was clearly positioning itself for a future diplomatic move by maintaining ties with all sides.

The USSR was to demonstrate a similar flexibility in its policy toward the Gulf war in the spring and summer of 1987. During the spring, Soviet-Iranian relations, which had taken a negative turn following the January 1987 Iranian offensive, continued to deteriorate. Moscow, apparently trying to exploit Arab unhappiness with the United States because of the Iran-Contra scandal, agreed to a Kuwaiti request to charter three Kuwaiti tankers as if to demonstrate that if the United States would not aid the Arabs in time of need, the USSR would. Yet just as the United States was later to encounter problems with Iran because of its reflagging operation, so too was the USSR. Thus in May a Soviet dry cargo ship was attacked by rockets and machine guns, and a tanker was hit by a mine.[96] These incidents elicited an angry Soviet response, with Deputy Foreign Minister Vladimir Petrovsky, after returning from a tour of Kuwait, the United Arab Emirates, Oman, and Iraq, noting in an interview with *Moscow News* that the "USSR reserved the right to act according to international law (i.e. use self-defense) if provocative actions with regard to Soviet ships were repeated."[97] But Iranian attacks on Soviet ships were not the only irritants in the Soviet-Iranian relationship in the late spring. Moscow complained not only about pro-Iranian forces in Afghanistan rejecting the Afghan government's appeal for a cease-fire but also about an article in the Iranian newspaper *Jomhuri e-Eslam* which claimed that the Soviet republics of Tadjikistan, Turkmen, and Uzbekistan, as well as some districts in Georgia, were originally Iran's national territory and ought to be liberated.[98] The USSR also emphasized its opposition to Iran's efforts to export Islamic fundamentalism. Andrei Gromyko, speaking to a visiting Arab delegation in late April, asserted that "no state had the right to interfere in the internal affairs of another, regardless of pretext," and a Moscow Radio Peace and Progress broadcast in Persian to Iran in early May noted sarcastically, "Tomorrow Afghanistan or even Turkey may be attacked on the basis of nonsensical pretexts such as a threat against traditional Islamic dress."[99]

Yet despite the sharp Soviet criticism of Iran, Soviet-Iranian relations were to take a major turn for the better in mid-June, when Moscow once again sought to improve ties with Iran, although it would appear that as in the past Iran was once again exploiting the USSR for its own purposes. The cause of the Soviet policy change was the U.S. decision not only to reflag eleven Kuwaiti tankers but also to protect them with a flotilla of the U.S. Navy, which would convoy the ships from the Strait of Hormuz to Kuwait's territorial waters. Moscow saw in this a major American effort to improve its ties with the Arabs after Iran-Contra, and, on the basis of its own experience with Iran, most likely as a source of U.S.-Iranian tension. Given Moscow's earlier concern that Iran's need for weapons would, as in the Iran-Contra affair, lead it to a rapprochement with the United States, any U.S.-Iranian tension over American assistance to Kuwait, a major ally of Iraq in the Iran-Iraq war, could only be welcomed. At the same time, however, as the Iran-Iraq tanker war escalated, Moscow had to be concerned that the United States would use the reflagging operation not only to redeem itself in the eyes of the Gulf Arabs but also to obtain the naval and air bases it had long sought in the Gulf. In addition, were Moscow overtly to tilt to backing Iran in the Iran-Iraq war, the USSR ran the risk of alienating Gulf Arab states like Kuwait and Saudi Arabia which it had been diplomatically courting. This must also have appeared to Moscow to be an opportune time to win the influence in the Khomeini regime it has long sought. Iran was isolated as never before under the Ayatollah with not only the United States opposing Iran's regime but most of the Arab world and Britain and France as well. For this reason Moscow moved openly to improve relations with Iran, while at the same time seeking to end the Gulf war and get the American fleet out of the Gulf. In doing this, however, Moscow sought to avoid alienating either the Gulf Arabs or the United States, which it had been urging to cooperate in solving regional conflicts such as the Iran-Iraq war.[100] This would be a very difficult diplomatic task.

Moscow's first move to improve relations with Iran came during a Tehran visit by Yuli Voronstov, now a Soviet deputy foreign minister, in mid-June. During his visit to Tehran Voronstov emphasized four major points: the USSR's interests were not parallel to those of the United States in the Gulf; the United States was planning projects against both the USSR and Iran in the Gulf; the USSR did not want foreign (non-Gulf) military forces in the Gulf; and the USSR had a great deal of respect for the Iranian revolution.[101] The Soviet representative also discussed industrial projects that Moscow was interested in helping Iran to develop, including the expansion of the capacity of the Isfahan metallurgical complex to 1.9 million tons and the completion and expansion of the Montagen power station.[102] In discussing these issues Moscow appears again to have been seeking to broaden the level of state-to-state economic relations which it hoped would lead to improved political relations, if not with the Khomeini regime then with its successor.[103]

Vorontsov's reception was relatively warm, although Iran's parliament speaker Hashemi Rafsanjani reportedly told Vorontsov that the United States had used the USSR's "small action" in the Gulf as an excuse for adventurism. Nonetheless, in an English-language broadcast over Tehran Radio—a possible effort by Iran to signal the United States that if it pushed Iran too hard the latter might move into the Soviet camp—Iranian Prime Minister Hussain Musavi noted that Iran wanted "clear-cut and friendly relations with the USSR within the framework of [Iran's] principles" and he expressed the hope that "the policies of the two anti-imperialist countries would be coordinated both at the regional and international levels."[104] Nonetheless, it was clear that on the issues of the situation in Afghanistan and the Iran-Iraq war, Tehran would not change its position. A Tehran Persian-language broadcast noted that when Iranian President Ali Khamenei met Vorontsov, in addition to calling for "an expansion of relations based on friendship and sincere cooperation" and "totally endorsing" Vorontsov's remarks about Soviet anxiety over U.S. hegemony and its presence in the Gulf, Khamenei repeated the "firm Iranian position on the evacuation of Soviet troops from Afghanistan" and stated that "our resolve to punish the [Iraqi] aggressor has become firmer in every way"—a statement unlikely to give Moscow much encouragement that Iran was considering an end to the war.[105]

Nonetheless, following Vorontsov's visit to Iran and later to Iraq, on July 3 Moscow issued a major new policy statement on the Iran-Iraq war. In a clear demonstration of the similarity of Soviet and Iranian views on the issue, the USSR called for the withdrawal of all foreign ships from the Gulf and called for Iran and Iraq to refrain from actions that threatened international shipping, for a cease-fire and the withdrawal of all troops to internationally recognized borders, and for the U.N. secretary general to play a "substantial role" in achieving a just settlement. That the Soviet effort was in large part an anti-American propaganda device, however, is evident from the commentary accompanying the proposal:

The United States wants to exploit the present alarming situation in the Persian Gulf area to achieve its long harbored plans of establishing military-political hegemony in this strategically important area of the world that Washington is trying to present as a sphere of U.S. vital interests.

As to several Soviet warships staying in the Persian Gulf to whch they
in Washington refer, they have to stay in the Gulf for they accompany
Soviet merchant ships and have nothing to do with the heightening of
tension in the area.[106]

As might be expected, Iran greeted the Soviet proposal that foreign
forces leave the Gulf as a "positive" one, and during a visit to Moscow
in mid-July, the Iranian deputy foreign minister, Mohammed Larijani,
discussed economic cooperation, including oil and gas. Soon after
Larijani's departure, on July 20, 1987, the U.N. Security Council unanimously adopted Resolution 598, which called for an immediate cease-
fire in the Iran-Iraq war and the release of prisoners of war. It tilted
somewhat toward the Soviet view by entrusting the U.N. secretary
general with a mediating mission and urging all other states to "refrain
from any act which may lead to further escalation and widening of the
conflict" (Moscow was later to claim that the United States had violated
this article by building up its forces in the Gulf). Finally, responding
to Iran's continuing desire to get Iraq condemned for starting the war,
Moscow succeeded in inserting an article suggesting that an "impartial
body" of inquiry determine responsibility for the conflict. Because the
document was slanted toward the Soviet position, it is not surprising
that Moscow praised it, although the United States was soon to emphasize the need for sanctions against Iran for its failure to agree to a
cease-fire.[107]

Following the U.N. resolution, Moscow adopted a strategy of delaying any attempt to impose sanctions on Iran in an obvious effort to
win Iranian goodwill. Thus Soviet propaganda began to assert that
the U.S. naval buildup in the Gulf was as great a cause of tension as
the Iran-Iraq war and a violation of the Security Council resolution.
At the same time, however, perhaps concerned that the United States
was winning influence among the Arab states of the Gulf, Moscow
warned them that the Gulf could become a second Vietnam, intimating
that just as Vietnam suffered massive destruction at the hands of the
United States, so too might the Arabs if they got too closely involved
with Washington.[108]

Moscow's courting of Iran continued with an evenhanded reporting
of the riots in Mecca in late July, and Vorontsov made another visit to
Tehran in early August. According to the Iranian version of the visit,
Khamenei told Vorontsov that "our people will continue the war on the
ground borders until the downfall of the aggressive Iraqi regime"—a
blunt rejection of Soviet efforts to achieve a cease-fire. Still, Iran
needed the USSR to block follow-up U.N. Security Council action,
including sanctions, against it. So the Iranians made further gestures
to give Moscow the feeling it had won influence in Tehran. Thus

during Vorontsov's visit there were discussions about the export of Iranian oil through the Black Sea and other areas of economic cooperation, and deputy Foreign Minister Larijani praised Iranian-Soviet relations as "progressing and developing at a very good level."[109]

As Soviet-Iranian relations improved, so too did U.S.-Arab relations as a result of the growing U.S. military presence in the Gulf—as was ruefully noted by *Pravda* in late August. During this period Moscow sought to portray Iran as more moderate than it actually was. A Tass broadcast on August 9 stated that Iran's U.N. representative had said Iran did not plant mines in international waterways and asserted that Iran had not specifically rejected U.N. Resolution 598.[110]

By early September, with tension in the Gulf rising and Iran still rejecting a cease-fire despite the mediating efforts of the U.N. secretary general, Arab criticism of Moscow began to mount. A delegation of the Arab League headed by a Kuwaiti official came to Moscow on September 7. Moscow sought to blame the rise in tension on the U.S. buildup in the Gulf and proclaimed its full support for U.N. Resolution 598. The final communique described the talks as having taken place in a "businesslike atmosphere" with a "frank exchange of opinions." This wording clearly meant there had been serious disagreement.[111] Moscow's sensitivity to Arab charges that it was protecting Iran was reflected in a September 9 *Pravda* article which condemned "attempts to cast a shadow on the Soviet Union's policy and drive a wedge in its relations with the Arab states."

Yet at the same time Moscow was trying to reassure the Arabs, it was entertaining the Iranian deputy foreign minister, Mohammed Larijani, who had come to Moscow for talks on September 9. Commentators in Tehran noted that the two countries had agreed in principle on the project for an Iranian oil pipeline through Soviet territory to the Black Sea and had also agreed to draw up plans for building a railway network in eastern Iran and for joint shipping in the Caspian Sea.[112] Clearly, Iran was offering Moscow an increased economic stake in Iran in return for its support in the United Nations against the United States, which Moscow continued to prove willing to do. Indeed, when the United States destroyed an Iranian speedboat laying mines in international waters, Moscow gave the Iranian view of the incident, claiming the ship was carrying food. Still, as tension—and Arab criticism of the USSR—rose, Moscow employed yet another diplomatic device. Soviet Foreign Minister Shevardnadze called for a U.N. force to replace U.S. and NATO forces in the Gulf.[113] Such a ploy, if successful, might reduce Iranian-U.S. tension, but it would also reduce U.S. influence in the Gulf, an important plus for Moscow. Not surprisingly, the United States rejected the suggestion. Many U.S. observers pointed out that U.N. forces have historically been effective as peacekeepers after a war has ended, not in the midst of an ongoing conflict, as the history of the U.N. force in Lebanon (UNIFIL) demonstrated. In addition, there were questions such as command responsibility and rules of engagement that had to be worked out, clearly a time-consuming process that would delay consideration of sanctions.

Iran was showing a measure of appreciation for the Soviet policy, which included getting the Security Council simultaneously to look into the causes of the Iran-Iraq war to posit blame (an Iranian demand), which was article 6 of Resolution 598, and to work out a cease-fire.[114] Thus on October 1, the Iranian ambassador in the USSR gave a press conference in which he praised the USSR for wanting to pull Soviet troops out of Afghanistan and criticized the United States for wanting to continue. Two weeks later, the Soviet airline Aeroflot resumed flights in Tehran. Then, in mid-October, when the United States placed an embargo on virtually all imports from Iran, the Iranian oil minister visited Moscow and signed an agreement in principle for the supply of Iranian oil for processing at Soviet refineries.[115]

The USSR also took the Iranian side during the two U.S.-Iranian military confrontations in October, and Soviet Foreign Ministry spokesman Genady Gerasimov called the U.S. attack on Iran's offshore oil platform on October 19 a "violation of the U.N. charter." Nonetheless, Moscow also sought to shore up its relations with the Gulf Arabs using, as it had in the past, its special relationship with Kuwait to try to accomplish this objective. Thus on October 15, during a visit to Moscow by Kuwait's oil minister, Ali al-Khalifa, the two countries signed a bilateral cooperation agreement.[116] If Kuwait, despite its unhappiness with the Soviet tilt toward Iran, had arranged Khalifa's visit to Moscow in the hope of deterring Iran, it failed. Indeed, the day before the agreement was signed, October 14, Iran fired a missile into Kuwait, which hit a tanker located in its port. Moscow's response to the Iranian act took the form of a *Pravda* statement condemning the attack as "unacceptable from the standpoint of international law, politics and morality."[117]

Arab displeasure with the USSR grew. Iraqi Foreign Minister Tariq Aziz, speaking at a news conference at the United Nations on October 2, rejected the Soviet effort simultaneously to effect a cease-fire and to set up a commission to determine responsibility for the war, and even though Moscow was Iraq's primary arms supplier, an Iraqi official was quoted as saying, "There is a mini-crisis in our relations with the Soviet Union.[118] Yet Moscow tried once again to achieve an end to the war. At the end of October Yuli Voronstov traveled to Iraq, Kuwait, and Iran, but the Iranians signaled their unwillingness to end the war by launching a missile at Baghdad while Vorontsov was still in the Iraqi capital. Following Vorontsov's return to Moscow, the Iranian prime minister, Hussein Musavi, appeared to put a final end to Vorontsov's effort to get Iran to accept U.N. Security Council Resolution 598 by publicly stating, "We have no hope that the U.N. can do anything about the war."[119]

Musavi's negative comment coincided with the opening of the Arab summit in Amman, Jordan, in early November. The Gulf war dominated the conference. Its opening was punctuated by an Iranian missile strike against Baghdad, and in the meetings the Arabs strongly condemned Iran in most of their resolutions.[120] The central decision of the meeting—to allow each Arab state to decide on its own about restoring diplomatic relations with Egypt—was a major defeat for Soviet efforts to keep Egypt isolated in the Arab world because of its peace treaty with Israel. The Arabs had decided that, despite Camp David, Egypt was needed as a counterweight to Iran. Indeed, in rapid succession, Saudi Arabia, Kuwait, the United Arab Emirates, Bahrain, Qatar, North Yemen, Morocco, and Tunisia restored ties with Egypt. Relatively little attention was paid to the Arab-Israeli conflict at the summit because the threat from Iran transcended the Arab world's previous primary preoccupation. *Pravda's* Middle East commentator, Pavel Demchenko, sought to put the best possible interpretation on the conference, noting that it was a step toward Arab unity and that it had endorsed the Soviet proposal to convene an international conference on the Middle East. Yuri Glukhov, also writing in *Pravda,* took a somewhat more negative view, noting that "the meeting's documents do not contain a single word condemning the policy of U.S. imperialism" and that Egypt was given "an opportunity to emerge from isolation, but there was no rehabilitation of Sadat's policy of separate deals."[121]

Moscow soon began to make diplomatic moves to try to compensate for the events at the Arab summit, which it saw as a gain for the United States. Thus in addition to repeated calls to Iran to end the war, Gerasimov, in a press briefing on November 30, went beyond the previous Soviet position on the Iran-Iraq war by stating that the USSR would be prepared to have a U.N. naval force not only escort ships in the Gulf but also act to implement sanctions. Gerasimov coupled this offer with a demand that Western nations enact legislation to prohibit both overt and covert trade in arms with any nation that violated U.N. Resolution 598. To some Americans, mindful of the time it would take to get such legislation passed, this appeared to be yet another delaying tactic by Moscow. Other analysts again raised the problem of command and control inherent in any such U.N. force.[122] Nonetheless, Iran took the Soviet policy change seriously—and in a highly negative manner. Thus on the eighth anniversary of the Soviet invasion of Afghanistan, Iran permitted a group of Afghan demonstrators to attack the Soviet consulate in Isfahan.[123] Moscow lodged a "strong protest" with Iran, claiming that the attack had been carried out by a "group of fanatical elements from the Afghan counterrevolutionaries who are based in Iran." One week later, a commentator on Iranian television took a highly caustic view of the change in Soviet strategy and warned Moscow not to continue its new policy:

> The Soviet Union feels that because of the possible threat to them posed by the continuation of the war, the reactionary Arab leaders are daily inclining more and more toward the United States and the West. The culmination of this inclination could be seen in the Amman conference and the GCC summit. The Russians feel that if they continue their previous line, they may lose the astronomic loans from the Arabs and their future economic-political presence in Arab countries. They also feel that if they do not react more strongly toward Iran, the Americans will become the only defender among the Arab reactionaries, and this will pave the grounds for the United States to take strategic steps where the future of the Middle East is concerned. At this juncture, the Soviet Union has altered its stand; it is gradually moving away from its previous position toward a more overt stand on the war. At the same time it is trying, as much as possible, to postpone the moment of decision.
>
> Moscow's request to the U.N. Secretary General to pay another visit to the region stems precisely from this. But is this a logical policy at a time when the Americans are still prepared at the slightest smile from Tehran to sell out all the Arabs for the sake of establishing a small relationship with Iran? What will the Russians gain from this stand? The United States understands very well Iran's sensitive role in the region and if, under such conditions, the Russians join in the arms embargo, they will destroy all the bridges that have been built so far. Moreover, because of their intrinsic fear of communism and the natural compatibility between their systems and capitalism, the Arabs will certainly not turn toward the Soviet Union. The only outcome of the Russians' act can be that the Americans will benefit and their position will be strengthened.
>
> The strength that Iran has shown in the past year in the Persian Gulf proves the seriousness of the remarks by our officials that if such a plan is implemented, all Persian Gulf ports will become obsolete. If the Russians go along with the Americans in this, they will be repeating the same mistake they once made when they leased their tankers to Kuwait. The difference, though, is that it is easy to make up for some mistakes, but difficult or impossible to do so for others.[124]

In addition to its announced change of policy on the sanctions issue, and perhaps reacting to another overwhelming defeat in the United Nations on the Afghanistan issue, Moscow moved to assuage Arab unhappiness with Soviet strategy in other ways as well.[125] Thus it took a harder line on relations with Israel,[126] and as if to make clear that there would be no Soviet-American deal on the Middle East at the expense of the Arabs at the Reagan-Gorbachev summit, the Soviet U.N. ambassador, in late November, reiterated the Soviet call for the PLO to participate fully in an international conference on the Middle East.[127] Perhaps acknowledging the inevitability of Egypt's rejoining the Arab mainstream, Moscow sought to make the best of the situation and signed a cultural protocol with Egypt for the exchange of films and television programs on October 22. Less than a week later, Soviet consulates were reopened in Alexandria and Port Said.[128] At the end of December Moscow signed a long-term trade pact with Egypt that doubled the trade between the two countries.[129] Even more important, however, Egypt became a regular stop on Soviet diplomatic trips to the Middle East, with important visits by Voronstov in October 1987 and Karen Brutents in January 1988,[130] as Moscow may have hoped to pull Egypt away from the United States to a more neutralist position.

The main Soviet diplomatic effort, however, came with the visit of King Hussein of Jordan to Moscow in late December, a visit the Soviet media sought to portray as an important example of Soviet-Arab friendship. *Pravda* described the talks as taking place in an atmosphere of "mutual understanding" and noted an "in-depth exchange of views." But there were clearly areas of disagreement, most probably on the Iran-Iraq war. Hussein, after making a major gesture to Moscow by rejecting U.S. plans to solve the Arab-Israeli conflict without the help of the USSR, urged Gorbachev to accept an embargo on weapons shipments to Iran. Gorbachev hedged on this issue, noting only that the USSR was "not against discussion" of the embargo in the U.N. Security Council. The Soviet leader then sought to cast blame on the United States, doubting whether "those who are shouting louder than anyone else for an embargo, and who, by the way, were found to be delivering arms secretly to Iran, are ready to observe it."[131]

Fortunately for Moscow, at the time of Hussein's visit, a major Middle East development at least partially diverted Arab attention from the Iran-Iraq war and back to the Arab-Israeli conflict. The Palestinian uprising (Intifada) began in Gaza on December 8 and quickly spread to the West Bank. Initially, Moscow seemed as surprised by the uprising as the Israeli government, although the USSR quickly moved to exploit it for propaganda purposes. Thus a Soviet government report linked the Israeli "repression" of the protesters with the newly signed U.S.-Israeli military cooperation agreement, and Moscow sought to exploit the U.S. abstention on a U.N. Security Council resolution condemning Israeli actions on the West Bank and Gaza.[132]

Yet aside from condemning Israeli policy and constantly linking the United States to Israeli actions, Moscow took no substantive action in regard to the uprising until mid-January, despite Arab urging.[133] To be sure, there were Palestinian solidarity meetings, a World Federation of Trade Unions (WFTU) declaration, a statement by Soviet Moslems, condemnation from the Afro-Asian Peoples Solidarity Organization, and even a message from Gorbachev to Arafat noting that the "violent measures Israelis were using against the Palestinians aroused anger and indignation in the Soviet people."[134] The Gorbachev message also noted that "one must not ensure one's own rights and security by flouting the rights of others"—a statement that foreshadowed his later remarks to Arafat in Moscow that the PLO had to take into consideration Israel's security needs. In addition, perhaps concerned that its delegation in Israel might be terminated by Israeli officials demanding a reciprocal Israeli mission in Moscow just at the time when it was of the highest importance for Soviet officials to have accurate information on what was going on in Israel, Moscow agreed in principle in mid-January to receive an Israeli consular delegation, although no date was set for the visit, and Gerasimov, in a press briefing, stated that the resumption of Soviet-Israeli relations would be possible "within the process of a Middle East settlement."[135]

The major Soviet response to the uprising came six weeks after it had begun. On January 20, Soviet Foreign Minister Shevardnadze wrote a letter to the U.N. secretary general, in which he called for the Security Council to begin consultations at the foreign minister level both to establish and to start up a mechanism for an international conference on the Middle East.[136] This was an effective propaganda ploy for Moscow because both Israel and the United States rejected the Shevardnadze proposal and the Arab states generally supported it.[137] Nonetheless, the United States was galvanized by the Palestinian uprising to the point that Secretary of State Shultz, after first dispatching Philip Habib and Richard Murphy to the Middle East, set out himself on what was to be the first of four trips in the winter and spring to bring about a peace agreement. Moscow's negative public reaction to the peace efforts of the American envoys generally emphasized two points. First, the U.S. efforts were just another attempt to make a "separate deal," like the Camp David agreement, while in the process diverting attention from the Palestinian uprising. Second, with Moscow increasingly supporting Arafat and the PLO following the Algiers PNC conference, the USSR asserted that U.S. efforts to claim that the uprisings were "spontaneous" were merely an effort to undermine and discredit the PLO. Indeed, on the latter point, PFLP leader Naef Hawatmeh, invited to Moscow in early February by the Afro-Asian Peoples Solidarity Organization and interviewed in *Izvestia*, noted: "The aim of all these allegations is clear—to discredit the PLO

as allegedly not enjoying authority and influence among the population of the occupied territories and instill mistrust of this organization.
To our deep regret, some Arabs have fallen into this propaganda
trap."[138] In addition, Soviet propaganda, which all along had been
linking Israel's repression of the Palestinians on the West Bank and
Gaza to U.S. support of Israel, charged that the U.S. plan to close
the PLO mission to the United Nations was yet another U.S. anti-
Palestinian and anti-Arab action.[139]

As the U.S. position weakened in the Arab world, the Soviets were
strengthened by yet another development—Gorbachev's announcement in early February that he was pulling Soviet troops out of Afghanistan. The Soviet occupation of Muslim Afghanistan had been highly
unpopular in the Muslim world, especially in its Arab segment, and
such nations as Saudi Arabia and Iran perceived a strategic threat
from the Soviet occupation. Consequently, the Soviet withdrawal could
be expected to improve relations both with the Arab world and with
Iran, and Gorbachev sent special envoys to virtually every Arab state
to inform them of the withdrawal and to seek their aid in assisting it
by using their influence to get Pakistan and the United States to agree
to Soviet conditions for the withdrawal at the Geneva talks.[140] Reportedly, in his messages to Arab heads of state, Gorbachev also warned
them against accepting the Shultz Middle East peace plan and stated
that the withdrawal from Afghanistan "would help the USSR devote
more time to other Middle East problems like the Gulf war and the
Palestinians."[141]

Shultz was having a difficult time during his journeys to the Middle
East. Although no side, including Syria, gave an out-and-out "no" to
his plan (which consisted of a foreshortened autonomy period and
talks between Israel and its neighbors at a ceremonial international
conference), there was little support for it outside of Shimon Peres
and Hosni Mubarak, with Shamir, Syria, and Jordan, to say nothing
of the PLO, which denounced the plan, opposing it. As it became clear
both that the Palestinian uprising was continuing and that Shultz's
efforts had proved unsuccessful, with another U.S.-Soviet summit on
the horizon, Moscow took a more active and somewhat more positive
role in Middle East diplomacy, again seeking to convene an international conference. Thus in its description of the meeting between
Shevardnadze and the seven-man Arab committee that came to Moscow in mid-March to discuss Middle Eastern problems, Tass, emphasizing that Israel had to withdraw from *all* occupied territory, also stated
that the participants in the talks agreed on the need to ensure the right
of all states and peoples of the region to a safe existence and expressed
the view that in evaluating the U.S. (peace) proposals, the main crite-

rion should be the extent to which "they accord with the task of achieving a comprehensive and lasting Middle East settlement with due regard for *the balance of interests of all the parties* involved in the conflict."[142] The Tass report also noted that the sides agreed that the international conference "should be a permanently functioning forum within the framework of which talks would be held and *mutually acceptable decisions taken*" (emphasis added). Then Gorbachev, meeting in early April with the general secretary of the Italian Communist party, Alessandro Natta, appeared further to soften the Soviet position on renewing diplomatic relations with Israel when he stated that "within the framework of preparing to hold the (international) conference, a way will be found also toward renewing normal relations between the USSR and Israel." In an obvious effort to demonstrate that coercion would not be used at the conference, Gorbachev reportedly noted that "the most varied multilateral and bilateral talks could take place within it" and, instead of calling for PLO representation, referred only to representatives of the Palestinian people.[143]

The main Soviet signal to Israel was to come during PLO leader Yasser Arafat's visit to Moscow in early April. During talks with Shevardnadze and Gorbachev, the PLO leader was told that Israel's interests, including its security interests, along with those of the Palestinians, had to be taken into consideration in any peace settlement. Specifically, Gorbachev noted, according to a Tass report:

> The Palestinian people has extensive international support and this is the earnest of the solution of the main question for the Palestinian people— the question of self-determination. Just as *recognition of the State of Israel and account for its security interests*, the solution of this question is a necessary element of the establishment of peace . . . in the region on the basis of the principles of international law.
>
> The Soviet Union, Mikhail Gorbachev said, persistently works for a just and all-embracing settlement *with due account for the interests of all— both Arabs, including Palestinians, and Israel*. It is prepared to interact constructively with all the participants in the peace process.[144] (Emphasis added).

Although Gorbachev's comments may have been aimed at convincing Israel it had nothing to fear from an international conference, it would appear that Arafat, despite his assertion that this was "the most successful of all his visits" and that there was "complete unity of views," did not like all that he heard.[145] Thus not only did the Tass statement note that there was a "businesslike atmosphere" (the usual Soviet term for very low-level agreement), but Arafat, after leaving the USSR, asserted that Gorbachev did not ask him to recognize Israel, an assertion that would appear to be inconsistent with both the tone and the content of the Tass statement.[146] Arafat may have been irked by Gorbachev's unwillingness to state that the PLO was the sole legitimate representative of the Palestinian people or to use the term *Palestinian state*; the Soviet leader limited himself to the more ambiguous *self-determination*. These may well have been further tactical gestures to the Israeli leadership, which was united on its opposition to the PLO and to a Palestinian state, if on little else, as well as to the United States, which also opposed the PLO and a Palestinian state. Indeed, in an interview with the Kuwaiti newspaper *al-Siyasah*, a Soviet Foreign Ministry official, Alexander Ivanov-Golitsyn, responded to a question about a Palestinian state that "it was the first time the Soviet leadership did not discuss a Palestinian state. This is not a rescindment of the Soviet stand, but we believe some flexibility should exist." In response to a question about Palestinians who were dispossessed in 1948, he stated: "We as realistic politicians can only discuss the establishment of a state in the West Bank and Gaza. Palestinians living abroad can return to this state. Israel is a fait accompli. Talking about the repatriation of the 1948 Palestinians is something extreme."[147]

Gorbachev's gesture to Israel during Arafat's visit was accompanied by a further low-level improvement in relations between the USSR and Israel. Thus the Soviet Party Youth Organization Komsomol invited a group of Mapam (a left-of-center party, but noncommunist) youth to visit the USSR; Soviet radio operators were permitted to talk to their counterparts in Israel; a famous Soviet singer, Alla Pugachova, gave concerts in Israel; and Soviet Jews were allowed to visit Israel as tourists.[148] There was a brief cooling of ties after the assassination of Abu Jihad, which the Soviet media blamed on Israel and linked to the signing of a memorandum on security cooperation between the United States and Israel, in what appeared to be yet another example of Soviet disinformation aimed at weakening the U.S. position in the Arab world.[149] Still, Moscow welcomed the temporary reconciliation between Assad and Arafat that was precipitated by the assassination; Moscow Radio, in Arabic, hailed it as a "very important event."[150] Possibly because Moscow felt it had to demonstrate a tougher Middle Eastern stance in the aftermath of the Abu Jihad assassination (Abu Jihad was, after all, a close comrade of Arafat, who had just visited Moscow), Soviet negotiators took a hard line on the Middle East during Shultz's visit to Moscow in late April. Whatever the reason, Richard Murphy reportedly told Israel's U.N. ambassador Moshe Arad that the talks were "not productive" and the Soviets were "rigid" in their attitudes.[151]

By the beginning of May, however, with the summit less than a month away, Moscow again began to send signals to Israel. Thus

Shimon Peres made a surprise visit to Hungary—the first such visit by a major Israeli leader to a Soviet bloc state (other than Romania) since the 1967 war. Peres, who had been interviewed by the Hungarian government newspaper in April (a month after the formal establishment of a diplomatic interest section agreed upon in 1987), met with several top Hungarian officials, including the prime minister, Karoly Grosz.[152] Given the very close ties then existing between the USSR and Hungary, it is difficult to believe that the Soviet Union had not approved the visit, despite Shevardnadze's assertion at a news conference in mid-May that "the visit by the Israeli foreign minister to Hungary has no bearing on Soviet-Israeli relations. This was an independent step, taken within the framework of bilateral relations."[153]

From Hungary, Peres went to Madrid, to a meeting of the Socialist International, where, as in 1987, he met with Soviet officials. This time he was reportedly assured by Soviet Middle East specialist Alexander Zotov that the proposed international conference would not have the authority to impose a settlement. To make sure Shamir got the same message (lest he perhaps assume that Peres was using the meeting for partisan political purposes), Edgar Bronfman, who was visiting the USSR, was given a message to carry to the Israeli prime minister emphasizing the same point.[154] To improve the atmosphere further, there was another marked increase in the exodus of Soviet Jews, 1,086 leaving in April and 1,145 in May, both figures higher than any month since 1981.[155]

As the date of the summit neared, Moscow stepped up its diplomatic activity. On May 18 Peres met with the Soviet ambassador to the United States, Yuri Dubynin, in Washington, and was read a Soviet position paper on the Middle East.[156] Once again Peres was told that in Moscow's view, an international conference could not impose a settlement and that any negotiations must be based on U.N. resolution 242.[157] Dubynin again pressed the issue of Palestinian self-determination and promised to look into the delay in the Soviet issue of visas for Israel's consular delegation that was due to go to Moscow. A week later, Peres's adviser Nimrod Novik was told by Vladimir Tarasov, deputy director of the Soviet Foreign Ministry's Middle East Department, that Moscow would issue visas for the Israeli consular delegation after the superpower summit.[158] Peres, predictably, sought to get the maximum political benefit from the Tarasov statement, commenting that the USSR had come a long way in its relations with Israel. Shamir's supporters, also predictably, sought to minimize the move; Yossi Ben-Aharon, director general of Shamir's office, accused Peres of "constant theatrics" in depicting the USSR as moving toward a more favorable attitude toward Israel.[159] Shamir and his Likud backers were not the only ones skeptical about whether the Soviet position had really changed. A number of U.S. officials, including Secretary of State Shultz, expressed skepticism, and one American close to the Middle East negotiations remarked that Peres was engaged in "wishful thinking."[160]

It was perhaps to quiet such skeptics that Gorbachev, in his press conference following the summit (where little progress was made on the Middle East, although Reagan pressed the issue of Soviet Jewry), went further than ever before in seeking to reassure Israel that Moscow would take its interests into account at an international conference:

> We stand for a political settlement of all issues, *with due account for the interests of all sides concerned and, of course for the principled provisions of the relevant U.N. resolutions.* We are talking about the fact *that all the Israeli-occupied lands be returned* and the Palestinian people's rights be restored. We said to President Reagan how we view the role of the United States, but we cannot decide for the Arabs in what form the Palestinians will take part in the international conference. *Let the Arabs themselves decide, while the Americans and we should display respect for their choice.*
>
> Furthermore, *we ought to recognize the right of Israel to security and the right of the Palestinian people to self-determination. In what form—let the Palestinians together with their Arab friends decide that. This opens up prospects for active exchanges, for a real process.* Anyway, it seems to me that such an opportunity is emerging.
>
> I will disclose one more thing: we said that *following the start of a conference—a normal, effective conference, rather than a front for separate talks—a forum which would be inter-related with bilateral, tripartite, and other forms of activity, we will be ready to handle the issue of settling diplomatic relations with Israel.*
>
> We are thus introducing one more new element. This shows that we firmly stand on the ground of reality, on the ground of recognition of the balance of interests. Naturally, these are principal issues—the return of the lands, the right of the Palestinian people to self-determination. I should reiterate: *We proceed from the premise that the Israeli people and the State of Israel have the right to their security because there can be no security of one at the expense of the other. A solution that would untie this very tight knot should be found.*[161] (Emphasis added.)

When one analyzes the Soviet leader's statement, it appears to be a Soviet version of an "evenhanded" position on the Arab-Israeli conflict. Thus though Gorbachev called for the return of all lands occupied by Israel and the Palestinian people's rights of self-determination, he did not stipulate a specific role for the PLO at the conference, leaving that for the Palestinians and the Arabs to decide. In addition, he stated that Soviet-Israel diplomatic relations could be restored following the start of the conference and that the USSR recognized Israel's right to security. To be sure, much of what Gorbachev said was vague; nonetheless, the tone toward Israel was positive, as even Shamir recognized, noting in New York that Gorbachev was a "great man and a great leader" and that the tone of Soviet statements had changed.[162] He questioned, however, whether the substance of the Soviet position had changed, and he indicated that, having been invited to meet with Shevardnadze in New York, he would, as in the past, press for increased emigration of Soviet Jews to Israel and the restoration of diplomatic relations.

In deciding to arrange the Shevardnadze-Shamir meeting, the Soviet leadership seems to have been motivated by one major consideration. With Shamir's Likud party gaining in the polls against Labor, there was a good chance that Shamir would form Israel's next government, and Moscow may well have wished to signal its willingness to deal with him. The Soviets sent Shamir a further signal during the talks—which both sides publicly characterized as "useful and constructive"—by announcing the time of the forthcoming Israeli consular visit to Moscow (mid-July).[163] This enabled Shamir to demonstrate to the Israeli public that he too, not just Peres, could obtain benefits from Moscow. Several days later Israel agreed to renew the visas of the Soviet consular delegation in Israel for an additional three months, thus enabling Moscow to keep a diplomatic presence in Israel, and on July 28 the Israeli diplomatic delegation arrived in Moscow.[164]

As Moscow was trying to position itself diplomatically to deal with whichever major party emerged victorious in the Israeli election, developments in the Iran-Iraq war were posing both challenges and opportunities for the USSR. One of Moscow's goals in pulling out of Afghanistan was to improve its ties with Iran, but although the Khomeini regime welcomed the Soviet move and called it a "positive development," it nonetheless expressed reservations that it might be a ploy to keep the Najibullah regime in power and prevent the "Afghan Moslem people and revolutionaries" from controlling their own country.[165] Soviet Deputy Foreign Minister Vladimir Petrovsky flew to Iran on February 11 to explain the withdrawal to the Iranian leadership but was told by Iranian Foreign Minister Velayati that Iran expected that the Mujahadeen would have a "fundamental and decisive" role in the future of Afghanistan, which should be "independent and nonaligned."[166] Majlis speaker Rafsanjani apparently went so far as to offer Petrovsky a deal on this point, noting that "if you are determined to pull out of Afghanistan, we are prepared to assist you, so that after your departure there will be no U.S. domination in Afghanistan."[167] Although Foreign Minister Velayati was to give an overall positive evaluation to the Petrovsky visit, differences on the role of the Mujahadeen remained, and on February 23 the Afghan Muslim Council issued a strongly worded anti-Soviet statement in Tehran rejecting the idea of any compromise with "Soviet-inspired groups who are responsible for the social calamities in Afghanistan."[168] Yet another irritant in the Soviet-Iranian relationship at the time was what Tehran saw as Soviet acquiescence in U.S. attempts to achieve an arms embargo against Iran. The greatest blow to Soviet-Iranian relations, however, occurred at the end of February, when Iraq launched a missile attack against Tehran. The Iranian leadership denounced the USSR for supplying Iraq with the missiles, and Iranian protestors marched on the Soviet embassy in Tehran and the Soviet consulate in Isfahan, shouting "death to Russia."[169] Moscow denied supplying the missiles, but the Iranian leadership rejected the Soviet denials, and Rafsanjani asserted that the Iranian people would "never forget the Soviet Union's impudence" in supplying Iraq with missiles and said that "this will definitely affect our future relations" with the USSR.[170] Rafsanjani also asserted at a news conference that the Soviet Union was "currently pursuing a policy of hypocrisy and duplicity" by putting the missiles at Iraq's disposal and providing parts to modify the missiles and increase their range.[171] Meanwhile, Iran's Deputy Foreign Minister Larijani, also speaking at a press conference in Tehran, noted that on his recent trip to Moscow he "clearly told the Soviet President and Prime Minister that any missile or bomb given to the tottering regime of Iraq by the Soviet Union will first hit Tehran-Moscow relations before hitting Iranian soil."[172]

The Soviet Union, clearly troubled by the Iranian response to the Iraqi missile barrage, sought to assuage Iranian anger by leading an effort in the U.N. Security Council to achieve an end to the "war of the cities," although this effort was to prove ineffective.[173] One month later, Tehran denounced the U.S.-Soviet agreement on Afghanistan that was signed in mid-April because it did not include the Mujahadeen.[174] Moscow was to use another ploy to improve ties with Iran just a few days after the signing of the Geneva agreement on Afghanistan. Thus on April 10 it sought to exploit the U.S. attack on Iranian offshore oil platforms which followed the mining of a U.S. warship. Soviet commentators denounced the American attack, which quickly escalated into a battle between the U.S. and Iranian navies, with Tass commentators calling the attack "an act of aggression" and a "gangsterlike act." A Soviet Foreign Minstry spokesman, Vadim Perfilyev, labeled it a "gross violation of international law" taken in "total disregard for world public opinion."[175]

This ploy, however, did not appear to meet with too much success, as Tass news analyst Valery Vavilov somewhat ruefully acknowledged, when he deplored Rafsanjani's claim that the U.S. attack was part of a "coordinated campaign of the United States, the Soviet Union and Kuwait."[176] A Radio Peace and Progress broadcast, in Persian, to Iran on April 25 made this point more clearly, asserting that the Iranian mass media were claiming that the USSR was "hand-in-hand" with the United States in a coordinated effort to destroy the Islamic republic and that Iran was not a target of hostile actions agreed to by the Soviet Union and the United States. Moscow also deplored Iran's role in splitting Muslim unity through its refusal to end the war (diplomatic relations between Iran and Saudi Arabia had just been broken by Riyadh). Moscow Radio Peace and Progress went so far as to assert: "Those who support a protraction of the Iran-Iraq conflict hide their spiteful programs under the shield of religious slogans. They regard war as a decisive means in the struggle for leadership in the Islamic world. Such a policy can yield the most dangerous results under current international conditions."[177]

Indeed, the negative status of Soviet-Iranian relations was spelled out in detail by the Iranian newspaper *Kayhan International* on June 27 in an editorial:

> The Iranian nation and leadership have been alarmed at the rate Iraq's arsenals have been stock-piled after Gorbachev took the helm of power. Long-range Soviet missiles have rained on innocent Iranian civilians. Soviet MIGs are responsible for a very large number of Iranian non-military casualties. And these inhumane events have unfolded parallel to Mr. Gorbachev's image-building efforts at home and abroad. . . . As things appear to be, the Soviets have failed to win substantial influence in Tehran. Nearly 10 years of diplomatic, political and economic relations with the Islamic republic has surely not placed the Kremlin in a better position than the White House in the eyes of 50 million Iranians.[178]

Moscow was to try again to exploit a U.S.-Iranian clash in early July, when a U.S. cruiser, in the midst of a battle with Iranian gunboats, accidentally shot down an Iranian airbus civilian airliner. Soviet commentators condemned the action; one hinted that it was "premeditated aggression" and others, including *Pravda,* called it "cold blooded murder" and an attempt to intimidate Iran.[179] Most Soviet commentaries strongly endorsed the Iranian version of the incident. Moscow also sought to use the airbus affair to mobilize diplomatic pressure on the United States to pull its naval forces out of the Gulf—a goal shared by Iran.

Less than three weeks after its airliner was shot down, Iran agreed to a cease-fire in the Iran-Iraq war. Having suffered major losses on the battlefield between April and July 1988, including the loss of the Fao Peninsula, and in the face of both missile and gas attacks by Iraq, Iran changed its previous position and reluctantly accepted the cease-fire without conditions.[180] As might be expected, the USSR warmly welcomed an end to the war that had caused it so many problems in

the Middle East for the past eight years.[181] Voronstov immediately flew
to Tehran to consult with Iranian leaders and reportedly took the
opportunity to condemn the shooting down of the Iranian airliner as
an "act of barbarity" in another effort to undermine the U.S. position
in Iran and open a new page in Soviet-Iranian relations.[182]

Soviet-Iranian relations were to improve considerably once the Iran-
Iraq cease-fire took hold in August 1988 and the Soviets accelerated
their troop withdrawal from Afghanistan, which was completed in
February 1989. Soviet attention in the latter half of 1988 shifted back
to the Arab-Israeli conflict when, in a move that surprised many observers, King Hussein, at the end of July 1988, announced he was
severing Jordan's political ties to the West Bank. Whatever the king's
motivation, his action gave the PLO the opportunity to proclaim the
two-state solution to the Israel-Palestinian conflict which Moscow had
long been urging. After three and one-half months of deliberations
and numerous trips of PLO delegations to Moscow, in mid-November
1988 the Palestine National Council proclaimed the establishment of
the state of Palestine alongside of—not in place of—Israel, albeit somewhat ambiguously. Israelis, who had just given a narrow 40 to 39
victory to the Likud party over Labor, did not fully trust the PLO's
change in position, and neither did the United States, which continued
to call for a clearer exposition of the PLO's position on terrorism and
recognition of Israel and refused to give Arafat a visa to come to the
United States. The U.S. action precipitated a vote in the United Nations
to move the U.N. debate over Palestine to Geneva. In Geneva, however,
Arafat uttered the correct words, and in mid-December, the United
States began an official political dialogue with the PLO.

The Soviet reaction to these events reflected both its continued
efforts to cultivate Israel (and the United States) while urging a rapid
convening of the international conference on the Middle East. Thus,
instead of formally recognizing the Palestinian state, Moscow recognized only the proclamation of the state, a move probably aimed at
partially assuaging the Israelis while at the same time acknowledging
the important diplomatic move taken by the PLO.[183] The USSR also
welcomed the beginning of the U.S.-PLO dialogue, although the official Soviet statement noting the beginning of the dialogue seemed also
to reflect concern that the United States might exploit its dialogue with
the PLO to work out an Israel-Palestinian settlement much as it had
worked out an Israeli-Egyptian settlement in the 1970s in a process
that left the USSR on the diplomatic sidelines. For this reason the
Soviet statement urged the rapid convening of an international conference, a theme Soviet Foreign Minister Shevardnadze was also to press
during his trip to the Middle East in February 1989.[184]

In any case, the opening of the U.S.-PLO dialogue is a good point of departure for examining the thrust of Soviet policy toward the Middle East under Gorbachev.

In the first three and one-half years of Soviet policy toward the Middle East under Gorbachev, it would appear that, unlike many other areas of Soviet foreign and domestic policy, there was far more continuity than change. Thus, as under Brezhnev, Andropov, and Chernenko, Gorbachev called for an international conference to solve the Arab-Israeli conflict and continued to adhere to a three-point plan for settling the conflict: the total withdrawal of Israeli forces to the pre-1967 war boundaries; the right to exist of all states in the region, including Israel; and the establishment of a Palestinian state on the West Bank and Gaza. The only changes Gorbachev made in Moscow's strategy on the peace process were to call for a preparatory committee made up of the permanent members of the U.N. Security Council to make the necessary arrangements for the peace conference and for a more flexible policy toward Israel.

A second major area of continuity between Gorbachev and his predecessors was Moscow's unwillingness to challenge either American or Israeli military actions in the region in such a way as to provoke a direct confrontation. Thus just as Brezhnev did not oppose the Israeli invasion of Lebanon in 1982 or the American troop deployment there, and Andropov did not come to Syria's aid when its troops in Lebanon were attacked by U.S. forces in December 1983, so too Gorbachev stood by while American planes twice bombed Libya in 1986.

In each of these cases, Moscow sent weapons to the targeted group before the military action occurred (artillery to the PLO in Lebanon; SAM 5s and SS-21s to Syria; and SAM 5s to Libya), but this increased military commitment did not deter the attacks and may actually have helped precipitate the Israeli invasion of Lebanon in 1982 and the U.S. attacks on Libya in 1986.

A third area of continuity was Moscow's unwillingness fully to back either Syria or the PLO during their many confrontations. Brezhnev, during the Lebanese civil war in 1976, was caught between Assad and Arafat; so was Andropov in 1983 when Syrian forces were pushing Arafat out of Lebanon; and so too was Gorbachev during the camps' wars of 1985 and 1986–87 when the Lebanese Shiite militia, Amal, which was supported by Syria, sought to prevent Arafat's followers from reestablishing their positions in Lebanon. The most Moscow was able to do in each of these situations was to urge a PLO-Syrian reconciliation.

A fourth major area of continuity was Moscow's continuation of its

zero-sum game competition for influence with the United States in the
Middle East, despite all the talk about "new thinking" and "balance of
interests" in Moscow in solving the problems of the Third World. This
continuity is particularly evident when one examines Soviet policy
toward the Iran-Iraq war under Gorbachev. Like his predecessors,
Gorbachev tried—and failed—to end the Gulf war, which caused numerous problems for Soviet strategy in the Middle East. The cease-
fire that ended the war in August 1988 was the result of Iranian
war weariness and defeats on the battlefield, not Soviet diplomacy,
although the weaponry supplied to Iraq by the USSR played a role in
the Iranian decision to accept a cease-fire. To be sure, Gorbachev
demonstrated more diplomatic flexibility than his predecessors in dealing with Iran, although it is an open question whether he was any
more successful. Thus in 1986, Iran made a series of gestures to the
USSR which Moscow eagerly reciprocated, only to learn that Iran had
exploited the Soviet drive for influence to mount major offensives
against Iraq. Moscow then sought to exploit the Iran-Contra crisis by
denouncing Iran and championing the Arabs against it, going so far
as to agree to charter three Kuwaiti tankers. Once the United States
took a major initiative to redeem itself for Iran-Contra by reflagging
eleven Kuwaiti tankers and building up its naval armada in the Gulf,
however, Moscow switched positions again, trying to exploit the rise
in U.S-Iranian tension to enhance its own position in Tehran. Its peace
initiative of July 3, which was full of anti-American propaganda, and
its efforts to delay the imposition of U.N. sanctions against Iran clearly
reflected the pro-Iranian bias in its policy. Moscow's policy alienated
the Arab states of the Gulf but won it very little new influence in Iran.
Indeed, relations between the Soviet Union and Iran appeared to fall
to their lowest point since Gorbachev took power, when, in March
1988, the Iranian leadership blamed Moscow for supplying Iraq with
the missiles it used to bombard Tehran, although Soviet-Iranian relations were to improve once the war came to an end. In any case, the
overtly anti-American policy of the USSR in the Gulf from the U.S.
reflagging of Kuwaiti tankers in July 1987 to the cease-fire one year
later would appear to make a mockery of Soviet efforts to demonstrate
"new thinking" in the solution of such Third World crises as the Iran-
Iraq war.

   Although there were major areas of continuity in Soviet policy toward the Middle East, there was (in addition to an attempt to improve
Soviet-Egyptian relations) one major new initiative under Gorbachev—a clear change in Soviet policy toward Israel. Thus there was a
sharp upsurge in Soviet Jewish emigration, reaching 3,652 in December 1988, the highest monthly total since 1981. In addition, all the

prisoners of Zion were released from jail, and some were permitted to go to Israel. Finally, Moscow stepped up its formal diplomatic contacts with Israel. This process began in July 1985 with a secret meeting between Israeli and Soviet ambassadors to France and continued in 1986 with public consular-level talks in Helsinki, Finland, in August and an extended meeting between Peres and Soviet Foreign Minister Shevardnadze, at the United Nations in September. The pace of contacts increased in 1987 with numerous meetings between Soviet and Israeli officials, culminating in April with a six-hour meeting between Peres and the Soviet delegation to the Socialist International Department, Karen Brutents. Moscow's dispatch of a consular delegation for a prolonged visit to Israel in July 1987 and its permitting Warsaw Pact allies Poland and Hungary to reestablish diplomatic relations with Israel, albeit at the low level of diplomatic interest sections, were other signals of its interest in improving relations with Israel, as were Shevardnadze's meeting with Shamir in New York in June 1988 and Moscow's willingness to receive an Israeli consular delegation in July 1988 and its promise to resume diplomatic relations with Israel once a peace conference got under way.

To explain these changes under Gorbachev, two major factors seem most important—Middle East politics and Soviet-American relations. When Gorbachev took office, the Middle East peace process appeared to be well under way as a result of the Hussein-Arafat agreement of February 1985 and U.S. efforts to broker a Palestinian-Jordanian negotiating team acceptable to Israel. Consequently, Gorbachev, a far more flexible leader than his predecessors, felt an opening to Israel was necessary for Moscow to enter the peace process from which it had been excluded since 1973. Although the peace process came to a halt because of the rise in Middle East terrorism and the break between Hussein and Arafat, Moscow continued its contacts with Israel, in part because it was seeking Israeli support for an international peace conference, which Gorbachev, like his predecessors, felt was the best way to resolve the Arab-Israeli conflict (and enhance the Soviet position in the Middle East in the process), and in part because Moscow, seeing an escalation of Syrian-Israeli tension resulting from Syria's involvement in terrorist attacks against Israeli aircraft, may have wished to deter a possible Israeli attack on Syria. By the fall of 1986, the threat of a Syrian-Israeli war had receded, but Moscow saw the opportunity to go on the diplomatic offensive in the Middle East when the Iran-Contra scandal dealt a major blow to the U.S. position in the region. Consequently, Gorbachev stepped up Soviet efforts to convene an international conference on the Middle East, and these efforts involved expanded contacts with Israel.

Fortunately for Moscow, Soviet interests in convening an international conference were reciprocated by Peres, who saw in such a meeting, particularly after he stepped down as prime minister, a means of
bringing down the National Unity government and moving Israel to
new elections. Yet in advocating such a conference and claiming that
important changes had taken place in Soviet policy, such as its promise
not only not to allow an international conference to impose a settlement on Israel but also to take Israeli interests into consideration at
the conference, Peres left open a series of questions to which the
Soviets, in speaking to different audiences (Israeli, Arab, U.S.) had
given very ambiguous answers. To be sure, Gorbachev had now promised to settle the issue of reestablishing diplomatic relations with Israel
once the international conference had begun. This was a considerable
change from previous Soviet positions, which had gone so far as to
refuse to consider reestablishing diplomatic relations until after Israel
had withdrawn from all occupied territories. In addition, Gorbachev's
public comments to Israel's most implacable enemies, Syrian President
Hafiz Assad, to whom the Soviet leader urged a political (not military)
settlement of the Arab-Israeli conflict and who was told that the lack of
Soviet-Israeli diplomatic relations was "abnormal," and Yasser Arafat,
who was told that recognition of Israel and concern for its security
would have to be part of any peace settlement, could be pointed to by
Peres as significant changes in Soviet policy. The Israeli foreign minister could also point to the increase in Jewish emigration, the release
of prisoners of Zion, and the reestablishment of interest section diplomatic relations with two of Moscow's East European clients, Poland
and Hungary, the latter of which Peres paid a formal visit to in May
1988—the first such visit by an Israeli leader to a Soviet client state
since the 1967 war. Nonetheless, despite these moves, the Soviet Union
continued to take an ambiguous position on two of the key questions
involved in the peace process. First, would Moscow be satisfied with
merely a formal role at the international conference or would it demand the right for the conference as a whole to approve any
agreements reached in the bilateral or multilateral talks between Israel
and her neighbors? The Soviet Union's change in terminology from
calling for an "authoritative" conference to calling for an "effective"
conference does not end its ambiguity on this question. Second, would
Moscow back PLO representation at the conference, which to Israel
was still anathema? Having invested a considerable amount of effort
in helping bring some of the disparate factions of the PLO back
together, and given the increased prestige of the PLO because of the
Palestinian Intifada (uprising) in the occupied territories, it appeared
unlikely that Moscow would throw away the political capital it had

gained in the organization by excluding it from an international conference, particularly after the Palestine National Council's vote for a two-state solution in November 1988 and the beginning of the U.S.-PLO dialogue in December 1988. Indeed, Gorbachev's comments at the postsummit press conference in June 1988 that the Palestinians themselves and the other Arabs would decide Palestinian representation seemed to be a tactical deflection of the question, as did his call for Palestinian "self-determination" rather than for a Palestinian state. The ambiguity of the situation fitted Moscow's goals perfectly; so long as there was no conference, it could continue to pursue a variety of policy options simultaneously (Israel, PLO, Arab states) without having to commit to anyone, while giving the impression of being actively involved in the peace process, a policy that was calculated to bring Moscow dividends not only in the Middle East but in the United States as well. This was the case because Moscow's opening to Israel, along with its policy toward Soviet Jewry in 1987 and 1988, seemed aimed at influencing public opinion in the United States.

Following the CPSU party conference in February 1986, with his position in the party reinforced, Gorbachev set about to undertake major economic and political reforms in the USSR. To succeed in his program, however, particularly at a time of declining hard currency earnings because of the drop in oil prices, Gorbachev clearly wanted to slow down the arms race to free resources for Moscow's lagging economy. He was also interested in getting credits from the United States, as well as investments in joint enterprises, and this necessitated changes in the Jackson-Vanik and Stevenson amendments. Because Moscow had long overestimated Jewish influence in the United States and understands the close tie between American Jewry and the state of Israel, Soviet gestures to Israel, coupled with the increased exodus of Soviet Jews, seemed aimed at improving the Soviet image in the United States for arms control purposes and to position Moscow for U.S. trade benefits. Indeed, the invitation to National Conference on Soviet Jewry President Morris Abram to visit Moscow and his willingness to support changes in the Jackson-Vanik and Stevenson amendments if the Soviet Jewish exodus increased indicated that Moscow was actively using the issue of Soviet Jewry (as well as the appearance of an improved relationship with Israel) to improve its standing in the United States.

In sum, however, though Moscow has demonstrated considerable diplomatic flexibility in dealing with Israel and with the Iran-Iraq war during the period since Gorbachev took power in March 1985, there appears still to be far more continuity than change in Soviet policy toward the Middle East. Increased diplomatic flexibility does not nec-

essarily mean substantive policy change, and Moscow, under Gorbachev, shows no sign of changing its basic goals in the region or many
of the means used to achieve them. The region remains a central area
of U.S.-Soviet competition in the Third World, and the so-called new
thinking in Soviet foreign policy has not yet penetrated very far into
its activities in the Middle East.

Notes

1. The main representatives of this school of thought are Dennis Ross and
Uri Ra'anan. See, for example, Ross, "The Soviet Union and the Persian Gulf,"
Political Science Quarterly 99 (Winter 1984–85): 615–35.
2. The main representatives of this school are Galia Golan and George
Breslauer. See Golan, *Yom Kippur and After: The Soviet Union and the Middle
East Crisis* (London: Cambridge Univ. Press, 1977), and Breslauer, "Soviet
Policy in the Middle East, 1967–1972: Unalterable Antagonism or Collaborative Competition?" in *Managing U.S.-Soviet Rivalry: Problems of Crisis Prevention,*
ed. Alexander L. George (Boulder, Colo.: Westview Press, 1981), pp. 65–105.
3. See Robert O. Freedman, *Soviet Policy Toward the Middle East since 1970,*
3d ed. (New York: Praeger, 1982).
4. These readmissions were reported in the *Washington Post,* Feb. 3, 1985,
and the *Jerusalem Post,* Aug. 6, 1985, respectively.
5. The arms agreement is mentioned in a report by Jonathan Randal,
Washington Post, Jan. 7, 1985. Jordan's difficulties in obtaining weapons from
the United States, which escalated in 1985 because of the American Congress's
opposition, helped Hussein keep open his options with the USSR.
6. For a Soviet evaluation of the "evils" of the Numayri regime and its
initial hopes for the new Sawar-Dahab government, see V. Bochkaryov,
"Exit Nimeri: What Happens Now?" *New Times* (Moscow), no. 17, 1985, pp.
10–11.
7. Kaddafi was the first foreign head of state to visit Sudan's new government. See reports by Christopher Dickey, *Washington Post,* Apr. 16, July 9,
1985; Clifford D. May, *New York Times,* July 10, 1985; Bill Keller, *New York
Times,* Aug. 1, 1985; and Neil Chase, *Washington Post,* Aug. 16, 1985.
8. See *Pravda,* Jan. 16, 1985, and Dmitry Volsky, "Behind the Prosective
Israeli Pull-out from Southern Lebanon," *New Times,* no. 5, 1985, pp. 14–15.
9. Arafat was quoted on Rabat (Morocco) Domestic Service in Arabic, Aug.
7, 1985 (*Foreign Broadcast Information Service: Middle East and South Asia* [hereaf-
ter *FBIS:ME*], Aug. 8, 1985, p. A-4).
10. This was the usual term Moscow employed to decry intra-Arab conflict.
11. See reports by John Kifner, *New York Times,* May 25, June 12, 1986,
and *New Times,* no. 23, 1985, p. 15.
12. There was a report in *al-Ray al-Am* on June 4, 1985, that Moscow has
sent a "strongly worded" message to Amal leader Nabih Berri (*FBIS:ME,* June
7, 1985, p. A-1). As might be expected, Moscow warmly praised the cease-fire
(*Pravda,* June 20, 1985).
13. For an analysis of Soviet behavior in this crisis, see Robert O. Freedman,
"The Soviet Union, Syria and the Crisis in Lebanon," *The Middle East Annual,
1983,* ed. David H. Partington (Boston: G. K. Hall, 1984), pp. 103–57.

14. *Pravda,* June 22, 1985; *Izvestia,* June 24, 28, 1985; Tass, in English, June 19, 1985, and Damascus Domestic Service, in Arabic, June 19, 1985 (*FBIS:USSR,* June 20, 1985, pp. H-1, H-2).

15. *Al-Qabas* (Kuwait) cited in *FBIS:ME,* June 24, 1985, p. i.

16. Reagan press conference, *Washington Post,* Feb. 22, 1985; article by Henry Trewitt, *Baltimore Sun,* Feb. 20, 1985 (the talks were between Assistant Secretary of State Richard Murphy and the head of the Soviet Foreign Ministry's Near East Division, Vladimir Polyakov); report by Bernard Gwertzman, *New York Times,* Feb. 22, 1985.

17. Reports by David Ottaway, *Washington Post,* May 31, 1985, and Jim Hoagland, ibid., June 8, 1985.

18. For an excellent survey of Soviet-Israeli relations, see Arthur J. Klinghoffer, *Israel and the Soviet Union: Alienation or Reconciliation* (Boulder, Colo.: Westview Press, 1985).

19. This is particularly true on the issue of Soviet Jewry. See Robert O. Freedman, "Soviet Jewry and Soviet-American Relations: A Historical Analysis," in *Soviet Jewry in the Decisive Decade, 1971–1980,* ed. Robert O. Freedman (Durham, N.C.: Duke Univ. Press, 1984), pp. 38–67.

20. The denial is in English, July 20, 1985 (*FBIS:USSR,* July 22, 1985, p. H-2); the speech is in Jerusalem Domestic Service, in Hebrew (*FBIS:USSR,* July 19, 1985, pp. H-1, H-2).

21. See comments by Soviet chargé d'affaires in Kuwait, Vladimir Zentchner, as reported in KUNA on July 23, 1985 (*FBIS:USSR,* July 26, 1985, p. H-1), and comments by Leonid Zamyatin, head of the International Information Department of the Communist Party Central Committee, as reported in KUNA, July 27, 1985 (*FBIS:USSR,* July 29, 1985, p. H-1).

22. *Novosti* report, cited in *New York Times,* Aug. 7, 1985. See also Moscow Radio Peace and Progress, in Hebrew, July 22, 1985 (*FBIS:USSR,* July 23, 1985, p. H-3).

23. Report of Peres's comments in article by Michael Eilan, *Jerusalem Post,* July 22, 1985.

24. For analyses of the diplomatic background of the summit, see the articles by Christopher Dickey, *Washington Post,* Aug. 6, 1985, Mary Curtis, *Christian Science Monitor,* Aug. 7, 1985, and Judith Miller, *New York Times,* Aug. 7, 1985. For a description of the issues concerning Moscow, see O. Fomin "The Casablanca Summit," *New Times,* no. 34, 1985, pp. 10–11; *Pravda,* Aug. 7, 1985; and Tass report, in English, Aug. 8, 1985 (*FBIS:USSR,* Aug. 9, 1985, p. H-1).

25. Article by Jean Gueyras, *Le Monde,* Aug. 11, 1985, quoted in *Manchester Guardian Weekly,* Aug. 25, 1985.

26. *Manama Wakh,* in Arabic, Aug. 8, 1985 (*FBIS:ME,* Aug. 8, 1985, p. A-8).

27. Fomin, "Casablanca Summit."

28. Moscow Radio, in Arabic, "Window on the Arab World" (Alexander Timoshkin), Aug. 10, 1985 (*FBIS:USSR,* Aug. 12, 1985, p. H-1). For a background analysis of this development, see the report by Thomas Friedman, *New York Times,* Oct. 18, 1985. A preliminary version of the agreement was broadcast over Israeli radio on October 5, 1985. Poland, which also wished to influence U.S. Jewish opinion, had its own reasons for making this move, but it could not have done so at that time without Moscow's approval.

29. Quote in *Jerusalem Post,* Oct. 6, 1985. See reports by Michael Eilan and

Joshua Brilliant, *Jerusalem Post*, Oct. 31, 1986, and Judith Miller, *New York Times*, Oct. 26, 1985. The rumor was renewed after a December 1985 visit by Bronfman to the Soviet capital (*Washington Post*, Dec. 23 and 24, 1985). Bronfman was closer to Prime Minister Peres than to Foreign Minister Shamir, who often took a dim view of the World Jewish Congress president's quasi-diplomatic activities.

30. On the rise in terrorism, see the report by Thomas L. Friedman, *New York Times*, Oct. 3, 1985. A major seaborne attack on Israel in late April, authorized by Arafat's deputy Khalil Wazir (Abu Jihad) was prevented when the Israeli navy sank the PLO ship carrying the guerrillas (G. Jefferson Price, *Baltimore Sun*, Apr. 23, 1985, and Reuters, *Jerusalem Post*, May 10, 1985).

31. Reports by Christopher Dickey, *Washington Post*, Sept. 27, 1985, Bernard Gwertzman, *New York Times*, Aug. 27, 1985, and David Ottaway, *Washington Post*, Apr. 16, 20, 1985. Algeria was, of course, also interested in driving a diplomatic wedge between Morocco and the United States, which shared Algeria's displeasure with the 1984 Libyan-Moroccan treaty.

32. Moscow International Service, in Arabic, Oct. 2, 1985 (*FBIS:USSR*, Oct. 4, 1985, p. H-3).

33. Report by David Hirst, *Manchester Guardian Weekly*, Nov. 3, 1985.

34. To make matters worse for the PLO, Farouk Kaddumi claimed at the United Nations that there was no evidence of Klinghoffer's murder. For the British agreement see Associated Press report, *Washington Post*, Sept. 21, 1985; *FBIS:ME*, Oct. 15, 1985, p. i, and Oct. 16, 1985, p. i; and report by Jo Thomas, *New York Times*, Oct. 15, 1985. It was rumored that Hussein was seriously considering dropping Arafat (report by John Kifner, *New York Times*, Oct. 27, 1985).

35. Report by Nora Boustany, *Washington Post*, Oct. 3, 1985. Gorbachev was asked during a Paris news conference whether Moscow was as helpless as Western states in dealing with Beirut kidnappings (*Pravda*, Oct. 5, 1985).

36. Reports by John Kifner, *New York Times*, Oct. 1, 1985, and Ihsan Hijazi, ibid., Oct. 2, 1985.

37. Reports by Ihsan Hijazi, *New York Times*, Oct. 5, 31, 1985, Nora Boustany, *Washington Post*, Oct. 5, 1985; Reuters report, *Jerusalem Post*, Oct. 22, 1985; reports by Elaine Sciolino, *New York Times*, Dec. 10, 1985; and Michael Berlin, *Washington Post*, Dec. 19, 1985.

38. Report by Bernard Gwertzman, *New York Times*, Oct. 31, 1985.

39. Report by Walter Ruby, *Jerusalem Post*, Nov. 17, 1985. Vlasov was the deputy Soviet spokesman at the summit. Yevgeny Primakov made the same point at another press conference in Geneva (KUNA, Nov. 16, 1985 [*FBIS:USSR*, Nov. 18, 1985, p. H-7]).

40. Quoted in report by Asher Wallfish, *Jerusalem Post*, Nov. 19, 1985.

41. Report in *Jerusalem Post*, Dec. 4, 1985. The head of the Soviet delegation to the Israeli Communist Party Conference, Mikhail Menashev, however, said Herzog's attendance would not influence Russia's policy on the exit of Soviet Jews or hasten the renewal of diplomatic ties (*Jerusalem Post*, Dec. 8, 1985).

42. Reports by Ihsan Hijazi, *New York Times*, Nov. 20, 1985, and by David Ottaway, *Washington Post*, Nov. 8, 1985. For the text of Reagan's speech, see *New York Times*, Oct. 25, 1985.

43. Arafat was particularly suspicious. See report by Ihsan Hijazi, *New York Times*, Nov. 20, 1985.

44. Moscow Radio International Service, in Arabic, Nov. 17, 1985 (*FBIS:USSR*, Nov. 19, 1985, "Reportage on the Reagan-Gorbachev Summit," p. 3).

45. Report by Bob Woodward and Lou Cannon, *Washington Post*, Dec. 21, 1985.

46. *Pravda*, Oct. 16, 1985 (*FBIS:USSR*, Oct. 16, 1985, p. H-3). ibid., Oct. 13, 1985 (*FBIS:USSR*, Oct. 15, 1985, p. H-6).

47. See report by Bob Woodward, *Washington Post*, Nov. 3, 1985.

48. Report in *New York Times*, Apr. 3, 1985; Reuters report, *Washington Post*, Apr. 13, 1985. Kaddafi denied hosting the radio station but praised its message, and the available evidence indicates that it was located in Libya.

49. Quoted in report by Bob Woodward and Lou Cannon, *Washington Post*, Dec. 21, 1985.

50. Reports by Thomas L. Friedman, *New York Times*, Nov. 20, 1985, William Claiborne, *Washington Post*, Dec. 16, 27, 1985, and *New York Times*, Dec. 27, 1985; Moscow Radio, in French, to Maghreb states, Dec. 28, 1985 (*FBIS:USSR*, Dec. 30, 1985, pp. H-2, H-3); reports by Christopher Dickey, *Washington Post*, Apr. 29, 1985, and Hirsh Goodman, *Jerusalem Post*, May 8, 1985.

51. See Norman Cigar, "South Yemen and the USSR: Prospects for the Relationship," *Middle East Journal* (Autumn 1985): 782–83.

52. See Mark N. Katz, "Civil Conflicts in South Yemen," *Middle East Review* 19 (Fall 1986): 7–13; and David Pollock, "Moscow and Aden: Coping with a Coup," *Problems of Communism* 35 (May–June 1986): 50–70.

53. Associated Press report, Dec. 5, 1986, cited in Bohdan Nahaylo, "The USSR and South Yemen One Year after the January Events," *Radio Liberty Report* 72/87 (Feb. 23, 1987): 1.

54. Tass, Feb. 10, 1987, cited in ibid., p. 4.

55. For the text of Gorbachev's speech, see *Pravda*, Feb. 26, 1986. His foreign policy emphasis was on Soviet-American, Soviet-European, and Soviet-Asian relations, in that order.

56. For an analysis on Soviet-Libyan relations at the time of the U.S.-Libyan clashes, see Robert O. Freedman, "U.S.-Libyan Crisis—Moscow Keeps Its Distance," *Christian Science Monitor*, Apr. 24, 1987.

57. Quoted in report by Celestine Bohlen, *Washington Post*, Mar. 26, 1986.

58. For an analysis of the events leading up to the Soviet-Israeli talks, see the article in the *Jerusalem Post*, Aug. 5, 1986. The Soviet warning to Libya and Syria came during visits to Moscow by Syrian Vice-President Abdel Khaddam and Libya's No. 2 leader, Abdel Jalloud, in May.

59. Moscow was less happy, however, at King Hussein's crackdown on Jordan's Communist party and his arrest of leaders of the Jordan-Soviet Friendship Society, which the USSR may have feared might be the first step to a deal with Israel (*Pravda*, May 29, 1986).

60. For the Soviet view of the talks, see the Tass report, in English, Aug. 19, 1986 (*FBIS:USSR*, Aug. 20, 1986, p. CC-1). For the Israeli view, see Helsinki Domestic Service, in Finnish, Aug. 18, 1986 (*FBIS:ME*, Aug. 19, 1986, p. I-1), and Tel Aviv, Israeli Defense Forces Radio, in Hebrew, Aug. 18, 1986 (*FBIS:ME*, Aug. 19, 1986, pp. I-1, I-2).

61. See the report by Bernard Gwertzman, *New York Times*, Sept. 23, 1986. In his U.N. speech, Shevardnadze noted that Israel owed its existence "to, among others, the Soviet Union," and reiterated Moscow's call for a preparatory committee "set up within the framework of the Security Council to do

the necessary work for convening an international conference on the Middle East."

62. See John Tower, Edmund Muskie, and Bren Scowcraft, *The Tower Commission Report* (New York: Times Books, 1987), esp. pp. 36–39.

63. See report in *Washington Post*, Feb. 5, 1986.

64. For a survey of Soviet-Iranian interactions in 1987, see Bohdan Nahaylo, "Moscow and Tehran: Cultivating Mutual Interests Without Budging on Political Differences," *Radio Liberty Report*, no. 47/87, Feb. 3, 1987.

65. For the text of the Soviet statement, see *Izvestia*, Jan. 9, 1987 (*FBIS:USSR*, Jan. 9, 1987, p. H-1). On January 16, *Izvestia* condemned Iran for "stubbornly rejecting" appeals for a cease-fire and insisting on "war until victory" and replacing the Iraqi regime.

66. *Pravda*, Jan. 29, 1987. On February 15, 1987, *Izvestia* reported Gromyko's criticism of Iran's policy on the war and its aid to the Afghan rebels.

67. For a background analysis of Soviet policy toward Khomeini's Iran, see Robert O. Freedman, "Soviet Policy Toward the Persian Gulf from the Outbreak of the Iran-Iraq War to the Death of Konstantin Chernenko," in *U.S. Strategic Interests in the Gulf Region*, ed. William J. Olson (Boulder, Colo.: Westview Press, 1987), pp. 43–80.

68. Tass, Jan. 21, 1987 (*FBIS:USSR*, Jan. 22, 1987, p. H-1); *Izvestia*, Feb. 16, 1987.

69. Quoted in report by Wolf Blitzer, *Jerusalem Post*, Feb. 20, 1987.

70. Report by Benny Morris, Yossi Lempkowicz, and David Horowitz, ibid., Feb. 24, 1987.

71. For the text of this document, see *FBIS:ME*, Mar. 23, 1987, pp. 1–3.

72. Reuters report, *New York Times*, Mar. 20, 1987. In May 1987, 871 Jews, the highest monthly total in six years, left Russia.

73. Quoted in National Conference on Soviet Jewry Report, Apr. 1, 1987.

74. Quoted in report by Walter Ruby and Andy Court, *Jerusalem Post*, Apr. 2, 1987.

75. See Jerusalem Radio Domestic Service interview with Soviet Foreign Ministry spokesman Genady Gerasimov, Apr. 2, 1987 (*FBIS:ME*, Apr. 2, 1987, p. I-1). See also the article by Henry Kamm, *New York Times*, Apr. 3, 1987.

76. Report by Joel Greenberg, *Jerusalem Post*, Mar. 27, 1987.

77. Reuters report, *New York Times*, Mar. 29, 1987. China's permanent U.N. representative, Li Luye, met with the director general of the Israeli Foreign Ministry, Abraham Tamir. See also the report by David Landau and Walter Ruby, *Jerusalem Post*, Mar. 29, 1987.

78. Jerusalem Radio Domestic Service interview with Soviet Foreign Ministry spokesman Genady Gerasimov, Apr. 2, 1987 (*FBIS:ME*, Apr. 2, 1987, p. I-1); Jerusalem Radio Domestic Service interview with Peres, Apr. 2, 1987 (*FBIS:ME*, Apr. 3, 1987, p. I-1). Peres noted other changes in Soviet policy, including the release of nearly all the prisoners of Zion, the rise in exit permits from 100 to nearly 500 a month, and Soviet statements in diplomatic meetings that they wanted improved relations with Israel.

79. Jerusalem Radio Domestic Service, Apr. 5, 1987 (*FBIS:ME*, Apr. 6, 1987, p. I-1), and *Jerusalem Post*, Apr. 5, 1987.

80. Quoted in report by John Tagliabue, *New York Times*, Apr. 10, 1987.

81. Jerusalem Radio Domestic Service, Apr. 8, 9, 1987 (*FBIS:ME*, Apr. 9, 10, 1987, pp. I-1, I-3).

82. This information, reported by "sources close to Peres," was discussed

in the *Jerusalem Post*, Apr. 10, 1987, in the report coauthored by Wolf Blitzer, David Horowitz, Jonathan Karp, and Robert Rosenberg.

83. Jerusalem Radio Domestic Service, Apr. 7, 1987 (*FBIS:ME*, Apr. 8, 1987, p. I-3).

84. Report by Lea Levavi and Asher Wallfish, *Jerusalem Post*, Apr. 10, 1987; Israeli Defense Forces Radio interview with Yitzhak Shamir, Apr. 13, 1987 (*FBIS:ME*, Apr. 13, 1987, pp. 1-4–1-5).

85. *Izvestia*, Apr. 27, 1987.

86. For the text of Gorbachev's comments, see *Pravda*, Apr. 25, 1987.

87. Al-Ray al-Am interview with Soviet official Alexander Ivanov (*FBIS: USSR*, June 8, 1987, p. E-5).

88. Quoted in report by Thomas Friedman, *New York Times*, May 8, 1987.

89. Jordan's denial came in a statement by Prime Minister Zaid al-Rifai. The text of the denial was printed in the *Jerusalem Post*, May 5, 1987. According to David Shipler, *New York Times*, May 12, 1987, Jordan had reportedly agreed to a limited role for the USSR in the conference, which would be convened by the secretary general of the United Nations based on U.N. Resolutions 242 and 338. There were widespread rumors that Peres and King Hussein had met secretly in London in April 1987.

90. Report by Glen Frankel, *Washington Post*, May 15, 1987.

91. *Izvestia*, Aug. 11, 1987, and numerous Moscow Radio Peace and Progress Hebrew-language broadcasts to Israel in July and August 1987.

92. Jerusalem television, Aug. 17, 1987 (*FBIS: Near East/South Asia* [hereafter *FBIS:NE/SA*], Aug. 18, 1987, p. AA-1); *Rose al-Yusuf* (Cairo), Aug. 17, 1987 (*FBIS:USSR*, Aug. 20, 1987, p. E-3); Radio Moscow, in Arabic, Aug. 21, 1987 (*FBIS:USSR*, Aug. 24, 1987, p. E-2).

93. *New York Times*, Oct. 2, 1987, reported that Peres demanded full diplomatic relations because of the Soviet Union's importance in world politics. Report by John Goshko, in *Washington Post*, Oct. 1, 1987.

94. Report by Moshe Zaq, *Ma'ariv*, Sept. 28, 1987 (*FBIS:NE/SA*, Oct. 1, 1987, p. 22).

95. *New York Times*, Oct. 13, 1987.

96. Tass, May 25, 1987 (*FBIS:USSR*, May 26, 1987, p. H-1).

97. Tass, June 3, 1987 (*FBIS:USSR*, June 4, 1987, p. E-1).

98. *Izvestia*, June 1, 1987; Moscow World Service, in English, May 20, 1987 (*FBIS:USSR*, May 20, 1987, H-2). See also Moscow Radio, in Persian, to Iran, May 27, 1987 (*FBIS:USSR*, June 9, 1987, p. E-7).

99. *Pravda*, Apr. 30, 1987; Moscow Radio Peace and Progress, in Persian, to Iran, May 8, 1987 (*FBIS:USSR*, May 11, 1987, p. H-3).

100. As part of the "new thinking" being proclaimed in Moscow, Soviet academics and other officials urged the United States to join in efforts to control regional conflicts rather than engage in zero-sum game competition for influence. (See presentation by a Soviet academic delegation headed by Nodari Simoniya, of the Institute of Oriental Studies, and Aleksey Vasiliev, USA-Canada Institute, University of Maryland, Oct. 21, 1987).

101. *FBIS:NE/SA*, June 15, 1987, p. AA-1, and Tehran Domestic Service, in Persian, June 13, 1987 (*FBIS:NE/SA*, June 15, 1987, p. S-1).

102. Tehran Domestic Service, in Persian, June 14, 1987 (*FBIS:NE/SA*, June 15, 1987, p. S-1).

103. Freedman, "Soviet Policy Toward the Persian Gulf."

104. Tehran Domestic Service, in Persian, June 14, 1987 (*FBIS:USSR*, June

15, 1987, p. S-2); Tehran *IRNA*, in English, June 14, 1987 (*FBIS:NEA*, June 15, 1987, p. S-2).

105. Tehran Domestic Service, in Persian, June 15, 1987 (*FBIS:NEA*, June 15, 1987, p. S-3).

106. *Pravda*, July 4, 1987 (trans. in *FBIS:USSR*, July 6, 1987, pp. E-1, E-2).

107. Tehran *IRNA*, in English, July 18, 1987 (*FBIS:USSR*, July 20, 1987, pp. E-3, E-4; the text of the resolution is in *New York Times*, Sept. 25, 1987; *Pravda*, July 22, 1987.

108. Tass, in English, July 22, 1987 (*FBIS:USSR*, July 23, 1987, p. E-1); article by Alexander Bovin, *Izvestia*, July 31, 1987; Radio Moscow, in Arabic, Aug. 1, 1987 (*FBIS:USSR*, Aug. 3, 1987, p. A-4).

109. *Pravda*, Aug. 4, 1987; Tehran Domestic Service, in Persian, Aug. 3, 4, 1987 (*FBIS:NE/SA*, Aug. 4, 1987, pp. S-11, S-12).

110. *Pravda*, Aug. 24, 1987; Tass International Service, in English, Aug. 9, 1987 (*FBIS:USSR*, Aug. 10, 1987, p. A-4); Tass, in English, Aug. 24, 1987 (*FBIS:USSR*, Aug. 25, 1987, p. E-3).

111. Tass, in English, Sept. 8, 1987 (*FBIS:USSR*, Sept. 9, 1987, p. 24); *Pravda*, Sept. 10, 1987. See also Paris AFP, Sept. 10, 1987 (*FBIS:USSR*, Sept. 11, 1987, p. 15). For a somewhat different view of Soviet policy toward the Iran-Iraq war, see Galia Golan, "Gorbachev's Middle East Strategy," *Foreign Affairs* 66 (Fall 1987):57. Golan believes that Moscow took a "fully supportive role" in U.N. efforts to bring about an end to the war.

112. Tehran Domestic Service, in Persian, Sept. 8, 1987 (*FBIS:USSR*, Sept. 9, 1987, pp. 22–23).

113. Moscow Radio, in English, Sept. 23, 24, 1987 (*FBIS:USSR*, Sept. 24, 25, 1987, pp. 35, 37).

114. Report by Michael J. Berlin, *Washington Post*, Oct. 16, 1987.

115. Tass International Service, in Russian, Oct. 1, 1987 (*FBIS:USSR*, Oct. 2, 1987), p. 15; *Izvestia*, Oct. 18, 1987; Tass, in English, Oct. 20, 1987 (*FBIS:USSR*, Oct. 21, 1987, p. 5).

116. *Pravda*, Oct. 21, 1987. The agreement called for the creation of a permanent Soviet-Kuwaiti commission on economic, scientific, and technological cooperation in the areas of oil, pipeline transport, irrigation, trade, health protection, and other fields (Tass, Oct. 15, 1987 (*FBIS:USSR*, Oct. 16, 1987, p. 35).

117. *Pravda*, Oct. 17, 1987.

118. Report by Elaine Sciolino, *New York Times*, Oct. 3, 1987.

119. *Washington Post*, Oct. 31, 1987. Musavi quoted in AP report, *New York Times*, Nov. 6, 1987.

120. For the text of the Amman summit resolutions, see Baghdad INA, in Arabic, Nov. 12, 1987 (*FBIS:NE/SA*, Nov. 13, 1987, pp. 23–25).

121. *Pravda*, Nov. 14, 15, 1987 (the latter trans. in *FBIS:USSR*, Nov. 19, 1987, p. 20).

122. Tass, Nov. 30, 1987 (*FBIS:USSR*, Dec. 1, 1987, p. 7). For a discussion of the U.S. reaction to the Soviet offer, see the reports by David Ottaway, *Washington Post*, Dec. 16, 1987, and David Shipler, *New York Times*, Dec. 29, 1987.

123. Report by Celestine Bohlen, *Washington Post*, Dec. 28, 1987.

124. *Pravda*, Dec. 28, 1987; Tehran television, in Persian, Jan. 8, 1988 (*FBIS:NE/SA*, Jan. 12, 1988, p. 83).

125. On November 10, 1987, the U.N. General Assembly voted 123 to 19

(with 11 abstentions) for the withdrawal of foreign forces from Afghanistan. In 1986, 122 states voted in favor of the troop withdrawal (report by Paul Lewis, *New York Times*, Nov. 11, 1987). The roll-call vote was also reported in the November 11, 1987, issue of the *New York Times*.

126. Moscow, for example, rejected a U.S. plan to have a meeting of Israel and a Palestinian-Jordanian delegation at the Reagan-Gorbachev summit. See Moscow television program "The World Today," October 29, 1987, reiterating Shevardnadze's statement following the October 1987 visit of Shultz to Moscow that "rumors and talk to the effect that the USSR is not supporting the Arabs are fictitious and groundless from start to finish" (*FBIS:USSR*, Nov. 2, 1987, p. 31). See also the report by Thomas L. Friedman, *New York Times*, Nov. 7, 1987; Israeli Defense Forces Radio, in Hebrew, Nov. 19, 1987 (*FBIS:NE/SA*, Nov. 19, 1987, p. 30).

127. Tass, Nov. 24, 1987 (*FBIS:USSR*, Nov. 24, 1987, p. 16).

128. Tass, Oct. 22, 28, 1987 (*FBIS:USSR*, Oct. 23, 29, 1987, pp. 23, 36).

129. Reuters report, *New York Times*, Dec. 28, 1987.

130. Tass, in English, Jan. 4, 1988 (*FBIS:USSR*, Jan. 5, 1988, p. 24).

131. *Pravda*, Dec. 21, 23, 1987 (the latter trans. in *FBIS:USSR*, Dec. 23, 1987, p. 31).

132. *Pravda*, Dec. 20, 24, 1987.

133. Tass, Dec. 28, 1987 (*FBIS:USSR*, Dec. 29, 1987, p. 42), reported a meeting between Vorontsov and a group of Arab diplomats on December 26, 1987, to discuss "the dangerous situation in the Israeli-occupied Palestinian territories."

134. Moscow Domestic Service, Jan. 16, 1988 (*FBIS:USSR*, Jan. 19, 1988. p. 37).

135. Tass, Jan. 26, 1988 (*FBIS:USSR*, Jan. 27, 1988, p. 9); Jerusalem Domestic Service, Jan. 20, 1988 (*FBIS:USSR*, Jan. 20, 1988, p. 19); Gerasimov quoted in Tass, Jan. 19, 1988 (*FBIS:USSR*, Jan. 20, 1988, p. 5). Perhaps as a signal to Moscow, the Israeli Foreign Minister had granted only a one-month extension to the visas of the Soviet consular delegation in December 1987 (interviews at Israeli Foreign Ministry, July 1988, and U.S. embassy, Moscow, Jan. 1988).

136. *Izvestia*, Jan. 22, 1988 (*FBIS:USSR*, Jan. 22, 1988, p. 23).

137. Article by Pavel Demchenko in *Pravda*, Feb. 2, 1988.

138. *Pravda*, Feb. 9, 26, 1988; *Izvestia*, Feb. 6, 1988 (*FBIS:USSR*, Feb. 12, 1988, p. 36).

139. Tass, Feb. 11, 1988 (*FBIS:USSR*, Feb. 18, 1988, p. 24).

140. Tass, International Service, Feb. 19, 1988 (*FBIS:USSR*, Feb. 22, 1988, p. 39).

141. KUNA (Kuwait), Feb. 23, 1988 (*FBIS:USSR*, Feb. 24, 1988, p. 29).

142. Tass, Mar. 18, 1988 (*FBIS:USSR*, Mar. 21, 1988, p. 30). A Tass report on April 4, 1988 (*FBIS:USSR*, Apr. 5, 1988, p. 22) noted that the USSR had no "fundamental objections" to the intermediate steps preferred by the United States, but "such steps can yield a positive result only in the context of a comprehensive settlement."

143. Moscow Domestic Service, Apr. 3, 1988 (*FBIS:USSR*, Apr. 4, 1988, p. 13). See also Reuters report, *Jerusalem Post*, Mar. 31, 1988.

144. Tass, Apr. 9, 1988 (*FBIS:USSR*, Apr. 11, 1988, p. 26).

145. Moscow Domestic Service, Apr. 9, 1988 (*FBIS:USSR*, Apr. 11, 1988, p. 27).

146. AP report, *Jerusalem Post*, Apr. 13, 1988.

147. *Al-Siyasah* (Kuwait), Apr. 26, 1988 (*FBIS:USSR*, May 2, 1988, p. 35).

148. The Mapam visit is mentioned in report by Michael Yudelman, *Jerusalem Post*, Mar. 8, 1988. Three days later, the *Jerusalem Post*, reported a meeting between an Israeli and a Soviet diplomat at the United Nations at which the Soviet diplomat reportedly stated that the PLO terrorist attack on an Israeli bus in early March was a "tremendous mistake" and openly wondered if the PLO had any coherent policy. The radio contact is mentioned in a report by Jonathan Karp, *Jerusalem Post*, Apr. 15, 1988. For a wry comment on the Pugachova tour, see the article by former Refusenik Yosef Begun, *Jerusalem Post*, Apr. 14, 1988, calling for more Israeli artists to tour the USSR. Gorbachev's purpose in allowing tourism may have been to lessen the pressure from Soviet Jews to leave the country permanently.

149. Tass, Apr. 22, 1988 (*FBIS:USSR*, Apr. 25, 1988, p. 38). For the text of the memorandum of agreement, see the *Jerusalem Post*, Apr. 22, 1988.

150. Moscow International Service, in Arabic, Apr. 25, 1988 (*FBIS:USSR*, Apr. 26, 1988, p. 23).

151. Report by Menachem Shalev and Wolf Blitzer, *Jerusalem Post*, Apr. 29, 1988.

152. For a description of the interview, see AP report, *Jerusalem Post*, Apr. 15, 1988. For a description of the Peres visit, which Hungary played down, see the report by Menachem Shalev and Lisa Billig in *Jerusalem Post*, May 10, 1988, and the article by Henry Kamm, *New York Times*, May 10, 1988.

153. Tass, May 12, 1988 (*FBIS:USSR*, May 13, 1988, p. 7).

154. *Jerusalem Post*, May 11, 1988; report by Bernard Josephs, ibid., May 16, 1988.

155. Report by David Remnick, *Washington Post*, June 9, 1988. See also the report by Philip Taubman, *New York Times*, May 18, 1988.

156. For the reported text of this document, see the *Jerusalem Post*, June 10, 1988.

157. Report by Wolf Blitzer, *Jerusalem Post*, May 19, 1988.

158. Jerusalem Post Diplomatic Staff Report, *Jerusalem Post*, May 25, 1988.

159. Report by Glenn Frankel, *Washington Post*, May 25, 1988.

160. Report by Wolf Blitzer, *Jerusalem Post*, May 20, 1988.

161. *Pravda*, June 3, 1988 (*FBIS:USSR*, June 3, 1988, p. 9).

162. Reports by Elaine Sciolino, *New York Times*, June 7, 1988, and Wolf Blitzer, *Jerusalem Post*, June 9, 1988.

163. For the Shamir-Shevardnadze talks, see the reports by Don Oberdorfer, *Washington Post*, June 10, 1988; Elaine Sciolino, *New York Times*, June 10, 1988; and Menachem Shalev, *Jerusalem Post*, June 12, 1988. According to Israeli Foreign Ministry sources, however, Shevardnadze was "disappointed" by his talks with Shamir (interview, Israeli Foreign Ministry, July 1988).

164. Report by Menachem Shalev and Asher Wallfish, *Jerusalem Post*, June 13, 1988; AP report, *New York Times*, July 29, 1988, and report by Gary Lee, *Washington Post*, July 29, 1988. The chief rabbi of the city of Rehovot in Israel, Rabbi Simha Kook, was given a visa to visit the Soviet Union in late June 1988 even though he put on his visa application that the purpose of his visit was to "teach Jewish law and visit synagogues" (*Jerusalem Post*, June 24, 1988).

165. Tehran *IRNA*, in English, Feb. 10, 1988 (*FBIS:NE/SA*, Feb. 11, 1988, p. 56).

166. Tehran Domestic Service, in Persian, Feb. 14, 1988 (*FBIS:NE/SA*, Feb. 16, 1988, p. 61).

167. Tehran television, in Persian, Feb. 12, 1988 (*FBIS:NE/SA*, Feb. 18, 1988, p. 61).

168. Tehran Domestic Service, in Persian, Feb. 18, 1988 (*FBIS:NE/SA*, Feb. 19, 1988, p. 44); Tehran *IRNA*, Feb. 23, 1988 (*FBIS:NE/SA*, Feb. 23, 1988, p. 65).

169. Tehran Domestic Service, in Persian, Feb. 22, 1988 (*FBIS:NE/SA*, Feb. 23, 1988, p. 65). For a description of the demonstrations, see Tehran *IRNA*, Mar. 4, 1988 (*FBIS:NE/SA*, Mar. 4, 1988, p. 55), and *IRNA*, Mar. 6, 1988 (*FBIS:NE/SA*, Mar. 7, 1988, p. 57).

170. Quoted in *FBIS:NE/SA*, Mar. 21, 1988, p. 1.

171. Tehran television, Mar. 24, 1988 (*FBIS:NE/SA*, Mar. 25, 1988, p. 57).

172. Tehran *IRNA*, in English, Mar. 6, 1988 (*FBIS:NE/SA*, Mar. 7, 1988, p. 59).

173. Tehran *IRNA*, Mar. 9, 1988 (*FBIS:NE/SA*, Mar. 9, 1988, p. 60).

174. Tehran *IRNA*, in English, Apr. 14, 1988 (*FBIS:NE/SA*, Apr. 15, 1988, p. 55).

175. Tass, Apr. 20, 1988 (*FBIS:USSR*, Apr. 20, 1988, p. 12); Tass, in English, Apr. 20, 1988 (*FBIS:USSR*, Apr. 21, 1988, p. 3).

176. Tass, in English, Apr. 19, 1988 (*FBIS:USSR*, Apr. 20, 1988, p. 13).

177. Moscow Radio Peace and Progress, Apr. 25, 1988 (*FBIS:USSR*, Apr. 26, 1988, p. 22); ibid., May 12, 1988 (*FBIS:USSR*, May 13, 1988, p. 17).

178. *Kayhan International*, June 27, 1988 (*FBIS:NE/SA*, July 13, 1988, p. 54).

179. Moscow Radio, in English, July 7, 1988 (*FBIS:USSR*, July 8, 1988, p. 29); *Pravda*, July 15, 1988; *Krasnaya Zvezda*, July 10, 1988 (*FBIS:USSR*, July 14, 1988, p. 5).

180. See Khomeini's statement, Tehran Domestic Service, July 20, 1988 (*FBIS:NE/SA*, July 21, 1988, pp. 41–53). See also James Bill, "Why Tehran Finally Wants a Gulf Peace," *Washington Post*, Outlook Section, Aug. 28, 1988.

181. Moscow Radio, in Persian, July 18, 1988 (*FBIS:USSR*, July 20, 1988, pp. 22–23).

182. Tehran *IRNA*, July 21, 1988 (*FBIS:NE/SA*, July 22, 1988, p. 48).

183. *Pravda*, Nov. 19, 1988. Gerasimov gave a legalistic argument for the Soviet Union's limited recognition, stating, "our practice knows no precedents when a state would be recognized while its territory was under foreign occupation and which had no government at the moment of recognition" (Tass, Nov. 24, 1988 [*FBIS:USSR*, Nov. 25, 1988, p. 5]).

184. *Pravda*, Dec. 18, 1988.

2

U.S. Policy and the Middle East, 1985–1988

The Impact of the Iran-Contra Affair

Barry Rubin

U.S. Middle East policy during the Reagan administration's second term dealt with continuing regional crises when opportunities seemed to arise for making progress. One pair of initiatives involved the Persian Gulf—the Iran arms deal and the reflagging of tankers. Diplomatic activity on the Arab-Israeli conflict primarily occurred in two periods—the 1985–86 diplomacy arising from the Jordan-PLO joint communique and the 1987–88 efforts following the development of a Palestinian Arab uprising in the West Bank and Gaza Strip.

The Iran Arms Deal Controversy

The Reagan administration followed a consistent policy on the Iran-Iraq war from the time it took office in 1981—official neutrality combined with a tilt toward Iraq. This posture avoided entanglement in the fighting, kept open the possibility of future rapprochement with Iran, and reduced the chance that Iran would be pushed into an alliance of convenience with Moscow. Some U.S. allies, including Egypt, France, Jordan, and Saudi Arabia, aided Iraq whereas others, notably Israel, Pakistan, and Turkey, kept channels to Iran open through overt or covert trade and diplomacy.

The U.S. favoritism of Iraq helped prevent that country's defeat. Washington gave Baghdad trade credits and intelligence. In addition, large amounts of weapons and military training were provided to improve the Gulf Arab monarchies' defense capabilities. No impediment was placed on U.S. allies selling arms to Iraq, but Washington discouraged allies from selling arms to Iran.

As President Reagan began his second term in January 1985, Iran was much on his top advisers' minds. They had an exaggerated fear of a Soviet takeover and more rational concerns that Iran might defeat Iraq and spread Islamic revolution. The White House found particularly frustrating its inability to free American hostages held in Lebanon by Iran-backed terrorists. But the prospect of either rapprochement with Iran or serious retaliation against it seemed most unlikely.

At this unpromising moment in the spring of 1985, Iranian emissaries approached Israel claiming to be moderates with a desire to move their country toward the West. The Israelis passed their Iranian contacts to Washington. Reagan was informed of these initiatives. National Security Council (NSC) consultant Michael Ledeen was sent to meet Manuchehr Ghorbanifar, an Iranian arms merchant, and mid-level officials linked to Majlis speaker Rafsanjani. The Iranians asked to buy arms and promised to arrange the release of American hostages in exchange.[1]

Despite its own arms embargo against Iran, the U.S. government gave permission to Israel to send 504 TOW antitank missiles to Iran in August and September 1985. On September 14, the day of the last shipment, the Reverend Benjamin Weir, an American hostage in Lebanon, was freed.

Hoping to win the release of all the hostages, the U.S. government next approved a shipment of 120 Hawk antiaircraft missiles to Iran. Israel sent the first 18 missiles in November but, because they were not the latest model, the Iranians returned them. Matters were further complicated, however, because Lieutenant Colonel Oliver North of the NSC staff used excess money from Iran's payments to obtain arms for the U.S.-backed Nicaraguan guerrillas, the Contras.

The administration was now split over whether to try again, Secretary of State Shultz and Secretary of Defense Caspar Weinberger opposing any further sales to Iran and National Security Adviser Admiral John Poindexter and CIA Director William Casey supporting them. Reagan signed a "Finding" authorizing the sales; the NSC took over running the program.

In February 1986, the United States sold an additional thousand TOWs to Iran. North also supplied intelligence designed to convince Tehran of a Soviet threat. Additional funds were generated and used for the Contras and other covert operations around the world. But again Iran did not live up to the U.S. expectation that it would free all the remaining hostages.

A third round of exchanges with Iran was attempted beginning in May 1986. Hawk missile parts would be offered to Iran on the condition that all American hostages in Lebanon be released. Robert McFarlane, the former national security adviser, traveled to Tehran with the

first load of Hawks. There he met Iranian officials, albeit at a much
lower level than he had expected. No agreement was reached, and he
judged the mission a failure.

Hopes were reignited when, on July 26, another American hostage,
Father Lawrence Jenco, was released. Although McFarlane had
warned the Iranians that no further arms would be sent, the administration again conceded and sent more Hawk parts after Jenco was
freed.

In September 1986, the NSC began negotiating with a new "Second
Channel," apparently members of another Iranian faction linked to
Prime Minister Musavi. The American negotiators promised to press
the Kuwaiti government to release seventeen imprisoned Shiite terrorists, members of the Iranian-backed al-Dawa group, held for a series
of bombings in December 1983. North and retired General Richard
Secord, handling logistics for the Iran and Contra operations, told the
Iranians that the United States would help them remove Iraqi leader
President Saddam Hussein and would defend Iran against Soviet
aggression. These commitments had not been approved by the president. Five hundred more TOWs were supplied in late October and a
third hostage, David Jacobsen, was released on November 2, 1986.[2]

The President's Special Review Board (the Tower Commission),
investigating the affair, summarized the motive for these activities:

> First, the U.S. government anxiously sought the release of seven U.S.
> citizens abducted in Beirut . . . held hostage by members of Hezbollah, a
> fundamentalist Shiite terrorist group with links to the regime of the
> Ayatollah Khomeini.
>
> Second, the U.S. government had [an] interest in establishing ties to
> Iran. Few in the U.S. government doubted Iran's strategic importance or
> the risk of Soviet meddling in the succession crisis that might follow the
> death of Khomeini. For this reason, some in the U.S. government were
> convinced that efforts should be made to open potential channels to Iran.
>
> Arms transfers ultimately appeared to offer a means to achieve both
> the release of the hostages and a strategic opening to Iran.

The commission concluded that the operation was "directly at odds"
with other important policies, including the administration's stance on
terrorism and the Iran-Iraq war. The hostages became the dominant
concern, surpassing and even contradicting any effort to rebuild the
bilateral strategic relationship. Arms sales created "an incentive for
further hostage-taking [and] could only remove inhibitions on other
nations from selling arms to Iran. This threatened to upset the military
balance between Iran and Iraq, with consequent jeopardy to the Gulf
states and the interests of the West in that region [and] rewarded a
regime that clearly supported terrorism and hostage-taking. They

increased the risk that the United States would be perceived, especially in the Arab world, as a creature of Israel. They suggested to other U.S. allies and friends in the region that the United States had shifted its policy in favor of Iran. They raised questions as to whether U.S. policy statements could be relied upon." And in the end, the offer did not free the hostages.[3]

A separate congressional investigation noted:

—The United States armed Iran, including its most radical elements, but attained neither a new relationship with that hostile regime nor a reduction in the number of American hostages.
—The arms sale did not lead to a moderation of Iranian policies . . . and Iran to this day sponsors actions directed against the United States in the Persian Gulf and elsewhere.
—The United States opened itself to blackmail by adversaries who might reveal the secret arms sales and who, according to North, threatened to kill the hostages if the sales stopped.
—The United States undermined its credibility, with friends and allies, including moderate Arab states, by its public stance of opposing arms sales to Iran while undertaking such arms sales in secret.[4]

The administration maintained that it was acting to gain influence in Iran and to help moderate factions rather than merely to free hostages. On November 13, 1986, Reagan explained in a national address that he had sought "to renew a relationship with the nation of Iran, to bring an honorable end to the bloody six-year war between Iran and Iraq, to eliminate state-sponsored terrorism and subversion, and to effect the safe return of all the hostages. . . . The United States has not swapped boatloads or planeloads of American weapons for the return of American hostages." Instead, he stated, only one planeload of arms had been sent to confirm his negotiators' credentials.[5]

There was overwhelming public disapproval of the affair on a variety of grounds. The administration's behavior blatantly contradicted its own stated policy of not negotiating with terrorists and discouraging other countries from selling arms to Iran. Terrorists would be encouraged to take more hostages; allies would be discouraged from taking a tough line against terrorism and from refusing to provide Iran with weapons.

On strategic grounds, the policy seriously misestimated the Soviet threat to Iran, the state of the Iran-Iraq war, and U.S. interests. On procedural grounds, it was amateurishly implemented; White House lines of authority and decision-making methods were found to be inadequate. Undersecretary of State John Whitehead told a hearing, "We in the State Department found it difficult to cope with the National Security Council's operational activities."[6]

Constitutional objections were raised over the systematic exclusion of Congress from information or involvement in these decisions. The president had even ordered CIA Director William Casey in January 1986 not to submit these covert operations to the congressional intelligence committees for approval. The diversion of money for the Nicaraguan Contras, contrary to Congress's refusal to permit aid, also seemed an act of bad faith. On legal grounds, questions were raised about the use of U.S. funds and weapons, the enrichment of private individuals, and the destruction of official documents.

National Security Adviser John Poindexter and NSC staff member North were ousted on November 25 following disclosure of the diversions. White House Chief of Staff Donald Regan resigned a few weeks later. Hearings were conducted by the specially appointed Tower Commission, a House-Senate committee, and an independent prosecutor. The congressional committee's hearings were televised and widely discussed during the summer of 1987.

The president rejected the more substantive criticisms. "What is driving me up the wall," he complained, "is that this wasn't a failure until the press . . . began to play it up. I told them that publicity could destroy this, that it could get people killed. They then went right on."[7]

The number of American hostages held by terrorists in Lebanon actually increased during the course of the secret U.S.-Iran contacts despite the release of three people in exchange for arms. This fact reinforced the assertion that concessions to terrorists only encouraged them to carry out more attacks. Those still held in 1988 (with the date of kidnapping in parentheses) were Terry Anderson, chief Middle East correspondent for the Associated Press, and Thomas Sutherland, an administrator at the American University in Beirut (1985); Frank Reed, head of the Lebanese International School, and Joseph Cicippio, deputy controller of the American University of Beirut (September 1986); Edward Tracey, an itinerant poet (October 1986); and Professors Allen Steen, Jesse Turner, and Robert Polhill (January 1987).

Many observers felt that the arms-for-hostages deal with Iran made it harder for the United States to urge other countries to take a tough line against terrorism. Earlier, sympathy for Americans held in Lebanon had produced widespread approval for active government efforts to obtain their release. But, according to polls, the Iran affair hardened popular opinion against making concessions to terrorists.

The Iran-Contra scandal was generally regarded as the Reagan administration's most politically costly error.

Deepening Engagement in the Persian Gulf: Reflagging

The U.S. policy of avoiding direct involvement in the Gulf was based both on the desire to avoid entanglement in the Iran-Iraq war and rejection by the local Arab states of an increased U.S. presence, which they feared might be damaging to them.

By 1987, however, the administration believed that new developments warranted a change in strategy. The main U.S. objectives in the region were to block Soviet control or influence; to deter Iran from attacking or fomenting Islamic fundamentalist revolutions; to ensure the export of oil at levels required by the United States and its allies; and to protect Gulf security and friendly regimes.

By the summer of 1987, high U.S. officials believed that these four interests were critically endangered by Kuwait's request that Moscow lease it three ships. Washington reversed its earlier lack of enthusiasm about putting Kuwaiti tankers under the U.S. flag.

The sequence of events was as follows. On November 1, 1986, Kuwait told the Gulf Cooperation Council that it would seek international protection for its tankers. On December 10 the Kuwaitis inquired about the technical requirements for reregistering tankers to fly the U.S. flag. The first query on possible reflagging came on January 13, 1987. About the same time, the United States learned that Kuwait was discussing a similar arrangement with the Soviets.

On January 23, Reagan restated his commitment to maintain the free flow of oil from the Gulf when the White House informed Congress of the proposed sale of a squadron of F-16 fighter planes to Bahrain and of Bradley fighting vehicles to Saudi Arabia. Six days later the State Department told Kuwait that it could reregister the ships and, on February 6, that the United States would protect them. Kuwait applied for reflagging on March 2 and was offered protection five days later. Kuwait agreed on March 10 and the administration informed Congress of the offer on March 12. On April 2, Kuwait formally accepted the offer.[8] The point of these three rounds of exchanges was to work out the agreement between the White House and Kuwait before Congress or the U.S. public was informed.

The administration then stated its case boldly. If the United States did not act, said National Security Adviser Frank Carlucci, our allies "will be faced with either giving in to Iranian intimidation or accepting Soviet offers of protection, and not just for shipping." Secretary of State George Schultz spoke in apocalyptic terms: "The worst thing that can happen to the United States is to be sort of pushed out of the

Persian Gulf. . . . One of the worst things in the world that could happen would be to find the Soviet Union astride the supplies of oil to the free world." President Reagan summed up: "In a word, if we don't do the job, the Soviets will."[9]

Attention was also drawn to the Gulf by a dramatic event on the night of May 17. An Iraqi Mirage fighter plane fired an Exocet missile into the U.S. Navy guided missile frigate *Stark* about seventy miles northeast of Bahrain, resulting in the deaths of thirty-seven crew members. The Iraqi government said the attack was a mistake, and the U.S. government accepted an apology.

The controversy over reflagging took on both procedural and policy aspects. The administration was criticized for not presenting Congress with CIA assessments warning that a U.S. naval presence might lead to armed conflict but providing only the Defense Intelligence Agency's far more optimistic assessment.

In addition, there were questions about whether congressional approval for reflagging was needed and whether the War Powers Act applied. Many legislators felt uncomfortable with the new Gulf policy. In the colorful words of Representative Toby Roth (R., Wisc.), "At best the Persian Gulf is a snakepit and we're going to be bit again." Senator Dale Bumpers (D., Ark.) said, "There's not one member of this body that doesn't know we're courting disaster . . . that a lot of sons aren't going to come back from the Persian Gulf." Even the relatively hawkish Senator Sam Nunn (D., Ga.) said the plan "poses substantial risks" of violent confrontation with Iran. Nunn concluded that the United States had "vital strategic interests" in the Gulf but that they were "not being substantially challenged at this time."[10]

The administration denied that the War Powers Act, which required that the president report to Congress within forty-eight hours when U.S. troops are in danger of hostilities, had jurisdiction in this case. Under the act, he must remove the troops unless Congress approved the military operations within sixty to ninety days. Many Democrats wanted to apply the law to the situation in the Gulf. A Republican filibuster blocked action for several weeks, and the Senate finally refused by a 50 to 41 vote to invoke the act.

But Congress also had tremendous respect for the president's role as commander in chief and fear of appearing indifferent to a Soviet advance in such a critical region. Representative Lee Hamilton (D., Ind.), chairman of the House of Representatives Foreign Affairs Subcommittee on Europe and the Middle East, said: "I think the Congress would approve the President's policy in the Gulf if it was called upon to vote. Part of the reason is that there's no clear alternative."[11] Once convoying began, the committee members largely accepted the argument that the United States could not revoke such a commitment.

The general public took a similar attitude. Asked if they supported a U.S. military presence in the Gulf to protect the free flow of oil, 75 percent of those polled agreed and only 24 percent disagreed. They were less sure of the U.S. ability to defend itself in the Gulf—46 percent had "a great deal of confidence," 42 percent "some confidence," and 12 percent little or none. Asked if the United States should take all possible steps, including the use of force, to ensure an adequate supply of oil, those queried agreed by a 57 to 39 margin. They approved of "U.S. ships escorting those reflagged oil tankers even if the U.S. ships risk being attacked" by only 53 to 44 percent.[12]

Many wondered whether the reflagging and convoying were necessary or beneficial. Even Secretary of the Navy James Webb questioned, in a tough memo, whether it was wise to send a force without clear military objectives. Former Secretary of State Henry Kissinger wrote: "The odd aspect of the crisis is that nothing significantly new has happened. The rate of attacks continues about at the level of last year, when no Western country—including the United States—bothered to protest, and the United States was clandestinely shipping arms to Iran. The best evidence that there is no new threat is that ship insurance rates for the Gulf have not changed appreciably in 1987." Yet despite this lack of urgency, "America thus risks being drawn into an expanded military role that cannot be decisive."[13]

The Soviet threat was also arguably overstated by the administration. Kuwait's apparent strategy was to play off the superpowers against each other, avoiding dependence on either one while trying to align both of them against Iran. When their small gesture set off alarm bells in Washington, even the Kuwaitis seemed bemused. "The United States' problem," commented Sulayman Majid al-Shahin, undersecretary at the Kuwaiti Foreign Ministry, "is that the mentality of Hollywood tends to influence it sometimes. As for Soviet tankers, these have been quietly sailing in the Gulf for some time. So what has changed?"[14]

The second main U.S. objective was to bring the war to an end and thus reduce the possibility that the fighting might spread or that Iran could intimidate the Gulf monarchies. On May 7, 1987, the United States announced its willingness to support sanctions against any country refusing to cooperate in ending the war. On July 20, the U.N. Security Council unanimously passed Resolution 598 calling for a cease-fire, withdrawal of troops to the international boundary, and a political settlement to the war. It seemed likely that another resolution would soon be passed involving sanctions, including an arms embargo, against Iran for refusing to comply.

The Iranians, however, outmaneuvered U.S. diplomacy by pronouncing themselves ready to accept a cease-fire if the United Nations found Iraq responsible for starting the war. Yet because of the continued domination of Khomeini's hard line, this might be only a first step. Once negotiations began, Iran could use Iraq's war guilt as justification for demanding the ouster of Saddam Hussein's regime. Tehran also courted Moscow, persuading the Soviets not to support sanctions. Although the administration repeatedly stated its belief that the Soviets would support the resolution, the Soviets preferred to block the U.S. embargo effort in the hope of gaining influence in Iran.[15]

The third U.S. objective was the continued free flow of oil from the Gulf, which provided about 66 percent of Japan's imported oil and 40 percent of Western Europe's petroleum. Despite the numerous attacks, mainly by Iraqi planes and most often against Iranian-flag boats, and the dozens of seamen killed, ships suffered relatively minor damage and a glut of tankers made shipping companies eager to undertake the Gulf run. Oil prices generally fell, and there was still so much petroleum available that OPEC was hard-pressed to hold down production.

Reflagging Kuwaiti tankers did not greatly contribute to protecting this commerce because U.S. warships ignored Iranian and Iraqi attacks on non-U.S.-flag ships. The administration was far more successful, however, in gaining support from its West European allies. Britain, France, Italy, and other countries followed the U.S. lead by sending naval forces to convoy tankers.

Finally, the administration stressed the need to preserve U.S. credibility. Washington's basic assumption was that the Gulf Arab states would fully cooperate with the United States when persuaded that it was serious and consistent in protecting them. But the Arab states' policy was largely an independent variable based not on a yearning for U.S. guardianship but on the rulers' domestic and regional political requirements. They wanted American help in ending the war without providing too much assistance to the United States or risking their own direct involvement in the war.

Defending the need for credibility, Assistant Secretary of State Richard Murphy argued in his May 1987 congressional testimony that "in the light of the Iran-Contra revelations, we had found that the leaders of the Gulf states were questioning the coherence and seriousness of U.S. policy in the Gulf along with our reliability and staying power. We wanted to be sure the countries with which we have friendly relations—Iraq and GCC states—as well as the Soviet Union and Iran understood the firmness of our commitments."[16]

Murphy also assessed positively the actual operations in the Gulf: "To date, Iran has been careful to avoid confrontations with U.S. flag vessels when U.S. Navy vessels have been in the vicinity. U.S. Military Sealift Command and other commercial U.S. flag vessels have transited the Gulf each month under U.S. Navy escort without incident. We believe that our naval presence will continue to have this deterrent effect. Iran lacks the sophisticated aircraft and weaponry used by Iraq in the mistaken attack on the USS Stark. Moreover, we will make sure in advance that Iran knows which ships have been reflagged and are under U.S. protection."[17]

This situation continued as the Iranians went around the Americans instead of attacking them, mined Kuwaiti and Gulf waters, and used Silkworm missiles to strike at Kuwait and hundreds of small speedboats for stepped-up attacks on tankers flying the flags of countries not participating in the convoys.

The GCC states also continued to evince great doubt about the nature of U.S. credibility in the face of both the superpower conflict and the threat from Iran. For example, the United Arab Emirates paper *Al Wahdah* said that the war must be ended "to ensure that the Gulf is not converted into a U.S. and Soviet arsenal under the pretext of protecting their military presence and strategic interests."[18] Kuwait's ambassador to Washington complained that "Iran is now settling its score with America at the expense of Kuwait." The GCC states were reluctant to offer the United States minimal military facilities even when the U.S. Defense Department said assistance was forthcoming. Kuwait, for example, would not allow minesweeping helicopters to take off from its territory. Nonetheless, the administration drew comfort from the fact that the 1987 Amman Arab summit supported the measures Kuwait was taking in its defense, an implicit endorsement of the U.S. presence.[19]

The GCC's revision of its traditional position opposing the presence of any U.S. warships in the Gulf was, indeed, a dramatic change brought about by the war and fear of Iran. AWACs surveillance planes based in Saudi Arabia and P-3 reconnaissance aircraft taking off from Kuwait provided vital intelligence for the convoys. But the need to base U.S. Sea Stallion mine-hunting helicopters on ships made it harder to clear the obstacles, particularly in the upper Gulf, though Kuwait reportedly allowed a U.S. barge with antiaircraft weapons to moor in Kuwaiti waters. In private conversations, American officials and officers indicated their dissatisfaction with the level of GCC assistance.

The administration's official policy, provided by Defense Secretary Caspar Weinberger, promised that the U.S. protection of ships was "not part of an open-ended unilateral American commitment to defend all

nonbelligerent shipping in the Persian Gulf." Rather, "We're there to
ensure that there will be the free passage of vitally important cargoes
in international waters." As part of the "normal course of patrolling,"
U.S. military forces would "make sure of no additional minelaying"
or attempts "to interfere with the free passage of navigation." Most
important was to ensure "that Iran did not succeed in being dominant
in the Persian Gulf by intimidating and bullying the Gulf states, and
that the Soviet Union did not become, in a sense, the protector of these
vital supply routes."[20]

The first convoy entered the Gulf on July 22. The U.S. Navy force
in the Gulf included eleven warships and seventeen supply, patrol, or
minesweeping craft with about four thousand personnel. Another
sixteen ships, including an aircraft carrier and battleship with twelve
thousand crew members, remained outside the straits. The operation
cost an estimated $15 to 20 million per month.

In a mid-September speech to the United Nations, Reagan called
on Iran to accept a cease-fire "clearly and unequivocally." At the September 25 U.N. Security Council meeting, the Soviet Union blocked
an Anglo-American effort to introduce a mandatory arms embargo
against Iran.[21] Four days earlier, U.S. helicopters sighted the *Iran Ajr*,
an amphibious landing ship, dropping mines in the Gulf fifty miles
northeast of Bahrain in international waters. American forces attacked
and seized the ship. Some twenty-six crew members were captured
and later returned to Iran. Three Iranians were dead and two were
missing. A second military incident took place on October 8, when
U.S. helicopters sank three Iranian gunboats after they allegedly fired
at a helicopter fifteen miles southwest of Iran's Farsi Island. At least
two Iranians were killed. Thereafter, the Iranians were more careful
to avoid impinging on the U.S. rules of engagement that permitted
ships to fire if they determined that an approaching ship or plane had
"hostile intent."[22]

"We do not wish to get into a conflict with the United States and we
say so explicitly," explained Iran's parliamentary speaker Rafsanjani.
American policy makers concluded that this was indeed Iranian policy
but also had to take into account the continuing fiery rhetoric emerging
from Tehran. One Iranian statement, for example, alluded to terrorist
attacks on the U.S. Marines and embassy in Beirut; "We are ready to
repeat the events of Lebanon which resulted in their flight."[23]

On October 17 the reflagged tanker *Sea Isle City* was hit off Kuwait
by an Iranian Silkworm missile. The American captain was wounded.
According to orders governing the convoy, U.S. protection did not
apply within Kuwait's waters. Nevertheless, the attack required some
response. U.S. forces warned Iranian personnel to leave an Iranian oil

platform in the Gulf being used as a communications station and then destroyed it.

The United States thus showed its ability to convoy the eleven ships and to muster support from European allies. But the wider problems remained unsolved. A GCC leader commented, "The whole issue is out of focus when one talks about accompanying or escorting ships. The issue is the war and how to end it." A Saudi official complained that the United States was merely "administering pinpricks." "Hitting small boats doesn't matter. What matters is that the American military presence, in order to be justified by us, must insure our total security by insuring Iran to total paralysis."[24]

Yet this very end was being accomplished by other factors. Iran had no strategy for winning the war militarily: Tehran's troops could achieve no breakthrough, Iraq refused to buckle under the pressure, and Iran itself was undergoing extensive economic and psychological strain.

In this context, the Iranian perception—despite, or because of, its exaggerated worry—that U.S. forces had entered the war on Iraq's side was a further factor. After Iraqi offensives in 1988, increasing numbers of leaders in Tehran proposed to Ayatollah Khomeini that the war be ended. On July 4, 1988, during a U.S.-Iran naval confrontation, an overflying Iranian passenger aircraft was misidentified as a fighter plane and shot down by an American warship with extensive loss of life. The pro-cease-fire forces in Iran used this event to argue that the war must be ended or the United States would escalate attacks on Iran.

Thus U.S. support had reassured the Gulf Arab states, allowing them to protect their own sovereignty and deter Iranian aggression. The U.S. naval presence had strengthened Washington's ties to the GCC states and also played some role in bringing the Iran-Iraq war to an end.

Arab-Israeli Peace Process

The idea of resolving the Arab-Israeli conflict is understandably attractive for U.S. policy makers. Success in negotiating peace would bring great honor on the mediator and simplify the problems for U.S. Middle East policy. U.S. attempts to mediate—and failure to resolve—the Arab-Israeli conflict might seem to produce acrimonious reactions in the area, yet it was still universally acknowledged that only Washington could foster a peaceful settlement.

But the very factors that invite U.S. involvement also make it a complex, frustrating endeavor. In addition to the long, bitter, and entangled conflict, U.S. mediation faces three additional difficulties. First, not only do the Arab states and Israel have conflicting objectives but so do the Arab states themselves. Syria is determined to sabotage negotiations that would allow a Jordanian role on the West Bank or the entrenchment of an independent PLO. King Hussein and Yasser Arafat compete to dominate any future Jordan–West Bank federation. The United States must consider whether concessions to Syria or the PLO—its enemies and Soviet allies—might weaken U.S. allies and strengthen Moscow's regional position.

Second, there are conflicts within each state over its bargaining position and goals. Jordan would like to have the West Bank back but does not want to pay the price of recognizing Israel. Israel wants peace but not at the price of a PLO state that might be more threatening than the current situation, and the Likud prefers to retain the territory. Arafat would like to have his own West Bank state but hesitated to recognize Israel or designate stand-ins for talks because he feared Jordanian domination, Syrian revenge, and a split in his own ranks.

All these difficulties are interlocked. It is hard to envision a diplomatic solution without Syrian participation but almost impossible to see any framework or outcome that would please Damascus and still be acceptable to Israel, Jordan, or the PLO. King Hussein cannot step forward to negotiate without Arafat and, apparently, could not persuade the PLO leader to make concessions either, until the PLO leader, under the pressure of the Intifada, did so in November and December 1988. Consequently, the U.S. government tended to focus on other, more pressing—or promising—areas of the world except when regional developments forced action or gave hope that activism might succeed.

During the Reagan administration's eight years in office, its Middle East policy went through six distinct phases.

From January 1981 to August 1982, the administration downplayed the Arab-Israeli conflict's relative importance to concentrate on Persian Gulf security issues emerging from the Iranian revolution, the outbreak of the Iran-Iraq war, and the Soviet occupation of Afghanistan. Events culminating in the Israeli invasion of Lebanon made a change in focus both necessary and potentially opportune.

From September 1982 to May 1983, the administration pursued an activist policy aimed at settling the Lebanese civil war and the Arab-Israeli conflict. The Reagan plan proposed a Jordanian–West Bank federation as a framework for Palestinian self-determination and suggested that Israel yield territory in exchange for Arab recognition and some border modifications. These U.S. efforts failed. Syria refused to withdraw from Lebanon; Lebanese political factions could not resolve their differences. U.S. Marines in Beirut were killed, provoking domestic criticism. Meanwhile, Israeli Prime Minister Menahem Begin, PLO leader Arafat, and Jordan's King Hussein rejected Reagan's plan.

Disillusioned with these efforts, the administration entered a period of low activity until February 1985. This was a natural course given the recent failures and disillusionment. Only an initiative by regional forces, reasoned U.S. policy makers, would make American involvement worthwhile.

That event came when the February 1985 Jordan-PLO accord ushered in a fourth period. Washington sought formation of a joint Jordanian-Palestinian delegation willing to deal with Israel, creating a basis for direct negotiations that would produce a solution within the context of the Reagan plan. After King Hussein abandoned this effort in February 1986, another lull ensued until the Palestinian Arab uprising in the territories began a sixth era in November 1987, continuing into the administration's final year.

The 1985 Jordan-PLO communique called for an exchange of "land for peace," the acceptance of conditions "cited in U.N. resolutions," total Israeli withdrawal from the West Bank, Palestinian "right to self-determination" but only in the framework of a Jordan-Palestinian confederation, and a joint Jordanian-Palestinian delegation to an international conference.

As soon as the communique was announced, however, individual PLO leaders and the PLO Executive Committee demanded amendments, including a joint delegation of all Arab governments plus the PLO, independence for a PLO-led Palestinian state, criticism of the land for peace formula, refusal to recognize Israel or to accept U.N. Resolutions 242 and 338, and unwillingness to cede representation (even temporarily) to non-PLO Palestinians (even those willing to follow Arafat's orders).[25]

Thus the United States had to explore whether the PLO might accept U.N. Resolutions 242 and 338, negotiate seriously with Israel, abandon the use of terrorism, and agree to recognition of Israel. Arafat seemed too restricted by internal PLO conflicts, Syrian threats, fear of Jordanian control, ideological obsessions, and lack of control over his own organization to take such a major step. He was either seeking U.S. recognition without making concomitant concessions or seeking a stronger position—a military presence in Jordan or control over the West Bank—from which to continue a long-term revolutionary and terrorist campaign against Israel.

Successive U.S. administrations had preferred a Jordanian option precisely because they deemed an independent Palestinian state under Arafat's leadership as contrary to U.S. national interests. Policy makers believed that such a state would not be a stabilizing force in the region and that its revanchist ambitions against Israel or Jordan might bring further, chronic violence. The PLO's long alliance with the USSR and the radical stance of many of its leaders would threaten U.S. interests.

Nonetheless, the United States tried to solve the issue of Palestinian participation by giving the PLO a choice: either Arafat could find a way to indicate his willingness to recognize Israel or he could designate pro-Arafat, but non-PLO, Palestinians to represent his interests in preliminary exchanges.

Hussein and Arafat insisted on an international conference, including the U.N. Security Council members and all relevant Arab states, as the framework for negotiations. Washington and Jerusalem wanted direct negotiations, arguing that an international conference would be doomed to failure. Damascus could be expected to wreck it by pushing the Arab side toward intransigence. Moscow could seek Arab favor and undermine moderates by raising maximalist demands. These considerations had led the Carter and Reagan administrations to abandon a U.S.-USSR-chaired Geneva meeting. Since the major asset for a U.S. policy of reducing Soviet influence was Washington's monopoly as mediator, bringing in Moscow seemed counterproductive.

On a May 1985 visit to Washington, King Hussein presented a comprehensive plan for advancing the process, a blueprint demonstrating both promise and weaknesses:

1. The United States would meet a Jordanian-Palestinian delegation, including Palestinians who were not PLO members but who would take orders from the PLO.

Israel worried that such a step would constitute U.S. recognition of the PLO without any commensurate Arab concession. Israel wanted no PLO members involved and argued that members of the Palestine National Council (PNC) should be counted as such. The administration was willing to meet a group, even including PNC members, but only if there was a guarantee that it would produce progress toward direct negotiations.

Asked to submit the names of potential Palestinian participants, Hussein requested a list from Arafat. The PLO's response in July was disappointing, consisting—even after Jordanian vetting—almost entirely of PLO activists. When Peres accepted two proposed delegates, the PLO withdrew their names. Washington, too, found the PLO-Jordan list contrary to its position and even to Hussein's formula.

2. After a U.S. meeting with a joint delegation, Washington would accept Palestinian self-determination through a confederation with

Jordan. Arafat, according to Hussein, would then announce his willingness to recognize and negotiate with Israel by accepting U.N. Resolution 242. The United States could never obtain PLO confirmation of Hussein's claim. Arafat's top colleagues repeatedly contradicted the king's assertion, making Washington skeptical about PLO intentions and Hussein's ability to deliver on his own plan.

3. After the exchange of recognitions, Hussein proposed another U.S. meeting with a Jordanian-Palestinian delegation that would include PLO officials to discuss the details for an international peace conference. But steps 1 and 2 appeared unlikely to work, and the U.S. government was, in effect, asked to recognize the PLO and accept an international conference without prior assurances of any new PLO policy or eventual direct negotiations.

4. An international conference of the five Security Council members plus Israel, the PLO, Jordan, Egypt, and Syria would convene to make a peace agreement. The United States, opposed to an international conference, preferred that the fourth stage be direct talks between Israel and a Jordanian-Palestinian delegation.

Responding to Hussein's ideas, Israeli Prime Minister Shimon Peres issued a plan on June 11 for a Jordanian-Palestinian-Israeli summit with U.S. participation. The Security Council members would endorse it without participating themselves. The administration thought the gap had narrowed considerably but was still unable to resolve the problems of the joint delegation, PLO recognition of Israel, linkage between Hussein's proposed steps, and direct negotiations even within an international conference. A better offer from Hussein and Arafat was needed, but none was forthcoming.

The administration's hopes were pinned on Hussein's September visit to the United States. It proposed a large arms sale to Jordan if the king gave assurances on his diplomatic intentions persuasive to Congress. Hussein made clear his willingness to accept U.N. Resolutions 242 and 338 and to negotiate with Israel at an international conference that would be an umbrella rather than a substitute for direct talks. But Hussein's visit disappointed the administration. He brought no new ideas for resolving the impasse on the joint delegation and would not publicly end the state of belligerency with Israel. The peace process seemed stalled after eight months of intensive efforts. When Congress postponed considering an arms sale, the White House did not forcefully object.

Meanwhile, a dramatic series of events involving terrorism further stymied an already staggering peace process. In June 1985, Shiite fundamentalist hijackers seized a U.S. airliner and took it to Beirut. An

American passenger was murdered and thirty-nine others were held for seventeen days. The hijackers demanded that Israel free Shiite militiamen and terrorists captured in southern Lebanon. But Israel was already in the process of releasing them, and the real issue seemed a battle among Shiite groups to claim the credit. Although officially continuing to refuse concessions to terrorists, the administration urged Israel to release the prisoners. The hostages were then let go.

The crisis showed the nation's fixation with terrorism. Media coverage reached unprecedented proportions, and polls showed that most Americans wanted the hostages freed even it meant giving in to terrorist demands.

The U.S. response to Libyan support for terrorism was more direct. Libya was implicated in the December 1985 machinegunning of passengers at the Rome and Vienna airports. In March 1986, Libyan forces attacked U.S. naval maneuvers in the Gulf of Sirte. In the ensuing confrontation, Libyan patrol boats were sunk and onshore radar installations were destroyed. After a bomb on a TWA plane killed four Americans over Greece and one in a West Berlin discotheque killed a U.S. soldier, the Reagan administration retaliated by bombing Libyan installations and Kaddafi's personal compound in April 1986.

A series of terrorist attacks in September and October 1985 had a direct effect on the peace process. After the brutal September 25 murder of three Israelis in Cyprus, Israeli planes bombed PLO offices in Tunisia on October 1. Six days later, terrorists from a PLO group hijacked the Italian cruise ship *Achille Lauro*, murdering an elderly, crippled American. U.S. fighter planes later forced an Egyptian airliner carrying the terrorists to land in Italy, where the three terrorists were tried and convicted, although the leader, Mohammed Abbas, was allowed to leave.

The *Achille Lauro* affair made the PLO seem less attractive as a negotiating partner and less credible as a moderate force. A planned meeting between a joint Jordan-PLO delegation and Great Britain, which seemed like a dress rehearsal for the long-awaited U.S. meeting, fell through after the PLO refused to authorize its delegates to sign a statement implying willingness to recognize Israel.

Chances for a breakthrough dimmed considerably, even after Peres conceded that direct talks could be held in conjunction with an international forum and hinted that he would accept PLO delegates if that group's policy changed.

Following King Hussein's announcement that the joint communique initiative was dead, the administration entered a fifth period. Negative experiences with the region in general and with the peace process in particular made the White House feel that the area was a patch of quicksand. The lack of clear opportunities or clear dangers coupled with the urgency of other issues pushed the Middle East onto the back burner.

Both Peres, now Israel's foreign minister, and Egyptian President Hosni Mubarak pressed for an international conference, forcing the United States to consider the idea more seriously if not enthusiastically. Thus, beginning in February 1987, Reagan and Schultz spoke of considering an international conference as a way to stimulate direct talks. In June, Shultz agreed to invite Soviet participation in such a project. He suggested that the U.N. secretary general invite Israel, the Arab confrontation states, a Jordanian-Palestinian delegation, and the Security Council's permanent members to an opening session. There would be no veto or imposed settlement.

On the Palestinian problem, Shultz stated: "The Palestinians must be involved in the peace process if it is to mean anything. There isn't any question about that. [But] it's also true there isn't a role in the peace process for people whose tactics are violent and refuse to renounce violence, who refuse to recognize that Israel is there as a state, and [instead they must be] ready to talk and try to make peace."[26]

The eruption of demonstrations in the Gaza Strip and West Bank in December 1987 led to an upsurge of U.S. activity. Shultz's new plan, presented in January 1988, combined elements of the Camp David accords, the Reagan plan, King Hussein's proposals, and Peres's ideas. Negotiations would begin as soon as July over granting limited autonomy to the West Bank and Gaza Strip. These terms would be implemented during a three-year transition period.

An international forum of the five U.N. Security Council members— the United States, USSR, Great Britain, France, and China—would convene to launch these talks but would have no veto over the results.

These negotiations would be followed within six months—regardless of whether they were complete—by peace talks, also in the context of an international event. Governing principles for these negotiations would be the exchange of "territory for peace" and U.N. Resolutions 242 and 338. Although Shultz did not publicly stress the nature of Palestinian representation at these meetings, he preferred that it be in the form of a joint Jordanian-Palestinian delegation. He also, at times, seemed to suggest that a meeting co-hosted by the United States and the USSR might be acceptable instead of the broader five-party structure.

Egypt, Jordan, and Israeli Foreign Minister Peres supported the plan while Israeli Prime Minister Shamir, Arafat, and the Syrians were critical. Jordan, however, began to speak about a separate Palestinian delegation, and Shamir questioned the timetable, international forum, and territory-for-peace formula. According to Shamir, the future of the territories would be determined in the peace negotiations rather than before they took place.

Meanwhile, however, the uprising itself was affecting the stands of the different parties, particularly that of the PLO. The Nineteenth Palestine National Council meeting in November 1988 passed a resolution which took a big step toward moderation. The language was judged too ambiguous in Washington, though, and the United States continued its long-established policy of refusing to meet with the PLO until that organization clearly recognized Israel's right to exist, accepted U.N. Resolutions 242 and 338, and rejected the use of terrorism. When Yasser Arafat applied for a visa to come to New York and address the United Nations, Shultz refused on the grounds of the PLO leader's continued involvement in terrorism, including attacks on Americans.

Nonetheless, secret negotiations were conducted through third parties—particularly Egypt and Sweden—on what Arafat would have to say to meet the U.S. requirements. Even though an understanding was reached, Arafat fell short of his promised statement in a December 1988 speech before the U.N. General Assembly, which had moved to Geneva for the session because of the U.S. rejection of a visa to Arafat; but he stated the agreed formulations at a press conference the following day. The United States quickly initiated a "substantive dialogue" with the PLO in Tunis. The Arab-Israeli peace process had entered a new phase, made possible by U.S. firmness as well as by events in the region itself.

Conclusion

Despite the inevitable vicissitudes and uncertainties of Middle East politics, then, the overall strategic and political situation in the region was not unfavorable to U.S. interests during this period. Even the Iran-Contra blunder, which caused humiliation for the administration, damage to its counterterrorist policy, and domestic political repercussions, had little affect on the U.S. regional position. Terrorism, often aimed against Americans, hypnotized the media and caused a terrible loss in human terms but hardly destabilized the United States's fundamental standing in the Middle East. Islamic fundamentalism had proved incapable of mounting successful or even serious revolutionary challenges to friendly regimes. The Lebanese civil war raged on, but the nightmare of absolute Syrian domination had faded. The bloody Iran-Iraq war ended in a cease-fire in August 1988, but without endangering the Persian Gulf's oil exports. Most significant, the United States retained a wide variety of allies and was seen as the only plausible mediator of the Arab-Israeli conflict and protector of the Gulf Arab states. The USSR's influence on both fronts remained extremely limited.

Although the strong U.S.-Israel relationship was reinforced by Reagan's personal thinking, a key role in this trend was also played by the power of experience. Officials like Shultz had been genuinely frustrated by their efforts to negotiate seriously with the Arabs, to bring the PLO into the diplomatic process, to gain assistance from Saudi Arabia, and to improve relations with states such as Syria and Libya.

U.S. regional objectives were defined by four principles: limit Soviet influence while maximizing its own, encourage regional stability against the danger of war or radical revolution, support and strengthen allies, and seek the continued supply of oil at reasonable prices. As always, there were numerous points of danger and tensions, but the overall picture on these four concerns was reasonably positive.

Some U.S. experts argue that the strong U.S.-Israel relationship jeopardized all of these policy goals. They predict imminent Marxist or fundamentalist revolt and the loss of the United States's position in the region unless policy is drastically changed to incorporate a quick solution to the Arab-Israeli conflict on Arab terms. Nearly four decades of experience demonstrated the fallaciousness of this argument and led U.S. policy makers to reject it, though it still has appeal for some academics and analysts.

In fact, Washington's relative edge in the East-West competition rested on an ability to maintain good relations with a variety of Middle Eastern countries—Israel, Egypt, Jordan, Saudi Arabia, and even Iraq. This situation, in turn, was based on the United States's unique military, political, economic, and technological resources. Whether the issue was mediating the Arab-Israeli conflict or providing the needed training, equipment, and guarantees to underpin Persian Gulf security, the United States enjoyed powerful advantages.

Notes

1. The source for the breaking of the story was an article in *al-Shira*, Nov. 3, 1986. See *Daily Report* (hereafter *DR*), Nov. 6, 1986, pp. 11–3.

2. John Tower, Edmund Muskie, and Brent Scowcroft, *The Tower Commission Report* (New York: Times Books, 1987), p. 73.

3. Ibid, pp. 18–19, 63.

4. *Report of the Congressional Committees Investigating the Iran-Contra Affair,*

[House Report 100–433, Senate Report 100–216] (Washington, D.C., 1987), p. 12.

5. Department of State, "U.S. Initiative to Iran," *Current Policy*, no. 890, Nov. 13, 1986.

6. *Washington Times*, Nov. 25, 1986.

7. *Washington Post*, Dec. 1, 1986.

8. Clyde Mark, "The Persian Gulf, 1987: A Chronology of Events" (Washington, D.C.: Congressional Research Service, 1988).

9. *Washington Post*, June 17, 29, 1987.

10. *Washington Post*, June 3, 30, Sept. 19, 1987.

11. Christopher Madison, "A Reflagged Policy," *National Journal*, Nov. 28, 1987.

12. *Washington Post*, June 3, 1987.

13. Henry Kissinger, "Wandering in the Gulf," *Washington Post*, June 21, 1987.

14. *DR*, June 30, 1987, p. J2.

15. See Chapter 1, on Soviet policy, by Robert O. Freedman in this volume.

16. Text in U.S. Department of State, "International Shipping and the Iran-Iraq War," *Current Policy*, no. 958, May 19, 1987.

17. Ibid.

18. *FBIS: Middle East and Africa*, May 20, 1987, p. C-6, and Oct. 27, 1987, pp. 16–17; *Washington Post*, June 26, 1987, p. A-25.

19. *DR*, May 20, 1987, p. C-6. See also *Washington Post*, June 26, 1987, p. A-25; Ambassador Sa'ud Nasir al-Sabah, Kuwait News Agency, Oct. 26, 1987, in *DR*, Oct. 27, 1987, pp. 16–17; see also *DR*, June 23, 1987, p. J-1.

20. *New York Times*, Sept. 23, 26, 1987.

21. *Washington Post*, Oct. 18, 1987.

22. See, for example, Loren Jenkins, "Iranians Attack Ship Near American Convoy," *Washington Post*, Nov. 12, 1987.

23. *Economist*, Aug. 29, 1987; *Washington Post*, Aug. 13, 1987.

24. *Washington Post*, Oct. 11, 1987; *New York Times*, Oct. 16, 1987.

25. These issues are analyzed in detail in Barry Rubin, *The PLO's Intractable Foreign Policy* (Washington, D.C.: Washington Institute for Near East Policy, 1986).

26. *Washington Times*, Oct. 16, 1987.

3

Western Europe and the Middle East since the Iran-Contra Affair

Robert E. Hunter

Introduction and Background

To understand what happened in Western Europe at the time of the revelations about U.S. arms sales to Iran, it is important first to explore some of the background of European involvements in the Middle East, as well as some recent history of U.S.-European relations with regard to that region.

Until recent years the concept of European involvement in the Middle East related almost entirely to the acts of individual states and four in particular: Britain, France, Germany, and Italy. Each has had its own historical associations and patterns of action concerning individual countries in the region, and each differs from the others in its view of individual features or the region as a whole. These differences have been well cataloged and analyzed elsewhere and need not be dwelt upon at length here, although some relevant points will be made later.

The importance of the role played by individual states in the Middle East is highlighted because, from the perspective of discussing foreign policy, the term *Europe* has had little relevance but rather has been an expression relating to a congeries of states only loosely tied together in their ability to act collectively abroad. During the past three decades, there has been some progress toward developing the concept of European unity, but not much compared to the requirements of being able to express a collective personality with regard to either a defense or a foreign policy.

Nevertheless, even considering limits on common action, there has begun to be a growing European personality in foreign affairs encompassing the twelve countries that now make up the European Community. This personality is being expressed through an institution called

European Political Cooperation (EPC), which has no formal mandate based on the Rome Treaty of 1956. Rather, it has been created along the way as the members of the Community have wanted to try their hands at developing practices in an area that, after all, contains the essence of sovereignty—how states or collections of them relate to the outside world. And European Political Cooperation will continue to expand in scope as the result of the Single European Act, which provides for increased cooperation in this area, including some regarding broader aspects of security.[1]

As European Political Cooperation has developed, it has begun to move the European purview beyond that of individual states in apprehending the Middle East. Indeed, it has had a stronger emphasis on that region than on any other off the European continent for the simple reason that it has proved easier for the various member states of the European Community to agree on approaches to issues beyond Europe, with which most of these member states are involved, than to agree on matters nearer to home. In fact, within Europe itself, during the early years of EPC the twelve were able to agree on common positions at the various review conferences of the Conference on Security and Cooperation in Europe (CSCE) but on little else. Even on a divisive issue of signal importance within Europe—Cyprus—EPC has found itself sorely pressed to agree on anything constructive.

The Community's collective efforts in the Middle East have had two dimensions. One has been the so-called Euro-Arab Dialogue, which has not gone very far and has not proved to be a strong reed for either European or Arab states to lean on.[2] For the Arab states of the Persian Gulf—the collection of Arab states for which the Euro-Arab Dialogue was designed—the principal interest has been in having a forum with a political focus and, oftimes, one that would permit a good deal of lobbying about issues related to the Arab-Israeli conflict. The interest of the West Europeans in the Euro-Arab Dialogue, by contrast, has almost exclusively had an economic focus, namely, how economic relations can develop to mutual benefit and in particular to the benefit of European industry and exporters.

The other aspect of European Political Cooperation with regard to the Middle East has been the Arab-Israeli conflict. The high-water mark of West European cooperation was the Venice Declaration issued by the European Council summit meeting in June 1980, although there have been further actions and statements since then, consistent with that declaration.[3] Most notable was the declaration at the Madrid meeting of the European Council in June 1989.[4]

The Venice Declaration—as well as later EPC statements—departed significantly from key tenets of U.S. policy.[5] In particular, it argued that the Palestine Liberation Organization would "have to be associated with negotiations" over the West Bank and Gaza. Further, it called for the Palestinian people to be able "to exercise fully its right to self-determination" with the full understanding that this would imply the creation of an independent Palestinian state. These are not trivial points—the first calls on the United States to violate an undertaking to Israel about the conditions under which it would deal with the PLO (a point rendered moot since the start of a U.S.-PLO dialogue in December 1988), and the second presupposes the outcome of any negotiating process. Indeed, regarding the differences between the United States and the West European allies, which are also members of the European Community, it is important that European Political Cooperation was conceived in part to try to create some European foreign policy personality distinct from that of the United States.

The Arab-Israeli Conflict

The Arab-Israeli conflict has historically produced differences of viewpoint across the Atlantic. First, the Middle East is much closer geographically to Western Europe than it is to the United States. To a great extent, proximity tells in foreign policy, and the West Europeans are always concerned with what happens in the Middle East, even at times when the United States remains relatively aloof. Second, there is always a question in West European minds about the effects of Arab-Israeli conflict on East-West relations. Traditionally, the Europeans have worried not just about the possibility of confrontation between the United States and the Soviet Union—a possibility that has decreased remarkably since the conclusion of the Egypt-Israeli Peace Treaty and the evolution of new Soviet leadership—but also about the impact that untoward events in the Near East might have on any prospects for East-West detente in Europe. Third, compared to the United States, the countries of Western Europe have long been far more concerned about the flow of oil from the Middle East and the relative balance of Western relations with regional countries, as between Israel and the Arabs. There has been European concern about United States diplomacy in the European backyard, where events would affect the allies' interests but they would have no direct involvement in shaping those events or the policies that bring them about. Of course, in part it has been a matter of choice that the allies have little impact on the policies of the United States toward the Arab-Israeli conflict—they are willing for America to take the diplomatic lead. But that does not keep them from, at times, being concerned about U.S. policy. This set of attitudes culminated in the Venice Declaration.

West European concern about U.S. policy toward the Arab-Israeli conflict slackened in the early 1980s, however, when there was an oil glut and the Arab states became far more concerned with what was happening in the Persian Gulf and in Iran. The result of this process was seen at the Arab summit in Amman, Jordan, in the fall of 1987, when confrontation with Iran was declared to be more important than the Palestine problem—a declaration that most observers believe was the principal proximate cause of the uprising on the West Bank and Gaza: the Intifada. This diversion of attention to the Persian Gulf also had an impact on attitudes in Western Europe, lessening pressures on the United States to act in Arab-Israeli peacemaking.

In general throughout much of the 1980s, a paradox existed: the U.S. administration was not particularly concerned about seeking peace between Israel and its neighbors, and the West Europeans placed less pressure on the United States to change its positions than they had during the heyday of the Camp David accords. The oil glut only partly explains this seeming paradox. It was also important that there was very little U.S.-led peace process for the allies to try to affect.

The Intifada, along with changes in the PLO's declared attitude toward terrorism and its recognition of Israel, however, changed the context of West European attitudes toward the U.S. role in Arab-Israeli peacemaking. After Chairman Yasser Arafat renounced terrorism and seemed both to recognize Israel and to accept United Nations Security Council Resolution 242, the United States and the PLO opened a formal dialogue in Tunis. And although the new U.S. administration did not introduce a new master plan for the resolution of the Middle East conflict, the beginning of this dialogue signaled a greater U.S. interest in Middle East peacemaking than had been true for most of the Reagan years.

The West Europeans welcomed these developments and tried to encourage further PLO moderation. Thus, despite strong protests from France's Jewish community, in the spring of 1989 Yasser Arafat visited Paris and was received by President François Mitterrand.[6] The Europeans made no concerted effort to push the peace process forward, however, and were content once again with letting the United States take the lead.

During the early part of the decade, several of the West European allies also demonstrated a willingness to cooperate with the United States in some special areas. First and perhaps most significant was the creation of the Multinational Force and Observers (MFO) in the Sinai Desert, designed to provide a symbol of the separation of the Egyptian and Israeli armies within the context of the peace treaty. Yet four West European states—France, Italy, the Netherlands, and the United

Kingdom—agreed to join the MFO only after the assassination of Anwar Sadat in October 1981 and after it had become clear that the global oil glut would continue indefinitely.[7] It had thus become politically safer to provide this implied endorsement for the Camp David accords and the Egyptian-Israeli peace treaty than when they were concluded.[8]

There was also allied cooperation in Lebanon. France, Italy, and Britain all have concerns in the eastern Mediterranean and—for differing reasons and to differing degrees—joined with the United States in the Multi-National Force (MNF) that returned to Lebanon in September 1982 after the massacres at the Sabra and Shatilla refugee camps. The French have long considered themselves to have a special relationship with Lebanon, dating back several hundred years. During the early part of the decade, the Italians saw opportunities for their country to be a special ally of the United States, thereby gaining more attention and playing a greater role in allied deliberations. And the British—who never did have a sizable contingent of forces in Lebanon—were anxious not to be left out of a venture in which some of their Continental allies were taking part.

The acquiescence of the West European allies that took part in the MNF was also seen as a way of prompting the United States to take a greater role in Arab-Israeli peacemaking. European interest in achieving such a peace rose briefly because of the reaction in the Arab world to the Israeli invasion of Lebanon. Even so, the preoccupation of the Arab states—and especially the Gulf Arabs—with the Iran-Iraq war reduced their political pressure on the Europeans to act on the Arab-Israeli front. At this time, the Arabs were more interested in gaining, and to a considerable degree received, European assistance to meet the challenge from Iran.

The Persian Gulf

At the eastern end of the Middle East, there has also been a history, antedating Iran-Contra, of intra-allied relations that helped to condition reactions in Europe to the revelations in November 1986 about U.S. arms sales to Iran.

Most important have been two factors shaping U.S.–West European relations over Persian Gulf questions. First, the West European states have a greater need to secure oil from the region than has the United States. With the exception of a few countries, such as Britain and Norway, which have access to North Sea oil and gas, the West European requirement for Persian Gulf oil will continue to be absolute well into the next century. This need will continue to influence West European attitudes toward the Persian Gulf and its politics. Nevertheless, even though the United States is less dependent than Western Europe on Persian Gulf oil, it does not have the option of abstaining from any crisis that would seriously affect the flow of oil because the unity of the global oil market would make any such stoppage felt in the United States almost immediately, and an oil stoppage would pose serious risks to the security of America's allies. The Europeans are about ten times more dependent than is the United States on Persian Gulf oil in total energy usage, but that makes little difference in the management of an alliance.

The second factor, however, is that dependence on oil is not reflected in the sharing of responsibilities within the West for regional security. The West European nations have long been and are likely to continue being willing to see the United States take the lead in the Persian Gulf. Yet at the same time, there have been significant differences of viewpoint across the Atlantic with regard to developments in the region that might cause difficulty for Western interests, shared or otherwise.

There are differences, for example, between most European countries and the United States regarding the threats to Western interests that might arise within the Persian Gulf region. Until the last few years, when it began to see Iran as the key threat to its interests in the region, the United States tended to focus on external threats involving military force and with a connection to projections of Soviet power. The West Europeans, in general, have worried more about internal developments and political and economic threats—especially instabilities within countries—and regional factors other than the role of the Soviets. There have also been some differences of opinion among the European countries. Most of them—notably West Germany and Italy—did not subscribe to the French policy of giving near-total support to Iraq during most of its war with Iran. Of course, during that eight-year conflict, there has been some greater coalescence of transatlantic attitudes because of the threat posed by the war and the challenge the Iranian revolution posed to the security of the Gulf Arab states. Even so, the United States has generally been more concerned than its European allies about the prolongation of the conflict.

This differing perspective on the Persian Gulf and the rest of southwestern Asia has led to a difference in viewpoint concerning the appropriate responses. In general, the West European allies have put emphasis on pursuing political and economic approaches, at least in the first instance. In the United States, by contrast, there has been a greater predilection to consider military action and presence as being important. This generalization holds true even though the French, and to a degree the British, have maintained some fleet presence in the region for many years—a point that Britain, in particular, made during the patrolling of the Persian Gulf in 1987–88, in part to minimize the idea that there had been a ratcheting up of the Royal Navy's involvement.

Finally, there has been some disagreement within the alliance about which countries should take responsibility for preserving Western interests in the Persian Gulf—even when it can be agreed that there are common interests and agreed-upon challenges to them. The West Europeans have clearly wanted the United States to take the lion's share of the responsibility. Thus they were reluctant at the end of the 1970s to see applications of sanctions against Iran during the hostage crisis and against the Soviet Union over the invasion of Afghanistan.

Terrorism

From the late 1970s until the present, Middle East terrorism has had a critical impact on the way West European countries and the United States have viewed the Middle East and has helped shape their respective policies.

Beginning with the seizure of the U.S. embassy in Tehran in November 1979, terrorism and hostage-taking became a major preoccupation in the United States. This concern intensified with each incident that, through television, was brought into the American living room. Terrorism became a key factor in U.S. foreign policy. For many West Europeans, however, this preoccupation has always seemed a bit puzzling. Much of Western Europe has experienced indigenous terrorism that has led to a certain insensitivity, whereas in the United States, terrorism (as opposed to other forms of violence) is not a local phenomenon. Many West Europeans also noted that the locus of much of the Middle East–born terrorism was in Europe—in their cities and airports, not those of the United States. Indeed, Europeans, proportionately, bore more of the brunt of political terrorism.

In working on remedies to terrorism, there also tended to develop a difference of viewpoint across the Atlantic. In the United States, most emphasis was placed on a dual strategy of trying to prevent terrorism through better intelligence and security and on dealing with its effects, including possible military retaliation. Almost everywhere in Western Europe far greater emphasis is placed on trying to reduce the causes of terrorism. And in Europe, the premier cause of Middle East–born terrorism is believed to be the unresolved Palestinian problem.

In April 1986, the United States bombed Libya as an active and tangible means of combating terrorism. This event produced perhaps the most serious split of perceptions between the United States and its Western allies concerning one another's actions since the Suez crisis of 1956. This split affected both governments and public opinion, with the notable exception of French popular attitudes, which on balance supported the U.S. action. Yet the United States was still not deeply engaged in Arab-Israeli peacemaking efforts, nor did it seize upon the spate of terrorist incidents to become more involved. Not surprisingly, the gap in attitudes between the United States and its European partners widened, and a crisis built over the terrorism question. The problem was exacerbated in Britain, in particular, which in late 1986 accused Syria of masterminding an effort to blow up an El Al Airliner. The United States refused to follow Britain's lead in severing diplomatic relations with Syria, a refusal that was resented by Britons, who believed that their country had earned U.S. understanding by supporting the Libya raid.

Then in November 1986, the world learned that the United States had not been practicing the antiterrorist policy it had been preaching—especially the cardinal principles of "no negotiations, no deals"—but instead had been attempting to trade arms to the Iranian regime of the Ayatollah Khomeini in exchange for the release of some American citizens held hostage in Lebanon. The Reagan administration gave many explanations for its actions, including the perfectly valid and correct argument that it valued the independence and integrity of Iran as a vital interest and wished to encourage elements in Iran that were inspired more by nationalism than by Islamic ideology. But few people were swayed by this argument. Particularly in Western Europe, where both government and public opinion were still concerned over the Libya raid, the news struck like a bombshell.

Ironically, however, the Iran-Contra affair let the air out of the terrorism balloon as far as the United States was concerned. In effect, American public opinion came to understand that it had been misled by officials in Washington and even by the president, who had argued that the U.S. government could act decisively against terrorism. That had never been true; terrorism had not been eliminated, and Americans traveling abroad could not feel fully secure. American vulnerability to Middle East terrorism had sprung primarily from this dichotomy between expectations and the ability of the U.S. government to deliver on them. The revelations about the arms sales to Iran, however, suddenly told the American people that the administration was not adhering to an antiterrorist policy based on rigid refusal to negotiate but was pursuing appeasement.

Remarkably, however, this revelation reduced expectations and thus U.S. vulnerability to terrorism and may be a major reason why the number of terrorist incidents involving Americans decreased markedly. In January 1987, three Americans and an Indian who was a U.S. resident were seized in Beirut. Rather than becoming another cause célèbre, this incident raised the question, Why were they there?

Over time, West European concern about Middle East terrorism receded. As U.S. concerns about and reactions to terrorism went down, so too did West European concern that the United States had to take a more rigorous role in Arab-Israeli peacemaking lest the Americans should do something that, from a European perspective, would be counterproductive, silly, or worse. Nevertheless, the connection between terrorism and West European pressure on the United States to be vigorous in Arab-Israeli peacemaking could again become a significant issue in U.S.-European relations.[9]

The Impact of the Iran-Contra Scandal

The Iran-Contra revelations had a major and immediate impact in Western Europe. The first reaction was part shock, part cynicism. Initially, there was a sense of disbelief that the United States, especially the Reagan administration, could have violated its declared intention not to negotiate with terrorists. This feeling was intensified by memories of the pressures put on West European governments to take stronger actions against Middle East–born terrorism such as sanctions against Libya in early 1986 and to cooperate in the bombing raid against Libya despite their misgivings. They also recalled the heaping of moral opprobrium on their heads by more than one U.S. administration spokesman. On another level, however, European cynicism came from an awareness, based on bitter experience, of the difficulties of holding a firm line against negotiating or compromising with terrorists. The revelations also came only a month after the U.S.-Soviet superpower summit in Reykjavik, which had produced a profound unease about America's conduct of East-West relations and reinforced a widespread belief that U.S. foreign policy was prone to excesses.

At the same time, the knowledge that, in its own policy, the United States had been violating its admonitions to others removed any opprobrium that might accrue from others taking similar actions. At once, it seemed to be permissible in the eyes of the United States—despite efforts by the Reagan administration to pretend that nothing had changed in policy—to be seen negotiating to secure the release of hostages. Indeed, not only were any future European negotiating efforts legitimized but so were any that had already taken place and, in some cases, had been condemned by the United States.

The impact of this change in attitudes was seen in 1987 and 1988, when Britain and France began negotiating with Iran and others about the fate of their citizens held hostage, and West Germany kept a weather eye out for opportunities to reach compromises. Thus West Germany was reluctant to take firm legal action against one of the purported hijackers of TWA flight 847 in June 1985, when he came into West German custody late the following year; and his trial did not begin until mid-1988, after the fever of U.S. anger about terrorism had sharply declined. Nevertheless, West German nerve held, and the hijacker was convicted and incarcerated.

Of course, these West European countries have never developed the emotional attitudes toward Iran that colored U.S. behavior, in large part because of the history of U.S.-Iranian relations after 1978. Ironically, the "betrayal" of the common Western positions by the British and French—as the United States had done with Iran-Contra—enabled them to improve relations with Iran and thereby have some influence in producing the August 1988 cease-fire in the Iran-Iraq war. Whatever the merits of not succumbing to extortion based on hostage-taking—and there are many—the larger purpose was aided by the British and French departure from the standard.

This reaction came later, however. At the time, the revelations about Iran-Contra led the United States to increase pressures on its allies to keep their distance from Iran. As a result, the Western attitude toward Iran generally became one of confrontation. Meanwhile, those Iranian nationalist leaders who were relatively pragmatic were largely discredited by the same revelations—a "Washingtongate" among the ruling clergy in Iran. To restore their revolutionary credentials, they had at least to sound tough, hence, the emergence of a confrontational attitude on Iran's part, as well.

Thus during the first year after Iran-Contra, relations between Iran and both Britain and France deteriorated still further and included major diplomatic clashes. In July 1987, the French government decided to prosecute an Iranian embassy employee, Vahid Gordji, on charges of involvement in terrorist attacks carried out in France. Gordji claimed diplomatic immunity and refused to leave the Iranian embassy precincts. The French police surrounded the embassy to prevent him from escaping.[10] The Iranian government retaliated by accusing the first secretary of the French embassy in Tehran of spying, and the Iranian police surrounded the embassy. Thus began the so-called war of the embassies, which led to the rupturing of diplomatic relations between Iran and France.[11]

The crisis was not resolved until December 1987, when Iran and France began a process of reconciliation. The war of the embassies ended after France agreed to expel several members of the Iranian opposition, the Mojahedin-e-Khalgh. Then, in May 1988, the three remaining French hostages were released in Lebanon. Shortly afterward, France declared that it was resuming diplomatic ties with Iran.

A similar situation arose with Britain, which expelled an employee of the Iranian consulate in Manchester on charges of shoplifting. In retaliation, Iran expelled four British diplomats, and bilateral relations deteriorated. Britain's handling of the shoplifting incident reflected the hardening of overall Western attitudes toward Iran, and Britain became outspoken on the issue of the imposition of a U.N.-sponsored arms embargo against Iran.

Only after it became clear in Iran that its military situation was badly deteriorating did it begin again to reach out to London, Paris, and other Western capitals. And when it did, memories in Western Europe of Iran-Contra lessened the effectiveness of U.S. pressures to keep its allies from reciprocating.

The Iran-Contra affair had other effects on the Western alliance and on antiterrorism efforts. Thus cooperation across the Atlantic on antiterrorism slackened from the high point after the U.S. attack on Libya when it was necessary to prove to the Americans that West Europeans were taking effective action against terrorism. This did not necessarily mean that the allies were doing less, only that it was possible to consider appropriate steps to take rather than judging the political impact in the United States.

In addition, the Iran-Contra revelations reduced Washington's moral position in trying to limit the flow of arms to Iran in a renewal of the so-called Operation Staunch that had been pursued by the United States in an effort to force Iran to the bargaining table. Because the United States was not prepared to follow its own strictures, the reasoning in Europe went, there was no reason for the Europeans to do so. It has been argued that this attitude helped prolong the Iran-Iraq war, but there is little supporting evidence. Any impact on Iran's military capability that came from opening a bit wider the door of arms sales—and that by only a crack—was more than offset by the new willingness of the United States to become actively engaged in the Iran-Iraq war. When it came time to decide whether to reflag eleven Kuwaiti tankers and to protect them against Iranian attacks —attacks undertaken in response to deliberate Iraqi provocations—the United States undertook this duty in part to demonstrate to the Arab states of the Persian Gulf that the arms sales to Iran had been an aberration, not part of a settled policy.[12] And, in part spurred on by the political humiliation of the Iran-Contra affair, the Reagan administration became more active militarily on Iraq's side—co-belligerent in all but name—and began striking Iran hard militarily when there was the provocation or pretext to do so.

The projection of U.S. naval power into the Persian Gulf and the ensuing military encounters between Iran and the United States finally convinced Iran of the futility of continuing the war and led it to accept U.N. Security Council Resolution 598. As a result, a cease-fire on land and sea was declared on August 20, 1989.

Following the cease-fire, a mood of self-criticism and questioning of past policies enveloped Iran. One result was an effort to improve its relations with West European countries, which led to reestablishment of full diplomatic relations with Britain in September 1988. On November 27, 1988, the West German foreign minister visited Tehran, and on February 5–6, 1989, the French minister of foreign affairs did so.[13]

This policy of opening to the West, however, was not supported by all factions in Iran, and the radical elements continued to fight a rearguard action. The publication of the book *Satanic Verses* by Salman Rushdie and the outbreak of the so-called Rushdie affair offered the radicals the opportunity to reverse the course of Iran's Westward-looking policy.

After the Ayatollah Khomeini pronounced his death sentence on Rushdie, the European Community countries recalled their ambassadors from Tehran and, shortly afterward, Iran broke diplomatic relations with Britain. Yet as the Rushdie affair began to die down and Iran and its Middle East allies took no action to execute Rushdie, some Community members began to return their ambassadors to Tehran. After Khomeini's death, the French and German ambassadors also returned.

The Iran-Contra revelations about U.S. violation of its own strictures on the flow of arms to Iran spurred an ongoing U.S.–West European competition within the region. For many years, there have been very strong commercial and arms sales rivalries between the United States and Western Europe, which in the ordinary course of events will become far more intense in the years ahead. The United States has faced a dilemma of selling arms to the Gulf Arab states because of the possibility that these weapons could then be used against Israel. Thus the United States has wanted to be able to have some control over the disposition of weapons sold within the region and to limit the sales of some types of weaponry. In recent years, however, an increasing share of these sales has gone to West Europeans—an $18 to 30 billion agreement between Britain and Saudi Arabia in 1988 being the most notable—and the United States has not been in any position to exercise control over the weapons and their use. This exacerbation of the arms situation is partly a result of the Iran-Iraq war and even of Iran-Contra—that is, the pressures on the United States to sell more arms to Gulf Arab states as one proof that it was not supporting Iran, followed by intensified domestic political opposition in the United States to some of these sales. The European allies that are in the arms business are not subject to the same domestic pressures to consider the impact of weapons sales on regional balances. These competitions will continue, and in the wake of the final battles in the Iran-Iraq war—including the use of poison gas—the strains and tensions within the Western alliance over arms sales policies could be considerable.

Finally, the revelations about Iran-Contra hardened attitudes in Western Europe about another issue: the potential use of bases on the Continent for U.S. military actions elsewhere. Coming against the background of the arms-for-hostages dealing, the bombing of Libya, which took place at about the same time as the U.S. contacts with Iran, seemed even more bizarre to most Western Europeans and even more self-serving on the part of the Americans. But this was not just a matter of denying future opportunities for the United States to use military bases for a repetition of the Libya raid—that had already been more or less ruled out by the public reaction, even in Britain, whose government had cooperated with the United States. It could also affect attitudes toward the projection of U.S. military power from Western Europe, for any purpose, beyond the area defined by the North Atlantic Treaty. This could also include efforts by U.S. forces to intervene in a crisis or conflict in the Middle East unconnected with terrorism. Already in the 1973 Yom Kippur war, only predemocratic Portugal among the West European allies had permitted the United States to use bases for the military resupply of Israel. Following Libya and Iran-Contra, the chances that the allies would be accommodating seemed even slimmer. Indeed, in operating from Europe toward the Middle East, the United States is likely to have problems in using its military forces on a contingency basis, a regular basis, or a spot basis. And any such development would bring greater questioning in the United States about the relative merits of keeping so many forces on the Continent if they could not easily and readily be used for U.S. military purposes elsewhere that, in the American mind, are in the common Western interest.

This is not a new issue. For years, the European allies have been concerned with U.S. actions and policies that go beyond Europe. They have seen these actions as distracting attention from European problems and as potentially getting the United States in over its head, embroiling the alliance in matters that are not common interests for all members. And there is the possibility of complicating detente in Europe.

Indeed, this set of concerns does more than anything else to explain why the West European allies were willing to take part in the effort to protect shipping in the Persian Gulf in 1987–88 against attacks by Iran. None of the allies was particularly enthusiastic. All understood that there was no major threat to Persian Gulf shipping or to the flow of oil; fewer than 1 percent of all tankers had been attacked, about 70 percent of them by Iraq. But in time, five West European states did send ships: Britain, France, Italy, Belgium, and the Netherlands (Britain and France were only augmenting their naval presences). West Germany, prohibited by law from projecting military power beyond the North Atlantic Treaty area, did not join in, but it did agree to take up some of the naval slack in the Mediterranean caused by the departure of allied vessels for the Persian Gulf. And at least two states—Belgium and the Netherlands—acted through the Western European Union, in part to provide some multinational cover and in part to help strengthen that fledgling institution of defense cooperation among European states.

The allies helped the U.S. Navy in the Persian Gulf in large part because of the American reactions observed at the time of the Libyan bombing. There was hope in Western Europe of gaining some standing in Washington so as to be able to take part in and influence U.S. policy decisions over the Persian Gulf. In addition, there was concern that, should the United States be left in the lurch—no matter how flawed its Persian Gulf policy might be—there could be further strains in transatlantic relations, recriminations against West Europeans by the American public, and even the removal of some U.S. forces from Europe. So with some reluctance, the five allies joined the United States in the Persian Gulf, even though they were not totally in tune with U.S. assessments of what was happening or what should be done.

Thus as memories of Iran-Contra faded from the European perspective, there remained a desire to see responsibility rest in Washington, not on the European continent, for protecting Western interests in both the zone of Arab-Israeli conflict and the Persian Gulf. Yet the allies were far more willing to give advice than to accept responsibility. They gave minor cooperation to the MFO and the MNF and the sending of ships to the Persian Gulf, but no European state and certainly not the European Community collectively was willing to pay the price of being an active participant in critical Middle East diplomacy. This was particularly true with regard to Arab-Israeli peacemaking, the price of which is denominated in terms of actions to demonstrate commitment to the legitimacy and survival of the state of Israel, including a willingness to sell it arms. This no West European state would do. Indeed, as the Intifada has intensified, it has become even less likely that any West European state would seek an active role in Arab-Israeli peacemaking and, in the process, secure its legitimacy with Israel by entering into an arms supply relationship.

The Soviet Factor

During the last several years, and particularly during the past decade, there has also been a considerable difference of viewpoint—or at least of perspective—across the Atlantic concerning the role of the Soviet Union. During the years in which a U.S.-Soviet confrontation over the Arab-Israeli conflict was still possible (as, in some form, seemed the case during the wars of 1956, 1967, and 1973), there were naturally considerable West European fears about the way the United States was conducting policy both in the region and directly with the Soviets. A U.S.-Soviet confrontation, for whatever reason it came about, would have profound implications for European security.

In the Persian Gulf, meanwhile, there tended to be a difference of opinion across the Atlantic about the degree of danger to Western interests being posed by the Soviet Union. Thus, following the Soviet invasion of Afghanistan, the United States was hard-pressed to gain support from its allies for sanctions against the Soviets, and, even when they were put in place, it gained little to show for its efforts. It was not just that the West European allies were concerned about the risks of American overreaction, they were worried that the problems of a far-away quarrel might be felt closer to home. Indeed, U.S. strategy during those years was based on the premise that a Soviet military attack against Iran might lead to either horizontal or vertical escalation—either changing the place of U.S.-Soviet conflict or introducing tactical nuclear weapons. Nor did the allies share U.S. concerns about the role the Soviet Union was likely to play in regional events and potential for conflict. For the allies, local conditions and regional rivalries, which, save for the Iran-Iraq war, were more political and economic than military, led them to depreciate the threat from the Soviet Union.

With the advent of Mikhail Gorbachev as Soviet leader, there began to be a narrowing of U.S. and West European perceptions of the role of the Soviet Union in the Middle East. The risk of war between Israel and Egypt—and with it, the risk of a U.S.-Soviet confrontation—had already gone down precipitously. In southwestern Asia, the risks of a Soviet invasion of Iran had gone down, presumably as Moscow had begun to count the cost of its Afghanistan venture. And then, in 1987, it began moving toward an eventual military withdrawal, which was finally completed in February 1989.

West European perceptions of potential change in the Soviet Union still ran ahead of American perceptions. This was especially notable because of desires in Western Europe to see a renewal of detente and because of the sudden rise of Gorbachev's popularity as peacemaker, especially in contrast to the U.S. president. European attitudes toward events in the Persian Gulf could not change much in response to Gorbachev because the Soviet Union had not been seen as central to European concerns about the region, but that was less true in the zone of Arab-Israeli peacemaking.

For the first several months of 1988, and until July 31, when Jordan's King Hussein withdrew from the peace process and turned over any remaining mandate to the PLO, the United States was actively engaged in a peacemaking effort known as the Shultz plan, after the U.S. secretary of state. One element of that plan was the notion of an international conference, including local parties to the conflict and some combination of outside countries, perhaps the five permanent members of the United Nations Security Council, but certainly the Soviet Union as well as the United States. In theory, this arrangement—the modalities of which were never worked out—would provide Hussein with a protective political umbrella, guarding him against recriminations from Palestinians and Arab enemies, particularly Syria.

In the United States, there was considerable ambivalence about such an international conference, even though it was formally blessed by the Reagan administration. The counterargument was that the Soviet Union's intentions should be tested before it was invited to take part in an international conference for Arab-Israeli peacemaking, lest Moscow use the opportunity either for mischief-making in general, or at least to isolate Israel and the United States at key moments in negotiations. But there was no such ambivalence throughout most of Western Europe: most Europeans stood foursquare behind the position of the Israeli foreign minister, Shimon Peres, and opposed that of the prime minister, Yitzhak Shamir, in regard to Soviet participation in peacemaking. The idea of including the Soviets was seen as a natural outgrowth of other developments in East-West relations and also, for some observers, a potential spur to a laggard United States. This last point took on added cogency because of the uprising on the West Bank and Gaza, which reintroduced considerable urgency into West European attitudes about peacemaking.

In any event, the prospect grew of some friction within the Western alliance about the potential role of the Soviets within the Middle East, and especially regarding Arab-Israeli peacemaking. At the same time, however, the allies were still not prepared to take an active role in peacemaking and thus did nothing to bring about an international conference. Yet with the U.S. opening to the PLO at the end of 1988, plus the advent of a new American administration that showed signs of more engagement than its predecessor in Arab-Israeli peacemaking, European agitation for a Soviet role subsided. In addition, it appeared that the Soviet Union was prepared to be helpful to the process—it was instrumental in getting Arafat to meet the U.S. conditions for a dialogue—without a formal role.[14]

A U.S. Program for Relations with Western Europe in the Middle East

During the next few years, European attitudes toward the Middle East will be strongly influenced by what the United States does in the region. This is particularly true regarding generalized perceptions of U.S. standing and influence, its commitment to preserving Western interests, and its activism. Thus the Bush administration should follow a nine-point program with the regard to the Middle East, both for the sake of U.S. interests directly in the region and for the sake of developing effective relations with its West European allies. Some of these policies it has already adopted.

First, it has been important for the United States to reassert its commitment to Arab-Israeli peacemaking, not just because of what has been happening on the West Bank and Gaza, but also because of the need to manage effectively U.S.-European relations beyond the area that formally defines the North Atlantic Alliance—so-called out of area. This commitment to renewed peacemaking efforts, which seemed implicit in actions by the Bush administration during its first several months, is necessary in part because of the strains that could develop within the alliance if the United States refuses to resume this responsibility and also because of the potential impact of the terrorism issue if that tactic continues to be pursued against American citizens by one or more Middle East groups, as happened in July and August 1989. At the same time, it is important for the United States to gain West European assurances that they will abstain from undercutting U.S. peacemaking diplomacy because, as long as the United States has that responsibility, it must also have considerable latitude in making key judgments about the timing and substance of peacemaking.

Second, the United States should test the Soviet Union before allowing it into Arab-Israeli peace talks, much less encouraging it to take part. This point does not relate just to the proper conduct of U.S.-Soviet relations and to the need for due caution in judging the evolution of policy and goals under Gorbechev. The United States must also ensure that it is not raising undue expectations in Western Europe or being stampeded into acceding to Soviet involvement because of European pressures. At the same time, the Bush administration has gained by taking the initiative in Europe on arms control and on beginning efforts to try to ameliorate some of the most noxious elements of East-West division. But judging where to deal with the Soviets and where to be reluctant to deal is an important part both of managing East-West relations and of managing the Western alliance.[15] The United States has to balance its concerns in the Middle East with the problems of prosecuting detente in Europe; in effect, it is necessary to keep the West Europeans from running away with this issue.

Third, the United States needs to challenge its European allies to recommit themselves and to reinvigorate the so-called division of labor. This was the policy adopted in 1979, after it was proposed by West Germany at U.S. instigation, to share responsibility for providing economic support for countries in and near the Middle East region, most notably Turkey, Egypt, and Pakistan. Lebanon should also be a major recipient of West European economic support, especially after the demonstration of its impotence in the July–August 1989 hostage crisis. If the allies cannot or will not become directly involved in Arab-Israeli peacemaking in a supportive fashion, they should at least be counted upon to pay a considerable portion of the economic support price that must underpin effective efforts to resolve conflict and promote development. Their doing so will also be helpful with the broader burden-sharing question within the Atlantic alliance, where there is increased U.S. concern that the allies should spend more on collective security.

Fourth, the United States should continue to limit its military exposure in the Persian Gulf so as to reduce risks, demonstrate that the policy of 1987–88 worked, and show the increased sensitivity that is needed to deal with the one indisputable problem that the United States has had with Iran—the potential spread of Islamic fundamentalism. Obviously, the prosecution of Arab-Israeli peacemaking relates fundamentally to this object, and pursuing it accords well with U.S. goals in working with its European allies, in particular reducing the risks of transatlantic tension over the projection of U.S. military power from Europe to the Middle East. U.S. forces have indeed been reduced from the high of the tanker war, but the principle is nonetheless sound.

Fifth, the United States should be wary of taking any steps that would press Iran in the direction of a Soviet embrace, and it should encourage allied attempts to improve relations with that country. This would mean a reversal of U.S. policy, but it is facilitated by the cease-fire in the Iran-Iraq war and the emergence of a new, more nationalist and pragmatic regime in Iran, led by Hashemi Rafsanjani, whose first priority seems to be to rebuild his shattered nation. The struggle for power in Iran continues, however, and one aspect of the outcome will be the relative influence of the Soviet Union in Iran and, by extension, on Iranians in Afghanistan during the political competition in that country.

Sixth, the United States needs to take the lead in working out rules regarding arms sales to the Persian Gulf region, particularly regarding high-tech weapons. The Soviet Union has shown some willingness to do so, and the West European allies should be drawn in along with other countries, such as China. This is particularly important with regard to the new influx of ballistic missiles, and the Missle Technology Control Regime, agreed among some Western states, is a useful beginning.

Seventh, the United States and its European allies need to develop clearer understandings about the nature of their economic competition in the Middle East, expecially when there is risk that it will move in the direction of an undue emphasis on military goods.

Eighth, the United States needs to work far more effectively with its West European (and Japanese) allies to reduce their collective vulnerability to another oil cutoff. The trends, at least in the United States, have all been in the wrong direction since the Reagan administration backed away from many of the useful efforts that were begun by its predecessor. Otherwise, the risks for the West and for the alliance are considerable.

Ninth and finally, the United States needs to work within the NATO alliance to develop a rational structure for dealing with out-of-area problems. Any cooperation should be organized on a bilateral or multilateral basis—not within the formal structures of the alliance— partly in an effort to guard against a reappearance of what in the last administration was called U.S. global unilateralism but which the Bush administration seems to have abandoned. There also needs to be agreement on the ways and means for the United States to be able to use allied military facilities for Middle East contingencies well before there is any need to act. In this case, the allies need to be more forbearing of U.S. needs, for example, to be able to project power to the region in the event of a crisis.

These nine prescriptions do not exhaust the subject. But they do take account of the major developments in policies and attitudes toward the Middle East, on the part of the West European states and their American partner, that have taken place since Iran-Contra. They offer the basis for a reasonable set of transatlantic relations regarding the Middle East during the 1990s.

Notes

1. See, for example, "L'Acte unique europeen," commentaire par Jean De Ruyt, *Etudes Europeennes* (Brussels: University of Brussels, 1987), pp. 219–52.

2. The Community also "attaches importance to the strengthening and development of relations with the Maghreb, particularly following the establishment of the Arab Maghreb Union." See the declaration of the European Council meeting in Madrid, June 26–27, in *European Community News*, no. 21/89, June 28, 1989.

3. See, for instance, Robert E. Hunter and Geoffrey Kemp, rapporteurs, *Western Interests and U.S. Policy Options in the Middle East: A Joint Policy Project of the Atlantic Council of the United States and the Middle East Institute* (Washington, D.C., 1988), pp. 13 and 17.

4. See "Declaration on the Middle East," Annex 1 of Political Cooperation Section, from the declaration of the European Council summit meeting in Madrid, June 26–27, 1989, in *European Community News*, no. 21/89, June 28, 1989.

5. See "Declaration by the 17th European Council on the Euro-Arab Dialogue, Lebanon, Afghanistan and the Situation in the Middle East (Venice, 12/13 June 1980)," in *European Political Cooperation (EPC)* 4th ed. (Bonn: Press and Information Office of the Federal Government, 1982), pp. 202–6

6. On Arafat's trip to Paris, see "Arafat Says Mitterrand Meeting 'Fruitful,' " *Foreign Broadcast Information Service: Western Europe;* May 3, 1989.

7. See "Statement by the Ten on the Participation of Member States in the Sinai Peace Keeping Force (London, November 23, 1981)," in *European Political Cooperation (EPC)*, p. 294.

8. For the European Community's lukewarm endorsement of the Egyptian-Israeli peace treaty, see "Statement by the Nine on the Egyptian-Israeli Peace Treaty (Paris, March 26, 1979)," ibid., p. 163.

9. With the uprising on the West Bank and Gaza since 1987 (the Intifada), European concerns about Arab-Israeli peacemaking have increased. There have been statements on the issue by the European Community in the context of European Political Cooperation, notably in January 1988 and June 1989, but neither included a new departure from U.S. policy and neither was presented with intensity. For the most recent statement, see "Declaration on the Middle East."

10. See "Affaire Gordji: Teheran Nargue Paris," *Le Point*, July 6, 1987.

11. See "France-Iran: Le bras de fer," *Le Point*, July 20, 1987.

12. See testimony of Michael H. Armacost, under secretary of state for political affairs, to the Senate Foreign Relations Committee, June 16, 1987.

13. On the visit of the French minister, Roland Dumas, see "The New French Connection," *Middle East Economic Digest* 33 (Feb. 17, 1989); on West German Foreign Minister Hans-Dietrich Genscher's visit, see "Bonn Agrees to Consider Financing Request," ibid. 32 (Dec. 9, 1988).

14. Thus this point was omitted from the EPC declaration at the Madrid European Council meeting in June 1989. See "Declaration on the Middle East."

15. See Robert E. Hunter, "A Rule of Thumb for Inviting the Soviets to Talk," *Christian Science Monitor,* July 28, 1988.

Part Two

Regional Political Dynamics

4

Arab Politics and the Iran-Contra Affair

Jerrold D. Green

Introduction

The impact of the Iran-Contra affair on Arab politics has been minimal. This is not to say that the Arab world was unaffected by America's hypocritical and shortsighted attempt to provide Iran with weapons in exchange for Americans held hostage in Beirut. Still, the credibility of the United States is consistently so low in the Arab world that there is little that can be done to make it worse. The significance of Iran-Contra for Arab politics does not lie in its qualities as a discrete political event. Instead it should be emphasized that in recent years Arab politics have been dominated by two separate although interrelated issues: the Iran-Iraq war and the Palestine question. The impact of Iran-Contra can best be understood, therefore, not as an isolated political development but rather within the context of these dominant political considerations.

The moderate Arab regimes with which the United States maintains its closest relationships all share a profound fear of the Islamic Republic of Iran and particularly of its charismatic leader, Ayatollah Ruhollah Khomeini. Even after the death of the Ayatollah in 1989 no Arab moderates support Iran and its has been widely and automatically assumed that the United States shared this perspective. This presumed American antipathy toward post-Pahlavi Iran was premised on two sets of factors. First, for its own reasons, the United States was opposed to the Islamic Republic. The Iranian revolution and expulsion of the shah, the takeover of the American embassy, and Khomeini's unremitting hostility to the United States and support for anti-American groups and causes seemed to guarantee continued American opposition to Iran for many years to come.[1] Second, America's closest friends in the Arab world opposed Iran, and it seemed logical that the United States would support its friends. To put the issue somewhat more narrowly, it seemed obvious that petroleum producers and consumers shared a common foe in Ayatollah Khomeini, whose attempts to export the Islamic revolution were potentially disruptive to commerce. Because the Gulf oil producers and the United States/Western alliance/Japan all shared a commitment to a stable Gulf (read unimpeded access to oil), American opposition to Iran, its radical policies, and its unpredictable leadership seemed a foregone conclusion.[2]

From an Arab perspective, America's primary flaw is that it is unreliable and apparently irrational. This irrationality results from American support for Israel. The Arabs are not uncomfortable with this support per se because they have grown accustomed to it. What they find irrational is its character. From their perspective, it is inconceivable that Israel is permitted to pursue policies counter to American interests and that the United States appears powerless or unwilling to influence or deter Israel. Furthermore, to many Arabs it seems that the raison d'être for uncritical American support of Israel can be found in the domestic political sphere, not in the international geopolitical one. Thus Arab political elites have become unusually keen observers and students of American elections, activities on Capitol Hill, and the like. Despite these problems, Iran's bellicose opposition to Zionism and vociferous support for the Palestinians permitted the moderate Arab leadership to conclude that Israel would have no greater affection for the Islamic Republic than did anyone else in the region. These factors appeared to suggest that American support for the Arab moderates would be assured because Israel would be as opposed to Iran as would Saudi Arabia and the others. The Iran-Iraq war was one arena in Middle East politics in which the Arab-Israeli conflict would not intrude. Furthermore, Israel was a major beneficiary of this war because the conflict prevented collective Arab-Islamic action against the Jewish state. Thus it was assumed that the United States would be able to define and pursue its interests in the Gulf with comparative ease. Finally, this interest was articulated and codified by a continuing American commitment to the Carter Doctrine, which was promulgated in the aftermath of the Soviet invasion of Afghanistan to prevent the Soviets from taking advantage of the regional power vacuum that developed in the wake of the fall of the shah. Because the Soviets were militarily bogged down in Afghanistan and were pursuing primarily diplomatic initiatives in the Gulf region, it soon became clear that the primary threat to regional security was not Moscow but Tehran. Therefore, the Carter Doctrine was an appropriate response to the fall of the shah although it anticipated the wrong threat.

Logic does not always prevail in the Middle East, nor in Washington for that matter, as the unanticipated linking of the Arab-Israeli conflict with the taking of American hostages in Beirut and the Iran-Iraq war soon demonstrated. Iran-Contra became a factor in Arab politics because of the impact it had on seemingly unrelated issues elsewhere in the region. Indeed, the influence of Iran-Contra on Arab politics is instructive and interesting precisely because it demonstrates how tightly linked seemingly unrelated issues in the Middle East can be.

The Rise and Fall of the Palestine Issue
in Arab Politics

The years from 1985 to 1988 can be crudely broken down into two phases in which the status of the Palestine issue within the Arab world was directly proportional to the Iran-Iraq war. The stronger Iran became, the less important the Palestine question became to regimes that feared for their own stability. Roughly speaking, from 1985 through the first half of 1986, the Palestine issue enjoyed great attention throughout the Arab world; from the second half of 1986 through 1987 its importance plummeted. This situation was reversed somewhat in 1988, when Palestinian insurrection against Israel in Gaza and on the West Bank forced the Arab world once again to devote some of its attention, resources, and energies to the fate of the Palestinians.

On February 11, 1985, Jordanian radio announced that King Hussein and Yasser Arafat of the Palestine Liberation Organization had reached agreement on a formula for a joint Jordanian-Palestinian program for the Middle East. This agreement contained an introduction emphasizing that it "emanates from the spirit of the Fez Summit . . . and from United Nations resolutions relating to the Palestine question."[3] What is *not* stated but should be emphasized is that this agreement became possible because of Palestinian decision making that was heavily influenced in this period by the Israeli invasion of Lebanon, the virtual destruction of the PLO's military capability, and, presumably, the unwillingness of any Arab power to help the PLO, which was trapped in Beirut by the surrounding Israeli army. It is important to emphasize the degree to which the Palestinian leadership was scarred by the ease with which the PLO was left to its fate in Beirut by Arab powers whose commitment to the Palestinians was primarily rhetorical rather than substantive. It is with these events in mind that the Jordanian-PLO agreement should be understood and analyzed, for the PLO did not easily recover from the shock of its abandonment by the Arab world to the Israelis.

The agreement contained five provisions: a call for Israeli withdrawal to its pre-1967 borders; commitment to Palestinian self-determination; resolution of the problem of Palestinian refugees; resolution of the Palestine question in all its aspects; and the convening of an international peace conference that would include the five permanent members of the United Nations Security Council and all parties to the conflict, including the Palestine Liberation Organization, which would participate as part of a joint delegation with Jordan. Although by most standards this draft agreement seems to deviate but little from prior statements by the Palestinians and Jordanians, it does have one new twist that was potentially promising. The willingness of the PLO to participate in a joint delegation with the Jordanians appeared to provide a way around the Kissinger-imposed prohibition on American dealings with the PLO. That is, by allowing Jordan to "front" for the PLO, the PLO would be represented but in a subtle fashion that *could* allow American and Israeli participation. It is this element which most pleased King Hussein, who viewed the accord as a significant step forward. Conversely, it outraged significant numbers of Palestinians, including senior members of the PLO, who felt that Arafat's willingness to subjugate a Palestinian presence at an international conference to a Jordanian one created a dangerous precedent that might lead to the obsolescence of the PLO. Thus, almost immediately after it appeared, the declaration was the subject of intense debate among and between the Palestinian and Jordanian leaderships, each of whom came to interpret the ambiguous fifth point in a different and self-serving fashion.

On a visit to the United States in May 1985, King Hussein took pains to convince American audiences that the agreement represented a significant step forward. At the same time, he attempted the impossible: to portray simultaneous PLO participation in *and* absence from an international peace conference. To American audiences he went much farther than did the original text of the declaration in making reference to his commitment to "the return of the captured territories of 1967 in exchange for recognition of Israel's right to exist within secure and recognized borders."[4] This emphasis on Israel, mentioned repeatedly and directly by the king to Americans, differs from the oblique mention of Israel in the actual text of the agreement in which it appears by name only once and as an "occupier of Arab territory."

Hussein's attempt to have it both ways undercut his effort in virtually every camp. The promulgation of this rather unremarkable agreement unleashed tremendous hostility, embarrassment, and defensiveness among much of the Palestinian leadership, which was aghast at Arafat's apparent ceding of PLO prerogatives to the organization's primary competitor, Jordan's King Hussein, never a great friend of the Palestinians or the PLO to begin with. Thus, only two days after the announcement of the agreement, Farouk Kaddumi, the PLO's equivalent to a foreign minister, in an interview on Radio Monte Carlo, stated, "The PLO will not mandate, authorize, or deputize other parties to share representation." He went on categorically to reject Security Council Resolution 242, the Camp David accords, the Reagan plan, and anything that would deprive the Palestinian people of anything less than full self-determination.[5]

While the PLO was trying simultaneously to kill and promote its agreement with Jordan, Hussein continued his futile attempt to interest the United States in his scheme. The Reagan administration was adamant in its opposition to an international peace conference because such a meeting would allow the Soviets an unacceptable diplomatic role in the Middle East. There was less unanimity in Israel, where the Peres faction of the National Unity government was in favor of an international peace conference and the Yitzhak Shamir portion unalterably opposed to it. Having met secretly with King Hussein, reportedly in London, Shimon Peres was eager to keep alive a plan that he presumably helped the king to develop.[6]

The response throughout the Arab world to the Hussein-Arafat agreement differed. The Egyptians called it a breakthrough because it expressed the PLO's new-found commitment to a peaceful resolution of the problem, but it was condemned by radical Palestinians in Damascus. Yet just as Syria opposed the agreement, Iraq supported it. From the Iraqi perspective this was readily understandable, for by supporting the Jordanian-Egyptian position, Iraq was positioning itself to solicit greater Egyptian support in its war with Iran. Indeed, the Iraqi gesture of support was a harbinger of things to come for on March 18, 1985, Egypt's Hosni Mubarak met with King Hussein in Amman, and the two made a surprise visit to Baghdad to show support for Saddam Hussein in the Gulf war. This was the first visit by an Egyptian leader to Iraq since 1979. It signified the formal welcome of Egypt back into the Arab fold, despite its agreement with Israel, and foreshadowed the impending and gradual diminution in import of the Palestine question in the face of the Iranian threat to regional stability. It cannot be overemphasized that the primary concern of every regime in the region is its own longevity. Iran's increasing strength could pose a threat to such regimes, but ignoring the Palestinians would not. Indeed, Arab regimes have historically been ambivalent about supporting the Palestinians, who were more often regarded with suspicion than empathy by regimes committed to maintenance of the status quo rather than to change. Thus the eclipse of the Palestine question by the Iranian threat represents a well-known syndrome in Arab politics.

Throughout the spring of 1985, the PLO and Jordan tried desperately to generate enthusiasm and support for their joint scheme. Although both King Hussein and Yasser Arafat visited a variety of Arab capitals, individually and in tandem, success continued to elude them. And their "agreement" began to unravel as the PLO continued to redefine the accord's more ambiguous elements in a fashion that would in effect have nullified the agreement in its entirety. By trying simultaneously to support and disavow the agreement, Arafat was engaging in the contradictory political behavior that has historically been a hallmark of his leadership of the Palestinian movement. His olive branch and gun balancing act allows him to seek support in the West and among the moderate Arab leadership through diplomatic efforts, whereas to keep radicals within the Palestinian movement and elsewhere in the Arab world at bay, he supports armed struggle and terrorism.[7] Although neither is terribly convincing, one could argue that Arafat has remained in power despite remarkable adversity and thus his strategy has proven successful. Yet success is a relative term, and there are many who feel that Arafat's political longevity has been at the expense of the Palestinian movement, whose progress in recent years has been minimal.[8]

In August 1985, seventeen representatives of the twenty-one member Arab League convened in Casablanca for an emergency meeting. Somewhat surprisingly, Libya attended the meeting, which was boycotted by Algeria, Lebanon, South Yemen, and Syria. Despite intensive efforts by Jordan and Egypt, the meeting concluded without an endorsement of the Arafat-Hussein agreement. The meeting's final communique took no firm action on the Arab-Israeli conflict, but it did condemn Iran for prolonging the Gulf war. Somewhat later in August, a countermeeting was held in Damascus at which the foreign ministers of Iran, Libya, and Syria called for the creation of a Palestinian state in all of Palestine and condemned the "Arafatist capitulationist policy."[9] Diplomatic activity within the region intensified as attempts were made to close the chasm that had split the Arab League and led to two competing meetings rather than a single unified one. Yet, true to form, Palestinian diplomatic activity was accompanied by an increase in military action as well. Terrorism escalated and culminated on September 25 with an attack on an Israeli yacht moored in the Cypriot harbor at Larnaca. Three Israelis on board were killed.[10] After a ten-hour siege, the three gunmen, two Palestinians and one Englishman, surrendered to the Cypriot authorities. The following day King Hussein spoke at the United Nations and noted that Jordan was prepared to negotiate with Israel under the auspices of a U.N.-sponsored international conference. He also met with President Reagan, who praised Hussein for his "courageous support for peace" even though the

United States remained steadfastly opposed to any international forum that would include the Soviet Union.[11]

The situation in the Middle East continued to deteriorate as Israel responded to the attack on the yacht in Cyprus by an air attack against PLO headquarters in Tunis. In the October 1 raid, almost fifty people were killed. Mubarak and Hussein strongly condemned the raid and promised to continue the search for peace, yet the attack so outraged the Arab world that for the peace plan, a nonstarter from the outset, success was even more elusive. The gap grew wider when the Italian liner *Achille Lauro* was hijacked a week later. After surrendering unconditionally to the Egyptians, the Palestinian hijackers were flown out of the country by the Egyptians and were themselves skyjacked to Italy by the United States. Tensions between Egypt and the United States were greatly increased because the United States felt that Egypt had not told the full truth about the whereabouts of the terrorists and the Egyptians bitterly resented the "diversion" of their unarmed passenger plane by American military aircraft. Finally, on October 13, the British government abruptly canceled a scheduled meeting with a Jordanian-Palestinian delegation, and hopes for the Arafat-Hussein plan were dashed again.

The Impact of the Arafat-Hussein Agreement on Arab Politics

The Hussein-Arafat plan contributed to the fragmentation of an Arab political order that was already badly divided. Shifting alignments and realignments already existed in the Arab world so that certain political issues are often used by various regimes as a means to enhance their preexisting interests and to weaken their foes in the broader conflicts and political alliances that characterize the region. For example, Egypt supported the Arafat-Hussein agreement because it no longer wanted to be penalized for its separate peace with Israel. Its isolation as a consequence of Camp David would be minimized or even terminated if Egypt could convince others to go along. Iraq supported Egypt in its encouragement of the PLO-Jordan agreement, not because it had any great enthusiasm for peacemaking with Israel, but because Iraq sought Egyptian support against Iran. Given the quality and size of the Egyptian military, such support was not trivial. Egypt wanted to support Iraq against Iran because, like other moderates in the region, it feared attempts by Iran to play on regional and domestic political difficulties to foment the type of revolution that brought Khomeini to power. Mubarak has not forgotten that President

Sadat was assassinated by Islamic fundamentalists and that the fundamentalists continue to enjoy support, popularity, and influence in
Egypt. Thus a vanquished Iran could help Egypt keep Islamic fundamentalism at bay. In short, apparent inter-Arab cooperation on certain
issues might have little to do with the issue being cooperated on and
much to do with the differing political goals and character of the
parties working together.

    The year 1985, which began with optimism and attempts to improve
the Arab-Israeli situation, ended with a flurry of terrorist activities,
confusion, and bitter recriminations by all parties in the Middle East.
In early September Iraq, Jordan, and Syria agreed to hold meetings
in Jiddah to resolve their differences in preparation for the thirteenth
Arab Summit scheduled for November. Around this time rumors
surfaced that Shimon Peres and King Hussein had met in Paris.[12]
Sensing a shifting diplomatic climate, Arafat opted for caution and
began to talk of withdrawing support for the PLO-Jordanian peace
initiative about which he already appeared to be ambivalent. Syrian-
Jordanian negotiations began in earnest, and it quickly became apparent that Shimon Peres was unable to persuade the members of his
coalition or even the United States that an international peace conference was in Israel's interest. After the spate of terrorist activity in
Cyprus, the *Achille Lauro* affair, and various bombings, stabbings, and
other incidents in Israel, the political climate in Jerusalem was clearly
not conducive to the conciliatory and diplomatic approach promoted
by Peres and Hussein. Hussein also feared going too far out in front
of the Arab leadership because he did not want to be perceived to be
undercutting Yasser Arafat and the PLO. At the end of 1985 an
Egyptian airliner was hijacked by Abu Nidal's followers. An attempted
rescue by Egypt backfired, and fifty-seven passengers lost their lives.
Slightly more than a month later, Abu Nidal's group staged an attack
against the El Al counters at the Rome and Vienna airports. Although
condemned by the PLO, these actions made Peres's support for an
international peace conference an even more remote possibility than
before. Ironically, neither could he "deliver" the Israelis nor Arafat
the Palestinians. Hussein never spoke for anyone other than himself.

    In February 1986 King Hussein formally abandoned the abortive
agreement with the PLO. After two weeks of discussions with Yasser
Arafat, he charged that the PLO leader had broken his word after
Hussein had extracted key concessions from the United States regarding PLO participation in the conference. In reality, Hussein extracted
little because neither the United States nor the Israelis, with the exception of Peres and his followers, had been enthusiastic about the idea

of an international peace conference. The split between Jordan and the PLO or, more specifically, between Hussein and Arafat, widened appreciably when the king called on the Palestinians to decide who should lead them in an effort to prevent the Israelis from permanently annexing the West Bank. Although Hussein asserted that he would continue to recognize the PLO as the sole and legitimate representative of the Palestinians, he also said he would recognize other modes of representing Palestinian interests as well. This not-so-veiled reference to circumventing the PLO led to an attack on Hussein by Salah Khalaf of the Fatah Central Committee, who called the Jordanian-PLO agreement dead as long as Hussein tried to bypass the PLO. Hussein responded by closing the PLO liaison office in Amman and expelling seven PLO officials from Jordan for "activities likely to endanger the state." These activities heralded the beginning of a war of attrition between Jordan and the PLO in which the Jordanian government used virtually every means at its disposal to exert pressure on the PLO. The Jordanians confiscated the passports of Palestinians expelled from the West Bank by Israel and imposed a boycott of major West Bank newspapers that were critical of Jordan's policy toward the PLO. At the same time, they ordered the arrest of thirty-four Palestinian journalists on the West Bank, if they entered Jordan, for writing material critical of the policies of King Hussein. Hussein even began negotiations with Syria's Hafiz Assad, a longtime opponent of both the Jordanian monarch and of Yasser Arafat. On July 7 the authorities ordered twenty-five Fatah offices throughout Jordan closed on grounds of national security and Arafat's number two, Khalil al-Wazir (Abu Jihad), was expelled from Jordan. Harassment was soon transformed to an all-out attack on the PLO as it became clear that Israel was supporting Jordan's attempt to subvert the organization by allowing the reopening of a Jordanian bank on the West Bank. The opening of a financial institution gave the king a degree of leverage in the occupied territories that might permit him to generate support for himself and opposition to the PLO.

That Jordan and Israel had found a common enemy became readily apparent to West Bank Palestinians, and students at Bir Zeit University burned pictures of King Hussein at a mock funeral held for Palestinian students who had been killed at a demonstration at Yarmuk University in Jordan. As the Jordanian-PLO rivalry intensified, concern arose throughout the Arab world. At an Arab foreign ministers' meeting in Fez in May 1986, unsuccessful attempts were made to repair the damage. Somewhat earlier, a meeting of major Palestinian groups was held in Algiers, and although there had been a tentative reconciliation within the movement, there was no improvement in ties with Jordan. The ministers in Fez could not agree among themselves about how to proceed, and the deadlock remained.

Fragmentation persisted in other quarters of the Arab world as well. Iraq and Syria, which had made tentative overtures to each other, soon found themselves in disagreement. Although Jordan tried to play a diplomatic role between the two, Hussein was soon too preoccupied with his conflict with the PLO to be of any significant help. On July 21 Shimon Peres made a surprise visit to Morocco, where he received a cordial welcome from King Hassan.[13] Because Peres was accompanied by a delegation of Israeli policy makers and journalists, his visit should have promoted significant comment and speculation, but somewhat surprisingly it did not. One would think that the highly publicized visit by an Israeli leader to an Arab country other than Egypt would merit positive attention in the West while raising hackles in the Arab and Islamic world. Remarkably, this was not the case. Libya's Muammar Kaddafi predictably criticized King Hassan for his de facto recognition of Israel, but Egypt's Hosni Mubarak publicly supported the king. And though Syria broke diplomatic ties with Morocco, the Saudis opted only for mild criticism of the king and lamely complained about not having had prior knowledge of the meeting. This general unwillingness to take serious, concerted action against Morocco highlights the political lassitude that gripped the Arab world in this period. Any legitimization of Israel by an Arab state adversely affects the Palestinians, whose goal it is to foster the isolation of Israel by her surrounding Arab neighbors. By ignoring this restriction, Morocco in effect trivialized the Palestinian issue as well as the status of Israel as an enemy of Arabs everywhere.

In reality, what King Hassan did was hardly without precedent in the Arab world although he acted in a more public fashion. Since Golda Meyerson (later Meir) secretly met with Jordan's King Abdallah in November 1947, there have been contacts between Israelis and Arabs.[14] For example, the Israeli invasion of Lebanon in 1982 was initiated after collaboration between the Israeli government and the Gemayel family in Beirut.[15] Elements within the Sudanese government helped Israel to bring Ethiopian Jews to Israel. Peres and King Hussein rendezvous regularly in Europe. During the Iran-Contra scandal, it was revealed that Israel and Saudi Arabia collaborated in shipping arms to Iran. The point is that individual Arab politicians and regimes have always been able to turn a blind eye to the sins of the Zionist state when dealings with Israel were in their interest. Others in the Arab world will castigate those who deal with Israel, not necessarily because they oppose the relationship with Israel, although they certainly may, but because there may be some other problem in their relationship in which criticism for dealing with Israel could be useful.

The best example of the flexibility which Arab governments can bring to bear vis-à-vis dealings with Israel is the experience of Egypt. Its separate peace treaty with Israel virtually excommunicated the largest and most populous state in the Arab world from the Arab camp and kept it isolated for several years. When Egypt's peace with Israel became routinized, the magnitude of its sin was diminished somewhat. Nonetheless, there were significant disruptions to the relaxation of Arab criticism of Egypt such as during the 1982 Israeli invasion of Lebanon, after Israel's attack on the Iraqi nuclear reactor in Baghdad, after Israel's bombing of PLO headquarters in Tunis, and after the assassination of Abu Jihad. These Israeli actions all promoted significant popular outrage and opposition to Israel throughout the Arab world and, by extension, against Egypt, for Egypt indirectly abetted Israel in its actions by maintaining a peace treaty with the Jewish state. By not challenging Israel militarily, Egypt, which has the largest and most powerful army in the Arab world, implicitly allows Israel the security to undertake other adventures such as the invasion of Lebanon, which, some Arabs claimed, might not have been possible if Israel had been obliged to be militarily vigilant against Egypt. Despite all these objectionable activities on the part of Israel, however, the Arab governments can be forgiving, not out of any affection for Israel but for reasons of self-interest. Objectionable actions by Israel will not be excused, but they can be overlooked by an Arab world that has more than enough problems of its own. This triumph of individual nationalisms over transnationalisms (e.g., Pan Arabism) demonstrates that the Arab world is immunized against yet still allergic to Israel.[16] Israel can be temporarily ignored but never permanently forgotten. The troubling factor in this equation is that although active warfare with Israel is relatively low on the agenda of virtually all Arab governments in the region, there is still too great a sensitivity to Israel to go the Egyptian route. This means that no Arab leader will unilaterally make peace with Israel as did Sadat. Although Jordan and Israel have not engaged in major military hostilities since 1967, they have also not been able to end their conflict. The absence of war does not mean peace.

What all this tells us about inter-Arab politics is that although the political maturity of most Arab regimes is beyond question, the ideology of the region has not kept pace with its political practices or realities. The days when the observer of Middle East politics would ask, "Where is today's coup?" appear to be over. Most regimes in the region have been in power far longer than many realize. And the one factor that unites them all is their commitment to the pursuit of their national interests as they define them. In every case this national interest is deemed synonymous with maintenance of the status quo, political stability, and the retention of power by prevailing political elites. Nothing is allowed to stand in the way of these permanent and inflexible goals. Unfortunately for the Palestinians, this has meant that their cause has generated far more enthusiasm than action.[17] For this reason, the Palestine cause was handily displaced on every political agenda by the Iran-Iraq war.

Iran and the Eclipse of the Palestine Issue

Increasing Palestinian disunity and growing concern among the moderate Arab states about the situation in the Gulf began to grow simultaneously. In January 1987 the foreign ministers of the Gulf Cooperation Council met for two days in Riyadh. The primary issue on their agenda was the Gulf war, and they collectively expressed their commitment to the Islamic Conference Organization (ICO) meeting scheduled for Kuwait later in the month. At the ICO meeting, twenty-one heads of state were present, as well as lesser delegates from twenty-three other Islamic countries. Iran was conspicuously absent. And although Yasser Arafat met with King Hussein, Hosni Mubarak, and others at the meeting, the final communique embedded its normal reference to a resolution of the Palestine question within a variety of other issues of Islamic and regional concern such as calling for an end to the Iran-Iraq war, Soviet withdrawal from Afghanistan, and so forth. It was clear that Iran's actions in the Gulf were of far greater concern than was the Palestine question, whose resolution was as remote and unattainable as ever. One beneficiary of all of this was Egypt, whose support against Iran was considered so valuable that its separate peace with Israel became progressively more easy to ignore. Indeed, in April 1987 the secretary general of the Arab League, Chadli Klibi, announced in Tunis that the league was prepared to welcome Egypt back into the fold, thus implicitly legitimizing Egyptian policy toward Israel while highlighting the fact that the Arab world needed Egypt at least as much as Egypt needed it.[18]

Sensing their growing isolation and impending marginality, members of the Palestinian leadership came to realize that unity was the best strategy, and a meeting was called to resolve their differences. Four days after the Arab League's announcement of reconciliation with Egypt, Yasser Arafat, George Habash, Naef Hawatmeh, and other Palestinian dignitaries met in Algiers to plot strategy and reconcile their not inconsiderable differences. As a price for this new-found unity, Arafat privately announced his abrogation of the 1985 PLO-Jordanian accord. And a week later the Palestine National Council (PNC) convened its first unified meeting in more than two years under the leadership of Arafat. On April 21 the PLO's ten-member executive committee officially, formally, and with great fanfare abrogated its (read Arafat's) 1985 accord with Jordan. In return, Arafat was re-elected chairman of the PLO.

The reunification caused barely a ripple in the Arab world. Although a spate of diplomatic shuttling and meetings occurred, primarily on the part of the Jordanians, who are invariably unnerved by any expression of Palestinian unity, the situation remained basically the same. And a series of events elsewhere in the region wrenched attention away from the Palestine issue in a particularly dramatic and, for the Palestinians at least, damaging fashion.

On July 23, 1987, Iranian Hojjat al-Islam Mehdi Qarrubi, the head of Iran's Mecca-bound pilgrims, led a massive unity rally in Medina.[19] On July 31, there was a confrontation between Saudi paramilitary police and Iranian pilgrims who began a political demonstration in front of the Grand Mosque in Mecca. Reports on casualties varied, although the number four hundred was generally accepted; almost three hundred of those killed were members of the Iranian contingent. The disturbances sent shock waves throughout the *ummah* (Islamic world) because political demonstrations, riots, and the loss of life at Islam's holiest spot were inconceivable to Muslims throughout the world. The symbolism of this horrible confrontation was unmistakable to Muslims everywhere.

Since the Iranian revolution, the hostility and competition between Iran and Saudi Arabia has been evident, acrimonious, and steadily increasing. The regimes of both countries have engaged in bitter competition for the role of Islamic state par excellence, and neither has emerged as a clear winner. Each had inherent advantages. Saudi Arabia is the birthplace of Islam and the home of its two holiest places, Mecca and Medina. The Prophet Muhammad was born in Arabia, and as the cradle of Islam and home of its two holiest places, Saudi Arabia occupies a unique place in the hearts of Muslims everywhere. Muslims throughout the world face Mecca (Saudi Arabia) to pray several times a day and the Quran enjoins them to make a pilgrimage to Mecca at least once in their lives if they are able. The Saudi ruling family/ruling elite has effectively capitalized on this unique attribute and has strenuously worked to create a seamless web between their political hegemony and the central Islamic role and character of the country they rule. For the most part, they have been more than successful in playing this role, and most Muslims historically viewed the royal family not merely as members of a conventional political elite but as the guardians of the holy places imbued with certain special responsibilities and characteristics that distinguish them from more conventional politicians elsewhere. The Saudis have tried to enhance this advantage by making Saudi Arabia a uniquely Islamic country. Unlike other states that may be Muslim but not necessarily Islamic because, although Muslims constitute the majority of the population, the country is not formally governed on the basis of Islamic law (e.g., Egypt, Syria, Indonesia), Saudi Arabia made genuine efforts to create an Islamic state run in accord with the Shari'a. Thus the *ulema* play an active role in state management, and until recently Saudi Arabia was clearly the closest thing to a genuine Islamic state.

In 1979 the Iranian revolution catapulted a relatively unknown cleric, Ayatollah Ruhollah Khomeini, to power. One of Khomeini's first acts was to change the name of the country to the *Hukumat-e Islami Irani* (the Islamic Republic of Iran). His goal, as he saw it, was to do in Iran what the Saudis tried to do or, in his opinion, pretended to do, in Arabia. This meant that, according to Khomeini, the Saudis were cynically and hypocritically using Islam to promote their own political and economic interests. Thus Saudi Arabia, according to Khomeini, was not a truly Islamic state or society but a sham. We need not delve too deeply into this conflict within an Islamic context for our primary concern is with its temporal rather than spiritual manifestations. It must be emphasized, however, that it promoted a very real and extremely serious competition and conflict between Iran and Saudi Arabia which involved elements of religiopolitics (leadership of the *ummah*), ethnicity and nationalism (Arab versus Persian), spirituality (Sunni versus Shi'a Islam), political orientation (pro-U.S. versus nonaligned), geopolitics (dominance of the Gulf), ideology (what type of Islam will prevail, the role of Arabism), and regional conflict (different solutions for Lebanon). In short, Iran and Saudi Arabia disagreed on virtually everything.[20] The riots in Mecca highlighted these differences and promoted disunity and shock in the Islamic world in almost equal measures. In the inter-Arab realm these events highlighted the temporary eclipse of the Palestine issue by the "Iranian threat," whose existence came to dominate regional Arab politics, American Middle East policy, and so forth.

By bringing its struggle for regional dominance and its hatred for the Saudi royal family right into Mecca, the stronghold but also potential Achilles' heel of the Saudi royal family, Iran sent an unambiguous message to the Arab world about its intentions and also its methods. These crucial events can best be understood within the context of events occurring immediately before the Mecca disturbances (America's reflagging of Kuwaiti vessels, the arms-for-hostages deal with Iran) and events after the disturbances (the Arab Summit in Amman, insurrection on the West Bank and Gaza). For from an intra-Arab perspective the Mecca riots provide an important chronological watershed for examining the weakening of Saudi Arabia's Islamic hegemony, the rearranging of the Arab political agenda, and the reshaping of the Palestine issue culminating in insurrection on the West Bank and Gaza.

Both Sides Against the Middle: Reflagging and the Iran-Contra Affair

In the months preceding the disturbances in Mecca, the United States pursued two parallel but ultimately contradictory policies. One was very public, the other very private: reflagging Kuwaiti oil tankers, after secretly providing arms to Iran to effect the release of American hostages held in Beirut, presumably by pro-Iranian Shi'a groups. Put somewhat more plainly, the United States was siding with one side in the Iran-Iraq war after siphoning weapons to the other.

Although the Iran-Contra fiasco has been widely written about elsewhere, a brief review of events surrounding the American arms transfer should prove useful.[21] In December 1983 truck bombs were exploded at the American and French embassies in Kuwait. Subsequently, the Kuwaiti authorities arrested seventeen members of an Islamic fundamentalist group who were ultimately sentenced to long prison terms. Their compatriots decided the best way to force their release was to take American hostages, and Beirut quickly emerged as the easiest place to do so. Over the next several years, numerous Americans were seized, including journalists, employees of the American University of Beirut, the CIA chief of station in Beirut, and an American military officer attached to the United Nations peacekeeping forces in Lebanon. Two days after the embassy bombings, the United States announced Operation Staunch, which was an effort to prevent the transfer of arms to Iran.

In May 1985 a consultant to the National Security Council (NSC), Michael Ledeen, met with Prime Minister Shimon Peres to discuss Iran.[22] Peres had asked Ledeen to obtain American approval for an arms transfer to Iran in response to an Iranian request. National Security Adviser Robert McFarlane agreed.[23] In conjunction with CIA National Intelligence Officer for the Middle East Graham Fuller, the NSC prepared a National Security Decision Directive which proposed that the United States relax its global arms embargo against Iran. The ostensible reasons for this directive were to deter Ayatollah Khomeini from turning to the Russians and to effect the release of CIA station chief William Buckley from his kidnappers in Beirut. After reading this policy recommendation, Secretary of Defense Caspar Weinberger wrote, "This is almost too absurd to comment on."[24]

Prolonged analysis of the reasons for this radical shift in American policy lie beyond the scope of this essay. Basically, however, America's 180-degree shift from Operation Staunch to providing arms to Iran can be attributed to a desire to effect the release of CIA station chief William Buckley, who was brutally tortured while in captivity; a desire to effect the release of other American hostages held in Beirut; a willingness to please the Israelis; and a means to raise money that could be used to support the Contras in light of the reluctance of the United States Congress to do so. From the perspective of Arab politics, the most relevant considerations were America's willingness to provide arms to Iran covertly despite Operation Staunch. Furthermore, the Israeli connection was of great interest and concern to the Arabs.

The United States has never enjoyed great credibility in the Arab world. Most Arab states also question America's rationality vis-à-vis its relations with Israel, for it is clear that the Israeli role in Iran-Contra was more than advisory. A significant number of Israeli policy makers felt that over the long run Iraq was a greater threat to Israel than was Iran. These officials believed that Iran and Israel share one factor in common—neither is Arab. Thus the two might bind together because of their common Arab antipathy to these ethnically different regional powers. Despite Khomeini's opposition to Israel, it was felt by such Israelis that after his demise the new and possibly frail Iranian leadership might view relations with Israel as in its own interests because the benefits of dealing with Israel could outweigh their ideological costs. Despite Iraq's new-found moderation (such as establishing ties with the United States and rekindling relations with Egypt despite Camp David), this Israeli school of thought argued that Iraq's fundamental goals had not changed and that Iraq was feigning moderation to generate support against Iran. Once Iraq won the war, it was argued, it would revert to its previous unremitting opposition to the Jewish state. Cleverly appealing to the desire of the Reagan administration to continue its support of the Contras, as well as benefiting from McFarlane's ignorance about Iran, and the rest of the Middle East for that matter, this pro-Iranian stream of the Israeli government was able to persuade Washington to support arms transfers to Tehran.

The Reagan administration made several crucial blunders, the most obvious of which was confusing American hostages in Beirut with those held in Tehran during the Carter presidency. Reagan was eager to avoid the fate of Jimmy Carter, whose handling of the hostage issue contributed to Reagan's victory. There is a crucial distinction, however, between official hostages like those in the embassy in Tehran or William Buckley *and* private citizens who foolishly and *voluntarily* visited Beirut that apparently eluded President Reagan and his advisers. Arab leaders were incredulous that American foreign policy would go against America's own interests simply for some potential good headlines. Furthermore, by exchanging weapons for hostages, the United States encouraged further terrorism for after its capitulation, the United States had more of its citizens taken hostage. As one Israeli scholar, who clearly did not belong to the pro-Iran clique discussed above, wrote at the time: America's "arms-for-hostages deal constitutes a clear deviation from established policy adopted for broader reasons of national interest, regional stability and international order. They violate the principle of not yielding to terrorism and ignore the compelling need to prevent Iran from winning or escalating its war with Iraq. Sacrificing the national interest for the sake of a few hostages could hardly be justified."[25] Although written by an Israeli, these words clearly and accurately reflect the anger and incredulity evident throughout much of the Arab world at America's hypocritical and counterproductive actions. Nine days earlier, on November 3, 1986, the Lebanese periodical *Al-Shiraa* revealed that McFarlane, North, and others had secretly visited Tehran. It was not long before the entire story unraveled and it became widely known that the United States and Israel had secretly been funneling arms to Tehran.

Meaningful American diplomatic activity in the region ground to a halt while the Arab world shifted virtually all its attention to the Gulf and the actions of Iran. Even the Soviet Union was able to benefit from America's duplicity. Its sporadic negotiations with Israel continued while at the same time it enhanced its attempts to improve its diplomatic profile in the region, particularly in the Gulf, where it enjoyed diplomatic ties only with Kuwait, the United Arab Emirates, and Oman. Initiating normalized relations with as many countries in the Middle East as possible became a primary goal of the Soviets, and America's maladroit efforts in arming Iran indirectly aided them.

As revelations about America's arms-for-hostages effort continued to appear in early January 1987, the House and Senate both set up committees to look into what became known as the Iran-Contra affair. The Reagan administration desperately began to seek a way to distract attention from the humiliating scrutiny under which it had fallen. Iran-Contra represented a major failure for it had not ingratiated the United States with the Iranian "moderates" nor had it promoted the release of significant numbers of hostages. Furthermore, it had provided the Soviets with a point of entry into the diplomatic life of the region and alienated the Arab regimes that were most important to the United States. From an American perspective, the replacement of the Palestine issue with the Gulf war was potentially promising because the United States was not well equipped to deal with the Palestine issue. Yet rather than taking advantage of the respite, the United States instead found a new and totally unnecessary way to irritate the Arabs and further damage its prestige in the region. Distrust of the United States was so great that Iraq, in January 1987, accused the United States of providing it with false information about Iranian military concentrations before an Iranian military offensive the year before. Criticism of the United States by other Arab regimes was at times more muted but nonetheless very real. Finally, Kuwait, perhaps inadvertently, provided a desperate United States with a partial way out of the problem.

Throughout the winter of 1986–87 Kuwaiti ships increasingly became targets of Iran. Kuwait sided with Iraq in the war but was particularly vulnerable to attack because of its small size and the corresponding weakness of its navy. Rather than accepting American offers to provide naval convoys to protect its shipping, the Kuwaitis instead proposed that their oil tankers be reregistered in the United States and thus travel under the American flag. This would minimize a visible and large American military presence in the Gulf while at the same time providing Iran less vulnerable targets, for attacks on American shipping would certainly be more risky to Iran than would attacks on defenseless Kuwaiti ships. To increase the attraction of the scheme, the Kuwaitis let it be known that if the United States did not see fit to reflag the vessels, they would turn to the Soviets, who had expressed a willingness to provide support.[26]

Invoking the Soviets accomplished what the Kuwaitis had intended, for the United States formally expressed opposition "to any formal Soviet role in protecting Kuwaiti shipping in the Persian Gulf."[27] The United States decided almost instantly to accept the scheme. Throughout the spring the United States, Saudi Arabia, and Kuwait cleared the Gulf of mines laid by Iran, and in July, the first of eleven Kuwaiti ships registered in the United States and flying the American flag sailed toward Kuwait. They were accompanied by American warships, and the passage was uneventful although the tanker *Bridgeton* did sustain some damage after hitting a mine. From Washington's perspective the reflagging was a success— it firmly placed the United States on Iraq's side in the war with Iran and showed that despite its arms transfers to Iran the United States was still a loyal friend to the Gulf Arab states. This was the Reagan administration's primary goal as it tried with only limited success to live down the Iran-Contra scandal.

As events in Washington continued to unfold, the Arabs forgave but certainly could not forget America's recent involvement with Iran.

By placing half of Kuwait's tanker fleet under the American flag, Reagan made an important gesture both to the Arabs and to the Iranians. Typically, however, the Arabs, in this case Kuwait, accepted American support in a somewhat ambivalent fashion. For at the time of the reflagging the Kuwaiti press was rife with statements reaffirming Kuwait's independence, its neutrality, its self-sufficiency, and so forth. What this highlights is a basic axiom of Arab politics—it is acceptable to need American support; it is unacceptable to admit such a need, at least in public. The reasons for this ambivalence lie in a complex amalgam of new nationalisms, old rivalries, and an understandable reluctance to admit the obvious—that relying on Israel's biggest supporter is better than jeopardizing national security. Historically this has promoted a relationship based on what has been termed the just-over-the-horizon mode of deterrence. The United States, through the Rapid Deployment Force, later called the Central Command, was destined to ensure the security of the weak but wealthy Arab oil producers in the Gulf region. American troops could not be stationed in the region, however, but *near to it* so they could be deployed in time of emergency, save the friendly but weak regimes the U.S. supports, and then quickly withdraw. This camouflaging of U.S. support was meant to promote a low American profile in the region. After the initiation of the Iran-Iraq war, conditions changed. Kuwait required more direct and permanent American involvement, and thus the re-flagging scheme was created. Yet the states in the lower Gulf region were less than enthusiastic about this arrangement for although, like Kuwait, they were loyal to Iraq, they are geographically vulnerable to Iran. Nonetheless, all states in the region agree that being too closely identified with the United States is bad. As we shall see, the worst of all possible worlds was soon to emerge, as the rekindling of the Palestine issues *and* a worsening of tensions between Iran and Iraq occurred simultaneously.

The Amman Summit and the Return of the Palestine Question

The Arab world continued to downplay the Palestine issue for several reasons. First, Arab unity was needed so as to generate as much support for Iraq and opposition to Iran as possible. Second, active American support was needed, and a high-visibility Palestine issue made American involvement politically more costly. Despite the cynicism of Arab governments, the Arab masses maintain a high level of support for the Palestinian people and a concomitant degree of hostility to Israel and, by extension, to Israel's friend and supporter the United States. If the Palestine issue abated, U.S. support could more easily be solicited and accepted. Third, Egypt remains a key element in the Arab world despite having betrayed it by making a separate peace with Israel. As long as the Israeli-Palestinian conflict could be shunted off to the side somewhat, Egypt would be able to take its place in the Arab world again. This was impossible, for example, during the Israeli invasion of Lebanon, when Egypt was a virtual pariah in the Arab world. Thus, to promote Arab unity and permit Egyptian support, the Palestine question had to be put on hold.

As the situation in the Gulf continued to deteriorate, an Arab summit was scheduled for Amman. Although Muammar Kaddafi boycotted the summit, labeling it a U.S.-inspired plot to isolate Iran, there was significant enthusiasm for the meeting throughout the Arab world. On November 8, 1987, the first major Arab League summit in five years to be attended by almost twenty-two heads of state was convened. Its main agenda item was the creation of a unified Arab stand against Iran. Iraq's rival, Syria, tried to head off such action while the moderates, led by King Hussein, sought to have Egypt reintegrated into the Arab world. At a submeeting, the Gulf Cooperation Council countries supported this initiative. Only Syria opposed admitting Egypt back into the Arab League; most other states recognized that Egyptian support against Iran was essential. Significantly, Israel and the Palestine issue were virtually ignored at the meeting for these subjects would not have been compatible with the league's "political rehabilitation" of Egypt. Yasser Arafat and Hafiz Assad vainly tried to keep the Palestine issue high on the agenda, but because the meeting was convened to address events in the Gulf, this focus remained dominant. Although the four-day meeting ended without a decision to readmit Egypt to the Arab League, the delegates did agree that each Arab state could decide for itself whether to reestablish bilateral ties with Egypt. Within hours, the United Arab Emirates announced the resumption of full diplomatic ties with Egypt. In the following weeks numerous states also resumed ties, among them Iraq, Kuwait, Morocco, North Yemen, Mauritania, Saudi Arabia, Bahrain, and Qatar.

The significance of the summit was that for the first time the Palestine issue was clearly and unambiguously relegated to a subordinate position on the Arab agenda. Not only did the Iranian threat supersede it but the reintegration of Egypt into the Arab world further minimized its importance. Indeed, the English-language translation of the summit's resolutions neglected to mention the PLO as the sole and legitimate representative of the Palestinian people, although this standard phrase was present in the Arabic version. Yasser Arafat accused the Jordanians of intentionally leaving it out. Most informed observers feel that it was intentionally deleted to humiliate Arafat, whose status at the summit was far lower than it had ever been. His host, King Hussein, had not yet fully recovered from his anger over the 1985 "agreement" with Arafat, which the king felt the PLO head had not honored. Thus the temptation to exact revenge from Arafat by embarrassing him in front of more than twenty Arab heads of state, in Hussein's own capital city, must have proven irresistible to the king. The Amman summit was of tremendous significance because it portrayed Iran as a greater threat to the Arab world than Israel, permitted Egypt's reentry to the Arab world despite its separate peace with Israel, and relegated the Palestine question to second-class status. For the moment at least, Arab unity appeared to have returned to the Middle East and pragmatism to have triumphed over ideology.

Most Palestinians were unsympathetic to attempts by the Arab leadership to subordinate the Palestine issue to the Iranian threat. Given the historical ambivalence of the Arab states on the Palestine question, such neglect was not without precedent, and Palestinians are acutely sensitive to it. Yet this time something was different. The public humiliation of Arafat as well as the ease with which the summit participants were able to circumvent the Palestine issue were deeply troubling because they did not bode well for future progress in ameliorating the problem of the Palestinians. At the same time, the situation in the occupied territories continued to deteriorate. The Israeli government remained deeply divided and paralyzed but continued to squabble over the merits or demerits of an international peace conference. Sporadic Israeli-Soviet negotiations continued with Israel formally establishing ties with such East Bloc countries as Hungary and Poland. The feeling of isolation among West Bank/Gaza Palestinians grew as they saw no progress for them on any front or support from any quarter.

Although the subsequent uprising in the occupied territories is generally thought to have begun on December 9, 1987, when a car driven by an Israeli crashed into a truck and killed four Arabs, it is important to realize that the preceding months were rife with conflict. For example, in just the second half of October 1987, fifty Palestinians were arrested for being members of Islamic Jihad, the newspaper *Al-Quds* was ordered closed for two years, the editor of *Al-Sha'b* was put under house arrest, attempts were made to deport Mubarak Awad to the United States, Bethlehem University was closed, and there were riots in Gaza. The perceived abandonment of the Palestinians by the Arab

League occurred in the context of uncertainty and conflict on the West Bank and in Gaza. What is significant is that this instability mushroomed into unbridled insurrection against Israel with concomitant loss of life. We can assume that the hardening of the Israeli occupation when combined with the displacement of the Palestine issue by Iran at the Amman summit created a situation in which the Arabs living under Israeli rule felt that they had been completely abandoned by everyone. That was why conflict with Israel in this period grew so dramatically in scale and intensity.

The PLO was as taken by surprise by the Intifada as was Israel, yet it is evident that the uprising significantly closed the gap between the Palestinian leadership outside of the territories and the new leaders and activists that developed within. A detailed review of the Intifada is beyond the scope of this essay; but it is important to emphasize that the Palestinians, once they saw their cause being pushed aside, were able to correct this situation quickly enough to avoid being ignored by their friends, their enemies, and those elsewhere with little direct interest in their cause. Indeed, an outgrowth of the Intifada was an emergency Arab summit called by Algerian President Chadli Ben-Jedid in Algiers in June 1988. Although the stated reason for the meeting was the uprising on the West Bank, the outcome was not totally satisfactory to the Palestinians. Arab financial support for the PLO was not appreciably increased nor was sole responsibility for raising or disbursing these funds given to the PLO. Indeed, even criticism of America's Middle East policy was largely avoided and long-standing Arab financial commitments to the PLO were not formally renewed. The Algiers summit again demonstrated that Arab support for the Palestinians still remained embedded within a larger set of concerns with each state placing its own perceived interests before those of the Palestinians.

On July 30–31, 1988, King Hussein took the surprising step of formally relinquishing control of the West Bank to the Palestine Liberation Organization. In August the PLO Central Committee announced a special PNC meeting to discuss the implications of King Hussein's unanticipated move. On November 12 the PNC opened its meeting in Algiers and proclaimed an independent Palestinian state on the Gaza Strip and West Bank. The following month Yasser Arafat, after being denied a visa to enter the United States, addressed a special U.N. meeting in Geneva. While in Geneva he formally renounced terrorism and recognized Israel's right to exist. The United States almost immediately abrogated its long-standing prohibition against dealing with the PLO and approved Arafat's rejection of terror and recognition of Israel as complying with American requirements for recognition of the

PLO. The United States announced an intention to open a diplomatic dialogue with the PLO through its ambassador to Tunisia, Robert Pelletreau. U.S. recognition of the PLO began a new era in Middle East politics.

Conclusion

The Iran-Contra fiasco was only indirectly a significant element in Arab politics. America's support for Iran ultimately allowed it to be pulled unwittingly, if temporarily, into the Arab camp. Both the Arab world and the United States were sidetracked by Iran; for each Iran became a central rather than a peripheral concern. An unintended consequence was the rise in visibility of those Palestinians living under Israeli occupation who correctly felt that this shift in Arab and, to a lesser degree, American priorities negatively affected them by diverting attention from their plight. The Amman summit may have been a step forward for Arab unity, but it signified a major step backward for the Palestinians. And as the Arab world disengaged, Palestinians grew increasingly more desperate and bold. In their diffuse but well-organized uprising, they have managed to shame and outrage the Arab world, to generate almost universal sympathy, and to confuse an already divided and demoralized Israeli populace. This uprising and its final outcome are likely to remain central features of Middle East politics in the immediate future.

From 1985 to the present, the Middle East has been convulsed with the dual, parallel problems of the Gulf war and the Arab-Israeli conflict. For a while the two tended to manifest themselves separately. What came to pass was the worst of all possible worlds, the manifestation and possible expansion of both crises at the same time. Ultimately, the Iran-Iraq war wound down and settled into a cease-fire and an uncomfortable period of hostility without actual fighting. The manner and effectiveness with which all parties dealt with these changing configurations dominated regional politics for some time. And indeed, we can only begin to anticipate the future course and significance of these problems within the context of the following events and possible developments: the success of the Bush presidency and its policies in the Middle East; the ability of Israel's Likud coalition to remain whole; the willingness and ability of the Palestinian leadership on the West Bank/Gaza to avoid armed conflict while sustaining the Intifada; the outcome of intermittent U.S.-PLO negotiations; the ability of Iraq and Iran to maintain the peace; the political succession struggle in Iran in the wake of Ayatollah Khomeini's death; the situation in Lebanon; and apparent improvements in the status, role, and influence of the

JERROLD D. GREEN

Soviets in the region. In the 1990s it is more than likely that the political character, stability, and direction of the Middle East will stem from the conflicts and political forces that I have discussed here.

Notes

1. Among analyses of American-Iranian relations see James A. Bill, *The Eagle and the Lion: The Tragedy of American-Iranian Relations* (New Haven: Yale Univ. Press, 1988); Rouhollah K. Ramazani, *The United States and Iran: Patterns of Influence* (New York: Praeger, 1982); Barry Rubin, *Paved with Good Intentions: The American Experience and Iran* (New York: Oxford Univ. Press, 1980); Gary Sick, *All Fall Down: America's Tragic Encounter with Iran* (New York: Random House, 1985); John Stempel, *Inside the Iranian Revolution* (Bloomington: Indiana Univ. Press, 1981); and William Sullivan, *Mission to Iran* (New York: Norton, 1981). Other useful works include Robert E. Huyser, *Mission to Tehran* (New York: Harper & Row, 1986), and Anthony Parsons, *The Pride and the Fall, Iran 1974–1979* (London: Jonathan Cape, 1984).

2. The term *Gulf* is meant to circumvent the politically pregnant yet analytically unnecessary appellations *Arabian* or *Persian Gulf*.

3. The complete text of the PLO-Jordan agreement is published in *Palestine Perspectives*, no. 14 (Mar. 1985): 6.

4. While in the United States, King Hussein delivered a speech at a national conference of Arab-Americans (May 4, 1985) and another at the American Enterprise Institute in Washington, D.C. (May 31, 1985). The full texts of both speeches are published in the *Journal of Palestine Studies* 14 (Summer 1985): 15–22.

5. See *Palestine Perspectives*, Mar. 1985, for the full text of the interview with Farouk Kaddumi.

6. For a discussion of King Hussein's "secret" ties with Israel, see Steven Posner, *Israel Undercover: The Secret Warfare and Hidden Diplomacy in the Middle East* (Syracuse: Syracuse Univ. Press, 1987).

7. For an analysis of Arafat's dual political personality, see the aptly titled book by Shaul Mishal, *The PLO under Arafat: Between Gun and Olive Branch* (New Haven: Yale Univ. Press, 1986).

8. Such dissatisfaction with Arafat has been repeatedly emphasized to the author in talks with Palestinians, primarily members of the intelligentsia, in the United States and Europe as well as on the West Bank, and in Jordan, Egypt, the Gulf, and elsewhere throughout the Middle East. The prevailing sentiment indicates that although Arafat's leadership appears to be characterized by a greater fondness for power than for action or decisiveness, he still functions as an important and unique symbol for Palestinians everywhere. This role as "father of his country" permits Arafat to be respected if not necessarily very popular among those politically sophisticated Palestinians who realize that his value as a symbol outweighs his liabilities as a decision maker. Because no one within the movement could currently perform Arafat's symbolic role, his political survival, if not effectiveness, is probably assured in the near term.

9. FBIS, Aug. 26, 1985, cited in the Chronology, *Middle East Journal* 40 (Winter 1986): 118.

10. There was great speculation about whether the Israelis were intelligence operatives as claimed by the Palestinians or tourists as argued by the Israelis.

11. The Reagan statement is from the *Washington Post*, Oct. 1, 1985, and is cited in the Chronology of the *Middle East Journal* 40 (Winter 1986): 116.

12. *New York Times*, Oct. 28, 1985, cited in the Chronology of the *Middle East Journal* 40 (Spring 1986): 308.

13. For an interesting discussion of Israeli-Moroccan relations, see Mark Tessler, "Moroccan-Israeli Relations and the Reasons for Moroccan Receptivity to Contact with Israel" (unpublished).

14. See Howard Sachar, *A History of Israel: From the Rise of Zionism to Our Time* (New York: Knopf, 1982), pp. 322–23, for a description of the Meir-Abdallah meeting.

15. For an analysis of this Israeli-Lebanese tie, see Ze'ev Schiff and Ehud Ya'ari, *Israel's Lebanon War* (New York: Simon and Schuster, 1984).

16. The literature on Pan-Arabism is both prodigious and varied. For a useful if somewhat extreme critique of the current political significance of Arabism, see Fouad Ajami, *The Arab Predicament* (New York: Cambridge Univ. Press, 1981). Although Ajami dismisses Pan-Arabism somewhat too readily for some, he does demonstrate how the Arab world can be anti-Israel while at the same time tolerating Israel because of the pressures of more immediate political exigencies. For an excellent analysis of how Arab foreign policy is made, see Bahgat Korany, Ali E. Hilal Dessouki, et al., *The Foreign Policies of Arab States* (Boulder, Colo.: Westview Press, 1984). Finally, for a discussion of whether Arab politics are particularly Arab, see Jerrold D. Green, "Are Arab Politics Still Arab?" *World Politics* 38 (July 1986): 611–25.

17. For a discussion of the role of the Palestine question in Arab politics, see Aaron David Miller, *The Arab States and the Palestine Question: Between Ideology and Self-Interest* (Washington, D.C.: CSIS Books, 1986).

18. *FBIS*, Apr. 9, 1987, cited in the Chronology, *Middle East Journal* 41 (Summer 1987): 417–18.

19. It is interesting to note that in the parliamentary elections of 1988, Qarrubi received the second largest number of votes. Clearly his efforts in Medina were appreciated both by members of the Iranian elite and by the electorate.

20. Saudi Arabia formally broke diplomatic ties with Iran on April 26, 1988. Significantly, this was during the holy month of Ramadan and on the eve of the season in which pilgrimages to Mecca are most common. Several days before ties were severed, Ayatollah Khomeini exhorted those making the haj to make a political statement and engage in demonstrations as they had the previous year. The Saudis were understandably concerned about this, and the Ayatollah's speech undoubtedly played a role in their decision to break ties.

21. Among the most useful works on the Iran-Contra affair, which include detailed chronologies of events as well as analyses, see Daniel K. Inouye and Lee H. Hamilton, *Report of the Congressional Committees Investigating the Iran-Contra Affair*, ed. Joel Brinkey and Steven Engelberg (New York: Times Books, 1988); National Security Archive, *The Chronology: The Documented Day-by-Day Account of the Secret Military Assistance to Iran and the Contras* (New York: Warner Books, 1987); and John Tower, Edmund Muskie, and Brent Scowcroft, *The Tower Commission Report* (New York: Times Books, 1987). A more interpretive work is Bob Woodward, *Veil: The Secret Wars of the CIA, 1981–1987* (New York: Simon and Schuster, 1987).

22. Ledeen was the author of a controversial book on Iran: Michael Ledeen and William Lewis, *Debacle: The American Failure in Iran* (New York: Knopf, 1981).

23. These events are discussed in National Security Archive, *Chronology*, pp. 98–101.

24. Inouye and Hamilton, *Report of the Iran-Contra Affair*, p. xviii.

25. Mark Heller, "When U.S. Policy Is Kidnapped," *New York Times*, Nov. 12, 1986.

26. For a useful analysis of the reflagging effort, see Barry Rubin, "Drowning in the Gulf," *Foreign Policy*, no. 69 (Winter 1987–88): 120–34.

27. "U.S. Opposes Soviet Role," *New York Times*, Apr. 15, 1987.

5

The Gulf Cooperation Council
Security in the Era Following the Iran-Contra Affair

Shireen T. Hunter

The aftereffects of the ill-fated U.S.-Iran arms deal, popularly known as the Iran-Contra affair, were felt strongly among the Persian Gulf Arab states, members of the GCC. The disclosure of the U.S.-Iran arms deal generated considerable anxiety among the Gulf Arabs regarding American resolve to prevent Iraq's collapse and to deter possible Iranian attempts to expand the war into their territories. Such a change in the U.S. attitude would have drastically altered their security environment and thus their assessment of their security needs and the best strategy to meet them.

This was the case because after the Islamic revolution and the elimination of Iran's stabilizing influence, the U.S. commitment to maintain the security of the Persian Gulf and to protect the Gulf Arab states had become the most important component of those states' security strategy. This U.S. commitment was first enunciated by President Carter within the context of the Carter Doctrine. Admittedly, the Carter Doctrine was developed in response to the Soviet invasion of Afghanistan. It was primarily intended to prevent a Soviet attack on Iran as a prelude to a Soviet advance toward the Persian Gulf. Nevertheless, its ultimate purpose was to defend the Arab side of the Gulf and U.S. interests there.

Following the enunciation of the Carter Doctrine, the U.S. administration proceeded to develop the military and political instruments needed for its implementation. The result was the creation of the U.S. Rapid Deployment Force, later expanded and institutionalized within the context of the U.S. Central Command.[1] When President Reagan took office in January 1981, he added to the Carter Doctrine what has become known as the Reagan corollary.

The central point of the Reagan corollary, as the U.S. president stated it, was that the United States would not permit Saudi Arabia to go the way of the shah and Iran. What this meant, in reality, was that the United States's strategy in the Persian Gulf was not only to prevent Soviet advances but to protect Arab regimes from potential internal and regional threats.

As the 1980s progressed, the much dreaded Soviet invasion of Iran did not materialize. But the Gulf Arab states faced a number of internal and regional security challenges, largely because of the contagious effect of Iran's revolution, plus active Iranian propaganda and subversion.

In November 1979 the Grand Mosque in Mecca was seized by a militant Islamic group. Although this group was Sunni and had no Iranian connection, it nevertheless exacerbated Saudi concerns. During most of 1980 there was significant agitation among the Shi'a populations of Saudi Arabia, Kuwait, and Bahrain. In December 1981, there was an aborted coup attempt in Bahrain, allegedly sponsored by Iran. In short, as the 1980s progressed, it became increasingly evident that, though potentially and in the final analysis, Soviet domination of Iran remained the most serious threat to U.S. interests in the region, for the Gulf Arabs internal and regional security challenges loomed larger.[2]

As a result, the United State's defensive and deterrent posture in the Gulf became increasingly focused on protecting the Gulf Arabs against more home-grown threats. Two other developments contributed to the shift in American focus from the Soviet threat to regional and internal threats to Gulf security.

The first was Iran's ability to turn the course of the Gulf war in the spring and summer of 1982 in its favor by forcing the withdrawal of Iraqi forces and by launching a counteroffensive of its own. This suddenly raised the specter of Iraq's defeat, the possible installation of an Islamic government in Iraq, and a joint Iran-Iraq threat to the survival of current Gulf regimes.

The second development was the course of events in Lebanon after the Israeli invasion of June 1982.[3] One of the consequences of the Israeli invasion was the greater radicalization of the Lebanese political factions, in particular the Shi'as, and the increase in Iran's influence among the Lebanese Shi'as. This development intensified U.S. and moderate Arab fears of the rise of Islamic militancy and the consequences of an Iranian victory not only for the Gulf region but for the entire Middle East. Therefore, by the beginning of 1984, the dominant view among U.S. policy makers was that the greatest threat to U.S. interests in the Middle East and to the security of its Arab allies was Islamic fundamentalism and not the Soviet Union.[4] The logical extension of this diagnosis was that the threat that the United States had to guard against, and gear its strategy to meeting, was Iran and not the Soviet Union. A significant upshot of this new assessment on the part of the United States was a decisive tilt of policy in favor of Iraq in the Persian Gulf war.

This shift in American outlook and policy, in turn, brought the views of the United States and the Gulf Arabs regarding principal sources of threat to Gulf security closer together. Although even before 1984 the United States had been involved in bolstering the Gulf Arabs' ability to meet internal and external security challenges, the GCC states, with the exception of Oman, had been reluctant to recognize their need for an American security umbrella and to cooperate openly with the United States.

The following two factors accounted for the Gulf Arabs' concern about openly cooperating with the United States:

1. Following the Iranian revolution and Egypt's isolation after the signing of the Egyptian-Israeli peace treaty, the radical forces in the Arab world were in the ascendant. All through 1979 and 1980 Iraq was in the forefront of the radicals' efforts to isolate Egypt and sabotage U.S. peace efforts. Feeling almost omnipotent, Iraq was behaving like a hegemonic power in the Persian Gulf. In 1980 Iraq published a so-called Arab Charter setting out the rules of conduct for the Arab states.[5] Regarding the Persian Gulf, a cardinal rule of this charter was to keep the Gulf free from superpower intervention so that Iraq would become the arbiter of events in the area. To make the Gulf Arabs' need for superpower protection unnecessary, Iraq even offered its help in meeting their security needs, and to make its offer of help acceptable, it indicated that it was loosening its ties to the Soviet Union.

2. Parallel with the rise in the radical Arabs' political influence, the Iranian revolution had aroused the passions of Muslims throughout the Middle East. The crucial point is that both of these political trends had strong anti-American components. In fact, one of the reasons for the animosity of radical Arab and Islamic political trends toward the Gulf leadership has been their close association with the United States and the West.

Therefore, it was only natural that the Gulf Arabs would find it difficult to cooperate openly with the United States. Thus Saudi Arabia, a close ally of the United States, criticized Oman for taking part in the U.S. Bright Star military operations in November 1981. The Saudi foreign minister, Prince Saud al-Faysal, said that this went against the principle of nonalignment accepted by all GCC members.[6] Yet, at the same time, the Gulf Arabs needed the U.S. protective umbrella more than ever before.

In the compromise that finally evolved, the Gulf states accepted the

U.S. security umbrella as long as it remained "over the horizon" and did not require basing American arms and military personnel in their countries. Other discrete cooperation in upgrading the Gulf states' ability to meet internal and external security challenges was also acceptable.

The creation of the GCC was another instrument devised to help the Gulf Arabs cope with their new security problems. The GCC would create an institutional framework within which the military resources of the strongest Gulf Arab country, Saudi Arabia, as well as those of Oman, could be marshaled for the defense of the smaller and more vulnerable Gulf states. Similarly, the United States could use the bilateral channels of cooperation already in place with Saudi Arabia and Oman to bolster the security of other Gulf Arabs. And indeed, this strategy was adopted and applied with considerable success.

The Gulf Arab countries developed the GCC Rapid Deployment Force. They also have made some progress toward creating a more coordinated defense system, as illustrated by the GCC military exercises known as the Peninsular Shield. Saudi AWACs were used to enhance the GCC's air defense capabilities, which illustrates the discrete security cooperation between the United States and other Gulf Arabs via the Saudi and Oman connections. The Saudi AWACs also helped Iraq in its war with Iran because the Saudis shared the information gathered by AWACs with Iraq. In short, by 1986 a web of direct and indirect cooperative activities had linked the GCC, the United States, and, to some extent, Iraq.

In addition, in 1984 the United States had begun a serious campaign known as Operation Staunch to stem the flow of arms to Iran in the hope of forcing it to accept a negotiated settlement to the Iran-Iraq conflict. Thus, though the GCC countries continued to put emphasis on their national and collective defense capabilities, and despite their problems in obtaining certain U.S.-made military equipment because of congressional opposition, the American connection had become the most important part of the GCC security strategy.[7]

Thus the discovery that the United States was engaged in secret negotiations with Iran and had even supplied it with arms was disquieting to the Gulf Arabs. But it was not so much the fact of U.S. contacts with Iran that disturbed the GCC states. It is unlikely that the Gulf Arabs were totally unaware of U.S.-Iranian contacts. Indeed, some prominent business figures with close ties to the Gulf Arab political leadership were involved in these contacts.[8] Nor was the idea of U.S.-Iranian contacts per se unbearable to them. Indeed, if these contacts could have led to a moderation of Iran's behavior, the Gulf Arabs would have been the first to benefit.

It is also worth remembering that 1985–86 was a period of relative thaw in Iran-Gulf relations. The Gulf Arabs were disturbed by the thought that the United States may have been tempted to make a deal with Iran at Iraq's expense or that a U.S.-Iranian deal may have indicated a slackening of U.S. resolve to protect the Gulf Arabs and to continue pressuring Iran so as to end the war in a way that would have led to the establishment of a regional balance of power in the Arabs' favor or at least an even balance. Another reason for the Arabs' negative reaction to the U.S.-Iran contacts was the role played by Israel, which the Arabs feared might indicate a resurrection of old Iran-Israel ties, albeit in a discrete manner.

Thus, after the Iran-Contra affair the strategy of the Gulf Arabs and those within the United States's policy-making community, who had all along opposed the so-called Iran option, became focused on how to use the Iran-Contra incident to develop a U.S. strategy built around the principles of pressuring Iran, excluding for a long time any dealing with Iran, and becoming more actively involved in the conflict on Iraq's side.[9]

Before elaborating on the details of this strategy, how it was implemented, and how successful it has been, I must stress the following points. There is often a tendency in all writing, either in the popular press or in more academic publications, to refer to the Gulf Arabs or the GCC as if they were a single political body with common views on every issue. Admittedly, the GCC's efforts to present to the outside world as unified a facade as possible and the general Arab practice of glossing over differences in their declaratory policy have contributed to these tendencies. To get a more accurate image of what is happening in reality, it is important to look beneath this facade.

Although the Gulf Arab states that formed the GCC shared many common traits, aspirations, and views, including significant security concerns, they are also very different from one another. These differences affect their perceptions of their interests and the best way of achieving them. In addition, there is significant rivalry and conflict of interest among GCC members. Because of regional conditions, these differences and rivalries have been somewhat muted in the past several years, but they do still exist. For example, in the spring of 1986 Bahrain and Qatar almost went to war because of a dispute about the ownership of Hawar Island.[10] It was only because of Saudi arm-twisting of both Qatar and Bahrain, over which Saudi Arabia exercises considerable influence, that war was averted. But the conflict is still unresolved.

Thus to get a correct picture of what is happening in the GCC in regard to regional security issues, it is important to look beneath the facade of joint communiques and study the action of individual Gulf

states. There have been considerable differences in the views and
perceptions of the GCC members regarding the seriousness of the
Iranian challenge, the Iran-Iraq war, and the best approach toward
Iran.

Several factors contribute to these differing views of Iran among
the Gulf states. One is geographical proximity. Kuwait, which is close
to both Iran and Iraq and was only an earshot away from the Gulf
battlefields, inevitably had a different perception of threat than one
better situated. The internal ethnoreligious makeup of individual Gulf
countries also affects their perceptions. Again, Kuwait's example is
instructive. Kuwait is the Gulf country with the largest and longest-
established Palestinian community. It also has a large, and mostly
disaffected, Shi'a population. The existence of this large Shi'a community makes Kuwait vulnerable to Iran's ideological challenge. In theory,
its vulnerability should have encouraged Kuwait to adopt a more
neutral stand vis-à-vis the Iran-Iraq war so as to protect itself against
Iranian manipulation of its Shi'a population. But Kuwait adopted a
totally different strategy for two reasons. First, Iraq's geographical
proximity and its ability to occupy parts of Kuwait have encouraged
Kuwait's extensive and multidimensional aid to Iraq. Second, a large
portion of Kuwait's Palestinian population consists of extreme Pan-
Arab nationalists, who are very influential in the Kuwaiti press. The
Pan-Arabists have been strong advocates of total and unconditional
support for Iraq, and many of them have links to Iraq.[11] Also, the Pan-
Arabists have traditionally been hostile to Iran, even before the Islamic
revolution and Iran's ideological threat to Kuwait.[12] The combination
of these factors has made it very difficult for Kuwait to remain neutral
in the Gulf war.

The United Arab Emirates, by contrast, do not suffer from these
handicaps and thus have been able to maintain a balanced posture
between the two combatants, despite significant pressure from Iraq.[13]
This has also been true of Oman, which currently has the best relations
with Iran. Even Qatar to some extent, despite its very close links with
Saudi Arabia, has managed to maintain tolerable relations with Iran.[14]

In addition to Saudi Arabia's legitimate fears of Iran's intentions, its
own power ambitions in the Persian Gulf region and the intense Wa-
habi dislike of the Shi'as, whom they consider heretics, have contributed to its attitude toward the war and relations with Iran. Again the
impact of this factor on Saudi-Iranian relations predates the Islamic
revolution and the Gulf war.[15] These factors, which have all along
been very important in determining the Gulf states' perception of
their regional security, their own security requirements, and their

attitude vis-à-vis relations with Iran have also determined their reaction to the Iran-Contra affair and their security strategy following it.

The U.S. Credibility Gap and Kuwait's Reflagging Strategy

The Gulf Arabs' fears about U.S. intentions after the disclosure of the U.S.-Iran arms deal were exacerbated because these disclosures occurred at about the same time Iran was engaged in the last of its major offensives against Basra. That was a time of heightened tension and anxiety in the Gulf. A few months earlier, in February 1986, Iran had captured the Fao Peninsula, and there were strong fears that the psychological impact of the Fao victory might so drastically undermine Iraqi morale as to lead to its internal collapse, if not military defeat.

The Fao victory had already led to a stiffening of the GCC position on Iran. This is not surprising because the capture of the Fao peninsula not only made Iraq's position more vulnerable but exacerbated Kuwait's security dilemma by giving Iran greater ability to pressure it. As a result, after the capture of Fao, the GCC issued one of its strongest warnings to Iran, stating that an attack on any of the GCC countries would be considered as an attack on all GCC members.

This shift in the GCC's attitude is especially important in light of the statement issued by the sixth GCC summit in November 1985. The communique issued at the end of the 1985 summit contained the most positive statement on the Iran-Iraq war thus far from the Iranian perspective. It seemed that the GCC states were trying to adopt a more evenhanded approach toward the war. Even if this was not exactly the GCC's intention, Iran choose to interpret it as such.[16]

Moreover, the GCC communique of 1985 was not an isolated affair in GCC-Iran relations. Quite the contrary; 1985 was a period of thaw in Iran's relations with the GCC. Even Iran's relations with Saudi Arabia had improved somewhat after Prince Saud al-Faysal, the Saudi Arabian foreign minister, visited Iran in May 1985. Relations with Kuwait, however, remained strained, particularly after the assassination attempt on the emir's life by elements suspected of having links to Iran. In short, coming as it did after the capture of Fao and just before the Iranian offensive against Basra, the disclosure of the U.S.-Iran arms deal intensified the Gulf Arabs' anxieties and reopened the perennial debate about U.S. credibility. Judged by the public statements of Gulf and other Arab officials, U.S. credibility in the Middle East region reached its lowest level since the fall of the shah in 1979 and the Israeli invasion of Lebanon in 1982.

The widening credibility gap between the United States and its Gulf and other moderate Arab allies also caused serious concern within U.S. policy-making circles. These concerns, in turn, led to efforts on the part of the United States to reassure its Gulf and other Arab allies.

The failure of the Iran policy also discredited the proponents of the thesis that the United States should try to establish a dialogue with Iran. U.S. Secretary of Defense Caspar Weinberger openly stated that there was no sense in a U.S.-Iranian dialogue unless there was a change of regime in that country.

Moreover, the proponents of more direct and active U.S. support for Iraq became more influential. The result was the development of a new U.S. strategy of increasing pressure on Iran. In addition to changes in the United States, however, the aftereffects of the Iran-Contra affair in Iran made the pursuance of a U.S.-Iranian dialogue extremely difficult, if not impossible.[17]

The new U.S. strategy entailed using the United Nations to bring pressure on Iran. The result of these efforts was the passage of U.N. Security Council Resolution 598 in July 1987. This resolution had the endorsement of all five of the permanent members of the Security Council. The resolution called for a cease-fire between Iran and Iraq, withdrawal to the internationally recognized borders, exchange of prisoners of war, and the start of negotiations for the conclusion of a peace treaty. In an apparent concession to Iran, the resolution provided for the establishment of a committee to investigate the origins of the war. But its most significant aspect was the provision that in the case of noncompliance by either of the belligerents, the Security Council would proceed with the imposition of sanctions, including an arms embargo on the recalcitrant party.

Ostensibly, the resolution was phrased in a way to make it attractive to Iran. The more widespread expectation, especially on the part of the United States, however, was that Iran would reject the resolution outright, thus enabling the United States to push aggressively for an arms embargo against Iran.[18] Nor was this expectation unjustified. The mere fact of the creation of the committee did not mean that Iraq would automatically be identified as the aggressor, a goal Iran had long pursued. Indeed, immediately after the passage of the resolution, the Iraqis made it clear that they had every intention of proving that Iran was responsible for the war.

Iran, however, did not reject the resolution outright. Rather, it expressed satisfaction with certain aspects of the resolution, thereby creating the hope that perhaps greater efforts by the U.N. secretary general could lead to a breakthrough. This Iranian reaction, plus improvements in Soviet-Iranian relations, frustrated the American strategy of pressuring Iran through the United Nations. The United States had to find another way of reassuring the Gulf Arabs and undoing the damage done to its Gulf ties.

Such an occasion was presented by the Kuwaiti request to the United States for reflagging of eleven of its tankers and offering them protection. The most widely accepted explanation for the Kuwaiti request has been that Iranian attacks on its shipping were increasing. The reasons given for U.S. acceptance of the Kuwaiti request have been more varied, ranging from a desire to prevent Soviet infiltration of the Persian Gulf to protection of freedom of navigation. For Kuwait, no doubt increased Iranian attacks on its shipping, in part in response to devastatingly successful Iraqi bombings of Iran's oil installations, had a role. But at no time had the Iranian attacks seriously interfered with Kuwait's oil exports and thus its economic well-being. One aspect of the Kuwaiti strategy, which has received little attention, is that it was very similar to the Iraqi strategy of internationalizing the Persian Gulf war by drawing in outside forces, particularly the two superpowers and the principal European powers.

This strategy began when Iraq initiated the tanker war in 1984. The logic behind the Iraqi tanker war strategy and the Kuwaiti reflagging exercise has been that they would either provoke Iran into actions that would trigger retaliation by the European powers or the superpowers, especially the United States against Iran, or it would lead the superpowers to impose sanctions on Iran that would paralyze its war-waging capability. The result, the Gulf Arabs and Iraq hoped, would be an Iranian defeat and the imposition of a humiliating peace on Iran, which might lead to internal disturbances or perhaps even a change of regime in that country. And, indeed, some U.S. policy makers and some among the expert community considered certain U.S. military action against Iran desirable.[19]

It is difficult to ascertain whether Kuwait had coordinated its reflagging strategy with Iraq, but the effects of the reflagging were favorable to Iraq. Moreover, although both Kuwait and the United States used the so-called shock of the Iran-Contra affair to proceed with their new strategy, there is some evidence that the Kuwaiti strategy predated the disclosure of the secret U.S.-Iran arms deal. For example, a U.S. Senate Foreign Relations Committee report, issued in October 1987, revealed that Kuwait had approached the United States and the Soviet Union in September 1986.[20] Be that as it may, what is important within the context of this study is the attitude of other GCC countries toward the Kuwaiti reflagging strategy. The GCC countries, as is their custom, tried to maintain a facade of unity. In private, however, there were significant differences of opinion among GCC members. For example,

Oman and the United Arab Emirates opposed Kuwait's strategy and U.S. reflagging of Kuwaiti tankers, which they feared could lead Iran to desperate actions against the Gulf states. Moreover, both the Gulf and other Arabs had mixed feelings about the U.S. role in the region.[21]

They also feared that U.S. pressure on Iran could lead Iran to turn to the Soviet Union. No doubt the Gulf states, notably Oman and the United Arab Emirates, had established their own lines to Moscow, but they nevertheless appreciated the Iranian buffer between themselves and the Soviet Union. These Gulf states were also worried about their future relations with Iran beyond the current crisis and the Iran-Iraq war. They realized that U.S. warships would not remain in the Gulf indefinitely. They were also aware that total alienation of Iran would not be in their long-term interest.

Iranian officials tried to impress this point on the Gulf states. Prime Minister Musavi, for example, said that the Gulf states must remember that the United States would eventually have to leave the Gulf, but these states had to live with Iran for a long time. There was also fear of increased Iranian-inspired subversion in the Persian Gulf.[22]

Amid the tensions arising from the Kuwaiti request and Iranian efforts such as conducting the so-called martyrdom maneuvers, the Omani foreign minister visited Tehran in hopes of preventing the United States from acceding to the Kuwaiti request. During this visit the speaker of the Iranian Parliament, Hashemi Rafsanjani, declared that Iran and Oman should be jointly responsible for the security of the Strait of Hormuz. The Iranians also sent messages to Kuwait that if it withdrew its reflagging request, Iran would not attack Kuwaiti ships. Because Iranian attacks were not the only, or even the principal, reason for the Kuwaiti request, these messages went unheeded.

The reflagging commenced, and at one time the United States had close to forty naval vessels in the Persian Gulf. The European countries also made some contribution to the naval buildup in the Persian Gulf.[23] Yet Kuwait's reflagging strategy and the United States's willing cooperation with it have been only partly successful. The judgment on the success of the reflagging operation would, of course, depend on an assessment of its objectives.

In the beginning, a variety of reasons ranging from the protection of international shipping to the prevention of Soviet infiltration of the Gulf and the reassuring of the Gulf Arabs were cited for the U.S. reflagging operation. These certainly were primary objectives. But both Kuwait and the United States hoped that U.S. naval presence in the Gulf would have an effect on the course of the Iran-Iraq war.

The Kuwaitis and the Saudis hoped that Iran would do something foolish, such as attack an American warship, which would lead to massive U.S. retaliation. But Iran did not take on the United States. Nevertheless, when an Iranian missile accidently hit the reflagged Kuwaiti tanker *Sea Isle City*, the United States retaliated by bombing an Iranian oil platform.

Although neither Kuwait nor Saudi Arabia said anything publicly, they thought the U.S. retaliation against Iran was not strong enough. But the United States had good reasons for not launching a massive military strike against Iran, among them the fear of escalation and getting bogged down in a protracted conflict with Iran and uncertainty about the Soviet reaction.

After the *Sea Isle City* incident and until the April 1988 encounter, both the United States and Iran scrupulously avoided unduly provoking each other and avoided a massive military confrontation. For a long time the reflagging did not affect the course of the war and then not decisively; it did not force Iran to accept a negotiated peace, and it did not solve the Gulf Arabs' security dilemma. Nor did it lead to open security cooperation between the GCC and the United States. Both Saudi Arabia and Kuwait refused to grant military facilities to the United States, even though this attitude raised the ire of the U.S. Congress.

In this period, those Gulf Arabs who managed to maintain reasonable relations with Iran fared better. Oman, for example, helped prevent an undue escalation of the U.S.-Iranian confrontation by discretely acting as an intermediary between the two countries. For example, the bodies of the Iranian crew killed by a U.S. helicopter gunship were flown to Oman, and Iranian officials retrieved them in Muscat. In short, the way the reflagging episode began and the approach of individual GCC members toward it once more proved that beneath the facade of GCC unity, there were significant differences in their perceptions of the nature and magnitude of threats to their security, including those emanating from Iran, and the best way of coping with them.

The Mecca Incident and Saudi-Iranian Crisis

Since the advent of the Islamic revolution in Iran, the behavior of Iranian pilgrims during the hajj ceremonies has become a security problem for Saudi Arabia and a source of tension in Saudi-Iranian relations.

The Iranians have used the hajj ceremonies to spread their revolutionary message among other Muslims. They have also used this occasion to criticize what they call imperialism, Zionism, and Arab reaction, although they avoid criticizing Saudi Arabia by name. Nevertheless, the Saudis have felt nervous about the impact of Iranian activities on their internal security. There have also been allegations that the Iranians have on occasion tried to smuggle firearms into the kingdom.

In response, the Saudis in the past criticized Iran for using the hajj for political purposes, which they argue is against Islam. Their taking this position is ironic because Saudi Arabia, more than any other Muslim country, has used Islam for political purposes, namely, for legitimizing power domestically and for expanding influence abroad. The Saudis have also on occasion limited the numbers and range of activities of Iranian pilgrims. At no time, however, had the Saudi police used firearms against Iranian pilgrims. But during the hajj in July 1987, the Saudi police opened fire on Iranian pilgrims and killed four hundred of them. At first the Saudis denied that firearms had been used and accused the Iranian pilgrims of carrying knives and trying to attack the police. They also claimed that the Iranian pilgrims had died in the stampede that followed police intervention. Later on, however, Iranian officials displayed the bullet wounds in the victims' bodies, which proved that the Saudis had indeed used firearms.

The behavior of Iranian pilgrims had always been a source of tension between the two countries, but both of them were reconciled to it. Thus the question arises, Why did the Saudis overreact to Iranian protests during the 1987 hajj? The answer is that after the disclosure of the Iran-Contra affair, and particularly after the Kuwaiti reflagging strategy, the mood of the Saudi Arabian leadership had shifted to one of confrontation toward Iran. Saudi overreaction to an event that had become more or less routine was part and parcel of a U.S.-Arab strategy of putting pressure on Iran after what they perceived to have been the failure of a policy of engaging it in a dialogue. It is not farfetched to say that the presence of the U.S. Navy in the Persian Gulf may have contributed to the Saudi decision to take a tougher stand against Iran. At the same time, the Iranians, who did not want to take on the United States and were feeling pressured as a result of the Kuwaiti reflagging ploy, tried to use the pilgrimage protests to intimidate Saudi Arabia and Kuwait. Thus the Iranian overplaying of the hajj protest contributed to the Saudi decision to take a tougher stand because the Saudis did not want to appear to be intimidated by Iran.

The Mecca incident created a great deal of tension between Iran and Saudi Arabia. During the GCC summit in 1987, King Fahd, harshly criticized Iran, saying that it should stop imposing its ideas on the Gulf states—these ideas were alien to their Arab and Islamic character. In the same speech, he admonished Iran to make peace with Iraq and join the fight against Israel.[24]

Iranian officials warned the Saudis that the deaths of the Iranian pilgrims would not go unanswered. But with the buildup of the U.S. naval presence in the Persian Gulf, Iran was in no position to take retaliatory measures against Saudi Arabia.

Certain Arab countries, including Syria, tried to ease the tensions between the two states. The GCC, as could be expected, was supportive of Saudi Arabia and critical of Iran. Nevertheless, there were gradations of criticism from individual Gulf countries reflecting their overall approach to dealing with Iran. Although the Mecca incident did not lead to a military confrontation between Iran and Saudi Arabia, it began a process of deterioration in Saudi-Iranian relations that finally led to the Saudi decision in April 1988 to break diplomatic relations with Iran.

Arabs Unite Against Iran: Egypt's New Role in the Gulf

For some time the Iran-Iraq war had been an Arab-Persian war in all but name. From the very beginning, Iraq, to harness Arab support for itself, portrayed the war against Iran as the so-called defense of Arabism and the Arab nation against the racist Persians.

Arab states financed Iraq's war, provided logistical and intelligence support, and contributed military advisers and volunteers. Iraqi prisoners of war captured by Iran included a significant number of other Arabs. Nearly 2 million Egyptians working in Iraq kept the Iraqi economy going. Moreover, all through the war the Arab and Gulf press called for a much more open Pan-Arab response to Iran, including the invocation of the Arab Defense Pact.

Several efforts were made to convene an Arab summit totally devoted to the consideration of the Iran-Iraq conflict which would ratify and sanctify already substantial Arab support to Iraq. Because of intra-Arab differences, including those about how to handle relations with Iran, such a gathering was not possible until November 1987. Even at the Amman summit in November 1987, Arab states did not adopt a totally unified and clear stand either against Iran or on other issues such as the readmission of Egypt into the Arab fold. But those Arab states that had reservations about these issues did not voice them openly, and the summit gave the appearance that the Arab world was uniting against Iran and bringing back Egypt.[25]

Egypt did indeed come out the winner from the Amman summit. At its close, the GCC countries reestablished diplomatic relations with Egypt Shortly after that, President Husni Mubarak visited the Gulf Arab states. In the meantime, it was widely speculated that the Gulf

Arabs would resume financial aid to Egypt and that Egypt would export military equipment to the Gulf states. Egypt has since frequently been mentioned as having accepted new responsibilities in the defense of the Gulf as a counterweight to Iran. This is an ironic turn of events because in the 1960s Saudi Arabia appealed to Iran to act as a counterweight to Egypt.

Not all the Gulf states were equally enthusiastic about Egypt's new role or about portraying an image of the Arab world ganging up against Iran. Thus, for example, Oman and the United Arab Emirates indicated to Egypt that they would prefer that President Mubarak not go to Iraq immediately after his Gulf tour because they did not want the trip to appear as an anti-Iranian exercise. Saudi Arabia and Kuwait were more eager to involve Egypt directly in the Gulf security arrangements. Growing Egyptian-Gulf security cooperation may have had something to do with the Saudi decision to send back the Pakistani military contingent that had been in the kingdom since 1981. The official excuse given for this decision was the presence of a significant number of Shi'as in the Pakistani contingent, but a more important reason was that Pakistan had made it clear that its troops would not participate in a war against Iran. Yet according to press reports, although Saudi Arabia never thought of going to war against Iran, Iran had not overruled such a possibility. No doubt all these considerations contributed to the Saudi decision. But the introduction of the Egyptian factor into the Gulf states' calculations about their security must also have affected the Saudi decision.

Thus far, however, the details of an Egyptian-GCC security cooperation have not been worked out or formalized, and there still are significant differences of opinion among the GCC members stemming to a great extent from the Gulf Arabs' different views of Iran and the best way to deal with the Iranian challenge.

U.S.-Iran Military Clash, Rupture of Saudi-Iranian Diplomatic Ties, and Iraq's Capture of Fao

By the end of 1987, the situation in the Persian Gulf seemed to be stabilizing. Military confrontation between Iran and the United States had been avoided, and the two countries seemed to have established some kind of strategic signaling to avoid confrontation.

This relative stabilization and the high cost of maintaining a large naval presence in the Persian Gulf led the United States to reduce the number of its ships there. U.S. Gulf policy seemed to have been moderately successful, although its impact on the war had been minimal. The Gulf Arabs had been reassured of the U.S. commitment to their security, and a military conflict with Iran had been avoided.

While the Gulf war was still going on, particularly in the northern front in the Kurdish areas, it had become obvious that Iran's military thrust had been stalled. There were also growing indications that it might be possible to negotiate an informal cease-fire to the war within the United Nations. Moreover, the Palestinian uprising in the West Bank and the Gaza Strip had focused Arab and international attention on the Arab-Israeli conflict and away from the Persian Gulf.

This period of relative calm in the Persian Gulf was very short-lived. Iraq, sensing Iran's military weakness and concerned about the diversion of international attention from the Gulf scene, in March 1988 once more launched massive and indiscriminate attacks on Iranian cities with Soviet-made missiles whose range had been extended. Iran retaliated in kind, albeit on a much smaller scale because it lacked adequate weaponry. The stepped-up Iraqi attacks on Iranian cities were accompanied by gassing of the residents of the Iraqi Kurdish town of Halabja as punishment for their cooperation with Iranian troops and autonomy-seeking Iraqi Kurdish rebels.

Both of these developments had negative consequences for Iraq's diplomatic position. The Soviet Union, which was embarrassed because Soviet-made missiles were hitting Iranian cities, called on the United Nations to halt the war of the cities. The Iraqi atrocity of gassing its own civilian population brought even the United States to criticize the Iraqi action, although it softened this criticism by accusing Iran of also having used chemical weapons.

In the West European media criticism of Iraq was even stronger. A subtle shift seemed to be taking place in international public opinion with the growing realization of Iraqi excesses. Two developments, however, reversed this trend: the hijacking in April 1988 of a Kuwaiti passenger plane by a group of extremist Lebanese Shi'a and the damaging of the USS *Roberts* by a mine in the Persian Gulf waters the same month. The hijacking undid whatever benefits Iran might have gotten out of the shift of opinion against Iraq because allegations were made regarding Iran's involvement in the incident, although no conclusive or even strong circumstantial evidence of Iranian involvement was provided. The second incident was far more consequential. Initial U.S. reaction to the damaging of the USS *Roberts* was that the mine that hit the *Roberts* had been laid much earlier, probably during the early part of the Kuwaiti reflagging episode in 1987. Later on, the United States decided that the mine had been laid more recently and retaliated by bombing two Iranian oil platforms that exported about 150,000 barrels of oil per day. Unlike the previous occasion in 1987, when the Iranians had taken American bombing of the Rustam oil field without retaliating, this time the Iranians fired back. As a result, the United States bombarded Iranian naval vessels, destroying three frigates, or as some reporters put it, a third of the Iranian navy.

Later the United States tightened the screws on Iran by deciding to offer protection to neutral shipping in the Gulf, thereby offering Iraq a "free-fire zone" against Iran. As the U.S.-Iranian confrontation intensified, the attitude of the Gulf Arab states, particularly Saudi Arabia, against Iran also hardened. In April 1988, Saudi Arabia broke diplomatic relations with Iran.

The Saudi decision was apparently related to the 1988 hajj ceremonies and was aimed at discouraging large numbers of Iranian pilgrims from going to Saudi Arabia. Immediately after the rupture of Saudi-Iranian diplomatic relations, it was speculated that other Gulf Arab states might follow suit. Such a development did not occur. On the contrary, Shaikh Zaid, the United Arab Emirates president, stated that they thought it was better to have relations with Iran than not to have them.[26] This statement reaffirms one of the principal points of this essay—that it is not advisable to approach GCC-Iranian relations or other issues related to Gulf security as if the GCC were a single political unit and always acted in a totally unified manner. Rather, there have been and will continue to be subtle, and at times not so subtle, differences in these nations' approach toward Iran and other security issues in the region.

The hardening of the Gulf Arab attitude toward Iran also reflected the changing balance of power in the Gulf with the increased U.S. military presence and the reverses suffered by Iran in its war with Iraq, dramatically illustrated by the recapture of the Fao peninsula by Iraq in April 1988. Despite these reverses, however, until early July 1988 there were no signs that Iran was prepared to accept a cease-fire based on Resolution 598. Then in July 1988, an Iranian passenger plane was hit by a missile fired by the USS *Vincennes*, killing 299 passengers. This incident had a traumatizing effect on Iranian public opinion. Many Iranians came to see the war as changing from one with Iraq—or even the Arab world— into one with the United States, a confrontation they knew they could not win. As a result of this experience, public pressures inside Iran to end the war increased.

Despite inflammatory rhetoric from the Ayatollah Khomeini, Iran did not take any rash actions against the United States. Rather, it sought vindication for its grievances through the international organizations. It got no satisfaction either in the United Nations or in the International Civil Aviation Organization (ICAO), which illustrated Iran's international isolation. In its report, however, the ICAO declared the U.S. guilty of gross negligence. The United States declared that the incident was the inevitable result of Iran's inflexibility and the warlike conditions of the Persian Gulf and said its actions were taken in self-defense.[27] Some U.S. commentators, however, held the provocative posture of the U.S. Navy in the Gulf responsible for the incident.[28]

The cumulative effect of U.S. military actions against Iran and its military reverses finally forced it unconditionally to accept Resolution 598, and on August 20, 1988, a U.N.-sponsored cease-fire came into force between Iran and Iraq.

Post-Cease-fire Developments

The most significant result of the Iran-Iraq cease-fire has been the reassertion of the old pattern of Arab-Iranian and intra-Gulf Arab relations. The last months of the war left Iran militarily far the weaker of the two belligerents. Thus in their old practice of maintaining a balance between the two largest Gulf powers, most GCC countries began to improve their ties with Iran. Kuwait, once freed from the pressures of war, moved quickly to mend relations with Iran and send its ambassador back to Tehran. Oman's and the United Arab Emirates's relations with Iran grew warmer, and there were talks of closer economic cooperation. The Iranians, however, stated that for continued improvement, the Gulf states must make up for past behavior by helping in the peace process.[29] Iran's relations with Saudi Arabia remained strained over the issue of the number of Iranian pilgrims allowed to come to Saudi Arabia for the hajj.

After the cease-fire, it became clear that Iraq, emboldened by its victories, intended to become the principal Gulf power by, among other things, increasing its naval power and presence.

Because Iraq's coastline in the Persian Gulf was limited, it had been pressuring Kuwait to lease Bubiyan Island and refused to finalize the demarcation of borders.[30] Iraqi ambitions have increased the Gulf Arab states' concerns, although these anxieties have not been publicly voiced. It was, perhaps, to assuage these concerns that Iraq and Saudi Arabia signed a nonaggression treaty.[31] Another reason for the treaty may have been to ease Saudi concerns over Iraq's joining Egypt, Jordan, and North Yemen in creating the so-called Arab Cooperation Council (ACC). The Saudis were particularly concerned about the membership of North Yemen in the ACC.[32]

Soviet-Gulf Relations After the Iran-Contra Affair

In 1985, the Soviet Union scored a major diplomatic victory when Oman and the United Arab Emirates declared that they were establishing diplomatic ties with the Soviet Union. This success was the fruit of extensive Soviet efforts at courting the Gulf states over a long period of time.[33]

At the time there was every indication that in due course Saudi Arabia would also establish relations with the Soviet Union. In 1984 Saudi Arabia and the Soviet Union became involved in what has been called "soccer diplomacy" when the Saudi soccer team visited Moscow. Since then, there have been other visits by Saudi Foreign Minister Prince Saud-al-Faysal and Oil Minister Hisham Nazir to Moscow. These contacts created the expectation that after the withdrawal of Soviet troops from Afghanistan, the two countries would establish diplomatic relations.

The disclosure of the U.S.-Iranian arms deal was initially perceived to have helped the Soviet Union's position with the Gulf states. This scandal was expected to show that the Gulf Arabs could not rely solely on the United States and that ties with the Soviet Union could be a valuable asset even in their dealings with Iran. Soviet propaganda had focused on what it characterized as U.S. treachery. Kuwait's request to the Soviet Union to lease it some of its tankers and Soviet acquiescence seemed to indicate that Soviet-Gulf ties would benefit from the Iran-Contra fallout.

The U.S. decision to reflag eleven Kuwaiti tankers and the dispatch of U.S. naval forces to the Persian Gulf changed the situation. First, U.S. actions caused serious anxiety in Iran, prompting it to try to improve its ties with the Soviet Union. The Soviets responded favorably to Iranian overtures and Iranian and Soviet officials made several visits to each other's capitals.

The buildup of the U.S. and European naval presence in the Persian Gulf created a common interest between Iran and the Soviet Union— to seek the withdrawal of these forces from the Persian Gulf.[35] Moreover, as a result of improvements in Soviet-Iranian relations, the Soviet Union refused to go along with the idea of the U.N. Security Council imposing an arms embargo on Iran. This Soviet attitude angered the Gulf states, especially Kuwait and Saudi Arabia. The Gulf press began to ask what game the Soviet Union was playing in the Gulf. Other Arab states also voiced dismay at Soviet behavior. King Hussein of Jordan, for example, during his trip to Moscow, indicated to the Soviets that they might be damaging their future prospects with the Arabs if they continued to prevent the imposition of an arms embargo on Iran.[36]

Yet the Soviets still refused to endorse the embargo. Their attitude apparently was based on the calculation that potential gains in Iran might be higher than those in the Gulf, because it was unlikely that for the foreseeable future that they would be able to replace the United States among the GCC members even if they opened embassies in all of them. Also, though the Soviets value the chance to establish a greater presence in the Gulf states, the Arabs also need the Soviets both for dealing with Iran and in handling the Arab-Israeli conflict. Thus their ability to penalize the Soviets because of their relations with Iran is limited. Nevertheless, Moscow tried to reassure the Gulf Arabs about Soviet ties with Iran, and its efforts kept Soviet-Gulf relations from deteriorating too far, although the pace of their improvement was slowed.

The end of the Persian Gulf war eliminated one of the principal problems in Soviet-Iranian relations. Immediately after the cease-fire, the Soviets offered to mediate in the peace talks, but Iran refused and opted for U.N. mediation. The Soviets also admitted to their past mistakes vis-à-vis Iran and vowed to make up for them.

In the months following the cease-fire, Soviet-Iranian relations improved a bit but not spectacularly because Iran focused its attention on improving its ties with the West. The withdrawal of Soviet troops from Afghanistan in February 1989 removed a significant obstacle to better Soviet-Iranian relations. Meanwhile, the outbreak of the so-called Rushdie affair following the publication of the book *Satanic Verses* and the Ayatollah Khomeini's pronouncement of the death penalty against its author on the grounds of blasphemy and apostasy created a major crisis in Iran's relations with the West and enhanced its receptiveness to Soviet advances. As a result, Soviet Foreign Minister Eduard Shevardnadze visited Tehran and met with the Ayatollah Khomeini.[37] Both sides stated that after this meeting Soviet-Iranian relations entered a qualitatively different era.

Then on June 2 the speaker of the Iranian parliament and presidential candidate Hashemi Rafsanjani visited Moscow. During this visit, far-reaching agreements on economic cooperation were reached between the two countries and the USSR even undertook to help Iran strengthen its defensive capabilities.[38]

Closer Soviet-Iranian ties are likely to displease the Gulf Arab states, especially Saudi Arabia, but the Soviets seem to have calculated that having close relations with Iran is more important to their interests, both within their own Asiatic republics and in South Asia. Also, after several years of courting the Gulf Arabs, the Soviets seem to have realized that even under the best circumstances they would not be able to replace Western influence in the Gulf, whereas they have a strong chance of consolidating a significant foothold in Iran.

Moreover, closer Soviet-Iranian ties should not necessarily harm the USSR's prospects with the Gulf Arabs but might instead prompt them to seek better ties with Moscow, in part as a means of protection against potential Iranian pressures. This kind of consideration had in the past played a role in Kuwait's establishing ties with the Soviets as a means of getting protection against Iraqi and Palestinian pressures, in view of the latter's close Soviet links.

Conclusion

The Iran-Contra affair initially was very disquieting to the Gulf Arabs and made them uncertain about U.S. commitment to their security. Thus as part of their security strategy, the Gulf Arabs used the United States's embarrassment over the Iran-Contra affair and the scuttling of U.S.-Iranian rapprochement to move U.S. policy toward closer identification with Arab security concerns and interests. Judged by the record, as explained in this essay, that policy has been quite successful. The United States has become far more deeply involved in the security of the Gulf Arabs, but they have not had to make any concessions to the United States, such as offering basing facilities, which could be politically costly to them.

The projection of the U.S. naval force into the Persian Gulf finally helped bring the Iran-Iraq war to an end. The Gulf Arabs also succeeded in involving Egypt in the region's security calculations, thus improving the balance of power in their favor and against Iran. Relations with the Soviet Union, however, remained somewhat stagnant after the dramatic advances of 1985. Relations with Iran worsened in the immediate aftermath of the Iran-Contra affair. But they improved after the end of the war and the establishment of the cease-fire. Indeed, after the cease-fire, the old pattern of Arab-Iranian relations has gradually reasserted itself.

Most important, the post-Iran-Contra evolution of GCC policies on a number of issues has demonstrated the centrality of the United States in GCC security calculations and to a large extent in their approach to key regional issues, especially the Iran-Iraq war and relations with Iran.

Notes

1. For a study of these and other related issues see Anthony H. Cordesman, *The Gulf and the Search for Strategic Stability* (Boulder, Colo.: Westview Press, 1984); and Thomas McNaugher, *Arms and Oil: U.S. Military Strategy and the Persian Gulf* (Washington, D.C.: Brookings Institution, 1985).

2. For an excellent and balanced discussion of the Iranian challenge to the GCC countries and their response to it, see R. K. Ramazani, *Revolutionary Iran:*

Challenges and Responses in the Middle East (Baltimore: Johns Hopkins Univ. Press, 1986).

3. For a study of the Middle East regional scene after the Lebanese crisis of 1982, see Robert O. Freedman, ed., *The Middle East after the Israeli Invasion of Lebanon* (Syracuse: Syracuse Univ. Press, 1986).

4. The assistant secretary of state for Near East and South Asian affairs expressed this view in testimony to the House of Representatives Committee on Foreign Affairs.

5. See Shireen T. Hunter and Robert E. Hunter, "The Post–Camp David Arab World," in Robert O. Freedman, ed., *The Middle East since Camp David* (Syracuse: Syracuse Univ. Press, 1984), pp. 79–102.

6. See *Washington Post*, Nov. 11, 1981.

7. For example, Kuwait could not obtain U.S. Stinger missiles from the United States. On the GCC effort to cope with its new security environment, see J. E. Peterson, "The GCC and Regional Security," *American-Arab Affairs*, Spring 1987, pp. 62–69.

8. One of these individuals was Adnan Kashoghi.

9. See Eric Hoogland, "Factions behind U.S. Policy in the Gulf," *Middle East Report*, 18 (Mar.–Apr. 1988): 29–31. According to Hoogland, "while the 'Arabists' are unified in their perception of the threat posed by Iran, there is less consensus on how that threat should be contained. One camp supports active measures, including the use of military force in order to convince Iran to cease efforts to export its revolution." (p. 31).

10. See "Government Issues Statement on Dispute with Bahrain," *FBIS/Middle East* (hereafter *FBIS:ME*), May 1, 1986, "King Fahd Reportedly Contains Bahrain-Qatar Dispute," May 2, 1986, and "King's Swift Action Cited," May 5, 1986.

11. See the article in *al-Anba* reproduced in *FBIS:ME*, Dec. 18, 1986.

12. See R. K. Ramazani, *The Persian Gulf: Iran's Role* (Charlottesville: Univ. Press of Virginia, 1973).

13. Iraq has been particularly hard in its criticism of Dubai, which all through the war has maintained extensive commercial relations with Iran. The Iraqis have gone so far as to call Dubai a traitor to the Arab nation.

14. For example, during the Bahrain-Qatar dispute, Iran supported Qatar. See *FBIS:ME*, "Iran Reportedly Siding with Qatar," May 19, 1986.

15. See Judith Pererra, "Together Against the Red Peril: Iran and Saudi Arabia Rivals for Superpower Role," *Middle East*, May 1978, pp. 16–27.

16. For example, the speaker of the Iranian parliament, Hashemi Rafsanjani, said that "for the first time they [the GCC] did not praise Iraq, and did not say that Iran does not want peace but Iraq does. Rather, they emphasized that they must have better relations with Iran." See *FBIS:South Asia*, Nov. 1, 1985.

17. One reason for this difficult situation was that those in the Iranian leadership who were involved in the dealings with the United States were put on the defensive. To redeem their revolutionary credentials, they must not advocate a dialogue with the United States. Despite these considerations, for a few months after the disclosure of the Iran-Contra dealings, the speaker of the Iranian parliament, Rafsanjani, tried to leave the door open to future contacts. See Shireen T. Hunter, "Beneath the Surface of Iran's Relations with the West," *World and I* 2 (Nov. 1987):89–90.

18. See Gary Sick, "What Do We Think We Are Doing in the Gulf War?,"

Washington Post, Apr. 24, 1988. According to Sick, "the U.N. resolution had deliberately been written by the United States to support the Iraqi position and to be unacceptable to Iran."

19. See, for example, Laurie Mylroie, "The Superpowers and the Iran-Iraq War," *American-Arab Affairs*, no. 21 (Summer 1987):15–26.

20. See R. K. Ramazani, "The Iran-Iraq War and the Persian Gulf Crisis," *Current History* 87 (Feb. 1988):62.

21. See "Mixed Feelings about U.S. Role in the Gulf," *New York Times*, Apr. 10, 1987, and "Nervous Arabs Voice Doubts on U.S. Gulf Policy," *Christian Science Monitor*, Nov. 30, 1987.

22. See "Iran Presses Gulf States to Resist U.S. Naval Build-up," *Financial Times*, June 1, 1987.

23. "Gulf Pact Set by Britain, Italy, France," *Washington Post*, Jan. 24, 1988. See also the chapter by Robert Hunter in this volume.

24. See "Saudi Asks Iran to Rejoin Fight Against Israel," *Washington Post*, Dec. 28, 1987, and Alan Cowell, "Saudi King Accuses Iran of Hampering Fight with Israel," *New York Times*, Dec. 28, 1987.

25. See "Saudis Seeking an Arab Alliance Against Iran," *New York Times*, Oct. 15, 1987, and "Syria Joins Other Arab States in Rebuking Iran on War," *Washington Post*, Nov. 12, 1987.

26. See *Middle East Economic Digest* 32 (May 20, 1988):14.

27. See "World Aviation Panel Faults US Navy on Downing Iran Air Jet," *New York Times*, Dec. 14, 1988, p. 8; Admiral Crowe's statement that Iran was responsible for the incident, *Washington Post*, Aug. 20, 1988.

28. See Gary Sick, "Failure and Danger in the Gulf," *New York Times*, July 6, 1988.

29. See "Commentary Views G.C.C./Conference Cooperation," *FBIS:NE/SA*, Sept. 7, 1988, p. 16.

30. See "Non-Interference Accord Signed," *FBIS:NE/SA*, Mar. 28, 1989, p. 21.

31. See "Saykh Said: Some Issues with Iraq 'Outstanding,' " *FBIS:NE/SA*, Feb. 16, 1989, p. 27.

32. See "Report on 'Concealed Crisis' with Egypt Denied," *FBIS:NE/SA*, Feb. 8, 1989, p. 15.

33. On Soviet-Gulf relations, see Stephen Page, "The USSR and the Gulf States," *American-Arab Affairs*, no. 20 (Spring 1987):38–56.

34. See various issues of *FBIS:NE/SA*, during summer and fall 1987 and the chapter by Robert O. Freedman in this volume.

35. See, for example, Andrei Gromyko's statement to the Iranian ambassador in Moscow, *FBIS:USSR/International Affairs*, Dec. 7, 1987.

36. During his visit to Moscow, King Hussein complained about the Soviet Union's attitude. See *Washington Post*, Dec. 23, 1987.

37. See "Shevardnadze, Khomeini Meet in Tehran," *Washington Post*, Feb. 27, 1989.

38. On Rafsanjani's visit and Soviet-Iranian agreements, see "Rafsanjani Leads Iran Out of Quarantine," *Financial Times*, June 21, 1989, and "Iran-Soviet Agreement 'Worth over $6bn,' " *Financial Times*, June 26, 1989.

6

Iran and the United States
"Islamic Realism"?

R. K. Ramazani

Few developments since the eruption of the Iranian revolution have had more profound significance for the foreign policy of Iran than the U.S.-Iran secret arms deal.[1] That the deal could occur reveals that the revolutionary regime is capable of pursuing the national interests of the Iranian state despite its Islamic idealism. It also reveals that in the pursuit of such interests revolutionary Iran is capable of dealing with the United States, the Great Satan.

The primacy of realism in Iran's foreign policy despite its rhetorical stridency is nowhere so graphically demonstrated as in its policy toward the United States since the arms deal was first exposed in November 1986. I shall suggest in this essay that in spite of the embarrassment the disclosures caused, the Iranian leaders have firmly retained the option of normalizing relations with Washington. This realistic approach seems all the more remarkable in view of the unprecedented confrontation between Iran and the United States as a result of the Reagan administration's decision to intervene in the Persian Gulf with the most massive deployment of U.S. naval forces anywhere in the world since the Vietnam war.

The Iranian "Cover-up"

The Iranian leaders to a man denied that Iran had purchased arms from the United States. They had considered it necessary to deal with Washington as secretly, indirectly, and cautiously as possible. One of the first questions the Iranians asked Robert C. McFarlane during his visit to Tehran was whether the Americans "could keep a secret." Ironically, as it turned out, the faction that leaked the news of McFarlane's visit to *Al-Shira'*, a Lebanese magazine, was an extremist one led by Mehdi Hashemi.

Iranian leaders appeared to be technically correct in denying that arms had been purchased from the United States; they had built a two-tiered level of deniability into their covert relations with Washington. First, they had dealt with the United States largely through arms dealers. The principal intermediary was Manuchehr Ghorbanifar, an Iranian businessman, who had been deeply involved in five of the six arms transactions and on whom the NSC and the CIA had relied heavily even though he had failed a CIA-administered polygraph test. The other major intermediary was Albert Hakim, an Iranian-born American businessman, who became involved in the transactions only in January 1986. He was antagonistic toward Ghorbanifar and claimed to have much better access to Iranian leadership through a "second channel," a "relative" (reputedly Hojatolislam Hashemi-Rafsanjani's). Second, although Iranians met and talked directly with U.S. officials in May 1986 during McFarlane's visit to Tehran and on other occasions such as in Frankfurt in February and October 1986, it is still not clear whether any Iranian leader talked directly to U.S. officials.

In an ingenious move, the day after the disclosures, Hashemi-Rafsanjani took advantage of the symbolically important date of November 4 to divulge McFarlane's visit to Tehran. On that date in 1964, Ayatollah Khomeini had been exiled by the shah, and November 4 became, in the eyes of the pro-Khomeini factions, the dawn of the Islamic revolution. He mocked the McFarlane visit, telling the Iranians a colorful story about how the Americans had arrived in Tehran without Iran's permission, carrying Irish passports and bringing a cake and a Bible. Allegedly, they were arrested and held in custody during their stay in Iran, and Ayatollah Khomeini, Hashemi-Rafsanjani claimed, had instructed the Iranian leaders, "There should be no talking with these people and do not receive their message, but find out who they are, what their designation is, and who sent them." The reason for these instructions and the extremely cautious approach of the Iranian leaders in dealing with the United States was the fear of public reaction to open and direct contacts with the U.S. government. Talking to U.S. leaders, after all, had destroyed the provisional government of Mehdi Bazargan in November 1979. In trying to deny such talks, Rafsanjani asked, "How could we meet and talk to you [U.S. representatives]! Have we forgotten that Brzezinski met our ad interim government in Algiers and our ad interim government has been [?swept aside] and now you have come inside our house, our country intending to meet us? Could our nation be asleep in such matters?"[2]

Once President Reagan broke his silence in a televised speech to the nation on November 13, 1986, the Iranian leaders resorted to stronger denials. The following day President Ali Khamenei refuted the allegation that U.S. officials had started talks with Iranian officials eighteen months earlier, saying that they might have held these talks with others, "with international smugglers perhaps. This has nothing to do with us." Regarding President Reagan's remark about talks between the U.S. team and Iranian officials during McFarlane's visit to Tehran, President Khamenei said, "It is a mere lie" and claimed that no "diplomatic talks" had been held between the McFarlane groups and any Iranian officials at any rank and that only a few Iranian "intelligence officers" had talked with them to obtain information. "This is not called diplomatic talks. If you call these information officers, 'officials,' it is up to you."[3] He also said that Iran was in possession of tapes that contained details of these talks and that if it were deemed necessary, he would publish them.

The publication of the Tower Commission report occasioned another outburst of Iranian denials and charges against the United States. Hashemi-Rafsanjani said on March 13, 1987, that material in the report quoting Iranian officials "are all lies." Calling the report "desperate efforts" by the White House to establish ties with Iran, he charged that the report contained items aimed at provoking the Soviets against Iran and vice versa. The main purpose of this move was to mar Irano-Soviet relations and "to involve us in a war with our northern neighbor." President Khamenei said on March 20, 1987, that from the day the scandal was exposed American leaders gave the American nation and the world one lie after another. The Tower Commission report, too, concocted stories, "some of which contained truth, but which are largely fictional." He identified three U.S. objectives in its dealings with Iran: the release of American hostages, the establishment of relations with Iran, and the acquisition of a foothold against the other superpower and America's arch rival, the Soviet Union.[4]

The Iranian cover-up involved more than denials; it entailed the suppression of a potential parliamentary investigation. On November 17, 1986, the evening newspaper *Resalat* reported that Foreign Minister Ali Akbar Velayati had been asked to explain to the public what exactly had transpired regarding Iranian-U.S. relations. It added that the Majlis, which held anti-Americanism to be one of their most important revolutionary principles, "wanted to know which officials and authorities decided to establish links" with Washington. Three days later, Ayatollah Khomeini personally intervened to quash an eight-man parliamentary demand for an investigation. On November 20, 1986, he declared that Americans had come back to Iran and "presented themselves meekly and humbly at the door of this nation wishing to establish relations. They wish to apologize for their mistake, but our nation rejects them. This is an issue, an issue greater than all your other victories." Without naming the deputies, he admonished them: "You should not set up radicals and reactionaries. You should not create a schism. This is contrary to Islam. It is contrary to faith and contrary to fairness. Do not do such things." That was the end of the matter. In true Iranian style, there were no wrenching hearings, no sensational investigations, and no protracted judicial prosecutions. The move of the eight deputies who had dared to demand an investigation was characterized as "irresponsible" by a majority of the Majlis deputies who wrote Khomeini to express their regrets for the acts of their fellows and to stress their own allegiance to Khomeini and his line.[5]

The Greater Blow

The Reagan administration dealt an even greater blow to Iran's relations with the United States when it decided to reflag eleven Kuwaiti oil tankers. That decision was said to have been motivated by the U.S. embarrassment in front of its Arab friends, who suddenly discovered that Washington had been secretly selling millions of dollars worth of arms to Iran. But this was not the real reason behind the decision. The principal reason for reflagging was the exaggerated concern of the Reagan administration with the potential projection of Soviet power and influence into the Persian Gulf.[6] On March 7, 1987, only five days after President Reagan learned that Kuwait and the Soviet Union had reached a deal to be signed in ten days, he decided to reflag Kuwaiti vessels. The supposed embarrassment of the U.S. officials had not earlier prompted any response to Kuwait's request for the reflagging of its ships, a request made as early as September 1986, unofficially in December 1986, and officially in January 1987.

Because the events regarding "Reagangate," to use the Iranian appellation, were still unfolding when the United States started escorting the Kuwaiti tankers, most observers mistakenly attributed Iran's angry attitude toward Washington to the continuous embarrassment of its leaders. On the contrary, a close scrutiny of the record reveals that Iran's anti-American rhetoric intensified only in March 1987, when President Reagan decided to reflag the Kuwaiti ships, and reached its peak only after July 22, when the U.S. Navy began escorting operations.

Before the first U.S. convoy was launched, the Iranian leaders had condemned both superpowers for planning to intervene in the Gulf. In trying to induce a U.S. decision to reflag their tankers, the Kuwaiti leaders played on the Reagan administration's obsession with the threat of the "evil empire" to the Gulf by getting the Soviets to lease them three vessels. As Stephen S. Rosenfeld aptly put it, "little Kuwait wins the brilliant and gutsy diplomacy award."[7] The Iranian leaders accused Moscow and Washington of hatching a "conspiracy" against the Iranian revolution, the purpose of which was to isolate, encircle, and ultimately destroy the revolutionary regime. In the words of Ayatollah Hussein-Ali Montazeri, the United States was trying to "impose peace" on Iran just as it had imposed war through its Gulf "deputy," the regime of President Saddam Hussein.

What outraged the Iranian leaders most of all was the unprecedented American naval buildup in the Persian Gulf. In July 1987, when the United States started escorting Kuwaiti tankers flying the American flag, the Joint Chiefs of Staff believed that eight warships plus the command ship *La Salle* would be enough. By the winter of 1988, however, U.S. navel strength in the Gulf had reached a peak of forty-eight ships, and when other Western naval forces are included, there were some eighty-two vessels in the Gulf and adjacent waters. All this was happening in Iran's backyard. How would the United States feel, wondered the Iranians, if the Soviet Union deployed a similar armada in the Gulf of Mexico? A mixture of myth and history over thousands of years has underpinned the perception that Iran's primacy in the Gulf is the sine qua non of its overall freedom from foreign control. The Iranian revolution added a new sense of religious primacy to Iran's ancient claim of political paramountcy in the Gulf. The American military intervention in the region was seen as threatening both.

Not since President Jimmy Carter admitted the shah to the United States in October 1979 had any American action triggered such an emotional outburst against the United States among Iranian leaders and their followers as did the American intervention in the Gulf. Ayatollah Khomeini was the first to express the Iranian fury. About a week after the journey of the first U.S. convoy through the Gulf began, he castigated the "criminal United States" as the leader of the "pagans and apostates of world arrogance" and called all Muslim pilgrims around the world to "disavow" America by conducting political marches and demonstrations during the hajj ceremony in Saudi Arabia. He urged the United States to conclude from his long and angry message that "military intervention in the Persian Gulf is not simply an experiment. It is a big step, a dangerous game. We, along with all the Muslims of the Persian Gulf region, interpret the superpowers' military presence as a prelude for invading the Islamic countries and the Islamic Republic of Iran."[8]

This vituperative message is universally, but mistakenly, thought to have provoked the tragic eruption of riots at Mecca on July 31, 1987, when hundreds of Iranian pilgrims died as the result of a clash with Saudi Arabian police. What really infuriated the Iranian pilgrims and

Khomeini alike was the pouring of massive U.S. forces into the Persian Gulf region. For months the Iranian leaders had hoped that logistical difficulties and congressional opposition would prevent the actual deployment of American forces. Once that hope was dashed, no one could predict how Iranian exasperation would express itself. In the meantime, Khomeini's hajj representative, Hojatolislam Mehdi Qarrubi, acquired, as in past years, the permission of Saudi Arabia for Iranian "political marches and demonstrations." Fearing violence, at the last minute the Saudis tried to pressure Qarrubi to cancel the planned marches, which he resisted.

Ayatollah Khomeini, also fearing violence, particularly because of the rage of the Iranian pilgrims over the U.S. military intervention in the Persian Gulf, urged more than usual in his hajj message that "the respected clergy, managers, and officials of the convoys and pilgrimage must make every effort to ensure that the hajj ceremonies will be conducted in a correct and orderly manner." According to Khomeini, the "House of Saud" sent him a message "thanking me for saying that there must be calm there [in Saudi Arabia]."[9] In 1979, the frenzied crowds, resenting President Carter's admission of the shah to the United States, had seized the U.S. Embassy in Tehran without the prior approval of Khomeini. By rioting in Mecca, they acted in violation of his specific instructions to avoid disturbances.

Although the obsession of President Reagan and Secretary of Defense Caspar Weinberger with the threat of the Soviet Union prompted the initial decision to intervene in the Persian Gulf, various objectives were attributed to the American policy afterward. In justifying his controversial decision, President Reagan inflated the U.S. objectives to the defense of Western freedom, security, and oil supplies against the Iranian threat. Secretary Weinberger claimed that the U.S. objective was to end the Iran-Iraq war or at least stop the tanker war. And the U.S. naval commander Rear Admiral Harold J. Bernsen said that the American objective was to "contain the war." Whatever the real U.S. objectives, in committing itself to protect the Kuwaiti oil tankers by military means, the United States, as seen from Tehran, was clearly siding with Iraq. Washington was no longer neutral either in the choice of its means or its objectives. Its naval escorts protected only the oil tankers of Kuwait, Iraq's close logistical and financial ally. The American intervention threatened to rob Iran of its major means of retaliating against Iraqi attacks on its oil exports and to prevent Iran from winning the war.

In response, Iran sought to obstruct the United States in the attainment of its objectives. The Iranian leaders continued to retaliate against Iraqi attacks on Iran's oil export by disrupting those of Kuwait and Saudi Arabia. At the same time, however, in single-mindedly pursuing its war against Iraq, Iran sought to contain the spread of the war to its Gulf neighbors so as to conserve its energy and resources. It also strenuously sought to avoid getting involved in a direct armed conflict with the United States.

The mining of the *Bridgeton,* a Kuwaiti supertanker flying the American flag, on July 24, 1987, set the stage for an indirect Irano-U.S. armed conflict. On September 21, 1987, the day before Iranian President Ali Khamenei was scheduled to address the United Nations General Assembly, a United States Navy helicopter fired on an Iranian vessel, *Iran Ajr,* which the Reagan administration said was laying underwater mines. Three Iranian crewmen were killed and two others were lost at sea. The twenty-six surviving crewmen were returned to Iran, and the ship was destroyed by American forces. The armed skirmishes escalated on October 16, 1987, when another American-flagged ship, *Sea Isle City,* was hit by an Iranian missile. But as contrasted with the *Bridgeton,* this ship was in Kuwaiti territorial waters instead of the high seas. Nevertheless, the United States retaliated on October 19, when navy destroyers shelled and set ablaze one Iranian derelict oil rig and American crewmen blew up two other Iranian rigs. Predictably, Iran retaliated on October 22 by firing a missile into Kuwait's Sea Island terminal.[10]

The Door Is Still Open

The disclosures of November 3, 1986, marked the end of eighteen months of clandestine and indirect Iranian-American relations and the beginning of eighteen months of open conflict. Remarkably, in spite of the confrontation, throughout this turbulent period the Iranian leaders retained the option of "normalization of relations," to borrow the words of Hashemi-Rafsanjani, with the United States. Neither embarrassment over the revelations nor the indirect armed conflict between the two countries in the Persian Gulf has destroyed that option. In his first speech of November 4, 1986, the day after the news of the McFarlane visit to Iran was disclosed, Rafsanjani said to the United States: "At the moment we are your enemy and you are our enemy. If you wish us to intercede on your behalf [to free the American hostages held in Lebanon], we have left the door open."[11]

But Hashemi-Rafsanjani left the door open for much wider issues than the narrow one of helping to obtain the release of American hostages. He left it open for the overarching objective of normalizing relations with the United States. He replied to questions from a CBS correspondent on January 28, 1987: "It was your government that was hostile to our people before the revolution, and to our people and government after the revolution. There is only one condition [for normalizing relations]—the United States must prove that it is not hostile to our people, government, and revolution." When the correspondent asked how the United States could show that it was not hostile to Iran, he replied: "The U.S. government should release our assets that have been unlawfully frozen in the United States. That would be one form of proof for us."[12]

The point here is not to enumerate the conditions of normalization of relations. Statements regarding such conditions have varied from time to time and from leader to leader. Even Hashemi-Rafsanjani's conditions have not always been the same. They have ranged from the unfreezing of Iranian assets to effecting changes in U.S. support of Israel. The point is that regardless of conditions and the person who suggests them, Iranian leaders have persistently retained the option of normalizing Iran's relations with the United States. In the aftermath of the disclosures even Ayatollah Hussein-Ali Montazeri, reputedly a foreign policy hawk, was quoted as saying: "If the United States truly changed its policies and methods, then it would be possible to establish ties. In this case relations would be between two independent countries and not between an oppressor and the oppressed."[13]

Even at the height of the armed hostilities in the Persian Gulf, the Iranian leaders did not see why the relations between the two countries could not be normalized. President Ali Khamenei continued to want to normalize relations with the United States even when the effects of his much heralded speech to the United Nations General Assembly appeared to have been ruined by U.S. charges that Iran had been caught red-handed laying mines in the Persian Gulf. In answering a correspondent of the *Tehran Times* on October 18, 1987, he said, "The phrase 'neither East nor West' does not mean not having friendly ties with the East or West. It can be interpreted as not accepting domination from the East or West." When the same correspondent asked: "If the United States were to halt its enmity and return Iranian assets, would these constitute conditions in which ties could be established?" The president replied: "Certainly there are conditions where our ties with the United States could be normalized. Of course, they include those conditions you have already mentioned, and perhaps there would be others."[14]

Why does the door remain open? The anti-Islamic advocates of a containment-of-Iran policy have an all-too-easy answer: Iran, they say, is using deceptive tactical maneuvers to achieve its anti-American strategic goals. Essentially, they use the argument that doctrinaire anti-Soviet advocates have used for decades against any sign of Soviet opening to the world. Mesmerized by their own rhetoric, the anti-

Iranian ideologues have managed to equate Iran, communism, and Islamic fundamentalism. To them, revolutionary Iran's "open-door" foreign policy is nothing but an opportunistic tactical hoax in the Leninist style. The same cynicism that disallows acknowledgment of the emerging realism of Mikhail Gorbachev's Soviet Union disparages any signs of a significant return to normalcy in the foreign policy of revolutionary Iran. Once a revolutionary, always a revolutionary, these cynics say. In such thinking, none of the great historical revolutions has ever changed or will ever change. Ideological rhetoric is the only guide to understanding the foreign policy of revolutionary states, and any changes in their pronouncements and practices that seem to deviate from the original tenets of their ideology are considered a ruse that only fools can take seriously.

The irony is that such a dogmatic view is not only ahistorical and antiphilosophical but egotistical. The Iranian revolution, like all great historical revolutions, claims universal validity for its message. The French Revolution claimed universal value for the ideals of the Enlightenment—liberty, equality, and fraternity. The Russian Revolution promised world socialism and a classless society. The American Revolution declared certain inalienable rights to life, liberty, and the pursuit of happiness for all peoples, not just for Americans. Yet, according to these ahistorical cynics, it is all right for Americans to want, in Wilsonian terms, "to make the world safe for democracy," but it is wrong for Iranians to want to make it safe for Islam. In other words, the only ideological claim to uniqueness that they can allow is American "exceptionalism" and to no other nation will they cede the right even to dream its own dreams. What is more, their stale formula of containment, they believe, is the only way to handle revolutionary states, whether they preach international communism, Islamic fundamentalism, or any other "ism." They consider that any other approach to such states amounts to appeasement and will surely lead to disaster.

Yet the Iranian revolution, like other revolutions, has had to adjust the theory and practice of its foreign policy to the realities of the mundane world because of the pressures of its own particular circumstances. Iran's open-door foreign policy has been the by-product of the effects of its domestic revolutionary politics and its protracted war with Iraq.[15] Having eliminated their "liberal" ideological and political rivals, led by Mehdi Bazargan and Abolhasan Bani-Sadr, the followers of the Khomeini line managed, by late 1982, to consolidate power and monopolize legitimacy in the name of Islam. By that time the Khomeinists had managed to turn the tide of war against Iraq and thus matched domestic political success with triumph on the battlefield. Khomeini took note of this important change in Iran's internal and external circumstances and for the first time adjusted his ideological stance accordingly. At the height of the hostage crisis, when Iran was isolated internationally as a consequence of Western diplomatic and economic sanctions, Khomeini was prescribing isolation: "We must become isolated so that we can become independent" (*ma bayad monzavy shavim ta mostaqel shavim*). In the new circumstances in December 1982, however, he forcefully urged Iran's return to the community of nations, saying that the revolution had ended and Iran needed "stability" and "reconstruction." A week later he was calling, for the first time, for an end to Iran's "hermit" status in world affairs.[16]

This landmark call was the foundation on which President Khamenei based his proclamation about Iran's new "open-door" foreign policy on July 20 and August 6, 1984. He said "Iran seeks to have rational, sound and healthy relations with all countries" so as to serve both Iran's national interest and the spread of its ideology. Reportedly, he said, "there were two objectives behind establishing such relations. The first one was to establish reciprocal ties for securing the needs of the country. The second motive was that it will enable us to convey our message. Even if we were able to meet all our needs and expectations domestically, we should not close the doors of the country." He stressed that he was stating "the expressed wish of Imam Khomeini." A few months later that wish was spelled out. On October 29, in a major speech to the Iranian foreign minister and Iran's diplomatic representatives abroad, Khomeini said: "We should act as it was done in early Islam when the Prophet . . . sent ambassadors to all parts of the world to establish proper relations. We cannot sit idly by saying we have nothing to do with governments. . . . It is inadmissible to common sense and to humanity that we should have no relations with other governments, since it would mean defeat, annihilation and being buried right to the end. . . . So my advice to you is to strengthen your relations wherever and in whatever country you are." On November 2, 1985, again addressing the Iranian foreign minister and diplomatic representatives abroad, he said, "We do not want to live in a country which is isolated from the rest of the world. Today's Iran cannot be that way. Other countries cannot close their borders to others either; it would be irrational. Today the world is like one family, one city. In the present world circumstances, we should not be isolated."[17]

The juxtaposition of the concept of the national interest and Islamic ideology in these fundamental proclamations of the Iranian leaders still leaves unanswered the most difficult question of all: which is the central guide of the foreign policy of revolutionary Iran? Is it the national interest of the Iranian state or the transnational interest of the Islamic *umma* as interpreted by Khomeini? With Khomeini's downgrading of the concepts of nation-sate (*watan*) and nationalism (*melli-gara'y*), these questions take on added significance. Nationalism, he says, "contradicts Islam." "Although Islam respects the national home as a place of birth," he adds, "it does not consider it as its equal. The foundation is Islam . . . and those who sow the seeds of discord amongst the Muslim people in the name of nationalism are the soldiers of Satan, the agents of the superpowers, and the opponents of the Holy Quran."[18] The centrality of Islamic values was also stressed by other Iranian leaders such as former Prime Minister Musavi, who believed that the Iranians wanted to establish a new Islamic "system of values" independent of East and West and under which the Iranians could "organize their relations with other countries, nations and liberation movements."[19] Overzealous revolutionaries criticized such declarations in protesting Iran's expanding relations not only with the East and the West but even with such pro-Western countries as Turkey. They considered the extensive commercial and economic relations with Western or pro-Western or Eastern or pro-Eastern governments as a deviation from Islamic principles and the doctrine of "neither East nor West."

One of the best answers to such extremist critics and to the more basic question of the relative importance of ideology and national interest in the formulation and execution of Iran's foreign policy was to be found in an important, but universally overlooked, interview by Hashemi-Rafsanjani. In an exclusive interview with a correspondent of *Kayhan Hava'i* on April 6, 1987, he said, "It is not that we have ignored [by having relations with Germany and Turkey] our own [Islamic] principles. Of course, conditions in the world, the war, urgencies, necessities, and so on impose some limitations on us—which means we do not always have the power to choose. *I believe our principles are obeyed, but in some cases we may be limited and we may have to forego some of these principles.*"[20] What this means is that even before Khomeini's death Iranian leaders defined their national interests neither exclusively in terms of power, state, or nation nor merely of Islam or the Khomeini line. Rather, they acknowledged in principle the importance of both "raw power" and "faith power" in making and implementing Iran's foreign policy, and if and when their ideology stood in the way of pursuing their national interests, the latter must prevail. But they do not hesitate to combine the two.

Such a foreign policy is undergirded by an Islamic realism, no matter how contradictory this may sound to a Western ear. What impelled an Ayatollah Khomeini to change the Khomeini line and thus avoid the stifling effects of a rigid ideology was a flexible and eclectic intellectual heritage which is as old as Iranian history. It springs from the deep cultural ethos of both pre-Islamic and Islamic Iran, from the coexistence of Shi'ism and Iranianism in the Iranian sense of national identity. Ideological flexibility has been a salient feature of the Shia cultural tradition, even among Shia "jurisprudents" (*fuqaha*) and philosophers (*falasefeh*). Reason (*'Aql*) being a principle of Shia jurisprudence (*fiqh*), Shia scholars have for centuries used "practical principles" (*usul-e 'amaliyyeh*) in an innovative blending of Islamic principles and practical considerations.

Pre-Islamic Iranians were also concerned with blending practical exigencies and ethical principles in the conduct of foreign policy, although these principles were not rooted in a religious tradition. According to Ada B. Bozeman, the Iranians posed "for the first time in historically known terms" the problem of moral principles and national interest in foreign policy. She says that in the sixth century B.C., when the tyranny of empires plagued community life everywhere, the Persian Empire, vaster than any preceding empire west of China, attained "universal" peace for some two hundred years in large part as the result of a tolerant respect for the cultural diversity of its subjugated peoples. Furthermore, "this Persian policy of tolerance was suggested by statesmanship rather than by the religious ethic of the sixth century B.C." The Iranian, or "Islamic," revolution has not destroyed this ancient heritage of statesmanship.

Today the same basic values that have for centuries shaped Iranian statecraft are changing both the theory and the practice of Iran's foreign policy. Theoretically, its two fundamental tenets of "neither East nor West" and "the export of the Islamic revolution" are being reinterpreted. Iranian leaders now insist that the first does not mean having no relations with either East or West. Rather, it only means that Iran will tolerate "neither Eastern nor Western domination" (*nah salteh-ye sharq, nah salteh-ye gharb*). And the second tenet does not mean that Iran should try to export its revolution at any cost and by any means. If the export of the Islamic revolution should appear to be hurting the interests of the Iranian state, it should cease. The pragmatic leaders rationalize that without a powerful Islamic republic, Iran cannot export the Islamic revolution, which they believe it must do through the example of what Khomeini called its "Islamic ethical behavior." Exporting the revolution by the "sword" or by force, Khomeini stressed, is no export at all.

Pragmatic Realism

Iran's emerging Islamic realism is essentially pragmatic in nature, as evidenced by Tehran's relations with the East and the West. So long as the Soviet Union continued to supply arms to Iraq during the Iran-Iraq war and Russian troops were in occupation of Afghanistan, the prospects of improving Iran's relations with the Soviet Union were poor. But when the cease-fire took effect and the Soviet forces withdrew from Afghanistan, the relations between Tehran and Moscow improved dramatically in spite of their ideological differences. Rafsanjani's visit to Moscow in June 1989 formalized an unprecedented expansion of Iran's economic, commercial, and technical ties with the Soviet Union. The two nations even entered into a military relationship.

The newly expanded Irano-Soviet relations were severely tested, however, in January 1990, when Soviet troops opened fire on Azerbaijanis in Baku, killing and injuring many people. Iranian Azerbaijanis undoubtedly sympathized with their Soviet ethnic cousins. Iran's spiritual leader, Ayatollah Ali Khamenei, emphasizing their religious ties, said, "Our Muslim brethren, forcefully kept away from Islam for 70 years, are once again showing their Islamic feelings."[21] The Iranian foreign ministry expressed "deep regret" over the Soviet use of force, stressing that Iran "seriously wants the Soviet government to halt the violent encounter with the people of Azerbaijan and resolve the issue by employing peaceful means."[22] This, however, was as far as Iranian leaders would go in exporting the Islamic revolution. Any serious attempt to inflame the rebellion of the Soviet Azerbaijanis across the border would not only have violated the mutual Soviet-Iranian commitment to noninterference in each other's internal affairs—a principle that was firmly nailed down during Rafsanjani's visit to the Soviet Union—but, more crucially, would have jeopardized budding Soviet economic and military relations with Iran at a time when Iranian leaders desperately needed to maintain these relations in the pursuit of their postwar economic and military reconstruction.

The pragmatic restraint of the Iranian officials seemed all the more remarkable in the face of the ideological stridency of the radical idealists, who would have liked Iran to smuggle arms and men across the border into the Soviet Union in support of the Azerbaijani rebels. Iran's former interior minister, Ali Akbar Mohtashemi, who had just been elected to parliament, wrote in the daily *Kayhan* that Gorbachev "is now holding the Marxist sword of Lenin and Stalin in one hand and the poisonous bayonet of the American White House in the other, taking aim at the heart of Islam and Muslims." Iran's pragmatic leaders not only ignored such provocative pronouncements but went out of their way to keep the border quiet. They actually took the initiative in cooperating with Moscow. President Rafsanjani instructed Foreign Minister Ali Akbar Velayati to try to mediate the conflict, "to solve problems and end bloodshed and violence." Iran's ambassador to Moscow, Nasser Nubari, immediately met with Soviet Foreign Minister Eduard Shevardnadze, discussed the situation along the Soviet-Iranian frontier, and "expressed the mutual desire to develop border relations in trade, the economy, culture and humanitarian areas."[23]

The same practical considerations that impelled Iran's normalization of relations with the East probably underpin its desire to improve relations with the West by helping to achieve the release of Western hostages held in captivity in Lebanon. The same imperative of economic and military reconstruction that pushed Tehran toward Moscow propelled it even more toward Western capitals. Soviet markets for Iranian goods and Soviet financial credit for Iran paled in comparison with potential Western aid if the American and other Western hostages were released with Iranian assistance. Before Iran's acceptance of a cease-fire with Iraq, pragmatic streaks in Iranian foreign policy emerged for the first time, and it became clear to Iranian leaders that unless they ended the war with Iraq and helped with the freeing of Western hostages, Iran would have little chance of fully reentering the international community of states. Now, despite the ending of the war, Iran still remains a pariah state, largely because of the unresolved hostage issue. In early 1990 there were still eighteen Western captives in Lebanon, including eight Americans, four Britons, two West Germans, two Swiss, an Italian, and an Irishman.

Just as ideological rhetoric masked Iran's real economic and financial needs in its refusal to inflame disturbances among fellow Shi'a Muslims in Soviet Azerbaijan, it camouflaged these same needs in making overtures to the West on the hostage issue. In both cases Iranians invoked "Islamic humanitarianism" in support of their conciliatory attitude. On February 22, 1990, the pro-Rafsanjani newspaper *Tehran Times* called for prompt freedom for the captives in Lebanon. Four days later, it quoted Iran's top Shi'a Muslim justice as saying that his country opposed the taking of hostages, terrorism, and air piracy because "they are contrary to Islamic and humanitarian principles."[24] Three days earlier Sheik Mohammad Hussein Fadlallah, reputedly the spiritual leader of Hezbollah, the main umbrella group that holds Western hostages, had urged his followers, "We have to think of finding realistic and humanitarian means to free the foreign hostages." There was little doubt by mid-March 1990 that President Rafsanjani genuinely wanted to help with the release of the hostages in the interest of developing economic ties with the West. He sent his brother Mahmoud Hashemi to Damascus to coordinate Iranian and Syrian efforts to free the hostages, and upon his return to Tehran President Rafsanjani told journalists that Iran wanted to solve the hostage problem, adding, "My feeling is that the issue of the hostages is moving towards a solution."[25]

Despite Rafsanjani's optimism, the militant elements continued to oppose the resolution of the hostage problem. On March 10, in a scathing article in the newspaper *Kayhan*, Deputy Ali Akbar Mohtashemi urged those holding the captives to "continue in this hostage cold war" because freeing them would "unleash the blood-drinking wolves [American officials]."[26] Two days later, Ahmad Khomeini, the son of the late Ayatollah, while denying that Iran was directly implicated in the holding of hostages said, "The United States is wasting its time" if it is trying to open channels to Iran. He also said that "the United States will never see the day when the Islamic Republic will make concessions to Washington."[27]

The division between the pragmatic realists and the radical idealists on the hostage issue revealed the fundamental inability of the Iranian leadership to achieve consensus on the nature of the revolutionary regime and its foreign policy.[28] Despite a decade of conflict with the United States, the pragmatic leaders of Iran managed to retain the option of normalizing relations with Washington. But the hard-liners continued to block any meaningful realization of that option. For this reason as well as the expected increased participation of Western Europe in world affairs in the 1990s, the pragmatic leaders of Iran may well put the normalization of relations with the United States on the back burner for the time being and attempt to improve relations with West European nations. Such a move, in turn, may well pave the way for the resumption of normal relations between Tehran and Washington in the future. In the meantime, the current spate of rumors and denials about secret discussions between Tehran and Washington may be expected to continue, as may eventual normalization of relations between the two capitals despite the doomsday predictions of the hard-liners.

Notes

1. The significance of the arms deal may best be appreciated in the context of the pragmatic tendencies in Iran's foreign policy, which I first identified on September 8, 1985, with the publication of "Iran: Burying the Hatchet," *Foreign Policy*, no. 60 (Fall 1985): 52–74. See also the paperback edition of my *Revolutionary Iran: Challenge and Response in the Middle East* (Baltimore: Johns Hopkins Univ. Press, 1988), esp. pp. 253–69.

2. See *Foreign Broadcast Information Service, Daily Report, South Asia* (hereafter *FBIS:SA*), Nov. 5, 1986.

3. Ibid., Nov. 14, 1986.

4. Ibid., Mar. 13, 20, 1987.
5. Ibid., Nov. 18, 20, 25, 1986.
6. See R. K. Ramazani, "The Iran-Iraq War and the Persian Gulf Crisis," *Current History*, Feb. 1988, pp. 61–64, 86–88.
7. *Washington Post*, May 22, 1987.
8. See *FBIS:NE/SA*, July 30, 31, 1987.
9. Ibid., Aug. 3, 25, 1987.
10. For details, see Ramazani, "Iran-Iraq War."
12. *FBIS:SA*, Jan. 28, 1987.
13. Ibid., Nov. 10, 1986.
14. *FBIS:NE/SA*, Oct. 20, 1987.
15. See Ramazani, "Iran," and *Revolutionary Iran*.
16. *FBIS:SA*, Dec. 27, 1982.
17. Ibid., July 31, Aug. 7, Oct. 30, 1984, Nov. 4, 1985.
18. See vol. 11 in the series of collections entitled *Dar Jostaujooy-e Rah Az Kalam-e Imam, Meligara'y* (Tehran: Mo'asseseh-ye Amir Kabir, 1983–84).
19. *FBIS:SA*, July 8, 1981.
20. Ibid., Apr. 17, 1987; emphasis added.
21. *New York Times*, Jan 21, 1990.
22. *Washington Post*, Jan 21, 1990.
23. *New York Times*, Jan 23, 25, 1990.
24. Ibid., Feb. 27, 1990.
25. *Washington Post*, Feb. 24, Mar. 8, 1990.
26. Ibid., Mar. 12, 1990.
27. *New York Times*, Mar. 14, 1990.
28. For details of this theme see R. K. Ramazani, ed., *Iran's Revolution: The Search for Consensus* (Bloomington: Indiana Univ. Press, 1990).

7

Iraq Emerges

Frederick W. Axelgard

A diplomat posted to the U.S. embassy in Baghdad in recent years once described the difficulty he had encountered in trying to read up on the country to which he was newly assigned. His summary comment on the wide-ranging literature search of public sources he and his wife had conducted for relatively up-to-date materials was that they found thirty to fifty sources on Iran for every one that they found on Iraq. One could speculate endlessly about the reasons for this large discrepancy or just as readily reject the implication that the availability of materials on Iran and Iraq should somehow be comparable. Yet this experience describes a real condition—that Iraq, by and large, has been a distant and obscure point of limited interest to the West generally and to Americans in particular.

But if developments in the period covered by this study (1985 to 1988) are any indication, this condition may be on the verge of change. During these years, Iraq acquired an indisputable familiarity, if not notoriety, even among the less politically aware portions of the American public. In 1986–87, Iraq, to its chagrin, was at or very near the center of a succession of full-blown crises in U.S. foreign policy. The most prominent of these was the Iran-Contra scandal, stirred by the secret U.S.-Israeli collaboration to sell weapons to Iran, which was engaged in a bitter and bloody war with Iraq. Then, in May 1987, well before the political storm from Iran-Contra had subsided, an Iraqi jet looking for Iranian targets in the Persian Gulf mistakenly fired two missiles at the USS *Stark*, killing thirty-seven U.S. servicemen. Finally, the massive deployment of American naval forces in the Gulf that began just weeks after the *Stark* incident was debated hotly because it appeared to involve the United States in the Iran-Iraq war on Iraq's side.

It is an understatement to say that the intense exposure these crises gave Iraq was without precedent. Iraq had been "off the screen" of serious U.S. interest for nearly thirty years. Its last moment in the limelight was the July 1958 revolution, which had uprooted Iraq's monarchy and sent shock waves through the entire pro-Western superstructure in the Middle East. Then, after a decade of no significant interaction, Baghdad severed diplomatic relations with Washington because of its alleged support for Israel during the June 1967 war. The restoration of these ties in November 1984, though important, was not expected to result in much more than tentative efforts to expand the scope of U.S.-Iraqi interests with what appeared to be a maturing leadership in Baghdad.[1]

But the exchanges of ensuing years proved to be more intense than expected. In the following pages, I attempt to set forth why this was the case by undertaking an analysis of Iraq's management of its domestic and foreign affairs between 1985 and mid-1988. This analysis shows an Iraq seeking not only to meet the challenges associated with its war with Iran but to rise above the confusion that had plagued its domestic and international affairs for many years. It is premature to predict the outcome of this process, but if Iraq succeeds, future U.S. diplomats will almost certainly have a good deal more to read (and write) about Iraq.

Internal Developments

Although the war with Iran is not the focus of this study, that conflict above all else determined that the course of internal developments in Iraq from 1985 through mid-1988 was one of extremes. Iraqi fortunes and spirits sunk to their lowest level in several years between early 1986 and early 1987. This period of depression and crisis began with Iran's seizure of the Fao peninsula at the southern tip of Iraq and continued through the revelation of secret U.S.-Iranian arms deals, to Iran's conquest of lands near Basra in perhaps the bloodiest fighting of the entire war, which finally wound down in April 1987. The catastrophic tenor of these times for Iraq was enhanced by a collapse in world oil prices, which caused a crisis for Baghdad's source of revenue for its war effort and economic development.

By the middle of 1988, however, virtually all of these dire circumstances had been reversed. Signs of a possible reprieve for Iraq accelerated as 1987 wore on: the U.N. Security Council unanimously passed Resolution 598, calling for an end to the Gulf war and threatening sanctions if either party did not comply; a Western armada, pushed into being by Washington, entered the Gulf in force to protect the international shipping lanes, leading to military hostilities between Iran and the United States; finally, at the end of the year, Iran failed to muster enough manpower and material to launch its annual "final offensive" against Iraqi territory. The momentum in the war then seemed to swing in Iraq's favor after surprising counterattacks (in April and May 1988, respectively) drove Iranian revolutionary guards from the Fao peninsula and their dearly won positions near Basra. Meanwhile, new oil pipelines and the partial rebound of crude oil prices left Iraq with a revenue outlook of up to $15 billion for 1988, roughly twice the level of its income just two years earlier.[2]

The pressures generated in Iraq by the wide vacillations in the war almost certainly posed the stiffest challenge the ruling Ba'th party had faced since it came to power in Baghdad in 1968. As had been the case ever since Saddam Hussein became president and chairman of the Revolutionary Command Council (RCC) in 1979, the linchpin of the campaign to keep Iraq politically viable was his manipulation of power. The first instrument of Hussein's power was his effective internal security apparatus (often referred to collectively as the *mukhabarat*), which retained its reputation among Iraqis and international human rights groups for its effective suppression of any meaningful political opposition.[3]

Nor was there a letup in the fostering of the personality cult around Saddam Hussein, which had been actively promoted since the earliest days of the war. The thrust of this campaign continued to be to depict Saddam as the "struggler-hero" and the father figure who embodied Iraq's national will to survive the onslaught by Iran. His ubiquitous image adorned everything from giant placards in public squares to the watchfaces worn by most of the government officials one encountered, as well as local currency and children's school notebooks. Though the cult is thoroughly alien to Western tastes and criticized by some as a sign of weakness,[4] others have argued that "to all intents and purposes, it has worked: inasmuch as they do not surrender, Iraqis have accepted his leadership and, moreover, have accepted the notion that this was and is a defensive war which Saddam Hussein would gladly end were it not for the intransigence of the regime in Tehran."[5]

Although in the months after the loss of the Fao peninsula there was a rash of rumors about assassination plots and coup attempts, there was little concrete evidence of effective opposition to Saddam Hussein during the period examined here. The outside world did, however, learn of one disturbing incident which upset the image of airtight security that surrounds the Ba'thist regime. It occurred in September 1987 in the small town of Baquba, northeast of Baghdad. Extremists, believed to be either Shi'as from the violent al-Da'wa opposition movement or Kurdish insurgents, attacked a government parade that was being watched by official dignitaries and foreign diplomats. Scores of deaths and injuries reportedly resulted from the attack. Despite this embarrassment to the regime, the isolated nature of the incident and the lack of follow-on actions tended to reinforce the impression that no broadly based campaign against Saddam had taken hold in the country.[4]

Viewed from the perspective of mid-1988, several other recent developments of importance in Iraq—economic as well as political in nature—merit comment. The relationship of Iraq's Shi'a and Kurdish subcommunities to the Sunni-Arab-led state has been a source of concern since its inception in the early 1920s but never more so than during the war with Iran. As the war approached the end of its eighth year, it seemed apparent that the issue of these two communities' identification with the state and their relations with the Ba'thist government had taken very different turns. The Shi'is, who form a majority of Iraq's population, have by all indications refused to identify with the Shi'a Islamic revolution in Iran. This much seemed clear after several years of conflict, during which Shi'a soldiers and the Shi'a civilians of southern Iraq bore the brunt of absorbing the military and ideological challenge presented by Iran and gave no sign of any serious division of loyalty. Analysts are not of one mind over whether the reasons for the Shi'is' solidarity with the regime are primarily positive (the result, for example, of strong nationalist sentiments or acceptance of Saddam Hussein's leadership or the lavishing of government expenditures to refurbish Shi'a shrines and expand economic and social programs in Shi'a areas) or negative (induced by fear of the regime's internal security apparatus).[7]

Irrespective of the reasons one adduces for it, the political quiescence of the Shi'a community in Iraq stood in sharp contrast to the difficulty the regime experienced with its Kurdish population after 1985. Up to this point in the war, the ability of the Kurdish separatist movement to take advantage of the regime's preoccupation with the war had been limited by internal divisions in its ranks. In 1983, forces from the Kurdish Democratic party (KDP, led by the sons of the late Mustafa Barzani) joined Iranian troops in operations against government positions in northern Iraq. Forces from the other major Kurdish faction, the Patriotic Union of Kurdistan (PUK, led by Jalal Talabani), worked with Iraqi troops to resist these advances.[8]

Early in 1985, however, Saddam Hussein broke off a months-long negotiation with Jalal Talabani. These talks had reportedly produced an agreement on Kurdish demands for greater autonomy and a portion of the oil revenues generated in northern Iraq, but the oft-postponed announcement of the accord never took place. The precise

reason for the failure of these negotiations was never made public—
Kurdish sources charged the regime with negotiating in bad faith, and
Iraqi officials close to the talks suggest that Talabani's tactics changed
when Iran launched an offensive at the beginning of 1985.[9] The
estrangement between the PUK and the Iraqi government intensified
and became complete when Talabani overcame years of bitter rivalry
and suspicion with the KDP and decided to join ranks against the
Saddam Hussein regime. The announcement of this reconciliation
was made in Tehran late in 1986, indicating as well a de facto alliance
between the burgeoning Kurdish front and Iran.[10]

In apparent coordination with Iran's major offensive against Basra,
the PUK joined with Iranian troops early in 1987 to carry out several
apparently successful attacks in the northern border areas. The government's response to these developments had broad implications for
a large segment of the Kurdish community in northern Iraq. In the
spring of the year, it began a sustained campaign of razing Kurdish
villages and relocating large numbers of inhabitants to other regions
of Iraq.[11] By the end of the year, the severity of the regime's response
had created so much dissension among the Kurdish community that
Talabani warned that a general uprising among the Kurds of northern
Iraq was a distinct possibility.[12]

Although such an uprising did not occur, events in northern Iraq
in early 1988 nevertheless took a decided turn for the worse for
both the Iraqi regime and the Kurds. Iranian troops, again in close
cooperation with Kurdish guerrillas, launched a surprise offensive
against population centers in Iraqi Kurdistan. The success of the
operation quickly became apparent. Iran claimed that one hundred
thousand Iraqis, in an area centered on the town of Halabjeh, had
been "liberated from the clutches of the Ba'thist Iraqi regime and are
now with the Islamic Republic of Iran." Moreover, it was expected that
Iraq's transfer of troops to deal with the new crisis in the north—
including defense of approaches to the Kirkuk oil fields and the vital
Darbandikhan dam—would clear the way for Iran's long-postponed
offensive against Basra.[13]

But in an action that drew an outraged response around the world,
Iraqi government forces struck back by using chemical weapons. Independent press representatives who visited Halabjeh under Iranian
escort shortly after the attack found little to discredit Tehran's claims
that from three to five thousand people, the majority civilians, had died
from exposure to mustard gas and cyanide.[14] Washington condemned
Iraq's use of chemical weapons, drawing praise from Iran in the process and a request to help in obtaining treatment for victims of the

188 FREDERICK W. AXELGARD

attack.[15] Subsequently, U.S. officials stated that there was evidence that Iran, too, had used chemical weapons at Halabjeh, but this did little to erase the incident's negative effect on Iraq's international image.

In summary, developments between 1985 and 1988 appeared to take the Kurdish issue in Iraq further from rather than closer to a resolution, whereas the consolidation of a national identity among Iraqi Shi'is seemed to have become a reality. In the wake of the Halabjeh incident and the campaign of razing Kurdish villages and relocating their inhabitants, the gulf between the regime and the Kurdish community was broad and deep. The prospect that Iraqi Kurdish leaders might be reconsidering their ties to Tehran following the spring 1988 Iranian setbacks at Fao and Chalamchah was the only source of optimism that a working relationship might eventually be resumed with the central government in Baghdad.[16]

In addition to surviving the war, the most important long-term developments in Iraq between 1985 and 1988 may well have been the drive to enlarge its oil-exporting system and the wide-ranging economic reforms initiated in 1987. Both efforts owed their initial intensity to war-induced expediency. Nevertheless, their significance in reducing Iraq's future vulnerability to external threats to its oil-export lifeline and raising domestic productivity and initiative is likely to extend well beyond the end of the war with Iran.

The expansion of Iraq's oil-export capacity since 1984 proved to be remarkable and was decisive in enabling the country to withstand the draining impact of the war. Methodically and aggressively, Iraq increased oil exports from just over 900,000 barrels per day (b/d) in 1983 to a level three times that high in the closing months of 1987.[17] These gains were realized by building and expanding oil pipeline capacity across Turkey and Saudi Arabia. Iraq developed its trans-Turkey capacity to a level of 1.5 million b/d by upgrading the pumping capacity of the existing Kirkuk-Ceyhan pipeline to 1 million b/d in 1984 and by completing a 500,000 b/d pipeline to Ceyhan in 1987. Plans were then pushed forward to double the capacity of this second Turkish pipeline to 1 million b/d. In addition, a pipeline due to be completed at the end of 1988 would send 70,000 b/d of Iraqi crude to a refinery at Batman, Turkey. A proposal was made early in 1988 to add a second, 300,000 b/d pipeline to Batman.[18] In total, projects existing and planned as of mid-1988 would result in nearly 2.4 million b/d of Iraqi crude oil exports to and across Turkey.

A major breakthrough in Iraq's oil export outlook occurred in 1985, when it opened a pipeline connecting its southern oil fields to Saudi Arabia's east-west Petroline. Exports through this spur (referred to as IPSA I) reached their maximum capacity of 500,000 b/d in early

1987. Just months later, contract approval was given to proceed with construction of IPSA II, a wholly Iraqi pipeline to the Red Sea, which will give Iraq an overall trans-Saudi export capacity of 1.6 million b/d by the end of 1989.[19].

A final vital project was construction of a second strategic north-south pipeline within Iraq, which was begun in 1988. This project promised to galvanize the oil-security philosophy underpinning the entire Iraqi pipeline system. Its capacity (like that of the existing "strategic" line) to carry oil northward or southward will enable Iraq to transfer large amounts of oil from either of its major producing regions to either the trans-Turkey or trans-Saudi pipeline systems as political and economic circumstances may deem necessary or expedient. When completed, this 900,000 b/d strategic line might also turn Iraq's system into a partial safety valve for the industrial world because it would have the potential to reduce significantly any oil-supply pressures caused by a possible suspension of oil traffic through the Strait of Hormuz.[20]

A second important development in Iraq's economic sector was Saddam's energetic and wide-ranging reform program, ushered in at the beginning of 1987 once the crisis year of 1986 was past. Saddam invested his personal authority extensively in a bid to reshape the Iraqi economy through deregulation and expansion of the private sector, while reducing the role of the state sector and the influence of the Ba'th party in economic activity.[21]

The scope of the reforms being pursued in Iraq makes them difficult to summarize. One key step, taken early in the process, was the abolition of Iraq's comprehensive labor law—one of the most dramatic transformations of social policy in two decades of Ba'thist rule. It ended the guarantee of a job for all adult laborers but reinstated the freedom to choose one's mode of employment.[22] Privatization of public sector initiatives has proceeded most rapidly in agriculture, an area in which all state-owned enterprises were expected to be sold off by the summer of 1988. Meanwhile, private companies in all sectors have seen the removal of key foreign exchange controls as a prod to greater economic activity. Overall, Saddam's emphasis on productivity and profitability—with the open admission that twenty years of socialism in Iraq had not worked to expectation—provoked comparisons with the reforms made in Britain under Margaret Thatcher.[23]

Saddam also attacked the inefficiency caused by the proliferation of an unwieldy bureaucratic superstructure. Pointedly, one of his most decisive reform speeches, driving home the need to cut back the size and closely monitor the effectiveness of the statist system, was made to local government officials.[24] Thereafter, a host of major changes were made, featuring most prominently the merging of some ministries, the abolition of others, the complete elimination of the layer of "state organizations" that had been interposed between government ministries and the public sector industrial and commercial operations they oversaw. According to Iraq's Planning Ministry, a total of 811 departments and state organizations had been eliminated or merged by mid-1988 in an effort to overhaul the state bureaucracy.[25] The directors of the remaining state enterprises were said to be free of all legal restrictions that hindered them from taking the steps they deemed necessary to enhance output and productivity.[26]

The best measure of the significance of the internal developments described here will be whether they survive into the post–Gulf war period and how they affect that transition. After Iraq's battlefield successes in the spring of 1988, it seemed that conditions within the country were being openly evaluated from the perspective of the postwar era. The reforms described above, for example, became a lens through which to anticipate the postwar revitalization of the country. Indeed, high-ranking Ba'thist officials encouraged the view that these reforms were part and parcel of Saddam's longer-range vision of Iraq's development, rather than merely a response to war-induced requirements for greater efficiency and productivity.[27]

There were also definite political overtones to this interpretation of Iraq's recent reforms. The same Ba'thist officials argued that the forward-looking measures of economic liberalization also constituted steps toward political liberalization. They held that in a Third World context, it is axiomatic that economic reforms must precede meaningful political evolution. In making such suggestions, Iraq's leadership seemed to be admitting the need for postwar political adjustments. Indeed, it would appear that the peacetime task of granting greater political freedom to a population that has made great sacrifices in the cause of national survival will present the Saddam Hussein regime with a formidable political challenge. Even the oblique nature of their few direct comments about political reform—a hint that a new constitution to replace the provisional one of 1970 had been drafted and an off-the-cuff observation that Saddam actually "doesn't believe in the one-party system" of government[28]—suggested that Iraq's leaders may have anticipated fundamental political changes.

External Developments

In the same way that it affected internal developments, the war dictated that Iraq's fortunes in international affairs between 1985 and 1988 would be very much an up-and-down experience. The nadir for Iraq was, of course, the secret U.S.-Israeli collaboration to sell arms to

Iran. The apex was the vigorous international campaign in the months after Iran-Contra, led by Washington, which resulted in the unanimous passage of Security Council Resolution 598 in July 1987 and the deployment of a massive armada of Western ships in the Gulf. The avowed purpose of these ships was to contain Iranian actions against international shipping. But they were arguably more successful in reassuring Iraq's Gulf Arab allies of the West's commitment to their security and as a signal to Iran that it would not be permitted to overthrow the strategic balance in the Gulf.

Though it varied widely, Iraq's international experience in this period was held together by a common thread: its plight was consistently at the focal point of world attention and international policy concern. In part, this was a result of circumstances beyond Baghdad's control. But also in part, it resulted from the policy Iraq had pursued vigorously since 1984 of raising the international stakes in the war by attacking Iranian oil targets in the Gulf. All in all, this condition marked a dramatic shift for a country which only a few years earlier was relegated to obscurity, both strategically and politically, by most Western powers.

Iraq and the Superpowers

A fundamental premise of Iraq's persistent effort to internationalize the war—or more precisely, to raise the international stakes of Iran's insistence on continuing the war—was that the international community, and the superpowers in particular, could end the conflict if they wanted to. The effort to move Washington and Moscow to take such a course of action was Iraq's most important, most successful, and yet most frustrating foreign policy initiative during the period under review here.

By 1985, Iraq had already made progress in its efforts to focus the superpowers' attention on its difficult wartime situation. After ceasing direct military support for the first two years of the war, the Soviet Union responded in 1983 to Iraq's urgent requests to resume major arms shipments. Soviet-Iraqi diplomatic exchanges, which had been strained for some time, escalated sharply during 1984. Moscow added the sweetener of financial support, on concessional terms, for several major economic projects in Iraq, including a nuclear power facility. Finally, there was also an unsuccessful but appreciated Soviet attempt to persuade Syria to drop its alliance with Iran and thereby eliminate much of the regional pressure on Iraq.[29]

With respect to the United States, Iraqi Foreign Minister Tariq Aziz had pressed Secretary of State George Shultz early in 1983 for U.S.

support of strong U.N. action—including the threat of Security Council sanctions for noncompliance—to end the war.[30] But American concern was not galvanized until several months later, when Iraq procured sophisticated air-attack weaponry from France and announced its intent to launch a major campaign against Iranian economic targets, including oil installations in the Gulf. Washington quickly became involved and helped bring about Security Council Resolution 540, which was passed at the end of October 1983. This call for an end to the war was accepted by Iraq but rejected by Iran, which helped lead the National Security Council to draw the policy conclusion that Iran was responsible for the continuation of the war.[31] As a result of this sequence of events, Washington initiated Operation Staunch, an effort to persuade Western countries not to sell arms to Iran, thereby reducing the Islamic Republic's capability to wage war.

The restoration of full diplomatic relations between Baghdad and Washington in November 1984 indicated Iraq's satisfaction with U.S. cooperation in addressing its war-related concerns. It was followed early the next year by another key development, the start-up of Washington's practice of providing intelligence data on Iranian military deployments to help Iraq defend itself. Predictably, there were signs that the Soviet Union was not happy with the U.S.-Iraqi rapprochement. These signs included Soviet equivocation on the question of supplying aircraft to Iraq, lack of concern over Syrian and Libyan transfers of Soviet arms to Iran, and hints of a growing political dialogue between Moscow and Tehran. Iraq's sustained efforts to reassure (and gain reassurance from) the Soviet Union appeared to bear fruit in December 1985, when Saddam Hussein made his first visit to Moscow since becoming president of Iraq. One of the implications of this visit—that Iraqi policy, in the Soviet view, had regained an acceptable balance—may have been related to Saddam's then-recent and abrasive exchange with Secretary of State Shultz over Israel's bombing of the PLO headquarters in Tunis and the U.S. interception of an Egyptian airliner following the *Achille Lauro* incident.[32]

Despite these diplomatic maneuvers, Soviet-American discussions on the war (conducted from the U.S. side by the State Department) were initiated early in 1985, as part of a broader dialogue on regional conflict in the Third World.[33] Here was an indication that irrespective of the vagaries of its bilateral relations with the two superpowers, Iraq had succeeded in drawing their attention to the need to end the Gulf war. Furthermore, this Soviet-American dialogue continued at relatively consistent intervals throughout the period under examination.

The most meaningful installment in this exchange took place in

mid-1986, short months after Iran's stunning success in occupying the
Fao peninsula. In Stockholm at the end of June, Assistant Secretary
of State Richard Murphy made a proposal to his Soviet counterpart
for accelerating an end to the Iran-Iraq war. It consisted of two discrete
elements: an offer of a joint Soviet-U.S. communique denouncing the
war and calling for an end to hostilities; and the suggestion that the
superpowers should work together to prevent arms from reaching
Iran from either Western or Eastern bloc sources. For the first time in
this series of exchanges, the Soviet response to an American suggestion
was not an immediate dismissal.[34] The same basically nonnegative
attitude still prevailed when the American side checked back with the
Soviets in August.[35] Perhaps to avoid tainting the bilateral atmosphere
just before the Reykjavik summit, Moscow never explicitly rejected the
U.S. proposal. But once the annual convention of the U.N. General
Assembly began, it became clear that the Soviets were not willing to
play along. This disappointment explains why Secretary of State Shultz
sharply criticized the Soviet Union's position on the war when he met
with Gulf Arab foreign ministers in New York at this time.[36]

The tables quickly turned on Secretary Shultz when, just weeks later,
the Iran-Contra scandal erupted and threatened not only to upend
the U.S. position on the Gulf war but also to liquidate any sense of
trust in Washington by the Arab world at large. Even a summation of
the Iran-Contra scandal and its domestic and international impact is
beyond the scope of this essay, so intense was the shock and so extensive
were the deliberations and debate it occasioned. Still, it is instructive
to note that because of their pervasive focus on matters of policy
process, management style, and the diversion of funds to the Nicaraguan Contras, the public debate and the investigations conducted by
the Tower Commission and the select congressional committee gave
little if any consideration to the impact on Iraq and on its budding
relationship with Washington that might stem from the secret U.S.-
Israeli arms transfer to Iran.[37].

Similarly, the Iraqi government showed no desire to make an elabo-
rate public display of outrage over the Reagan administration's betrayal of its embryonic trust with Baghdad and at least two cardinal
features of its policy in the Gulf, namely, Operation Staunch and the
refusal to provide arms to either combatant in the Gulf war. Rather
than exacerbate what its diplomats had described as an extremely
embarrassing and difficult situation for the Reagan administration,
Baghdad decided to address its grievances in a restrained, primarily
private manner.[38] The foremost Iraqi concern expressed at this point
was reportedly the desire that the White House issue a presidential
statement clarifying the U.S. position on the war, which apparently

was fulfilled some weeks later when President Reagan condemned Iran for its continued support of international terrorism and its prosecution of hostilities against Iraq.[39]

It would be inaccurate, however, to suggest that strains in U.S.-Iraqi relations did not result from the Iran-Contra scandal. The most negative comments from Baghdad at the time were channeled through Taha Yasin Ramadan, Iraq's first deputy prime minister, who was known not to be a strong supporter of U.S.-Iraqi rapprochement. As Iran pushed forward in its threatening offensive against Basra in January 1987, with U.S.-supplied arms appearing to play a major role in its success, Ramadan leveled the charge that the U.S. arms sale to Iran was "expressive of a bigger U.S. program in the region aimed at conspiring with Iran against Iraq." This American plot, Ramadan charged, had included providing faulty military intelligence, which had led to Iraq's loss of the Fao peninsula one year earlier at the cost of thousands of Iraqi lives.[40] Significantly, this potentially damaging issue was never taken up by Saddam Hussein personally. And although Ramadan continued to make the charge after the U.S. embassy in Baghdad had strenuously denied it, the matter never imperiled the U.S.-Iraqi relationship.[41]

The equanimity maintained between Baghdad and Washington was attributable in no small part to the pace of developments in the Gulf and in U.S. policy related thereto in the first few months of 1987. For example, even as Iran was making penetrations near Basra, U.S. diplomats initiated the vigorous consultations at the United Nations that eventually resulted in the passage of Resolution 598 in July. Meanwhile, Washington accepted Kuwait's request to reflag eleven Kuwaiti oil tankers to gain some protection against Iranian attacks on Kuwaiti oil interests in the Gulf. Iraq was a clear beneficiary, politically, of these expressions of U.S. desire to contain Iranian advances in the Gulf. Although the large U.S. naval presence violated Iraq's long-standing opposition to the expansion of outside military influence in the Gulf, Iraqi officials sidestepped what had heretofore been a matter of ideological principle by refusing to criticize "brotherly Kuwait" for defending its national interests.[42]

In May, another crisis erupted when an Iraqi jet mistakenly fired its missiles at the USS *Stark*, killing thirty-seven American seamen, the first Americans to die as a result of the war between Iran and Iraq. The Iraqi government—with its ambassador in Washington, Nizar Hamdoon, playing a highly visible role[43]—deflected serious political damage by rapidly extending Saddam Hussein's written apology for the inadvertent attack and promising compensation to the families of the *Stark*'s victims.[44] The Reagan administration readily accepted Iraq's apology, although it pressed energetically for arrangements that would prevent the recurrence of a similar mistake. Moreover, it proceeded undeterred with plans to reflag the Kuwaiti tankers, which took effect in late July.

After Iran-Contra and during the fierce battle for Basra, Moscow moved to reassure Iraq of the strength and importance of Soviet-Iraqi ties. Soviet statements on the war emphasized Iraq's acceptance of international proposals to end the conflict by negotiation and called for international pressure on Iran to do the same.[45] A timely milestone in Soviet-Iraqi relations was passed when Iraq became the second country outside the East bloc to receive Soviet MIG-29 jets.[46] The Soviet Union threatened to make further political and military inroads into the Gulf during this period of turmoil when it, too, was asked by Kuwait to help protect its ships from Iranian attacks. Although Moscow responded to Kuwait quickly and affirmatively, the vast size and eventual multilateral nature of the U.S.-led armada far outstripped the Soviet response and stunted its political impact in the Gulf.

The Soviet Union cooperated in bringing about the unanimous passage of the toughly worded Security Council Resolution 598 on July 20, 1987. The resolution paralleled very closely the above-mentioned secret proposal which Washington had made in Stockholm a year earlier, inasmuch as it combined a demand for an end to the hostilities in the Gulf with a clear determination to proceed with sanctions against any party that did not comply. The passage of Resolution 598 undoubtedly marked the high point of several years of international efforts to curtail the bloody Gulf war. It also gave firm evidence of the degree to which Iraq had succeeded in maneuvering the superpowers into the "right" position on the Gulf war.

But Iraq's success was not conclusive. In the weeks and months after the passage of Resolution 598, Iran's diplomatic finesse in neither rejecting nor accepting the resolution played on the Soviet Union's desire to explore closer ties with Tehran during a period of hardening Iranian-American antagonism. Thus, though it had supported Resolution 598, Moscow equivocated on the notion of imposing sanctions with Iran. This ploy immediately introduced strains into Soviet-Iraqi relations. Initially, Iraq criticized "the shortsighted superpower opposing the imposition of sanctions against Iran," without naming the Soviets explicitly.[47] In time, the charade was dropped, as is evident from the following comments by Iraqi Foreign Minister Tariq Aziz:

> We call for a serious and principled commitment to Resolution No. 598. We believe that a true translation of such a commitment is to arrive at the correct conclusion and to acknowledge it—for I am sure, and you can quote me—that the Soviet Union and China have reached the conclu-

sion that Iran rejects Resolution No. 598. They know well that Iran rejected Resolution 598 before it was adopted. I have said this to . . . Soviet Foreign Minister Eduard Shevardnadze. . . . Therefore, I can say that the Soviet Union and China know that Iran does not accept Resolution No. 598 but do not want to admit it openly . . . because the admission of such a fact will deprive them of any pretext for not agreeing to the resolution calling for the imposition of sanctions on Iran, a resolution which—let us say until now—they have not wanted.[48]

The tone of Tariq Aziz's remarks bespoke a growing sense of realism about the limits of the existing diplomatic momentum for ending the war. This realism extended to the conclusion that there was no possibility of a softening of the Soviet position on sanctions against Iran until after Soviet forces completed their withdrawal from Afghanistan, owing to the danger that Iran would use its influence among Afghan resistance groups to complicate the withdrawal process.[49] But by the time Aziz's remarks were made, the U.S. posture had become more complex.

Following the Halabjeh chemical-warfare incident and Iraq's routing of Iranian forces from Fao—not to mention the massive damage U.S. ships inflicted on the Iranian navy in an encounter in April 1988—U.S. officials concluded that continuing to depict Iraq as the aggrieved party in the Gulf conflict was not a promising diplomatic strategy. As a result, the Reagan administration pressed Iraqi officials at the United Nations for a gesture of flexibility in Iraq's approach to Resolution 598. Presumably these proposals revolved around replacing Iraq's demand for a ceasefire-*cum*-withdrawal with a demand for a ceasefire-in-place because the liberation of Fao had eliminated a major territorial concern for Iraq. Iraq rejected the proposal. Nor did Vernon Walters, the U.S. ambassador to the United Nations, make any headway when he attempted to make the case directly to Iraqi leaders in Baghdad.[50]

In summary, then, between 1985 and 1988 Iraq experienced very active relations with the superpowers. On one extreme was its success in bringing both Moscow and Washington to acknowledge, persistently and openly, the importance of ending the Gulf war as a threat to international peace and stability. On the other extreme were the painful exhibitions of American and Soviet opportunism vis-à-vis Iran. What remained to be seen was whether Iraq's aggressive cultivation of the superpowers would set a pattern whose significance would extend beyond the end of the war itself.

Iraq in the Region

The other major development in Iraq's external relations was the evolution of its regional position. Iraq had already made significant progress in fostering a moderate image in regional politics before 1985. In the period under examination here, this process expanded significantly. Iraq became more deeply entrenched in relationships with moderate, status-quo countries in the region, while also provoking speculation about a seminal shift in its attitude toward the Arab-Israeli conflict.

Much has already been said about Iraq's ties with the two countries that were arguably its most important regional allies, Saudi Arabia and Turkey. Iraq could not have survived without the oil exports these two states—one the United States's closest ally in the Gulf and the other a member of NATO—allowed to transit in ever-increasing quantities. Iraq also deepened its ties to Kuwait with the completion of natural gas pipelines to this emirate in 1987. Beyond serving as outlets for Iraqi hydrocarbon exports, Saudi Arabia and Kuwait also provided Iraq with billions of dollars in financial support during these years, primarily by marketing 200,000–300,000 b/d of oil on Iraq's behalf.[51]

Equally important to Iraq were the military, diplomatic, and political dimensions of these relationships. Kuwaiti ports, for example, channeled the bulk of the Soviet Union's military supplies to Iraq throughout this period. Kuwait's role in this activity provoked Iran to declare it a "co-belligerent" in the Gulf war. This set the stage for the surge in Iranian attacks against Kuwaiti oil tankers in 1986 and for the Silkworm missile attacks which Iran launched against Kuwait in the latter part of 1987. Saudi Arabia's most important military actions on behalf of Iraq were indirect, those taken in quiet cooperation with the Western naval armada that began patrolling the Gulf in 1987. It was taboo to discuss the extent and nature of the cooperation between the states of the Gulf Cooperation Council (led by Saudi Arabia) and these Western forces. Nevertheless, its reality became widely accepted and was an essential factor in making the American deployment in the Gulf politically viable in the United States and a stiff deterrent against Iranian aggressiveness in the Gulf.

Between 1985 and 1988, the Arab GCC states continued to be a source of vital political backing for Iraq, particularly in voicing support in international councils for the quickest possible end to the Gulf war. Although Iraq took care to maintain active political, commercial, and cultural relations with these states, Iranian actions—in particular, the occupation of Fao in 1986 and the riots in Mecca in 1987—were probably more decisive in galvanizing GCC attitudes toward the war. After its invasion of Fao put Iran within missile range of Kuwait, the GCC called on Iran to withdraw its forces and condemned "Iran's occupation of portions of Iraqi territory, and the breach of international conventions and the principles of good neighborliness and viola-

tion of Iraq's sovereignty and territorial integrity, which that occupation represents."[52]

It was after Fao that the GCC, led by Saudi Arabia and Kuwait,
resolved to pursue more actively Arab and international support for
action to end the conflict and the regional danger and tension emanating from it. By the time of the riots at Mecca eighteen months later,
however, these efforts had made little tangible progress. Moreover, in
the wake of these riots Saudi Arabia also failed in its efforts to get the
Arab states as a whole to take decisive action against Iran such as
collectively severing diplomatic relations with Iran.[53]

Iraqi and GCC efforts to focus the Arab League effectively on the
issue of the war finally bore fruit at the Amman summit conference
of November 1987. From Iraq's perspective, the accomplishments of
the conference were several, the most basic being that the Gulf war
displaced the Arab-Israeli dispute and the Palestinian problem as the
top priority on the inter-Arab agenda. The summit also voted to
condemn Iran in surprisingly strong terms (given Syria's reservations)
for its continued prosecution of the war. Furthermore, King Hussein
announced at Amman that Iraq and Syria had had a reconciliation "in
the full sense of the word." It was anticipated that the process of
resuming normal relations begun at Amman would bring about the
restoration of formal diplomatic ties between Baghdad and Damascus
in a matter of weeks.[54]

Like the passage of Resolution 598, the Amman summit represented
the consummation of years of intense effort by Iraq to generate diplomatic awareness and action on the war. Also like Resolution 598,
the enthusiasm of the summit was followed by disappointment. The
projected reconciliation between Iraq and Syria never took place. Early
in 1988, Syria and Iraq resumed their war of words, with Iraq charging
that Syria had failed to make any fundamental alteration in its relations
with Iran and had undermined rather than adhered to the unified
Arab stand developed at the Amman summit.[55] Furthermore, Iraq
found the outcome at Amman mitigated by the eruption of the Palestinian uprising in the occupied territories beginning in December
1987. By the time Arab heads of state met in Algiers in June 1988, it
was abundantly clear that Iraq's situation and the threat of the Gulf
war had slipped to a position of distant second in priority.

Finally, we turn to the question of Iraq's position with respect to
Egypt and Israel. The only major accomplishment of the Amman
summit which proved to be irreversible in the short run was the
vote to allow Arab League member states to restore their diplomatic
relations with Egypt on an individual basis. Iraq reopened its embassy
in Cairo immediately after the conclusion of the summit and was soon

joined by the majority of the Arab League in doing so. Its rapid action and the broad positive Arab response to the summit decision reflected years of effort by the Saddam Hussein regime to prepare the way for a reinstatement of Egypt in Arab ranks.

This effort had many dimensions, but Iraq's main interest in strengthening Egypt's position in the Arab world had to do with the military and political repercussion of the Gulf war. When Syria vaulted to the side of Iran in 1982, it divided the Arab world and left Iraq with a fundamental flaw in one of its most important arenas of support. To involve Egypt on Iraq's side was the only way to remedy this flaw. Moreover, Egypt was the only Arab country capable of posing as a strategic counterweight to Iran, and Iraq worked assiduously to promote such a posture. As early as 1982, Baghdad openly suggested the possibility of restoring diplomatic relations with Egypt, and Saddam Hussein and Hosni Mubarak commented on Egypt's possible role in alleviating the dangerous situation in the Gulf war.[56]

Although it apparently felt itself too strongly in need of the "shelter of Arab consensus" to break out on its own and resume formal ties with Cairo, Iraq pressed for Egyptian involvement at Arab summit gatherings. Nevertheless, Iraq hosted political, military, and commercial delegations from Egypt, including a visit to Baghdad by President Mubarak himself early in 1985. This gesture reinforced Iraq's positive and unique view of Egypt's importance only months after the rest of the Arab world had sharply criticized Jordan for unilaterally restoring relations with Egypt. Providing a tangible and forceful counterpart to these political maneuvers, Egypt by 1985 had become the third largest supplier of military hardware to Iraq, behind the Soviet Union and France.[57]

Until 1985, Iraq had also begun to show signs of moderation on its policy toward Israel and the Arab-Israeli conflict. It was once again in the critical war year of 1982 that Saddam Hussein told U.S. Congressman Stephen Solarz that "the existence of a secure state (or condition) for the Israelis" was necessary for regional peace.[58] Iraq had also given quiet encouragement to the dialogue between King Hussein and Yasser Arafat between 1983 and 1986, another indication of support for a negotiated Arab-Israeli settlement. Furthermore, Iraqi officials speaking in Washington sought to project Iraq as having secondary importance to Arab-Israeli issues because it had no direct role in the conflict.[59]

In the end, though, these gestures had no practical effect on the Arab-Israeli peace process and were ignored or minimized in Israel with virtual unanimity. But following the explosion of the Iran-Contra controversy, there appeared to be a renewed interest in Iraq on the part of some Israelis and Israel supporters. The shift in mood was foreshadowed in a *New York Times* opinion piece that admonished Israel for "treating Iraq as an intractable foe" when it had been moving away from the Arab radicals and might, after its war with Iran ended, follow Egypt's pattern of making peace with Israel.[60] The atmosphere was stirred further when Iraqi ambassador Nizar Hamdoon gave an interview to the newsletter of the Israeli lobby in Washington in which he stated Iraq's "hope" that there would not be another Arab-Israeli war.[61]

In the months that followed, there were signs of a significant debate in Israel over policy toward Iran and Iraq—the new feature being emergence of a pro-Iraqi voice. Foreign Minister Shimon Peres sounded an early note in the dialectic when he told the General Assembly that he supported U.N. efforts to stop the Gulf war. He was quickly contradicted by Defense Minister Yitzhak Rabin, who declared that Israel retained a long-term strategic interest in Iran and that the United States had been manipulated by Iraq into a weak position in the Gulf. This exchange occurred amid persistent reports that a fundamental review of Israeli policy toward the Gulf war was under way and that growing (but still minority) support for Iraq was producing a new, balanced view of the conflict.[62] By the close of the period under review, there had been no clear resolution of this debate. Nevertheless, the mere fact that the merits of a constructive view of Iraq were being openly and vigorously discussed in Israel marked a breakthrough of no small proportions.

Conclusion

The years 1985 to 1988 were filled with turmoil for Iraq in its domestic and foreign affairs. To resume the theme adopted in the introduction to this essay, the developments described above seemed to chart a fitful emergence for Iraq into a new era of economic and, possibly, political reform. They also led Iraq to break tentative new ground in its international policies with a vigorous balancing act between the superpowers, while also provoking a modicum of new thinking in Israel about its regional role.

The next step must be to watch how Iraq emerges from the Gulf war, which has been the midwife to whatever change has taken place in the country.

That transition will determine whether Iraq's emergence from obscurity and appearance on the "screen" of serious U.S. policy interest proves to be permanent or ephemeral. Only then will it become clear whether Saddam Hussein's management of Iraq's internal and external affairs during the war has provided sufficiently for a transition from a war footing that will enable Iraq to revitalize itself from within and project a clear, positive definition of its regional and international role to the outside world. The true measure of Iraq's emergence is yet to be made.

Notes

1. Frederick W. Axelgard, *U.S.-Arab Relations: The Iraq Dimension* (Washington, D.C.: National Council on U.S.-Arab Relations, 1985), p. 27.
2. *Middle East Economic Digest* (hereafter *MEED*), Jan. 2, 1988, p. 7.
3. See U.S. Department of State, *Country Reports on Human Rights Practices* (Washington, D.C.: U.S. Government Printing Office, 1986–88), for annual reports on Iraqi human rights in the years 1985–87.
4. Ofra Bengio, "Iraq," in *Middle East Contemporary Survey: Volume IX, 1984–85*, ed. Itamar Rabinovich and Haim Shaked (Boulder, Colo.: Westview Press, for the Moshe Dayan Center for Middle Eastern and African Studies of Tel Aviv University, 1987), p. 462.
5. Ralph King, "The Iran-Iraq War: The Political Implications," *Adelphi Papers* 219 (Spring 1987): 11. See *Washington Post*, Jan. 25, 1987, for a similarly positive assessment of the Iraqi national consensus behind the war.
6. *New York Times*, Sept. 22, 1987.
7. See Frederick W. Axelgard, *A New Iraq? The Gulf War and Implications for U.S. Policy* (New York: Praeger, for the Center for Strategic and International Studies, 1988), pp. 20 – 29.
8. Author's discussion in late 1983 with officials of the State Department and the (then) U.S. Interests Section, Baghdad.
9. *Washington Post*, July 29, 1985; author's discussions with Iraqi officials in Baghdad, May 1988.
10. Chris Kutschera, "Inside Kurdistan," *Middle East*, Sept. 1985, pp. 10–12; *Financial Times*, Jan. 8, 1986; *MEED*, Nov. 1, 1986, p. 2, Nov. 15, 1986, pp. 20, 23; and *Economist*, June 13, 1987, p. 44.
11. *Economist*, June 13, 1987, p. 44; my discussions with a member of a U.S. Senate delegation that visited northern Iraq in August 1987. There were also allegations at this time that the Iraqi regime had attacked Kurdish positions in northern Iraq with chemical weapons.
12. *Kayhan al-Arabi* (Tehran), Nov. 5, 1987, as translated in Joint Publications Research Service, *Report for Near East and South Asia* (hereafter *JPRS*), Jan. 20, 1988, pp. 19–24.
13. *MEED*, Apr. 2, 1988, p. 8.
14. Ibid.; *Washington Times* and *Financial Times*, Mar. 23, 1988.
15. *Washington Post*, Mar. 25, 1988; *Christian Science Monitor*, Apr. 1, 1988.
16. *Washington Post*, May 4, 1988.
17. *Petroleum Intelligence Weekly*, June 6, 1988, p. 2, reports that Iraqi oil exports reached a peak of 2.8 million b/d in November 1987.
18. *Arab Oil and Gas*, Apr. 16, 1988, p. 15; Ibid., Apr. 1, 1988, p. 10.
19. American Embassy, Baghdad, "Foreign Economic Trends and Their Implications for the United States: Iraq," Feb. 1988, p. 10.
20. *Middle East Economic Survey* (hereafter *MEES*), May 9, 1988, p. A-5; *Financial Times*, May 10, 1988; *Arab Oil and Gas*, June 1, 1988, pp. 5–7.

21. *MEED,* Aug. 15, 1987, pp. 6–7.

22. Ibid.

23. *Middle East International,* Oct. 1, 1987, pp. 14–15; *Financial Times,* Oct. 1, 1987.

24. Iraqi News Agency (INA), July 13, 1987, as cited in *JPRS,* Sept. 14, 1987, pp. 1–19. This speech was one of several landmark events that gave critical momentum to Iraq's economic reform movement. For a wider reading of the concepts behind this movement, see Saddam Hussein, *Economy and Management in Socialist Society* (Baghdad: Dar al-Ma'mun, 1988), trans. Naji al-Hadithi.

25. *MEED,* June 17, 1988, p. 20.

26. American Embassy, Baghdad, "Foreign Economic Trends," p. 8.

27. *Middle East International,* June 24, 1988, pp. 19–20.

28. Author's conversations in Baghdad, May 1988.

29. Author's discussions in Baghdad, Dec. 1983; Dennis Ross, "Soviet Views Toward the Gulf War," *Orbis* 28 (Fall 1984): 438, 440–41; *al-Majallah* (London), Mar. 31, 1984, as cited in *JPRS,* May 21, 1984, p. 1.

30. Reuters Northern European Service, May 13, 1983.

31. *New York Times,* Jan. 11, 1984; Richard M. Preece, "United States–Iraqi Relations," Washington, D.C., Congressional Research Service, Report No. 860142F, July 30, 1986, p. 12.

32. Bengio, "Iraq," pp. 477–79.

33. *Washington Times,* Feb. 15, 1985.

34. Author's discussions with U.S. and Iraqi officials, July–October 1986.

35. *Los Angeles Times,* Aug. 9, 1986.

36. *New York Times,* Oct. 2, 1986.

37. I have written elsewhere that "the debate kindled by revelation of the Iran arms sales has displayed the same weakness—obsession with domestic politics—which apparently led the Reagan Administration into a desperate attempt to trade arms for the release of American hostages" ("Deception at Home and Abroad: Implications of the Iran Arms Scandal for U.S. Foreign Policy," *American-Arab Affairs* 30 [Spring 1987]: 5).

38. Iraq showed similar restraint in not publicizing the December 1987 expulsion of the defense attaché attached to the U.S. embassy in Baghdad for photographing Iraq-bound Soviet equipment while on a visit to Kuwait. The story did not become public knowledge until several months later (*Washington Times,* Apr. 20, 1987).

39. Author's discussion with Iraqi officials, Dec. 1986; *Middle East Policy Survey* (Washington, D.C., December 19, 1986); Statement by the President, Office of the White House Press Secretary, Jan. 23, 1987.

40. *Washington Post,* Jan. 27, 1987; *Wall Street Journal,* Jan. 13, 1987.

41. Repetitions of Ramadan's charge are recorded in *New York Times,* Jan. 19, 1987, and *Christian Science Monitor,* Apr. 15, 1987. The U.S. denial is described in *Washington Post,* Jan. 22, 1987.

42. Author's discussion with Iraqi officials, Apr. 1987.

43. The day after the *Stark* attack, Hamdoon gave some thirty press and broadcast interviews to express Iraq's apology and condolences, an effort that helped greatly to contain the damage the incident inflicted on U.S.-Iraqi relations.

44. *Washington Times,* May 19, 1987; *Washington Post,* May 22, 1987. For a useful summation of the impact of the *Stark* incident on U.S.-Iraq relations,

see Richard Mackenzie, "A Fatal Error, but a Stronger Bond," *Washington Times Insight,* July 27, 1987.

45. INA (Baghdad), Jan. 10, 1987 *(FBIS:ME,* Jan. 12, 1987, p. E-1). See also INA (Baghdad), Dec. 10, 1986 *(FBIS:ME,* Dec. 11, 1986, p. E-2). For a study of Soviet policy toward the Iran-Iraq war during this period, see the chapter by Robert O. Freedman in this volume.

46. *Al-Dustur* (Amman), Feb. 7, 1987, p. 1 *(FBIS:ME,* Feb. 9, 1987, p. E-1).

47. *New York Times,* Aug. 22, 1987.

48. *Al-Watan al-Arabi,* May 6, 1988, pp. 26–31 *(FBIS:ME,* May 10, 1988, Annex p. 4).

49. Author's discussion with Iraqi officials, Apr. 1988.

50. Author's discussion with U.S. and Iraqi officials, Apr. and May 1988.

51. Iraq is under agreement to replace this volume of oil at some later date. Kuwait and Saudi Arabia were also believed to have given direct financial subventions to Iraq. There have been no public comments to confirm the existence of such support for Iraq since the first months of the war, and speculation varies widely as to its amount.

52. *MEES,* Mar. 10, 1986, p. C-4. For a further analysis of GCC policy, see the chapter by Shireen Hunter in this volume.

53. *Middle East International,* Aug. 28, 1987, pp. 4–5.

54. A good summation of Iraqi-Syrian developments at the Amman summit is found in the Jordanian foreign minister's interview with *al-Mustaqbal* (Paris), Nov. 21, 1987, trans. in *JPRS,* Jan. 20, 1988, pp. 2–5.

55. Saddam Hussein began to express open disappointment at the unfulfilled promise of the Amman summit in early January 1988. See *Voice of the Masses* (Baghdad), Jan. 6, 1988 *(FBIS:ME,* Jan. 7, 1988, pp. 29–33).

56. *Washington Post,* Dec. 30, May 21, 1982; *New York Times,* May 25, 1982.

57. Bengio, "Iraq," pp. 481, 474.

58. INA (Baghdad), Jan. 2, 1983 *(FBIS:ME,* Jan. 4, 1983, p. E-10). This transcript gives the content of an interview actually conducted in August 1982.

59. *MEED,* Nov. 30, 1984, p. 18, reports Tariq Aziz making this point to members of the U.S. Congress.

60. *New York Times,* Mar. 11, 1987. The author was Alfred Moses, vice-president of the American Jewish Committee.

61. *Near East Report,* Aug. 17, 1987, p. 132.

62. National Public Radio, "All Things Considered," Oct. 26, 1987; *Washington Post,* Oct. 29, 1987; *New York Times,* Nov. 2, 1987.

Part Three

National Perspectives

8

Israel's National Unity
Solution or Stalemate?

David Pollock

Introduction

Israel under the National Unity government of late 1984 through 1988 presented a mirror image, in many ways, of the country's experience during the preceding period. In the first part of this decade, foreign policy drove domestic politics; but lately things have been the other way around. Thus the 1982 war in Lebanon left the Jewish state's security situation essentially unchanged but triggered an internal political upheaval that lasted through mid-1985 with high-level resignations, mass protests, early elections, and aggravated economic crisis.[1] The most recent period, by contrast, began with a successful focus on domestic problems under a broad coalition between the country's two major rival political groups. But the delicate internal political balance precluded any decisive external initiatives. The result was that the country took on an unaccustomed air of normalcy—until internal Arab-Jewish conflicts exploded and revived the prospect of changes in the security sphere.

It was on the home front that Israel scored its most notable achievement during this period, with an impressive economic turnaround in 1985. And it was also on the internal front that Israel confronted its most serious new problem: the Palestinian Intifada (uprising) in the occupied West Bank and Gaza that began in December 1987 and persisted through the following year. In between these two developments that framed the four-year tenure of the National Unity government there was, as will be shown below, a good deal of motion but little real movement in either foreign or domestic policy. The period was punctuated by revelations of Israel's role in the Iran-Contra affair, but this isolated episode did nothing to alter the basic stalemate.

It is a truism that the foreign policies of most states begin at home.

In Israel's case, ironically, an erosion of national consensus on some basic security issues has made this proposition truer than ever before. Indeed, despite Israel's image as an embattled state bent single-mindedly on security, the reality has lately been one of a divided polity driven (if that is the right word for partial paralysis) by domestic political considerations.

This essay will develop that theme. It will begin by setting Israel's internal political context and then explore how it in turn affected the initial issues facing the National Unity government, longer-term regional and extraregional diplomacy, and finally the current controversies and future prospects confronting the country as it entered a "midlife crisis" in its fortieth year.

Domestic Political Context

The central fact of Israel's internal affairs lately is the paradox of a "National Unity" government in a polarized political system. So delicate and fragmented (the latter a product of "pure" proportional representation) was the electoral balance in 1984 that neither party— the left-of-center, more "dovish" Labor, or the right-of-center, more "hawkish" Likud—could put together a workable majority in the Knesset (Israel's parliament), even in coalition with like-minded smaller parties. The uniquely pragmatic expedient adopted in September 1984 to deal with this deadlock was a rotation agreement between the leaders of Israel's two major rival parties. Shimon Peres, leader of Labor, would preside as prime minister over an evenly split Labor-Likud coalition for two years, while Likud's Yitzhak Shamir served as foreign minister; afterward, the two would switch positions.

This "house divided against itself," defying most predictions, stood for four years, the maximum period between elections allowed by Israeli law. Its unexpected longevity went beyond the mere desire on all sides to hold on to power. Rather, the National Unity coalition also answered a widespread and persistent popular desire to put partisan squabbling aside and get on with urgent tasks. Public opinion, as measured in many polls, overwhelmingly supported continuation of this hybrid governing arrangement during most of its tenure. The public was equally united in the priority assigned to internal (especially economic) issues on which Labor and Likud proved willing and able to work together. Foreign policy issues, by contrast, were both more divisive and less urgent in common perception. Israelis were most often split down the middle on the core question of trading territory for peace. They were eager for peace talks but very skeptical about their value and generally complacent (at least until mid-1988) about maintaining the status quo. Moreover, straw polls consistently showed a roughly even balance between the two leading political parties, leaving neither one confident enough to risk an early election.[2]

Policy outcomes flowed from these underlying factors. On many issues, primarily internal ones, on which there was a working consensus, the coalition was capable of surprisingly cooperative and therefore effective action. But on other important issues—including fundamental foreign policy choices—Israel's government was constrained by continuing elite and popular divisions and followed only a temporizing, tentative, or at times even openly two-headed approach.

Another result of the Labor-Likud "cohabitation" was a tendency toward fragmentation or extremism in what remained of the parliamentary opposition. (In a further irony, the country's delicate overall political balance and the uncertain coalition loyalties of many small parties precluded concrete movement on the perennial issue of reforming an electoral system that put a premium on factionalism.) On the far left/dovish side of the spectrum were the Mapam party (newly splintered from Labor) and the Citizens' Rights movement, which held 9 out of 120 Knesset seats between them. At the opposite extreme, with 5 seats, was the ultranationalist Tehiya party, which supported outright annexation of (rather than Likud's preferred autonomy for) the occupied territories. Even further to the right was Rabbi Meir Kahane's Kach party, which explicitly advocated expelling the Arabs under Israel's control. Kach's 25,000-plus votes in 1984 entitled it to just one seat in parliament; but it enjoyed a diffuse sympathy for its basic attitude from as much as half the Israeli Jewish public, according to reliable surveys. And then, outside the mainstream of Israeli politics, were two nationalist/protest parties mainly representing around half of Israel's 750,000 Arab citizens—the Democratic Front for Peace and Equality (Hadash) and the Progressive List for Peace, with a combined 6 mandates in the Knesset.[3]

The role of such factions, though fractious and difficult, suggests a significant and stabilizing measure of co-optation(or at least channeling) of Israel's extremes into the existing political system. Nevertheless, there remain hard-core, organized militant groups, whether Jewish or Arab nationalist, that are prone to potentially dangerous extraparliamentary or even violent action. In particular, many adherents of Gush Emunim, the Bloc of the Faithful that champions Jewish settlement in the overwhelmingly Arab occupied territories, reject their own government's authority to order any withdrawal from those areas. The full implications of this challenge have never been tested, in part

because the specter of a showdown is alarming to all sides. But that
in itself imposes an additional constraint on Israel's already limited
domestic room for maneuver on this critical issue.

The tendency toward fragmentation on the margins has also affected the religious parties, four or more of which competed for
the allegiance of the orthodox 10 to 15 percent of Israel's Jewish
electorate—and three of which were included in the governing coalition.[4] (There is, in addition, a tiny but vocal minority of ultraorthodox
anti-Zionists who reject participation in the state.) From time to time,
the facade of National Unity was briefly disrupted by this camp's
parliamentary initiatives. In mid-1988, for example, the Knesset witnessed another in a long series of failed attempts to add one word
(kahalakhah) to Israel's Law of Return, which offers citizenship to all
Jewish immigrants, so as to exclude any but orthodox conversions
to the faith. But the same factors that cemented the "marriage of
inconvenience" between the major parties prevented the religious
ones from bringing down the government on such issues, as had
occasionally happened in the past.

In fact, the most visible religious skirmishes during this period took
place not in the parliament but in the streets, where localized tensions
with the secular majority flared episodically over such issues as Sabbath
traffic or movies, "obscene" posters, and "blockbusting" in segregated
orthodox neighborhoods. Such confrontations were especially frequent in Jerusalem, where the ultraorthodox constitute about one-
fifth of the city's Jewish population (quadruple their proportion in the
country as a whole). In 1986, as worse troubles receded from popular
consciousness, religious conflict rivaled Arab-Israeli and even economic issues as Israel's perceived number one problem.[5] The solution,
as in the past, was the practical expedient of enforcing law and order
while offering scattered symbolic concessions to orthodox feeling without ever clarifying the ambiguous status of Judaism in the fundamentally secular Jewish state.

By contrast, ethnic friction between the Sephardi (Oriental) and
Ashkenazi (Western) halves of Israel's Jewish population has recently
abated. The former remained disproportionately loyal to Likud, the
latter to Labor. But the main reason for this polarity was not, as many
have assumed, that the Sephardim are overwhelmingly "hawkish"; in
reality, surveys have consistently placed the "ethnic gap" on foreign
policy issues at a relatively modest 10 to 20 points. For example,
one mid-1988 poll showed half the Sephardi community favoring
territorial concessions for the sake of peace, while nearly two-thirds
of Ashkenazim took that position. When differences in income and
education are taken into account, the purely ethnic factor in the contest

over foreign policy shrinks even further. So the disproportionate
(roughly two-to-one) Sephardi preference for Likud or other right-
wing parties reflects socioeconomic protest and lingering charismatic
or traditional, quasi-religious appeal at least as much as it does the
fabled hard-line Sephardi attitude toward Arabs. Whether Labor can
overcome this gap with an enhanced appeal to Sephardim on personality or other issues will be a crucial question as Israel looks toward new
national elections in November 1988.[6] Indeed, Labor sought to deal
with this problem by allotting 30 percent of its "safe seats" to Sephardim on its 1988 election list.

Leftovers

Once the 1984 elections and consequent coalition bargaining were
over, the first year of the National Unity government was largely
devoted to urgent problems inherited from the preceding administration. Top priority, in popular and official attitudes alike, was assigned
to Israel's economic crisis, the chief symptom of which was accelerating
inflation running well into triple digits (400 percent). After some
early and ineffectual half-measures, a drastic austerity and economic
recovery program was announced in July 1985. Its implementation
was facilitated both by the absence of significant parliamentary opposition and by an emergency transfusion of $1.5 billion in cash (above
and beyond the routine $3 billion annual grant) from the United
States. By year's end, dramatic improvement was registered. Inflation
was quickly cut by a factor of ten, dropping still further in 1986, and
the country enjoyed two years of slow but steady renewed economic
growth. This progress continued to require close monitoring at the
working level, but inflation no longer preoccupied public and top-
level government attention.

Halfway through 1988, however, the Israeli economy sank back into
the doldrums, with macroeconomic indicators pointing back in the
direction of marginal decline. The culprits were the direct and indirect
costs associated with an ongoing Palestinian uprising in the occupied
territories, coupled with a modest resurgence of the twin evils of
inflation and organized (Jewish) labor troubles. But even then, Israel's
economy had a long way to go before approaching the chaotic environment and pervasive sense of crisis of the disastrous 1984–85 episode.
The Labor-Likud coalition could thus be credited with putting the
country's economic affairs back on a relatively stable course.

A very different, if no less difficult, issue on which the incoming
coalition responded efficiently to strong internal impulses to do something was the extrication of Israeli forces from Lebanon, where they

had been bogged down since the 1982 war. In January 1985, the cabinet voted to complete Israel's unilateral withdrawal, and the last major combat units were back across the border almost exactly on schedule in June. They left behind a few hundred military advisers and intelligence agents, a practice of occasional limited incursions, and a roughly six-mile-wide "security zone" patrolled by a local client force—a reorganized (but still mostly Maronite) South Lebanon army now commanded by Antoine Lahad.

Three years later, this arrangement had proved itself to general Israeli satisfaction. There were still potentially hostile Hezbollah forces encamped in South Lebanon and increased numbers of Syrian troops and PLO guerrillas from various factions moving back into that country further north—but they were all busy fighting each other. Sporadic rocket attacks and infiltration attempts targeted at Israel continued but inflicted no civilian and few military fatalities during this entire period. Lebanon's larger problems appeared as far from resolution as ever. But the Israeli government—heartily seconded by public opinion—had clearly abandoned its ill-fated attempt to restructure all of Lebanon more to its liking. In the meantime, the "nuisance threat" from the north was no longer viewed with great concern.[7]

On other fronts, however, Palestinian attacks and Israeli reprisals kept the National Unity government heavily engaged toward the end of its first year. The most sensational such sequence in 1985 was the murder of three Israelis in the Cypriot port of Larnaca in August, Israel's bombing of PLO headquarters in Tunis in September, and the Palestinian hijacking of the Israel-bound cruise ship *Achille Lauro*, and subsequent American capture of the terrorists' getaway plane in October. Other incidents (none of which, as usual, had any lasting political effect) followed in 1986, including a failed attempt to blow up an El Al passenger jumbo jet in London. By that time, though, with Israel well on the way out of both its economic and its Lebanese quagmires, Prime Minister Peres was already occupied with a more ambitious effort to address the underlying Arab-Israeli dispute.

The Peres Peace Plan

Indeed, once installed in office, Shimon Peres had lost little time in starting to explore a "Jordanian option" for an Arab-Israeli compromise settlement. This was a long-standing Labor party preference that had gotten a heavily qualified endorsement in the coalition agreement with Likud. By the middle of 1985, with Israel's most immediate problems resolved, Peres forged ahead with a two-pronged peace strategy. On the ground, Israel began to encourage, in quiet cooperation with

Jordan, a series of limited improvements in the "quality of life" for Palestinians under Israeli rule, including the opening of an Arab bank, appointment of Arab mayors, and initiation of new development projects funded from Amman. Some progress was recorded, but even these relatively apolitical measures soon faced local opposition as mere cosmetic gestures that would only perpetuate Israeli and/or Jordanian occupation. A chilling reminder of this opposition was the March 1986 assassination of Zafer al-Masri, the new Israeli-appointed and Jordanian-approved mayor of Nablus, the largest city on the West Bank.

In the diplomatic arena, meanwhile, Peres publicly endorsed (in an October 1985 U.N. address) a modified version of King Hussein's proposal for an international Arab-Israeli peace conference. For the next three years—and probably for another several years to come—an enormous amount of public and private diplomatic maneuvering would center around the "modalities" and "authority" of such a venture. Beyond the obvious problem of obtaining detailed U.S., Soviet, and other prospective participants' agreement, a major sticking point, as always, was the issue of Palestinian representation. Peres and Hussein sought separately, aided by active if indirect American probing, to finesse the issue by arranging a PLO "green light" for "non-PLO" Palestinians to join a Jordanian delegation, possibly on the basis of the February 1985 Hussein-Arafat understanding. The effort was slowed but not stopped by yet another collapse, in February 1986, of the desultory diplomatic dance between Hussein and Arafat, with the latter apparently yielding to internal PLO objections to an entente with Jordan. In the summer of that year, as the clock ran out on Peres' rotation as prime minister, his diplomacy assumed a frenetic pace. He held cordial yet inconclusive summit meetings in quick succession with two of the most moderate Arab heads of state—King Hassan of Morocco, in July, and President Mubarak of Egypt, in September. The latter meeting produced a joint proclamation that 1987 would be "the year of negotiations"; but no such negotiations came to pass.

A major underlying hurdle, of course, was that Israel's government was at least as divided as the PLO over the terms for peace talks. All along, the Israeli debate over negotiating procedures masked a much deeper debate over substance. An international conference, to put it bluntly, implied Israeli willingness to consider "territorial compromise" in "Judea and Samaria"; the Likud half of the government was therefore against it. Peres might have taken a chance and sought a new electoral mandate to pursue his project. Polls showed a solid majority of Jewish Israelis behind it, and Peres himself was then at the peak of his personal popularity, with around a 70 percent approval rating. But he faced a political "Catch-22"—had he forced new elections over the conference issue, his popularity would have been undercut by charges that he was reneging on the rotation agreement—and Labor's edge in electoral straw polls appeared too close for comfort. So Peres characteristically opted for caution and switched places with Shamir on schedule in October 1986.

Even that change did not derail Peres's quest for his elusive diplomatic objective. In a semisecret April 1987 meeting in London with Hussein, the two agreed on a formula for a limited international conference with no formal PLO participation. But Israel's policy-making ten-man "inner cabinet" predictably deadlocked on this proposal along straight Labor versus Likud party lines, and there the matter seemed to rest for the remainder of that year.

Shamir Takes over Again

With the cabinet clearly deadlocked on the international conference issue, Shamir, back again as prime minister, could afford to play a waiting game—and he was a past master at that. His chief rivals within Likud, ministers David Levy and Ariel Sharon, posed no immediate threat. The Israeli public, like its government, was split down the middle on possible peace terms, but most saw little urgency in the entire issue. Indeed, most Jewish Israelis, according to all the polls, remained generally satisfied with the coalition's handling of both domestic and foreign affairs and were content to leave the diplomatic ball in the Arabs' court.

As Peres nevertheless kept up his attempts to push a peace process forward, Israelis and outsiders alike were treated to the spectacle of an Israeli prime minister and foreign minister publicly pursuing two very different agendas. In the spring of 1987, to take but one example of this phenomenon, Shamir openly wished Peres's failure on one of the latter's many trips abroad to explore the prospects for an international conference; Peres, in slightly more civil fashion, returned the compliment. Some Israelis voiced dismay at such unseemly exchanges, but only a minority of either the public or the parliament wanted to bring the matter to a head by calling for early elections. So complacent was the overall atmosphere that many in Israel actually appeared to welcome a prolonged broadcast news strike in the autumn of 1987; indifference to politics was a refreshing change.

On the external front Shamir could rest secure in the knowledge that both the Americans and the Arabs were preoccupied with other, more pressing conflicts. In June, the twentieth anniversary of Israel's territorial conquests had passed with barely a ripple of protest or even public notice. In November, an Arab summit in Amman—little more than an hour's drive from "occupied Jerusalem"—demoted the PLO and the Palestine question to distinctly second billing and focused instead on shoring up a common Arab front against Iran. Altogether, in the words of one acute observer of the local scene, the only danger to Israel seemed to be sheer boredom.

Israel and the Iran-Contra Affair

In these deceptively serene circumstances, word leaked out in November 1986 that Israeli arms dealers and government officials had collaborated for over a year with American, Iranian, and even Arab counterparts in a plan to sell arms to Iran and divert some of the proceeds to the Nicaraguan Contras. An inordinate amount of attention has since focused on who first suggested this idea. In fact, throughout what soon came to be known as the Iran-Contra scandal, Israel was as usual neither the master manipulator nor the selfless agent of American policy.

Israel's side of this story has not been officially released, but details from the American side have been amply documented in journalistic reports, congressional hearings, and so on.[8] Suffice it to say here that both American and Israeli motives were mixed, and those two sets of motives, though overlapping, were not congruent. Israel shared with the United States the desire to keep open back channels and cultivate "moderates" in Iran. In this respect, at least, Jerusalem presumably saw itself as performing another small strategic service for Washington. But Israel also had ulterior motives—keeping a lucrative arms market, preserving the safety of the Jewish community of Iran, and keeping Iraq off balance and at war. For these reasons, one can only surmise, Israeli agents and middlemen counseled patience and persistence to their American colleagues even when early overtures to Tehran made little progress.

The entire scheme, of course, collapsed when it was leaked to the press, probably by a disgruntled Iranian faction via Syrian and Lebanese intermediaries. Its unraveling caused considerable if ultimately temporary political trouble in the United States. In Israel, however, the consequences were minimal. There was almost no public or parliamentary outcry. In the foreign arena, Israel lost little in Iran, if only because there was so little left to lose; and the war that pitted two of its enemies against each other ground on anyway, to Israel's silent satisfaction, for nearly two more years.

Most important, relations with Israel's vital American ally emerged unscathed. Despite obvious American dismay at the debacle and a few early and unauthorized attempts to divert the blame for it on to Israel, that country's involvement was generally viewed as a more or less well-intentioned and atypical blunder. It signaled the dangers of too careless a use of the close American-Israeli connection, without casting great doubt on that connection itself. Within the year, attention on both sides turned back to broader areas of convergence or divergence in U.S. and Israeli interests and policies.

In the meantime, a related regional development of great potential significance occurred in August 1988—a cease-fire that abruptly halted the eight-year war between Iran and Iraq. The implications of this sudden peace for Israel are still unclear but are likely to be limited for a good while. There have, for example, already been some subtle or indirect signals exchanged between Baghdad and Jerusalem that hint at a disavowal of actively hostile intent in this new regional equation. Yet the prospects for a major thaw (based perhaps on their common enmity with Syria) in the intense if mostly arm's-length antagonism between Israel and Iraq remain dim. And though Gulf issues play some part in Israeli foreign policy and even in American-Israeli relations, that policy and those relations will revolve as always around issues much closer to home.

The American Connection

Most discussions of American-Israeli relations begin with American domestic politics, in which those relations are anchored in a bedrock of broad public support and effectively mobilized political action. This favorable combination persists, despite a (possibly temporary) decline in Israel's public image and some division or anguish in the organized Jewish community. Palestinian protests dominated the media in early 1988.[9]

Israel's domestic politics also contributed to the absence of major diplomatic controversy with Washington in two different ways. In the beginning of this period, Washington understood and actually applauded Israel's belated concentration on internal (especially economic) rather than external problems. Afterward, the United States seemed resigned to the diplomatic deadlock imposed by the divided National Unity government of the Jewish state. Meanwhile, to put it crudely, the West has plenty of oil and generally good relations with Arab governments and does not need to demand a price from Israel. American policy makers had still another motive for caution—the perceived "lesson of Lebanon" in 1982–84 was to avoid excessive entanglement in Arab-Israeli diplomacy.[10]

Instead, the Reagan administration focused on further codifying and concretizing bilateral "strategic cooperation" with Israel in such areas as intelligence exchanges, weapons research and development, and regional military planning. Such steps were no longer merely unilateral cosmetic, confidence-building, or campaign-oriented gestures. Rather, U.S.-Israeli strategic cooperation gradually evolved during this period into an expanding and increasingly institutionalized network of tangible, if still marginal, mutual benefit.[11] The symbolic climax of this process came in late 1987, with the official conferral on Israel of "NATO-like ally" status. Indeed, for the first time in memory, such cooperation overshadowed traditional Arab-Israeli issues for a while. It seemed safe, and even tactically sound, for Washington to assign much lower priority to pursuit of an inevitably controversial peace process in the largely dormant Arab-Israeli dispute.

Until the Palestinian uprising, then, there were few serious trouble spots in American-Israeli relations during President Reagan's second term. One glaring exception was the late 1985 arrest and subsequent conviction of Jonathan Pollard, an American Jewish civil servant, on charges of spying for Israel. Washington treated this breach of confidence with exemplary gravity. Nevertheless, after some difficult moments, both governments seemed satisfied that the episode was an aberration in an established pattern of mutually useful intelligence exchanges, and any lingering damage was contained.[12] Much more serious, because of its lasting potential for controversy, were American objections to Israel's abuses in enforcing its occupation against Palestinian protests and, in the final analysis, to the very existence of the occupation. There was nothing fundamentally new about this; the United States had routinely gone on record against Israeli settlements, security practices, and permanent presence in the occupied territories on and off for twenty years. But such issues suddenly became more salient as the level of violence rose in 1988, and they seemed certain to roil relations regardless of which leaders took office in both countries after elections in November of that year.

Indeed, if American-Israeli relations were especially harmonious during the preceding three years, it was partly because the Arab-Israeli conflict was quiescent at the time. Washington could thus concentrate on cooperation with Israel in other areas, building upon underlying sympathy, growing (if sometimes also grudging) appreciation of that country's strategic value, and an official American worldview that stressed security issues in an East-West adversarial context. These factors will surely temper any future showdown between Washington and Jerusalem over regional issues. In this connection, one topic on which both capitals will continue to consult closely is the new Soviet overtures to Israel, which have the potential either to complicate

American-Israeli relations or to serve some common interests of all three parties.

Better Ties with the Soviet Bloc

One international development of considerable potential importance during this period was the incremental expansion of Israeli contacts with the Soviet Union, with which diplomatic relations had been broken during the 1967 Six-Day war. Informal, indirect, and intermittent contacts had naturally been maintained ever since, but their newly serious nature, steady pace, and above all generally positive substance or at least spirit constituted a qualitative change. For both sides, the ultimate objectives of this process remained distant but alluring. For Israel, the prize was a combination of greater access to Soviet Jews, enhanced international acceptance, and some indeterminate measure of Soviet restraint in and perhaps even constructive mediation of the intractable Arab-Israeli dispute. Moscow, for its part, sought more balanced and therefore greater influence on the region, greater stability or at least predictability in an occasionally dangerous and very costly nearby "proxy" conflict, and smoother overall relations with Israel's close American ally.

For both parties, too, the potential costs or complications of rapprochement for each side's existing alliances or sensitive domestic and foreign policy positions are likewise considerable. There is, however, a fundamental asymmetry between the two in this respect. From the Soviet standpoint, better relations with Israel are not a high priority, nor are they likely to involve any truly vital national interest, at least not directly. But for Israel, exactly the reverse is true.

Given this background, it is not surprising that both sides bargained hard and probed each other's intentions gingerly.[13] What is surprising is how much movement actually took place between 1985 and 1988; the sequence is no less significant for being a bit slow. By mid-1988, a Soviet consular delegation came to Israel and an Israeli one went to Moscow. Soviet Jewish emigration had climbed back to the level of about a thousand per month, even though the vast majority went to America rather than Israel. Some celebrated Refuseniks, including Anatoly Sharansky, had been released. All this activity was accompanied by some startling shifts in Moscow's public diplomacy, crystallized in Mikhail Gorbachev's observation to Syrian President Assad that the Soviet-Israeli diplomatic rupture was "abnormal."

Throughout this process, Israel's own domestic politics played an interesting and little-noticed part. Peres, unlike Shamir, could accept the key Soviet demand for inclusion in an international Mideast peace conference because he was in principle not averse to the territorial concessions such a conference would certainly promote. For that reason, the Soviets at first courted Peres and neglected Shamir. The result was a curious exercise in which Peres generally played up, while Shamir played down, every favorable nuance in the evolving Soviet position. But in the end, Israel's internal political balance swung the Soviets around; they seemed to have realized that Shamir was in a strong position, and they sent Foreign Minister Shevardnadze to meet him for the first time in June 1988 at a United Nations conference in New York. Shamir, for his part, apparently understood that progress on ties with the Soviet bloc was popular with his own public without the need to change his position on the conference issue one iota.

All this suggests that further improvement in Soviet-Israeli relations, along with more direct Soviet involvement in Arab-Israeli peacemaking, is likely, but also likely to be difficult. Many thorny obstacles remain, ranging from the international conference conundrum to the more mundane details of direct flights for Soviet Jewish émigrés, levels of diplomatic representation, and the like. The constraints imposed by Soviet-Arab and American-Israeli relations and by domestic politics on all sides are severe. On that basis alone, a complete East-West reversal of Arab and Israeli alliances—as has happened in a few other regional conflicts since the early 1970s—can be confidently ruled out. A concerted Soviet-American effort to impose a solution on recalcitrant local adversaries is less preposterous but still very unlikely. Indeed, given each of the superpower's limited influence on its respective regional clients, it is doubtful that either Washington or Moscow, separately or even together, holds the key to Israeli policy.

Other Bilateral Relations

An early goal of Peres's conciliatory foreign policy posture was an improvement in relations with Egypt, which had fallen to their lowest peacetime level in the wake of the Lebanese war. The overall parameters of this relationship were clear. It would perforce be at least correct because Egypt no longer had or sought a war option against Israel, while emulating her American connection. At the same time, Egyptian-Israeli relations could hardly be warm, or even "normal" as envisaged at Camp David, for a host of reasons: stalemate on the Palestinian question, Egypt's push to rejoin the Arab fold amid internal Islamic and nationalist pressures, and Israel's lack of any compelling leverage to press for major changes, all combined with the inevitable minor irritants arising between two proud, wary, and formerly hostile neighbors. Within that overall framework, however, there could still be some

movement in either a positive or a negative direction, and the period
under discussion saw both.

There was first a thaw in this "cold peace," despite the murder of
several Israeli diplomats and tourists on Egyptian soil and Egyptian
frustration at Israel's apparent satisfaction with a separate peace. Israel
finally agreed, after the usual squabbling between Labor and Likud,
to submit the trivial but symbolically significant Tabah border dispute
to arbitration; Egypt restored ambassadorial status to its chief diplomat
in Israel; and Mubarak at last agreed to host his Israeli counterpart
for a summit meeting.[14] But this progress was halted when the peace
process went back into deep freeze, the Tabah dispute languished
in legal maneuvers, and the Palestinians erupted into violent mass
protests.

On other fronts, with a new government at the helm, the Lebanese
misadventure largely over, its own economic house in much better
order, and the luxury of respite from immediate security concerns,
Israel turned a bit more attention further afield. Neighbors and superpowers aside, the years 1985–88 witnessed on balance a measure of
Israeli success in developing better relations with extraregional states.
A few minor breakthroughs were scored in black Africa. Togo, Camer-
oun, and the Ivory Coast restored diplomatic ties with Israel, and
other countries quietly expanded commercial and other links. On the
sensitive related issue of ties with South Africa, influenced by U.S.
congressional action, the Israeli government in mid-1986 imposed
limited restrictions on bilateral military and selected other contacts—
without rupturing the considerable existing network of diplomatic and
commercial exchanges.[15] Elsewhere, even in distant Latin America,
Israel maintained a surprisingly widespread presence, with emphasis
on oil and arms sales and other forms of security cooperation.[16]

Relations with Western Europe, still Israel's largest trading partner,
were generally kept on an even keel. Politics eventually intruded even
here; a new trade agreement, for example, was stalled by the Palestinian uprising. Resolution of this issue was linked, literally, to the choice
of shipping labels for West Bank and Gaza produce. By mid-1988, a
typically innocuous compromise was in the offing on this symbolic
expression of European displeasure with Israel's anti-Intifada tactics.

But the newest and most intriguing developments in bilateral ties
occurred in East Asia, long an area of scant Israeli presence. Trade and
academic, cultural, and diplomatic exchanges with Japan increased
noticeably, albeit from a very limited base.[17] Still more noteworthy was
a gradual, discreet, yet unmistakable expansion of unofficial Israeli
commercial, scientific, and reportedly specialized military contacts
with the People's Republic of China.[18] For the Chinese, this contact

was part of an effort to upgrade their international economic and technological position and to balance their newly active pursuit of arms markets and political influence in other regional states (including both belligerents in the Iran-Iraq war).

For the Israelis, too, these global contacts were valued mostly for economic and even psychological reasons. But in a region that has proved resistant to a *Pax Americana* or any other imported notions of stability, Israel has also been determined to diversify its marginal outside sources not just of income but also of legitimacy and security, as much as changing circumstances will allow.

National Security Issues

Throughout the period under discussion, as over the entire past decade, Israel enjoyed a comfortable margin of regional strategic superiority, primarily because of a combination of its own better use of military equipment and manpower and Arab distraction or disarray. The Gulf states were almost totally preoccupied with Iran and largely bereft of the "oil weapon"; the Arab radicals were mostly isolated, at odds with each other, or busy with internal or other crises. Among the classic "confrontation states," Egypt had opted out of an Arab war coalition; Jordan, too, continued to maneuver semisecretly to explore diplomatic rather than military options vis-à-vis Israel; and even Syria respected the "red lines" restricting its active hostility toward the "Zionist enemy." Israel's deterrent strength, of course, went a long way toward explaining why much of the Arab world seemed increasingly disposed to settle for something like the pre-1967 situation.

As a result, Israeli debates over national security issues in 1985–87—for all their sensational aspects—focused on limited, essentially internal matters having less to do with basic strategy than with problems of political accountability, bureaucratic coordination, resource allocation, or professional standards. There were the Pollard and Iran-Contra affairs. Also in this general category were the Shin Bet (Security Services) affair, involving the 1984 murder of two captured Arab terrorist suspects, and its attempted coverup and exposure; the Vanunu affair, involving the 1987 "defection" and subsequent kidnapping, trial, and imprisonment of a technician who leaked secrets about Israel's well-known but unacknowledged nuclear weapons capability; and several other, less publicized and less important cases.

In each case, the government's initially clumsy responses were soon "fixed" in consultations of the "Prime Ministers Club" (Peres, Shamir, plus former prime minister and now defense minister Yitzhak Rabin). The typical solution was a narrowly defined investigation leading to quiet resignations or transfers; political repercussions were contained by the widely shared responsibility for the embarrassment or error. Surveys showed that the Israeli public was disturbed by these events— but not enough to press for a broader, more open, or higher-level investigation.

On one national security issue, however, Israel's government eventually decided—by the closest of margins—to defy both public opinion and organized interest group pressure. This was the decision to cancel Israel's expensive effort to produce its own advanced jet fighter, the Lavi.[19] The decisive factors in this painful reversal were a combination of a swing vote in the cabinet by the austerity-minded finance minister, Moshe Nissim; strong and sustained American lobbying to drop the U.S.-financed and supplied project; and growing doubts within Israel's military establishment about the wisdom of diverting so much money to one high-profile acquisition at the expense of other looming strategic concerns.

Chief among those was the mounting unconventional threat of long-range missiles and chemical warfare. The Iran-Iraq war had relaxed regional inhibitions against the use of such weapons and suggested that they could have a significant effect on both battlefield position and political will. A further dimension of danger was the emergence of new buyers and sellers, demonstrated most vividly by revelations in early 1988 of a Chinese-Saudi missile deal. Although that posed no immediate threat, Israel viewed Syrian acquisition of similar systems with greater apprehension.

To counter such threats, Israel sought to maintain its deterrent capacity for retaliation (whether in kind or in sufficient measure by other means), while exploring defensive "technical fixes" like the development of a better antitactical ballistic missile system (ATBM). For the time being, at least, Jerusalem could also take some comfort in Moscow's reluctance to equip Syria's dream of "strategic parity" with Israel and in the vestigial international political constraints on the first use of unconventional weapons.[20] On balance, then, Israel could expect to keep its qualitative military edge. But while Israeli planners were preoccupied with these long-range and long-term challenges, the country suddenly confronted a new, very different, and much more immediate security dilemma.

Trouble in the Territories

The quiet first three years of the National Unity coalition proved, of course, to be the proverbial calm before the storm when a popular

Palestinian uprising against Israeli occupation broke out in early December 1987. This outburst of two decades of pent-up resentment reflected a growing sense of utter and endless neglect, symbolized by the short shrift accorded the Palestinians by both an Arab and a superpower summit in the previous few weeks. Other catalysts that enraged or emboldened some Palestinians to act included a November incident in which an Arab commando in a hang glider managed to penetrate Israel's defenses and kill six soldiers before being shot himself and a fatal traffic accident in Gaza that was rumored to be an act of deliberate Israeli revenge. Probably more important, though at somewhat greater remove, were Israel's release of over a thousand Palestinian activists in a typically lopsided prisoner exchange in 1985 and a growing demographic reservoir of educated but unemployed Palestinian youths deprived, since around 1983, of the emigration safety valve by new restrictions in Jordan and the Arab Gulf states.

Still, given all the underlying animosities on almost every dimension of Israeli-Palestinian interaction (social, political, economic, religious, and so on), the wonder is not that the uprising took place but why it took so long in coming. And because it did, it caught nearly everyone—Israelis, outsiders, and not least the Palestinians themselves—by surprise.

In retrospect, as always, one can see that some warning signs had already been apparent, more so in popular perceptions than in most "expert" assessments. One respectable effort to survey West Bank/Gaza Palestinians a year earlier, for example, had revealed overwhelming nationalist and pro-PLO (and also significant Islamic fundamentalist) sentiment, along with remarkably high approval of violent protest, particularly among young adults.[21] Other polls taken at around the same time among Jewish Israelis found surprisingly high public concern over the Arab-Jewish demographic balance, along with a very widespread feeling that traveling in Arab areas was unsafe.[22] Such apprehension was in part responsible for a slowdown (or even reversal, judging by some sources) of the momentum of Jewish settlement across the old Green Line in 1987, even before the uprising, for the first time in twenty years.[23]

Even so, the scope, intensity, and most of all the persistence of Palestinian protest proved unexpected. Rather like the "October earthquake" of the 1973 war, this new challenge, though much less threatening in any immediate sense, rudely shattered an interlude of Israeli complacency and compelled the government and armed forces to improvise a hasty response.

The Palestinian Uprising: A Tactical Appraisal

The Palestinian uprising (Intifada in Arabic) is generally viewed as beginning on December 9, 1987, with a series of anti-Israeli demonstrations that developed into large-scale riots in Gaza. From there mass protests quickly spread across the length and breadth of the West Bank, including, for the first time in almost twenty years, East Jerusalem. Through August 1988, with only sporadic lulls, protests included strikes, demonstrations, stone-throwing, arson, and occasional acts of or attempts at terrorism. In another striking departure from past patterns, most of these activities were apparently coordinated by an anonymous Unified National Leadership operating inside the territories and publicized in a series of locally drafted leaflets. It was not until several months later that the PLO organization in exile began to catch up with this new-found display of grass-roots initiative.

Israel, also caught off guard, at first responded in the classic military manner with live fire. Within a month, however, as Palestinians continued their protests and Israelis came under mounting outside pressure to reduce the number of deaths, less lethal methods of riot control (tear gas, rubber bullets, billy clubs, and stepped-up patrols) were employed. Still other methods adopted by Israel's army ranged from beatings to forcible strikebreaking, school closings, curfews, selected cutoffs of power and supplies, economic harassment (such as severe restrictions on the transferral of funds from abroad), demolition of suspected activists' houses, harsher censorship, a few deportations—and presumably also the assassination in Tunis of Khalil al-Wazir (Abu Jihad), Arafat's deputy and chief of PLO military operations.[24] Arguably the most effective measure, at least as a stopgap, was the detention of more than five thousand Palestinians, most of them for an indefinite time.

For the Palestinians, the price of this retaliation in economic hardship and personal suffering was high. Each month, on average, about one person per day died in these disturbances. Hundreds more were wounded over the entire period.

Israel, too, paid a price, in a different coin—international criticism, increased mobilization of reserves, and direct and indirect economic losses estimated as high as $1 billion over the six months in question. But only a handful of Israelis were killed or seriously injured. Everyday life went on normally almost everywhere inside the Green Line almost all the time. Only in the capital of Jerusalem, where three hundred thousand Jews lived in close proximity to one hundred thousand Arabs on opposite sides of the old border, was there a noticeable and sustained rise in tension—and even there the problem was largely confined to the Arab side.

By midyear, it appeared that Israel had managed to contain if not defeat the Intifada. Incidents (including fatal ones) continued, but large-scale protests were on the wane. The international media, often blamed by Israelis for fanning the flames and irresponsibly damaging the country's reputation, were gradually losing interest in the story. Most of the 120,000 or so Palestinian laborers employed in Israel had drifted back to work. Even some of the "collaborators" threatened by the "resistance" were now refusing to resign. Sullen compliance with new restrictions and regulations (about taxes, identity papers, and the like) was again the norm. And even some of the latest clandestine leaflets (notably numbers 18 and 20) seemed to scale back Arab demands and offer conditions for ending the uprising; in the cruel logic of power, that was interpreted as a sign of Palestinian weakness or fatigue.

Equally reassuring to Israel was the generally passive response among the country's 750,000 Arab citizens to the unrest across the Green Line. Mass demonstrations of solidarity in Israeli Arab towns and neighborhoods, as "Peace Day" in December and again on "Land Day" in March, were more disquieting to many Jewish Israelis than more distant troubles. Yet such events, along with isolated individual acts of sabotage, turned out to be the exceptions rather than the rule. The vast majority of Israeli Arabs, though clearly torn, had just as clearly concluded that they had too much to lose and too little to gain from joining in active protest. They at least could opt to work within Israel's basically democratic system for full equality and even for national rights for their fellow Palestinians.

Also, no doubt because of Israel's limited human losses, there was less internal debate over tactics among the political leadership, the military command, or the public than during the much more costly Lebanese war. Public opinion stayed solidly behind harsh security measures. Defense Minister Rabin, who coined the unfortunate slogan "force, might, and blows" to guide Israel's reaction to the uprising, became the most popular cabinet figure. From a tactical standpoint, then, the Intifada posed no clear and present danger to Israel's security. The situation may still simply stabilize at a higher plateau of resistance and repression.

Nevertheless, Rabin himself has been emphatic in conceding that in the end there can be only a political, not a military, solution to the Intifada. Even some Likud leaders say a new political approach is necessary. So even as the uprising simmers on, a look beyond its purely tactical aspects is already in order.

The Palestinian Uprising: Political Implications

Things will never be quite the same for Israel after the Intifada—
but just how different will they be? Certainly, the uprising demolished
the myth that occupation would forever be easy. Yet the cost may
still seem bearable, indeed preferable to something worse or more
uncertain. It is thus too soon to tell whether this crisis represents a real
turning point or just a temporary trial—or, more likely, something in
between—the "end of the beginning," to quote Winston Churchill
completely out of context, of Israel's occupation.

It is at least clear that, contrary to common impression, Israeli public
opinion, which remains hard-line on tactical measures, has *not* reacted
to the Intifada by adopting a more "hawkish" view on underlying
political issues. Rather, reliable surveys show that Jewish Israelis are,
if anything, somewhat more "dovish" than before on the core question
of "land for peace"; a clear majority now supports that concept. A
majority is now also willing to negotiate with the PLO if it renounces
terrorism and recognizes Israel.[25] Yet the Labor and Likud camps are
still running neck-and-neck in all the straw polls.[26] More mainstream
voices speak of "transferring" the Arabs themselves, instead of their
territories, away from Israel. Indeed, about half the Jewish public
continues to view this as a desirable albeit unrealistic option, suggesting
a frustrated and confused but very widespread impulse simply to get
rid of the problem.[27] And public opinion is often fickle and always
indirect in its impact on official policy.

For once, a fair amount depends on the Palestinians' own initiative.
Although they have attracted everyone's attention, it remains to be
seen how long and at what level they can keep up the pressure. Moreover, they have yet to translate this achievement into a political program that is at once credible and flexible enough to elicit a more
favorable Israeli response. A case in point is the remarkably conciliatory June 1988 document authored by Bassam Abu Sharif, Arafat's
press spokesman, which offered to reciprocate Israeli recognition.
Some Israelis admitted that this was a departure worthy of serious
probing. But most politicians and pundits, even among the moderates,
chose to dismiss it as nothing new—either because the statement was
insufficiently authoritative, or because it continued to insist on an
independent PLO-led state, or both.[28] A similar fate befell public hints
in August from Abu Iyad (Salah Khalaf), a senior PLO leader with a
hard-line reputation, that his organization was indeed preparing to
accept a two-state solution.

With this mixed picture, the only clear-cut political impact of the
Intifada on Israel so far was to put the United States back into the

peace process, with a proposal that was quickly dubbed the Shultz initiative. This was a clever new blend of old ideas, centering around the legendary U.N. Resolution 242 principle of land for peace—now with a Jordanian/Palestinian (but not necessarily PLO) partner. In substance, it was similar to the September 1982 Reagan plan. What was added was an "interlocking" procedure that attempted to integrate the requirements of all sides—a limited international conference, a transition period rather like accelerated Camp David autonomy, and early negotiations on the final terms for peace.[29]

As with any compromise proposal, this one suffered from the defect of its virtues; anything that has something for everybody is hard for anybody to accept. The timing, too, was ironic. The same crisis that had prompted this burst of high-level American statecraft also boosted the PLO at Jordan's expense and made the Likud half of Israel's government more determined than ever to stand fast. And coming so soon before American and Israeli elections, it was almost inevitable that the Shultz initiative would run into difficulty.

Nevertheless, in the first half of 1988, Shultz made four separate trips to the region to promote the plan. Predictably, the lack of Jordanian or Palestinian acceptance helped let Israel off the hook. Israel's government, like the others, neither accepted nor rejected the proposal, although comments by Peres and Shamir indicated, just as predictably, that the former was favorably and the latter unfavorably disposed. American officials responded by accusing Arab and Israeli "radicals" alike of working against peace.

To some Israelis, all this was vaguely reminiscent of earlier episodes when such challenging obscured an absence of effective American action. To be sure, the lame-duck Reagan administration had neither the time nor the inclination to push its own peace plan too hard. But there was also a parallel to 1976, when Washington diplomatic and "think-tank" talk about the Palestinian cause was suspended for election season but picked up by the next administration.[30] Shultz himself hinted strongly at this scenario during his June 1988 Mideast visit. Six months later there would also be a new government in Israel—and once again internal Israeli politics would provide a crucial piece of this intractable puzzle.

In the midst of this unsettled but seemingly stalled situation; King Hussein dropped a (figurative) bombshell by announcing on July 31, 1988, a new series of steps to disengage Jordan from both the diplomatic and the day-to-day fate of the Palestinians in the West Bank and Gaza. As all sides attempted to sort out the implications of this move, it appeared to be a double and even a triple-edged sword. On one hand, it intensified the pressure on Israel, on the local Palestinians, and on the PLO to deal directly with each other; on the other hand, it removed a convenient buffer, conduit, and "legal fiction" for all three parties; at the same time, no one could be certain just how or even how long this new situation would develop. Inside Israel, Likud trumpeted this move as vindication of its claim that there never was or could be a Jordanian option for Judea and Samaria. Labor struggled to redefine its platform accordingly. But neither party conveyed a clear sense of what the next steps should be, and neither seemed poised to gain a decisive advantage as both looked toward the crucial election in November. Indeed, even though the Palestinian uprising had already set in motion a series of shifts on all sides that, in principle, could break the diplomatic deadlock, the inconclusive nature of Israel's internal policy and political debates over responses to the uprising indicated that a new configuration had not yet crystallized.

Thus Israel's November 1, 1988, national election produced (to almost nobody's surprise) another virtual tie between Likud, which captured 40 Knesset seats, and Labor, which got 39. Also evenly matched were the splinter parties on the left (Citizens' Rights movement, Shinui, and Mapam) and on the right (Tehiya, Tzomet, and Moledet). The Zionist political mainstream remained deadlocked between its two major potential blocs, with neither able to muster even the bare majority in the 120-member parliament needed to govern on its own. The handful of mandates garnered by Arab nationalist protest parties, representing about half of Israel's growing Arab minority, were usually left out of practical coalition calculations.

Quite the opposite was the case with Israel's Jewish religious parties, which once again emerged as a pivotal swing group in the Knesset. In fact, the only real surprise in the 1988 election was the jump in their representation from 12 to 18 seats. Ironically, it was precisely the fragmentation and aggravated rivalry among four competing religious parties (Shas, the National Religious Party, Agudat Yisrael, and the tiny new Degel HaTorah) that helped boost this camp's overall electoral turnout. As Likud and Labor each scrambled to win these parties over, the usual hard bargaining over pocketbook, patronage, and to some extent policy issues dragged on. Once again, orthodox partisans pressed particularly hard on the sticky if largely symbolic issue of nonorthodox conversions to the faith (the "Who is a Jew?" controversy). This time, however, the leaders of both Labor and Likud were subjected to strong counterpressures on this issue from the American Jewish community. Moreover, neither major Israeli party relished the prospect of being at the mercy of fractious minor partners in a narrow coalition.[31]

In the end, after almost two months of especially complex and confusing coalition negotiations, Labor and Likud were again compelled to paper over their differences and join forces in another National Unity government. The three main religious parties, not to be left out, predictably swallowed their pride and once more jumped on the bandwagon at the last minute.

But in 1988, unlike the previous coalition agreement, the compromise tilted toward Likud. Shamir was named prime minister, with no rotation in prospect. The foreign ministry, too, went to Likud stalwart (and Shamir protégé) Moshe Arens. Peres settled for the important but thankless job of finance minister for a deficit-plagued government with a stagnant national economy. Rabin, now the most popular politician in Israel for his tough if still unsuccessful measures against the Intifada, stayed on as defense minister. These four, plus three additional ministers each from Likud and Labor, made up an evenly split policy-making "inner cabinet."

One could hardly have designed a government by committee more likely to promote political paralysis. Yet the Israeli government could not simply do nothing; the pressures for movement or at least motion on urgent problems were too great. The Palestinian uprising, with its daily toll of Arab and weekly trickle of Jewish casualties, ground on in a quieter but still deadly and disruptive fashion. Senior Israeli commanders openly conceded that a purely military solution was unattainable.

On the diplomatic front, too, the status quo appeared increasingly untenable. In November 1988, the PLO-led Palestine National Council formally accepted, for the first time, the principle of partitioning Palestine into separate Arab and Jewish states; and Arafat followed up at a Geneva press conference the following month with a statement repudiating terrorism and recognizing the right of "all states in the region, including the [newly declared] state of Palestine and Israel," to live in peace. More important, the United States immediately responded by opening an "official, substantive dialogue" with the PLO, on the grounds that it had finally fulfilled the conditions spelled out in Kissinger's 1975 understanding with Israel on this supremely sensitive subject. In early 1989, the administration of newly elected U.S. President George Bush decided not only to pursue the American-PLO dialogue but also to suggest publicly and privately that it expected Israel to reciprocate moderate Palestinian declarations with some constructive peacemaking moves of its own.

The Israeli government, though, remained under severe internal constraints in coping with this new challenge. The 1988 coalition agreement, for example, explicitly ruled out negotiations with the PLO; and a weary Israeli public still did not believe, to use a still current biblical metaphor, that the PLO "leopard had changed its spots." The dominant Likud half of Israel's government—in this case reflecting a distinct minority in public opinion—continued to reject the notion of trading any more land for peace, the cornerstone of most peacemaking efforts ever since the 1967 war. In May 1989, after several months of discussion, the divided Israeli cabinet managed to approve a new, lowest-common-denominator four-point peace initiative, including improvement in Egyptian-Israeli relations, progress toward peace with other Arab states, international rehabilitation for Palestinian refugees, and a West Bank–Gaza election plan for Palestinian representatives to interim peace talks.

It was the last item, quickly dubbed the "Shamir-Rabin election plan," that immediately garnered both the most international attention and the most American support. But progress even on this modest first step was soon stymied by a combination of conflicting interpretations of key details, second thoughts among Likud's leaders about their own proposal, and deep-seated ambivalence about the plan within the PLO and the local Palestinian population alike. By November 1989 diplomatic discussions had degenerated to a debate about whether American, Israeli, and Egyptian officials would meet to consider the character of a possible Palestinian delegation to a committee on arrangements for electing representatives to preliminary peace negotiations.

At that point, a year after the last election in Israel, it was clear as never before that the country's artificially mended internal split was a key factor in this obscure equation. Labor's "doves" and Likud's "hawks" were growing equally restless in their enforced political cohabitation, and there was increasing talk about breaking up the coalition. But all the straw polls showed that, though Likud retained a slight edge, a new election would probably produce a similarly inconclusive outcome. As the Intifada approached its second anniversary, the historic Palestinian-Israeli conflict was more acute and open—but perhaps also more open to resolution—than at any time in at least a generation. And yet would-be peacemakers still faced the herculean, if not utterly hopeless, task of sheperding the peace process through the thickets of Israel's fractured internal political landscape.

The longer-term prospects are, almost by definition, even more uncertain. Nevertheless, the preceding analysis of Israel's recent experience does suggest some conclusions about its future, which the following section will explore.

Conclusion

The preceding discussion has emphasized the crucial role of domestic politics in Israel's foreign policy over the past several years. A glance back at this period suggests that the brightest and darkest areas in the picture—economic recovery and Palestinian uprising—were both essentially internal. And because of the relatively stable strategic environment, the delicate internal political balance, and the new Palestinian activism inside the country, Israel's foreign policy is likely to remain driven by domestic developments.

Yet there is also a larger sense in which Israel's foreign policy, indeed its very existence, is a function of its internal situation. If Israel has so far met the challenges of a hostile environment, it is primarily because of its domestic political cohesion and material development and only secondarily because of support from its friends and distraction or division among its enemies. That combination of favorable factors promises to prevail for quite a while. The longer term, however, is again an open question.

From that perspective, everyone has a favorite analogy for Israel, drawn at will from a wide geographical and historical canvas. The Palestinians still cite the specter of South Africa, of nineteenth-century European imperialism, or even of the Crusaders to describe the current "artificial" and "doomed" situation of the Jewish state, and they look to the Algerian model of popular revolt or to armed struggle à la Saladdin for their salvation. Among Israelis, Likudniks invoke the Holocaust and the Bible to legitimize their pursuit of power and territory; Laborites counter by claiming to discern in their rivals the misguided messianism of Bar-Kokhba. Outside optimists foresee a future Benelux model or even a Swiss-style confederation for Israelis and Palestinians. Pessimists predict a Mideast version of Northern Ireland that will degenerate over time into another Lebanon, or at best a variant of the enduring instability and bitterness of the Indo-Pakistani partition.

One should not expect any of these scenarios to materialize any time soon. To be sure, the Middle East in general and the Arab-Israeli conflict in particular are famous for dramatic shifts. But if the recent history of the region teaches anything, it is that instability often achieves its own equilibrium so that an inherently precarious situation can persist for a very long time. The choice of which path Israel will follow has not yet been made—though the Israelis are slowly drawing closer to a decision, if only by default.

For, as the events in 1988 demonstrated, the Arab-Jewish demographic problem is no longer hypothetical. Both the ratio of Arabs to Jews and the price of maintaining Jewish control have risen appreciably, and there is no end in sight. By the end of the 1990s, assuming present demographic trends continue—and there is every reason to expect they will—there will be about 1 million Palestinians just in Gaza, plus another million and a half in the West Bank (not to mention still another million Arab citizens of Israel inside the pre-1967 Green Line). The number of Arabs, in other words, will nearly equal the projected Israeli Jewish population of something over 4 million.

Such numbers alone never tell the whole story, yet they do add considerable weight to the argument that Israel's security, in the broadest sense, would be better served by trading land for peace instead of holding on to the territories at all costs. A majority of Jewish Israelis already share this view, but that majority is still narrow, volatile, and politically ineffectual. And ultimately it is only the Israelis themselves, as the analysis above makes clear, who can decide the issue that is at once the heart of their domestic and their foreign policy. Until they do, the outlook is for more muddling through with solutions to some of Israel's other problems, at the expense of continued stalemate on the central Israeli-Palestinian dilemma.

Notes

1. For an analysis of the 1982–85 period along these lines, see my chapter "Israel since the Lebanon War," in *The Middle East since the Israeli Invasion of Lebanon*, ed. Robert O. Freedman (Syracuse: Syracuse Univ. Press, 1986).

2. For relevant public opinion polls during this period, see, e.g., *Ma'ariv* (Tel Aviv), July 18, 1985, Feb. 28, 1986, Jan. 27, 1987; *Yediot Aharonot* (Tel Aviv), May 15, 1987; *Jerusalem Post*, Sept. 13, 1985, Jan. 30, 1986; *Ha'aretz* (Tel Aviv), Sept. 22, 1985.

3. An excellent overview of Israel's parties and electoral system can be found in Asher Arian, *Politics in Israel: The Second Generation* (Chatham, N.J.: Chatham House, 1985), esp. chaps. 5 and 7.

4. For a report on the role of these parties in the early National Unity coalition, see *Jerusalem Post*, Nov. 22, June 18, 1985, Feb. 10, 1986; *New York Times*, June 13 1986.

5. See, for example, *Jerusalem Post*, May 29, 1987; *Ha'aretz*, June 15, 1988.

6. For a discussion along similar lines, see Maurice M. Roumani, "The Sephardi Factor in Israeli Politics," *Middle East Journal* 42 (Summer 1988): 423–35.

7. *Washington Post*, May 8, 1987.

8. Among the better concise treatments of Israel's role in and reaction to the Iran-Contra affair are those in the *New York Times*, Dec. 23, 1986, and Jan. 12, Feb. 2, and Feb. 27, 1987.

9. For an expert Israeli view of this issue, see the analysis by Professor Eytan Gilboa in *Ha'aretz*, June 8 and 9, 1988. Also see the remarks by Shamir on this issue as reported in *Davar*, Feb. 4, 1988.

10. See, e.g., Martin Indyk, "Reagan and the Middle East: Learning the Art of the Possible," *SAIS Review* 7 (Winter–Spring 1987): 111–38.

11. For sympathetic analyses of these developments, see Steven L. Spiegel, "U.S. Relations with Israel: The Military Benefits," *Orbis* 30 (Fall 1986): 475–98; Stuart E. Eizenstat, "Formalizing the Strategic Partnership: The Next Step in U.S.-Israeli Relations," Washington Institute for Near East Policy, Policy Paper 9, Mar. 1988.

12. *New York Times,* Mar. 15, 30, 1987.

13. For examples of the initial circumspection in Soviet public diplomacy on this sensitive issue, see *The Soviet Union and the Middle East* (Jerusalem: Center for Soviet and East European Research, Hebrew University), 11, no. 8 (1986); 5–7. See also the chapter by Robert O. Freedman in this volume.

14. See the detailed analyses of Egyptian-Israeli relations by Ann Mosely Lesch, *Universities Field Staff International (UFSI) Reports,* nos. 33, 34, 35 (Indianapolis, 1986).

15. *Jerusalem Post,* Feb. 13, 1986, Aug. 13, 1987; *Davar* (Tel Aviv) Feb. 20, 1987.

16. *Ha'aretz,* July 31, 1985; *Israel Economist* (Tel Aviv) 42 (Feb. 1986); *Ha'aretz,* June 22, 1987.

17. *Israel Economist,* 42 (Oct. 1986).

18. *Koteret Rashit* (Tel Aviv), June 26, 1985; *Israel Business* (Tel Aviv), no. 413 (Dec. 1985); *Jerusalem Post,* Mar. 27, 1987; *Ha'aretz,* June 21, 1987.

19. See the *New York Times,* May 30, July 2, 14, 1986. For an excellent summary of the Lavi debate, see Thomas L. Friedman, "A Skirmish over Israel's New Jet," *New York Times,* July 20, 1986, p. F-4.

20. See, e.g., *Jerusalem Post,* Aug. 7, 1987; Seth Carus, *NATO, Israel, and the Tactical Missile Challenge,* Research Memorandum 4 (Washington, D.C.: Washington Institute for Near East Policy, 1987).

21. Mohammed Shadid and Rick Seltzer, "Political Attitudes of Palestinians in the West Bank and Gaza Strip," *Middle East Journal* 42 (Winter 1988): 16–32; see also the comments on this poll by Richard Murphy, U.S. assistant secretary of state for the Near East and South Asia, in *Developments in the Middle East, October 1986,* Hearing before the Subcommittee on Europe and the Middle East, Committee on Foreign Affairs, U.S. House of Representatives, 99th Cong. 2d sess., Oct. 8, 1986, pp. 49–50.

22. Author's interviews with leading Israeli pollsters, Sept. 1986 and Sept. 1987.

23. See, e.g., *Ha'aretz,* May 29, 1987; and, esp., *Koteret Rashit,* Apr. 11, 1988.

24. For one account of that operation, see *Jeune Afrique* (Paris), Apr. 27, 1988, pp. 17–21.

25. See polling results in *Ma'ariv,* June 21, 1988; *Yediot Aharonot,* June 22, Aug. 4, 1988.

26. See, e.g., *Davar,* July 17, 1988; *Yediot Aharonot,* June 24, July 29, 1988.

27. See the perceptive commentary by Haggai Eshed, "Split National Personality," *Davar,* June 28, 1988. See also *Ha'aretz,* June 8, 1988; *Jerusalem Post,* Aug. 12, 1988.

28. See the diverse comments reported in Israel's three leading dailies, *Yediot Aharonot, Ma'ariv,* and *Ha'aretz,* June 23 and 24, 1988.

29. For a brief recent official U.S. assessment of this proposal and related peace process issues, see statement by Assistant Secretary Richard Murphy, published as "Review of U.S. Policy in the Middle East," *Current Policy No. 1097* (Washington, D.C.: U.S. Department of State, 1988).

30. For one Israeli view of this prospect, see editorial in *Jerusalem Post,* Aug. 25, 1988.

31. For a study of the role of the religious parties in Israel's 1988 election campaign and postelection coalition bargaining, see Robert O. Freedman, "Religion, Politics, and the Israeli Elections of 1988," *Middle East Journal* 43 (Summer 1989): 406–22.

9

The Palestinians

From the Hussein-Arafat Agreement
to the Intifada

Helena Cobban

Introduction

The period of Palestinian political history from early 1985 through the end of 1988 was marked primarily by the eruption of the Intifada (uprising) of the Palestinians of the occupied territories from December 1987 on. To understand the origins and dynamics of the Intifada it is necessary to review Palestinian developments both inside and outside the occupied areas throughout the years that preceded it. This study should throw some light on key questions concerning the Intifada, including not only Why did it break out? but also, and more important, Why was it sustained so long? and What was the relationship between the leadership of the Intifada inside the occupied areas and the PLO leaders outside?

In 1983, as I finished my book-length study of the Palestine Liberation Organization, one of my key conclusions was, "The years from 1977 onward were marked by an accelerated shift in the centre of gravity of the Palestinian movement from those of its components operating outside the Israeli-held areas closer towards those resisting Israel from within."[1] By December 1987, it seemed clear that this shift had effectively been completed, though the resident Palestinians still stressed the loyalty to the PLO that had been the dominant trend in their politics since at least 1974, and at key junctures during the early months of the Intifada they continued to stress the unity of both their own and the diaspora wings of the Palestinian movement.

To explore the relationship between the politics of the Palestinian diaspora and that of the resident Palestinians during the period 1985–88, I will first address each of these aspects of Palestinian politics separately and then attempt to show how they came together during the Intifada.[2]

A Diplomatic False Start, November 1984–July 1986

In November 1984, the mainstream group of PLO and Fatah leaders who remained loyal to PLO Chairman Yasser Arafat took a historic decision. For the first time since Fatah had entered the PLO in 1968, they would run the organization without insisting on consensus support from all its factions. With this decision made, they convened the seventeenth session of the Palestine National Council (PNC) in Amman, Jordan, despite the clear opposition of Syria, the Syrian-backed Fatah dissenters, and most of the PLO's non-Fatah constituent groups. Until June 1986, the Fatah/PLO leaders would continue to pursue nonconsensual politics as far as it would lead them.

The seventeenth PNC session attracted a total of PNC members that was claimed by participants to number 261—just over the 252 members required to form a PNC quorum.[3] Absent from the meeting were two members of two opposition coalitions that had grown up over the previous eighteen months. The first of these coalitions, the National Alliance, had been put together under the direct sponsorship of the Syrians, with whom Arafat had been in a state of open confrontation since mid-1983. This coalition included the Syrian-inspired rebels from inside Fatah, under the leadership of Saed Musa Muraghah (Abu Musa); Syria's two longtime client groups inside the Palestinian movement, al-Saiqa and the Popular Front for the Liberation of Palestine—General Command (PFLP-GC); and a small rump group called the Palestinian Popular Struggle Front (PPSF). The second opposition coalition was not so closely controlled by Syria—this was the Democratic Alliance, which grouped the Popular Front for the Liberation of Palestine (PFLP), the Democratic Front for the Liberation of Palestine (DFLP), the pro-Moscow Palestinian Communist party (PCP), and a wing of the tiny Palestine Liberation Front (PLF) led by Talaat Yaacoub.[4]

Despite the absence of these groups, the seventeenth PNC was able to conduct the normal range of PNC business. On November 29, 1984, it elected eleven members to the PLO Executive Committee. The winning list contained Arafat himself as chairman, two other Fatah members, the leaders of two small pro-Iraqi PLO factions (the Arab Liberation Front and the second wing of the PLF, led by Mohammed Abbas), and six pro-Arafat independents. Five seats were left vacant "for the independent Palestinian factions which, for various reasons, could not attend the PNC session."

In a lengthy welcoming address to the session, Jordan's King Hussein had invited the PLO to join him in pursuing a peace initiative based on U.N. Security Council Resolution 242, stressing the resolution's endorsement of the principle of exchanging territory for peace.[5] Arafat's reaction to this proposal was to stress that it "is a procedure for action, not substance for action. . . . As for resolutions 242 and 338, which were accepted by Jordan and Syria, they were among the concepts to which Jordan committed itself. We will plan our future action and agree as much as possible on all steps."[6]

Despite continuing differences between Arafat and Hussein, the PNC announced that it would move the PLO's headquarters to Amman. This move further riled the Syrians, who feared there was now some prospect of Jordan and the PLO entering a peace process that would exclude them. In December 1984, the PLO's representative in Italy and pro-Arafat PLO Executive Committee member Fahad Qawasmeh were shot dead by killers thought to have been sent into action by the Syrians.[7] Assad meanwhile stepped up his support for the Shiite Amal militia, which was trying to eliminate the PLO's remaining base of support in West Beirut and South Lebanon. But he was unable to deter the Fatah leaders from expanding their operations in Jordan, which they saw as a major route into the Palestinian population of the Israeli-occupied West Bank and Gaza. This was especially true of Arafat's second-in-command, Khalil Wazir (Abu Jihad). In his capacity as head of Fatah's "Eastern region," he used his new base in Amman to continue building Fatah's networks in the occupied territories, where popular resistance to the Israeli occupation forces had been mounting significantly since 1982.

Throughout the weeks that followed the seventeenth PNC, Arafat and Hussein continued to discuss approaches to a peace settlement. On February 11, 1985, they concluded an agreement which called for convening an international peace conference. The agreement endorsed the land-for-peace principle and called for the establishment of a federal or confederal relationship between a future Palestinian entity and Jordan.[8] The two sides then spent the next eight months pursuing the realization of an international conference. Their ability to accomplish this aim was, however, heavily constrained by three factors: the continuation of serious disagreements between them over interpretations of the February 11 agreement; the staunch opposition of Syria, which was still basking in its victory over the United States and Israel in Lebanon; and the opposition of the United States and Israel to the international conference formula and to any negotiating role for the PLO.

The Jordan-PLO disagreements came into the open within days of the conclusion of the February 11 agreement, when Jordanian Premier Ahmed Abeidat stated that the agreement committed both parties to the creation of a joint negotiating team at the future conference and to the establishment of a firm federation between Jordan and the future Palestinian state. Senior PLO/Fatah officials Farouk Kaddumi and Salah Khalaf countered that their interpretation was that the PLO remained the "sole legitimate representative" of the Palestinian people and that an independent Palestinian state would have to be formed in the occupied territories before any link could be established between it and Jordan.[9] Despite these differences, Jordan and the PLO continued to pursue their joint diplomatic initiative. (The PLO leadership apparently backed down on the issue of the joint negotiating team and agreed to postpone resolving the issue of the relationship between the future Palestinian entity and Jordan until a later date.)

In March 1985, the Syrians countered the Jordan/PLO moves by winning the PFLP over into a new coalition with the existing members of the National Alliance, which was now renamed the Palestinian National Salvation Front (PNSF).[10] It was significant that the Syrians were not able to bring into the new coalition the two Palestinian groups most clearly identified with Soviet policies in the region—the PCP and the Democratic Front for the Liberation of Palestine (DFLP). This failure indicated that the Soviets still preferred to keep their options open between Assad and Arafat on the Palestinian issue.

In addition to Hussein, another key player in Arafat's diplomatic plan at this stage was Egyptian President Hosni Mubarak. (His inclusion was another reason why the Syrians opposed Arafat.) In May 1985, U.S. Secretary of State George Shultz held discussions with government leaders in Israel, Jordan, and Egypt; he afterward described the immediate diplomatic task as being to "find people who are truly recognized as representing the Palestinians and who also have a background which would be acceptable to the negotiating process."[11] In pursuit of this aim, by mid-July, the PLO had reportedly submitted a list of twenty-two Palestinians to the Jordanians for consideration as the Palestinian component of the future delegation. The Jordanians passed seven of these names on to the United States, which relayed them directly to the Israeli government. On July 16, the Israeli cabinet rejected the seven as unacceptable, but one week later, Peres was reported to consider two of them—East Jerusalem editor Hanna Siniora and Gaza attorney Fayez Abu Rahme—acceptable as negotiating partners. For its part, the United States reportedly considered four of the named Palestinians acceptable.[12] At this stage, both the United

States and Israel remained opposed to the idea of a full international conference that would give the Soviet Union an entreé into the Arab-Israeli peace process.

By late summer, the slow-moving diplomatic project of 1985 seemed to be stalling badly. In early August, Hussein and Arafat failed to win endorsement of their plan from an Arab summit meeting in Casablanca; the meeting's final communique restated Arab support for the Fez peace plan of 1982, which had called for the establishment of a Palestinian state in the West Bank and Gaza.[13] (The Syrians and four additional states boycotted this meeting, which was called with the express purpose of discussing Amal's Syrian-backed assaults on the Palestinians in Lebanon. In the end, even those who attended the summit failed to condemn Amal outright.) Then, later that month, U.S. Assistant Secretary of State for Near Eastern Affairs Richard Murphy traveled to the Middle East, planning to meet with a joint Jordanian-Palestinian delegation that was awaiting him in Amman. (The Palestinian members of the delegation came from the list of seven.) At the last minute, however, Shultz instructed Murphy not to meet the delegation, pending assurances from its members that they would immediately follow up this meeting with the direct meeting with Israelis that Shultz wanted to sponsor. Unable to give this assurance, the joint delegation dispersed. At the U.N. General Assembly the following month, King Hussein gave assurance of his readiness to talk directly with the Israelis. But that assurance had been given on the understanding that, in return, the U.S. administration would help win Congress's approval for the $1.9 billion arms deal Hussein badly wanted. After Shultz reneged on that understanding, Hussein rapidly started backing away from the entire peace process as it had been conducted until then. In October, evidence that Hussein was building bridges back to the Syrians emerged clearly when his newly appointed Premier, Zaid Rifai, started conducting talks with his Syrian counterpart.

By October, other Palestinian and Israeli actions were shooting the fledgling peace process out of the sky. On October 2, the Israeli air force undertook a long-distance air strike against the PLO's buildings in Tunis, killing a total of sixty-five people, including twenty Tunisian civilians. The Israeli chief of staff confirmed later that Arafat himself, who by chance was away from the building, had been the target of the attack, which was planned as a retaliation for the killing of three Israelis in Cyprus the previous week.[14] Six days later, a four-man commando group from Mohammed Abbas's wing of the PLF hijacked the Italian cruise ship *Achille Lauro* while it was en route to Ashdod,

Israel. On October 9, after taking the boat toward Syria, the hijackers surrendered to the authorities in Port Said, Egypt. It then emerged that the previous day, they had shot dead a disabled American Jewish passenger, Leon Klinghoffer. Most of world opinion was outraged at this barbarity, and U.S. Navy pilots forced the plane carrying the hijackers to Tunisia to land instead in Italy, where the hijackers were brought to trial. This sequence of events seriously damaged the political acceptability in the United States of a PLO leadership that refused to dissociate itself from the activities of Executive Committee member Abbas.

On October 14, Arafat further undermined the diplomatic project when he apparently refused to give another two PLO Executive Committee members, Muhammed Milhim and Bishop Iliya Khuri, authorization to sign a statement that would enable them to attend a meeting with British Foreign Secretary Sir Geoffrey Howe. This statement, required by the British as a precondition to the meeting, would have committed the signatories to searching for a peaceful resolution of the Arab-Israeli conflict based on Security Council Resolutions 242 and 338.[15]

By the end of 1985, it must have been clear to the PLO leaders that their rapprochement with Hussein was leading nowhere in the broader diplomatic field and would probably soon also be in peril with respect to the political base they had been able to establish in Jordan. In addition to mending his fences with Syria, the king was stepping up the contacts with Labor Alignment politicians in Israel that he had maintained throughout the more than thirty years of his reign. Labor Premier Shimon Peres was riding high in Israeli polls after the popular withdrawal from Lebanon and after largely curing the Israeli economy of its spiraling inflation. By late October, reports were surfacing in the Israeli press that at a meeting in London earlier in the month, Hussein and Peres had agreed to establish some kind of de facto condominium on the West Bank.[16] Over the two years that followed, Hussein was coordinating his policies with both Syria and Israel, despite the continuing hostility between these two. He was thus less in need of the PLO's political support than hitherto; and indeed, his coordination with both his new partners was based in part on joint pursuit of *anti*-PLO policies.

The political situation in late 1985 and early 1986 must have seemed relatively bleak to the PLO leaders. They were engaged in increasing confrontation with Jordan, in addition to their long-standing battles with Israel and Syria, and the only possible bright spots on the horizon were their continuing relationships with Iraq and Egypt (neither of which was in a position to give full political and military support to the

PLO), the ability of the Palestinian fighters to hold out against Syria's clients in Lebanon, and the slow escalation of the anti-Israeli resistance movement in the occupied territories.

The PLO leaders tried as long as they could both to cling to the relationship with Jordan, which allowed them to keep in close touch with the occupied areas, and to keep the faltering peace process alive. In November 1985, Arafat visited Egypt and tried to make amends for the turmoil following the *Achille Lauro* affair by publicly announcing that the PLO was opposed to all forms of terrorism and would henceforth restrict its use of force against Israel to actions inside the areas occupied by Israel.[17] (There was, however, some remaining ambivalence over whether this "Cairo Declaration" signaled an intention to restrict such operations to areas occupied in 1967, or whether it also allowed operations inside Israel's pre-1967 borders.)

In late January 1986, Arafat visited Amman in a last-ditch effort to patch up the relationship with the king and to restart the diplomatic process with the United States. He failed. On February 19 the king delivered a lengthy speech that reviewed his diplomatic efforts over the years, including the period since the conclusion of the February 11, 1985, agreement. This speech spelled out several instances in which the United States had not been diplomatically forthcoming, but Hussein reserved his final opprobrium for the PLO leaders, announcing, "We are unable to continue to coordinate politically with the PLO leadership until such time as their word becomes their bond, characterized by commitment, credibility and constancy." The speech effectively abrogated the February 11 agreement, and in having it broadcast in full on the Jordanian television network, which was widely watched in the occupied territories, the king was making a clear bid to win Palestinian opinion there over to his point of view.[18]

In April 1986, Hussein persuaded Colonel Atallah Atallah (Abu Zaim), who was a PLO assistant chief of staff, to defect to his camp.[19] With Hussein's backing, Atallah claimed that he represented Fatah and PLO legitimacy. When Jordanian security forces started imposing increasingly harsh restrictions on the PLO organizers who remained in the country, Atallah's fledgling group started taking over the PLO's various facilities there. The PLO leaders were conciliatory toward Hussein as long as they could be, but by June they began to speak out publicly against him. On July 7, the Jordanians shut down the twenty-five Fatah offices that remained in the country and expelled Khalil Wazir. Hussein tried to maintain that these steps were not aimed against the PLO as such and pointedly left the PLO offices in Jordan open. But opinion in the vital Palestinian constituency of the occupied West Bank appeared to back Arafat on this issue—throughout the

West Bank, student demonstrators took to the streets to burn Hussein in effigy.[20]

Escalation in the Occupied Territories, Late 1984–Summer 1987

By the end of 1984, the Palestinian population in the occupied territories included an estimated 787,000 in the West Bank, 510,000 in Gaza, and 120,000 in East Jerusalem.[21] The expanded Jerusalem municipal zone was formally annexed to Israel in 1968, and its Palestinians were allowed some participation in the political process at the municipal level. Residents of the other occupied areas, by contrast, were ruled by a military government that by the end of 1984 had enacted a total of more than eleven hundred military orders controlling every aspect of daily life. Under the auspices of the military government, a total of 104 Israeli settlements had been set up by the end of 1984, in contravention of the provisions of international law. Outside of the Jerusalem area, these settlements had a population of 42,600 settlers by the end of 1984, up from 27,500 one year earlier.

The major reaction of the Palestinians of the occupied areas to the protracted offensive against the PLO in Lebanon in 1982 had been to step up their own campaign of nonviolent and violent acts against the occupation forces. The Israeli researcher Meron Benvenisti has noted that, in the five years preceding 1982, the average incidence of Palestinian "disturbances"—apparently including only nonviolent—had been at the level of 500 per year, but 4,400 such incidents were recorded in 1982–83, and the annual level never dipped below 3,000 throughout the five years following 1982.[22] Alongside these "violations of law and order," the Palestinians were escalating a campaign of violent acts inside the territories. Whereas between 1977 and 1982, West Bankers committed a total of 578 violent acts (an average rate of 119 violent acts per year), during the one-year period April 1983–March 1984, no less than 354 such incidents were reported.[23]

From late 1984 on, a series of developments fueled the violence in the territories. In the West Bank, the role of the militant Jewish settler organizations in escalating intercommunal tensions became increasingly clear. Between September 1984 and June 1985, trials were held in Israel for the network of settler militants known as the Jewish underground. Members of the underground were eventually convicted on charges of the attempted murder of Palestinian community leaders, including the 1980 attacks against elected mayors Bassam Shakaa and Karim Khalaf, the 1983 manslaughter of three students at Hebron's Islamic University, and a conspiracy to blow up the mosques in Jerusalem's sacred Haram al-Sharif (Temple Mount) area.

These trials rocked the settler movement, which had been unnerved by the failure of the right-wing Israeli parties to win an outright victory the year before and watched with distaste as possibilities of a Peres-Hussein peace process appeared to grow from November 1984 onward. Then, in late May 1985, the Israeli government agreed to an unprecedented prisoner exchange, and 1,150 Palestinian prisoners held in the occupied territories, Israel, and South Lebanon were exchanged for 3 Israeli soldiers held by Ahmed Jibril's PFLP-GC. Six hundred of the released Palestinians were allowed to return to their homes in the territories and in Israel. The settler militants, who had been testing the Israeli political winds for some weeks, then went on an unbridled rampage in many towns and villages in the West Bank in an attempt to force as many as possible of the released prisoners to leave. As Benvenisti described it, "The conclusion could not be escaped that the army and police had abdicated peacekeeping functions in the West Bank to roving bands of settlers."[24]

The Palestinians defended themselves as best they could and on occasion tried to retaliate against both the settlers and the army. On July 30, 1985, an Israeli civilian employee of the Israeli Defense Forces (IDF) was shot dead in Nablus, the fifth Israeli to die that year as a result of violence in the territories. Three Palestinians had apparently been killed in the territories in the same period.[25] The reaction of the Israeli cabinet was swift. On August 5, it reinstituted two punishments—deportation and administrative detention (that is, detention without trial for up to six months)—that the Likud government had used scarcely at all. Between August and December 1985, 31 Palestinians were deported and 131 had been placed in administrative detention.[26] The IDF continued the practice of demolishing or sealing the family homes of Palestinians found guilty of security-related offenses. These measures failed to stem the cycle of violence. Six more Israelis were killed in Palestinian-related incidents before the end of 1985 (and eight more, all IDF soldiers, died in a barracks fire in Shiloh that may or may not have started accidentally); five Palestinians were also killed in that period.[27]

In late November 1985, the Israelis tried a new tack, appointing a local businessman, Zafer al-Masri, as mayor of Nablus.[28] Masri's appointment was thought to have been carried out in close coordination with King Hussein, as part of Israel's longer-range plans to engage Jordan in a condominium-type arrangement in the occupied territories. It was protested vociferously by the PFLP and other left-wing Palestinian groups, but the Fatah leaders did not condemn it openly and indeed seemed to give the move some low-key backing. (Fatah was still eager to avoid the final break with Hussein, which was looming closer.) Then, in March 1986, the new mayor was assassinated. Responsibility for this act was claimed by the PFLP and by the extremely violent Palestinian grouplet led by Sabri al-Banna (Abu Nidal). Fatah was able to capitalize on the outrage felt toward the killing by the majority of Nablus citizens. Pro-Fatah activists turned Masri's thousands-strong funeral into a virtual Fatah rally, at which the outlawed Palestinian flag was prominently displayed and slogans were chanted against the PFLP and Syria's President Hafiz Assad, as well as against Hussein and Israel.[29]

The fate suffered by Masri did not deter the Israelis from trying to continue to institutionalize their rule over the West Bank. In August 1986, Premier Peres suggested that Israel should allow the West Bankers to vote directly for representatives to Jordan's rubber-stamp parliament in Amman. This proposal, which seemed to be part of the planned Israeli-Jordanian condominium, was strongly opposed not only by all factions of the PLO but also by Peres's partner in the coalition government, Yitzhak Shamir. (Under the coalition's operating agreement Shamir would rotate into the premiership in October.) In September and October, the Israelis appointed four more Palestinian mayors to other municipalites in the West Bank but with little rhetoric about the political meaning of the move, and these mayors came to no physical harm. Then in November, the Cairo-Amman Bank was allowed to open the branch in Nablus that had been promised one year previously. Operating under the dual authority of the Israeli and Jordanian banking authorities, it was the first offshoot of an Arab banking organization to be allowed to do business in the territories since Israel occupied them nineteen years earlier.[30] In November, too, Hussein announced the launching of a Jordanian-sponsored development plan for the West Bank, through which he promised to use U.S. Aid for International Development (AID) funds to improve the quality of life of the Palestinians under occupation.

Though the Israeli and Jordanian governments appeared to be making some headway with their political plans for the territories in 1986, a poll conducted among the Palestinians there in July and August of that year showed that support for Arafat and the PLO was still strong. In the poll, which was conducted under the auspices of the East Jerusalem daily al-Fajr and western news organizations, 71.1 percent of the 1,024 scientifically selected respondents declared that their preferred leader from the proferred list was Yasser Arafat, with only 3.4 percent choosing King Hussein. Asked to name their preferred Palestinian leader, 78.6 percent named Arafat, and the PFLP's Habash was the second with 5.6 percent. No other Palestinian leaders attracted even 2 percent in this vote.) Asked which body or bodies best reflected the political preferences of those in the Palestinian area, 71.2 percent responded by naming the PLO's current leadership. And asked whether they believed the PLO to be the sole legitimate representative of the Palestinian people, 93.5 percent of the respondents answered affirmatively.[31]

The pollsters noted the evident popularity within the West Bank and Gaza of both Arafat and the PLO. They also drew two conclusions that had extreme significance for their policy implications: "The lack of correlation between income and political attitudes suggests that improving economic conditions will not necessarily result in the moderation of political attitudes" and "The current leadership of the PLO is far more moderate than the Palestinian population residing in the West Bank and Gaza."[32]

Police statistics showed that the Israeli-Jordanian initiative had brought little real change to the occupied territories in 1986. Although only five Palestinians were deported that year, 1986, thirty-seven were served administrative detention orders, and the forty-eight demolitions and house sealings nearly equaled that of 1985.[33] The rate of political killings of Palestinians in the territories also apparently escalated sharply in the year beginning in April 1986.[34]

Meron Benvenisti has listed three waves of violence that rocked the occupied territories in the winter of 1986–87. The first, which brought a week of violence to all the Palestinian-occupied territories, including East Jerusalem, was sparked by a fight in December 1986 between IDF soldiers and students at Bir-Zeit University that left two students dead. Two months later, another wave of violence erupted in response to the deportation of a student from the Gaza town of Khan Yunis who was accused of leading Fatah's youth movement (al-Shabiba) there. This unrest was brought under control after all five West Bank universities were closed by the Israeli authorities. The third outbreak ended with ugly exchanges between West Bankers and Israeli settlers during which an Israeli woman and child were killed by a petrol bomb and settlers went on the rampage again in Qalqilya.[35]

In his analysis of the mounting Palestinian violence in the occupied territories in 1986–87, Benvenisti noted, "There is no doubt about the grass-roots origin of most violent actions." He concluded, "Though the overwhelming majority support the nationalist stances of the PLO, the Palestinian population is now acting of its own accord."[36] By the summer of 1987, it had also become clear that the Palestinians resident in all three parts of their homeland that were under Israeli occupation—the West Bank, Gaza, and East Jerusalem—were, with some support from Israel's own population of franchised Palestinians, increasingly acting as a unified political entity despite some continuing tension between Islamic and secular nationalist factions in Gaza and despite the Israelis' attempts to make the people of East Jerusalem consider themselves as somehow distinct.[37]

Two events took place in late June 1987 that were symbolic of what was happening to the population of resident Palestinians. On June 21, locals presumed to be Palestinian militants burned two cars belonging to East Jerusalem editor Hanna Siniora. In addition to being identified as a pro-Fatah spokesman in Jerusalem, Siniora had earlier launched an innovative proposal (apparently with some tentative backing from the Fatah leaders outside) that the Palestinian Jerusalemites should seek to make a big impact in the next municipal elections.[38] But he was unable to win much favorable response from his community, and after his cars were burned, he quietly agreed to shelve his plans.

The other event was a one-day strike, staged on June 24 by the Arab municipalities inside Israel proper to protest discrimination against them in public spending. This strike was widely observed in the Israeli Palestinian communities. It was significant that many Palestinians from the occupied territories joined the strike.[39]

PLO Reunification, August 1986–November 1987

After the Jordanian authorities shut down Fatah's offices in the country in July 1986, the Fatah leadership had to reconsider a policy that had involved taking great (their critics would say excessive) political risks, including forcing an open split in the PLO, to regain a base in Jordan. For the next eighteen months, the mainstream PLO found itself in the uncomfortable position of trying to battle both Syria and Jordan, while also keeping up its historic confrontation with Israel. One of the first tactics it adopted was to try to mend the internal schism that had plagued it since 1983.

In March 1985, the Soviets had adopted an agnostic stance on the Palestinian issue, as between the mainstream Fatah leaders and the Syrian government. Now, in the summer of 1986, they were among the first to whom the Fatah leaders turned in their pursuit of intra-Palestinian reconciliation. In August 1986, the Soviets sponsored a series of discussions in Moscow that reportedly involved both PNSF representatives and pro-Arafat loyalists. Nothing came directly of those talks, but the following month the two pro-Moscow Palestinian groups, the DFLP and the PCP, joined with Fatah in issuing a statement in Beirut which declared that the Jordanian-Palestinian accord of February 1985 "is no longer valid and does not constitute the base of the PLO policy." After an October 1986 meeting in Cairo, these three parties joined with the Arab Liberation Front (ALF) and the pro-Fatah wing of the PLF in declaring that they would promote national unity and work to convene a new session of the PNC. Though the PFLP did not attend the Cairo meeting, its secretary general and historic leader George Habash met with Khalil Wazir in Prague in mid-November, and contacts between Fatah and the PFLP continued thereafter.[40]

Ironically, the anti-Palestinian policy pursued in Lebanon by the Syrian government was the most effective motor of intra-Palestinian reconciliation in this period. In the fall of 1986, the Amal campaign against the Palestinians in Lebanon escalated to a new pitch, and Amal gunmen threw a tight siege around the large Rashidiyeh refugee camp in September 1986 and around the two refugee camps near Beirut over the two months that followed. In early February 1987, residents of the Beirut camp of Bourj al-Barajneh would ask their religious leaders for permission to eat the flesh of human corpses because those of dogs, cats, and mules "had already all been consumed."[41]

Amal's escalation against the Palestinians backfired badly, both for Amal itself (which succeeded only in scaring its Lebanese opponents into forming an effective countercoalition) and for its Syrian sponsors.[42] These latter may have hoped that their support of Amal would pressure the Palestinians into opposing Arafat and lining up behind the pro-Syrian Palestinian factions, but they actually achieved the exact opposite. Once they came under fire from Amal, Palestinian fighters who had been sent into the camps by the Syrians because of their supposed pro-Syrian leanings rapidly joined with the Arafat loyalists to defend their hard-pressed neighborhoods; they also sent increasingly strong messages to their leaders in Damascus urging a swing away from support of Syria.[43]

The Algerians and Libyans were also working behind the scenes to bring about Palestinian reconciliation. Fatah central committee member Salah Khalaf (Abu Iyad) met with the leaders of the DFLP and PCP in Algiers in February 1987. Representatives of the DFLP met with representatives of the PNSF factions in Tripoli, Libya, the following month. Representatives of all Palestinian factions then started gathering in Algiers from April 13 onward. On April 20, the eighteenth session of the PNC was formally opened there. Those who participated in all six days of its proceedings included Fatah, the PFLP, the DFLP, the ALF, the PPSF, both wings of the PLF, and the PCP, which was formally admitted to the PNC for the first time. The representatives of Abu Nidal's group (Fatah—Revolutionary Council) attended only for a portion of the opening day before they walked out.[44] The only groups that did not attend were those that were irrevocably wedded to the Syrian line—Saiqa, the PFLP-GC, and the faction Abu Musa had taken out of Fatah. President Assad made a formal visit to the Soviet Union at the time of the session, and in a joint statement at the end of the visit he and General Secretary Mikhail Gorbachev expressed their formal support for "unity in the ranks of the Palestinian resistance movement."[45] But Assad had done nothing to help this process along, and the Soviets had so many other matters to discuss with him that they did not allow his noncooperation on this issue to prevent the visit from taking place.

On April 26, the PNC session wound up its proceedings by voting unanimously for the fifteen-man list proposed for the new Executive Committee and by passing a series of important resolutions. The Executive Committee was composed of Arafat and two other Fatah Central Committee members, the PLF's Mohammed Abbas, and representatives of the PFLP, DFLP, ALF, PPSF, and PCP, along with six generally pro-Fatah independents.[46]

The eighteenth PNC's resolutions started with an affirmation of "the Palestinian Arab people's national inalienable rights to repatriation, self-determination, and establishment of an independent state on the Palestinian national soil whose capital is Jerusalem" and of the PLO's role as "sole legitimate representative for our people." The fifth resolution recorded the PNC's continued rejection of Resolution 242 because it "ignores the Palestinian people's national inalienable rights." In its eighteenth resolution, the PNC supported "the convocation of an international conference within the framework of the United Nations . . . to be attended by the permanent member states of the U.N. Security Council and the parties to the conflict in the region, including the PLO, on equal footing with the other parties." This resolution stressed that "the international conference should have full powers."[47] In resolutions on policy toward the Arab states, the PNC reaffirmed that "any future relationship with Jordan should be based on confederal bases between two independent states." And it entrusted the new Executive Committee with the task of "defining the bases for Palestinian-Egyptian relations," spelling out that this should be done in accordance with successive PNC resolutions, "especially those of the 16th session."[48] (At its sixteenth session, held in Algiers in February 1983, the PNC had resolved that the PLO should not restore relations with Egypt until the latter renounced the Camp David agreements.)

The last of these resolutions was the most immediately controversial because it provoked the official Egyptian observer delegation to walk out of the conference and the Egyptian government to close fourteen PLO offices in Egypt. The big issues that were the sticking point in the broader diplomatic game continued to be (as they had been since 1977) the role of the international conference and the nature of Palestinian representation at it.

In the months after announcing his break with the PLO in February 1986, King Hussein had made a limited amount of progress in winning Shimon Peres and the United States around to a grudging admission that some form of "international event" might accompany the direct Israeli-Arab talks that Israel and the United States insisted should lie at the heart of any future peace process. In October 1986, however, Peres had turned the Israeli premiership over to the Likud's Yitzhak Shamir, who remained stubbornly opposed to any international involvement in Arab-Israeli peace efforts. Peres became foreign minister, and he used this position to continue his peace overtures toward Hussein, as well as toward the Soviet Union, which, under Gorbachev's leadership, looked as though it were more interested in engaging actively in Mideastern diplomacy, including with Israel.

In April 1987, Peres held a semiclandestine meeting in London with Hussein, at which they formulated a joint plan according to which a purely ceremonial international conference would be convened under U.S. auspices. But when Peres tried in mid-May to force a general election in Israel on this issue, he failed to win the necessary support in the Knesset. So Hussein's attempt to pursue a peace process independent of the PLO failed, just as his earlier effort to do so in collaboration with the PLO had done, and prospects of any imminent diplomatic breakthrough on the Arab-Israeli issue had dissipated by the beginning of summer.

In the months that followed, Hussein turned the main focus of his attention to the bloody seven-year conflict in the Persian Gulf. He was now on good terms with both Iraq and Syria (which gave Iran significant diplomatic support) and hoped to be able to effect a reconciliation between these two countries. The main vehicle he sought to use to this end was the convening of an emergency Arab summit meeting in Amman.

Arafat was among the many Arab political leaders who attended this summit, but the meeting's focus was evident from the very first day, November 8, when Hussein in his opening remarks made extensive mention of the Gulf war before making any reference to the Arab conflict with Israel.[49] Two days later, Arafat was reported to have boycotted a state banquet because he felt he had not been accorded due privilege under protocol by his hosts. After three days of closed sessions, Arab League secretary general Chadli Klibi read the summit's closing statement, in which five paragraphs on the situation in the Gulf preceded the two and a half paragraphs on the Arab-Israeli conflict.[50] The summit passed a resolution reaffirming the participants' support

for the Fez peace plan and calling for an international peace conference on the Middle East in which all parties to the Arab-Israeli conflict,
including the PLO would take part on an equal footing. In addition,
it made a provision for Jordan and the PLO to resume the work of the
joint committee responsible for distributing Arab aid to the occupied
territories, which had previously been disrupted by Hussein's decision
to funnel Jordan's aid into the territories on a unilateral basis.[51]

On balance, however, the summit was not a success for the PLO.
Arafat failed to win any meaningful reconciliation from Assad, although he met with him there. And the summit gave a clear indication
to the whole world, including Israel, that the consensus of Arab states
was much more concerned with the situation in the Persian Gulf than
it was with the Palestinian issue. The conclusion reached by most
veteran Western observers of the Arab-Israeli conflict as of the end of
November 1987 was that, with the Arab states preoccupied elsewhere
and U.S. and Israeli elections coming up the following year, there was
little change of making diplomatic progress on the Palestinian issue
over the months that followed. Nor, the common wisdom had it, was
there any particular need to do so.[52]

The Intifada: Roots and Effects, Summer 1987–April 1988

The Palestinian Intifada (uprising) broke out on a massive scale in
the Israeli-occupied areas on December 9, 1987. But its seeds had been
sown throughout the more than twenty years of the occupation and
were increasingly evident in the months leading up to December.

In late July 1987, an Israeli army officer was shot dead in Gaza. The
IDF Southern Command imposed a tight curfew on the area, and at
least three hundred Palestinians were arrested for questioning. In
August and again in September, the Palestinians of East Jerusalem
staged a widely observed commercial strike and labor stoppage to
protest new government measures against the Palestinian-owned Jerusalem Electric Company. In September, an IDF patrol shot dead a
Palestinian stone-thrower in the Balata refugee camp near Nablus.
From October onward, the security situation in all the occupied areas
deteriorated further. On October 1, three Gazans were shot dead when
they tried to run an IDF roadblock, and five days later four Gazans
and a Shin Bet officer were killed in a shootout. On October 12, a
woman was shot dead by troops in Ramallah.[53] In early November,
and again at the end of the month, the IDF clamped a curfew on
Balata refugee camp, sending in tough Border Patrol units who report-

edly beat and terrorized camp residents. On November 10, a seven-teen-year-old girl was shot during a stone-throwing incident in Gaza. One month later police arrested four Israeli settlers in connection with her killing.[54] The veteran Israeli analyst Ze'ev Schiff had warned throughout 1987 that the security situation in the occupied areas was not stable. In February 1988, he chastised the Israeli intelligence community for having failed, in the period before December 1987, to understand "what is happening in its own home court, in its own bedroom."

On December 8, four more Palestinians were killed when their truck was rammed by an Israeli-driven vehicle. This turned out not to be just one more in the continuing series of incidents in the territories—it was the precipitating event of a remarkable outpouring of popular resistance that remained unstaunched two years later. On December 9, Palestinians throughout the Gaza area took to the streets by the thousands to protest the death of the four; they threw a hail of stones onto the few IDF positions in the Gaza Strip. Stranded IDF patrols lost control of the street, and they opened fire in an increasingly indiscriminate fashion. Within a day, the riots had spread to the West Bank and the Greater Jerusalem area, and by December 18, seventeen Palestinians had been killed by the IDF, but the troops were no nearer to restoring order. Adding fuel to the fire on December 15, Minister of Commerce Ariel Sharon ostentatiously moved into a new apartment in the Muslim Quarter of East Jerusalem. The following day, a general strike shut down the entire Arab sector of the city. On December 18, riot police tear-gassed three hundred Muslim worshipers in Jeru-salem's sacred Haram al-Sharif area, which contains the al-Aqsa Mosque.[56] Then, on December 21, Israeli Palestinian community lead-ers called a general strike in solidarity with the residents of the territor-ies, in which the Druze residents of the occupied Golan region also participated. The widespread observance of this strike sent a new tremor of fear through many Israelis.[57]

By the end of 1987, the IDF still had not quelled the Intifada, and both sides settled into a new state of hostility in which each tried a range of tactics to increase its advantage over the other, or—failing that—to wear it down. In late December, IDF chief of staff Dan Shom-ron instituted new forms of riot-control training for his troops. On January 13, four Palestinians thought to be leaders of the Intifada were expelled to Lebanon. On January 19, Defense Minister Yitzhak Rabin ordered troops in the territories to start beating demonstrators, but the slick new wooden riot sticks issued for this purpose were often used in a vicious and uncontrolled way, which merely served to increase the hostility of the Palestinians. The IDF resumed its practice of shooting demonstrators by the end of the month, but the beatings also continued. Refugee camps and other areas were placed under intermittent lengthy curfews, and the rate of arrests and administrative detention orders escalated steeply.[58] By the end of April, five thousand Palestinians had been sent to hastily constructed jail camps, and seventeen hundred of them were held under administrative detention orders.

The Palestinians responded in a variety of innovative ways, aiming to keep the Intifada alive. By the beginning of January, reports were surfacing about a new secret leadership body, the Unified National Command of the Uprising (UNCU), and, in a development of extreme significance for the Palestinians, UNCU's operations appeared to be suported both by the mainstream PLO leadership and by the remaining pro-Syrian groups operating out of Damascus. In the first weeks of the Intifada, the Syrians set up a powerful new transmitter south of Damascus whose broadcasts came out under the name of al-Quds Palestinian Arab Radio. On January 14, al-Quds broadcast what was described as "Call Number Two issued by the National Command for the Escalation of the Uprising." Six days later, the PLO's Voice of Palestine, transmitting from Baghdad, broadcast the text of another UNCU call, this one distributed in Gaza.[59] Over the following weeks, there was a small amount of criticism aimed by the Voice of Palestine against the al-Quds station and vice versa, and there appeared to be some slight differences in the texts of the UNCU calls as broadcast by each of these stations. But in general, the broadcasts showed remarkably little intra-Palestinian rancor. Al-Quds voiced no discernible open criticism of Yasser Arafat, and the operational parts of the UNCU calls were broadcast in much the same terms on both stations.

With the UNCU calls, which continued to appear at regular intervals until at least early June, the Intifada took on a much higher level of organization and sophistication. For example, "Call Number Two" designated January 15 as a "day of unity and solidarity in commemoration of the martyrs of the uprising." The call instructed Palestinian workers to attend work as much as possible on days not specially designated as strikes and called on drivers of buses and taxis to observe three days of nationalist strike. By the time UNCU's fifth call was issued at the end of January, its instructions included an appeal for a boycott of Israeli goods. This tactic was advocated again in the sixth UNCU call, which also called for "the immediate resignation of the appointed municipal councils as a prelude to holding democratic elections at the appropriate time" and for boycotts on tax authorities and the pro-Jordanian news paper al-Nahar.[60]

UNCU's sixth call also included another innovation—a list of six provisional demands for the uprising, presumably as an interim step on the road to the PLO's goal of creating an independent Palestinian state in the occupied territories. According to the Voice of Palestine, these demands included the withdrawal of the IDF from populated areas, releasing the prisoners and detainees, suspending the emergency regulations, and holding free elections for the Palestinian municipal councils. In the version of the call broadcast by al-Quds, however, this last demand was omitted.[61] Subsequent calls ordered occupants of the territories to refrain from using the few firearms kept clandestinely in their possession. Despite the great provocations to which they were subjected, the resident Palestinians observed this limit with great discipline through at least the end of April, with the exception of a single incident on March 30 in which a soldier was shot dead in Bethlehem. In a separate incident earlier in March, three Palestinians who had infiltrated from Egypt were killed, along with three Israeli hostages, in a firefight after they had hijacked a bus traveling to Dimona.

In an article published in the middle of February, Israeli journalist Tzvi Gilat gave an assessment of the dynamics of the Intifada that rang relatively true. Gilat reported that the leadership of the UNCU was a covert group with fifteen members, three from each of the prominent streams of local politics—Fatah, the PFLP, the PFLP-GC, the communists, and the Islamic activists:[62]

> The Palestinian society in the territories is constructing a new pyramid. The people are at the base of the pyramid. . . . At the top are the spokesmen, the famous personalities, those who are exposed to the media. Today, more than ever before, the top of the pyramid must be sensitive to the power and desires of the base, otherwise they will begin to totter. . . . The questionmark, the new leadership, is in the heart of the pyramid between the base (the people) and the turret (the spokesman). This is the glue. This is the element that shapes and funnels the gust of wind blown by the people. One can only guess who is in this bloc. One cannot tell with certainty.

The writer judged that "all parts of this pyramid, which is now being built, are in contact with the PLO leadership. The PLO is testing the Palestinian society in the territories and vice versa.[63]

What, then, was the role of the PLO in the first months of the Intifada? It was clear that the PLO leaders had not instigated the uprising by instructing the Palestinians of the territories to launch it on such and such a day. But the level of confrontation had been building up inside the territories throughout the previous five years, and throughout these lower-level confrontations the PLO groups with followers active on the inside had been perfecting their methods of organization, their communications, and their tactics. Thus the clandestine networks were in place by December 1987 to maximize, sustain, and channel the anger that had been building up among the resident Palestinians throughout the two decades of Israeli occupation. It should be stressed that the political stance of the clandestine networks, as enunciated repeatedly in the UNCU calls, stated strongly that the PLO remained the sole legitimate representative of the Palestinian people. It rejected both the idea that community leaders of the territories could negotiate on any national-level Palestinian issues in the absence of any external PLO-backed component in the negotiating team and the idea that King Hussein or any of his supporters could represent the Palestinians. This reflected, of course, the standard PLO position on Palestinian representation.

The clandestine networks—many of which had been painstakingly put together by Fatah's Khalil Wazir—then showed themselves, throughout the early months of the Intifada, remarkably capable of adapting to the rapidly changing situation. Some tactics were dropped (as apparently was the call for the resignation of the municipal councils at one point); others were picked up or adapted. In the first days of the riots, for example, calls from Jerusalem intellectuals for a boycott of Israeli products were met with derision from the refugee camps, but by late January, this tactic had been officially adopted by the UNCU, and residents of the refugee camps set about planting victory gardens to lessen their dependence on Israeli produce.

At some stage, apparently in the latter half of January, the Israeli Palestinian Knesset member Abdel-Wahhab Darawsheh (who resigned from the Labor Alignment in protest over Rabin's policy of beatings) proposed to East Jerusalem Palestinians that they form a negotiating team to pursue the provisional demands that were starting to be enunciated formally in the UNCU calls. This proposal was transmitted to the PLO leaders, who agreed on the membership of a team of public figures from the territories and on a list of fourteen provisional demands that would be presented to the Israelis.[64]

The first formal presentation of these demands was made to no less a person than Secretary Shultz, in a meeting he conducted in Washington on January 27 with Hanna Siniora and Fayez Abu Rahme. In the memorandum Siniora and Abu Rahme presented to Shultz, they affirmed "our people's unbreakable commitment to its national aspirations," stating that "these aspirations include our people's firm national rights of self-determination and of the establishment of an independent state on our national soil under the leadership of the PLO, as our sole legitimate representative." The memorandum said that the Palestinians called for the convening of an international con-

ference, which would be attended by all interested parties, including
the five permanent members of the Security Council, and the PLO
"as an equal partner." Before listing the provisional demands, the
memorandum stated that "we call upon the Israeli authorities to comply with the following list of demands as a means to prepare the
atmosphere for the convening of the suggested international conference." The demands were then listed in full. They more or less encom-
passed the demands to be stated in UNCU's sixth call on February 5,
but they also included more abstract measures such as that Israel
should "abide by the 4th Geneva Convention" and overtly political
matters such as that the restrictions on contacts between the resident
Palestinians and the PLO should be removed.[65]

It is not known whether Shultz transmitted these demands to the
Israelis, but the Israelis did nothing discernible to pursue the matter.
Shultz tried to arrange another meeting, with a broader group of
resident Palestinians, when he traveled to the Middle East in late
February. Although Arafat at first reportedly agreed to this meeting,
he reversed his position after urgent communications from the clandestine UNCU activists in the territories, who wanted to underline the
principle that resident Palestinians should not deal with Palestinian
issues separately from diaspora Palestinians.[66] Thus, when Shultz invited a number of local Palestinians to a meeting in Jerusalem on
February 26, no one turned up. A subsequent meeting in Egypt,
between Shultz and "acceptable" Palestinians from inside and outside
the occupied territories, to which the secretary reportedly "had no
objection," failed to materialize because the Palestinians did not have
enough advance notice.[67] Shultz did meet with two diaspora Palestinians of middle-level political importance in late March, in Washington,
but he tried to downplay the connections these individuals (both of
whom were Palestinian-American professors) had with the PLO, although one of them, Ibrahim Abu-Lughod, had been elected to the
PLO's intermediate body, the Central Council, at the PNC session the
previous April.

By April 1988, the peace process Shultz had belatedly launched in
the Israeli-Palestinian conflict was showing serious signs of stalling, a
victim both of its failure to budge Prime Minister Shamir from his
rejection of any negotiations and its ill-directed focus on obtaining a
leading role for Jordan. (There were still some hopes that the secretary
might make progress during a visit to the region in early June.) The
situation in the territories meanwhile remained tense; and as had often
happened over the previous years, the Jewish settler militants were
playing their part in keeping tensions high. On April 6, two armed
adult settlers organized and led a "hike" of settler teenagers, which

took them through the Palestinian village of Beita. When Palestinian youths started to stone the approaching group, at least one of the armed adults started firing and killed one of the stone-throwers. A melee broke out, during which this settler accidentally shot and killed a fifteen-year-old girl hiker before himself being stoned insensible by relatives of the dead Palestinian. As the melee died down, the Israeli group was escorted into the village, while villagers called ambulances. Despite the facts behind this encounter (which were later released by the IDF), the militant settlers vowed heavy vengeance on the villagers for the girls's death. Their calls were backed at the rhetorical level by Shamir and at the operational level by the justice minister (who called for razing the entire village to the ground) and to a lesser extent by a pressured IDF command. The IDF ordered the demolition of fourteen houses in Beita (although they later apologized for one of these demolitions) and arrested many villagers, naming six of them for deportation.[68]

On April 16, Shamir's government further escalated the war against the Palestinians by launching another raid against PLO facilities in Tunis, killing Khalil Wazir. When news of his killing reached the occupied territories, violent riots erupted spontaneously there, and fourteen Palestinians were killed while the IDF tried to regain control of the streets that day. Wazir's killing proved, as had all previous Israeli tactics, unsuccessful in breaking the remarkable spirit of the Intifada.

The surviving PLO leaders got some solace for the loss of Wazir by the opportunity it finally afforded Arafat to win what he hoped would be a meaningful reconciliation with the Syrians. Wazir was buried in a tumultuous funeral ceremony in Damascus, but Arafat refused to attend the funeral because he was still uncertain of the honor the Syrians would accord him in their country. By the time he did visit Syria a few days later, his supporters seemed relatively assured that he had won significant political concessions from Assad. But evidence that the PLO's differences with the Syrians had not all been resolved emerged in early May, when fighting once again erupted between pro-PLO and pro-Syrian factions in the Beirut refugee camps.[69]

The Palestinian Political Initiative, July–December 1988

By the summer of 1988, it was clear both that the Intifada was deeply embedded in Palestinian society and that no return to the status quo ante December 1987 was easily conceivable and that the underground networks in the occupied territories were increasingly driving the politics of the PLO's exile-based leadership. Moreover, the direction in which the resident Palestinians were driving the leadership had shifted throughout the spring of 1988. In February, pressure from the residents' networks had forced Arafat to reverse his original decision to let Siniora meet Shultz, but by mid-July, Dutch Foreign Minister Hans Van den Broek was meeting a group of Palestinians in East Jerusalem that included—along with Siniora—a number of other individuals with impressive credentials in the nationalist movement and presumed links to important underground networks.[70] Also in the group was Faisal al-Husseini, an intellectual whose credentials as head of the Arab Studies Center in Jerusalem were surpassed only by his role as an intermediary between the underground networks and such local veterans of diplomatic contacts as Siniora and by his personal history as the son of legendary Palestinian nationalist leader Abdel-Qader al-Husseini, who had been killed in the fighting around Jerusalem in 1948.

During the Arab League summit meeting held in Algeria in early June 1988, Arafat adviser Bassam Abu Sharif had circulated a document that called for direct talks between Palestinian and Israeli leaders and for a resolution of the conflict based on an unequivocal two-state solution. This document defined the PLO's ultimate aim as being "a free, dignified, and secure life not only for our children but also for the children of the Israelis."[71] It was generally assumed that Abu Sharif circulated this document only after getting permission from Arafat himself. (Abu Sharif's position within the movement was somewhat ambiguous organizationally because he had broken definitively with the PFLP a few years earlier after a long career as PFLP spokesman, but he also lacked the trust of many longtime Fatah members. As a result, he was more dependent than most other PLO activists on the direct goodwill of the organization's chairman.) The Abu Sharif document was thus widely seen as an Arafat trial balloon. Nevertheless, it incurred the wrath of many PLO activists, including Abu Sharif's erstwhile colleagues in the PFLP.

For a while after its publication, it was not clear what reaction the document would provoke from the underground organizers in the occupied areas. By the end of July, however, it seemed that the resident organizers' reaction to the ideas expressed in it had crystallized into some degree of qualified support. At a meeting with Israelis sponsored by the Peace Now organization (and attended by the U.S. consul-general in Jerusalem), Faisal al-Husseini said that the paper represented "the PLO's wish for a just peace" and that it was "100 percent sincere." Urging the Israeli government to deal directly with the PLO, he said, "There has to be mutual recognition by both sides."[72]

At the end of July, a firm indication came from another quarter that if the Israeli government sought a negotiated settlement to the conflict over the occupied areas, it would ultimately have to deal with the PLO. This was the message when King Hussein went public with a speech ambiguously dissociating himself from the conflict over the West Bank and Gaza.[73] Hussein's speech had several important consequences. It forced the United States to start to look for ways of overcoming its thirteen-year refusal to deal politically with the PLO. It removed from the PLO leaders any last excuse for not seriously considering the question of the political future of the occupied territories. (This effect was further intensified by Hussein's decision to cut off thousands of the salaries he had been paying to individuals in the territories, which forced the PLO to try to find ways to replace the income lost by the affected families.) And, possibly, Hussein's move contributed to the poor showing in November's general elections in Israel of the Labor party, which for forty years had based its Palestinian policy on close coordination with Jordan.

Many figures from within the occupied areas were meanwhile intensifying their campaign to win formal PLO backing for the ideas expressed in the Abu Sharif document. In early August, Bir Zeit philosophy professor Sari Nuseibeh published an article urging the Palestinian leadership "to take advantage of the historical opportunity to which the Intifada had given birth . . . and to translate it into a political product, to establish the independent state on the land which was occupied in 1967."[74] The significance of this article was increased because it was published in the prominent pro-Fatah weekly *al-Yawm al-Sabi*, indicating that important forces within Fatah were lining up behind the views expressed.

Also in early August, Israeli government sources leaked details of some of the papers that had been confiscated when, shortly after the Peace Now meeting, Faisal al-Husseini had been once again detained without trial. According to the leaks, one of the confiscated documents had been a draft of a Palestinian declaration of independence. In a commentary on the Husseini document, Nuseibeh noted, "As far as I know, the idea of a declaration of independence in these areas was first floated in recent times in 1980. The idea was again presented for discussion at the beginning of the uprising. Some intellectuals even wanted to incorporate the January 14th statement of 14 points in such a declaration."[75] Nuseibeh also noted that discussion of declaring an independent Palestinian state became much easier following the publication of articles on the subject in the local press by the visiting American Jewish scholar Jerome Segal.

The campaign for PLO adoption of the declaration of independence gathered momentum among both the resident and the exile wings of the movement. By November, Arafat and his colleagues were ready to take the issue to a full PNC session; this session, the council's nineteenth, was convened in Algiers on November 12. At it, Arafat read out the text of the independence declaration that had been hammered out in the discussions of the preceding weeks. The declaration stated, "The PNC declares in the name of God and in the name of the Palestinian Arab people the establishment of the State of Palestine over our Palestinian soil—over our Palestinian soil—and its capital holy Jerusalem."[76] The declaration, which was adopted unanimously by those present, based its claim for the legitimacy of the new state on "U.N. resolutions since 1947," including the partition resolution of 1947 whose validity had never previously been accepted by any Palestinian political group.

At the close of the session, the PNC issued a political statement that, for the first time ever, included no reference to the need for armed struggle and for the first time was not prefaced by an explicit endorsement of the PLO's controversial charter. In the statement, the PNC called for convening an international conference on the Palestinian issue that should be "held on the basis of United Nations Security Council resolutions 242 and 338 and the assurance of the legitimate national rights of the Palestinian people."[77] For the first time at a PNC, a real vote was taken on the text of the political statement. The leadership won this vote by a count of 253 to 46.[78] But the dissenters, who were mainly followers of historic PFLP leader George Habash, made it clear that they would continue to act as a loyal opposition within the PLO, rather than leaving its embrace for an alliance with Syria.

By eschewing the reference to armed struggle and the PLO charter that hitherto had been customary in PNC statements and by including a positive if still indirect reference to Security Council Resolution 242, Arafat apparently hoped that he had fulfilled the requirements the United States had kept in place since 1975 as a precondition for any direct political contacts with the PLO. One week later he applied for a visa to visit New York, where he planned to address the United Nations General Assembly. Secretary Shultz personally approved the decision to turn down the visa request.[79] The General Assembly then voted to move its discussion of the Palestinian question to Geneva so the PLO chairman could attend. In an impassioned speech to the assembly on December 13, Arafat referred to the PNC's call for holding an international conference on the twin bases of Resolutions 242 and 338 and "the safeguarding of the legitimate national and political rights of the Palestinian people, foremost among which is its right to self-determination."[80]

Arafat's reiteration of the PNC language failed to persuade Secretary Shultz to reverse his judgment that the PLO still had not adequately met the 1975 conditions for talks. In a press conference the following day, however, Arafat spelled out the PLO's "acceptance of resolutions 242 and 338 as the basis for negotiations with Israel within the framework of an international conference." The PLO chairman also said that "we totally and absolutely renounce all forms of terrorism, including individual, group and state terrorism." At this point, Shultz finally relented. He declared in Washington that the United States was now "prepared for a substantive dialogue with PLO representatives."[81] Shultz also pointed out that the United States did not recognize the PNC's declaration of an independent Palestinian state. But the thirteen-year barrier to direct communication between the two sides had been breached, and U.S. Ambassador to Tunisia Robert Pelletreau opened talks with a PLO team there shortly afterward.

Conclusion

The above survey of Palestinian political developments in the period from early 1985 through December 1988 shows the continued relevance of PLO decision makers to the course of the Palestinian movement and the Israeli-Palestinian conflict.

Arafat, Wazir, and their supporters took what was in Palestinian terms a sizable political risk when they decided in November 1984 to split the movement in pursuit of their collaboration with King Hussein and the political base this allowed them in Jordan. By the summer of 1986, however, it seemed that, in overt political terms at least, they had led the loyalist part of the PLO into a dead end—they found themselves opposed by both Syria and Jordan, deeply embattled in Lebanon, and with key parts of the "legitimate" PLO coalition, including both the PFLP and DFLP, still in firm political opposition. It was at this stage that the Soviets played an important role—along with the Algerians and Libyans—in helping the loyalists put the traditional coalition back together again. The resident Palestinian activities also reportedly played a significant role in promoting these efforts through their contacts with the groups involved. By April 1987, the Palestinian (as opposed to strictly pro-Syrian) parts of the PLO coalition had been put together again, and the PLO groups were thus in a strong position to coordinate their actions when the Intifada broke out at the end of the year.

Inside the occupied territories, the years from 1985 through 1987 saw a continued bubbling of the Palestinian nationalist movement, which was spurred on by many factors, including the military administration's continued stifling of Palestinian political and economic processes, the economic squeeze between a faltering Israeli economy and the decrease in economic opportunity in the Gulf, and continued harassment by the militant Israeli settlers. Throughout this process of nationalist fermentation (which has yet to be adequately described), coalitions were forming and breaking between the various strands of the nationalist movement, including the various strands within Fatah (coordinated by Wazir), the PFLP, DFLP, and communist networks, and the different groups of Islamic fundamentalists. But there was an increasingly clear consensus on opposition to Jordan, which hardened after Hussein broke with the PLO in 1986. The different networks in the territories were meanwhile finding new ways of working together, and their effectiveness would be clearly demonstrated from December 1987 on.

The eruption of the Intifada and its institutionalization throughout 1988 had a profound impact both on relations between the Palestinian movement and other relevant actors and on the balance within the movement.

The first results of the Intifada on relations between the Palestinians and the Arab states were to strengthen the political power of the PLO leadership in its dealings with the Arab regimes. This effect was most pronounced with respect to Jordan but was also discernible with respect to Egypt and Syria. In the case of Jordan, King Hussein had spent the two years prior to December 1987 competing with the PLO for influence in the West Bank and, to a lesser extent, in the Palestinian diaspora. After the eruption of the Intifada, he moved rapidly toward a posture of renouncing responsibility for the West Bank that was formalized effectively in July 1988. The eruption of the Intifada almost immediately forced Syria's clients in the Palestinian movement to mute or at least soften their rhetorical attacks against the PLO leadership, and by April 1988, the Syrian government was finally forced to move at least partway toward a reconciliation with Arafat. In the case of Egypt, the Intifada pressured President Mubarak to redouble his efforts to convene an international Mideast peace conference with PLO participation. His persuasion was reportedly one of the key factors in Secretary Shultz's reactivation of his Mideast diplomacy in the spring of 1988.

For the Arab states as a whole, the Amman summit of November 1987 had relegated the Palestinian issue, and with it the PLO, to the margins of Arab concern. The outbreak of the Intifada abruptly reversed that trend. Iraq's achievement of successive battlefield victories over Iran and finally of a cease-fire agreement with Iran in August 1988 substantially assuaged Arab fears over the situation in the Gulf that had dominated the Amman summit and freed up correspondingly more Arab attention for the Palestinian question.

The Intifada succeeded in moving the Palestinian issue to the top of the political agenda in Israel. But it still was not clear in 1988 whether this could be expected to bring any rapid political gain for the Palestinians, or whether it might lead instead to a long-term hardening of Israeli attitudes against the Palestinians. Certainly, the Israeli general elections of November 1988 revealed some confusion in Israeli public attitudes over the Palestinian issue. Neither of the major blocs, Labor or Likud, was able to obtain a plurality of the votes, and in late December 1988 they formed a new coalition in which the policy on the Palestinian issue was still left intentionally undefined.

It was in the field of relations with the United States that, by the end of 1988, the Intifada had been able to register its most significant political gains to date. In its early months, the Intifada succeeded in activating a level of sustained American diplomatic engagement on the Israeli-Palestinian issue that had not been seen since the flurry of efforts to get the Camp David autonomy talks off the ground in 1979. Indeed, it could be argued that the three visits Secretary Shultz made to the region in the spring and summer of 1988 exceeded the commitment to Arab-Israeli peacemaking of any secretary of state since Henry Kissinger's shuttle diplomacy of 1973–74. In the end, though, Shultz's visits to the region were most important not for any immediate achievements they may have registered but because they set the stage for the most important Palestinian-American diplomatic breakthrough—the fine-tuned diplomacy that brought the PLO leadership and the U.S. government to the point of being able to resume direct contact in December 1988.[82] On both the U.S. and the PLO sides, the momentum pushing that diplomacy to a successful conclusion stemmed primarily from the new political environment created by the Intifada.

Some of the most significant long-term results of the Intifada, however, were those created within the Palestinian movement itself. The ability of the resident Palestinians to sustain their challenge to the occupation revealed the degree to which they now set the agenda for the entire national movement. The resident activists remained unanimous in their avowal that only the PLO leadership could represent them at the national level, but to an unprecedented degree they now found themselves able to dictate the direction PLO policy should take. This would not necessarily result in a softening in the PLO's position. Throughout the middle months of 1988, the residents appar-

ently did have a moderating effect on the content of the PLO leaderships's policy, but by the end of the year, there were some indications
that the communications coming to the leadership from the residents
were more in the direction of limiting the leaders' political moderation.

Regardless of changing nuance in the content of the communications from the resident Palestinians to the leadership, the major effect
of the Intifada was to ensure that the importance of these communications could no longer be downgraded by the PLO leaders as had
sometimes been the case before December 1987. These communications also resulted in the PLO giving more serious consideration than
ever before to the new tactics introduced into the movement by the
residents.

Ever since the 1969 takeover of the PLO by the militants of Fatah
and the other Palestinian guerrilla groups, these groups' concept of
armed struggle had constituted a cornerstone of PLO policy. But
already, in the very early weeks of the Intifada, the PLO Executive
Committee had taken a decision that armed struggle was *not* to be used
as part of the Intifada.[83] This decision was reportedly taken after full
consideration of the views of the organizers of the resident wing of
the movement. And its observance throughout 1988 was near total
even though it was generally assumed that a number of Palestinian
activists in the occupied areas had access to caches of secret weapons.
There was apparently only one occasion during the first thirteen
months of the Intifada in which a Palestinian *initiated an armed attack
against an Israeli*—this was when an IDF soldier on patrol was shot
dead in Bethlehem in March 1988.[84]

Virtually none of the resident activists was prepared to issue a public
and comprehensive renunciation of the PLO's traditional strategy of
armed struggle. But the residents clearly played a great role in winning
the Executive Committee's endorsement of the curtailment of the
applicability of armed struggle in their particular case. And as the
Intifada progressed, their communications helped to push the leadership toward the policy enunciated gropingly at the Algiers PNC and
then more unambiguously at the Arafat press conference in Geneva
in December, when "all forms of terrorism" were explicitly renounced.

As explained by Arafat in February 1989, this formulation included
a ban on all attacks against civilian targets anywhere, as well as attacks
against any military targets outside of Israeli-held areas.[85] The official
formulation would still seem to imply (at least at some theoretical level)
PLO approval of armed attacks against military targets in Israel and
the occupied territories. But the tactical decision not to use arms in
the Intifada had been taken in its early weeks and held firm throughout

1988. Some of Fatah's colleagues from other PLO member groups such as the PFLP and DFLP did try even after the Geneva declaration to mount armed raids against Israeli targets from across the demarcation line in South Lebanon. But the Israeli-backed South Lebanese army was able to block each of these attempts well north of the border with Israel so it remained unclear what or where their intended targets were, and Israeli military intelligence reported in early 1989 that Fatah itself had not attempted any such raids following the Geneva declaration.

Even after the end of 1988, it remained unclear whether the political initiative launched by the PLO in the latter months of that year would succeed in its aim of bringing Israel to a negotiation that would result in a substantial Israeli pullback from the occupied areas and the establishment of a Palestinian state from the areas vacated. But it was clear by year's end that the successful institutionalization of the Intifada had created—for all the actors involved—a new political environment that precluded any easy or quick return to the status quo ante. The Intifada had important consequences for any analysis of Palestinian political developments. It completely changed the political questions that were most pertinent concerning the Palestinian movement, primarily by shifting the constituency of resident Palestinians to the center stage of national politics. No longer would the central questions concerning Palestinian politics be those centered on the politics of the diaspora—which of the alphabet soup of Palestinian exile groups was up or down at any moment, which of the Arab regimes was supporting or opposing the PLO leadership at any particular point, and so on. The newly central questions would be those that focused, in the first instance, on political trends among the resident Palestinian constituency, and second, on relations between the resident spearhead of the movement and exile institutions, including the PLO leadership.

At the end of 1988, the degree of national unity and discipline within the resident constituency remained high, a significant tribute to the organizing abilities of the underground activists and the man who had trained many of them, Khalil Wazir. The degree of coordination between the residents and the PLO leadership also seemed effective because the Israelis were unable to find any way to achieve the aim revealed by several of their national leaders of splitting the resident Palestinians away from their loyalty to the exile leadership.

If these judgments seemed valid at the end of 1988, whether and how long they would remain so would continue to be a function of the complex, many-faceted interaction between the Palestinians and their Israeli neighbors/occupiers. The major achievement of the Palestinian nationalists was that, for the moment at least, they had brought this interaction unambiguously to the top of the agenda for both national communities.

Notes

1. Helena Cobban, *The Palestinian Liberation Organization: People, Power and Politics* (New York: Cambridge Univ. Press, 1984), p. 257.

2. This methodology is not entirely satisfactory, primarily because the history of the clandestine resistance groups inside the occupied areas remains to be clearly written. But as of December 1988, it is the best I can achieve.

3. For details of this session, see *Keesings Contemporary Archives* (London: Longmans, annual), 31 (1985):33492–94.

4. For details of the provenance of these groups, see Cobban, *Palestine Liberation Organization*, chap. 7.

5. See *FBIS:ME*, Nov. 26, 1984, p. A-17.

6. For this text, the list of Executive Committee members, and the text of the political statement endorsed at the PNC, see ibid., Nov. 30, 1984, pp. A-1–A-5.

7. See *Keesings* 31 (1985):33495.

8. For the text of the agreement as published by the Jordanian government later that month, see "Hikmat Releases 'Text' of PLO-Jordanian Agreement," on Amman Radio, Feb. 23, 1985 (*FBIS:ME*, Feb. 25, 1985, p. F-1).

9. See *Keesings* 31 (1985):33494. The Jordanian text referred to "an Arab confederation (*ittihad konfidirali 'arabi*) that is intended to be established between the two states of Jordan and Palestine" (see "Hikmat Releases 'Text' " (1985).

10. *Keesings* 31 (1985):34075.

11. Ibid.

12. Ibid., p. 34076. This *Keesings* account remains open to some question, however, because U.S. officials subsequently made clear that Nabil Sha'th, one of those *Keesings* said was acceptable in Washington, was not in fact, and the "Mr. Sbeigh" referred to by *Keesings* is hard to track down. Possibly, it is a reference to Palestine Central Council member Hasib Sabbagh, a banker and personal acquaintance of George Shultz.

13. *Facts on File*, 1985, p. 645.

14. The events of October 1985 are usefully summarized in *Keesings* 31 (1985):34076–78.

15. See ibid, p. 34078.

16. Ibid., p. 34079.

17. Ibid.

18. The full text of the speech is in *FBIS:ME*, Feb. 20, 1986, pp. F-1–16. The quote is on p. 16.

19. Atallah had started his military career in the Jordanian army but defected to the PLO during the fierce Jordanian-PLO fighting in September 1970.

20. See *Keesings* 31:(1985):34899.

21. The totals for the West Bank and Gaza come from Meron Benvenisti, *1986 Report* (Jerusalem: West Bank Data Base Project, 1986), p. 1. The East

Jerusalem figure is extrapolated backward from the figure given in Benvenisti's *1987 Report* (Jerusalem: West Bank Data Base Project, 1987), p. 1.

22. Benvenisti, *1987 Report*, p. 40. Benvenisti is not absolutely consistent in the categories he uses or even in the figures he gives for the same event in different editions of his *Report*, but the increase from 1982 onward is very evident.

23. Benvenisti, *1986 Report*, p. 63.

24. Ibid., p. 74. For further details of these events, see also *Keesings* 31 (1985):34010–12.

25. See *Keesings* 31 (1985):34011.

26. Figures from Benvenisti, *1987 Report*, p. 40.

27. See *Keesings* 31 (1985): 34011, 32 (1986): 34966.

28. The town's previous mayor had been Bassam Shakaa, both of whose legs were blown off by the Jewish underground in 1980. He was removed from office by the military government in March 1982, and since then Nablus had been controlled directly by an Israeli official.

29. See *Keesings* 32 (1986):34967.

30. See ibid., pp. 34967–68.

31. *Al-Fajr/Newsweek* poll report, pp. 2–5.

32. Mohammed Shadid and Rick Seltzer, "Political Attitudes of Palestinians in the West Bank and Gaza Strip," *Middle East Journal* 42 (Winter 1988):31.

33. Benvenisti, *1987 Report*, p. 40.

34. See ibid., p. 42. Benvenisti notes, "Official figures put the number of Palestinians killed during 1987 at 22, compared with 8 in 1986." This report was published before the sharply increased killing rates associated with Palestinian uprising, which started in December 1987, could be registered. Indeed, in this report, when Benvenisti quotes Israeli statistics directly, he generally defines 1986 as the year April 1985 through March 1986 and 1987 as the year April 1986 through May 1987, which makes accurate counting and comparison difficult.

35. Ibid., pp. 43–44. In an interview published in May 1988, Yasser Arafat dated the start of the Intifada in the occupied territories to October 24, 1986 (*FBIS:ME*, May 18, 1988, p. 5).

36. Benvenisti, *1987 Report*, pp. 41–44.

37. Observations from the summer of 1987 are culled from the author's visit to Israel and the occupied territories in July 1987.

38. Conversation with Hanna Siniora, Jerusalem, July 1987.

39. See "Chronology," *Middle East Journal* 41 (Autumn 1987):587.

40. See *Keesings* 33:(1987):34900.

41. Ibid., p. 35344.

42. For details of Lebanese-level developments, see ibid., pp. 35344–45.

43. The Syrians could have learned a lesson from what happened to their supporters inside the Palestinian refugee camps in Lebanon a decade earlier, after Syrian and surrogate forces attacked the camps in July 1976. See Cobban, *Palestinian Liberation Organization*, p. 72.

44. See *Keesings* 33:(1987) 35408–9.

45. *FBIS: Soviet Union*, Apr. 28, 1987, p. H-14.

46. For the lists of both the Executive Committee and the PLO Central Council members, see *FBIS:ME*, Apr. 27, 1987, pp. A-5 – 6. In June 1987, the two wings of the PLF reunited.

47. Ibid., p. A-8.

48. Ibid., p. A-9.

266 HELENA COBBAN

49. *FBIS:ME*, Nov. 9, 1987, p. 14.

50. For the report about the dinner boycott, see *FBIS:ME*, Nov. 10, 1987, p. 24. For the text of Klibi's statement, see ibid., Nov. 13, 1987, pp. 8–9.

51. Ibid., Nov. 16, 1987, p. 7–8.

52. This conclusion, common in Washington in November 1987, was also admitted to in retrospect by Shimon Peres's aide, Yossi Beilin, when he spoke at the Brookings Institution in February 1988.

53. See "Chronology," *Middle East Journal* 42 (Winter 1988):83–85.

54. "Chronology," ibid., 42 (Spring 1988): 273–75.

55. Ze'ev Schiff, "The Surprise and the Responsibility," *Ha'aretz*, Feb. 5, 1988, pp. A-1, 7 (*FBIS:ME*, Feb. 9, 1988, p. 37).

56. See the accounts of this incident in the *New York Times* and the *Washington Post*, Dec. 19, 1987. Written accounts of this incident, at which these two reporters apparently were not present, were sketchy, but television footage of it appeared to show worshipers tossing a smoking gas grenade back out of the Haram's al-Aqsa Mosque.

57. For accounts of the early days of the Intifada, see "Chronology," *Middle East Journal* 42 (Spring 1988): 275–77; *Facts on File, 1987*, pp. 927, 945–46, 967.

58. See *Facts on File, 1988*, pp. 2, 9, 27, 97–98.

59. See *FBIS:ME*, Jan. 15, 1988, pp. 3–4; Jan. 21, 1988, pp. 6–7.

60. *FBIS:ME*, Jan. 15, 1988, p. 4; Jan. 29, 1988, p. 11; Feb. 5, 1988, p. 3.

61. See ibid., Feb. 5, 1988, p. 4; Feb. 8, 1988, p. 3.

62. Tzvi Gilat, "The Leadership of the Uprising," *Hadashot* (Sabbath supplement), Feb. 12, 1988, pp. 35, 37 (*FBIS:ME*, Feb. 19, 1988, p. 30). There was some evidence that a different internal balance was in place in Gaza than in the West Bank.

63. Ibid., pp. 30–32 (*FBIS* pagination).

64. See *FBIS:ME*, Jan. 27, 1988, p. 30. Roni Shaqed of *Yedi'ot Aharonot*, stated that the suggested Palestinian delegation was to have thirteen members. Gilat, writing two weeks later, said that it would have had twelve members, "with an option to include two more." Gilat also listed who these should be (see Gilat, "Leadership of the Uprising," p. 33).

65. Text of Siniora and Abu Rahme memorandum handed to Shultz on January 27, 1988 as given to the author by Siniora. The Fourth Geneva Convention of August 12, 1949, prescribed conditions of fair and humane treatment for civilians in war, particularly those in areas of armed conflict or in enemy-occupied territory (J. A. S. Grenville and Bernard Wasserstein, *The Major International Treaties since 1945: A History and Guide with Texts* [London: Methuen, 1987], pp. 492–93).

66. Information from conversation with Hanna Siniora, Jerusalem, Apr. 1988.

67. For a partial account of this affair, see *Facts on File, 1988*, p. 140.

68. *Jerusalem Post* (daily), Apr. 10, 1988, pp. 1, 2.

69. *Facts on File, 1986*, p. 353.

70. For the names of those in the delegation, see Khalid Abu 'Akr, "Dutch Foreign Minister Meets with Palestinians," *al-Fajr* (Jerusalem), July 19, 1988 (*FBIS:NES-88-140*, July 21, 1988, p. 30).

71. For the text of the document, see Appendix L in William B. Quandt, ed., *The Middle East Ten Years after Camp David* (Washington, D.C.: Brookings Institution, 1988), pp. 490–93.

72. Joel Greenberg, "PLO Backers Endorse Abu Sharif Peace Bid," *Jerusalem Post,* July 28, 1988, pp. 1, 12 (*FBIS:NES 88-146,* July 29, 1988, p. 23).

73. See "King Husayn Speaks on 'Separation' from West Bank," in *FBIS:-NES-88-147,* Aug. 1, 1988, pp. 39–41.

74. Sari Nuseibeh, "A Call for a Discussion of the Stages of the Intifada and Its Horizons," *Al-Yawm al-Sabi'* (Paris), Aug. 1, 1988, p. 18.

75. Mahir Abu Khatir, "Academic Favors Declaration of Statehood," *al-Fajr* (Jerusalem), English ed., Aug. 14, 1988, pp. 16, 13 (*FBIS:NES-88-160,* Aug. 18, 1988, p. 26).

76. *FBIS:NES-88-220,* Nov. 15, 1988, p. 10.

77. *Al-Fajr,* English ed., Nov. 21, 1988, pp. 3, 14. The text broadcast by the Baghdad Voice of the PLO in Arabic at 1952 GMT on November 15 apparently failed to mention resolutions 242 and 338 at this point. See *FBIS:NES-88-221,* Nov. 16, 1988, p. 4; see *FBIS:NES-88-222,* Nov. 17, 1988, pp. 4–5, for a comparison of the Baghdad text and that published in *al-Ra'y* (Amman) on November 16, which did include the reference to the two resolutions.

78. Alan Cowell, "Arafat Urges U.S. to press Israelis to Negotiate Now," *New York Times,* Nov. 16, 1988, pp. A1, A10.

79. Robert Pear, "Shultz's 'No' to Arafat," *New York Times,* Nov. 28, 1988, p. 1.

80. "Excerpts from Arafat's Address," *New York Times,* Dec. 14, 1988, p. A12.

81. "Arafat: 'We are committed to peace, We want to live in our Palestinian State and let live," *Washington Post,* Dec. 14, 1988, p. A40.

82. Other writers will most likely provide more details of these efforts in the years to come. Watch, in particular, for a work in preparation by William B. Quandt.

83. Information confirmed to the author by Yasser Arafat in a personal interview, Tunis, Feb. 1989.

84. There were other occasions when Palestinian activists took up arms against compatriots suspected of collaborating with the IDF; at least two incidents were reported in which seemingly crazed Palestinians ran amok with knives, killing Jewish civilians in Tel Aviv and Jerusalem; and the true facts of what happened during the Beita incident of April 1988 may never be known. Nevertheless, the truth of the judgment as stated in the text seems indisputable, and the significance of what it reveals about the resident Palestinian community's sense of self-discipline in the face of extremely trying circumstances should not be underestimated.

85. Definition as stated by Yasser Arafat, Tunis, Feb. 1989.

10

The Importance of Being Hussein
Jordanian Foreign Policy and Peace in the Middle East

Adam M. Garfinkle

Whether by historical accident or by an act of providence, a small, weak, and oilless country stands at the vortex of the Arab-Israeli conflict. Without the participation of the Hashemite Kingdom of Jordan, Israel cannot have peace, nor can the Palestinians achieve minimal national satisfaction as most of them define it. And without Jordan, or use of its territory, the Arabs cannot wage a conclusive war against Israel.

Yet Jordan has never been the fulcrum of war or peace; by itself it is too weak to be either. The regional reality of no war, no peace, is thus in part a function of Jordanian reality. But this reality is not very fungible; Jordan can neither force closure on the conflict by going to war nor can it serve as a driving force for peace because every one of its neighbors is either much richer or much stronger or both. Yet by dint of geography, demography, and economic dependency, Jordan cannot absent itself from the Arab-Israeli conflict either, tactical feints to the contrary notwithstanding. King Hussein must keep trying against the odds, for the Arab-Israeli conflict is as dangerous to Jordan as it is to Israel.

King Hussein is a flexible man in an inflexible situation; no amount of pragmatism can lead Jordan out of its labyrinth without considerable help from other, improbable, sources. Although tactical feints such as those of July and August 1988 may occasionally suggest the opposite, Hussein must keep trying against the odds because the Arab-Israeli conflict is as dangerous to Hashemite Jordan as it is to Israel. An active Jordanian role is thus a necessary but not a sufficient condition for a Middle East peace. Jordan may be weak and dependent— certainly too weak by itself to deliver an Arab peace constituency—but that does not make it unimportant. Even great ships, after all, are steered by small rudders. Within a generally constrained situation, Jordan has options with important implications.

Inherent Constraints of Jordanian Policy

There are real constraints on what a small, nearly landlocked country with 3 million people can do. Jordan's situation is such that its foreign and domestic policies are functions of each other in such a way as to produce generally cautious, reactive, and incremental behaviors. Even actions that appear to be bold, such as Jordan's formal severing of its ties to the West Bank in July 1988, are not all that they seem. These constraints are a consequence of three related conditions. The first concerns the crucial relationship between the ruling Hashemite hierarchy and Jordan's largely Palestinian demography, a relationship that influences most if not all of Jordan's important public policy choices. The second revolves around Jordan's economic well-being, which still depends overwhelmingly on external subventions of various sorts. The availability of these subventions influences Jordan's internal political stability, for money is a powerful sociopolitical palliative in managing the domestic Hashemite-Palestinian nexus. The third concerns Jordan's internal and external security problems, which are largely defined and often exacerbated by the first condition and whose easement is financed through the second.

Jordanian policy since the creation of the state of Israel and the flow of Palestinians into the East Bank has sought to control and integrate Palestinians within the Hashemite realm. Unlike other Arab host countries, which were able to isolate and manipulate their Palestinian refugee populations, Jordan had little choice but to bend under their political and demographic weight lest it break from it. Because of its perilous demographic balance, Jordan takes a keen interest in a solution that precludes a fully independent Palestinian state. Jordan's core political interest in the Palestinian problem has thus been qualitatively different from that of all other Arab states with significant Palestinian populations; like Israel, the Hashemites view radical Palestinian nationalism as a mortal threat, whereas for other Arab states it falls somewhere between a nuisance and a challenge.

Before 1967 Jordan could not, and did not, depart from the rhetorical Arab consensus against Israel, even as it developed a working private modus vivendi with Israel. Hussein encouraged the Palestinians to focus their political aspirations on Palestine and identified symbolically with those aspirations even as he ensured through the creation of a crack internal security force that Palestinian paramilitary activities would not drag Jordan into combat with Israel. Most important, Hussein tried to get as many Palestinians as possible into the mainstream economy, to give them a concrete stake in the Jordanian status quo in hopes that a modicum of political loyalty would follow, and to move the country, especially the East Bank, toward economic self-sufficiency. In other words, the regime sought to Jordanianize the Palestinians.[1]

Between Hussein's ascendancy to the throne in 1953 and June 1967, the regime made much progress in this regard. Many Palestinians, including those in the East Bank, made comfortable lives for themselves within the Hashemite framework, particularly the roughly 30 percent who never lived in refugee camps.[2] Even for these Palestinians, however, being a Jordanian still required an act of political schizophrenia, and pretending that the Palestinians' stay in Jordan and their Jordanian citizenship were temporary became ever more difficult.[3] But hypocrisy is often the advanced wave of a new truth, and that was exactly the developing logic of the Palestinian situation in Jordan before the Six-Day war.

The 1967 war brought another two hundred thousand non-Jordanianized Palestinians into a truncated Hashemite realm, and Hussein was nearly back to square one. Having lost the war and the West Bank, he was in a poor political and poorer financial condition to get up off the mat. He almost did not get up. The transformation of the Palestine Liberation Organization after the war led before long to a PLO state-within-a-state in Jordan and then to civil war in 1970.[4]

The civil war was testimony to two fundamental truths. First, it showed that the de facto abdication of Jordan from the battle against Israel carried a high domestic price, especially to the extent that a recrudescent Palestinian national movement undermined Jordan's claim to carry Palestinian interests. But second, the failure of most Palestinians in Jordan, especially those of the 1948–49 generation, to fight for the PLO but either to remain neutral or to support the king, showed that to some degree the Jordanianization process was irreversible. Seeking a formal peace with Israel through direct negotiations was thus out of the question for domestic reasons alone unless pursued in close ranks with Egypt and Syria—an unlikely prospect. Pursuing a war was dangerous for other reasons. But disengagement was impossible, too, if the Jordanianization process was to continue and if Jordan hoped to be left in relative peace by its Arab neighbors. So Jordan was too weak inside to make peace, too vulnerable outside to make war, and too dependent on forces beyond its control to ignore tendencies toward either.

Although the particulars have changed over time, King Hussein's essential predicament has not. Jordan's situation still leads it to seek the maximum feasible Arab consensus so that Jordan does not have to choose enemies, or so that its enemies (especially, on occasion, Syria) do not choose it, using the Palestinian issue as a bludgeon. It leads Jordan to hope for financial stability and prosperity, for the more money that rolls through Jordan, the faster and the deeper the Jordanianization process can proceed, the more robust a deterrent military position it can maintain, and the larger an extended patronage network Jordan can afford in the West Bank. And it leads Jordan to oppose the recourse to war and ideological polarization, for the former leads it into the sharp teeth of the Israeli Defense Force and the latter leads it toward conflict with Palestinians and their allies outside, and still potentially inside, the kingdom. This is why, if there has to be a PLO, Jordan prefers Yasser Arafat to George Habash—not because Jordan and the PLO share any important long-range goals[5] but because Arafat is neither doctrinaire nor an organizational Leninist. This is why, if there has to be an Israel, Hussein prefers Labor to Likud, not only or perhaps even primarily because Labor wants to make peace by trading territory for a treaty but because it shares a pragmatic interest in assisting at least some Jordanian desiderata on the West Bank and because its policies do not threaten to foist ever more unJordanianized Palestinians across the river into Jordan.

The Jordanian Option and Its Discontents

This does not mean that the "Jordanian option"—defined generally as solving the bulk of the Arab-Israeli conflict by returning the greater part of the West Bank (and Gaza for the first time) to effective Jordanian control in return for a peace treaty—is impossible or that the king does not desire it. Assertions that the regime does not ever want to regain the West Bank, albeit under new conditions, because it does not wish to be saddled once again with too many angry, antimonarchical Palestinians are false. There are times when conveying the opposite impression helps the king manage his short-term problems and serve his longer-range objectives. But, in truth, Hussein wants the West Bank back, and for good reason. The Jordanian option in one version or another, if properly executed, is the only way that Jordan can free itself from the enervating contest with Israel, establish lasting comity with the Palestinians in its midst and reduce the danger posed by those outside, and have good relations with the United States all at once.

But, clearly, there are ways of pursuing a Jordanian option that could bring regional war and subversion from his better-armed and wealthier neighbors and civil war and chronic insurrection from his own still marginal Palestinian population. The king's interest in some formulation of the Jordanian option is conditional on a few key regional and domestic political factors.

First, Jordan needs a representative, legitimate Palestinian partner in this endeavor. Second, the king needs a supportive regional environment; at least he needs the absence of a conclusive veto from any stronger neighbor, namely Syria. Third, Hussein needs a political combination in Israel receptive to a Jordanian option; and, fourth, he needs the competent brokerage of the United States to consummate the deal. He needs not only some of these conditions but probably all of them simultaneously. Insofar as it is able, that is what Jordanian diplomacy aims to produce.

Most important is the Palestinian key. If the king is ever to sign an agreement that does not recover all of the occupied territories, he must have enough credibly representative Palestinians to accept part of the onus or he invites both his grandfather's fate and another civil war. Some analysts believe that Hussein has striven since the denouement of the Lebanon war in 1982, if not since his federation plan of March 1972, to coax or force real moderation from Fatah, believing that a combination of failure, fatigue, and fear would ultimately deliver Arafat to abandoning the PLO Charter and the ambition of either a fully independent Palestinian state or the regaining of Palestine beyond the West Bank and Gaza. Others have argued that Arafat could never do such a thing and that the king never expected him to, for the cadres he represents do not covet the West Bank but instead think of their home as being the Galilee and the towns of the coastal plain in Israel proper. If Arafat capitulated to such a compromise, epitomized by U.N. Security Council Resolution 242, he could not bring much of the PLO with him; instead, he would be replaced by someone in tune with the core PLO constituency that has never been to the West Bank and does not wish to go there.

Thus the series of negotiations between Hussein and Arafat in the years between the war in Lebanon and the outbreak of the Intifada were designed from the Jordanian point of view either to get Arafat to say yes and then proceed to a U.S.-brokered settlement on the basis of a Jordanian-Fatah political condominium, or designed to force Arafat to say no, the better for the king to recruit an alternative Palestinian political voice, a third force, from among the Palestinians of the occupied territories, to the same general end. Before December 1988, Arafat did not conclusively do one thing or the other.

Clearly, the eventual success of a Jordanian option would not finally end the Arab-Israeli conflict, and Jordan's problems with it, as long as significant sectors within Palestinian nationalism aim at recovering Israel proper. The king knows this, but precisely because Palestinian nationalism is a long-term, potentially lethal problem for the Hashemites, it requires a long-term strategy. Since the 1930s, the Hashemites have allied with those Palestinians willing to live with them and fought those who were not. Pursuing and especially achieving a Jordanian option is risky business, but the alternative is passivity and that is risky, too. Jordan's genuine exit from the conflict could mean losing the battle with the PLO in the West Bank and thus potentially empowering an irredentism strong enough to undo the Hashemite realm for good on the East Bank.

From the vantage point of the early 1990s, it seems clear that at points of maximum PLO weakness after 1982, Hussein entertained the first possibility—of getting Arafat to say yes—even while planning for the second, hoping to mix and match those he could entice away from Fatah with remaining pro-Jordanian forces in the West Bank. Perhaps Hussein concluded that the power of the third force in the territories would in turn deliver Arafat, lest he lose his most important future constituency. Perhaps he believes it still. The evidence suggests that between 1984 and the summer of 1988, the king pursued the latter option in a slow, patient, protracted strategy, the maximal aim of which was the Jordanian option without the PLO, the more relevant minimal aim of which was to maintain as much leverage as possible in the territories against any change in the status quo there. After the summer of 1988, the king's strategy was designed to force decisions and divisions in the PLO, push the PLO toward a West Bank constituency, watch how things turned out, and then judge what to do next.

Thus Jordanian policy between 1982 and 1988 was both ambitious for the longer term and defensively self-protective in the near term. Hussein knew that he was not loved in the West Bank and that much had changed in the last two decades. He clearly understood the symbolic power of the PLO there, especially after the Intifada. Yet the king also knew that in Middle East politics it is more important to be needed than to be loved and that other things had changed very little. There is an enduring logic in the Jordanian option: the road through Amman is the only way for the Palestinians in the occupied territories to end the Israeli occupation. Because of both Israeli and U.S. views of the problem, the king knows that he is the only game in town for any practical purpose. He has hoped that a conjunction of conditions— the weakness of the PLO and fears of irreversible or de jure Israeli annexation being the two most important—will one day convince the residents of the territories to turn to him at least in part for salvation and that when they do he will be able to seize the symbolic mantle of the PLO—and perhaps Arafat himself—to sanctify the procedure. By forcing the PLO to put up or shut up in the territories by "giving" it responsibility for them in July 1988, the king hoped to bring this day closer.

In the meantime, Jordan had other problems. One was Syria. Aside from the potential veto that Syria held over the peace process, it sat on the wrong side of the Gulf war and Arab politics in general. It also sat on the wrong side of superpower politics, bringing Soviet weapons, agents, and influence perilously close to Jordan. The way Damascus manipulated internal divisions in Lebanon both before and after 1982 stood as a sobering object lesson of what it might be able to do to Jordan if it ever succeeded in conquering and deploying the Palestinian national movement under its aegis.

Money was a problem, too. By the end of 1983, it was clear that the oil boom was over, at least for a while. Meanwhile, the increased urbanization, the dislocation of Jordan's real estate and financial markets, the huge trade deficit whetted by burgeoning appetites for imports—all a function of Jordan's go-between role in the oil economy—had stimulated new problems, including fundamentalist Islam, that required money to solve. These problems were revealed in the April 1989 riots that engulfed southern Jordan and by the results of the November 8, 1989, parliamentary elections.

The Gulf war and the problem of Iran, too, ranked higher in the Jordanian calculus of danger between 1982 and early 1988 than any aspect of the Arab-Israeli conflict. If Iraq had crumbled, Iranian power would have moved to Jordan's eastern frontier probably in the guise of a revolutionary, Iranian-allied Shi'a state. Fear of such a development explains in large part Jordan's ardent support for Iraq, its enthusiasm for reintegrating Egypt into the Arab domain, and its unbounded frustration with the Reagan administration over its gift of weapons to Jordan's new nemesis. That the United States has not only failed to arm Jordan adequately, as solemnly promised by the executive branch, was bad enough. But sending some of the very ordnance to Iran that had been denied to Jordan—including Hawk missiles—and then failing to get anything in return for them, was simply maddening to the Jordanians. They did not know whether to be humiliated at having such a naive and guileless ally or angry at having such a perfidious and feckless one.

Withal, the United States is still very important to Jordan; it is its protector of last resort. Jordan has a pledge, dating from November 1967 and repeated often since, of U.S. support for Jordanian recovery of the West Bank.[6] Jordan has a pledge of U.S. support for what is left of Jordan's territorial integrity short of that. The United States arms Jordan in the main, even though the king has purchased hardware from Western European countries and some weapons from the Soviet

Union. The U.S. and Jordanian militaries meet yearly, alternatively in the United States and in Jordan, and the respective intelligence agencies have good working relations. On another level, U.S. financial support for the United Nations affects whether Jordan gets a full or a half-full allotment of money from the United Nations Relief and Works Agency (UNRWA), which has been and remains important to Jordan's economy—up to $80 million per year. The Agency for International Development, too, has a large staff in Amman and does work deemed valuable by the government.

The point is that, as with Jordanian policy toward the PLO and assorted Palestinians, and toward Syria, Jordanian policy toward the United States has both proximate and more remote agendas, some of which concern the Arab-Israeli conflict and the peace process and some of which do not. Not all Jordanian policies are designed to achieve the political millennium. This situation is normal, natural, and inevitable given Jordan's circumstances; only the fishbowl-like obsession of many American observers with the so-called peace process obscures this simple truth.

The Jordanian-PLO Dialogue Before the Intifada

The best laboratory to watch the interplay of Jordan's foreign policy interests and constraints is that of the Jordanian-PLO dialogue that has been going on intermittently for many years. Not only does it shed light on Jordan's central political and diplomatic dilemmas, but it engages all other regional actors in one way or another, as well as peace brokers and would-be peace brokers on the international level.

The long-standing Hashemite effort alternatively to coopt and to weaken the Palestinian national movement is a carrot-and-stick methodology, with Jordan both identifying with Palestinian ambitions and encouraging them and simultaneously pressuring the Palestinian leadership away from independent paths and toward Jordanian influence, if not control. The regulating mechanism that often determines whether Jordan chooses the boot or the glove is the shape of regional politics. Jordan and Syria have competed for influence over the PLO in recent times; the weaker the PLO, the heavier the competition. Because Jordan and Syria do not see the same future, have different regional interests, and move in different superpower orbits, the PLO can usually survive this competition. On those rare occasions when Syrian-Jordanian relations have been good, the PLO has had real trouble.

Between the Lebanon war and the outbreak of the Intifada, there were four full oscillations in this basic pattern. First, Jordan's effort to seize or divide the PLO gained some success between late 1982 and

April 1983, when both the PLO and Syria were weakened by the war in Lebanon. Second, Syria struggled successfully against the Jordanian campaign, not by enticing the PLO toward it but by threatening it; the PLO stood in perilous, dispersed limbo from late 1983 and throughout much of 1984. Third, the PLO's isolation and dispersion, combined with Syrian antagonism, led it back toward Jordan, starting tentatively in mid-1984 and accelerating into 1985. Intense Jordanian-PLO jockeying for position continued for nearly two years, yielding apparent agreement and then retrenchment, while Syrian opposition stuttered because of its deep involvement in Lebanon and the failure of its Abu Musa faction to develop any real Palestinian constituency. Fourth, starting in late 1985, and hitting its stride in February 1986, Jordan commenced simultaneously an intensive anti-PLO campaign and an entente with Syria, both of which lasted into the spring of 1988, after which the Intifada's general effects engulfed regional politics.

In April 1988, false signs of a fifth phase emerged briefly, when Arafat traveled to Syria in the wake of the political funeral in Damascus of Khalil Wazir. But a PLO-Syrian reconciliation did not occur; indeed, quite the reverse took place—another war of the camps, the scene for which was again the shanties and refugee camps of Lebanon. King Hussein again strove to take advantage of PLO-Syrian enmity and the Intifada to challenge the PLO while it was weak and divided; Syria had again bloodied it and the Intifada threatened to marginalize it. Although circumstances differed, the fifth phase looked a lot like the third in many ways. I will discuss these phases in turn.

Phase One: 1982–1983

The Lebanese war reshaped the local constellation of power in the Arab East. Israel's Likud leaders had so intended it; their aim was to destroy the PLO in Beirut, the better to work their will in the West Bank. Ariel Sharon, in particular, sought a pliant, Christian Lebanon, a Jewish Greater Israel and, most portentous of all, a "Palestinian" Jordan. The scheme was misconceived and failed grandly. Lebanon did not become pliant or Christian; it became, and remains, ghoulishly chaotic, ever more vulnerable to Syrian penetration, and its warring religious groups are internally divided. A Jewish Greater Israel was always, and remains, beyond the prudent reach of Israeli capabilities. Finally, the ultimate irony: the war did evoke moderation in the West Bank, not for Israel's version of autonomy but for a renewed Jordanian role, precisely the sort of moderation Likud leaders most feared and Jordanian leaders most sought.

The Lebanon war frightened West Bankers, as well it should have. With the final Israeli withdrawal from Sinai in April 1982, many of them vaguely expected some progress toward peace on their behalf. Instead they bore witness to war in Lebanon, an "iron fist" in the territories, and then Sabra and Shatilla. Fear gathered into local pleadings to the PLO to allow King Hussein to take the lead in ending the occupation before it was too late. The September 1982 U.S. Reagan plan, which highlighted anew the Jordanian role, provided the framework of hope at that time. With the loss of Lebanon as a base of operations, and mindful of these pleadings, Arafat endeavored to test the king's willingness to readmit the PLO to Jordan. Jordan's price was clear and steep: Arafat's head, politically speaking.

The war in Lebanon aided Jordan in the regional competition over the Palestinian movement in many ways. First, it dispersed the PLO away from areas in Lebanon controlled by Syria, and it weakened Syria itself. Second, the war did not radicalize the Palestinians or the Arab states, as many had predicted, but brought forth a moderation demonstrated in particular by the Fez plan of early September 1982. Seeing these developments, Egypt pursued its reintegration into the Arab world, and its first point of contact was Jordan. And third, American policy was reenergized, and U.S. energies always elevate the Jordanian role both because of the inertia of diplomatic formulas and geopolitical logic.

Jordan promoted these developments. The king encouraged the United States, professed to see compatibilities between the Reagan and Fez plans (although there were few), talked explicitly about Israel's right to exist, and tried to entice the PLO toward him. The king also asked his patrons on the West Bank to put pressure on the PLO, although they needed little encouragement.

Arafat saw the writing on the wall after his first eviction from Beirut and gravitated toward the conservative Arab states. From afar, Arafat started a quiet dialogue with King Hussein, pursuing the possibility of basing Fatah in Jordan. Arafat met in Amman with the king from October 8 to 12, 1982, and said nice things about the Reagan plan. At the same time, however, Arafat tried to reestablish himself in Lebanon. Arafat had less room to maneuver than he thought, for Syria, though bloodied, was determined not to bow to either Israeli, PLO, or American desiderata. Syria began mustering its Palestinian allies to ensure that Arafat would not dominate the next Palestine National Council meeting, and it succeeded. Fatah began splitting under Syrian pressure, and in this environment the price for a firm Jordanian ticket to a U.S.-brokered settlement was too much for too little as far as Arafat was concerned. But for lack of a choice, Arafat continued to test out the king, trying to secure both an operational base and a way into Washington as near to his own terms as possible.

Arafat wanted to hold the Palestine National Congress in Amman, and he visited the king in Amman in November and again in December 1982 to discuss that and other matters. PLO radicals wanted to hold the PNC session in Damascus instead. Arafat countered with Tunis. It ended up, in February 1983, in Algiers. In the meantime, based on his conversations with Arafat, the king came to Washington in December 1982 with hopeful things to say, and he persuaded the Reagan administration that there was a chance that he could finally land Arafat, now in his most desperate condition ever, over U.N. Security Council Resolution 242. But Syria increased its pressure on the PLO, on Jordan, and on the Americans in Lebanon. Palestinian moderates were threatened and intimidated, Jordanian diplomats suddenly began getting shot in Europe and India, and the U.S. Marines in Lebanon found themselves targets of Syrian Druze and Shi'a proxies. Not surprisingly, the PNC meeting undercut Arafat.

Arafat in turn sent mixed signals to the king: he wanted to continue the dialogue but stay away from Amman lest he stir the wrath of his enemies. But the king summoned him. Finally, Arafat showed up on March 31, 1983, and began a week of brutal talks with the king. Hussein demanded serious commitment to the peace process, which meant Resolution 242 and essentially the subsuming of most Palestinian political interests beneath Jordanian ones. Hussein promised a base in Amman in return but little else. Arafat came close to agreeing but in the end he did not. On April 10, 1983, the Jordanians lost patience and ended the matter. But Arafat came close enough to convince the Syrians to increase the pressure still further and, now that Arafat had alienated Jordan, who would oppose them?

Phase Two: 1983–1984

Arafat smelled the political wind, and on May 4, 1983, he turned up in Damascus for the first time in eight months. His meeting with Assad supposedly "turned a new page in Syrian-PLO relations"; all it really did was express joint opposition to U.S. efforts in Lebanon. Arafat did have another motive; much as he distrusted the Syrians, he still needed a base next to Israel. He had failed to get one from Hussein and hoped to secure Syrian acquiescence to his carving out a new one in Lebanon. In mid-May, Arafat reorganized his remaining forces in Lebanon and began wheeling and dealing again amid Lebanon's many factions. This abraded against Syrian interests in Lebanon, and it was then, taking full measure of Arafat's weakness, that the Fatah mutiny began with Syrian knowledge and aid.[7]

Between June and September 1983, the PLO was one of many factions in Lebanon. But when Israel vacated the Shouf in September

1983 and the PLO tried to fill part of the vacuum, the mutiny took a decidedly military turn. Arafat and his minions were soon besieged in Tripoli by rival PLO factions and the Syrian army. On December 20, 1983, Arafat's second expulsion from Lebanon landed him in Tunis, this time for an extended stay. On the way, however, Arafat stopped off in Cairo, partly to snub the Syrians, partly to impress the United States, and partly to explore differences in Egyptian and Jordanian attitudes against the onslaught from Amman that would surely come.

On balance, the Fatah mutiny was an opportunity for Jordan. Had Arafat capitulated to Syria and become a Syrian stooge, it might have stimulated new thinking and organizing among Palestinians inclined toward moderation. That did not happen. But if the mutiny had convinced Arafat to throw in his lot with Jordan, which would have meant adopting a genuinely moderate attitude toward a settlement, that would have been fine for Jordan, too. But Arafat knew that tying himself to the Jordanians, and through them to the United States and Resolution 242, would have meant at that time yet another intra-PLO civil war, as well as abandoning the charter and the PLO's oldest constituency. Just as important, Arafat must have realized that even if he signed on with the king Syria could still exercise a veto over the peace process and even kill him if need be. So Arafat came as close to the king for protective purposes as he could in 1983–84, but in the end he demurred; he refused to let the Syrians or the Jordanians put him into checkmate, even though he was forced to lose some pieces to both. Syria did achieve a lesser goal: the mutiny's limited success, combined with the overturning of the U.S.-brokered Israeli-Lebanese accord and helping drive U.S. military force out of Lebanon, helped Syria regain its regional strength after the Lebanon war.

As Arafat walked the tightrope after the mutiny, Jordan ingratiated itself further with the Palestinians of the West Bank, taking advantage of the new consciousness in the territories after the Lebanon war. Jordan sought to demonstrate renewed authority over the territories such as when, in March 1983, a military court sentenced a number of West Bankers to prison terms for cooperating with the Israeli "village league" scheme. Above all, Jordan sought to persuade West Bankers that they shared a community of interests with Jordan in opposing the Israeli occupation and stemming the demographic erosion of the area. Jordan also gave wide publicity to any positive statements about the Jordanian role made by prominent West Bankers. And the government spread rumors in the wake of the breakdown of Jordanian-PLO negotiations in April that it was considering the constitutional reformulation of Jordan solely on the East Bank, leaving West Bankers either to defend their own interests alone against Israel or depend on the PLO.[8] This was not a serious threat at the time, but it reminded the West Bankers of practical constraints and interests. It had the desired effect on the West Bank but a dolefully predictable effect in Damascus. Even as the Syrians were attacking Arafat in Lebanon, they were shooting Jordanian diplomats and setting off bombs in Amman on a regular basis. On November 5, while the battle of Tripoli raged, the king accused Syria of trying to subvert and terrorize his country. Of course, he was correct.

Phase Three: 1984–1985

The weakness of the PLO, promoted by Syria, nevertheless whetted Hussein's appetite despite Syrian pressures on Jordan. The king had failed to land Arafat in 1983, but he had denied him shelter, forcing the PLO back to Lebanon to be despoiled and massacred by Syria's Palestinian and Lebanese allies. The Fatah mutiny drove Arafat toward Hussein even as it failed to displace him from the PLO leadership, and Arafat was not long in coming around. Almost as soon as Arafat arrived in Tunis from Tripoli, he recommenced contact with Jordan. The mutiny had hurt him, more than ever he needed a base close to Israel, and Arafat feared the progress that Jordan was making at PLO expense in the territories. The king knew that Arafat was far from able to deliver the PLO to a Jordanian option, even had he wished to do so, but he could deliver himself qua symbol, and that would have been victory enough for the effort. And so the deadly game began again, with Arafat and Hussein needing each other for different, antithetical purposes, each one betting that in the end he would prevail. Arafat refused to capitulate to the king's renewed demands, but he wobbled. On January 2, 1984, from Tunis, Arafat called for the rejection of the Reagan plan and for PLO-Jordanian cooperation over the West Bank.

The Jordanians kept up the pressure. After the 1974 Rabat Summit, constitutional life had been suspended in Jordan lest the structure of parliament represent a Hashemite claim over the West Bank. But Jordan never altered its constitutional arrangement and on January 16, 1984, the king renewed parliament in its original form, clearly expressing renewed claims in the West Bank. At the opening meeting of the parliament, Hussein called on the PLO to adopt a "practical framework" for peace, that is, a Jordanian framework. A few days later, seven new West Bank delegate seats were filled—all by Hashemite Palestinian patrons.

The most concerted Jordanian effort to date to seize Arafat and bring him into a negotiation with Israel under American auspices took place during the early months of 1984. The king and his court put on a full press. While maintaining the formal sanctity of the Rabat Declaration, the Jordanians did everything in their power to undermine it. Pilgrimages of prominent Palestinians from the West Bank arrived in Amman to plead the king's case with Arafat, all arranged by the royal palace. Jordanian statements now referred to the PLO as the "legitimate representative of the Palestinian people," conspicuously dropping "sole." The press stressed that the West Bankers were the silent majority, the people who mattered most. The revival of parliament was discussed as a solely internal matter with an insistence so artificial as to convey the very opposite. Jordanians recalled aloud their doubts about Rabat, noting repeatedly that Rabat had failed to produce any positive result. They explained that for practical purposes they could not abandon the West Bank lest Israel be unopposed in all its designs. Jordanian officials said that the 1950 "free will" declaration of unity still pertained legally "until the liberation" and that there was no contradiction between the 1950 unity agreement on the one hand and an "independent" PLO role on the other. Finally the king spoke broadly of history, destiny, Arabdom, and the graves of his ancestors in Jerusalem and Gaza.[9]

Jordan also began activating the Egyptian dimension of its strategy. Osama al-Baz, a confidant of President Hosni Mubarak, declared Egyptian support for Jordan's views of a PLO-Jordanian strategy. In February 1984, in Washington, both Hussein and Mubarak pressed the United States to open direct talks with the PLO; the motive was to have additional pressure brought to deliver Arafat to Hussein on Jordan's terms. But Washington demurred; after what had happened in Lebanon, few top officials wanted anything to do with the Middle East. All this activity got the PLO's attention. Khalid al-Wazir was dispatched to Jordan in late January to arrange the resumption of the Jordanian-PLO dialogue and, on February 26, Arafat showed up again in Amman.

For much of March, Arafat and Hussein continued to circumnavigate each other. Arafat evidently thought he had more bargaining power than he did; he resisted the king, and the talks again failed to settle on the details of how a Jordanian-Palestinian delegation would be composed and how it would operate. In the king's calculation, the weight of the argument might be settled by the United States; perhaps what Washington could give or threaten to take away from the PLO would finally do the trick. But Washington soon proved to be a major source of disappointment to Jordan.

Jordan had long sought to make the Reagan administration understand that establishing American credibility in the eyes of all sides was crucial to starting negotiations. Hussein's litmus test was the U.S. ability to get the Israelis to stop building and expanding settlements in the territories. If he could not do that, his own credibility as protector of the West Bank would be undermined. If he could not get that, he could not promise Arafat anything because he could not be sure there would be anything to give. As the king saw it, the United States was obligated to reward Jordan for its pragmatism, opposition to violence, and avoidance of the Soviet Union, and to help it establish credibility in the West Bank and the resultant power that would bring over Arafat. Jordan's very weakness obligated Washington to speak its case if it really wanted peace. During his meeting with President Reagan in Washington on February 13, Hussein thought he had extracted firm promises directly from the president over a number of issues, but within a month Jordanian expectations were shattered.

First, despite direct promises to the contrary, the United States withdrew from Lebanon under Syrian and Iranian pressure. If the United States would not stick it out for Lebanon, what might Hussein expect Washington to do for Jordan?[10] Besides, the U.S. presence in Lebanon guaranteed poor U.S.-Syrian relations, and that enhanced the prospect that if the Syrians began to cause real trouble for Jordan, Washington would help face it down.

Second, an arms deal for Jordan, though proposed by the administration, quickly evoked congressional opposition. The president then made his appeal on Jordan's behalf to a Jewish audience, urging American Jews who wanted peace to support the arms deal. From an American perspective, this was a practical and logical move. But from Jordan's perspective, it was a hurtful humiliation.

Third, Hussein had promised Arafat that he could get the United States to bring pressure on Israel to allow West Bank delegates to travel to the next Palestine National Council meeting. Only with those delegates would Arafat have a chance to win permission for a nexus with Jordan. Hussein thought he had a direct promise on this matter. But Washington brought no pressure, and a private letter in early March iterated that it would bring none, forcing Hussein to admit to Arafat that he could not deliver the Israelis even on this point.

Fourth, and more damaging, a second letter from the White House contained a polite but firm refusal to support, or even not to veto, the king's own U.N. draft resolution condemning Israel's West Bank settlements as illegal. (Some weeks later the United States vetoed the resolution.) As one Jordanian official put it: "While Washington was demanding on the one hand that Jordan participate in the peace process, on the other hand the administration refused to help Hussein reestablish his authority with the Palestinians."[11] It was actually worse than that; to put it bluntly, the king did not trust the administration's basic competence. The Jordanians could see that high officials in Washington had not a clue as to the particulars of Jordan's tactics regarding Arafat and the West Bank and that the president's word was subject to rapid and complete reversal. Hussein did not have to tax his imagination to understand what such a condition would mean in the middle of a difficult, detailed, and discreet negotiation with Israel.

If that were not enough, parliamentary elections on March 12 revealed, surprisingly and frighteningly, the power of Islamic fundamentalism in Jordan. Moreover, an economic recession was at hand thanks to the softness of the oil market and Jordan's own maladroit economic management. There was a general social tension in the air, bad times standing in ugly contrast to great expectations. It was not a propitious moment for a major foreign policy gambit. So on March 14 the king bitterly denounced the United States, refusing to join direct negotiations under American auspices. The peace process ground to a clattering halt when the last marines left Lebanon.

Arafat and Hussein met again in Amman on May 3, 1984, and discussed plans to hold the PNC there in November. In the meantime, Arafat strove to mend fences with other PLO factions to ensure that there would *be* a PNC meeting with most everyone in attendance. To prepare for the meeting, Arafat was willing to make marginal and cosmetic concessions to his peers. The Jordanians understood perfectly. The summer and fall of 1984 also witnessed a major improvement in Jordanian-Egyptian relations, in part because of Jordanian fears about the Gulf war. Finally, on September 25, diplomatic relations between Jordan and Egypt were restored—the first Arab restoration since Camp David. President Mubarak soon visited Jordan, and in May 1985 joint military maneuvers were held both in Egypt and Jordan.

By the fall of 1984, money had become an increasingly critical problem for Jordan, and it invariably influenced Jordan's regional politics—clear evidence of how dependent and porous Jordan's economic lifeline is. During the flush years of the oil boom, Jordan's budget culled more than 80 percent of its operating revenue from external subventions and remittances from Jordanian workers in the Gulf. By 1984, aid from the Arab states had fallen by more than half from the peak levels of 1978–79 (although remittances rose). Unemployment doubled in a single year, and the economic growth rate fell below the rate of natural increase for the first time in a decade.[12] Industrial and military procurement and infrastructural plans were based partly on an expected flow of revenue that never arrived, and it is no simple matter to cancel or delay major plans once they are made. For Jordan, soliciting money from more wealthy Arab neighbors is a time-honored tradition, and the king is a master at it; the problem in 1984 was that most discretionary Gulf oil revenue was earmarked for Iraq and little was left for Jordan. In the beginning, the Gulf war made money for Jordan, as Jordan became a land bridge to ferry war matériel to Iraq. But because there was less oil money to spread around, the war now became a financial liability to Jordan. So when, on May 30, 1984, the Kuwaiti National Assembly voted to reduce aid to Jordan, Syria, and the PLO by 39 percent in order to reduce the Kuwaiti budget deficit,[13] the king rushed to Kuwait to see whether Kuwait desired any assistance from Jordan as Iranian pressures against it increased. In June, fearing Iranian successes, but also increasingly depleted aid levels, Hussein offered Jordanian troops for the battle— implicitly, for a price.[14] And thus lives on the mercenary tradition of the Jordanian military developed by the British and cultivated by Sir John Bagot Glubb (Glubb Pasha) during the 1930s.

Phase Four: 1985–1988

The next major development in Jordanian-PLO relations was characterized by more of the same tactics that both parties had pursued in 1983 and early 1984. The Jordanian desire to hold the PNC meeting in Amman in November 1984 was motivated to advance the king's strategy of partly co-opting, partly displacing, the PLO. On the outs with Syria and physically out of Lebanon, Arafat had little choice but to accept the king's offer. King Hussein's performance at the PNC was meant to make life as uncomfortable as possible for Arafat and his deputies. As they squirmed in their seats while Hussein spoke of Resolution 242 and peace, Jordanian television beamed the scene into the occupied territories.

This anxious Jordanian-PLO duet had a predictable effect on Syria and drew a predictable response. Ismail Dawish, a relatively moderate associate of Arafat, was gunned down on a street in Rome. A few days later, a Palestinian inclined to cooperate with the king's endeavor and well placed to do so—Fahd Kawasmeh, the former mayor of Hebron— was assassinated in Amman. Arafat then began frequent public recitation of his rejection of Resolution 242, and Hussein, unable to work his way against Syria or to interest the United States in helping him with the Palestinians, threw up his hands in despair.

The PNC and the king's failure to secure U.S. support made two things clear. First, Syrian pressures on Arafat were working, slowly but surely. The split in Fatah was institutionalized and Assad now carried permanent leverage not only within the PLO but also within Fatah. This was not necessarily bad news for Hussein, for to the extent that Arafat concluded that his problem with Syria was not tactical and temporary but unconditional and permanent, the more appealing a nexus with Jordan would appear, notwithstanding the price. Arafat could not resist seeing his choices: Jordan could get him half a loaf, some independence, and let him live; Syria could get him nothing, offered him no independence, and was not beyond taking his life. The king pressed Arafat further, arguing that his refusal to heed the needs and views of Palestinians in the territories was tantamount to delegitimating the PLO's right to speak for the Palestinian cause. The king intimated, not for the first time, that he might enter into negotiations with Israel without the PLO, which would then soon find itself in the dustbin of history.

But to make this threat credible, the United States had to pay active attention to the conflict again; there had to be a prospect of a negotiation to enter to force matters, and that required more than Jordanian will. But it had become clear, that until Israel had extricated itself from Lebanon, neither Israel nor the United States would tackle the Palestinian problem. So when Israel announced its intention to withdraw unilaterally from Lebanon in January 1985, Hussein prepared for the next round, hoping as always for full success but expecting modest progress within a protracted process.

Intensive private negotiations between the king and Arafat resumed. Then suddenly, on February 13, the king announced dramatically a PLO-Jordanian accord based on Resolutions 242 and 338. The king implied that Arafat accepted these resolutions, renounced terrorism, and would strive for a political solution if only the United States would help out by talking with the PLO. King Fahd, keeper of the PLO bankroll, happened to be in Washington at the time—a neat little piece of political theater—and President Reagan, loving a good show, promptly pronounced himself delighted with the accord. But the State Department, having seen no document and having heard nothing from Arafat, awaited "clarifications." In the meantime, on February 20, Prime Minister Shimon Peres pronounced himself delighted, too, and offered to go to Amman to talk directly with the king.

Then on February 23, King Hussein published the text of the PLO-Jordanian accord presumably to force the issue one way or the other. Arafat was shocked, for the text showed that the king had tried to reel in Arafat and that Arafat allowed himself to be reeled far enough to get into deep trouble with his own Fatah lieutenants. But it was still not far enough for the United States to pronounce the PLO fit for negotiations. In truth, the February 13 agreement was merely a shift in the pattern of Jordanian-PLO competition, for although there was an "accord," there was almost no agreement on what it meant.

As matters seemed to sink back into a typical desultory routine, another surprise came forth, this time from Cairo. On February 26, President Mubarak called for direct negotiations between Israel and a Jordanian-Palestinian delegation. Mubarak did not specify the PLO, and this was a major change in Egyptian policy—or so it seemed. Everyone knew that the question of Palestinian representation was difficult, but many people thought it could be finessed, particularly because Arafat had not repudiated the February 13 accord. Peres quickly praised the Egyptian position and, for a change, things began to look up.

But it turned out that Mubarak had misspoken. A scheme devised by al-Baz called for a prior meeting between a Jordanian-Palestinian delegation and the United States in hope of persuading Washington about the character of Palestinian representation and then having the United States sell it to Israel. The Arafat-Hussein accord was supposed to be ambiguous enough to allow the United States to maintain to Israel that it would not be negotiating with the PLO and for Hussein to persuade his Palestinian constituencies that, yes indeed, that was exactly what it meant and that he, the king, had achieved it. Unfortunately, the Egyptians had failed to brief Hussein adequately before Mubarak misspoke; al-Baz went to Jerusalem to explain the foul-up to Peres while Hussein stewed. One of the reasons Hussein was annoyed was that he had his own private line open with Israel, this time through an influential group organized by Gene Haleby, his father-in-law, and the Egyptian gambit had the initial effect of confusing everything and everybody.

Despite the general mayhem, these events convinced the State Department that a new possibility had opened up to make progress. For the rest of the year, the United States tried to arrange direct negotiations between a Jordanian-Palestinian delegation and Israel. The American approach was to accept a meeting with a Jordanian-Palestinian delegation only if it led to direct negotiations and was not meant to substitute for them. If the meeting led to direct negotiations, the United States suggested it might be prepared to press Israel on who would be allowed to represent the Palestinians—if not, then not. Israel watched and worried. The Jordanians were agreeable to the trade: semiofficial U.S. recognition of the PLO in return for direct negotiations.

But King Hussein then raised another requirement: an international conference attended by the five permanent members of the Security Council. This requirement was absent from the previous round of diplomatic maneuvering and can be accounted for partly because of the Syrian factor. Ideally, the king would enter a negotiation with Arafat on one arm and Assad on the other. If he could not have Assad, and by 1985 it was clear he could not, then he could perhaps have some degree of protection against Assad by having the Soviet Union, which, for its own purposes, was amendable to the notion. At first Israel and the United States were opposed, but, soon facing a stalemate in the process, both Peres and U.S. Secretary of State George Shultz decided to explore the proposal. The condition, however, was the same: that an international conference not be a substitute for direct negotiations but a prelude to them.

This was just what the king hoped for and needed. Hussein proceeded to press Arafat on explicit endorsement of Resolution 242 and the question of direct negotiations. He hoped that Arafat's lack of a Syrian option, ironically for Damascus, would finally break Arafat's will. But Arafat resisted; he did not say no and he did not say yes. Instead he told the king, and the king told the United States, that he would accept Resolution 242 only in return for U.S. recognition of the Palestinian right to self-determination, a deal Jordan was reluctant to press in Washington.

There were other items on the table, too. When the king visited President Reagan in Washington in May, a major U.S. arms replenishment for Jordan was long overdue. But Hussein was told that unless he agreed explicitly to the principle of direct negotiations, any major arms deal was doomed in Congress. Hussein told the president that, at this stage in the process, while he was still trying to land Arafat, he could not do that. The president chose to press for an arms deal anyway, which ran into the predicted trouble in Congress. In the summer, Assistant Secretary of State Richard Murphy was dispatched to the region, in part to tell the king that things were not going well for him on Capitol Hill and to try again to elicit Jordanian agreement toward direct talks. The king tried to set the stage. In mid-July, he got from Arafat a list of seven Palestinians who might form the Palestinian part of a unified delegation. Hussein sent the list to Washington, and Washington sent it to Jerusalem, where two of the seven names were accepted after a few weeks of dithering and arguing within Israel. This represented a de facto, albeit once-removed, Israeli-PLO negotiation, a "shape of the table" stage of negotiation—trivial at first glance but essential all the same.

Arafat thought hard about all this "progress" and apparently concluded that he could not submit to the king. He continued to insist that Resolution 242 was unacceptable by itself because it concerned only the territories occupied in 1967 and would end the PLO's right to struggle for all of Palestine. If he forsook that, he himself might be forsaken. The Jordanians were hard bargainers throughout, leaving no space between an independent Palestinian state, which they vowed to prevent, and a "federation" in which the PLO would be the junior partner. But because Arafat lacked the option of renewing relations with Syria, he coveted the rocky relationship with Jordan just the same, particularly since it enabled Fatah to work more effectively in the occupied territories. Arafat waited and hoped for someone else to mess up the "progress," and it did not take long: thanks to Syrian threats and Saudi petulance, the August 1985 Casablanca Summit failed to endorse Hussein's strategy.

Israel also resolved to push Arafat off the fence, although not for the same purposes. After the murder of three Israelis in Cyprus in September, Israeli planes flew fifteen hundred kilometers on October 1 to raid the PLO headquarters outside of Tunis. Whether the raid was designed to pressure the PLO away from terrorism and toward Hussein or to elicit a PLO terrorist response that would prod Hussein to seek independent action with Israel, or whether it was just revenge bereft of a larger design, is not clear. In any event, one of Arafat's PLO allies from the Palestine Liberation Front (PLF), a small PLO affiliate, then organized the *Achille Lauro* incident of October 1985, an act of bad faith as far as Hussein and Mubarak were concerned. In the same month the PLO sabotaged a London meeting arranged by the king that was designed to extract PLO recognition from Britain in return for PLO accession to Resolution 242. Hussein was very angry; he summoned Arafat to the palace on October 28 and told him if he did not stop the duplicity, Jordan would pursue a negotiated settlement without the PLO.

Jordan had been playing its own double game, negotiating in private with Israel over West Bank arrangements and more portentous matters besides. Indeed, on October 4, Hussein and Peres had met in France just three days after the Tunis raid. Israel, for its part, was ready to promote this latter course, naming Zafer al-Masri, a prominent pro-Jordanian Palestinian from a prominent Jordanian political family, to be mayor of Nablus on November 26.

To make sure that Arafat lacked the option of returning to the Syrian fold, King Hussein commenced, after the Casablanca Summit, an effort to improve Jordanian-Syrian relations.[15] The aim was not only to isolate Arafat but to moderate Syrian support for Iran in the Gulf war. The Jordanians also hoped to persuade Syrians to stop shooting and bombing Jordanian diplomats and assets abroad. But the entente with Syria also suggested that Hussein had given up on direct negotiations or a dramatic breakthrough in the peace process. The events of 1985–86 fit into Hussein's protracted, patient Palestinian strategy well enough, but with an incompetent administration in Washington and Likud's rotation turn coming in Israel, it was no time to reach for the brass ring. In reality, the high diplomacy of 1985–86 was not as serious as that which had fallen down in 1984.

Thus when Arafat returned to Amman on November 13, 1985, he must have been worried about signs of a Syrian-Jordanian rapprochement and fearful of a private Hussein-Assad agreement to discard him and deal jointly with Israel over Golan and the West Bank. The king's simultaneous declarations of support for the PLO and a Palestinian state meant nothing in practice, for Hussein knew that the United States and Israel would prevent one. To make sure, Hussein opened negotiations with Israel through Richard Murphy in January 1986 on a wide range of topics.

Arafat kept trying to fob off the king, and the king demanded yet again that Arafat finally decide. For two long months Arafat refused to commit himself, and the king, announcing on February 19, 1986, that the PLO was not serious about peace, suspended the Jordanian-PLO accord. In July, Jordan shut all PLO offices in the country and expelled its representatives, including the Khalil al-Wazir, who had busied himself developing a network of cells in the occupied territories.[16]

The February severing of Jordanian-Fatah cooperation led to a political vacuum on the ground in the occupied territories. In that context, Jordan's not-so-subtle threat that it might proceed with the peace process without the PLO, but with a local third force, garnered much attention from some quarters. The first casualty of this tactic, however, was Zafer al-Masri, who was murdered in Nablus on March 2 by the Popular Front for the Liberation of Palestine. In this way the Syrians demonstrated an active presence in the occupied territories both to undermine the third force elective and to undercut Fatah, for Masri had obtained Arafat's permission before taking the job and Arafat had clearly failed to protect him.

After the breakdown of the Jordanian-PLO dialogue in 1986, the king could not have been sanguine about the prospects for a breakthrough in the peace process. The Israeli government was in the wrong hands, and if the king had any second thoughts about trusting the power of U.S. diplomacy, the Iran-Contra scandal put an end to them. Actually, what annoyed the Jordanians most was not the arms deliveries but a new demonstration of the inability of the United States to keep a secret. The Jordanians are connoisseurs of discretion, and the king knows that secrecy will be crucial to the beginning, middle, and even the end of any negotiated settlement. Yet the United States has failed repeatedly to demonstrate a devotion to professional, discreet foreign policy. In the wake of the Church Committee hearings in 1975, the king was identified as having been on the CIA payroll for years.

And at a sensitive time in 1984, secret preparations for a Jordanian Rapid Deployment Force for the Gulf were leaked, with disastrous consequences. So when Iran-Contra was revealed, the Jordanians were doubtless aghast but probably not surprised.

Only two things remained positive for Jordan in this period: its campaign to rebuild its patronage effort in the territories at the PLO's expense and progress in private understandings with Israel. From February 1986 until December 1987, Jordan campaigned for its own constituency on the West Bank, bent on weakening the PLO as much as possible.[17] Jordan maintained in public that there was a difference between a good PLO and a bad PLO, hoping to co-opt as many "good" PLO members as might be found. This is one reason why, on January 19, 1987, Jordan executed the convicted killer of Fahd Kawasmeh (a "good" PLO affiliate), a young man named Nayef Khalil al-Bayed, allegedly a member of the Democratic Front for the Liberation of Palestine (DFLP), a "bad" PLO group.[18] Executions are very rare in Jordan, but if Jordan hopes and expects Palestinians to speak its case in the occupied territories, it cannot allow the murder of those who do to go unavenged. Just as important, if the regime does not demonstrate its willingness to punish acts of terrorism and political assassination on its own soil, it knows that in a Middle Eastern environment, it invites more of them.

In every imaginable way after mid-1986, Jordan intensified its public relations and patronage efforts in the territories. Shimon Peres helped; the range of Israeli-Jordanian private cooperation expanded dramatically in 1987.[19] Peres and Hussein reached an advanced agreement on preparations for an international conference, signed in London on April 11, 1987.[20]

The U.S. government, too, helped Jordan reassert its influence in the territories by agreeing to funnel a portion of its development funds for the West Bank through Jordan and by having Ambassador Thomas Pickering broker the reopening of a branch of the Cairo-Amman Bank in Nablus to disburse the funds. All the while, Jordan maintained good relations with Syria, Egypt, Saudi Arabia, and Iraq—no mean feat.

But these efforts did not presage an independent Jordanian bid for a settlement, either in their Palestinian or their regional dimension. They constituted continuing pressure on the PLO from the residents of the territories to force Arafat to associate with the Palestinian constituency most closely aligned with Jordanian interests and influence. The regional efforts had more to do with fobbing off danger, extracting money, and deterring Iran. All of these themes came together at the Arab summit in Amman in November 1987, which aided Egypt's reintegration into the Arab world, moderated Syrian declamations of support for Iran, and pointedly ignored the Palestinian problem.

Phase Five: Jordan and the Intifada.

The fifth cycle owes its impetus to the Intifada, which began in December 1987. Within a few months, the Intifada seemed to reverse most of what little momentum there was toward moderation in the Arab world and among the Palestinians. West Bank Palestinians were able to tune in Radio Jerusalem, broadcasting from Damascus and organized by Ahmed Jibril's Popular Front for the Liberation of Palestine—General Command. Radio Jerusalem (Radio al-Quds) was as nihilistic an expression of Palestinian nationalism as there has been since before 1967—and it quickly became very popular. Arafat chased this new force even as Syria promoted it. PLO statements about Jordan and the Jordanian role became testy in direct proportion to Jordan's plummeting image in the territories.[21]

The Intifada seemed at the outset to set the stage for a possible Fatah-Syrian reconciliation, and Hussein was the odd man out both in the territories and, potentially, in the region. Arafat visited Hafiz al-Assad in Damascus on April 24, 1988, and it may have seemed to Hussein that a new cycle in regional politics was about to begin. But the recrudescence of the Palestinian war of the camps in Lebanon put an end to that.[22]

Things could have been worse for Jordan, therefore, but they were plenty bad enough without a PLO-Syrian alliance. The Intifada destroyed the value of much of Jordan's political and financial investment in the West Bank made since 1982. Moreover, any attempt to negotiate a way to an international conference with the Israeli Labor party was now impossible. The London Plan was put on the shelf; Hussein understood that, at least for a while, the Intifada would help the Israeli right. A year or two earlier, the royal court thought that the prospect of a diplomatic breakthrough toward a Jordanian option could be a key factor in Israeli domestic political evolution away from the ascending right. Shimon Peres certainly entertained that notion, or acted as though he did, and so did Avraham Tamir, the director general of the prime minister's office at the time of Peres's tenure and the man responsible for coordinating the London agreement. But this possibility was overtaken by the Intifada and Israel's inability to control and contain it quickly. So not only did the Intifada hurt Jordan's patronage-building campaign in the West Bank, it also reduced the power and the numbers of the most natural audience for any Jordanian peace diplomacy directed toward Israel.

The Intifada was not entirely bad news for Jordan, however. Although danger resided in the disruptive power of Palestinian nationalism both in the immediate and longer term, an opportunity lay in the exploitable divisions within the PLO generated by the uprising. The king played Jordan's hand with consummate skill.

Hussein may have been one of the few people who understood the Intifada from the beginning. The mobilization of a romanticized Palestinian vanguard was, after all, not entirely new to him—between 1968 and September 1970 it had made life in the Hashemite kingdom bitter and dangerous. It was not that he liked the Intifada, no matter what he said publicly. His attitude toward the *shebab* in the territories was probably similar to his grandfather's attitude toward the rank and file of the Arab revolt in 1936. As Abdallah put it then: "We are not concerned anymore with organized bands but with certain elements from the lower strata of the population. My opinion is that these have gone mad like a man bitten by a rabid dog. How can you negotiate intelligently with crazy people?"[23]

With Israeli television broadcasting the stone-throwing and the reprisals on a daily basis, Hussein worried that the disturbances would spread to the East Bank. One of the first things Jordan did after the uprising showed signs of lasting was to arrest twenty-three Palestinians formerly involved with the PFLP and the DFLP,[24] and the second was to ban demonstrations supportive of the Intifada. The guard on the refugee camps was doubled, people were tense, and domestic comity eroded.

So much for the bedrock pragmatism. Next came public relations. To reduce his exposure to the rising tide of Palestinian emotion, Hussein announced on May 8 that he would not negotiate for the PLO, essentially telling the West Bankers that if they wanted the PLO, they could have it for all the good it would do them.[25] Then, on July 28, the king ended a highly touted development plan. And three days later, Hussein announced that Jordan was not Palestine and severed administrative links to the West Bank, an area that it had ruled for eighteen years before the 1967 war.

The reaction to the king's gambit was mixed. The Israeli Labor party, then in the midst of an election campaign, said that the king's move was merely "tactical." Others insisted that this time the king was not being coy, and soon the chorus of common knowledge asserted that the Jordanian option in all its forms was dead.[26]

Both reactions were marred by an inappropriate either/or approach and missed a basic point. King Hussein cannot ignore developments in Palestinian politics any more than Yasser Arafat can ignore Jordan. Jordan is largely Palestinian every way except politically; Arafat knows there are more Palestinians in Jordan than anywhere else in the world. What happens on one side of the river must influence what happens on the other side. In this, nothing essential changed in July 1988. A total severance of Jordan's links to the West Bank was out of the question and remains so today. Jordan's formal severing was accompanied by much real severing, but most basic relationships persisted or were put into escrow. The bridges across the Jordan stayed open, trade continued albeit in a restricted form, the banks and courts worked, and Jordan's currency, passports, and most professional licenses remain valid although in altered forms. Some development funds never ceased flowing. The Cairo-Amman Bank branches remained open, and a new branch opened in Gaza after July 31, 1988.[27] Besides, if the king wanted a real "divorce" from the West Bank, he could have abrogated the 1950 "union" agreement, which is the legal basis in the Jordanian context for Jordan's claim to the West Bank, but he did not. He could have reorganized the parliament at that time instead of merely delaying new elections for a year and half. He could have formally suspended the West Bankers' Jordanian citizenship. He did none of these things.

Since the summer of 1988, one may see the Jordanian option as half empty or half full; it is not correct to assume that the glass has been shattered. Inside Jordan, Hussein has presided over a studied ambiguity; Palestinians who are Jordanian citizens have been thrust into a limbo designed to generate just the right amount of discomfort and rethinking about Jordan. Many other people are wondering, too. But there is no doubt that something did change, namely that the integration of Palestinians into the mainstream of Jordanian society has reached, in the king's view, a stable point of no return. Otherwise Hussein would not have done what he did in the summer of 1988 without fear of shattering the country's domestic peace. This is what was new; Hussein could shout out loud in the midst of the Intifada that "Jordan is not Palestine," that it has a separate, prior agenda of its own. The East Bank first attitude, reconfirmed by a cabinet shuffle of December 16, 1988, buoyed his most essential tribal and familiar constituency without provoking even a modicum of serious unrest. The unrest that did come, in April 1989, affected non-Palestinians in Jordan and had other, economic, causes.

Although many Palestinians on the East Bank certainly did not like it, there was not much that they could or, more important, really wanted to do about the July 1988 disengagement. For the time being, as Jordan solidifies its regime on the East Bank, the king worries more about being associated too closely with the mayhem on the West Bank than about not being closely associated enough. This is a real change.

In this limited sense, Jordan has separated itself from the torments of the Palestinian issue.

Outside of Jordan, little of essence has changed. King Hussein has adopted new tactics in the old struggle with radical Palestinian nationalism, a struggle that he cannot give up, even though the tide of popular sentiment in the region is flowing against him. Hussein intended in part by his formal severing of the West Bank from Jordan to force the PLO to a decision, and he did. Jordan offered incentives: the economic lure of confederation, access to Washington, help in establishing the PLO in the territories. Threats, however, were more obvious. Jordan's disengagement implied gains for the Unified Leadership of the Uprising at the PLO's expense. Also, almost completely unnoticed in the West, Jordan's withdrawal of financial resources and the curtailing of trade constituted an effort to weaken the economic base of the Intifada. And while Arafat pondered the king's move— visibly annoyed by it—the PLO was relentlessly attacked by Jordanian officialdom.[28]

The Jordanian campaign worked quickly. Hussein and Arafat met in Aqaba on October 22, 1988, less than two months after Hussein's dramatic announcement and just a few days before the Israeli election. Arafat agreed to coordinate strategy with Jordan, and the king announced himself fully satisfied with the results.[29] Arafat's deputy, Khaled al-Hassan, admitted that coordination between Jordan and the PLO "was a necessity that can't be ignored."[30] This was a plain admission both that the PLO could not go it alone and that needing Jordan carried with it a price "to be determined."

On January 7, 1989, Arafat came to Jordan to raise the Palestinian flag when the Hashemite kingdom raised the PLO office in Amman to the status of an embassy. The king has been around too long to have allowed such a thing to take place—and be carried on television— without extracting something in return. Exactly what Hussein got is not a matter of public record; *that* he got something not only flows from the logic and practice of inter-Arab relations but was apparent in striking, new language that Arafat used on that occasion not once or twice, but three times. Arafat declared Hussein's support "true, strong and important . . . for the Palestinian march toward regaining holy Jerusalem, God willing, to raise these two flags once again over the walls, minarets and churches of Jerusalem." Then, in answer to a reporter's question, Arafat again said: "God willing, this flag, together with the Jordanian flag, will be hoisted over Jerusalem soon." And in case anyone missed it the first two times, he said it again: "We proudly say that our PNC . . . in Algiers has clearly pointed to these distinguished relations between the Jordanian and Palestinian peoples. This is why I said a short while ago that the two flags will fly over Jerusalem."[31]

Hussein accepted the PLO's entreaties with the same two-pronged strategy he has used since at least 1982. He continued to insist in public that he had no interest in the West Bank and at the same time skillfully maintained Jordan's interests there. In late February 1989, for example, the Jordanian government established official accounts in the Amman Bank for every employee in the West Bank who joined the Jordanian civil service *after* June 1967. Into these accounts, the government deposited all the money "suspended" since July 1988. All civil servants had to do to claim the money and move it to a bank in the territories was prove that they still worked at their jobs. They could do so by registering either through a religious court or a chamber of commerce—both redoubts of Jordanian influence in the territories.[32]

So Jordan is not Palestine, but it is. Jordan does not compete with PLO, but it does. Jordan leaves the West Bank to the PLO, but it does not. Even the basic question, whether Jordan will or will not negotiate over the West Bank, is not clear. Hussein put it very cleverly and more than once: he will not negotiate over the West Bank unless the Palestinians ask him to do so. But does he mean all Palestinians or just some Palestinians? If some, how many, and which ones? He does not say—a formula that allows a reassertion of the Hashemite voice in the West Bank under any number of circumstances.

Some of what the Jordanians have done since July 31, 1988, is irreversible, if not administratively than psychologically. But the process of Palestinian state building is to some extent irreversible, too. Whether one calls Jordan's strategy tactical or not is beside the point; such a vocabulary cannot do justice to a situation in which Jordan and the PLO are allied against Israel's continued occupation of the West Bank but in which Israel and Jordan are allied to prevent the PLO from getting full control of it when the Israelis leave.

What matters is that the king concluded by 1988 that the dangers of a titularly independent but in fact semisovereign Palestinian state were less than the dangers of a confederated arrangement along the lines of the March 1972 United Kingdom plan and that only the former was feasible. This does not mean that there is no more Jordanian option or that the king does not care about the West Bank. Jordan's interests there are no more absent than a tree that sheds its leaves in winter is dead. It does mean that the extent and the instruments of Jordanian influence are much diminished and different than in the classical Jordanian option scenario of 1968–71 or the abridged one of 1972–86. That, in turn, means that any Jordanian assumption of influence and authority will have to coordinate that much more closely with Israel to make sure that any small Palestinian entity does not "get out of hand."[33]

The Algiers PNC: Jordan, the Absent Master of Ceremonies

The disengagement put the PLO in a terrible bind over the West Bank; Hussein gave it responsibility without power. The king, in essence, established the agenda of the Algiers Palestine National Council meeting in mid-November 1988, and PNC members found themselves in an unenviable predicament.

If the PLO had "accepted" the West Bank from Jordan only to terrorize Israel more effectively, the residents of the territories would have suffered most and the PLO would have failed. Hussein risked little because there was no chance that the PLO as constituted before Algiers could achieve even Arab support for an independent state in the West Bank, much less achieve the state. It would then have been clear to all that the only way to end the occupation was through Jordan, and the king would have gained at least marginally in the territories at the PLO's expense.

It might be thought that Hussein should have worried more about the leadership of the Intifada, which seemed anti-Hashemite, radical, and self-identified as the PLO. But Hussein has been around too long to mistake appearances for realities, political dramatics for real interests. The king knew that the interests of West Bankers diverge considerably from those of the PLO. Excepting those in refugee camps, West Bankers *are* home and want the Israelis to *go* home. PLO cadres for the most part think of their homes as being in Israel proper; they are *not* home, want to *go* home, and want the Israelis to go back to impossible places like Poland and tsarist Russia. Although full of themselves from standing up to Israeli might and mesmerized by their own stirring rhetoric, the leadership of the uprising necessarily has a different perspective than the PLO's. Just as PLO cadres care more about Jaffa (in Israel proper) than about Nablus (in the West Bank), those from Nablus care more about Nablus than about Jaffa. Many West Bankers are ready for a two-state solution in perpetuity. But even those who are not ready for real compromise are more moderate tactically because they are the ones now under occupation who would be redeemed politically sooner rather than later. That is why, in the king's view, the West Bank leadership, despite its temporary revolutionary radicalism, is likely to be more flexible than PLO "moderates" of the pre-November 1988 variety.

Thus if the PLO decided genuinely to moderate its extremism in hopes of a lasting political compromise with Israel, then the PLO would for the first time accept the residents of the West Bank and Gaza as its core constituency instead of Palestinians in Lebanon and elsewhere who yearn, not for the occupied territories, but for Israel itself. If the PLO opted for political compromise, it had to find a way to replace Jordan's considerable role in the West Bank and a way to pay for it. To negotiate peace, it had to convince America and Israel that its moderation was sincere. Hussein knew that neither one of these would be easy; a "new" PLO would need Jordan to help administer the West Bank, to talk to Washington, to approach Israel and negotiate with it, and to make peace with it. And, again, Arafat knew that the king's help would have a steep price.

The problem for the PLO at Algiers, therefore, was to avoid both being squeezed between Jordan and the leadership of the Intifada and to avoid a civil war, for, clearly, some of its members, supported by many prominent Arabs in the territories, wanted the PLO to declare an independent state and a government in exile while others saw such tactics as invalidating PLO claims to all of Palestine. Given these differences and dangers, the challenges were many. The first was to design a set of statements that would improve its standing in the territories; to do this, the PLO had to embrace the idea of a state in the West Bank and Gaza. But it had to do so without implying that the PLO was giving up the right to struggle for all of Palestine from the river to the sea, lest it detach the organization from its old core constituency and cede it to its internal opposition, led by George Habash's Popular Front for the Liberation of Palestine, emanating directly and by proxy from Syria. Another challenge was to avoid a government in exile that might transfer too much of its authority to the Intifada leadership.

So the PNC declared an independent Palestinian state and avoided naming a government in exile. It invoked Resolutions 181 and 242, but neither was clearly interpreted and both were encumbered by an assortment of verbal mystifications and vagaries. PNC declarations were too much for some, too little for others. They were too little for the United States, which denied Arafat a visa to visit New York. This, in turn, finally led Arafat to Geneva in December 1988, where, in the clearest terms ever, he said the magic words: yes to Resolutions 242 and 338, no to terrorism, and yes to recognition of Israel's right to exist.

In the end, Arafat was forced by the Intifada and by Jordanian diplomatic maneuvering to make decisions he had assiduously avoided for years. King Hussein deserves much credit for whatever modicum of progress there was in 1988–89 in the PLO's position. Thanks in part to Hussein's tactics, the PLO was pressed to a decision that Jordan and the United States had been trying to extract for years.

But Arafat's Geneva statement did not end PLO divisions or Jordan's effort to nurture them for its own ends. Today's PLO has three factions instead of two: rejectionists, "tactical" moderates of the Phased Program sort, and real moderates. Because it can hardly be assumed that this third group represents the majority, there is no reason to proclaim the PLO a positive force for peace. But there has been some progress. Certainly, the king of Jordan thinks so; Hussein has repeatedly praised Arafat's moderation and tried to extend and support it to prevent any backsliding. The U.S. decision to talk with the PLO in Tunis, which Hussein supported, was essentially a wager that this third faction existed, was growing, and could be encouraged to grow further and faster by American diplomacy.

Jordan in the Bush Administration

The Bush administration's initial Middle East policy was designed to keep the focus of action on the ground in the occupied territories and Israel in hopes that the local protagonists would finally make some decisions conducive to reconciliation.[34] The Israeli election plan of May 1989 was the organizational device for this general approach and a way to draw the PLO to its new, more potentially conciliable constituency through the deliberately thin U.S.-PLO dialogue in Tunis. The administration deliberately put off larger questions (final status issues) and broader questions (the role of the Arab states) in the belief that the process could not bear that much additional weight and still move forward. This is where Jordan does or does not come in.

Never has Jordan been more visibly absent from the grindings of the Middle East peace process than in the Intifada years of 1989–90. There are many reasons for this. There is the symbolic power of the disengagement, strengthened by the November 1989 elections in Jordan, which eliminated the West Bank from Jordan's formal political jurisdiction. There is also Jordan's limited political liberalization, which consumes political energies. There are Jordan's severe economic problems. Indeed, one of the reasons the Jordanianization process on the East Bank slowed in the late 1980s was that more money was earmarked for the West Bank. And again, there is the local tactical focus of U.S. policy.

Some observers have mistaken these conditions to mean that the United States government no longer considers Jordan important to the peace process in the longer term.[35] A Palestinian state is believed to be inevitable, and thus one can only interpret U.S. efforts to produce elections with Palestinian representations as dedicated to that end. But this assumption is wrong. Responsible U.S. officials understand the implications of a fully independent Palestinian state for Jordan, and when Secretary of State James Baker says that U.S. policy still opposes an independent Palestinian state, he means it. Because it also opposes permanent Israeli occupation or annexation, that leaves Jordan, as always, in one way or another as a bridge between the interests and positions of the Israeli and Palestinian sides.

There are two general conditions under which Jordan will return to a prominent role in the peace process. One is if major progress is made between Israelis and Palestinians, which will require the right combination of political moderation on both sides and fortuitous timing. Even if such moderation and good timing were to occur, negotiations can travel only so far and no farther without Jordan; Jordan is the only element in the peace process that can bridge the gap between Israel's insistence that there be no fully independent Palestinian state and Palestinians' insistence that there be precisely that. This is understood much better throughout the Middle East than it is in Washington or in European capitals. The other condition is a vast deterioration of the situation from Jordan's point of view, leading either to the prospect of a fully independent Palestinian state or, more likely, to a radical right-wing Israeli government bent on turning Jordan into a Palestinian state by expelling hundreds of thousands of Palestinians across the Jordan River.[36] The Hashemite kingdom would certainly intervene in the diplomatic process to the best of its ability to forestall either of these developments.

But neither great progress nor a vast deterioration of the situation is yet in view, the king's alarmist remarks about Soviet Jewish emigration to Israel notwithstanding. Until one or the other becomes more likely, Jordan will stay on the Arab-Israeli sidelines and tend to related matters of regional politics and domestic comity, which keep its hands full. On the domestic front, economic problems and the uncertainties of Jordanian *glasnost* are its main concerns, and here it is not just Palestinians the king needs to worry about but newly politicized East Bankers and Islamic fundamentalism in both East Bank and Palestinian political communities. In regional politics, Jordan remains close to Egypt and is improving relations with Iraq. Iraq is an oil-rich state whose resources Jordan needs to share to dig itself out of its economic morass. The king may also view Iraq as Jordan's strategic protector of last resort in the event of a Palestinian revolt on the East Bank stimulated by Israel (and possibly taken advantage of by Syria).

All in all, King Hussein, one of the world's premier and certainly its most senior tenured political juggler, will have to keep juggling a little longer. In the meantime, his successor—whether that remains his brother Hassan or becomes his son Ali—had better practice hard.

Notes

1. See Clinton Bailey, *Jordan's Palestinian Challenge, 1948–83* (Boulder, Colo.: Westview Press, 1984).
2. See Avi Plascov, *The Palestinian Refugees in Jordan, 1948–1957* (London: Frank Cass, 1981), p. 16.
3. This problem is discussed in Shaul Mishal, *West Bank/East Bank* (New Haven: Yale Univ. Press, 1978).
4. The transformation of the PLO means its essential capture by Fatah, its movement toward Marxism, and its reversal of the ideological assumption that the Arab states would liberate Palestine for the Palestinians, thus catalyzing Arab political redemption and unification. Instead, the PLO bequeathed to itself this vanguard role after the June war.
5. See Asher Susser, *Double Jeopardy: PLO Strategy Toward Israel and Jordan* (Washington: Washington Institute for Near East Policy, 1987).
6. See David Ignatius, "The 20-Year U.S.-Israeli Battle over Land for Peace," *Washington Post*, Apr. 10, 1988, p. B1.
7. These events are detailed in Adam Garfinkle, "Sources of the al-Fatah Mutiny," *Orbis* 27 (Fall 1983): 603–640.
8. See Asher Susser, "Jordan," *Middle East Contemporary Survey* (hereafter *MECS*) 7 (1982–83): 642–43.
9. For details and sources, see Susser, "Jordan," *MECS* 8 (1983–84): 520–22.
10. In the historical shadow, always, is the traumatic episode of September 19–23, 1970, when the steadfastness of the United States in Jordan's hour of need left much to be desired, appearances to the contrary notwithstanding. See my "U.S. Decision-Making in the Jordan Crisis of 1970: Correcting the Record," *Political Science Quarterly* 100 (Spring 1985).
11. See James MacManus, "Reagan Letter Fueled Hussein's Attack," *Washington Post*, Mar. 16, 1984, p. 16. See also "Interview: H. M. King Hussein," *Defense and Diplomacy* (June 1984): 19.
12. Jordan's economic morass is discussed in Susser, "Jordan," *MECS* 9 (1984–85): 497–500.
13. *Middle East Economic Survey*, June 4, 1984.
14. Jordan's King Hussein Offers Troops to Iraq," *Washington Post*, June 18, 1984, p. 19.
15. In November 1985, Jordan cracked down on Islamic fundamentalism in Jordan, arrested a few hundred, and later turned some over to the Syrians. Most Western commentary assumed that this gesture was dictated by Jordanian-Syrian relations, for Ikhwan based in Jordan had troubled Syria for years. More likely, it was based on Jordanian domestic security considerations dressed up to appear as something else. See Susser, "Jordan," *MECS* 9: 507.
16. The king's July demarche to the PLO was probably quickened by Israeli concerns, voiced in public and in private, about the nature of al-Wazir's activities in Amman. See "Sharon on Attacking Terrorist HQ in Jordan"

Jerusalem Post, July 30, 1985, pp. 1–2; "Concern Evinced about PLO Entrenchment in Jordan," Tel-Aviv, Israeli Defense Forces Radio, July 31,
1985, *FBIS:NE/SA*, Aug. 1, 1985, p. I2; and "Bar-Lev: Jordan Asked to Remove PLO Bases," Jerusalem Domestic Service, *FBIS:NE/SA*, Aug. 8, 1985, p.
I3.

17. See Shaul Ramati, "Hussein's Plan," *Jerusalem Post*, Sept. 13, 1986.

18. See "Jordan," *Country Reports on Human Rights Practices for 1987*, Report
submitted to the Committee on Foreign Affairs, House of Representatives,
and the Committee on Foreign Relations, U.S. Senate, by the Department of
State in accordance with Sections 166(d) and 502B(b) of the Foreign Assistance
Act of 1961, as amended (Washington, D.C.: U.S. Government Printing Office,
1987), p. 1200.

19. See, for example, Andrew Whitely, "Israel, Jordan in Secret Talks on
Water Row," *Financial Times*, Dec. 15, 1987, p. 18; Uzi Mahanaymi,
" 'Technical' Agreement Signed with Jordan," from *al-Hamishmar*, Jan. 21,
1987 (*FBIS:NE/SA*, Jan. 21, 1987, p. I1; and "Jordan Prepared to Open
University in West Bank," *Hatzofeh*, Jan. 25, 1987, p. 1 (*FBIS:NE/SA*, Jan. 27,
1987, p. I2).

20. For the original English text, see *Global Affairs* 4, no. 2, p. 114.

21. See, for example, "We, Jordan, and the Only Option," Baghdad Voice
of the PLO, Mar. 16, 1988 (*FBIS:NE/SA*, Mar. 17, 1988, p. 7).

22. The war of the camps came to an end in the fall of 1988, only to be
replaced by an intra-Shiite battle pitching Hezbollah against Amal.

23. Ladislas Farago, *Palestine on the Eve* (London: Putnam, 1936), p. 266.

24. See Ihsan A. Hijazi, "23 Palestinians Seized by Jordan; Plot to Subvert
Regime Is Charged," *New York Times*, Jan. 25, 1988, p. A9; and Geraldine
Brooks, "Jordan's King Deflects Unrest at Border," *Wall Street Journal*, May
10, 1988, p. 35.

25. See Alan Cowell, "Hussein Seeks to Placate Palestinians," *New York
Times*, May 9, 1988, p. A3.

26. Two examples include Arthur Hertzberg, "This Time, Hussein Isn't
Being Coy," *New York Times*, Aug. 9, 1988, p. 19; and Trudy Rubin, "Hussein's
Had Enough of West Bank Mess," *Philadelphia Inquirer*, Oct. 11, 1988.

27. See "Cairo-Amman Bank Branches to Remain Open," *al-Ra'y* (*FBIS:
NE/SA*, Aug. 10, 1988, p. 27); " 'Some' West Bank Projects Reportedly to Continue," Abu Dhabi, *al-Ittihad al-Usubi'i* (*FBIS:NE/SA*, Sept. 26, 1988, p. 25);
and "Cairo-Amman to Open Branch in Gaza," Dubayy, *al-Bayan* (*FBIS:
NE/SA*, Sept. 28, 1988, p. 5).

28. Dajani's remarks can be found in *al-Ra'y*, Sept. 10, 1988 (*FBIS:NE*,
Sept. 14, 1988, pp. 27–32).

29. See Alan Cowell, "Arafat Confers with Hussein on Ending Split," *New
York Times*, Oct. 23, 1988; and Cowell, "Parley in Jordan Is Said to Narrow
Split with P.L.O.," *New York Times*, Oct. 24, 1988.

30. See Alan Cowell, "P.L.O. Appeals to Israelis to Vote the 'Peace
Choice,' " *New York Times*, Oct. 25, 1988.

31. "Flags Hoisted: 'Arafat Speaks,' " Amman Television Service, in Arabic,
Jan. 7, 1989, *FBIS:NE/SA*, Jan. 9, 1989, p. 42.

32. *Al-Sha'b*, Feb. 28, 1989, p. 1.

33. For background, see Adam Garfinkle, *In Cold Embrace: Israeli-Jordanian
Relations* (New York: St. Martin's Press, 1990).

34. This topic is covered in more detail in my "Getting It Right? U.S.

Middle East Policy in the Bush Administration," *Jerusalem Quarterly*, no. 52 (Fall 1989). Parts of this discussion are derived from that essay.

35. See in particular, Graham Fuller, "The Palestinians: The Decisive Year?" *Current History*, Feb. 1990, pp. 53–56, 80–82, and his longer *The West Bank of Israel* (Santa Monica: RAND Corporation, 1989), RAND/r-3777-OSD, done for the Office of the Secretary of Defense.

36. See Daniel Pipes and Adam Garfinkle, "Is Jordan Palestine?" *Commentary*, Oct. 1988.

11

Syria and Its Neighbors

John F. Devlin

The Internal Scene

By the summer of 1985, the high level of political activity which had marked most of the period since the Israeli invasion of Lebanon had subsided. The Ba'ath party had held its Eighth Regional (Syrian) Congress early in the year, a meeting marked by extended debate over economic policy and by changes in the Regional Command. Rif'at al-Assad retained his position on it, but several of his supporters were dropped. He has lived in Europe most of the time since, and his adherents in Syria are reportedly of little influence. President Hafiz Assad was reelected for a third seven-year term in the customary uncontested election in Mary 1985.[1]

Elections for the People's Assembly, primarily a consultative body, in February 1986 produced a voter turnout of 42 percent, higher than in previous years. Women won 18 of the 195 seats, 50 percent more than they had won in the previous assembly.[2] In other respects the assembly seemed little different from its predecessors. In mid-1987, however, the assembly exercised a seldom-used prerogative. It questioned and criticized the performance in office of four ministers having economic portfolios and voted no confidence in three of them. All four resigned, and none received other positions, which ministers who have outlived their usefulness customarily have gotten in Syria.

When Assad selected a new prime minister on November 1 the nominee was Mahmud al-Zu'bi, who as speaker of the assembly had presided over the unusual critique of the ministers. The outgoing prime minister was appointed to head the National Security Bureau. Zu'bi's cabinet contained eleven new faces, although the two principal ministers with economic responsibility remained in office. Zu'bi himself, albeit a longtime party activist, is trained in agronomy, and his appointment was taken locally and abroad as an earnest of the regime's intentions to deal more forcefully with its economic problems, especially those in agriculture, which has been the subject of repeated promises of greater attention for years.

The inability of the regime to make the progress it wants on military buildup and agricultural, infrastructural, and industrial development simultaneously has been compounded by inefficiency and corruption. The sacking of four ministers is a signal of another new start at dealing with this group of issues. Draconian measures to reduce imports, instituted in 1986, have reduced the balance-of-payments deficit sharply. An additional help in this regard is increased domestic oil production, which has cut Syrian oil import requirements in half.[3] Data are not yet available to judge whether the new cabinet is making progress in bettering Syria's economic situation and in learning to live within its resources. The economic difficulties of recent years, which have included daily power cuts and shortages of ordinary consumer goods, have not, however, affected political stability. The regime's grip on the political structure remains strong.

The Geopolitical Framework

Stability of government has been a major factor in Syria's ability to function as an important actor in the eastern part of the Arab world. Ba'athists have governed the country for twenty-five years, since the coup d'état of March 8, 1963; Hafiz al-Assad has been the dominant figure for nearly eighteen of those years. He emerged as the winner of a multisided power struggle by ousting his last major rival in November 1970. The contrast between the Ba'athist quarter-century and the first seventeen years of Syrian independence is striking. In the earlier period, Syria was an arena in which stronger Arab states contested for victory. In the 1970s and 1980s, Syria has projected its power externally to promote its interests. It has, as the Arab saying puts it, moved *min lu'ba ila la'ib*—from a game to a player.[4]

The long-lived Assad regime operates in the context of Syria's location, of its modern history, and of what it perceives as its proper status in the Middle East. Syria is a state of the Levant. It belongs geographically to a central group of Arab polities—Jordan, Palestine, Lebanon—that have much in common. The Maghrib states, although participating in general Arab affairs, have their own regional interests. Egypt, the strongest of the Arab states and the only one that has shown itself able to lead the Arab world, is anchored in the centuries-old distinct history of the Nile Valley. Belonging neither to the Maghrib, nor to the Levant, nor to the Eastern Marches of Arabdom, it has a unique status, with which Syria must reckon. The Eastern Marches is a term that may be fairly applied to the region—Mesopotamia and the

Gulf—where Arab culture and language have existed uneasily for many centuries with Iranian culture and language. Since the Safavids made Shi'a Islam Iran's official religion, in contrast to the Sunni Islam of the majority of Arabs, an additional element of religious difference has been introduced. The introduction of the concept of nationalism from the West sharpened the difference even further.

Although there have long been disputes between Iran and the power controlling the lower Tigris-Euphrates Valley, under recent Iranian dynasties these consisted largely of customary quarrels over borders, fealty of tribes, or access to the sea. The rise of the Islamic Republic changed the terms of dispute. The Khomeini regime has consistently presented its state as *the* proper model for Muslims. Iraqi President Saddam Hussein has just as consistently portrayed the conflict between the two as a war between the Arabs and the Iranians. Aided by the intransigent manner in which Ayatollah Khomeini has insisted that the Islamic Republic of Iran's version of the Islamic state is the only legitimate one for Muslims to emulate and especially by Iran's aggressive behavior toward the House of Saud, the guardians of the two holy mosques, Saddam has been successful in gaining acceptance among Arabs of the Gulf and peninsula for his view that in the Iraq-Iran war Iraq is defending Arab interests and therefore that Arabs have a duty to support Iraq.

From the vantage point of Damascus, the Saddam doctrine that Iraq is defending all Arabs from Persian aggression is not persuasive. The Levant, that area known as Syria under the Ottomans and called in this essay geographic Syria,[5] has not historically been involved in Arab-Iranian differences as the eastern Arabs have been. For the Arabs of geographic Syria, the key twentieth-century issues have been securing independence and coping with the emergence of Israel in their midst.

The Ba'athist regime in Damascus has, in addition, an aspiration to be the dominant power in geographic Syria. It looks back to the immediate post–World War I period, when for a brief moment Damascus was the capital of an Arab nationalist state,[6] a moment that ended with the carving up of the area into Palestine and Transjordan, Syria and Lebanon. Among the eastern Arab states, Egypt and Iraq were and are the strongest; had Damascus remained the capital of a geographic Syrian state, that state would have been roughly equivalent in population and resources (save for oil) to Iraq. The hope of reconstituting geographic Syria inspired Syrian politicians in the interwar years but died out by the time Syria achieved independence in 1946, about the same time that pan-Arab nationalism was beginning its meteoric rise. Post–United Arab Republic (UAR) Syria's Ba'athist rulers have striven to dominate their immediate Arab neighbors. They have recognized that for their country to dominate its immediate environment, it must strive not to let either of the two regional Arab powers, Egypt and Iraq, gain preponderant, permanent influence in Jordan, Lebanon, or among the Palestinians.

Restoring the Jordanian Connection

Two Arab summit meetings define the manner in which Syria conducts its regional relations. At the first, in August 1985 in Casablanca, which Syria did not attend, the participants appointed a committee charged with the task of restoring relations between Syria and Jordan and between Syria and Iraq. The committee, Crown Prince Abdallah bin Abd al-Aziz of Saudi Arabia, a Tunisian representative, and secretary general of the Arab League Chadli Klibi, set promptly to work and convened a meeting of the Jordanian and Syrian prime ministers in Jiddah on September 16–17; the participants agreed on "steps to create a propitious atmosphere" for improving relations between Damascus and Amman.[7] A second prime ministerial meeting took place the following month, and it also went well. During the interval between the two meetings and in the weeks following the second one, the Jordanian press took a very positive tone toward Syria. The Syrian media were more restrained.

The issue on which Assad wanted satisfaction from Jordan was that of Jordan having allowed elements of the Islamic Front, primarily Muslim Brothers, to use Jordanian territory in the early 1980s for a safe haven during their insurrection against the Assad regime. Jordan had had very close relations with Syria in the mid-1970s but turned abruptly in 1980 to support of Iraq, which also had aided Assad's domestic enemies. That this was a key issue was signaled early in the mediation process by Saudi King Fahd. After referring to the Syrian and Jordanian prime ministers' desire "to surmount the obstacles that impede entente between the two countries," he said, "a long time has passed since sedition and problems which I regard as marginal were prevalent."[8] Whether King Hussein was ignorant of what had been allowed to happen in Jordan may be doubted; an Islamic publication, in a pro-Brotherhood article, found it "quite inconceivable that he [Hussein] has remained ignorant of the Syrian Ikhwan who fled to his country three years ago."[9] In an open letter to his prime minister, however, Hussein wrote, "Suddenly . . . we discerned what we had been ignorant of . . . some of those who had something to do with . . . [the] bloody acts [in Syria] were among us."[10]

Hussein's admission opened the way to close relations. In a joint communique issued at the conclusion of Prime Minister Rifa'i's visit to

Damascus a few days later, the two countries reached agreement on reviving the joint high command council which had been formed in a period of close cooperation in 1975 but had become moribund in the late 1970s.[11] The reconciliation was sealed with Hussein's visit to Damascus at the end of the year. Symbolic of the multifaceted nature of Syria's regional interest, only two days before the Jordanian king's arrival, the Assad regime had presided over the signing of a tripartite agreement among the principal armed contestants in Lebanon, which Damascus hoped would be the first step on the way to a settlement of the Lebanese crisis.

Syrian-Jordanian relations have remained good over the following two and a half years. Once reconciled with Hafiz Assad, King Hussein joined the ranks of those trying to clear the atmosphere between Syria and Iraq. From the timing of the Iraq-Syria contacts—the first was in the autumn of 1985—it appears that Amman's efforts to bridge the differences between its eastern and northern neighbors began even before the king's dramatic admission of November 10 made his reconciliation with Damascus certain. Jordanian and Saudi efforts to reconcile Iraq and Syria have not been able to get around the fundamental fact that Saddam Hussein's insistence that all Arabs must support Iraq's struggle against Iran is seen in Damascus as meaning that Iraq is deciding what Syria's Arab policy is to be. Syria, with its vision of being the preeminent power in geographic Syria, cannot accept a status subordinate to Iraq.

In the course of improving relations with Syria, King Hussein abandoned, in February 1986, a year-old cooperation agreement with Yasser Arafat. At the second summit in November 1987, which brackets the period under review, Arafat began a process of restoring ties with Jordan. In the aftermath of the uprising in the West Bank and Gaza, which began in December 1987, Arafat has once again been received in Damascus.

Iran and Iraq

There are many reasons why the Assad regime has sided with Iran against Iraq in their ongoing conflict. Among them are a dispute with the Ba'ath party in Iraq as to which is the legitimate inheritor of the original party's mantle. A second is the religious legitimacy that acceptance of Alawis as Ja'fari (Twelver) Shi'as by Shi'a religious leaders with Iranian credentials gives to the regime. A third has been economic aid in the form of free or underpriced crude oil for a Syria with serious balance-of-payments problems. A fourth, now much diminished, has been the benefits for Syria in Lebanon of Iranian militia forces there. Underlying all these is the Syrian regime's under-standing of the harm that would come to it from accepting Saddam's doctrine that Arabs have a duty to support Iraq against Iran. It would make Syria's stance as the principal state confronting Israel less believ-able. It would harm Syria in its efforts to dominate the Palestinian political formations. Most of all, it would imply acceptance of Saddam's superior status as an Arab leader and as a Ba'athist, as well as accep-tance of Iraq as a regional power superior to Syria.

For a regime whose head and many prominent leaders come from the Alawi religious sect, acceptance of Alawis as Muslims by persons qualified by position or learning to render such acceptance is of great importance. This is especially so because the urban Sunni Muslims, who dominated Syrian economic, social, political and, through their clients, Muslim religious life until the UAR period, have bridled at being replaced in these roles by Alawis, whom they consider socially inferior. Many Sunnis have asserted that Alawis are not true Muslims.[12] Nonetheless, Alawis have gradually gained acceptance as Muslims in Syria. Under the French mandate, separate religious courts for the community were established; the courts were initially staffed by Shi'a Qadis of the Ja'fari school of jurisprudence. The Ja'fari school was accepted as "equal to other [i.e., Sunni] recognized schools of law" by independent Syria in 1952. In 1973, the since-vanished Lebanese Imam Musa Sadr, who is of Iranian origin and related by marriage to Khomeini, formally endorsed the Alawis as Ja'fari Shi'a Muslims, an endorsement that was repeated by Ayatollah Hasan al-Shirazi in 1977.[13] The Khomeini regime continued to back Assad's government in its fight against the Muslim Brotherhood insurgency, despite Tehran's generalized calls for Muslims worldwide to rise against their op-pressors.

Iranian agreement to provide economic support was a key factor in the Syrian 1982 agreement to close its borders with Iraq and cut off nearly half of Iraq's crude oil export capacity. For some four years Iran provided Syria about 120,000 barrels of oil a day, one-sixth free of charge and the rest at mildly concessionary prices. Syria's failure to pay its bills caused interruptions in 1986. Beginning at the end of 1986, Syria's requirements for Iranian oil were halved because of increased Syrian domestic production. Iran continues to provide 20,000 barrels a day free of charge, and Syria may buy up to 40,000 barrels a day at market prices.[14] New oil production facilities in Syria will eliminate Syria's need to import any crude oil sometime in the first half of 1989, sharply reducing Iran's economic leverage on Syria.[15]

Iranian involvement in Lebanon in the form of irregular forces and influence on the Shi'a community was of considerable importance to

Syria in the early 1980s but has become more of a mixed blessing recently. Syria's preferred partner among the Lebanese Shi'a has long been Amal. The rise of the Shi'a Hezbollah (Party of God) as a significant domestic force in Lebanon has been a burden for Syria. The Hezbollah leaders have had their own lines of communication with Iranian religious leaders; moreover, they espouse the establishment of an Islamic republic in the country.[16] Syria's goal for Lebanon of "an independent, sovereign country inside its internationally recognized borders," to be achieved through reconciliation, cannot be harmonized with an Islamic Shi'a republic.[17] For the reasons just cited, however, especially those of religion and geopolitics, Syria treads circumspectly in dealing with Hezbollah. It has made very clear to the Shi'a militants that when Syria's critical interests are involved it will not hesitate to oppose them. Thus Syrian forces killed twenty-three Hezbollah militants when the Syrians moved in to establish security in Beirut in March 1987. Damascus has also backed Amal in its successful effort to drive Hezbollah gunmen out of Tyre and from villages in South Lebanon.[18] But Syria has not confronted the Shi'a fundamentalists and their Iranian backers over control of the suburban area of South Beirut, and it still allows a major Iranian/Hezbollah presence in the northern Biqa' around Balbek.

Among the more intriguing developments in Syria's external affairs has been the two-year effort by Arab leaders on good terms with both Baghdad and Damascus to arrange a reconciliation between Assad and Saddam. Arab leaders meeting at the Casablanca summit in August 1985 established a committee to ameliorate certain disputes between Arab states. Saudi Crown Prince Abdallah and the committee made fast work of their charge in regard to Syria and Jordan, effecting a reconciliation by the end of the year. No progress was made in the Syria-Iraq sector, despite two meetings of intelligence officers on the Syrian-Iraqi border, one in the autumn of 1985 and a second in March 1986.[19] The latter took place at Soviet urging.[20] At each of these meetings the Syrian officials proposed that reconciliation start from the charter of joint action that the two countries signed in 1978 and which had been scotched by Saddam's forcing Iraqi President Ahmad Hasan Bakr into retirement and taking sole control of Iraq.[21]

The Iraqis derided the Syrian approach as neither serious nor practical.[22] They should not have been surprised, however, for Syrian officials had made the same point on several occasions in the preceding half-dozen years. Reverting to the unity proposal is the Syrian regime's way of saying to Iraq that there is another way of looking at Arab issues beyond Saddam's insistence that Iraq is defending Arab interests and that other Arabs have a duty to support Iraq. It is a way of asserting that Syria, too, has interests in the region, such as the Arab-Israeli confrontation, and that it does not see following Iraq's lead as the way to promote those interests. The Iraqi regime, however, has insisted that Syria must accommodate to Iraq's view. As Saddam put it in a later interview, "Saddam Husayn was not expected to change, while Hafiz Assad was expected to change. Because he did not change, everything remained as it was."[23]

Once Syrian-Jordanian relations had gotten back to a level of cordiality, King Hussein took a hand in mediating between Iraq and Syria. Conditions were not favorable. Syria had blamed Iraq for a series of truck- and car-bomb explosions that killed "hundreds."[24] Iraq had asked the Arab League to consider whether Syrian and Libyan stands on Arab issues would cause the two states to lose league membership. King Hussein pushed ahead and was confident enough of the prospects to publicize a planned June 13, 1986, meeting between the respective foreign ministers. The meeting did not occur; Iraqi media attacked Syria on June 11. Baghdad had taken umbrage at the Syrian regime's receiving a stream of official Iranian visitors in the first week of June. The visitors had brought promises of economic assistance to Syria and of pressure on Hezbollah to moderate its obstruction of Syrian moves in Lebanon.[25]

Hussein and the Saudis continued their efforts to bring the two sides together, this time very discreetly. Only after Hafiz Assad and Saddam Hussein had met in late April 1987 in Eastern Jordan with Hussein and Abdallah present did word get out. Assad had just returned from a three-day visit to the USSR, and his Soviet hosts had urged his attendance.[26] Although getting the two presidents in the same room was a diplomatic triumph, once again nothing came of the effort. Assad, who had again asserted that the 1978 charter could be the only basis for renewed relations, and Saddam did not agree on anything. Neither did follow-up meetings of senior foreign affairs officials in May and June.[27] By early June the media war had started again with Baghdad's Ba'ath party daily al-Thawrah on June 3 referring to the "wicked tyrannical regime" in Damascus and linking Damascus's perfidy to its alliance with the "Magian/Zionist regime" in Tehran. Such media invective by both parties kept up until arrangements for the Arab summit meeting at Amman were completed.

The chief reason for convening a summit was the growing concern among eastern Arab states over Iran's conduct concerning the war with Iraq and, in particular, its refusal to accept U.N. Security Council Resolution 598's procedures for achieving a cease-fire and starting a process to end the war. Iraq wanted the summit to concern itself only with the Iran-Iraq war, but Assad was adamant that it must deal with other concerns, with "all matters of interest to the Arab nation." Both Lebanon and the Palestine issue were included in the meeting's final declaration in terms acceptable to Damascus. In addition, Syria joined in the summit's condemnation of Iranian occupation of Iraqi soil, of its nonacceptance of Resolution 598, and of its aggression against Kuwait.[28] Assad was less than enthusiastic about the summit's decision that restoration of relations with Egypt was a matter for individual states and not an "Arab" decision.

The summit provided the occasion for another attempt to reconcile the Iraqi and Syrian presidents. King Hussein convened a meeting of the two, which was attended by five others who had been involved at one time or another in the conciliation attempts authorized by the 1985 summit: Shaikh Zaid of the United Arab Emirates. Shaykh Jabir al-Ahmad of Kuwait, President Chadli Ben-Jedid of Algeria, President Ali Abdallah Salih of the Yemen Arab Republic, and Crown Prince Abdallah, who represented Saudi Arabia at the summit in place of his brother, the king. King Hussein helped bridge the distance between the Iraqi and Syrian leaders by publicly linking their respective major regional interests. "There is a relationship between the Arab-Israeli conflict on the one hand and the Iraq-Iran war on the other . . . Israel is helping Iran to acquire arms.[29] He specifically associated the Saudi crown prince with the success of efforts to bring Saddam and Asad together and improve relations and cautioned people not to expect speedy change in the two countries' relations. "The matter may require some time . . . [before] the situation returns to how it should be."[30]

Signs of caution about prospects for concrete manifestations of closer Iraqi-Syrian ties were in evidence even as the meeting drew to a close. The Iraqi first deputy prime minister, Taha Yasin Ramadan, was reservedly optimistic, detecting a favorable change in Syrian attitudes but warning that normal relations would depend on Syria's "practical deeds on the [Gulf] war following the summit."[31] Abdallah of Saudi Arabia responded to press speculation of an immediate restoration of diplomatic relations between Damascus and Baghdad by warning that he was "not sure" that such relations were imminent although he had hopes for the future.[32] And even though Syria agreed to the summit resolutions criticizing Iran, Foreign Minister Faruk al-Shara' stated that "all attempts to undermine Syrian-Iranian relations will fail completely." He further asserted that "Iran . . . is not an enemy of the Arabs."[33]

A renewed break, if break is the correct term to use for a fracture that had been set but had scarcely started to heal, occurred just two months after the Amman summit. It was occasioned by Syrian efforts to promote a dialogue between the GCC and Iran. Al-Shara' visited

Tehran and Riyadh both before and after the late December GCC
meeting. He and Syrian Vice-President Abd al-Halim Khaddam
toured Gulf capitals in early January. The Syrian efforts were favorably received by Jordanian Prime Minister Rifa'i: "There have been
contacts between the Syrians and the Iranians regarding the escalation
of the war, and "there was no Arab decisions [sic] to ask the Syrians to
do anything in particular but . . . every Arab country is doing all it can
in its own way for the joint common Arab purpose to [sic] drawing
this war to an end."[34] King Fahd, responding to a question about the
Syrian diplomat's visits to Iran and Riyadh said, "We thank the Syrian
officials . . . for their good initiative in this regard. We hope these
initiatives will have the best possible results in . . . serving the causes
of our Arabic and Islamic nation.[35] Saudi Foreign Minister Saud al-
Faysal insisted that the Syrians were not involved in mediation. "They
are making the effort, which we naturally welcome, as a step toward
easing tensions in the area. It is also in harmony with GCC resolutions."[36]

The Iraqis took a much different view. On January 21, Minister of
Culture and Information Latif Jasim stated forcefully that "nobody
has authorized the Syrian officials to carry out . . . a mediation . . .
[because] none of the Arabs trust their role." He added that the Amman summit was "clear in condemning the Iranian aggression . . . and
in calling for true Arab solidarity" and that the Syrian actions were
contrary to the spirit and resolutions of this summit.[37] Arab diplomats—most likely Iraqis—told a London Arabic paper that Iraq's
concern stemmed from Syria's effort to separate the GCC from Iraq
and to prevent the war from spreading rather than trying to stop it.[38]
Tariq Aziz repeated the message a few days later, and Saddam himself
indicated concern about the GCC having "faults," though he "believe[d] that there is increasing awareness [in it] that Iranians are
enemies of the Arab nation."[39]

By the end of January, the Baghdad radio had gone back to calling
Assad "an element of treachery, treason and harm to the . . . [Arab]
nation."[40] On February 3 Damascus resumed broadcasts of its Voice of
Iraq station. Iraq replied by putting the Voice of the National Alliance
for the Liberation of Syria back on the air on February 14.[41]

The impasse between the two Ba'athist states remains as it has been
for many years. Syria continues to emphasize its role as the principal
state confronting Israel. Its interest in opposing Saddam Hussein's
efforts to win broad acceptance as the Arab champion opposing Iranian efforts to conquer Arab territory has not diminished. The Iraqi
leader, however, is meeting with some success in these efforts; Saudi
Arabia broke diplomatic relations with Iran in April 1988.

There is a question whether Saudi financial support for Syria will be affected by the break in relations with the Islamic Republic. The Saudis have been providing Syria with about $500 million annually in aid for several years under an agreement originally made at the Arab summit following the Camp David agreements. At the time of the Amman summit there was speculation that the aid would not be renewed; it had been set for a ten-year period. There were also speculations that such aid was a matter to be arranged bilaterally, the implication being that Saudi Arabia would continue to honor its commitments with the understanding that the timeliness of transfers of funds might be affected by Syrian actions that were not in harmony with Saudi policies, as had occurred even under the 1979 summit agreement.

Damascus and the Palestinians

The Amman summit also set the stage for yet another restoration of relations between the mainstream Palestinian organizations, notably Fatah and its head, Yasser Arafat, and the Syrians. Four years earlier, guerrilla forces backed by Syria had driven Arafat and his men out of Tripoli. That action demonstrated clearly, if anyone needed to be shown, that the Syrian regime desired to permit the Palestinian guerrillas as little freedom of military and political action as possible, a policy it had followed for years.[42] By the time Israel withdrew its major forces from Lebanon in mid-1985 and concentrated on controlling its border security zone with its Lebanese client Antoine Lahad's forces, stiffened with Israeli military advisers and security service men, there were for all practical purposes no Arafat loyalist fighters active in Lebanon. Those that remained were lying low.

From Fatah's perspective, restoration of relations with Syria was of critical importance. It was the major state confronting Israel; other members of the Steadfastness and Confrontation Front—South Yemen, Libya, and Algeria—were useful only as political bases. Even while Syria was encouraging its allies in Lebanon to eliminate the remains of the Palestinian guerrilla presence there that were not under Syrian control, other leaders were talking of restoring ties. Salah Khalaf told a Kuwaiti newspaper early in 1986 that Palestinian leaders had decided to stop their media campaign against Syria.[43] He met with Rif'at al-Assad in Paris later that month and had a useful exchange.[44] Farouk Kaddumi declared a few months later that the way was being paved for better relations but added, with considerable foresight, that it would take a "strong impetus" to move matters beyond the talking stage.[45]

Syria was not to be pushed into restoring relations with Arafat and his group unless the terms of a restoration would benefit Syria. For more than a year no progress was recorded. Then in February 1987 Damascus sent its forces into West Beirut to put an end to the escalating violence there. A few weeks later Syrian troops took up positions around the Palestinian refugee camps, putting an end to the "war of the camps" that had raged intermittently for a year and a half, but with particular violence from October 1986. Amal militia had failed to break the resistance of the defenders, whose numbers had been bolstered by fighters returning through Maronite-controlled territory, a process facilitated by the bitterly anti-Syrian head of the Lebanese forces, Samir Ja'ja'. The move occurred two months before a meeting in Algiers of the Palestinian National Council at which two of Arafat's opponents, who had long enjoyed Syrian hospitality, joined him on the dias.[46] In late April Assad visited the USSR; during talks there General Secretary Gorbachev urged Syrian-Palestinian reconciliation and spoke positively of the need for an Arab-Israeli peace settlement.

The November 1987 summit meeting in Amman, preoccupied with the Gulf war and the issue of allowing individual states to reopen diplomatic relations with Egypt, advanced the cause of Syrian-PLO relations only slightly. The PLO radio in Algiers quoted "observers" as saying: "The conference did not reach a solution to existing disagreements between Syria and the PLO . . . Palestinian leader Yasser Arafat did not meet with the Syrian president."[47] Arafat, however, told a London newspaper, "We reached a decision at the Amman summit to restore relations once again with Syria. This took place after a dialogue between me and Syrian President Hafiz-al-Assad in the presence of Algerian President Chadli Ben-Jedid."[48]

Even though both parties felt under compulsion to make up because of the Palestinian uprising in the West Bank and Gaza that began in December 1987, the parties dragged their feet. It took a dramatic event—the killing of PLO leader Khalil al-Wazir in Tunis by Israeli commandos—to push the two parties together. Syria offered to have Wazir buried in Damascus. His funeral was attended by most senior Fatah leaders. And on April 25, five years after Assad had expelled Arafat from Syrian soil, the two sat down together in Damascus.

What does this restoration of relations mean? Were Assad and Arafat reconciled? The historical record points strongly to a negative answer. Assad, who has displayed a consistency of purpose in his external policies over nearly two decades, has certainly not deviated from his view that Syria's interests require that the Palestinian organizations be responsive to Syrian control lest they force it into a confrontation with Israel at a time and place not of Damascus's choosing. Arafat is trying to co-opt the spontaneous uprising in the occupied territories. Assad is also trying to influence it. Hence the two leaders have met and embraced for tactical reasons. Their fundamental differences remain, as the fighting that erupted in the Palestinian refugee camps near Beirut between pro-Arafat and pro-Syrian forces in June 1988 clearly indicated.

The new circumstances brought about by the uprising in the West Bank and Gaza complicate Syria's efforts to influence Palestinian behavior. The Palestinian groups directly beholden to Syria—Sa'iqah and Abu Musa's group—have minuscule followings there. Better relations with Arafat do not help much either. Even if he were disposed to cooperate meaningfully with Assad, the loosely structured organization that is directing the events in the occupied territories is run primarily by a younger generation grown tired of the travels and speeches of the "big Abus," as Arafat and his cohorts are sometimes derisively called. Syria has no influence with the Palestinian organizations that provide the organizational stiffening for the stone-throwers in Palestinian towns and villages. Damascus may help the uprising with radio broadcasts and other support, but it will in the near term at least be primarily a spectator at a game played by others' rules.

Lebanon: A Continued Impasse

Much has changed in the twelve years since Syrian troops moved into Lebanon in response to appeals from beleaguered Maronites. The old generation of communal leaders is dead—Rashid Karami and Kamal Jumblat at the hands of assassins, Camille Chamoun and Pierre Gemayel of old age—or sunk into octogenarian retirement as Sa'ib Salam is. Alignments among the communities and factions have shifted and reshifted. An Israeli invasion that was designed to change the face of Lebanon has come and gone. The once passive and despised Shi'a now demand political power commensurate with their status as the largest community.

Many changes have not been for the good. The Maronite leaders of the Lebanese Forces are as stubbornly intransigent in their insistence on traditional Christian prerogatives as the old leaders were. New leaders head a divided Shi'a community. Nabih Berri has not proved able to attract communitywide allegiance; perhaps no leader could do so in the Shi'as's present state of political development. Neither has he been able to build a militia able to compete with rivals. His competitor among the Shi'a, Hezbollah, armed and supported by Iran, is seeking an Islamic Republic in a country that is 40 percent Christian and whose Druze and Sunni communities reject the politico-religious organizational principles pioneered by Khomeini.

The three years since the Israelis pulled back into the security zone along their border have seen no major changes in the Lebanese situation. The principal communities control approximately the same area they did in 1985. Efforts by Amal to take control of Palestinian areas in South Beirut failed. Amal and Druze fighting became so intense that Syria was compelled to take over West Beirut's security with its own troops in 1987. Amal's effort in the spring of 1988 to take control of the Shi'a suburbs of South Beirut did not go well. Hezbollah's militia has shown itself to be formidable, and Syria has so far limited itself to a mediatory role. Central government is nonexistent in practice. Militia discipline is such that any trigger-happy youth can spark a day or two's fighting. More serious conflict follows real or fancied efforts by one group or another to improve a tactical position or avenge a defeat.

Despite this dismal situation, the Lebanese parliament was due to elect a new president in 1988. Amin Gemayel, by law, cannot succeed himself, and there are only seventy-odd living members of the ninety-nine-member parliament chosen in 1972. The National Pact of 1943 reserved the presidency for a Maronite, and several have indicated interest. The Lebanese political compact is so fragmented that Shi'a leaders have hinted at proposing one of their people for the post. The electoral process indicated the limitations on Syria's tactical control in Lebanon, but it is not likely to bring about fundamental change in the Lebanese situation. (For the dynamics of the Lebanese elections and their aftermath, see the chapter by Marius Deeb in this volume.) Syria has repeatedly urged a reconciliation among the communities and a redistribution of political offices. Gemayel has suggested a deal whereby he would accept modest political changes, chiefly a greater role for the cabinet, if the constitution is changed to allow him a second term. The Lebanese Forces have not budged, and Syria has not yet attempted to force the changes it sees as the only solution.

Israel

Most of the three years since Israel pulled its major combat units out of Lebanon have been preternaturally calm on the Syrian-Israeli front. The cease-fire line on the Golan Heights has been totally without incident, as has been the case since the successful conclusion of Kissinger's shuttle diplomacy in 1974. In Lebanon there appears to be a tacit agreement that Syrian ground forces will not move closer than about fifteen miles to the international border in the east and rather more than that near the sea. The United Nations Interim Force in Lebanon (UNIFIL) and the Israelis' border security strip fill most of this distance. Syria has moved forces for internal security reasons, as when it occupied the Biqa' village of Meshgara for a few weeks in 1986 to assert control over Palestinian factions there. In late 1985 it moved missile batteries so as to restrict the Israeli air force's freedom to overfly parts of Lebanon when it judged that the Israelis were being too aggressive by shooting down two aircraft flying in Syrian airspace.[49]

For a few months in 1986 the adjective *calm* would not have been appropriate, but they stand out in comparison to the rest of the period. Tension escalated in February, when Israel, acting on faulty intelligence, forced down a Libyan airplane which it believed was carrying senior PLO officials to Damascus. The passengers were in fact Syrians and Lebanese; one was the assistant secretary general of the Ba'ath party.[50] All were released. Later in the month an Israeli political figure reiterated Israel's claim that the Golan Heights belonged to Israel in language the Syrians considered especially forceful. Assad took the opportunity to insert a sentence in his speech to the newly elected People's Assembly: "If the Israelis work to put the Golan within their borders, we will work to put the Golan in the middle of Syria, and not on its borders."[51] An Israeli journalist interpreted this statement as indicating aggressive intent on Assad's part.[52] On April 18, British authorities arrested Nizar Hindawi for attempting to smuggle a bomb onto an El Al plane; they subsequently implicated Syrian diplomats in London and expelled three of them. In addition, through March and April there were recurrent stories that war was imminent. They reached a peak when reports that Syrian forces were preparing earthworks in the southern Biqa' hit the press in May. Journalists and some political figures took up the stories with zest.[53] But Israeli military figures, from a battalion commander on leave to the chief of staff, made it clear that they saw no Syrian preparations for hostilities in the short term.[54] Israel's preeminent civilian military analyst, Ze'ev Schiff, assessed the Syrian move as defensive, although he, like most others who commented, stressed that Syria's long-term aims could include war.[55] The media crisis evaporated. There have been no incidents between Syrian and Israeli forces, either in Lebanon or in the Golan.

Assad's goal of strategic parity with Israel remains a top priority, whatever the reality of accommodating to superior Israeli strength at the present or to its insistence on controlling a security zone in Lebanon. He said in early 1986, "We are working to achieve this [strategic] balance . . . peace will be difficult to achieve while Israel feels that it is more capable than the others . . . we have in mind . . . a strategic balance between Syria and Israel."[56] Assad added that his balance contained economic, social, and political factors as well as military ones. Despite the difficulties involved in following this path, there is no indication that Syria has any intention of abandoning it. A position of strength from which to deal with Israel and a sphere of influence over Lebanon, Jordan, and the Palestinians are complementary goals. To the extent that they are achieved, Syria will find itself able to deal with Iraqi ambitions.

The positions and attitudes of the superpowers are never absent from Syria's calculations about its policies in the area. Both are important to Damascus, albeit for different reasons. The USSR is Syria's principal source of arms, renders it political support, and is linked by a friendship and cooperation treaty. Under Gorbachev, the USSR has taken the position favoring normalization of relations among competing Arab groups such as Syria and the PLO, Syria and Iraq, and Arabs and Israel. There is, of course, much that is not spelled out in regard to the latter issue. The implication for Syria in this Soviet policy is that as long as the USSR maintains this position and remains more interested in good relations with the United States than in supporting Arab confrontation with Israel, as the Soviets earlier had been, it will be very difficult for Syria to attain at least the military parity that it desires.

For the better part of a decade the United States has usually preferred to leave Syria out of its Middle East calculations. The country is considered difficult to deal with, a sponsor of terrorism, and unyielding in its demands. Nevertheless, Syria's location, strength, and ambition make it a key player in the Levant. When it sees advantages, Syria is prepared to discuss and work with the United States. Washington is currently engaged in one of its periodic attempts to deal with major Middle Eastern issues, talking with Damascus on the Arab-Israeli issue and participating in an effort to promote political compromise in Lebanon. The scope of the efforts is unclear and the prospect of progress uncertain at best, but the two parties are in contact at a high level.

Concluding Observations

Since mid-1985, the bulk of what is of interest regarding Syria has to do with its relations with its neighbors. Domestically, during these years Syria experienced a period of unusual political tranquility, by historical standards, although it has continued to encounter serious economic problems. Highlights of the Assad regime's external affairs included the restoration of close ties with Jordan at the end of 1985, attendance at the Arab summit meeting in Amman in November 1987, a short-lived reconciliation with Iraq arranged at that gathering, failure to ameliorate tensions between Iran and the Gulf Cooperation Council states, and in the first half of 1988 initial steps toward reestablishing civil relations with Yasser Arafat and the mainstream PLO factions. All through the period Syria has continued to grapple with the intractable problems of its twelve-year involvement in Lebanon.

In the second half of 1988 three developments acted adversely on Syria's interests in the region. First, the collapse of Iranian military resistance and Tehran's acceptance of U.N. Security Council Resolution 598 allowed Saddam Hussein to claim victory. He immediately turned his attention to a variety of initiatives designed to advance his twin ambitions of making Iraq an influential power in inter-Arab affairs and of making himself, *a*, if not *the*, commanding Arab leader. Assad, who had supported Iran for Syrian geopolitical reasons, found himself in the unpleasant position of having backed the losing side. Moreover, Saddam's relentlessly articulated doctrine that through eight years of war Iraq had been defending Arabdom against Persian aggression had attracted growing support over the years. This was not always because of Arab belief in Saddam's views; Egypt's interest in supporting Iraq, for example, was a means of increasing Arab acceptance of the need for its return to full political membership in the Arab community. But broadening Arab backing of Iraq had the effect of increasing Syria's isolation within the Arab state system.

Second, Syria's position in Lebanon took a severe downturn. Amin Gemayel's six-year nonrenewable term as president of Lebanon ended in September 1988. With the hardening of attitudes in the principal Lebanese sectarian communities, agreement on a successor proved impossible to achieve. Damascus compounded the problem by trying to impose former President Suleiman Franjieh's candidacy on the "rump" Lebanese parliament. His identification with Syria and poor record in office made him unacceptable. When a less controversial but essentially powerless second choice was proposed by Syria in consultation with the United States, the Lebanese Forces physically prevented a parliamentary quorum from assembling. The outgoing Gemayel then appointed a "midnight prime minister," General Michel Aoun, minutes before his term expired on September 22.

This event signaled the end of the unwritten national covenant under which Lebanon had been administered since 1943. (The covenant provided for a Maronite president, a Sunni prime minister, and a Shi'a speaker of parliament.) Since September 23, there has been no president but two prime ministers—one a Maronite. The fragile symbols of a unified state that had survived a dozen years of civil war disappeared. Iraq, eager to punish Syria for its support of Iran, supplied arms and advisers to the Maronite faction led by Prime Minister Aoun. Thus stiffened in their resolve and disposed to blame Syria for all Lebanon's ills, the Maronites became even more determined to hold to the status and position they had enjoyed since the days of the French mandate.

The third development was the change in fortunes of the Palestinians and of the PLO leader, Yasser Arafat. The continuing ability of Palestinians in the West Bank and Gaza to keep the Intifada going in the face of Israeli efforts to repress it forced change on the PLO. At its meeting in November, the Palestinian National Council proclaimed an independent Palestinian state in the West Bank and Gaza. It also accepted U.N. Security Council Resolution 242, thereby indirectly recognizing the existence of Israel. A month later, Arafat met U.S. conditions for conducting a dialogue. Watching these developments, Palestinian organizations that had accepted Syrian support since 1983 began to drift back into the PLO mainstream, a process that accelerated in 1989.

As the new year opened, Assad had taken the first steps toward making the best of the changed circumstances. In late December, the Syrian president let it be known that he would not try to obstruct Egypt's reintegration into Arab councils. That accommodation progressed during the first months of 1989 as did, albeit more slowly, Syrian-PLO relations. In Lebanon, the stakes for Syria remain high and the possibility that it will salvage something from the carnage there appears less than two or three years ago. If one judges by the history of that unfortunate country since the mid-1970s, however, it may be a long time before a settlement emerges from the tangle its affairs are in.

Notes

1. John F. Devlin, "Syrian Policy," in *The Middle East after the Israeli Invasion of Lebanon,* ed. Robert O. Freedman (Syracuse: Syracuse Univ. Press, 1986), pp. 299–302.

2. Press Conference by Minister of Interior, Syrian Arab News Agency (SANA), Feb. 12, 1986 (*FBIS,* Feb. 13, 1986).

3. See John F. Devlin, "Syria and Lebanon," *Current History* (Feb. 1988): 77–78, for more detail on these domestic developments.

4. Yahya Sadowski, review of *The Struggle for Syria,* in *Middle East Journal* 42 (Spring 1988): 309.

5. Geographic Syria extends from the Taurus Mountains to the Sinai Desert and from the Mediterranean Sea to the Middle Euphrates and the desert. See *Encyclopedia Britannica,* 11th ed. (1911), 26: 305.

6. The nationalists of the World War I era thought of the Arab countries as those areas east of the Red and Mediterranean seas. During the interwar period, nationalists progressively redefined the boundaries of Arabdom, culminating in the Pan-Arab concept of an Arab nation extending from Morocco to the Zagros Mountains and the Gulf.

7. Crown Prince Abdallah, Radio Riyadh, Sept. 17, 1985 (*FBIS:NE/SA,* Sept. 26, 1985).

8. Riyadh, Saudi Press Agency, Sept. 22, 1985 (*FBIS:NE/SA,* Sept. 26, 1985).

9. *Arabia,* Jan. 1986, p. 25.

10. Amman television, Nov. 10, 1985 (*FBIS:NE/SA,* Nov. 12, 1985).

11. Damascus, SANA, Nov. 13, 1985 (*FBIS:NE/SA,* Nov. 14, 1985).

12. Umar F. Abd-Allah, *The Islamic Struggle in Syria* (Berkeley: Mizan Press, 1983), esp. pp. 42–48.

13. Martin Kramer, "Syria's Alawis and Shi'ism," in *Shi'ism, Resistance, and Revolution,* ed. Kramer (Boulder, Colo.: Westview Press, 1987), pp. 243–44, 247–49. Kramer argues that Sadr's move was "political, not theological." But history has shown that politics, as well as belief and practice, can determine orthodoxy. His distinction is too simple.

14. *Middle East Economic Digest,* Apr. 29, 1988, p. 28.

15. *Financial Times,* Mar. 10, 1988.

16. *Al-Sharq al-Awsat* (London), Apr. 24, 1988 (*FBIS:NE/SA,* Apr. 28, 1988).

17. Hafiz Assad, press conference, Radio Paris, Nov. 18, 1984 (*FBIS:NE/SA,* Nov. 19, 1984).

18. *Middle East Economic Digest,* Apr. 22, 1988, p. 35.

19. *Economist,* June 15, 1986, p. 35.

20. Iraqi Foreign Minister Tariq Aziz, cited in *al-Tadamun* (London), June 7–13, 1986 (*FBIS,* June 11, 1986).

21. See John F. Devlin, "Syrian Policy," in *The Middle East since Camp David,* ed. Robert O. Freedman, (Boulder, Colo.: Westview Press, 1984), p. 127 and n. 11, and the fuller discussion in Phebe Marr, *The Modern History of Iraq* (Boulder, Colo.: Westview Press, 1985), pp. 228–31. Both express doubt that there was a coup planned against the Iraqi regime. It is of interest that Syrian Defense Minister Mustafa Talas, in a signed article in the Damascus newspaper Tishrin, on March 7, 1989, accused Saddam Hussein of fabricating the charge that Assad was trying to overthrow the Iraqi regime and of ousting then Iraqi President Bakr, a man "who had unity flowing in his veins" (*FBIS,* Mar. 24, 1988).

22. Foreign Minister Aziz in *al-Sharq al-Awsat,* Mar. 30, 1986 (*FBIS,* Apr. 4, 1986).

23. *Al-Dustur* (Amman), Oct. 12, 1987 (*FBIS:NE/SA,* Oct. 14, 1987).

24. Damascus television, Mar. 18, 1986 (*FBIS:NE/SA,* Mar. 19, 1986).

25. *Al-Majallah* (London), June 18–24, 1986 (*FBIS:NE/SA,* June 24, 1986).

26. Kuwait, Kuwait News Agency, citing *al-Qabas* (Kuwait), May 4, 1987 (*FBIS,* May 4, 1987); *Middle East Economic Digest,* May 9, 1987, p. 20.

27. *Middle East Economic Digest,* June 6, 1987, p. 29.

28. *New York Times,* Oct. 13, 1987; ibid., Nov. 12, 1987, for excerpts from the final declaration of the meeting.

29. *Al-Ra'y* (Amman), Nov. 10, 1987 (*FBIS:NE/SA,* Nov. 12, 1987).

30. King Hussein's news conference, Amman television, Nov. 11, 1987 (*FBIS:NE/SA,* Nov. 13, 1987).

31. Interview in *Jordan Times,* Nov. 11, 1987 (*FBIS:NE/SA,* Nov. 12, 1987).

32. *Al-Anba'* (Kuwait), Nov. 11, 1987 (*FBIS:NE/SA,* Nov. 17, 1987).

33. Radio Monte Carlo, Paris, Nov. 13, 1987 (*FBIS:NE/SA,* Nov. 13, 1987).

34. *Jordan Times,* Jan. 4, 1988 (*FBIS:NE/SA,* Jan. 5, 1988).

35. *Al-Ahram,* Jan. 15, 1988 (*FBIS:NE/SA,* Jan. 20, 1988).

36. *Al-Mustaqbal* (Paris), Jan. 30, 1988 (*FBIS:NE/SA,* Feb. 1, 1988). The date as given in *FBIS* may be incorrect; internal evidence places this statement much earlier in January.

37. Baghdad, Iraqi News Agency, Jan. 21, 1988 (*FBIS:NE/SA,* Jan. 21, 1988).

38. *Al-Sharq al-Awsat,* Jan. 24, 1988 (*FBIS:NE/SA,* Jan. 27, 1988).

39. *Al-Ra'y* (Amman), Jan. 26, 1988 (*FBIS:NE/SA,* Jan. 27, 1988).

40. Baghdad, Voice of the Masses, Jan. 27, 1988 (*FBIS:NE/SA,* Jan. 28, 1988).

41. *FBIS:NE/SA,* Feb. 4, 18, 1988.

42. Devlin, "Syrian Policy," p. 308.

43. *Al-Siyasah* (Kuwait), Jan. 4, 1986 (*FBIS:NE/SA,* Jan. 9, 1986).

44. *Al-Majallah* (London), Jan. 15–21, 1986 (*FBIS:NE/SA,* Jan. 17, 1986).

45. Kuwait News Agency, Mar. 20, 1986 (*FBIS:NE/SA,* Mar. 21, 1986).

46. *New York Times,* Apr. 21, 1987.

47. Voice of Palestine, Nov. 12, 1987 (*FBIS:NE/SA,* Nov. 16, 1987).

48. *al-Tadamun,* Jan. 2, 1988 (*FBIS:NE/SA,* Jan. 6, 1988).

49. *New York Times,* May 19, 1988.

50. Ibid., Feb. 5, 6, 1986.

51. Radio Damascus, Feb. 27, 1986 (*FBIS:NE/SA,* Feb. 28, 1986).

52. Hirsh Goodman, "Assad's Threats Must Be Heeded," *Jerusalem Post,* International ed., Mar. 15, 1986.

53. See, for example, Karen Elliot House, "Israel Says War Threat with Syria Grows," *Wall Street Journal,* May 7, 1986, which reported the views of Israeli political figures.

54. *Philadelphia Inquirer,* May 18, 1986; *New York Times,* May 19, 21, 1986.

55. *New York Times,* May 25, 1986.

56. Damascus television, Feb. 18, 1986 (*FBIS:NE/SA,* Feb. 19, 1986).

12

Lebanon in the Aftermath of the Abrogation of the Israeli-Lebanese Accord
The Dominant Role of Syria

Marius Deeb

The key for understanding the situation in Lebanon since March 1984 is, first, to examine the views and attitudes of the various sectarian communities in Lebanon toward each other and toward regional powers. Second, it is necessary to discern the objectives of Syrian President Hafiz Assad in Lebanon because Syria has been the major external power in Lebanon since the withdrawal of the Multi-National Force during February–April 1984.

The Lebanese Sects: Their Stands and Viewpoints

I will first discuss the various Lebanese religious or more appropriately sectarian communities and analyze their position in 1988, beginning with the Shi'i community, which is the largest Muslim community and among the major seven sects or communities, namely Shi'i, Sunni, Druze, Maronite, Greek Orthodox, Greek Catholic, and Armenian, the largest single sect or minority in Lebanon. Until recently the Shi'i community has been dominated by Amal and Hezbollah, but the recent fighting between these two groups that began in April 1988 in southern Lebanon and continued during May and June 1988 in the southern suburbs of Beirut produced the unintended consequence of the strengthening of traditional Shi'i leadership whether represented by the Higher Shi'i Council or by the return of the Muqataji (Feudal) leader Kamil al-Assad to center stage.[1]

At least three levels of analysis are necessary to understand the outburst of fighting among Shi'is. First there has been an increase in armed attacks by Hezbollah against the South Lebanon Army (SLA) and Israeli-controlled security belt in southern Lebanon, which led to retaliation by the SLA and Israel. Thus the attempt by Amal to curb Hezbollah in southern Lebanon was aimed, despite its rhetoric, at alleviating the suffering of the people of southern Lebanon from this cycle of violence initiated by Hezbollah. Second, there is the unavoidable competition between the most powerful militias among the Shi'is of Lebanon, Amal and Hezbollah, for ascendancy and domination, which in the context of a militia-dominant situation (in contrast to the premilitia era) means inevitably the ability to expand the physical presence of a particular militia in a particular region. Because the stronghold of Hezbollah has always been the Biqa' region, where Amal's presence has been weak since June 1982, it is not surprising that Amal felt threatened by Hezbollah's inroads into southern Lebanon since 1985. The third level of analysis pertains to the roles of Syria and Iran in Lebanon. To end the fighting among Shi'is, Syrian President Assad and Iranian President Ali Khamenei had to communicate with each other and to intervene on behalf of their proxies.[2] Nevertheless, the conflict between Amal and Hezbollah cannot be depicted as a struggle between Syria and Iran because the strategic alliance between these two states is much more important than intra-Shi'i conflict in Lebanon. The relationship between Syria and Amal is very strong because Amal's leader Nabih Berri has become increasingly dependent on Syria for the supply of arms and political support. Iran's relationship to Hezbollah is similar, but because Iran has no common border with Lebanon, it has to rely on continued Syrian support for its role in Lebanon via Hezbollah. Furthermore, although Amal's relations with Iran have more often than not been strained, Syria's relations with Hezbollah since the latter's formation in the Baalback region in June 1982 have been correct if not cordial.[3]

What does Hezbollah want in Lebanon? What is its attitude toward the unabated conflict in Lebanon? Is it in favor of ending the conflict or is it in favor of its perpetuation? What reform, if any, does Hezbollah want in the political system of Lebanon? It is clear that Hezbollah wants the establishment of an Islamic state in Lebanon similar to that in Iran.[4] The majority of the Shi'is of Lebanon, however, find such a goal unacceptable, and this view is shared by the Sunnis and the Druze as well as the Christians (Maronite, Greek Orthodox, Greek Catholic, and Armenian). Hezbollah is also interested in the perpetuation of the conflict whether against the SLA in southern Lebanon or internally against the Lebanese state and its institutions. Thus Hezbollah has placed itself outside the pale of the politics of compromise and reconciliation. But one should not underestimate the value of Hezbollah to external powers that have used its members for terrorist operations, whether suicidal car-bombings or hostage-taking.

Amal is the major militia among the Shi'is of Lebanon but is fragmented in organizational structure, as is reflected in the attitude of its various local leaders with respect to the issue of ending the conflict as well as that of political reform. For instance Dawud Dawud, the late chairman of the Executive Committee of Amal, wanted to pacify the Lebanese-Israeli border and reach an understanding with the Israelis and the SLA.[5] He also wanted to end the conflict across the Green Line between West Beirut and East Beirut. Berri, on the other hand, cannot possibly entertain, let alone follow, such policies because he is too dependent on Syria and could easily be outflanked by the militant Hezbollah. Amal, on the whole, is inward-looking and in favor of the Lebanese identity when faced with a choice between Iran and Lebanon, in stark contrast to the attitude of Hezbollah's leaders such as Ayatollah Muhammed Husain Fadlallah. Amal's demands for political reform are reasonable, including a Shi'i vice-president who cannot succeed the president and a larger share than the Sunnis of the Lebanese parliament seats allotted to Muslims.

Before dealing with the Sunni Muslim community, it is necessary to discuss the political system of Lebanon as it existed during the period 1943–75, the so-called heyday of political liberalism because of the role of the Sunni Muslims in it. The founding father of Lebanon was Riyad al-Sulh, the first Sunni prime minister on the eve of independence, who envisaged through the National Pact (*al-Mithaq al-Watani*) a unique political system with three major aspects. First, the Lebanese government would be a partnership between Christians and Muslims, which would involve not simply the equal division of cabinet posts between Christians and Muslims and the allotting of certain posts to certain sects but the cooperation of the various sects in making major decisions. Numerical majorities were less important than a broad base of power that could guarantee the input of each community through some of its prominent leaders. Second, Lebanon would remain a society in which the basic freedoms such as the freedom of speech, the freedom of association, habeus corpus, and the freedom of worship would be safeguarded. The democratic parliamentary system would be one of the pillars of this free society. Third, Lebanon should both be part of the Arab world and open to the West.[6]

In spite of the conflict in Lebanon for the last thirteen years, the reforms envisaged by the major parties to the conflicts do not question these basic principles of the National Pact. This is true of the first reform document, the so-called Constitutional Document of February

1976,[7] and of the latest proposals put forward by President Gemayel, which Ambassador April Glaspie discussed with the various Lebanese politicians and with Syrian officials in the spring and summer of 1988. Hezbollah, as expected, is not part of these discussions, but Amal is, and the differences that have to be ironed out are whether the prime minister should be elected by parliament or chosen by the president, whether the president should preside over all cabinet sessions, and whether the unicameral political system should be transformed into a bicameral system. The leaders of Amal and other Shi'i politicians favor a Shi'i vice-presidency and the selection or election of the prime minister by members of parliament. They are not enthusiastic, however, about the establishment of a Senate, which is primarily a Druze demand.[8]

The Sunni community in Lebanon has lost some of its power partly because before August 1982 it relied on the PLO and was adversely affected by the evacuation of the PLO leaders and fighters in 1982–83. The Sunnis of Tripoli have been suffering for at least the last five years. In December 1983, PLO leader Arafat was forced to evacuate Tripoli, leaving much destruction in his wake, because Tripoli was the target of Syrian and PLO dissident shelling. In September–October 1985, an offensive launched by four Syrian-proxy militias, the Syrian Social Nationalist party (SSNP), the Lebanese Communist party (LCP), the Ba'th Organization party (BOP), and the Arab Democratic party (ADP) against Sha'ban's Islamic Unification movement, destroyed a considerable portion of the city, and the Syrian troops entered as ostensible mediators. The Syrian troops then began disarming the Sunni local militias, culminating in a massive roundup in December 1986.[9] In June 1987, the leading Sunni politician in Tripoli, Prime Minister Rashid Karami, was assassinated. West Beirut, another traditional stronghold of the Sunnis, did not fare better, for its leading militia, al-Murabitun, was decimated in 1984–85 by Amal and the Druze Progressive Socialist party (PSP). The Palestinian camps war of May–July 1985, May–June 1986, and October 1986–February 1987, which were initiated by Amal, brought more destruction to West Beirut. Since February 22, 1987, Syrian troops have moved to West Beirut in addition to the Shi'i militias of Amal, Hezbollah, and the Druze PSP, which had been present since February 6, 1984.

The only Sunni community that currently has a local militia of its own is Sidon, where Mustafa Sa'ad's militia cooperates with some groups of the PLO. Another militia is the Sunni Islamic Group (al-Jama'a al-Islamiya), which has tended to cooperate with Hezbollah within the framework of the Rally of Muslim Clergymen (Tajammu' al-'Ulama' al-Muslimin), dominated by Shi'i clergymen.[10] Thus, on the whole, the Sunnis of Lebanon are living under the sufferance of militias of other sects or under the Syrian army.

That the Sunnis have been deprived (except in Sidon) of their own militias has made their traditional leaders who are represented in the Islamic Gathering (al-Liqa' al-Islami) more prominent. The latter is composed of former prime ministers, Taqi al-Din al-Sulh, Sa'ib Salam, Rashid al-Suhl, former cabinet ministers and members of parliament representing West Beirut, Tripoli, 'Akkar, and southern Biqa' (Zaki al-Mazbudi, Jamil Kibbi, Nazim al-Qadiri, and Talal al-Mar'abi), and the Sunni religious establishment represented by Dar al-Ifta' and the Grand Mufti Shaikh Hasan Khalid (killed by a bomb in 1989).

Because it chooses not to command militias, the Islamic Gathering has consistently opposed all militias, demanding the return of the legitimate authorities to all regions of Lebanon, including West Beirut and Tripoli. It would like to continue the custom of the president of the republic choosing the prime minister, after consultation with the various parliamentary blocs. It would like to have a stronger premiership but in cooperation with the presidency. It greatly fears that if parliament were to elect the prime minister, the non-Sunni Muslims and external regional powers would have a greater say in that election than hitherto has been the case. Even though their coreligionists constitute the vast majority of the Arab world, in the last two years the Sunnis have begun to feel besieged by a militarily dominant Shi'i community in Lebanon supported by external patrons, namely Khomeini's Iran and Assad's Syria. The Sunnis' political links to Saudi Arabia, Iraq, and Egypt became stronger as a counterpoise to Syria and Iran. Domestically their secret talks and agreements with the Lebanese Front and President Gemayel, which probably cost Prime Minister Karami his life, reveal that the differences between the Sunnis and the Christians are not irreconcilable. Indeed, Karami told a leading Maronite politician who had worked for President Amin Gemayel, "Solve your problems with the Syrians and then there will be no problem between us."[11]

The Druze is the only Lebanese community that managed to score gains without any losses in the course of the conflict. The Druze of Lebanon are not simply a religious sectarian community similar to the Maronites, the Greek Catholics, the Sunnis, and the Shi'is. They are qualitatively different from any other religious or sectarian community. They are socially cohesive and had kept their traditional leaders since at least the seventeenth century.[12] By remaining loyal to the Jumblat clan or the Arsalan clan they have safeguarded their traditions and their own separate identity. Because the Druze constitute no more than 7 percent of the population in Lebanon, they must remain cohesive. Druze also live in Syria and Israel, but their role in Israel has not been significant because they are a very small proportion of the population. In Syria their role was significant in the 1920s, as attested by the Druze Revolt of 1925, and in the 1950s and 1960s, when they played a role in the various coups and countercoups that ended with the supremacy of the 'Alwais in the Syrian army since 1966.[13]

The role of the Druze in Lebanon has been very significant historically. For instance, the backbone of the Lebanese princedom under the Ma'nids and later under the Shihabs was the Druze feudal aristocracy.[14] The Druze of Lebanon take pride in their role in the formation of modern Lebanon. This is important because, unlike other minorities, they have a desire to rule. Therefore, it was not surprising that Kamal Jumblat (who was assassinated in March 1977) acted as the kingmaker during the 1950s and 1960s and led the major Muslim opposition, the Lebanese National movement (LNM), during the civil war of 1975–76.[15] Thus, only in Lebanon could the Druze leaders play a role out of proportion to their numerical strength in the population at large.

Kamal Jumblat's vision of Lebanon was rooted in the Druze community but transcended it by depicting Lebanon as the Athens of the Arab world which was threatened by a new Philip of Macedon and his army, Hafiz Assad of Syria.[16] A few months after the arrival of that army into Lebanon, Kamal Jumblat was assassinated. Kamal's son Walid Jumblat, who took the mantle of the Jumblat clan, the Druze community, and the LNM from his father, visited the latter's nemesis in Damascus, thus initiating a new policy based primarily on realpolitik. The Druze community was successful under the leadership of Walid Jumblat because he opened channels to a variety of external powers, ranging from Syria, Libya, the PLO, and the Soviet Union to Britain and Israel with the sole objective of serving the interests of the Druze community. With the help of Syrian logistical support, Soviet arms, non-Fatah PLO fighters, and Libyan financial support, Walid Jumblat managed to oust the Lebanese forces from the 'Alay and Shuf areas in 1983 and 1985, thus gaining control of a region that had been traditionally part of the Druze fiefdom but was inhabited by a majority of non-Druze people, most of whom were Christians (Maronite, Greek Catholic, and Greek Orthodox). The Druze also control the Hasbayya region (the easternmost area of the Security Zone under the SLA), and parts of the southern Biqa' region, where the Druze clans of Dawud and al-'Aryan hold sway.

Despite the eviction of at least two hundred thousand Christians from the 'Alay and Shuf regions, the relations between Walid Jumblat and some leading Christian politicians remained cordial. The Christian population of the birthplace of former President Camille Chamoun, Dayr al-Qamar, and its environs was spared, and he was buried there when he died in 1987. Danny Chamoun, Camille Chamoun's son and political heir, has excellent relations with Walid Jumblat, who has promised him that the Christian population can return to the Shuf and 'Alay when the conflict in Lebanon is resolved.[17] Walid Jumblat wants the presidency of the republic to remain in the hands of the Maronites, and he supported the candidacy of Antoine Ashqar, a Maronite who belongs to the PSP, not because Jumblat thought he would be elected but as a message to the Maronites that the custom of electing a Maronite president should be kept.[18] The Druze demand three reforms: the creation of a senate presided over by a Druze; the decentralization of the state bureaucracy so that the 'Alay and Shuf regions would be run by Druze in cooperation with members of other sects, with the Druze always having the final say; and that the Lebanese army should not be enlarged sufficiently to be able to threaten the Druze. They most fear the demographic superiority of the Shi'is, a fear shared by the Sunnis.

The Christian communities have more in common than do the three Muslim communities—the Shi'is, the Sunnis, and the Druze. There are, of course, religious differences among the Maronites, the Greek Catholics, the Greek Orthodox, and the Armenians, who are relative newcomers to Lebanon and have remained neutral in the intracommunal fighting since 1975. Although there are small Catholic and even Protestant Armenian communities, the Armenians are primarily Orthodox. There are four important characteristics of the Christian communities in Lebanon. First, the Maronites constitute a majority among the Christians as a whole. Second, they were instrumental, in cooperation with Druze, in the creation of modern Lebanon and therefore have always had an edge over the other Christian communities. Third, although the Christians have or had a presence in all regions of Lebanon, the Maronites also have been compact communities in certain regions of Lebanon, including Kisarwan, northern Matn, Byblos, Zgharta-Bsharri, and Jizzin. The Greek Orthodox are a compact community only in the Kura region, and elsewhere in Lebanon they have always been intermingled with other Christian or Muslim communities. The Greek Catholics have the city of Zahle as their major compact community; otherwise they are or were dispersed in the Zahrani-Sidon region, in Jizzin, Shuf, Baalback, and Beirut. Fourth, the religious differences among the various Christian communities have been played down and, more significantly, they have not been transformed into political or ideological differences. The religious differences cut across sectarian boundaries and depend more on the location of communities or parts thereof. For instance, because of the presence of the Syrian army, the compact community of Greek Orthodox of the Kura region is limited either to joining a pro-Syrian party such as the SSNP or the LCP or ceasing to be active politically. The compact Greek Catholic community of Zahle has been faced since September 1985 with the same limited options. Thus ideological leanings do not necessarily depend on the particular Christian sect to which an individual belongs, and this blurs the differences among the various Christian sects and enhances the role of the Maronites as leaders of the Christian community.

The diversity of opinions among the Christian communities has been both beneficial and harmful to them. Under normal conditions, that is, when there is no armed conflict, diversity of political views would be the epitome of democracy. But when the barrel of the gun is the order of the day, ideological diversity inevitably leads to clashes among the various militias.

At present the most powerful militia among the Christians is the Lebanese Forces under the leadership of Samir Ja'ja. The Lebanese Forces were, to a large extent, the creation of Bashir Gemayel, the younger son of Pierre Gemayel, the founder and president of the Kata'ib party, who would have been assured of a niche in the political establishment whether he had created the Lebanese Forces or not. Undoubtedly, Bashir Gemayel's transformation of the Lebanese Forces into a formidable power base by eliminating Tony Franjieh in 1978 (an action with the adverse consequences that the Franjieh–Lebanese Forces feud has been exploited by Assad to the hilt), and undermining Danny Chamoun's militia in 1980, and rendering the remaining militias, George 'Adwan's Tanzim and Etienne Saqr's Hurras al-Arz, subservient to the command of the Lebanese Forces, paved the ground for his ultimate goal of becoming president of Lebanon. Ja'ja inherited Bashir Gemayel's legacy and therefore was able to keep his position despite his military defeat in the 'Alay and Shuf battles with the Druze militia in September 1983 and the disastrous evacuation from the Zahrani-Sidon region in April 1985. The replacement in January 1986 of Elie Hubayqa, who signed the Tripartite Agreement of December 28, 1985, as the head of the Lebanese Forces, enhanced Ja'ja's prestige and healed the rift between the Lebanese Forces and the legitimate forces of Lebanon (the Shar'iya) as represented by the presidency and the regular Lebanese army.

Ja'ja has transformed the military backbone of the Lebanese Forces into a militia personally loyal to him. It is composed of militia members recruited from his own region of Bsharri, the outlying villages of the region of Zgharta, which has been the power base of his nemesis, former President Suleiman Franjieh, the Batroun region, and the Shuf

Mountains. It is estimated that this elite force has around six thousand members.[19]

Ja'ja, unlike Berri, does not depend on one external power but has developed good relations with the major Arab countries such as Iraq, Egypt, and Saudi Arabia, and even Arafat's PLO, while also maintaining his relationship with Israel.

The Lebanese Forces, under Ja'ja, want to end the conflict and are willing to accept reforms that would not eliminate or undermine the presidency or the regular Lebanese army as an institution. Here there is a basic contradiction. On one hand, Ja'ja and the Lebanese Forces are in favor of the Shar'iya but their institutions have developed at the expense of the legitimate authorities. Like Ja'ja, other Christian leaders have accepted the equal division of the seats of parliament between Christians and Muslims, a principle that has been embodied in all reform proposals since the Constitutional Document of February 1976.

In early 1988 the most powerful Christian leaders in Lebanon were President Amin Gemayel, Samir Ja'ja, Danny Chamoun, and Suleiman Franjieh. Because of the deaths of Gemayel's father in 1984 and of former President Camille Chamoun in 1987, he seemed to be assured of a leading role among the Christians even after his term ended on September 22, 1988. Samir Ja'ja, by virtue of his position as the commander of the Lebanese Forces, would be expected to have a say in the affairs of the Christian communities. Danny Chamoun, who became the leader of the National Liberal party even before his father's death, would also continue to play a leading role in the politics of Lebanon. Former President Franjieh, whose power is clan-based and confined to Zgharta and its environs, will be assured of his position in the political establishment. Franjieh believes that the salvation of Lebanon lies in developing close ties with Assad's Syria. Whether he espouses such a position out of conviction or necessity is difficult to determine. Nevertheless, Franjieh is a vehement defender of the presidency and has been unwilling to accept its transformation into primus inter pares, let alone be subordinated to the Council of Ministers.

President Amin Gemayel, Danny Chamoun, Samir Ja'ja, and other less prominent Christian leaders (deputies and former cabinet ministers) would accept the bolstering of the institution of the premiership or the Council of Ministers with some curbing of the prerogatives of the president of the republic on the condition that a comprehensive peace plan to end the conflict were put into place. In other words, their greatest fear would be to make concessions and then return to square one because of the rekindling of the conflict by local proxies of external powers.

In conclusion, the conflict in Lebanon is now ripe for resolution. This is evident from the moderation of demands by the various communities and the realization that the conflict has become counterproductive to all communities except the Hezbollah. The major reason for this realization has been an overwhelming economic crisis caused by the decline of the purchasing power of the Lebanese pound from 5.6 Lebanese pounds to the dollar in July 1984 to 670 Lebanese pounds to the dollar in August 1990. The Christians have been forced to retrench and have lost control of areas in Mount Lebanon and the Biqa' to the Druze militia and the Syrian army respectively. They no longer insist that the central government should assert its authority at the expense of the various militias if the latter would accept decentralization or canonization. This attitude is shared with the Druze, but the Shi'is, who are divided into three locations, southern Lebanon, northern Biqa', and Beirut, are less enthusiastic about such a solution. The Shi'is, who gained control of West Beirut at the expense of its Sunni and Christian population, would be forced to share power with Sunnis or lose power to the central government, which is unlikely to accept the role of militias in the capital even under a decentralization or canonization plan. The Druze are willing to return some of their gains if the quid pro quo were resolution of the conflict. The Sunnis are probably the most enthusiastic and the most ready to end the conflict. The Christians would come next in their support for ending the conflict because they have been dispelled of any illusions they had entertained that they might regain what they lost. Perhaps the only community whose members still entertain the hope of gaining more ground is the Shi'i community, especially those who have been entranced or enticed by the Iranian revolution.

Assad's Strategy in Lebanon

The school of thought that maintains that Syrian President Hafiz Assad has embroiled himself in a quagmire in Lebanon is incorrect because no power that wants to disengage would systematically seek the expansion of its military presence in the target nation. I posit the opposite hypothesis that the survival of the Assad regime in Syria has become increasingly dependent on the continued Syrian military presence in Lebanon. Although a detailed description of this hypothesis is beyond the scope of this essay, a brief summary of the thesis will be examined here.[20]

Assad's strategy in Lebanon stems from the minority status of his regime, whose raison d'etre has been confrontation with Israel. This confrontation serves three purposes. First, it "legitimizes" the rule of the 'Alawi minority, which has been regarded by the Sunni majority in Syria as heretical in character. Second, Assad has received subsidies from the Arab oil-producing countries. Third, it justifies the continued military dictatorship and the large budget allocated to the military, which in turn reinforces the 'Alawi domination of Syria because the 'Alawi minority is so socioeconomically backward that it could not keep its domination if Syria were to be transformed into an economically and politically free society.

Confrontation with Israel was the order of the day until May 1974 across the Syrian-Israeli border. But after the signing of the Golan Heights Disengagement Agreement of May 31, 1974, between Syria and Israel, Assad had to look elsewhere to project to the Syrian people the image of confrontation leader, which he was no longer able to project across the Syrian-Israeli border. It follows, then, that the non-pacification of the Lebanese-Israeli border has become an essential ingredient of Assad's strategy in Lebanon. By maintaining this low-intensity conflict in southern Lebanon, Assad has managed to draw Israel into Lebanon (the 1978 and 1982 operations and the establishment first of Major Sa'ad Haddad's Free Lebanon and then the Security Belt in cooperation with General Antoine Lahad's South Lebanon Army). The entanglement of Israel in southern Lebanon has served two Syrian purposes: first, as long as the conflict remains a low-intensity one, Assad has made Israel dependent on him to curb the militias he has unleashed against the Israeli-backed SLA forces; and second, it provides Assad with the pretext to keep his troops in Lebanon.

In sum, Assad has no interest in resolving the conflict among the Lebanese because Syrian troops would then no longer be needed in Lebanon. A still worse scenario would be an agreement between the Lebanese and the Israelis for the pacification of their border, which would undermine Assad's credibility as the foremost Arab leader confronting Israel. Because Assad has no illusion about his support in Lebanon, his troops have to remain on Lebanese soil to ensure that neither the domestic conflicts nor the conflict across the Lebanese-Israel border comes to an end. Syrian behavior in the 1984–88 period illustrates how Assad has carried out this policy.

From February 1984 to August 1988 a Syrian offensive was aimed at the gradual expansion of the deployment of Syrian troops so that Syria could regain what it had lost during the previous period, that is, 1978–82. These four and a half years are divided into four distinct subperiods.

First, the subperiod that immediately followed the abrogation of the May 17, 1983, Israeli-Lebanese Accord on March 5, 1984, witnessed

the Lausanne National Dialogue Conference, the formation of the
National Unity Cabinet in May 1984, the easing of tensions, the opening of the Beirut port and airport, and some of the passages between
East Beirut and West Beirut. This subperiod culminated in July 1984
(concomitant with the Israeli elections) in an optimistic mood that
swept the country.

The second subperiod, from August 1984 until January 1985, was
an interregnum, with ominous signs of what the future portended for
Lebanon. It witnessed the sacking and burning of the Saudi Arabian
consulate in Beirut, forcing Saudi Arabia to close down its embassy
there after Prime Minister Karami's visit to Saudi Arabia upon which
he had pinned high hopes. The car-bombing of the U.S. embassy
annex in 'Awkar in September 1984 was another reminder for those
countries that supported Gemayel during the period September 1982
to February 1984 that they would not be permitted to return to play
an active role in Lebanon. This subperiod also witnessed the Bakfaya
Retreat, sponsored by Syrian Vice-President Khaddam, which included the members of the Lebanese cabinet and President Gemayel
and was another attempt by Assad to gain time until the opportunity
arose to change the balance of power on the ground. This subperiod
ended with the Naqura talks (November 1984–January 1985) between
Lebanese army officers and their Israeli counterparts concerning unilateral Israeli security arrangements in southern Lebanon. This is what
actually took place during the period January to June 1985, when
Israel decided to make such a redeployment.

The Israeli redeployment marked the beginning of the third subperiod, starting in January 1985 and ending in January 1986. In pure
realpolitik terms, it was disastrous for Lebanon. The Israeli withdrawal, or redeployment, encouraged Assad to launch a protracted
military offensive using proxies to create conflict and then force those
who were engaged in the conflict to ask for Syrian troops to act as the
ostensible mediators. Realizing the far-reaching implications of the
Israeli decision, Assad has been on the offensive ever since.

The hijacking of TWA airliner 847 in June 1985 and Assad's exploitation of the incident led to a statement issued by the U.S. Department
of State, which was more in tune with Syria's role in Lebanon than
previous U.S. assertions in favor of the territorial integrity and sovereignty of Lebanon. Furthermore, in the wake of the release of the
TWA hostages, Syrian military observers entered West Beirut. Second,
a car bomb was placed in the city of Zahle, prompting the people of
Zahle to "invite" back the Syrian troops in September 1985, who had
been pushed out by Bashir Gemayel in 1981.

A similar attempt in the northern city of Tripoli was rebuffed by the leader of the Islamic Unification movement (IUM), Shaikh Sa'id Sha'ban, who refused to accept the return of the Syrian army to the city of Tripoli. Consequently, Syrian President Assad unleashed the militias of the Lebanese Communist party, the Syrian Social Nationalist party, the pro-Syrian Ba'th Organization party ('Asim Qansu), and the 'Alawi Arab Democratic party ('Ali 'Id) against Sha'ban's IUM in September 1985. Considerable parts of the city of Tripoli were destroyed, and the Syrian troops, after an absence of more than three years, reentered the city in October 1985 under the guise of mediators.[21]

Assad unleashed the Shi'i Amal militia in May 1985 against the Palestinian camps in Beirut and its suburbs. Amal's war against the Palestinian camps was destined to provide one of the major pretexts for Assad to send his troops to West Beirut.

Assad's relentless pursuit of the goal of regaining what he had lost during the period February 1978 to September 1982 made him push during this third subperiod for what was to be known as the Tripartite Agreement, which was signed in Damascus on December 28, 1985. Such an agreement was unthinkable before the Israeli redeployment of January–June 1985. The core of the contents of the Tripartite Agreement was first enunciated by one of Syria's closest allies, Nabih Berri, the leader of Amal, in a speech delivered in the city of Baalback on August 31, 1985.[22] After three months of intense negotiations under Syrian sponsorship, the Tripartite Agreement was signed in Damascus on December 28, 1985, by Nabih Berri, the leader of the Shi'i Amal movement, Walid Jumblat, the head of the Druze Progressive Socialist party, and Elie Hubayqa, the commander of the Christian Lebanese Forces. The reforms called for in the agreement were similar to those of the Syrian-proposed Constitutional Document of February 1976. The seats in parliament would be divided equally between Christians and Muslims. The prime minister would be selected by parliament rather than by the president of the republic, whose powers would be curbed. The number of seats in parliament would be doubled to 198, and new or vacant seats would be filled by nomination or election. The power-sharing arrangements between Muslims and Christians represented only one aspect of the agreement. It also provided mechanisms for ending the conflict. All militias would be disarmed and disbanded, to be replaced by the Lebanese Internal Security Forces. The central government would regain control of the country for a period of one year, although the Lebanese army would be sent back to its barracks for retraining by the Syrian army, which would be deployed anywhere in Lebanon when the need arose. It is important that the Tripartite Agreement was signed only by militia leaders whose sources of power were in regions of Lebanon not controlled by Syria. Parties and militias based in the Syrian-controlled areas, such as Hezbollah, the Syrian Social Nationalist party, and the Marada militia of former President Suleiman Franjieh, were not asked to sign the agreement. Thus it seemed that the Tripartite Agreement was designed primarily to undermine the national Lebanese army by making it a surrogate for the Syrian army and to legitimize the gradual reoccupation of Lebanon by Syria rather than resolve the conflict or divide political power among the various religious sects.

The fourth subperiod began in January 1986, when the Tripartite Agreement of December 28, 1985, was rejected by President Amin Gemayel and the new commander of the Lebanese Forces, Samir Ja'ja. During this period, which lasted until August 1988, Assad unleashed the Amal militia against the Palestinian camps in western Beirut and from October 1986 until February 1987 in southern Lebanon as well to silence any criticism from the United States and Israel of the expanded deployment of Syrian troops in Lebanon. In July 1986 a limited number of Syrian troops entered West Beirut, but when two pro-Syrian militias, the Druze PSP (in alliance with the Lebanese Communist party) and the Shi'ite Amal, clashed in February 1987, the Syrian troops entered West Beirut in full force, ostensibly to curb the militias of Arafat's PLO. In May 1988, the clashes between Amal and Hezbollah in the southern suburbs of Beirut led to the deployment of Syrian troops in these slum areas.

All these events show that there is a clear pattern: whether the clashes take place between pro-Syrian and anti-Syrian militias or between two pro-Syrian militias, the bottom line is always the expanded deployment of Syrian troops on Lebanese territory. This expansion tightens Assad's grip over Lebanon and reaffirms the ostensible role of Syria as a mediator in a never-ending series of conflicts. Whenever Lebanese officials try to communicate with one another, Syria intervenes. Thus when Prime Minister Karami was killed in June 1987 and the Speaker of the House Husayn al-Husayni spoke to President Gemayel about the matter, he was publicly rebuked by Syrian Vice-President Khaddam during Karami's funeral because he had violated the boycott imposed by Assad on President Gemayel following the rejection of the Tripartite Agreement in January 1986. President Assad had met President Gemayel during the Arab summit of June 1988 in Algiers but since January 1986 has not allowed the Lebanese Speaker of the House, al-Husayni, or Acting Prime Minister al-Huss to meet Gemayel.[23]

Two recent developments of paramount importance have weakened Assad's role in the Middle East, with possible implications for Lebanon:

Iran's acceptance of a cease-fire with Iraq, which has virtually ended the Iran-Iraq war, and the Palestinian uprising in the West Bank and the Gaza Strip, which has been going on since December 1987. Coupled with King Hussein's decision on July 31, 1988, to sever formal ties with the West Bank, the prestige of Arafat's PLO has sharply risen and this can only be at the expense of Syria and its Palestinian allies.

The decline of Assad's influence in the region will not augur well for Lebanon. Rather than weakening Assad's manipulation of his Lebanese allies, he will most probably use all means available, including military force and terrorism, to avoid a disengagement from Lebanon. Assad refused to accept any compromise candidate for the presidency of Lebanon during August–September 1988. He had two candidates, either former president Franjieh or the deputy from 'Akkar, Mikha'il al-Dahir, who would toe Assad's line. When the chances for electing Raymond Edde as the consensus candidate became great, Assad forced the Lebanese Speaker of the House to move the place of the presidential election to West Beirut so that Assad could prevent his election. The Reagan administration apparently went along with Assad and supported al-Dahir, possibly because of a deal over some American hostages held in the Syrian-controlled areas of Lebanon.

Indeed, the developments in Lebanon since August 1988 can be seen primarily as a result of the failure of the United States to stand up to President Assad, who sabotaged the attempt to elect a new president for Lebanon. Ambassador Richard Murphy, who was then the under secretary of state for South Asian and Middle Eastern affairs, completed his career by kowtowing to the Syrian president. Ambassador Murphy's negotiating abilities left much to be desired. No negotiations can be called negotiations if one side accepts in toto the position of the other side, and this is what happened in the U.S.-Syrian talks conducted by Murphy in 1988. Reportedly, Murphy was kept from seeing President Assad by Syrian Vice-President Khaddam and Syrian Minister for Foreign Affairs Farouk al-Shara' until Murphy totally accepted the Syrian position,[24] which was that Mikha'il al-Dahir was the only presidential candidate and that the elections were to be held in the old parliament building in downtown Beirut (rather than in Villa Mansour, which is located on the Green Line and has been the meeting place of members of parliament since 1976), an area under the control of the Syrian army. Most probably Murphy accepted Assad's conditions because he did not want to return to Washington empty-handed, and he was to retire soon. Murphy certainly did not want to give President Assad a free hand in Lebanon, but Assad perceived his agreement with Murphy as giving him that free hand, and that is why Assad has been on the offensive in Lebanon ever since. Assad had to act swiftly because of new developments such as the opening of passages between East Beirut and West Beirut in January 1989, which resulted in traffic jams when the enthusiastic Lebanese moved to and fro; the crackdown on the unpopular Lebanese Forces militia in East Beirut in February 1989 and the closing down of their illegal ports; and the pressure exercised by the Soviet Union on Walid Jumblat to allow the return of evicted Christians to the Shuf and 'Alay regions of Mount Lebanon in February and March 1989. It is not surprising, therefore, that Assad rekindled the conflict in Lebanon on March 14, 1989, using the flimsy pretext that Prime Minister Michel Aoun had imposed a siege on the illegal port of Jiyya, which is controlled by the Druze militia of Walid Jumblat's Progressive Socialist party. But when Prime Minister Aoun agreed to lift the siege of Jiyya in accordance with the resolutions of the Arab summit held in Casablanca during May 1989, which called for the lifting of all blockades and a permanent cease-fire, Syrian President Assad did not comply and continued to impose a blockade on and to bombard the areas controlled by Aoun.

There are six reasons rooted in developments during the period August 1988 to March 1989, for Assad's decision to commence a military offensive against Prime Minister Aoun and his Lebanese army. First, there is Assad's penchant for conflict. Contrary to his public declarations, Assad thrives on conflict, whether in Lebanon or in the region as a whole. Assad has neither domestic legitimacy nor anything tangible to offer his people. He came to power by force and continues to stay in power by force, and only the perpetuation of conflict could enhance his position and possibly create a role for him.

Second, Michel Aoun, the commander of the Lebanese army, who was appointed by President Gemayel as the interim prime minister on September 23, 1988 (when Gemayel's term expired), does not belong to any political party or faction; he represents a national institution. Because of his impeccable background and his actions against the much detested militias, his popularity rose by leaps and bounds. Assad has realized the danger to his regime's interests of a popular Lebanese leader who could mobilize the Lebanese to drive the Syrian army out of Lebanon.

Third, Assad failed in his bet that the Iran-Iraq war would continue indefinitely. His power in the region declined when the Iran-Iraq war came to a halt in August 1988 and Iraq emerged as a formidable military power. Fourth, Arafat's PLO stole the thunder from Assad by recognizing the state of Israel and renouncing terrorism on December 14, 1988. Assad could no longer claim to the Syrian people that he was in power to fight Israel and liberate Palestine. Fifth, Assad had to accept the return of Egypt to the Arab League with the Camp David agreements intact and with Egypt continuing to conduct full diplomatic relations with Israel. Thus Assad has been deprived of another reason for keeping the Syrian people under his military dictatorship, namely, fighting the separate peace treaty between Egypt and Israel.

Sixth, as Soviet policy has been gradually moving toward the resolution of regional conflicts in the Third World (e.g., Namibia, Cambodia, Afghanistan, and Angola), Assad feared that he would be under greater pressure to pull out of Lebanon. Assad's response to these developments since March 1989 has been to reactivate the conflict in Lebanon.

Prime Minister Aoun watched closely the failure of President Amin Gemayel's successive attempts to reach an agreement with President Assad to resolve the conflict in Lebanon. Aoun has tried since he took power to start a dialogue with Assad but to no avail. Aoun thus had no option but "to name the true evil"[25] behind that conflict and to declare a war of liberation against Syria.

Conclusion

The actions of Syrian President Hafiz Assad show that there is little hope for the resolution of the conflict in Lebanon. Despite the weariness of the various Lebanese factions and their willingness to end the conflict (as witnessed by the support for the candidacy of Raymond Edde), Assad has demonstrated by his usurpation of the power of most of the Shi'i, Sunni, Druze, and some Christian leaders that he would prevent resolution of the conflict by all means available. Assad will continue to use the Lebanese territories as a stage for attacking Israel across the Lebanese-Israeli border and as the arena where leading organizations engaged in terrorism such as Hezbollah and the Fatah-Revolutionary Council (Abu Nidal) would continue to recruit and train members. Thus, primarily because of Syrian policy, Lebanon is likely to be a caldron of conflict for the foreseeable future.

Notes

1. See *al-Nahar*, Sept. 9, 1988, p. 5.
2. Ibid., May 16, 1988, p. 1.
3. Marius Deeb, *Militant Islamic Movements in Lebanon: Origins, Social Basis and Ideology*, Occasional Papers Series (Washington, D.C.: Center for Contemporary Arab Studies, Georgetown University, 1986), pp. 2, 3, 22.
4. Marius Deeb, "Shia Movements in Lebanon: Their Formation, Ideology, Social Basis, and Their Links with Iran and Syria," *Third World Quarterly* 10 (Apr. 1988): 694–96.
5. Dawud was killed, with two other prominent leaders of Amal in southern

Lebanon, in an ambush in the Syrian-controlled Awza'i area south of Beirut on September 22, 1988 (al-Nahar, Sept. 23, 1988, p. 1).

6. Interview with Ms. 'Alya' al-Solh, June 29, 1988, Washington, D.C.

7. Marius Deeb, The Lebanese Civil War (New York: Praeger, 1980), pp. 85–88.

8. Interview with Ambassador 'Abdallah Buhabib, June 1988, Washington, D.C.

9. It is significant that the major underground organizations engaged in armed attacks against the Syrian troops are led by Sunnis from Tripoli, for example, the Liberation Brigade headed by Shaikh Kan'an Naji and the Ninth of February Movement composed of supporters of Khalil 'Akkawi, who was assassinated on February 9, 1986.

10. Deeb, Militant Islamic Movements, pp. 18–19.

11. Private conversation.

12. Marius Deeb, "Lebanon: Prospects for National Reconciliation in the Mid-1980s," Middle East Journal 38 (Spring 1984): 276.

13. Nikolaos Van Dam, The Struggle for Power in Syria, Sectarianism, Regionalism, and Tribalism in Politics, 1961–1980 (London: Croom Helm, 1981), pp. 67–123.

14. Iliya Harik, Politics and Change in a Traditional Society: Lebanon, 1711–1845 (Princeton: Princeton Univ. Press, 1968), pp. 12–73.

15. Deeb, Lebanese Civil War, pp. 60–98.

16. Kamal Joumblatt, I Speak for Lebanon (London: Zed Press, 1982), p. 67.

17. Conversation with Danny Chamoun, June 1987.

18. Al-Nahar, June 2, 1988, p. 1.

19. Private communication from a leading member of the Lebanese Forces.

20. See my forthcoming book Lebanon in the Turmoil of Inter-Arab Rivalries and Regional Conflicts.

21. Deeb, Militant Islamic Movements, pp. 9–10.

22. Al-Nahar, Sept. 1, 1985, p. 4.

23. Ibid., June 10, 1988, p. 1, 10.

24. Private conversation.

25. Alya al-Solh, "Nommer el mal," Le Monde, Apr. 25, 1989, p. 2.

13

Egypt Reenters the Arab State System

Louis J. Cantori

The Iran-Contra affair affected Egyptian foreign policy in the two conflict areas of the Palestinian question and the Persian Gulf. Iran-Contra plus the more general challenge to the credibility and effectiveness of U.S. foreign policy in the Middle East as a whole has had the subjective and perhaps more objective effect of making the U.S.-Egyptian relationship more equal. The successful Iranian ground offensive, the post-Iran-Contra tanker war, the flagging of Kuwaiti ships, and the U.S. naval deployment (the latter actions possibly in response to the ineptitude of the Iran-Contra policy) created an atmosphere of regional crisis that prompted nearly unanimous Arab state concurrence in the need to reestablish bilateral relations with Egypt. Such reentry into the Arab state system and regaining of its historical regional leadership role has implications for the leadership stability of President Mubarak and for peace and war in the region.

The argument presented here is that in attempting to strengthen himself domestically, Mubarak strenuously pursued a solution to the Palestinian problem in an effort to guide Egypt back into the Arab fold. He achieved his aim, however, not via the Palestinian issue but rather via the conflict in the Gulf. His Palestinian and Gulf diplomacy helped him gain another domestic objective—relief from the repayment of international debts—partly on the ground of Egypt's importance to the solving of regional crises.

The International and Regional Context of Egyptian Policy

There now exists a congruence between a less polarized and more power-diffuse international system and a less hegemonical and similarly power-diffuse Middle Eastern regional international subordinate system. The rigidities of the bipolar Cold War world have softened.

Ideology has receded and greater pragmatism in Soviet-U.S. relations evident regarding issues of nuclear confrontation and the desire of both nations to avoid engagement in regional conflicts. Confrontation has been replaced by diplomacy, and the latter has been supplemented by informal conversations.[1] In the Middle East this improved international situation is evident in the greater willingness of the United States to accept a Soviet role in the proposal for an international conference. The moderation of the Soviet regional position can be seen in its behind-the-scenes role in reportedly nudging Syria to agree to the principle of Arab state bilateral relations with Egypt. In addition, pressure was brought to bear on the People's Democratic Republic of Yemen to recognize Egypt following the Arab summit meeting in November 1987 in Amman, Jordan.[2]

This more pragmatic Soviet policy has had a further direct effect on Egyptian-USSR relations in that they have become normalized. From the July 1972 expulsion of Soviet advisers by Sadat, there occured a discernible shift from reliance on the East to reliance on the West and the United States. More recently, Soviet-Egyptian relations have prospered in the form of the resumption of previously interrupted development projects, the reestablishment of ambassadorial relations, the restructuring of the earlier military debt to the Soviets, and special barter trade agreements. In addition, Egypt has had access to Soviet military spare parts for its Soviet weapons inventory via Eastern bloc nations. Now the Soviets will supply such spare parts as well.[3]

This improvement in relations has been useful in enabling Mubarak to continue to adhere to the principle of "positive neutralism" and to fend off domestic critics that he is too dependent on the United States.[4] In fact, however, Egypt has benefited signficantly from annual American economic and military assistance presently set at $2.3 billion a year. This assistance began as compensation to Egypt for having signed the 1979 peace treaty with Israel and its loss of foreign assistance from moderate Arab states. Thus though touted as economic development assistance to Egypt, it was and is a political payment. Government of Egypt officials view it this way, although the U.S. Agency for International Development tends to emphasize the imperatives of development. These differing views have created some internal policy tension within the U.S. policy establishment.[5] The American political objective, after all, is to stabilize the Egyptian leadership, a goal, not surprisingly, shared by that government as well. One of the components of this assistance is the Public Law 480 Food for Peace program, which is a bone of contention in the political versus developmental tension on the U.S. side. The food is related to a further policy controversy from the U.S. perspective—a \$2 billion a year food subsidy. These programs are the equivalent of American social security for Egypt. They touch directly upon the issue of stability in reference to extreme economic need as evidenced in the national food riots of January 1977 in which over seventy persons died and the more limited but intense violence of the security police riot of February 1986.[6]

After 1979 and the Iranian revolution, Egypt became not only a component of an approach to the solution of the Palestinian problem but also the remaining state outside of Israel that could be a point of policy access to the Middle East region. Thus the U.S. concern with stability increased, with implications for both development and military assistance. U.S. weapons assistance of \$1 billion a year has made Egypt to a degree dependent upon U.S. technology. The Egyptians, however, have worked to lessen this dependency by diversifying weapons procurement, for example, purchasing French Mystere 2000s for the air force, Spanish frigates, Chinese submarines, and British guns for Soviet tanks. Symbolic of the closer relationship with the United States has been the annual Bright Star combined U.S.-Egyptian army maneuvers.[7]

On balance, the U.S.-Egyptian relationship has been mutually beneficial even if occasionally strained, as in the American hijacking of an Egyptian aircraft carrying the *Achille Lauro* hostage-takers to Tunis in 1985. The relationship is fragile, however, because of, among other things, increasing U.S. support for Israel, which puts Egypt into a trilateral relationship with Washington. Issues nominally of a bilateral character between Cairo and Washington or Cairo and Tel Aviv repeatedly became a "ganging-up" phenomenon with Israel using its special relationship to get Washington to put pressure on Egypt.[8]

The implications for Egyptian foreign policy of the changing nature of the Middle East international regional system need to be addressed. The decades of the 1950s and 1960s were dominated by the ideologies of anticolonialism and Arab nationalism and the rivalry for leadership. Egypt and Gamal Nasser were in the forefront of this conflict. The Arab defeat in 1967 changed the issues of the region from ideology to the retrieval of conquered territory. Sadat's decision to go to war to regain Egyptian territory and force the Palestinian issued gained him and Egypt great support in the Arab world. Sadat's early diplomacy of Sinai I (1974) and Sinai II (1975) and even the Camp David meeting of 1978 continued to enjoy support. The 1979 treaty with Israel changed everything, and Egypt became the virtual outcast of the Arab world. The Camp David protocol of 1978 had kept the Palestinians as the first priority. In the peace treaty, however, Sadat succumbed to the temptation of regaining Sinai and in doing so seemed to disregard the Palestinians as a regional issue. Under heavy domestic political pressure, Mubarak finally succeeded in restoring bilateral relations with nearly all Arab states; only Arab League membership still eluded him in 1988.[9]

The changed characteristics of the Middle Eastern subordinate system have assisted Mubarak in his objective. Presently, it has some of the characteristics of the international system itself in that power has become diffused and conflict less polarized. For example, Egypt and Israel remain militarily the most powerful, and Iraq and Syria approach them in force and advanced military technology. The consequence is a subordinate system with three conflict focuses (Lebanon, Palestinian-Israeli, and Gulf), but in the eastern Mediterranean, at least, the existence of the buffer areas of the occupied territories, Lebanon and Jordan, mutes major regional conflict.[10] In the 1980s Egypt could not be as hegemonic as it earlier had been and Egyptian diplomacy rather than personality and power were more effective. Even when there is less regional actor hegemony, the system still remains potentially politically explosive. In fact, the buffer areas of Lebanon and the occupied territories are not buffers in a passive sense of cordoning off conflict but rather ones that divert conflict and focus it within their respective boundaries. Viewed from this perspective, the two buffer areas remain full of an explosive potential that could rapidly involve all regional actors in direct deadly conflict.

The Primacy of Domestic Determinants of Foreign Policy

Unlike his predecessor Sadat, Mubarak is oriented primarily toward domestic politics and only secondarily toward foreign policy, in large part because, even after seven years in power, the confidence and legitimacy of leadership still elude him as does a sizable constituency of support. Initially he had benefited from the contrast with Sadat. He was calm, quiet, administratively and technically competent, and free from an aura of corruption. By 1983, however, he had been buffeted by the shock waves of the June 1982 Israeli invasion of Lebanon, the Shatilla and Sabra Palestinian refugee camp massacres in which Israel was deeply implicated, and the American-Israeli effort to impose the *diktat* of a Lebanon-Israeli peace treaty. Egypt was constrained in its reaction by both the 1979 peace treaty with Israel and the closeness of the U.S. economic and military assistance relationship.[11] With time, however, Mubarak's initially welcomed personal qualities have become less attractive. Increasingly there has come to be an awareness that he is a leader who reacts rather than proacts, one with whom policy initiative lies somewhere else in the external or internal environment. In sum, then, his leaderhip has become more fragile and domestically more vulnerable. His own intelligent assessment of the greater priority of domestic issues to the maintenance of his leadership position and to the advancement of his country cause one to look inward rather than outward to understand Egyptian foreign policy.

To understand the domestic potential for influencing foreign policy, however, there is a need to assess the nature of Egyptian politics and economics in the late 1980s. If presidential leadership is reactive and noncharismatic, it continues to function because of its basic intelligence and freedom from corruption. It is not because the latter is not present and important but because it has been tamed. This is the message of Mubarak's early show trial of a few particularly egregious corrupt individuals. Limits have been set to avarice and ostentatious corrupt behavior.[12]

Most important to the overall understanding of Egyptian politics is to see it as a political system with a soft center. Part of that softness has already been described as it relates to presidential leadership. Further contributing to this quality is the fashion in which two potentially competing political forces appear to have been politically neutered by being granted a semiautonomous status within the system. The first of these is the military.[13] It may be useful to analyze two components of the army. First, the subject of the army is elusive both for objective reasons of national security and also because, one suspects, for reasons of accountability. The army emerged from the 1973 war with a refurbished reputation, which in general it has been able to maintain until the present. This elusiveness of knowledge and continued reputation for professional performance remain especially true for the combat arms. A second component of the army, however, is what might be called its production and service aspect. The army has responded to the conditions of peace in recent years under the leadership of Field Marshal Abu Ghazzala (also minister of defense and deputy prime minister) with community service activities and civilian and military production economic activities. It is common to see army engineering units laying telephone cable to contribute to the recent dramatic improvement in phone service and being involved in road construction. In addition, however, the army has undertaken the manufacturing of weapons both for Egypt's own needs and for Middle Eastern and African customers.

Egypt's goal has been to attain greater military self-sufficiency, a development reinforced by the funding of other Arab states with a similar regional goal in mind. In the process Egypt has become a major arms exporter, which has implications for its own influence and for foreign exchange earnings. The political meaning of this process is that this segment of the army has become entrepreneurial. This position has been reinforced by an increasing movement into the production of civilian consumer goods such as refrigerators and televisions when military production facilities were underused, and such intermittent production makes economic sense.

The entire military production process has allegedly been required to be economically self-sufficient. Capital and land are loaned to the enterprise from within military resources, but these loans must be paid back, and contractual relations to the Egyptian army are competitive; even foreign companies are allowed to participate. In addition, the autonomy and presumably the profitability are motivated by foreign joint venture capital.

The economic autonomy of the army is said to carry over into the production of its food needs, which has political implications in that the economic competitiveness of the private sector is not alien to the army, and it is implied that the army can outdo the private sector in useful production. At least some of the considerable energies of the army are presently directed to such activities. This is not to deny the more conventional mission of the army defending Egypt's national security. It remains a strong and capable force, not only as a standing military force but also as a stabilizer of domestic violence and an exporter of Egyptian military expertise abroad. But it may have been politically neutralized to the extent that in the absence of deep-seated crisis, it is politically passive to the marginally relative strength of the presidency.[14]

Religious groups are a second important neutered political actor. It is difficult to generalize about this very diverse phenomenon, not only concerning Muslims but also Christians. Nonetheless, what is striking at present is what might be referred to as Islamic quietism, which appears to have come about in two ways particular to the legal and illegal categories of these groups. The legal groups consist of the literally thousands of essentially private voluntary groups that have always existed as the informal organizational backbone of Islam. These groups have historically consisted of mosque organizations, charitable groupings, and Sufi (mystical Islamic) brotherhoods. Added to these more traditional groups have been those providing health and more recently elementary educational (with government approval) services. Financial services in the Islamic investment companies have also become important as part of this process. They are said to be investing billions of dollars of savings.[15] Islamic revivalism in Egypt has thus expressed itself in a process of introversion. Religious practice and a supporting system of religious building construction and social services have caused an inward orientation and direction of energy whose practical effect is one of quietism.

A barometer of this quietism has been the political fortunes of the nominally illegal Muslim Brethren, an organization that was socially and economically "progressive" before 1952 but also engaged in political violence and assassination and has become more moderate from the 1970s onward. It continued its violent activities under Nasser, including an assassination attempt on him in 1954 and an abortive coup attempt in 1965. By the early 1970s, however, Sadat, in his search for support and legitimacy, released thousands of the Brethren from prison. Gradually from that time on, while remaining organizationally illegal but legally allowed to publish its journal, it has been courted politically, initially by Sadat, subsequently by the New Wafd party in the 1984 parliamentary elections, and more recently by the Socialist Labor party in the April 1987 elections, which gained the group thirty-two members of parliament. But even this movement toward the political center might not be the limit of its activities because even though the army as an institution supports the separation of religion and state as an aspect of its modern identity, it has courted the Brethren by issuing invitations to deliver sermons at religious observances within the military.[16]

In addition, however, an illegal clandestine and violent religious opposition has become evident since the mid-1970s. The death of Sadat at the hands of such a group is only the most dramatic instance of this phenomenon. This sentiment seems to have receded somewhat at the present time, perhaps because with the death of Sadat as a polarizing personality, and especially the diminution of corruption, the provocations have also declined. Equally important has been the energy with which Mubarak has pursued the Palestinian question, thus depriving the opposition of that issue as well. Contributing to this lack of saliency may be the co-opting of the religious issue and symbols by the legal Islamic groups. Even in the apogee of their activities in the 1970s, they elicited little or no popular support because of the recommitment of the masses as a whole to Islam. Continuing instances of violence have been localistic and isolated.[17] Quietism has further inoculated the population from their appeals. Finally, but by no means least, the security apparatus has been effective in repressing them.

Further contributing to the "soft center" characterization of contemporary Egyptian politics is its continued experiment with democracy, which began with Sadat's decision to permit the formations of "forums" (minbar pl. munabar, literally pulpits) in the single-party-dominated parliament from 1975 onward. Then these became parties in a multiparty system only to be harassed and repressed by him in 1980 and 1981.[18] Under Mubarak this democratic expression has been fuller and more genuine, especially in the parliamentary elections of 1984 and 1987. In addition, freedom of the press has expanded to the point that the press is the freest in the Arab world. None of the political parties, however, represent anything but segments of the dominant middle class in either rivalry or dialogue with one another. For reasons of their own dynamics or the operation of the electoral law or the government, the parties do not possess a penetrative organization or truly mass appeal.[20] As a result, they have produced neither organization nor leaders that are credible alternatives or replacements for the government.

This "softness" is accompanied in the opinion of many observers by the "hardness" of the domestic economic situation. The macroeconomic indicators point to an economy in acute distress based on an enormously negative balance of payments ($–6.37 billion in 1986) and a staggering indebtedness ($28.56 billion in 1986). In addition, growth in Gross Domestic Product appeared to have been near 1.6 percent for 1986. When profound inequities in the distribution of wealth are factored in, most analysts conclude that the situation is adversely affecting the masses of the population.[21]

The "hardness" of the weaknesses of the domestic economy is intimately tied to foreign policy because of Egypt's reliance on foreign economic assistance and its foreign indebtedness. U.S. economic assistance constitutes roughly two-thirds of such economic assistance. This assistance has resulted in controversies surrounding its administration. Gradually and specifically since 1985, some of the Egyptian complaints about the restrictiveness of the disbursement of funds have been responded to. More important has been the question of repayment of the economic and military assistance debt. By 1986, the payment due on the military debt alone was $500 million (principal and interest). At first, the United States spoke of stretching out the repayment period, but by November 1987 an agreement was reached allowing for a five-year grace period, followed by repayment over ten years at interest rates significantly reduced to 2–7 percent. This agreement has relieved Mubarak of significant pressure. More troublesome has been the problem of dealing with the management of Egypt's general debt, which has been between $3 and $6 billion a year in food, energy, and other subsidies. These structural features have repeatedly caused the International Monetary Fund (IMF), in its negotiations with the government of Egypt, to call for reforms. In January 1977 such reforms were agreed to, and more than seventy persons were killed in rioting all over the country. In May 1987 a standby agreement was reached for the gradual introduction of reforms, a limited float of the Egyptian pound, raising domestic interest rates, and the promise of about one-third of a billion additional dollars.[22] The implementation of even this carefully negotiated agreement has proven difficult for Mubarak and has created renewed strains with the IMF. In a pattern of behavior revealing of the interconnectedness of Egypt's foreign policy with its economic difficulties, Mubarak undertook a tour of European capitals in 1988 ostensibly to promote his foreign policy but in reality to stress his indispensability to a peaceful solution of the Palestinian question. The purpose was undoubtedly to force the IMF to relent further in its demands for economic reform.[23]

The microrealities, however, which determine real peoples' immediate political responses, indicate a more qualified political judgment. Wage rates in the countryside indicate very high income levels and a condition of labor scarcity. In addition, there is the safety-valve effect of continued high-paying jobs abroad, in Jordan, Iraq, and the Gulf, although the availability of Gulf jobs may have declined in recent years. The labor outflow creates the supply-demand situation that forces wage rates upward. This is also true in urban areas, especially among the semiskilled and the skilled. There is, of course, poverty in the urban areas among some segments of the unskilled population, but the government's food subsidy program has become more precisely targeted to lower-income areas. In addition, these elements receive benefits from the multiple Muslim charitable organizations that have come into existence.[24]

It is possible that dangers of political instability arise not from the dissatisfied masses but from the relatively deprived middle class. First, a large segment of the middle class is employed in the poorly paid public sector. As an increasingly prosperous private sector develops, it further exaggerates the salary differentials. Second, one of the consequences of the floating of the pound in the spring of 1987 and its continued relative stability was to make the luxury imported goods and spare parts upon which the middle class had become dependent outrageously expensive. Third, a real inflation of 30 percent (as opposed to the official figure of 15 percent) seems to have affected the heightened expectations of the middle class more than the masses. Fourth, more speculatively, the middle class had heretofore been able to receive the benefit of food subsidies. As the government more accurately pinpoints the delivery of this food to the truly needy, the middle class is "disadvantaged."[25] The political effect of this apparent relative deprivation is the search for a political remedy, and the remedy most talked about among Nasserists on the left and those on the right is the army. Those on the left see the army as somehow restoring a sense of purpose and direction to what they appear to feel is a rudderless political system. Persons on the right have a similar feeling of a need for coherence, discipline, and, above all, more efficient management of the mixed managed and market economy.

What are the foreign policy implications of the "soft center?" There is first the point that foreign policy becomes a way for a president without great personal authority generally to strengthen himself. A theme of post-1981 criticism of the government in the press and parliament has been the need to remedy the failure of the Egyptian-Israeli peace treaty of 1979 to address the issue of Palestinian justice. This had been a point of criticism by illegal Muslim groups before 1981. The Israeli invasion of Lebanon in 1982 and the uprising (Intifada) in the occupied territories since December 9, 1987, have further served to dramatize this past failure and the present weakness of the Egyptians in the aftermath of the 1979 treaty with Israel to do anything substantive about it.

Egypt, Israel, and the Palestinians

The 1979 peace treaty with Israel was entered into to gain the benefits of Israeli withdrawal from the Egyptian territory of Sinai and the economic benefits of revenues from the reopened Suez Canal, access to the oil fields of the Red Sea and Sinai, and the assurance of U.S. compensatory economic and military assistance for the cutting off of Arab aid. These were major benefits for Egyptian national pride and for the Egyptian economy. The strength of Egyptian nationalism required the return of Sinai, and the Egyptian economy in 1979 badly needed the treaty's revenue and economic assistance benefits. In addition, in 1979 Egypt was war weary. Egypt had been engaged in the Palestinian struggle since the 1936–39 uprising (via unofficial volunteers), the 1948–49 war (which contributed to the causes of the 1952 revolution), the 1956 war, the 1967 war, the 1969–70 war of attrition, and the 1973 war. The treaty held out the promise of a diplomatic settlement of the problem. Egypt was weary of being sapped of blood and treasure, and thus the treaty was greeted with strong popular support. At the elite level, however, its reception was mixed. Most important, the army accepted it. Prominent political figures, intellectuals, and Foreign Ministry officials did not because they viewed it as failing to address the Palestinian problem.

In the years since 1979 the formal commitment to the treaty has not wavered even though its popular support has atrophied for two reasons. The first is that from the popular point of view, Sadat had perhaps oversold its potential economic benefits. An economic bonanza for the Egyptian masses was unrealistic but anticipated. When it did not materialize immediately in the 1980s, support inevitably cooled. When the economy did improve in the microreality discussed above, it was not seen as related to the benefits of the treaty. At the elite level, support for the treaty has been further eroded by a critical view of Israel's ability freely to reap its own benefits, primarily the settlement and creeping annexation of the occupied territories of the West Bank and Gaza. It pursued this objective with relative impunity until at least December 1987 and the uprising of the Palestinian inhabitants of these territories because the treaty granted Israel the strategic military security of its southern flank, thereby freeing its military forces as a result of the neutralization of Egypt. As a consequence, Israel had also been able to initiate and retrieve itself from its military invasion of Lebanon. The most serious consequence of its defeat in Lebanon was the self-inflicted wound of internal dissension. Egyptian elite responses to these Israeli initiatives have been bitter and scathing. The Egyptian official description of the treaty as "cold peace" only partially reveals this sentiment. Although the Egyptian government scrupulously honors its obligations to the treaty, elite opinion has shifted from initial acceptance, to neutrality, to hostility. The Egyptian press is revealing of this criticism, as is personal behavior. Israeli contacts or presumed contacts are shunned. Egyptian officials, other than perhaps those in the Foreign Ministry, who are either by necessity or inclination in regular contact with Israelis, are rejected.[26]

The Taba issue has been barometric of the Egyptian-Israeli relationship. The dispute involves the location of a boundary set originally in 1906 between a British-dominated Egyptian government and the Ottoman Empire. In December 1981 the Israelis laid claim to a line some seven hundred meters west of the 1906 line, thus getting an attractive beach area at the northern end of the Gulf of Aqaba to the west of the Israeli port city of Eilat. While the area was under dispute, the Israeli government gave permission for the construction of a $20 million hotel and a set of beach cabins. The provocative nature of this decision has made the issue especially galling to the Egyptians, who regarded it as similar to the "facts" of Israeli settlement policy in the occupied territories. In the last hours before Shimon Peres had to step down as prime minister in September 1986, an agreement was signed to present the case to international arbitration, and simultaneously the Egyptian ambassador, who had been withdrawn in protest of the Shatilla and Sabra massacres in Lebanon, was returned. On September 29, 1988, the commission found in favor of Egypt.[27]

The actions of Israel are the direct cause for the decline in the acceptability of the peace treaty, but these actions also focus on the glaring failure of the treaty to address the question of justice for the Palestinians. This issue is important in itself, but from the Egyptian point of view it is related to the need to reestablish Egypt's historical role as the dominant power in the eastern Mediterranean. It is not necessarily restricted to Mubarak but is a widely felt sentiment.

Sadat was so personally responsible for and identified with the treaty that it provided his assassins with one of the motives for killing him. His death therefore depersonalized the issue to a significant degree and paved the way for the Arab leaders almost immediately to cease their regular condemnation of Egypt. The stage was thus set for Mubarak to begin a diplomacy of progressive normalization, first with the Third World states of the nonaligned movement, then with the Islamic conference, and finally with Arab states and actors themselves. He was also aided by changes on the part of the moderate Arab states that signaled flexibility in their attitude toward Israel, as was expressed in King Fahd's plan of September 1981 and reiterated at the Arab summit meeting at Fez, Morocco, in September 1982. The Reagan plan in the same month augured for a possibly active U.S. diplomacy on the issue, but the increasing involvement of the United States in Lebanon diverted U.S. attention. As U.S. policy became a direct hostage to the war, Egypt was provided with some opportunities to express its Arabism and within the provisions of the 1979 treaty to express its criticism of Israel.

U.S. policy became more and more mired in the events in Lebanon, culminating in a large number of U.S. military deaths, the deaths of officials and other Americans, the destruction of embassy buildings, and the taking of U.S. hostages. The U.S. effort to impose a peace treaty between Lebanon and Israel in 1983 without the consent of any other actors both in Lebanon (except the Gemayel faction) and especially in Syria resulted in the U.S. withdrawal from active diplomacy in the eastern Mediterranean for the next four years.

The war in Lebanon created an embattled Palestinian movement which had been a primary target of the Israeli invasion. King Hussein of Jordan, perhaps fearing the implications of Israeli success in this endeavor and thus increasing his own Palestinian problem, first in Lebanon and then in the West Bank and Gaza, began to attempt to achieve negotiations on the overall Palestinian issue. Egypt also saw this effort as a way out of its Arab world isolation and began to work cooperatively with Jordan. At least initially, Egypt probably had hopes of being able to use its close relationship with the United States to facilitate the process. What developed was a dynamic in which Egypt worked to get closer to Arafat and the PLO. Mubarak was assisted by the growing opposition within not only PLO ranks but his own Fatah organization, as well as by radicals rejecting Arafat's more moderate leadership. The combination of this weakening effect on his leadership led to the February 11, 1985, agreement between Jordan and the PLO to an international conference in which a joint Jordanian-Palestinian delegation would seek a confederation of Jordan and the West Bank and Gaza.[28] Egypt had already had a success in its reentry policy with the reestablishment of relations with Jordan in September 1984. Thus Egypt's supporting role in the emerging diplomatic effort in convening an international conference made up of the U.N. Security Council membership plus that of other parties seemed auspicious. For the moment, the PLO was enlisted as one key actor in the effort. Israel, however, remained problematical, as did U.S. acceptance of the effort. Prime Minister Peres of Israel signaled his sympathy for the initiative, but the opposition of Foreign Minister Shamir and Minister of Industry Sharon immobilized Israel. Therefore, U.S. commitment to the undertaking was crucial. In his visit to the United States in March 1985, Mubarak found that it was not going to play the role of active mediator and was told that the Arab states should engage in direct talks with Israel and then turn to the United States for assistance. This, of course, was a nonstarter.[29] The American reluctance was to be reinforced by the equivocations of the PLO about its original commitment. Such an attitude was typical of Arafat in that when faced with disunity in his own ranks, he would give it primary attention so as to assume the continued viability of his movement and his leadership. The June 1985 hijacking of the TWA aircraft to Beirut once again demonstrated how acts of political violence by small groups could succeed in diverting attention from major policy issues to those meaningful to the group itself, in this case the repatriation of Shiite prisoners from Israeli prisons.

The political violence in the latter half of 1985 was to seal the fate of the combined Jordanian-Egyptian diplomatic initiative. Although it was neglected by the Americans, it was a formidable attempt to orchestrate an international conference in which the role of the Palestinians would be disguised and the USSR would be an important but somehow less active participant. The Americans were presumably the key to Israeli participation, but once again this was a chimera. Even if for some unprecedented reason the United States should put pressure on Israel, it was doubtful that it could have altered the internal Likud-Labor imbroglio on what to do in the occupied territories. Further sabotaging the effort was the increase in political violence carried out by Palestinians, both Fatah and its rivals. This violence followed a familiar pattern. There was first the killing of three Israeli "tourists" by what was said to be a Fatah unit. Allegedly they were "spies" reporting on Fatah seaborne attacks on Israel, which Israeli security had been able to intercept. The violence was also probably Arafat's way of maintaining his credibility against internal radical critics for having "supped with the devil"—Hussein. Not for the first time when Arafat's leadership was questioned and his movement fragmented, his greatest policy priority was internally defensive rather than externally venturesome as the February 1985 accord called on him to be. Again, in a familiar pattern, the Israeli response played into Arafat's hands in the form of the October 1985 air attack on the PLO headquarters in Tunis, which reinforced the PLO's radical trend by further inflaming sentiment within the PLO. The *Achille Lauro* incident was possibly an effort to embarrass Arafat and to protest the February 1985 agreement with Jordan. The ship had already left Egyptian waters when its takeover was effected. Nevertheless, the Egyptian authorities undertook negotiations, which brought about an end to the incident with the loss of one American citizen's life. Mubarak had succeeded in establishing negotiations by promising to provide safe passage for the hijackers to Tunis for disciplinary action by Arafat. There was earlier precedent for such disciplinary action, but Mubarak was also perhaps attempting to provide an opportunity for world opinion to see the PLO acting responsibly. Egypt's effort to keep its eye on the big picture of a regional policy oriented toward peace was now sabotaged not by the Israelis but by the Americans. White House officials (North and Poindexter) chose to make of the incident a dramatic antiterrorism act by the United States.[30] The Egyptian plane was intercepted by American aircraft and forced to fly to Italy, where the hijackers were turned over to Italian authorities, although the leader of the group, Mohammed Abbas, was released and allowed to leave the country. The February 1985 agreement was at a practical end by this time, but the U.S. action put a final end to it and infuriated Egyptian public opinion in the process. A Palestinian radical group's hijacking of an Egyptian aircraft was to follow as the February 1985 effort sunk further into oblivion.

In February 1986, Hussein abrogated the February 1985 agreement. PLO-Jordanian relations then began to decline significantly with Hussein cracking down on PLO activities in Jordan during July 1986, even as the Israelis stepped up their repression in the occupied territories. An Arab summit meeting in Fez, Morocco, in May 1986 proved futile in mending the situation. So badly had the situation deteriorated that even Shimon Peres's July 21, 1986, surprise meeting with King Hassan of Morocco came to nothing. This meeting, nearly as dramatic as Sadat's 1977 trip to Jerusalem, caused tremors in the Arab world but no universal condemnation and little worldwide publicity. The situation had deteriorated too badly.[31]

The Egyptian diplomatic coordination with Jordan in the hope that its relations with both the United States and Israel could be constructive in a peace process had come to nothing. Thus, a settlement of the Palestinian issue as a way of regaining Egyptian honor and reentry into the Arab state system was frustrated. Although this honor remains to be refurbished in the absence of a role for it in a successful resolution of the Palestinian issue, reentry to the Arab world was to be facilitated from the unexpected direction of the Gulf.

The Gulf

Egypt's policy in the Gulf in contradistinction to that of the eastern Mediterranean has been largely economic in its motivations. Egypt sought to gain the moderate Arab states' support for reentry into the Arab system, but an important goal has been to benefit economically from its oil wealth via workers' remittances, trade and barter arrangements, military sales, and advisers and economic assistance.

Its policy in the Gulf was facilitated and accelerated by the Iran-Iraq war, which had been under way since 1980. Perhaps 80 percent of Egypt's 3 million migrant workers, upon whom Egypt had become dependent for about $3 billion a year in remittances, had gone to the Gulf to work even before 1980. In all of the countries except Iraq, these workers were semiskilled and skilled. It is said that nearly a million such Egyptians have gone to Iraq and have been offered Iraqi citizenship.[32]

In early 1987, however, the Iranians appeared to have the Iraqis on the ropes, and the Arab Gulf states were alarmed. In January the Gulf Cooperation Council met in Riyadh to review the situation and to prepare a common position for the Islamic Conference Organization meeting to be held in Kuwait at the end of that month. It was clear that the Gulf War had eclipsed the Palestinian question and had become the major security issue among the Arab states. In April, the secretary general of the Arab League announced that Egypt would be welcome back in the organization.[33]

Egypt was seemingly on the verge of its long-sought reentry into membership in the Arab system. Iran's military success was worrisome enough to cause an opening to Egypt as the most militarily powerful Arab state, but in addition there was also the November 3, 1986,

Lebanese magazine revelation that top American advisers had visited Tehran. As the story of the Iran-Contra affair unfolded in early 1987, it became very clear to the moderate Arab states of the Gulf that not only was American policy in the Middle East biased in the eastern Mediterranean conflict area in favor of Israel, but that it was also duplicitous in the conflict area of the Gulf.[34] As a result, Egypt figured prominently in moderate Arab thinking as the Arabs attempted to marshal their resources after their apparent abandonment by the Americans.

Viewed against this background, the subsequent American decision to reflag Kuwaiti ships can be reasonably interpreted as an effort to regain credibility with the Arab Gulf states. Meanwhile, however, concrete benefits and involvements for Egypt continued apace. Egypt already had sold Soviet military supplies to Iraq, along with such non-Soviet items as Brazilian-designed but Egyptian-made primary and intermediate jet training aircraft. These sales totaled a billion or more dollars in value. In addition, Egyptian military training missions were in Iraq in large numbers and also in Kuwait. In May 1987 the Gulf Cooperation Council authorized a billion dollars to reenergize the Arab Industrial Organization (a weapons-making facility based in Egypt), which had been largely moribund since the 1979 treaty. In August, the GCC asked Egypt to train its newly integrated army.[35]

Mubarak's acceptance speech before the parliament upon his reelection as president addressed Egypt's new Gulf role squarely.[36] This occurred on the eve of the success of Egyptian policy the following month at the November 1987 Amman summit meeting. Overall, it reflected his policy priorities as well as his position on specific foreign policy issues. Only about one-eighth of the speech dealt with foreign policy. Much more important to him were the pressing needs of the Egyptian economy and the need to continue efforts at implementing the IMF reforms of the previous spring.

Underlying his comments on foreign policy was a long list of references to the Arab world, which indicated Egyptian intellectual and policy leadership and interests in putting them forward. The Arab world should

1. arrive at a common security policy (implying Egyptian leadership)
2. retain its independence from foreign influence (i.e., follow Egypt's presumed example)
3. remain committed to the formal agreements of Arab nations such as the Arab League Charter and the Joint Arab Defense Pact (which Egypt vigorously claims to have done)

4. respect the principle of noninvolvement in other Arab countries' affairs (again like Egypt and unlike Libya)

5. agree on a formula of relations with the non-Arab nations of the region and reject regional expansion and hegemony (i.e., Egypt's peace treaty with Israel on one hand and supporting role in the Gulf on the other)

6. work for solidarity rather than unity because the former is more practical and realizable (Egyptian membership in the Arab community would frustrate such unity because of the treaty with Israel)

7. preserve its resources for developmental purposes (i.e., the oil-rich states should assist other states such as Egypt)

In turning to the conflicts of the region and Egypt's position on them, Mubarak first noted the Gulf and the need to accept U.N. Resolution 598. In specific reference to Kuwait he said, "We support Kuwait with our hearts and resources in defending its territory, sovereignty and the security of its sons." What he did not promise was Egyptian military assistance. The Palestinians ranked second in his priorities. He reiterated the Egyptian commitment to a U.N.-sponsored international conference with the PLO participation. He called attention to the Jordanian-Egyptian coordinated effort at achieving such a conference. Finally, he noted that a solution in Lebanon would necessitate the removal of foreign involvements (clearly making reference to Israel but also possibly to Syria.)[37]

The November 1987 Amman summit resulted in the decision to authorize Arab states bilaterally to resume diplomatic relations with Egypt. Almost immediately nine of these did, leaving only Syria, Algeria, and Libya failing to do so. The Egyptian perspective of this decision is summed up as follows.

According to Butrus Ghali, Egypt, at the Amman summit, was "present in its absence." Its return was the major preoccupation of Arab leaders, and to lean toward Egypt became irresistible after the first summit and in other conferences, for the Arab leaders realized that for the sake of realism, logic, and duty, they should consolidate the Arab order at its base and restore the strategic balance of which Egypt was a cornerstone.[38]

Although reference is made to the "Arab order," and this was the successful culmination of long and strenuous diplomacy, Egypt has a very realistic view of Arab unity. As Mubarak puts it, "We are talking about solidarity at this stage because we believe that it is not practical, given present circumstances, to speak of immediate, comprehensive Arab unity."[39] In other words, Arab solidarity presupposes a key leadership role for Egypt, but the hallowed objective of Arab unity for the moment at least is not realizable.

Mubarak and Hussein attempted to use Egypt's reentry into the Arab state system to rekindle movement on the Palestinian issue. This initiative occurred independent of but coincidental with the December 9, 1987, outbreak of the uprising. Thus, following the summit, Hussein went to Damascus on November 25 and then met with Mubarak in Cairo on December 6. The next day, Hussein was in Riyadh and then went on to the Gulf. There is some evidence that he was holding out the promise of a combined Jordanian-Egyptian deterrent force in the Gulf, perhaps in exchange for greater support in the pursuance of a convening of an international conference on the Palestinian issue.[40] Hussein's visit was followed by a tour by Mubarak of virtually all the Arab Gulf states and the Sudan and meetings with Saddam Hussein and Arafat in Baghdad and concluded with a meeting with King Hussein at Aqaba. It was against this background that Mubarak visited Washington in January 1988. An observer has said that on this visit Mubarak was in a nearly equal relationship with the American side. Contributing to this situation was undoubtedly the American realization that Mubarak was speaking for King Hussein as well and had met with some agreement from leaders in the Gulf states with whom he had conferred. Perhaps more important, the significance of the uprising was becoming clearer and probably caused the Americans to listen more carefully to Mubarak. Mubarak proposed a six-month moratorium on West Bank settlement and violence in the territories and preparations for an international conference.[41] American diplomacy may have been energized by the uprising and the need to grant some response and credibility to Mubarak. In the succeeding months both American envoys and Secretary of State Shultz were to make repeated trips to the region in an attempt to weld the 1978 Camp David proposals for Palestinian autonomy to Mubarak's idea of ceasing settlements and violence for six months followed by an international conference.[42] The American initiative was to fail because of the irrelevance of a warmed-up Camp David formula badly out of touch with changed realities. The Palestinians and the PLO would have to be addressed directly because of Jordan's distancing itself from the PLO in February 1986 and the subsequent uprising. In addition, Shamir, now prime minister of Israel, refused to accept the proposal. There was to be little result from the peripatetic U.S. policy through the winter and spring of 1988, except that it assisted Mubarak domestically in that the initiative was perceived as having originated with him.

The Uprising and the Iranian Acceptance of U.N. Resolution 598

The uprising occurred just as Mubarak and Hussein had renewed their efforts at orchestrating Arab support for an international peace conference. A more systematic commentary in an effort to link the as yet unsuccessful diplomacy to the event came in April, when Foreign Minister Abd al-Majid made a speech to the Peoples Assembly on the subject. He noted that there had been no more momentous an event since the 1973 war and the 1982 Israeli invasion of Lebanon. He then went on to say that Egypt "rejected" the occupation of the territories and "condemned" the Israeli repression. Egypt, he claimed, had shouldered the Pan-Arab responsibility in attempting a diplomatic solution. Mubarak in Washington had not only made proposals regarding an international conference but also had raised the question of Syria and its territory on the Golan Heights. The PLO had the "main" right to choose Palestinian representatives.[43] This statement and the ultimately unsuccessful broader Egyptian efforts took place against the background of recurrent domestic protests against Israeli policy.[44]

The Hussein and Mubarak policy received its final and most important definition when Hussein took the public position of washing his hands of a Jordanian role in the occupied territories.[45] As a result, the PLO was left to attempt to play a more overt financial and administrative role in the territories as well as one of leadership and diplomacy. The outcome was the de facto realization of the original Jordanian and Egyptian position, namely that the Americans and the Israelis would have to deal directly with the PLO.[46]

Events were to occur that dramatically spotlighted the necessity of direct dealings with the PLO. In October 1988 activities directly affecting the Palestinians took place. On November 1 the Israelis were to have national elections, and on November 15 the representative body of the PLO, the Palestinian National Conference, was to meet in Algiers. As background to these events, Mubarak and Hussein met in Aqaba with Arafat to attempt to signal their preference for a Labor victory through a revived Jordanian role in a diplomatic solution. In addition, however, it is likely that background preparations were also under way for the extraordinary meeting of the PNC which was to vote for Arafat's approval for creation of a Palestinian state, the recognition of Israel, the acceptance of U.N. Resolutions 242 and 338, the renunciation of terrorism outside of the occupied territories and Israel, and the desirability of a two-state solution to the conflict The November PNC was so dramatic in the context of the continuation of the Intifada that it heralded a new period in Middle Eastern diplomacy. It is sufficient to note that the sustained Jordanian-Egyptian diplomatic effort contributed to the creation of this new era and that subsequently Egypt came out in recognition of the newly declared Palestinian state, much to the displeasure of the Israelis. Even though the main impetus for the PNC declaration and Arafat's support of it was probably the necessity of the PLO adequately to respond to the policy initiative created by the Intifada, it could also be seen as a success for Egyptian diplomacy.[47] Again, Egypt joined with Saudi Arabia, Algeria, and Jordan to urge a single link of communication by the United States with the PLO. On December 14 the United States decided to establish such a link.[48]

The Palestinian issue thus came to a diplomatic turning point, and events changed for Egypt in the Gulf as well. Iran's 1988 acceptance of U.N. Resolution 598 calling for a cease-fire and negotiations affected Egypt's policy in the Gulf.[49] Whereas Egypt's role until then had been implicitly a security one, now that was less the case. Egypt would undoubtedly continue to be a reliable source of weapons. Egypt might very well benefit economically from the sale of basic construction materials and the supplying of semiskilled and skilled workers to assist in repairing war damage. The Iran-Iraq war had given Egypt an increased presence in the Gulf. It appeared unlikely that its military and economic ties would decline significantly as a result of the cease-fire.

Conclusion

A general conclusion supported by the foregoing analysis is that Egyptian diplomacy has reaped a significant success in rejoining the Arab state system as a result of both a deliberate policy and the fortuitous outbreak of the Iran-Iraq war. Egypt has worked industriously to play a leadership role in bringing about a diplomatic solution to the Palestinian-Israeli conflict. The very effort, however insufficient, largely because of forces beyond its control in the United States, Israel, and within the Palestinian Liberation Organization, has legitimated its claim to membership and leadership in the Arab state system. The continuing effort at diplomacy, however, in effect created a sympathetic backdrop for its formal acceptance by the vast majority of Arab states for the reason of the more geopolitically remote Gulf conflict. This success has momentarily assuaged Mubarak's domestic critics and strengthened his overall political authority. He has been able to relate policies that have focused on Egypt's economic concerns in the Gulf and a leadership role on the Palestinian question to the rescheduling of Egypt's Soviet, American, and international debt. It is also true, however, that the "soft" political center domestically in Egypt of a president without genuine widespread popularity and with only tenuous support from important political groups creates the potential for an unstable regime. The other dimension of this "softness" is that for the moment alternative leaders do not appear ready to come forward nor is there a concerted religious group with the capability of doing so. The army remains the only viable alternative institution, but it is budgetarily favored on one hand and diverted on the other toward developmental and economically productive tasks.

The foreign policy implications of a diplomatically unresponsive international and regional environment appear to be a stalemate resembling the domestic situation. But if the domestic situation remains vulnerable to economic shocks following from economic nonperformance or, more likely, IMF-imposed reforms, the regional international environment is much more hazardous. Although the Gulf conflict has reached a cease-fire, if not yet a diplomatic settlement, the same cannot be said of Lebanon and the occupied territories. In Lebanon, the imbroglio over the presidential elections has resulted in rival Christian military and Muslim claimants to political authority. Even more dangerous for renewed internal conflict and especially the direct conflict of outside powers has been the killing of the top Amal Shiite leadership in the south and the military campaign of the Christian General Michel Aoun, supported now by the Iraqis. With the south potentially destabilized, a UNIFIL peacekeeping force remaining perhaps only because of the Nobel Peace Prize to such U.N. units, Syria isolated regionally and confronted within Lebanon, and Israel besieged by the Intifada and its own internal political polarization, intense international pressure to solve the situation is fraught with the danger of regionwide conflict. As Israel escalates its own repression in the occupied territories from truncheons and broken bones to plastic bullets, wounds, and deaths, it also is contributing to the creation of explosive forces within an improved international diplomatic situation but one handicapped by a timid third-party U.S. policy role. Viewed from Cairo, which is plagued by its own domestic policy immobilism, the situation is dangerous. With the United States only just emerging from its own elections, the inevitable transition and learning period of a newly elected administration and policy cautiousness verging on nonactivity and with Israel internally divided with increasing Israeli settler violence as well as the continuation of the violence of the Intifada, the potential for a sharp, violent conflict of a magnitude and character to compel direct Egyptian diplomatic and perhaps military involvement remains. Egyptian reentry into the Arab state system has had its opportunities for the Egyptian leadership, but it perhaps inevitably will have its costs as well.

Notes

1. This view of the international system is sketched more formally by Ed Kolodziej, "Superpower Competition in a Divided and Decentralized International System," in *The Limits of Soviet Power in the Developing Nations*, ed. Roger Kanet and Kolodziej (London: Macmillan, forthcoming), brought to my attention by my colleague A. R. Norton, Department of Social Sciences, U.S. Military Academy, West Point.

2. *New York Times*, Nov. 12, 1987, regarding the summit, and Feb. 10, 1988, regarding the Peoples Democratic Republic of Yemen.

3. On the Soviet rapprochement, see Abdel Moneim Said Aly, "Egypt: A Decade after Camp David" in *The Middle East Ten Years after Camp David*, ed. William Quandt, (Washington, D.C.: Brookings Institution, 1988), pp. 89–90. For a Soviet view of overall USSR policy, see Evgeni M. Primakov, "Soviet Policy Toward the Arab-Israeli Conflict," ibid., pp. 387–409.

4. The Egyptian insistence on pursuing its own interests can be seen in its determination to get possession of a special alloy for missile construction in the United States even though this violated U.S. trade restrictions on shipment of strategic items. It also illustrates Egypt's determination to arm itself according to its own priorities. In this case there is an apparent joint project with the Argentinians to produce a conventional warhead missile to stay abreast of the technology developed in the region by Syria, Iran, Iraq, and Israel. This case, involving Egyptian military officers and American businessmen, appears headed for very discreet handling because it is possible that the number two person in Egypt, Defense Minister Abdel Halim Abu Ghazala, might be involved. In addition, the Israelis have been involved in similar dealings and, rather than prosecution, the United States has given the staff of the Israeli office involved in New York City diplomatic immunity. See Richard W. Stevenson, "U.S. Studying Cairo Links to Smuggling Plot," *New York Times*, Sept. 4, 1988.

5. See Marvin Weinbaum, "Politics and Development in Foreign Aid: U.S. Economic Assistance to Egypt, 1975–82," *Middle East Journal* 37 (1983): 636–55.

6. On these issues as well as a detailed political economy analysis, see Yahya Sadowski, "The Sphinx's New Riddle: Why Does Egypt Delay Economic Reform?" *American Arab Affairs* 22 (Fall 1987): 28–40.

7. Robert B. Satloff, *Army and Politics in Mubarak's Egypt* (Washington, D.C.: Washington Institute for Near East Policy, 1988), Table 1, "Sources of Egyptian Arms Imports, 1981–85," p. 9. Satloff notes that three-fifths of the arms imported were from non-U.S. sources (p. 10), but he does not make the point of diversification which his data bear out.

8. A recent example occurred when, after an agreement on sending the Taba dispute to an international arbitration commission had already been made with Shimon Peres when he was prime minister, the new prime minister, Yitzhak Shamir, persuaded Washington to ask Egypt to attempt renewed bilateral talks. This "trilateralism" is discussed by Ali E. Hilal Dessouki, "Egyp-

tian Foreign Policy since Camp David" in Quandt, ed., *Middle East Ten Years after Camp David*, pp. 105–9.

9. This transition from Sadat to Mubarak is detailed in Louis J. Cantori, "Egyptian Policy under Mubarak: The Politics of Continuity and Change," in *The Middle East after the Israeli Invasion of Lebanon*, ed. Robert O. Freedman (Syracuse: Syracuse Univ. Press, 1986), pp. 323–44.

10. This is the characterization of Leonard Binder, "Lebanon and the Regional State System," *Middle East Insight* 6 (Summer 1988): 27–33.

11. These constraints are elaborated upon in Cantori, "Egyptian Policy under Mubarak." See also Cantori, "Husni Mubarak," in *Dictionary of Middle Eastern Political Biography*, ed. Bernard Reich (Westport. Conn.: Greenwood Press, forthcoming).

12. John Waterbury notes this phenomenon in the transition from Sadat to Mubarak, *The Egypt of Nasser and Sadat* (Princeton: Princeton Univ. Press, 1983), pp. 378–79.

13. On the military, see Satloff, *Army and Politics*. Satloff makes a very important point regarding Egypt's semiautonomy. He notes that under Mubarak expenditures on the army have reversed Sadat's policy of budgeting cutbacks as a means of control and instead have nearly doubled as percentage of central government expenditure from 1981 to 1986 (p. 5).

14. This analysis is partly based on interviews and discussions in Cairo in July 1988.

15. On the investment companies, see Moneim Said Aly, "Egypt," p. 83. On the larger perspective of Islamic economic activities and the investment companies, see Alain Roussilion, "Secteur public et societes islamique de placement de fonds: La recomposition du systeme redistributif en Egypte," *Bulletin du Cairo* 23 (Premier semestre 1988): 277–322. The *Bulletin* is published by the Centre d'Etude et de Documentation Economique, Juridique et Sociale, under the directorship of Jean-Claude Vatin.

16. On the Muslim Brethren in the present period, see Gilles Kepel, *The Prophet and the Pharaoh* (London: Saqi Books, 1985), pp. 1–128. Their contemporary electoral and economic role in the investment companies is detailed in Abdel Moneim Said Aly, "Democratization in Egypt," *American Arab Affairs* 22 (Fall 1987): 20–21.

17. On the earlier pattern of religious violence, see Louis J. Cantori, "Religion and Politics in Egypt," in *Religion and Politics in the Middle East*, ed. Michael Curtis, (Boulder, Colo.: Westview Press, 1981), pp. 92–122. For the contemporary period, see Saad Eddin Ibrahim, "Domestic Developments in Egypt," in Quandt, ed., *Middle East Ten Years after Camp David*, pp. 50–56.

18. Raymond Hinnebusch, *Egyptian Politics under Sadat* (Cambridge, Eng.: Cambridge Univ. Press, 1985), pp. 186–222.

19. See Moneim Said Aly, "Democratization in Egypt," for an excellent comparative study of the 1976, 1979, 1984, and 1987 parliamentary elections.

20. The electoral law and the way it inhibits parties caused a controversy over the requirement that a party must gain 8 percent of the vote nationally before it can declare a single candidate elected to the parliament. This rather high figure precludes, for example, the left-of-center National Progressive Union from any parliamentary representation (it received 2.21% of the national vote in 1987). Similarly, the fall 1988 local elections were to be conducted according to the system of majority voting instead of the national formula of proportional representation. It has been said that this is to prevent any local

establishment of an Islamic republic. Yusuf Wali, secretary general of the government National Democratic party, secretary of agriculture, and deputy prime minister, commented that the parties were not equipped to contest local elections anyway (remarks made in a meeting on July 18, 1988). It is possible that left-of-center exclusion from the electoral process has contributed to leftist Nasserist acts of violence and assassination directed against Israeli and American diplomats in 1986 and 1987. The group responsible carries the name Egypt's Revolution and its leader, now a fugitive abroad, is Khaled Gamal Abd al-Nasser, the late president's oldest son (Ali E. Hilal Dessouqi, "Egyptian Foreign Policy Since Camp David" in Quandt, ed., *Middle East Ten Years after Camp David*, p. 99).

21. World Bank, *World Development Report 1988* (Washington, D.C., 1988), pp. 250, 252, for the figures on balance of payments and indebtedness, respectively. For the 1986 GDP growth figure, see American Embassy, Cairo, *Economic Trends Report: Egypt* (Cairo, 1987), p. 8.

22. This analysis is based on that of Herman Eilts, "The United States and Egypt," in Quandt, ed., *Middle East Ten Years after Camp David*, pp. 136–42, *Economic Trends Report*, and Sadowski, "Sphinx's New Riddle."

23. This reluctance by the Egyptian government is occurring even though, as one analyst has pointed out, the IMF terms were requested by the Egyptians themselves (Sadowski, "Sphinx's New Riddle," pp. 32–33). For background analysis of the relation of the continued IMF disagreement to the September 1988 European tour, see Alan Cowell, "Mubarak, in Europe, Stresses Role as Peace Broker," *New York Times*, Sept. 28, 1988.

24. This speculative analysis about microrealities is based on first hand observation in Minufiyya Province in the summers of 1987 and 1988, where average peasant wage rates are said to be between fe 15–20 a day when peasant laborers are available. Other observers confirm this phenomenon at least for the Delta area, if not Upper Egypt. Furthermore, there is a high expectation among analysts that petrodollar downturns in the region would result in a decrease in the demand for Egyptian workers abroad. In fact, however, there are no data to support this expectation. What may be occurring instead is a cessation of the increase of this demand and a leveling out of actual numbers of workers abroad.

25. Illustrative of this relative deprivation are answers to the informal and unscientific but revealing question, How much is meat? The typical middle-class response is t 12–15 a kilo ($5.50–$7.00) for beef. The same question to taxicab drivers elicits the response t 5–7 a kilo ($2.20–$3.30). An inspection of butcher shops in humble neighborhoods confirms the taxicab drivers' figures. The difference is probably a matter of middle-class versus lower-income neighborhoods and an acquired taste for beef fillet as opposed to lesser-quality cuts.

26. For a detailing of specific instances of violence and controversies in Israeli-Egyptian relations, see Ann Mosely Lesch, "Irritants in the Egyptian-Israeli Relationship," *Universities Field Staff, Inc. (USFI) Reports*, no. 34 (AML-4-86) (Indianapolis, 1986). A trenchant criticism of the Egyptian regime's failure either to pursue justice for the Palestinians or to deliver a truer democracy for Egyptians is found in Robert Bianchi, "Egypt," in "Domestic Determinants of Foreign Policy and Peace Efforts in the Middle East," ed. Iliya Harik and Louis J. Cantori, *Conflict* 8 (Spring 1988): 52–54.

27. For a discussion of the controversy, see Dessouki, "Egyptian Foreign

Policy," pp. 100–102, and the technical details of the arbitration commission's decision in *New York Times*, Sept. 30, 1988.

28. For this phase of Jordanian policy, see Aaron David Miller, "Jordanian Policy: The Politics of Limitation and Constraint," in Freedman, ed., *Middle East after the Israeli Invasion*, pp. 221–29. See also Don Peretz, "Jordan," in Harik and Cantori, pp. 55–56, and Emile Sahliyeh, "Jordan and the Palestinians," in Quandt, ed., *Middle East Ten Years after Camp David*, pp. 279–318.

29. On the Egyptian attitude, see Eilts, "United States and Egypt," p. 125.

30. Details of how the CIA and the National Security Agency listened in to President Mubarak's telephone conversations with his foreign minister during the incident gave North and Poindexter the detailed flight information needed to carry out the action (Bob Woodward, *Veil: The Secret Wars of the CIA, 1981–1987* [New York: Pocket Books, 1987], pp. 476–78).

31. *Washington Post*, July 24, 1986.

32. On workers and remittances, plus Gulf Arab tourism, see Moneim Said Aly, "Democratization in Egypt," pp. 84–87.

33. Quoted in *FBIS*, Apr. 9, 1987.

34. This Gulf state point of view plus the longer-term one of looming generational change in the leadership and estrangement from the United States in the Gulf was made by James Placke in a panel discussion of U.S. Gulf policy chaired by Judith Kipper at the Brookings Institution, Washington, D.C., July 27, 1988.

35. These Gulf press reports are in *FBIS*, May 16, Aug. 14, 1987.

36. Translation of radio broadcast, Oct. 12, 1987, in *FBIS*, Oct. 16, 1987; Arabic text in *al-Ahram*, Oct. 13, 1987.

37. Ibid.

38. Butrus Ghali, Minister of State for Foreign Affairs, *Achievements of Egyptian Diplomacy 1987* (Cairo: Ministry of Information, 1988), p. 26.

39. Mubarak, speech of Oct. 12, 1987, in *FBIS*, Oct. 16, 1987.

40. *Al-Ittihad* (Abu Dhabi), Dec. 10, 1987, reported that at the December 6 meeting of Hussein and Mubarak in Cairo, they had discovered a possible joint Jordanian-Egyptian intervention force in the Gulf to which Egypt would contribute fifteen thousand men (*FBIS*, Dec. 11, 1987).

41. *Washington Post*, Jan. 22, 1988.

42. Eilts, "United States and Egypt," pp. 125–26.

43. Text in *FBIS*, Apr. 6, 1988.

44. Described by Saad Eddine Ibrahim, "Domestic Developments in Egypt," p. 37.

45. *New York Times*, Aug. 1, 1988. This declaration only made conclusive what Jordan had decided in its break with the PLO in February 1986 but which U.S. policy had refused to accept. The process by which the PLO has finally emerged as the only possible negotiating party is detailed by Rashid Khalidi, "The Palestinian Liberation Organization," in Quandt, ed., *Middle East Ten Years after Camp David*, pp. 261–78.

46. Even though Hussein had withdrawn the so-called Jordanian option from the peace process, he and Mubarak continue to coordinate policy as evidenced in their early September 1988 meeting in Cairo, which took place as the PLO considered forming a provisional government in exile (*FBIS*, Sept. 6, 1988). In a pointed comment while in Germany on his European tour, Mubarak cautioned the PLO against either forming a government in exile or declaring an independent Palestinian state until after the November 1988

American and Israeli elections. He implied that such action might negatively affect these elections (*FBIS*, Sept. 30, 1988).

47. For the PNC declaration, see *New York Times*, Nov. 16, 1988. For the recognition of the Palestinian state and the reaction of the Israeli Defense Minister, Yitzhak Rabin, see *Washington Post*, Nov. 26, 1988.

48. *Washington Post*, Nov. 26, 1988; U.S. decision, *New York Times*, Dec. 15, 1988.

49. For an effort to reassess the Iraqi-Egyptian relationship, see Tony Horwitz, "Strong Rivalry Between Egypt and Iraq Could Re-emerge as the Gulf War Ebbs," *Wall Street Journal*, Sept. 9, 1988. Such a rivalry would appear unlikely in the more egalitarian atmosphere of the region at the present time and as Iraq attempts to continue its good relations with the Arab Gulf states against even a defeated Iran.

14

The Sudan since the Fall of Numayri

Peter Bechtold

Introduction

The Republic of Sudan straddles Africa and the Middle East and is geographically the largest country in both regions. Although not a major player in the Middle East proper, and certainly neither involved in nor affected in any major way by the Iran-Contra affair, the Sudan offers fascinating perspectives in many areas, including domestic and foreign politics.

It is a country worth studying, if only because its 597 tribes, speaking some 400 languages and dialects, and following a variety of Islamic, Christian, and Animist religious traditions, make it one of the world's most heterogeneous societies. Sudan also has one of the most democratic political cultures in Africa and in the Arab world. These two attributes combine to make political stability very difficult to achieve and to maintain. Indeed, the country experienced four different governments during forty months, ranging from the end of the Numayri military dictatorship through a year-long transitional government under mixed civilian-military leadership to a multiparty parliamentary democracy.

This essay will trace the fall of the Numayri regime in April 1985 and describe and analyze the major issues facing all Sudanese governments then and now.

The Fall of Numayri

Any analysis of the current situation must go back at least to April 1985, when the generally despised dictatorship of military strongman Ja'far Numayri came to an end after a surprisingly long run of almost sixteen years.

On April 6 the army commander in chief, Lieutenant General Abdul-Rahman M. H. Siwar al-Dhahab, took control of the country and dismissed President Numayri and all his aides while he was returning from a state visit to Washington. Some journalists attributed Numayri's downfall to the large-scale riots and street demonstrations in late March following the government's decision to cancel food subsidies in compliance with strong urgings from the IMF and major economic donor countries (especially the United States). Tens of thousands marched in the streets and shut down virtually all public utilities, including hospitals, radio, and air communications. The demonstrators included, among others, students, lawyers, trade unionists, postal workers, and many doctors, who refused to work in hospitals after observing up close the victims of Numayri's trigger-happy riot police. Mass support for the opposition numbered in the hundreds of thousands in the capital area alone. It could be argued that by the beginning of April, President Numayri's support had dwindled to less than 1 percent of the politically aware population of the country.

A brief summary of the decline of this regime may help us understand the post-Numayri era better.

The May Revolution headed by Ja'far Numayri—so named after the date of its occurrence in 1969—had rested initially on a loose alliance of "progressive forces" in opposition to the traditional elite of sectarian leaders, urban merchants, and rural tribal notables. The traditional elite had organized themselves one generation earlier in the major political parties—Umma, National Unionist party (NUP), People's Democratic party [PDP] (the latter two merging into the Democratic Unionist Party (DUP). These represented the major northern demographic groupings of the largely rural-based *mahdiyya* (Umma party) and *khatmiyya* (PDP) sects and the nonsectarian urban merchants, civil servants, and others (NUP), respectively. They uniformly condemned Numayri as an "illegitimate usurper" of power—illegitimate because of his overthrow of a democratic order which had a parliamentary multiparty system. This phrase had been used repeatedly by all leaders of the (since 1969) defunct political parties, and in particular by the most prominent of these figures, Umma party president and defacto leader of the Ansar sect, Sadiq al-Mahdi.

The Ansar movement had borne the brunt of the first large-scale violent confrontation with the Numayri regime in its home base on Aba Island in March 1970, and the blood spilled by Numayri's forces would never be forgotten by the House of Madhi or its followers. Their major rivals in the northern Sudan had been members of the *khatmiyya* sect, led by the house of Mirghani, whose policy after 1969 was to maintain a low-profile disassociation from the government, in the hope of avoiding the sort of crackdown administered to the Ansar.

A large number of nonsectarian intelligentsia had fled the country and taken up senior positions in Arab and African universities as well as international organizations. Many midlevel civil servants had similarly left for the relatively young oil-producing states of the Gulf and soon became the respected backbone of these states' local adminis- trations. Known as highly competent, trustworthy, and apolitical public servants and educators, these Sudanese made major and much ap- preciated contributions to oil-rich but manpower-poor Gulf states, and their remittances helped somewhat to alleviate the chronic foreign exchange deficits back home. At the same time, their general refusal to cooperate with the May Revolution after Numayri's invitation to return became an indictment of that government's lack of legitimacy at home and abroad, along with ever-growing charges of mismanage- ment and corruption.

Together, these three centrist groupings have traditionally held more than a two-thirds portion of the political power groupings in the Sudan. The rest has consisted of the more radical elements of the political spectrum, the communists and assorted socialists on the left, the Muslim Brotherhood on the right, and several regional blocs in the south as well as in the east and far west. A final category consists of the trade unions and other professional organizations and, in partic- ular, the armed forces.

At one time or another, Ja'far Numayri tried to co-opt all of these groups, usually by playing some off against others and periodically by trying to create splits within some, for example, the trade unions, southern politicians, and, significantly, in 1984, the Muslim Brother- hood, by favoring a hoped-for counterweight to its longtime leader, Dr. Hassan al-Turabi.

A brief review of these groups reveals that both wings of the Com- munist party of Sudan—earlier one of the most active in Africa and the Middle East—had been targeted as public enemy number one after the abortive putsch in July 1971, and it was forced to operate in small numbers underground or in exile. The Muslim Brotherhood was publicly banned in 1969 and its leaders were imprisoned. It was brought into the government in the late 1970s and participated in the formulation of Islamic legislation proclaimed in September 1983, although many details about the method and application of these laws have been disavowed by Muslim Brotherhood notables. Virtually all observers agree that Numayri sought to use the Brotherhood as a counterweight to other northern groupings and attempted to ride the crest of Islamic movements in the region as a whole. When the application of these laws by emergency courts aroused consternation in Western donor countries and among neighboring Muslim states, Numayri undid this alliance and arrested large numbers of Muslim

Brotherhood leaders on charges of treason. Perhaps he expected to gain approval from centrist groupings; in fact, he alienated one of his last remaining political allies. The timing coincided with the departure of U.S. Vice-President Bush from a state visit to Sudan, creating the image that Muslims were being purged on the order of the United States. When Sudan gained the release of $53 million of suspended U.S. economic aid, the quid pro quo seemed clear to many observers.

These developments had become all the more important because Numayri had lost just about all support from his erstwhile possibly staunchest allies, the leaders of Sudan's southern region, mostly Animist (approximately 70 percent) and Christian (about 25 percent) by religion. In a disastrously shortsighted decision, Numayri undid his arguably greatest achievement—the Addis Ababa Accords of March 1972, which had brought autonomy to the south and had ended almost seventeen years of civil war by the Anya 'nya rebels. He did so by ordering the redivision of the south into three provinces to placate primarily anti-Dinka sentiments in May 1983.[1]

Clumsy discussions about the "export" of "southern" oil into northern-based refineries and oil terminals convinced many southerners that the "northern government" in Khartoum was up to its old tricks of exploiting the south.[2] The introduction of Sharia law for the entire country—not merely the Muslim areas or populations—added to these suspicions. And, indeed, a small group of bandits who never accepted the 1972 accords announced the formation of Anya 'nya II in early 1983. More significant, however, was the emergence of another rebel movement, eventually known as the Sudanese People's Liberation movement (SPLM), and its military arm SPLA (A for Army) under Colonel Dr. John Garang de Mabior, growing out of the mutiny of three garrisons at Bor, Pibor, and Pachella in May 1983. Garang declared war on Numayri and received significant military assistance from anti-Numayri regimes in Libya and Ethiopia.

Finally, the senior ranks of the armed forces had experienced repeated purges and forced early retirements from 1969 on. Many members increasingly lost confidence in their government, and this professional alienation reached a climax in an international confrontation with the commander in chief in January 1982, followed by the dismissal of twenty-six senior officers, including the deputy commander in chief and vice-president of the republic. Rumors were rife, and have been ever since, about inroads by Muslim Brothers, Ba'athists, some communists, and others into the officer ranks.

The final straw for this observer was the execution of an elderly Islamic reformer, Shaikh Mahmoud Mohammad Taha of the Islamic Republican Brothers, in late January 1985 on grounds of heresy.[3]

Shaikh Mahmoud and his movement had been active though numerically insignificant at least since the 1950s and had been tolerated and ignored as harmless by all regimes and politico-religious groupings. Killing a seventy-six-year-old gentleman was seen not only as a violation of Sudan's unwritten law of political tolerance but as a violation of Islamic law, as was determined by an appeals court ex-post-facto. But in the most significant sense it demonstrated to one and all that Numayri had totally lost his senses, including his often admired political savvy, and therefore had lost whatever minuscule justification remained for remaining in power. The masses did not need to wait long for an excuse to take advantage of the inevitable next misstep. Dismissing available lessons from Egypt and Sudan, Numayri aligned himself with foreign benefactors against his impoverished citizenry in the capital area, ordered the removal of food subsidies, and departed on a three-nation visit while Khartoum was in turmoil. Fortunately for him, he never returned.

The Transitional Period

When General Siwar al-Dhahab seized control in Sudan on April 6, 1985, he did so not in the fashion of many African military dictators eager for power, but rather reluctantly as the senior ranking officer in the country and the titular leader of a small group of military activists who wanted to save Sudan from further political, economic, and military chaos. A state of emergency was declared, the constitution that had evolved during Numayri's rule was suspended, and the National Assembly and the sole legal party—the Sudan Socialist Union—were dissolved. Three days later the General Command of the People's Armed Forces announced the formation of a fifteen-member Transitional Military Council (TMC) as the de facto government "until elections for a democratic parliament could be held." The TMC was complemented two weeks later by a civilian cabinet of sixteen members, which represented all significant political orientations in the country opposed to the defunct Numayri regime. It was headed for the next twelve months by Dr. Jizuli Dafa'allah, the president of the country's Medical Association, who had been temporarily imprisoned under Numayri and was known to be a devout Muslim and nonparty nationalist.

The greatest achievements of the transitional regime were the removal of a most unpopular dictatorship without any bloodshed and the faithful execution of its primary commitment, stated early and often, to conduct honest and open elections for a constituent assembly within one year. Notwithstanding the doubts of many cynics abroad,

the elections were held almost exactly one year later and were contested by an astonishing forty-two political parties and groupings.
Taken together, these achievements deserve strong admiration, if one
only recalls the generally authoritarian atmosphere in most of Africa
and the Arab world and the inherent difficulties of creating the necessary machinery for electoral participation after sixteen years of virtually absolute rule during which political parties had been banned. The
fervor of Sudanese politicians who were finally again permitted to
organize politically in public and the mushrooming of parties and
affiliations complete with their own newspapers and other publications
could only be described as euphoric.

Unfortunately, to this observer, most politicians seemed so caught
up in the prospects for elections and democracy that they saw these as
ends rather than means toward solving the country's problems. As a
result, the politicians expended almost all of their energies on party
organization, voter registration, fund-raising, and so on, and the TMC
limited its role to maintaining public safety and ensuring the presence
of conditions for successfully holding elections. No one addressed the
country's most urgent problems of rebellion in the south, famine, and
debt relief, the constitutional issues of law (*Sharia* or secular) and
administration (centralized or confederated), and the overall dismal
condition of the economy. The politicians were too busy preparing
for their upcoming contests and the TMC considered itself to be
constitutionally unauthorized to make decisions on major issues, which
it insisted on deferring to the future parliament. But as others have
observed, difficult problems usually do not remain frozen in time but
tend to deteriorate further.

One good example has been the national economy. At the time of
Numayri's downfall, the foreign debt total (about U.S. $10 billion) had
actually exceeded Sudan's GDP for one year. Thus all available foreign
exchange had to be diverted for debt servicing of interest obligations,
and the Sudan government was repeatedly warned by its creditors that
it was about to go bankrupt.[4] All parties concerned agreed on the
gravity of the economic situation, but the TMC felt helpless to make
major reforms, and the civilian politicians declared that the debts
belonged to Numayri. There was some justification to this argument—
Numayri's economic policies and mismanagement had been beyond
the influence of almost everyone—but the country's international
credit rating plummeted further. Timing was also unfortunate. The
Arab Gulf states experienced dramatic declines in oil revenues in the
mid-1980s while simultaneously facing pressing obligations such as
financial support to Iraq in the Gulf war. The United States government was caught in the throes of the Gramm-Rudman budget deficit

legislation and was unable to meet even the assistance levels of previous years, although considerable humanitarian aid was delivered to famine-stricken areas.

Throughout the 1980s hopes had been high that the Chevron oil fields in southwest Sudan would eventually produce enough revenue for import substitution and for some additional export. Unfortunately, this potential source for reversing the economic deterioration has not yet materialized because the Chevron management was forced to halt construction on the pipeline from Bentiu to the projected refinery in Kosti (and beyond to the shipping terminal of Port Sudan) as a result of attacks on the work crews by members by the SPLA, especially in 1984. Here the link between economic recovery and domestic security becomes clear. The SPLM had targeted the pipeline construction before the coup mainly to prevent the possibility that "Chevron oil revenues would rescue the tottering Numayri dictatorship." John Garang's pronouncements to that effect, broadcast repeatedly from the clandestine SPLA Radio, were unambiguous.

Rebellion in the South

With the departure of Numayri almost everyone had hoped that SPLA fighting would cease, but that was not to be. Despite many apparently well-meaning overtures by Prime Minister Jizuli Dafa'allah to John Garang to meet at any available conference site, complete with verbal (via radio) and written (special letter) assurances that the new government had no intention of subjugating or discriminating against southerners, the latter refused to accept these promises as genuine. In broadcast after broadcast, the SPLM labeled the TMC as the "mere extension of Numayri's military dictatorship without Numayri." In retrospect, many observers agree that the first few months after the April uprising presented several golden opportunities for resolving the conflict between the central government and the SPLM/SPLA. It is difficult not to allocate the larger portion of blame to Garang's uncompromising hard line, resulting perhaps from incorrect intelligence transmitted by his informants in the capital area. Given the usual distrust between northerners and southerners in all locations, one can easily imagine that a (justifiably or not) hypersuspicious mind would misread or miscommunicate a potentially workable proposal. Yet Garang and his allies could point to Khartoum's refusal to lift the highly sensitive *Sharia* laws as a good faith gesture, something the TMC felt was the province of the Constituent Assembly and would be inappropriate for the TMC. Whether the TMC actually believed in this position is difficult to judge, but one suspects that the devout, leadership of Prime Minister Dr. Jizuli and TMC Chair General Siwar al-Dhahab felt uncomfortable about entering Sudanese history, and that of the Islamic world, as the individuals who undid *Sharia*.

The Libyan Factor

This equation was further complicated by the change in Libyan policy after the successful negotiations by the transitional regime with Colonel Kaddafi. He had been delighted to finance weapons purchases for his archenemy's (Numayri) enemies in the SPLA. The overthrow of Numayri produced visible appreciation by the Tripoli government in the form of an official visit to Khartoum, soon followed by a tanker shipment of free petroleum from Libya to Port Sudan. Subsequent visits by the new prime minister and the TMC deputies to Tripoli resulted in promises by Kaddafi to withdraw financial and material aid from the rebel movement in the South.

John Garang denounced this Libyan turnabout and even accused Kaddafi of dispatching some Libyan-piloted bombers to attack SPLA positions in a raid. He concluded that an "Arab conspiracy" had resurfaced, this time in the guise of a Khartoum-Tripoli axis, and ordered his still sufficiently equipped troops to continue fighting. This, in turn, visibly angered TMC Chair General Siwar al-Dhahab to the point of using harsh language and actions against Garang, thereby reconfirming the latter's previous suspicions.

I surmise that General Siwar al-Dhahab, obviously a Sudanese officer from the old school of unquestioning discipline and professional integrity, could not stomach what he must have viewed as insubordination by a lower-ranking officer. No matter if this speculation is correct, it was certainly clear that Garang and the TMC perceived events not only from different political and military but also cultural, psychological, and generational perspectives. In the end, deadlock was the result for the rest of 1985.

Foreign Policy

To the outside world, especially those unfamiliar with the history of Sudan's domestic politics, the major visible change after April 1985 came in the country's foreign policy posture. Throughout the 1980s especially, Ja'far Numayri had become increasingly identified with a Cairo-Washington axis, with a concomitant unconcealed hostility to the governments in Libya and Ethiopia. This posture sat particularly well with the American Congress, which appreciated Numayri's support for Egypt's Camp David policy (vis-à-vis Israel) and for America's strategic concerns in the Middle East symbolized by joint participation in Operation Bright Star military exercises on Sudanese territory and his outspoken opposition to the "terrorist madman" Kaddafi and the "Marxist dictatorship" of Colonel Mengistu Haile Mariam of Ethiopia. The payoff had been the elevation of Sudan to the largest U.S. aid recipient in Africa proper—second on the continent only to Egypt, which the United States treats administratively as a Middle Eastern state—and close coordination on special projects such as famine relief to Eritreans through eastern Sudan and the exodus of Ethiopian "Falasha" Jews through Sudan to Israel via Europe.

Regardless of the merits of these policies, individually or collectively, the student of independent Sudan's history knows that these policies, or any other bloc identification, were an aberration. They were fundamentally inconsistent with the country's traditional role as a "bridge" between Africa and the Arab world and as nonaligned in regional (i.e., Arab) and international (i.e., superpower) bloc formations. Since April 1985 Sudan has reverted, once again, to these traditional roles, not for ideological reasons but as the result of a sound analysis of its national interests. Prime Ministers Jizuli and, one year later, Sadiq al-Mahdi argued persuasively for the need to maintain dialogues with potentially dangerous regimes in Libya and Ethiopia to prevent their support for anti-Khartoum rebels, especially in southern and western Sudan. Also, too close an identification with an Egypt then still somewhat ostracized by the Arab League could be seen as an obstacle to acquiring desperately needed economic assistance from the petroleum producers of the Arab Gulf (and North Africa). Too close an identification with American strategic concerns could also undermine the legitimacy of the new government domestically.

As a result, the post–April 1985 governments have distanced themselves slightly from Cairo and Washington; for example, Sudan no longer participates in Operation Bright Star and has effectively canceled the Nile Valley Integration Project with Egypt. Meanwhile, the government has maneuvered toward the direction of the GCC states and has reestablished dialogues with nations with which relations had been strained or nonexistent such as Libya, Ethiopia, and the Soviet Union. It should be emphasized that these movements *do not* indicate an identification with, or even closeness to, these three states. On the contrary, virtually all publicly aware Sudanese feel a closer identification with Egypt than with other Arabs and with Western cultures rather than Eastern bloc states. But Sudan's government cannot afford to be seen as too closely identified with these groups because of the demographic configurations in Sudan and the resultant requirement for a careful balance of domestic and foreign groupings.

Sudan's foreign policy since independence has usually revolved around two major issues and one minor one. Bilateral relations with neighboring states have been primarily affected by the special problems of ethnic minority groups on both sides of Sudan's borders and the tendency of antiregime rebels to seek refuge in these neighboring states. Thus political refugees from Uganda, Zaire, Chad, and Ethiopia have been welcomed on Sudanese soil (along with about a million economic refugees), and Sudanese rebel groups have intermittently resided in these same countries. In the 1980s Libya could be added to this list for similar reasons, when the Libyan National Salvation Front was able to broadcast attacks against the Kaddafi government from Sudanese transmitters and anti-Numayri rebels were harbored, trained, and equipped in Libya.

A second major foreign policy determinant has been the constant need for Sudan to acquire economic assistance from any and all sources, ranging from international donors such as the United Nations Development Program (UNDP) and International Bank for Reconstruction and Development (IBRD) to governments as diverse as Saudi Arabia, the Peoples Republic of China, the United States, and Libya.

The above variables would normally result in a posture of positive nonalignment and friendly dialogue with all sides. The third issue, however, has tended to be potentially divisive: the question of transnational identification either with the Arab world or with Africa. It goes almost without saying that undue emphasis at one level could backfire by producing emotional backlash at the other. For example, any significant involvement by Khartoum with Arab causes such as Palestine or Iraq has usually resulted in alienation by southern groupings and not infrequently in a revival of their old connection with Israel via neighboring African states. Sudan's foreign relations have been most stable and most productive during those periods when the government in Khartoum was itself sufficiently broad-based and emphasized Sudan's unique identity as a heterogeneous society of an Afro-Arab character.

Domestic Politics

Even though the issues of foreign policy and economic performance have been of prime concern to the interested world beyond its borders, Sudan's politicians have tended to focus nearer to home. The overwhelming proportion of political energy in the Sudanese capital has been expended on government formation and coalition building and undermining under all regimes. This interesting, yet lamentable, state of affairs has been very much in evidence once again during the period since Numayri's downfall.

After the TMC announced its intention to prepare the country for parliamentary elections, and once the machinery had been assembled for the actual conduct of elections, the diverse interests of the various political groupings came into the open. Whereas everyone professed belief in the desirability of "democratic rule," there was considerable difference of opinion about format and timing. Three clusters of perspectives emerged: the well-known northern parties of the pre-Numayri era, who called for the holding of nationwide elections as soon as possible in as many districts as the security situation permitted; the majority of southern parties and some regional groupings in western Sudan who preferred postponing elections until public safety had been returned to all parts of the country; and some ideological groupings left of center who feared the reemergence of the discredited party infighting of the 1960s and either wanted elections based on professional rather than territorial constituencies or advocated continued interim rule until a constitutional conference had resolved the interlinked issues of law and regional insurrection. It seemed evident to this observer that, as in 1965, the National Alliance of Professionals feared that nationwide elections would return to power "reactionary parties" who would rob the alliance of the fruits for their efforts in toppling the military regime. Their only hope of maintaining political influence was to prevent, or delay indefinitely, elections based on territorial constituencies. For the same reasons, the traditional parties—Umma, DUP, and even the nontraditional National Islamic Front (NIF)—favored elections as soon as possible and argued for holding them in all districts even if the electoral turnout was low in parts of the south. Indeed, the latter probability was very much a part of their calculations in winning the odd seat when some southern ethnic group had entered into an electoral alliance with them. Most southern politicians and the "non-Arabs" of the north such as Nuba Mountain, Fur, and Beja groupings pleaded for the postponement on grounds of security and the need for prior resolution of constitutional issues. In reality, they were unprepared for early elections because their internal organizations were late off the mark compared to the Umma and NIF especially and sought therefore to delay proceedings a few months at least, in the hope of catching up with their rivals.

In 1985–86, as had been the case in 1964–65, the Electoral Commission had to determine whether free and fair elections could be held safely in that part of the south where an insurrection had been raging. And if the evidence were to militate in favor of partial elections for those areas unaffected by the fighting, would the principle of partial elections compromise the integrity of the entire process? In the hope of resolving this dilemma, a series of contacts between Khartoum and the SPLM/SPLA leadership had been established. After seemingly interminable delays and numerous contacts with different groups resulting in relatively little progress, the SPLM/SPLA settled on an "acceptable" partner for dialogue and met in late March 1986 with representatives of the National Alliance of Professionals in Koka Dam, some distance from Addis Ababa.[5] After four days of speechmaking and subsequent negotiations, the parties issued the Koka Dam Declaration on March 24, 1986. This declaration continues to serve as the sole policy position by the SPLM/SPLA for resolving outstanding issues with the Khartoum government; hence, it is worth listing the major features.

It called for the "creation of a new Sudan . . . free from racism, tribalism, sectarianism and all causes of discrimination and disparity" and for lifting the state of emergency, for repealing the September 1983 (Islamic) laws, for adopting the 1956 constitution as amended in 1964, and for the abrogation of military pacts signed by the previous regime. With regard to the military conflict in the south, both parties stated that they "genuinely endeavor to stop the bloodshed resulting from the war in the Sudan" and "call for a ceasefire" and subsequently for a constitutional conference to be held in Khartoum during the third week of June 1986 with an agreed-upon nine-point agenda.[6]

Almost immediately after the announcement of the Koka Dam Declaration, the SPLA commander in chief John Garang clarified his interpretations of that declaration at a high-level meeting of his top lieutenants that was reported by the clandestine SPLA radio. One significant aspect concerned SPLM/SPLA policy regarding the then imminent elections, which he termed "partial, therefore resulting in a partial government in Khartoum, representing one side of the country and . . . not in line with the people's hopes for building a new Sudan where no one will be taken for granted."[7]

The impression has lingered that John Garang and the SPLM leadership have considered the Koka Dam Declaration to be both a pronouncement of their philosophical views and a policy statement of their conditions for negotiation toward a resolution of the conflict with Khartoum. By contrast, the northern politicians seem to have seen Koka Dam as a necessary concession to Garang to persuade him to agree to a cease-fire, but not necessarily as a policy platform for the final resolution of the conflict.

As it was, the TMC had committed itself to turning power over to the civilians and Chairman Siwar al-Dhahab was in no mood to prolong TMC rule. True to his word that he looked forward to retirement one year after stepping in as the TMC chair, he saw the nation through the parliamentary elections, which were held in April 1986 throughout the north and in much of the south.

The 1986 Elections

As has been true since 1965, parliamentary elections in the Sudan took place in both territorial and "graduates'" constituencies. The former are based on geographic units, while the latter give "educated" voters a second vote by permitting postsecondary school graduates to choose several candidates from special lists grouped by geographical areas. In the 233 territorial constituencies actually contested—elections were postponed in another 33, mostly for security reasons in parts of the south—the Umma party predictably gained the most seats (100), followed by the Democratic Unionist party (DUP) with 63 and the National Islamic Front (NIF) with 28. The remaining 42 seats were distributed among regional parties, "independents," and 2 for the Communist party of Sudan (SCP).[8]

By contrast, the graduates' constituencies were won overwhelmingly by candidates of the fundamentalist right and the radical left. This is easily seen in the results from the six northern regions, which were unencumbered by security issues, where the NIF–Muslim Brotherhood forces took 22 out of 28 seats, the Communists 4, and the Umma party 2. In all voting for graduates' constituencies nationwide, the NIF–Muslim Brotherhood received 42 percent, followed by the Communist party of the Sudan with 19.2 percent, and the Umma party with 16 percent. It is noteworthy that the party with the legacy of an educated, nonsectarian, urban background—the DUP—received less than 10 percent of the overall vote.

A detailed analysis of the 1986 elections would require more space than this essay can provide, but a few major conclusions can be briefly stated. First, the most educated segment of Sudan's population clearly favored the two "most radical" parties, representing the Muslim Brotherhood and, to a much lesser degree, the Communists, in great contrast to the results of the territorial constituencies. Second, in the latter category, the victorious Umma party was most successful in relative and absolute terms in Darfur region, which is not only one of its historic bases but also the most impoverished of the six northern regions. Third, the NIF was clearly the party with the tightest organization. In the graduates' constituencies all its candidates won in the six northern regions and swept the top positions in every instance. In the territorial constituencies, the NIF benefited four times from the multiple candidates phenomenon. That is, a trademark of Sudanese elections has been the proliferation of candidates from one party in a given district because of the general absence of party discipline, sometimes resulting in the loss of that district because of vote splitting. Never once did the NIF enter multiple candidates. By contrast, the

Umma party lost 9 constituencies because of this phenomenon, although it benefited in two cases. The DUP lost 5 seats but gained 7,
primarily at the expense of Umma. Finally, the Sudan National party
gained one additional seat. Were one to allocate the seats strictly according to vote per party, the final tally among the front runners
would have been: Umma party 107, DUP 61, and NIF 24.

Parliamentary Government

Soon after the elections had been completed, a smooth transition to
the new form of government occurred. Professor Muhammad
Ibrahim Khalil of the Umma party was elected as speaker of parliament. That same day, May 6, 1986, the Constituent Assembly voted
for the chairman and four other members of the State Council, which
functions as the equivalent of head of state. The chairman has been
Ahmed al-Mirghani, who has been joined by another colleague from
the DUP, two members from the Umma party, and a southerner.[9]
Later that afternoon, Sadiq al-Mahdi, leader of the Umma party, was
elected as the new prime minister with 165 votes, as against 49 and 3
votes for the candidates of the NIF and Sudan Communist party,
respectively. After intensive and extensive negotiations with almost all
parties, the prime minister on May 15 presented his twenty-member
cabinet in which he assumed the post of defense minister. The other
eighteen slots went to the Umma party (7), DUP (6), four southern
parties (1 each), and the National Alliance of Professionals, which was
awarded the newly created Ministry of Peace and National Constitutional Conference Affairs.

On paper, this portfolio represented a nice touch, indicating sensitivity to the importance of national reconciliation. Similarly, the constellation of officials in the so-called national unity government revealed a
carefully thought-out balance. The elections had given the premiership to the House of Mahdi so the chairmanship of the State Council
went to the House of Mirghani[10] and the deputy prime minister and
foreign minister went to the Hindiyyah sect.[11]

It seemed both significant and symbolic that the prime minister in
his first official interview that very evening offered the southerners
complete freedom in choosing their preferred administration and that
their choice would be ratified by the central government. Meanwhile,
the chairman of the State Council had used the occasion of his first
interview to stress the closeness of Egyptian-Sudanese relations, a
matter of constant and now considerable concern to the northern
neighbor because of the traditional difficulties between Egyptians and
the House of Mahdi.

On paper this newly democratic government looked very promising, and hopes were high that if anyone could solve the major issues facing Sudan in the late 1980s, this particular group not only had the best chance to do so but also the required broad-based popular legitimacy. Unfortunately, the record of accomplishments during the following two years fell far short of these expectations.

Governmental Stability

It took Prime Minister Sadiq al-Mahdi several weeks to complete his cabinet. He faced the additional problem of detailed negotiations over both policies and the allocation of ministerial portfolios with several combinations of potential coalition partners. In the end, a centrist alliance of Umma party, DUP, and "moderate" southerners emerged, all of them opposed to the ideologically strident NIF and the Sudanese Communist party. One major issue in the deliberations and, indeed, in the preceding elections, had been the disposition of *Sharia* laws, which had been introduced by the Numayri regime in September 1983 and were applied on a national scale. Sadiq al-Mahdi had been the first prominent politician to declare his opposition in public to these laws repeatedly—well before the elections were held. Although many members of the DUP had voiced similar reservations closer to the elections, the party had not taken an official position on the matter and began to drag its feet about abrogating these laws once it had entered the government. One may speculate that the DUP stance reflected disorganization among the several factions of the party, concern about future voter reaction, particularly in view of strident NIF charges of "un-Islamic" conduct, or an opportunity indirectly to embarrass the prime minister through lack of cooperation in the hope of future gains at Umma party expense.

The NIF predictably championed the *Sharia* laws, which southerners saw as evidence of northern "cultural imperialism." Increasingly, Sadiq al-Mahdi became less outspoken about abrogation of *Sharia* per se and called for "alternative laws" based on "true Islamic values" to replace "Numayri's September laws." Many observers, including southern politicians and foreign governments, became impatient with the spectacle of apparently conflicting statements, repeated many times in various formats and extending over what seemed like an inordinate number of months. The issue first came to a head in September 1988, when the coalition government submitted to parliament a draft bill for "new Islamic legislation."

The Rebellion

To the SPLM, however, these developments were proof that the Mahdi government was not making a serious effort to meet southern grievances. This notion was further reinforced when the central government decided to arm militias among tribesmen in areas bordering on SPLA strongholds, especially in southern Kordofan and Darfur, where there had been historic rivalries with Dinkas. Predictably, both sides rationalized their positions—Khartoum reminded all parties that the central government had an obligation to maintain "law and order" and to "protect innocent citizens endangered by the rebel outlaws." The SPLM/SPLA justified its continued fighting because the Khartoum "government demonstrated its bad faith by these actions." Thus fighting did continue sporadically; yet at the same time, out of public view, some dialogue through intermediaries traveling to East African cities continued just as sporadically. A cynical observer could refer to this situation as "an acceptable level of low-intensity violence," acceptable perhaps because of the long-standing traditions of sporadic tribal warfare between the Dinka in southwest Sudan and the adjacent Rizeigat and Messirriyah tribes. In this context, even the occurrence of unusually large "massacres" there in March, August, and September 1987 was not entirely surprising, although they were dutifully deplored by all parties.[12]

That characterization, however, could not be used to describe another event that left deep psychological scars among many. On the morning of August 16, 1986, a civilian Sudanese airliner was shot down just after takeoff from Malakal[13] airport by a SAM-7 missile fired by the SPLA; all fifty-seven passengers and a crew of three perished. During the next several days the SPLM/SPLA not only acknowledged the act but blamed the Khartoum government for ignoring the SPLA warning that it would shoot down any aircraft, military or civilian, regular or on a famine relief mission. It justified this policy by claiming that relief planes (and subsequently train and truck convoys) were used to smuggle weapons to the army or to supply food to government soldiers rather than famine victims. Interestingly, the SPLA statement insisted that this measure "should not be perceived as being directed against the Koka Dam negotiation process."[14]

A different response came from Khartoum, where the prime minister branded Garang and his movement "terrorist," and his chief spokesman in parliament declared the act the "language of war" and said, "This is the language the government will use from now on in dealing with Garang and his movement, the SPLA."[15] The government felt that John Garang had turned down all reasonable proposals for meetings and discussions of mutual problems. Even so, as an act of good faith, Khartoum decided to keep the door for dialogue open despite these earlier rejections. But the shooting down of the civilian airliner and the self-righteous defense of this act justified slamming that door shut and putting the onus for reopening it on the other side.

From the SPLM/SPLA perspective, however, the central issue has been adherence to the Koka Dam Agreement of March 1986. This document called for the "creation of a new Sudan . . . free from racism [read Arab versus African discrimination], tribalism, sectarianism and all causes of disparity." The last phrase clearly refers to a rejection of political organizations based on sectarian identity (read Umma party, DUP) and regionalism (read Nuba Mountain, Beja, Fur, and other party groupings). Other clauses about the "basic problems" being national problems rather than north-south issues, plus John Garang's repeated calls for a radical socialist Sudan point to the SPLM's quest to redefine not only the conflict (as other than North versus South) but also the solution. This solution denies at a minimum the legitimacy of the April 1986 elections and, in general, the legitimacy of the existing party structure. That such a policy would be unacceptable to the northern parties was obvious inasmuch as it would lead to their dissolution. Yet, given the demographics of the country and the re-sulting preponderance of political power of northern-based parties, southerners have no realistic chance of coming to power within the system. At the same time, because the central government is unable to defeat the rebellion by military force alone, the stalemate between northern politicians and southern rebels could go on forever.

New Coalition

A new government was formed and sworn in on May 15, 1988, ending almost nine months of coalition stalemate. During the most recent segment of that period, the government operated without a cabinet and consisted of the State Council for official functions. The daily tasks of ministries were performed under the administration of their respective undersecretaries. The new coalition of May 15, known as the "government of national salvation," included all political factions in parliament except the Communists. The cabinet was enlarged to twenty-six portfolios, partly to make room for five members of the NIF, including its leader Dr. Hassan A. al-Turabi as minister of justice and attorney general. Another five posts were given to southerners representing one party each, six went to the DUP, and ten to the Umma party. Presumably, the purpose of this alignment was to strengthen the hand of the central government vis-à-vis the rebellion and to show a united front for the (hoped-for) upcoming negotiations with the SPLM/SPLA leadership. The move clearly represents a gamble, inas-much as the placing of NIF ministers in (for them) key positions such as justice, education, and public communications should signal a hardened stance toward John Garang's positions and might cause him to refrain from negotiations.

The events of summer 1988 would seem to validate this hypothesis. A flurry of negotiations on all levels broke out—among coalition partners in the government; among southern groups such as SPLM, Anya Nya II, and the government opposition Union of Sudanese African Parties (USAP); and among well-meaning intermediaries such as Egypt, Ethiopia, and Uganda.

During late August, high-level talks between the SPLM/SPLA and the coalition government took place in Addis Ababa. Meanwhile, elements of the Anya Nya II forces joined the SPLA and others confronted it. Military battles increased and reports of their outcomes were conflicting. The various political groups seemed to be becoming further polarized.

The government of Ethiopia clearly tried to link the Eritrean issue with the rebellion in southern Sudan, a ploy vehemently opposed in public by Sudanese leaders. The government of Kenya was accused by Khartoum of aiding the SPLM/SPLA. Egyptian mediation between Addis Ababa and Khartoum seemed to lessen tension, but Sudanese mediation between Libya and Egypt and a poorly handled declaration by some government officials in support of a "unity merger" with Libya—opposed by others in government—reinforced negative stereotypes of Sudan's leadership both at home (in the south) and abroad.

Most important of all were two simultaneous developments: first, the new *Sharia* laws placed before parliament on September 19 after a drawn-out fight in the Council of Ministers met with immediate and negative reaction from southerners in government and outside. Second, the promise of top-level negotiation between the prime minister and John Garang under the auspices of Uganda's President Yoweri Museveni held out hope that an end to conflict might finally be negotiated. Several meetings were planned only to be frustrated by Garang's failure to turn up at the last moment.[16]

To make matters worse, the country's central region suffered the worst flooding in memory during mid-August 1988, further straining already inadequate communications and resource management. Human suffering in north and south had finally reached the capital area, and it exceeded anything known in Sudanese history. The only bright spot in this ominous picture was the apparent consensus by all parties that a constitutional conference should be held before the end of the year, at which time all outstanding issues would be discussed.

Foreign Affairs

The general orientation of Sudanese foreign policy since April 1985 has already been discussed in an earlier section. What remains now is to look at Sadiq al-Mahdi's particular orientation during his two years in power, as seen against the constraints of the aforementioned problems of the economy, the SPLA rebellion, and an uncertain coalition government.

Like many Sudanese leaders before him, Sadiq al-Mahdi enjoyed making his own foreign policy. Unlike some, he seemed to be well qualified to do so because of his extensive travels during the past thirty years and his frequent dialogues with foreign leaders and other public personages on the international lecture circuit. Sadiq was particularly sought after as a public speaker while out of power—or in exile—from 1967 to 1985, not only because of his position as Umma party leader but also because of his erudition and his demonstrated intellectual acumen as an Oxford University graduate.

It became clear early in his administration that Sadiq al-Mahdi wanted to reverse the policies followed by Ja'far Numayri during the last decade of the latter's rule. Toward that end, his first two official visits abroad were to Libya and the Soviet Union in early August 1986. Six weeks later he left for Saudi Arabia and then the United States (he also addressed the United Nations in New York) and paid an official visit to the United Kingdom on his return. Because much symbolism is attached to the order of official visits in the Arab world, Sadiq's message was clear—Sudan's affiliation with the Cairo-Washington axis had ended, but the two superpowers had been given equal time, as had the two potentially most important Arab economic donors (and political enemies). The Soviet Union responded with a trade agreement in November 1986, which was added to in early 1987, along with provision of some aid for economic projects.

The United States extended some economic aid but less than at previous times, in part because of the worldwide reduction in the U.S. aid budget but also because of misgivings about Sadiq's visit to Libya. Interestingly, according to the only publicly available information, aid promised by Libya and Saudi Arabia was not forthcoming until the end of 1987.[17]

The Sudanese prime minister traveled officially to Tehran in December 1986 as a self-appointed mediator in the Iran-Iraq war. His detractors noted that he visited Persian Tehran before Arab Baghdad (much later) and that he found time for an official visit to Italy (and to the Vatican) in 1986, but not for one to Egypt.

The uneasy relations between Cairo and the new government in Khartoum were also characterized by numerous pronouncements in both capitals about the state of earlier economic and military accords—now apparently in limbo—and public disagreements about Sudan's demands that Egypt extradite former President Numayri, who was to be tried in Khartoum for crimes against the state. Even though the

Council of State Chairman Mirghani paid Egypt an early official visit (resulting in a protocol of cooperation in July 1986), both parties saw this act as an extension of traditional ties between Cairo and the DUP/ Khatmiyya sect, as contrasted with the traditional tension between Egypt and the House of Mahdi. In the event, reservations and consternation gave way to a warming of relations; and a trade protocol was signed by the two neighboring states. Since that time, contacts have increased considerably and Sudanese relations with Libya cooled proportionately; and in March 1988 the first reported consignment of Egyptian military aid was shipped to Sudan.[18]

There can be no doubt that the United States urged the Sudanese government to ban Libyan military forces from Darfur province (adjacent to Chad). The Libyan claim that their units were engaged only in economic assistance in famine-stricken areas was strongly disputed by the U.S. government. The Sudanese regime was clearly uncomfortable about any Libyan presence on its soil yet remembered that the Tripoli government had been the first, and for a long time the only, regime after Numayri's fall to aid Sudan economically (by sending an oil tanker to Port Sudan) and militarily (against the SPLA when Khartoum needed logistical and air support). The triangular relationship between Khartoum, Cairo, and Tripoli has been fascinating to observe. It is based on carefully controlled tension among the three, yet it enabled Prime Minister Sadiq to use his good offices to reduce confrontations between Egypt and Libya to the extent that Cairo decided to withdraw its military units from the Libyan border.

In late 1988 Sudan had a "brotherhood charter" with Egypt, a commitment from Kuwait to provide its oil needs for the next four years, and close ties with Saudi Arabia, symbolized by massive disaster aid.[19] In addition, the prime minister traveled to Japan, Jordan, and the People's Republic of China during the last quarter of 1987, and all three visits were reported to have yielded some economic benefit.

Outlook

A brief glance at the Sudan's history since independence reveals that all the problems discussed in this essay still persist; the only differences are in style and tactics of rule.[20]

From the perspective of the International Monetary Fund/World Bank and measured by real income per capita, the national economy has been in almost constant decline since the middle years of the Abboud government (1959–64). From a more localist point of view, some positive developments have taken place. The "rush to development" from 1974 on started agricultural schemes and related manufacturing plants, especially in cotton and sugar, but the process has been uneven at best and has given rise to unrealistic expectations at worst. This has been especially true of the campaign to turn Sudan into the "foodbasket" of the region, a plan whose realization becomes less likely with each passing year. Unmet economic expectations have particularly aggravated southern leaders, who have felt—unjustifiably, so far—that their region possesses considerable wealth, which lamentably could not be developed because of Khartoum's failure to channel adequate resources to the south.

Another perennial problem has been the relationship between the center and the periphery, and this is likely to continue for some time. Thirty years ago, the issue was seen primarily as the so-called north-south conflict, even though many observers and politicians already recognized similar problems existing in the far west and the eastern region. The Addis Ababa Accords of 1972 temporarily addressed one major issue—the relationship between the north/center as a unit and the south as a unit. But many related problems such as regional versus local government, especially within the south, tax collection, and revenue sharing were ignored. Provincial governors have consistently been appointed from the capital, and yet Sudan is one of the world's largest countries with one of the most heterogenous societies. Even the proper function of the traditional leader (e.g., *nazir, sheikh, omda,* and so on) versus the civil servant in local government has not been adequately clarified. In this sense, John Garang's announced platform of restructuring the country's constitutional arrangement must be taken seriously, even though the more immediate crises call for stopping the military rebellion and for deciding on the role of Islamic versus some other law for the nation.

These issues, plus the challenge of forming a truly national government in a political culture characterized by factionalism, will continue to demand the greatest political energy for any government in Khartoum. Most observers and even practitioners repeatedly draw parallels to an earlier period of postmilitary rule. Indeed, there have been remarkable similarities between the events of October 1964 and April 1985 and between the two subsequent transitional periods after each overthrow of a military regime. Yet, there are some important differences. One is that now modern weapons are easily available to various groups throughout the country, which introduces not only a quantitative and qualitative escalation of intercommunal violence but also an international dimension through the suppliers of these weapons. This is a completely new phenomenon in Sudan's political history, and no one is sure of its portents.

Another change has been the internationalization of political ideologies. For example, the National Islamic Front is no longer made up solely of members personally educated and recruited by Turabi and a few aides; it also includes thousands of individuals who have been exposed to new publications, pamphlets, and video and audiocassettes from distant locations. On a more limited scale, a similar argument can be made for the new activist southern leadership, which is no longer confined to an in-group of mutually familiar graduates of Christian mission schools but draws on many southerners educated and politicized in many different countries.

Moreover, foreign weapons and foreign ideas are now for the first time actively spread by some agents of foreign governments, ranging from Iran to Libya, from Syria to Israel. The old days, when Sudan was self-contained like a traditional *zarriba* within which all items were locally familiar and controllable, are clearly gone.

Finally, and in contrast to the 1960s, the world as a whole no longer focuses much on Third World issues, as distinct from those with global implications. As a result, most countries like Sudan are judged by the major powers on their strategic role, which determines economic assistance more often than does demonstrated need. The Sudanese government will be hard put, despite its potentially real strategic assets, to convince major donor nations in the West and in the Arab world that it should receive the substantial external support it needs if it is to have any realistic chance to resolve all its other problems.

Notes

1. Numayri took this action although many non-Dinka southerners opposed redivision.

2. The Chevron-developed oil fields near Bentiu were technically just inside the southern region, and the proposed refinery at Kosti was relatively nearby but inside the north, as is the country's only functioning port facility at Port Sudan, which was projected as the oil terminus.

3. His accusers would disagree with the appellation *reformer* and insist on their term *heretic*. Shaikh Mahmoud's philosophy is contained in the book *The Second Message of Islam.*

4. The IMF and "Club of Paris" donor nations especially held this view.

5. This group was officially referred to as the National Alliance for National Salvation.

6. See Haim Shaked and Yehudi T. Ronen, "The Republic of Sudan—1986," in *Middle East Contemporary Survey, 1988,* ed. Itamar Rabinovich and Haim Shaked (Boulder, Colo.: Westview Press, 1988), pp. 585–86.

7. Radio SPLA, Mar. 29, 1986 (*FBIS: NE/SA,* Apr. 1, 1986).

8. Subsequently most independents were recruited to join the two leading parties.

9. They were Muhammad al-Hassan Abdallah Yasin (DUP), Idris al-Banna and Ali Hassan Taj al-Din (both Umma party), and Dr. Pacifico Lado Lolik.

10. Ahmed is brother of the DUP patron Muhammed Osman al-Mirghani.

11. Al-Sharif Zayn al-Abdin a-Hindi.

12. In March 1987 several hundred Dinka men, women and children—some say as many as a thousand—were killed at Ad-Daien in southern Darfur by a mob of Rizeigat tribesmen (Amnesty International, *Sudan: Human Rights Developments since 1985* [New York: Amnesty International 1988], p. 5). On August 11–12, 1987, and again during September 6–11, 1987, between one and two thousand Dinka civilians were reportedly killed by army and militia forces in Wau, Bahr el-Ghazal Province. This massacre followed an attempted missile attack on a government aircraft and was accompanied by the killings of Fertit militiamen by Dinkas (ibid.).

13. Capital of Upper Nile, the northernmost province of southern Sudan.

14. *FBIS*, Aug. 18, 1986.

15. Sudan News Agency (*FBIS: NE/SA*, Aug. 19, 1986, p. Q2); Sudan News Agency (*FBIS: NE/SA*, Aug. 21, 1986, p. Q5).

16. Meetings were arranged by former Nigerian President Obasanju and by Dr. Francis Deng, a former senior Sudanese diplomat, in Zurich, Addis Ababa, and Harare; each time Garang agreed to come but backed out.

17. *FBIS: NE/SA*, Dec. 23, 1987, p. 25.

18. *FBIS: NE/SA*, Mar. 21, 1988, p. 16.

19. *FBIS: NE/SA*, July 1, 1988, pp. 11–12. Saudi Arabia sent 126 planeloads of relief aid (*FBIS: NE/SA*, Aug. 25, 1988, p. 8).

20. For a more detailed analysis, see Peter Bechtold, *Politics in the Sudan* (New York: Praeger, 1976), esp. chaps. 9–10.

15

Turkey Between the Middle East and the West

George E. Gruen

Introduction

A recent *New York Times* article about Turkey was titled "The Turks Finally Ask: Are We Europeans or What?"[1] But since Mustafa Kemal Ataturk transformed the remnants of the Ottoman Empire into the modern, Western-oriented Republic of Turkey, the Turks have been asking themselves this question. In his first address to the parliament as prime minister in 1983, Turgut Ozal said that Turkey should be seen as a "natural bridge between the West and the Middle East."[2] Maintaining a balance between these two very different cultures is not an easy task, and the Turks are divided about which culture to claim as their own. Although Prime Minister Ozal committed the Turkish government to liberalizing the economy, restored Western-style electoral politics, and vowed to maintain a secular state, there is still some debate over how Turkey should relate to three basic elements of Western society: democracy, secularism, and a free market economy.

This debate occurs in the context of a complex political situation in Turkey, with regard both to domestic and international issues. Ankara is tied to NATO and is pursuing stronger ties with the European Community. Yet the Turks feel that the United States and the NATO countries have failed fully to appreciate Turkey's importance as a strategic ally.

The Iran-Contra affair had only a limited effect on Turkish-American relations. Not surprisingly, the Turks were distressed to learn that the United States had been using Turkish airspace to deliver covert arms shipments to Iran. The Turks have their own problems with terrorists, and they have maintained a firm policy of no concessions. Although the Turks have extensive diplomatic and, more important, economic dealings with both Iran and Iraq, they have refused to sell weapons to either side. Ankara was upset and embarrassed that Washington had essentially taken Turkish acquiescence for granted, despite reported Turkish government protests. Headlines in the popular press declaring "CIA duped Turkey" reflected the Turkish feelings. Washington's handling of the affair also damaged American credibility. The Reagan administration not only proved unfaithful to its friends, it also revealed incompetence and lack of sophistication in the conduct of its foreign policy. In keeping with their customary pragmatism, the Turks took no steps to convert their displeasure into retribution, but in the long run this incident may increase Turkish doubts about U.S. reliability as an ally in a crisis. (Recognizing this problem of credibility, Reagan administration officials took pains to stress that the Iranian arms-for-hostages deal was an isolated incident and an aberration from the tough American stand against terrorists.)

Yet even before the Iran-Contra scandal, Turkish foreign policy planners had taken steps to hedge their bets. To avoid becoming linked exclusively to the West, the Turkish government has cautiously cultivated relations with the countries of the Middle East and with the Soviet Union. The Turks are ever mindful of the Soviet presence on their borders and are careful to maintain correct, if not warm, relations with their powerful neighbor. Islamic revivalism among the youth in Turkey has created some pressure for policies that are more closely aligned with those of the Arab states, and the growing network of financial connections with the Middle East reinforces this trend.

Internally, the Turkish authorities have moderated the fervently anticlerical stand adopted by Ataturk. Although more than 99 percent of the country's population is Muslim, Turkey's political elite has maintained Ataturk's secular outlook and his belief in the separation of church and state. Since the 1980 military intervention, the government has moved to reestablish and strengthen democratic institutions. Still, Ankara has limited the openness of the political system, claiming that the continuing threat posed by extremists on the right and left and by militant separatist groups within Turkey requires legal restraints.

Clearly, the Turks have not yet decided precisely what they want their society to be like. Democratic institutions are in place, but they are not yet firmly rooted in all segments of Turkish society. The Turks look toward Europe and the United States for economic, political, and military support. But this is not a one-way street—Turkey is important to the Western countries because of its location, its active participation in the NATO alliance, and its moderate role in Middle Eastern politics.

The Domestic Situation
Politics: Democracy and the Military in Turkey

Mustafa Kemal, the World War I general who built the Turkish republic out of the ruins of the Ottoman Empire, left a paradoxical legacy. On one hand, Kemalism dictates that sovereignty rests with the people. On the other hand, the army, which sees itself as the guardian of the Kemalist principles, has arrogated to itself the right and the responsibility to intervene whenever it appeared that the people were making the wrong choice. This contradictory inheritance helps to explain one of the most peculiar features of the Turkish political landscape—the periodic intervention of the military, followed by the return to civilian rule. In this way the Turkish army differs from most Middle Eastern and Third World countries, where military dictatorships tend to perpetuate themselves.

The 1987 elections represent the latter part of a cycle that started with the military intervention of 1980. The late 1970s were a devastating time for Turkey—the sharp increase in oil prices put a heavy strain on the economy, inflation was terrible (in 1980, inflation for wholesale prices averaged 108 percent), strikes were frequent, and the violence caused by militants of the left and right claimed up to twenty lives a day.[3] In September 1980 the army, in a bloodless coup, ousted the civilian government and installed a military regime that ruled until 1983. Holding true to the army's mandate as the guardian of the state only during emergency periods, the military government led by General Kenan Evren held limited elections in 1983 (the three candidates who were allowed to participate were approved by the military government) and turned the government over to the victor, Turgut Ozal, even though he was not the military government's favored candidate.

In the fall of 1987, Prime Minister Ozal's government administered a referendum in which the Turks were asked whether the politicians who had been banned from the 1983 elections should be permitted to run for office again. Ozal favored continuing the ban because he shared the military's view that these politicians, who had participated in the ineffective governments during the tumultuous 1970s, should be held responsible for Turkey's fall from democracy into chaos. By a very slim majority, the voters in the obligatory referendum voted to abolish the bans. Some opposition politicians interpreted this as a vote of confidence in the ability of a civilian government to run the country. Other observers pointed to the closeness of the vote as an indication that the people were torn between a desire for democratic freedoms and a fear of a return of extremist elements. Professor Serif Mardin of Istanbul's Bosporus University argued that "the referendum, instead of uniting the population, divided them."[4]

The national election that followed on November 29 was contested by seven different parties. Ozal's right-of-center Motherland party won 36.3 percent of the vote. The left-of-center Social Democratic–

Populist party (SDPP) of Erdal Inonu, son of Ataturk's successor Ismet Inonu, came in second with 24.7 percent. Suleyman Demirel's True Path party (TPP) came in third with 19.1 percent. The TPP is the successor to the Justice party, which was outlawed in the 1980 military intervention. It had replaced the Democratic party of Adnan Menderes, which had been dissolved by the 1960 military junta. Demirel and Ozal have competed for the center and right of center of the Turkish electorate. To prevent a return to political fragmentation and weak coalition governments dependent on extremist fringe groups, the new constitution and election law imposed a 10 percent threshold of the national vote before a party could win seats in parliament. The effect was to give Ozal a disproportionately high and virtually unshakable majority of 292 out of the assembly's 450 seats. The SDPP won 99 and the TPP 59.[5]

Extremist Groups Lose Ground

Bulent Ecevit's Democratic Leftist party, successor to the Republican People's party, was a prime casualty of the new law. Although receiving more than 2 million votes, 8.5 percent of the total, Ecevit was excluded from parliament, beaten out for the left-of-center vote by Inonu. The new law worked effectively to eliminate the extremist fringe parties from the parliament. The Welfare party of Necmettin Erbakan received 7.2 percent of the vote or 1.7 million out of more than 24.6 million ballots cast. From 1972 to 1980 Erbakan had led the National Salvation party (NSP), which appealed to conservative voters by combining calls for a return to Islamic values with emphasis on modern technology (Erbakan had earned an engineering degree in Germany) and by championing the cause of provincial merchants against the power of the large conglomerates based in Istanbul. In foreign policy, Erbakan favored closer ties with the Islamic nations, blamed "international Zionism" for Turkey's economic problems, and called for Turkey to break off all relations with Israel. In a Jerusalem Liberation Day rally in Konya on September 6, 1980, NSP demonstrators had called for the restoration of the caliphate, refused to sing the Turkish national anthem, carried anti-Semitic signs, and burned the Israeli, American, and Russian flags. Some Turkish observers believed that the Konya rally was the last straw for the Kemalist army officers and prompted their military intervention a few days later.[6] The fortunes of the National Salvation party and its successor, the Welfare party, are a good barometer of the extent to which Islamic religious revival is translated into primary political party affiliation.

Prime Minister Ozal has tried not to alienate the religious voters. He is a pious Muslim who has made the pilgrimage to Mecca and, at the beginning of his political career, even flirted with the National Salvation party. Although he too has favored improved relations with the countries of the Middle East and increasing Turkish involvement in the Islamic Conference Organization, Ozal and the Motherhood party remain within the bounds of secular political institutions and shun Islamic fundamentalism of either the Khomeini or Muslim Brotherhood type. The high point of the NSP was in 1973, when it won 11.8 percent of the vote. It gained prestige from being included in coalition cabinets but fell to 8.5 percent of the vote in 1977. The Welfare party, the NSP's successor as champion of Islamic traditionalism, polled only 4.8 percent in the local elections of 1984 and 5.6 in the by-elections of 1986. Its 7.1 percent in the November 1987 parliamentary elections thus indicated a gradual increase but was still far below Erbakan's high point of 1973.

Erbakan has attempted to capitalize on the widespread Turkish popular outrage over reported Israeli mistreatment of the Palestinians in efforts to quell the uprising in the West Bank and Gaza, which broke out in December 1987. He and his party have organized popular rallies ostensibly directed against Israel but with Islamic and anti-Semitic themes prevalent and with most of the participants dressed in conservative Islamic attire, including the veil or *chador* for the women, not only in the Istanbul area but in cities in eastern Anatolia such as Trabzon, Bingol, Siirt, and Van, where the population is generally conservative Islamic with some Arab, Persian, and Kurdish elements. Erbakan's actions have aroused critical comment from the secular press. The police have arrested some demonstrators for engaging in illegal demonstrations and for carrying inflammatory slogans on their placards.

The Turkish government has pledged that any violations of law during the demonstrations "will be strictly dealt with, and perpetrators will be brought to justice." This statement was in a response by Dr. Sukru Elekdag, Turkey's ambassador in Washington, to an expression of concern by Theodore Ellenoff, president of the American Jewish Committee, about anti-Semitic signs with words such as "the blood of the Palestinians will be on the head of the Jews" and "Turkey will be the grave of the Jews" carried during an Islamic fundamentalist demonstration in Istanbul on March 20, 1988. Ambassador Elekdag added that "divergence of views, however extremist, are inevitable in a pluralistic democratic society." The demonstrations in question were arranged, he said, "by a small fringe group outside the mainstream of Turkish political and social life." Elekdag reaffirmed his government's commitment to Turkey's long-standing tradition of tolerance and peaceful coexistence and its "firm stand against any religious or ethnic hatred in any segment of its populace."[7]

Erbakan's efforts to stir up anti-Israeli and pro-Palestinian feeling have not been notably successful in attracting new followers to his party. According to a public opinion poll published on March 25, 1988, if elections were held at that time, the Welfare party would slip from the 7.2 percent it received in November 1987 to 6.2 percent. It may well be that Erbakan used the Palestinian uprising in a desperate effort to raise his party's flagging fortunes.[8]

The other extremist right-wing party, the ultranationalist Nationalist Labor party (NLP) has fared even worse. The NLP is the successor to the protofascist Nationalist Action party led by Alparslan Turkes, a former army colonel, who has advocated Pan-Turkism and the political unification of Turkey with the Turkic-speaking populations of the Soviet Union and China. The NLP received only 2.9 percent of the vote in the November 1987 elections. Far-left splinter groups received less than 1 percent. Thus though Turkey continues to have its radical elements, the great majority of the electorate divide their votes among the parties in the center of the political spectrum.[9]

In a bid to test how far the Turkish government would go in extending political freedoms, two exiled Turkish communist politicians, Haydar Kutlu and Nihat Sargin, returned to Turkey shortly before the election to establish a Turkish United Communist party. Kutlu and Sargin were accompanied by a number of European parliamentarians. The Turkish reaction was strong, both to the presence of the Europeans and to the proposal to establish a communist party. Turkish authorities pointed out that since the early days of the republic, Turkish law has banned extremist parties, both religious and political, from participating in Turkish politics. In an interview shortly before the elections, Necmettin Karaduman, the speaker of the parliament, explained this position: "Under article 14 of the Constitution, basic freedoms and rights cannot be observed to establish a state based on the concept of the dominance of a social class over the other . . . endangering the secular republic and to create discrimination in religion, language, race or sect . . . we think that our democratic order will be harmed if extreme left or right parties function."[10]

Both Prime Minister Ozal and President Evren said that at some time in the future fundamentalist and communist parties might be allowed to compete in Turkish elections but that presently the Turkish people were afraid that participation by such radicals could return Turkey to the chaos of the 1970s.

The continuing danger of extremism was again brought home to the Turkish people in June 1988, when Prime Minister Ozal was wounded and narrowly escaped death in an assassination attempt while he was addressing a convention of his motherland party. The gunman, Kartal Demirag, had recently escaped from prison, where he was serving a sentence for attempted murder. He had been involved with the Grey Wolves, an extreme right-wing terrorist group affiliated with Colonel Turkes's Nationalist Action party, which the army outlawed in 1980. Demirag was known as an admirer of Mehmet Ali Agca, the Turk who shot and wounded Pope John Paul II in 1981. It was reported that both men had copied verses from the Koran before perpetrating their acts of violence. There was speculation that Demirag was part of a larger conspiracy, and seven fringe groups ranging from the Communist Kurdish Labor party to the Revolutionary Officers Organization and various rightist and Muslim factions all claimed responsibility. Whatever the truth, the assassination attempt underscored the need for vigilance against extremist groups still lurking beneath the surface of Turkey's democratic political system.[11]

Another reason for the rejection of radical parties is the fear that they encourage foreign involvement in Turkish politics. Although the Iranian government reportedly supported Ozal's Motherland party in the elections, Iranian officials—including Khomeini—have publicly voiced their support for an Islamic revival in Turkey. Among the literature being distributed by the Iranians in Turkey are pamphlets in Turkish and English entitled *Eskiya Ataturk* or *Ataturk the Scoundrel*. These pamphlets quote from a speech by Ayatollah Khomeini on August 24, 1986, which attacked the alleged view of the Sunni *ulema* that "every scoundrel in power should be obeyed." Charging that Ataturk commanded the people not to pray, Khomeini asks, "Whom shall we listen to—to God or to Ataturk the Scoundrel?" The Turks are also concerned that a Turkish Communist party might become a fifth column for the Soviet Union.[12]

More immediately, Turkish authorities were angry that Kutlu and Sargin had drawn the Europeans into what, in their view, should have been an internal matter. The timing of the whole affair was particularly bad because Turkey had just applied, on April 14, to become a full member of the European Community. After the two were jailed in preparation for trial, European involvement escalated. The *Wall Street Journal* reported that they were being represented by "a team of 420 lawyers from Britain, West Germany, France and elsewhere," as well as human rights observers. One of the latter, Lord Tony Gifford of the British House of Lords Human Rights Group, said the trial would affect Turkey's bid to enter the EEC.[13] The Turks feel that many Europeans still identify them with the "Terrible Turk"—the savage warrior from the East—and that Kutlu and Sargin reinforced this perception by drawing attention to the ban on the Communist party instead of to the progress Turkey has made. In addition, Ankara does not think that whether Turkey permits a Communist party to exist should have any influence on Turkey's admission to the European Community.

Human Rights Issues

The Kutlu-Sargin affair also brought up the question of human rights abuses in Turkey, because the two political leaders claimed that they had been tortured. The pending application to the EEC makes the Turks particularly sensitive to accusations of human rights violations; in the past European groups have been very critical of Turkey's human rights practices. The Helsinki Watch 1987 report on human rights in Turkey concluded that there had been some improvements in the human rights situation in Turkey since its visits in the early 1980s, especially with regard to freedom of the press and freedom of association, but instances of torture and inhumane conditions in Turkish jails continue to be reported. The report noted that although the government has taken steps to improve human rights, Turkish law provides inadequate legal guarantees for individuals. After applying to the EEC, however, the Turkish government agreed to permit its citizens to petition the European Commission of Human Rights with individual complaints. In June 1988 Amnesty International "congratulated" the Turkish government for signing and ratifying the European Convention Against Torture but added that "much remains to be done." As its ties to the West deepen, it is likely that there will be more pressure on Turkey to increase the rights guaranteed to its citizens.[14]

The most sensitive human rights situation in Turkey involves the Kurdish minority in southeastern Turkey. The problem is also a political one: since the beginning of the republic, the Turkish government has completely denied the distinctive cultural and ethnic heritage of the Kurds for fear of encouraging separatist tendencies among this large minority (the Kurds make up an estimated 8 to 10 percent of the Turkish population, although some believe the figure may be closer to 20 percent).[15] Kurds are not allowed to give their children Kurdish names, are forbidden to publish in Kurdish, and are prosecuted for identifying themselves as Kurdish in official and unofficial settings.[16] In fact, no amount of repression has succeeded in snuffing out Kurdish rebelliousness. Kurdish guerrillas have staged a series of raids and bombings, mainly in the southeastern region of Turkey. The Marxist Turkish Workers party (PKK), which seeks to carve an independent or at least an autonomous Kurdish state out of eastern Anatolia, has acknowledged receiving material and logistical help from Syria and the Soviet Union. An estimated eleven hundred persons have been killed in PKK clashes with Turkish forces over the past four years.[17] Until recently the Turkish government refused even to acknowledge that there was a "Kurdish problem." Caught between the government and the guerrillas, the Kurds are becoming increasingly radicalized. The Turkish authorities hope that through a program of rapid agricultural and industrial development in eastern Anatolia, spurred by the new Ataturk dam on the Euphrates, they will be able to assimilate the Kurds into Turkish society and control their separatist tendencies.

A dramatic new development further complicating Turkey's relationship to the Kurds occurred in the summer of 1988. Taking advantage of a cease-fire with Iran in August, the Iraqi army launched a full-scale campaign against Iranian-backed Kurdish rebels in northern Iraq. In Baghdad's brutal attempt to wipe out the sixty-year-old rebellion once and for all, the regime of Saddam Hussein reportedly made widespread use of chemical weapons, including poison gas, against Kurdish villages. By early September some sixty thousand Iraqi Kurds had fled across the border, seeking refuge in Turkey. Turkish and Iraqi troops at the border almost came to blows when Ankara refused an Iraqi request for the same right of "hot pursuit" that Turkish forces had repeatedly invoked since 1984 to strike at PKK bases in northern Iraq.[18]

Although the Turkish authorities were initially reluctant to admit the refugees, who presumably included militant Kurdish nationalists who could stir up further trouble within Turkey's own Kurdish community, they knew that turning the refugees away would lead to many thousands of additional deaths, as well as to further unfavorable publicity in the West. Prime Minister Ozal received the support of the opposition parties in parliament when he explained that providing refuge for the Kurds was consistent with humanitarian traditions deeply rooted in Turkey's Islamic and Ottoman heritage. Ozal pointedly recalled that "500 years ago, at a time when religious differences were so sharp that people were burned for their religion, our ancestors accepted the Jews who escaped from the Spanish Inquisition."[19] Turkish authorities were hopeful that their humanitarian treatment of the Kurds would help improve their image in the West. At the same time, however, they stressed the economic hardships Turkey faced. Ozal estimated the cost of providing shelter for the refugees at a minimum of $300 million and appealed to the West to "help us a little by accepting some of these people" and by providing financial assistance. At a press conference in Diyarbekir after touring Kurdish camps in the area, Ozal said that the Kurds did not wish to return to Iraq and it was unthinkable to force them to return against their wishes. He appealed to "the democratic countries of the West who always claim they respect human rights: 'Can you take half of these people within your respective quotas?' If they fail to receive these refugees, we will see who respects human rights and who does not." In an interview with the *Wall Street Journal,* Ozal also called upon the superpowers to assume the responsibility for stopping the use of chemical weapons, which had added a new dimension of horror to regional conflicts.[20]

Retired Professor Fahir Armaoglu charged that Ozal's move to accept the Kurds, "even at the risk of disrupting Turkey's relations with Iraq," was "prompted by hopes of benefiting from the voting potential in southeastern Anatolia," where many of Turkey's Kurds lived, "not by 'humanitarian' motives."[21] To prevent the Kurdish asylum program from further souring relations with Iraq, the Turkish authorities insisted that their medical teams had not found conclusive evidence of poison gas injuries among the refugees and rebuffed a U.N. inquiry on the matter. Iraq is Turkey's major supplier of oil, and Baghdad still owed Turkey more than $2.75 billion for goods and services provided during the Iran-Iraq war.[22]

The Turkish Economy: Attempts to Become Integrated into the International Market

The economic crisis of the late 1970s, brought on by increasing oil prices coupled with a high demand for imports and a deepening shortage of foreign exchange, was one of the catalysts for the military intervention of 1980. Turkey was saved from defaulting on its loans by a combination of aid from the European Community and the United States and by the intervention of the IMF. Turkey's debt burden was lowered, but, as a result of these measures, the Turkish government had to undertake an austerity program, which resulted in rising interest rates and decreasing wages, social benefits, and government subsidies. In addition, the IMF pressured Ankara to open the Turkish economy to the forces of the international market.[23]

As head of the State Planning Office, Turgut Ozal designed the economic stabilization program that helped put Turkey on the road to economic recovery in January 1980. The 1980 plan changed the orientation of the Turkish economy away from a policy based on import substitution and pervasive state control toward one based on exports and the free market. The government implemented its new policy by establishing a flexible exchange rate, liberalizing interest rates and prices, reducing subsidies to state enterprises, creating export incentives, and enforcing a tight money policy. In his role as prime minister, Ozal has continued to press for economic liberalization. He has taken the further step of offering to the public shares in state economic enterprises, thus opening these protected industries to market forces. By and large, Ozal's economic policies have had good results. Between 1980 and 1986 GNP growth averaged 4.6 percent, and the rate for 1986 alone was 8 percent. In 1987 it was still a healthy 6.8 percent, the highest among the Organization for Economic Cooperation and Development (OECD) countries. From 1979 to 1987, the dollar value of Turkey's exports quadrupled, reaching $10 billion. But this growth was achieved at a heavy price. Foreign debt soared from $18 billion in 1983 to over $38 billion in 1988. Annual interest on this debt is currently over $7 billion.

After slowing in the early 1980s, consumer price inflation rose to 55 percent during 1987 and approached 80 percent per annum in September 1988. The worsening economic situation has also led to some decline in Ozal's popularity. Chronic unemployment has also been a problem, with rates ranging from 15 to 20 percent in recent years. Finally, the decline in purchasing power in the Middle East, both because of falling oil prices and because of the Iran-Iraq war, has caused Turkey's markets in the Middle East to shrink.[24]

Another important element in Turkey's decreasing economic relations with the Middle East has been the loss of contracts with the oil-producing countries. Between 1980 and 1984, contracts with the Muslim countries almost quadrupled to reach a high of more than $14 billion. The major trading partners have been Libya, Saudi Arabia, Iraq, Jordan, and Kuwait. Adding Turkish workers' remittances from Middle Eastern countries, the total inflow amounted to $1.3 billion a year. Both sources of funds have decreased since the mid-1980s, but in 1987, the Libyans began to pay their debts to Turkey and, as a result, contacts with Libya are again expanding. Libya also imported new Turkish workers in late 1987; the total number of Turks currently working there is estimated at thirty-five thousand.[25]

In 1986 exports decreased 6.3 percent in dollar value and the trade deficit increased to $3.5 billion. In 1987 that figure was almost $4 billion. According to one analysis, Turkey's current economic policy is driven by its goal of bringing the Turkish economy into parity with those of the European countries. According to Prime Minister Ozal, 65 to 70 percent of Turkey's exports are now going to OECD countries. The composition of exports has also changed from being primarily agricultural. Industrial products constituted 80 percent of Turkey's exports in 1987. Turkey must improve its economy to ensure that it will be accepted into the EEC. Turkey's low per capita income, currently about $1,200 a year, and high birth rate and unemployment raise fears in Europe that allowing Turkey to become a full member of the EEC—it has been an associated member since 1963—would strain the Community's social funds and aggravate its unemployment problems as a result of a new influx of Turkish workers. Ozal counters that by developing its own industrial base at home, Turkey will become an asset rather than a liability to its European partners. Still, as a developing country, Turkey will continue to need infusions of foreign capital to build the kind of infrastructure the European countries all possess.[26]

The Balancing Act: Turkey's Foreign Relations

Turkey, NATO, and the Superpowers: A Brief Background

Simply looking at a map gives one an idea of why Turkey is important to the NATO alliance. Turkey is the only NATO member that shares a long border with the Soviet Union (Norway has a short border with the USSR); Turkey guards one-third of NATO's thirty-six-hundred-mile border with the Warsaw Pact nations. Turkey also controls the Bosporus and the Dardanelles, the only waterway between the Black Sea and the Mediterranean. From this strategic location, facilities in Turkey provide 25 percent of NATO's intelligence on Soviet military preparations and nuclear activities. A total of twenty-six bases and other facilities provide NATO with a range of intelligence and military functions, including an air base at Incirlik in southern Turkey that acts as a staging area for U.S. fighter bombers, a seismic station near Ankara that measures Soviet nuclear tests, a radar warning and space monitoring station at Pirinclik, and warehouses for fuel and military supplies at Yumurtalik and Iskenderun.[27]

Turkey officially joined NATO in 1952, but the Turks had openly committed themselves to Europe and the West by the end of World War II. In 1945, Turkey rejected Soviet demands for territorial concessions and joint defense of the Turkish straits. Two years later, Turkey became one of the cornerstones of the Truman Doctrine under which the United States pledged financial and political assistance to countries "resisting attempted subjugation by armed minorities or by outside pressure."[28] Turkey showed its good faith by sending troops to assist the United States in Korea in 1952.

The Truman Doctrine marked the beginning of a period in which Turkish–United States relations were very strong because the two countries shared a similar view of the Soviet Union. Turkey was to be the barrier to any Soviet attempt to expand further into Asia or to attack Europe from the south. To enhance its ability to protect Europe and the Middle East from the "Soviet threat," Turkey became a member of the short-lived Middle East Command and the Baghdad Pact.

President John F. Kennedy's unilateral decision to remove the obsolete Jupiter missiles from Turkey during the Cuban missile crisis of 1962 upset the Turkish government but did not significantly affect relations. The Cyprus question, which disrupted relations within the NATO alliance, caused more damage. When communal friction on the island reached a dangerously high level in the middle of 1964, Ankara notified Washington that it intended to intervene under its rights according to the 1960 Treaty of Guarantee. President Lyndon Johnson sent a letter to Prime Minister Ismet Inonu warning the Turks not to use American-made equipment in any action on Cyprus and telling Inonu that if the Turks provoked "Soviet intervention," Washington would have to consider whether it was obliged to protect Turkey.[29] The letter was leaked to the press; the Turks were stunned at the sudden revision of long-standing U.S. commitments.

In July 1974, in response to a Greek-led coup on Cyprus, whose leader proclaimed his intention to unite the island with Greece, Turkish forces invaded the island and a month later occupied more than a third of Cyprus. In October 1974 the U.S. Congress suspended all military assistance and sales to Turkey. In June 1975 the new caretaker government, under Suleyman Demirel, responded by suspending most U.S. base privileges in Turkey.

In addition to the fighting over Cyprus, Greece and Turkey have also disagreed about territorial control of the Aegean. In 1982, for example, Greece violated provisions of the 1923 Treaty of Lausanne and remilitarized an island at the western end of the Turkish Straits. Although Greece withdrew from active participation in the NATO military command from 1974 to 1980, at least partly in protest over the Cyprus issue, Turkey continued to play a role. Turkey began to hedge its bets by improving its diplomatic relations with the Soviet Union and the countries of the Middle East. By late 1975 the United States was backing away from the embargo (in October of that year, Congress exempted from the embargo deliveries contracted for before the effective date of the embargo). In February 1979, arms shipments were resumed. The Soviet invasion of Afghanistan reinforced Turkey's commitment to NATO, and in 1980, the United States and Turkey negotiated a new Defense and Economic Cooperation Agreement.

Relations with the Soviet Union: Keeping the Russians at Arms' Length

The Turks maintain a distant but proper relationship with the USSR. Having fought a number of wars against their powerful neighbor, the Turks are careful not to antagonize the Russians, even though they act as NATO's southeast outpost on the Soviet Union. For their part, the Soviets reportedly have secretly supplied Kurdish and Armenian separatist movements and have built up concentrations of Soviet troops in the Caucasus, along the Turkish border. Yet the Soviets seem as eager as the Turks to maintain peaceable relations, and under Gorbachev the two countries appear to be undergoing a rapprochement.[30] In the fall of 1987, two Turkish warships visited the Soviet Union for five days, and the two countries have been holding talks about building trade and financial cooperation.[31] In addition, after the INF treaty negotiations, the Soviets sent a special envoy to Turkey to discuss the treaty with the Turkish government.[32] Soviet officials also went out of their way to explain that a remark Mikhail Gorbachev made concerning the balance of conventional forces in the southern wing of NATO was not meant to threaten Turkey by implying that Turkey's conventional forces were stronger than those of the Warsaw Pact in the region.[33]

The Turks, for their part, have limited the availability of both NATO and U.S. facilities in Turkey so as to keep a low profile vis-à-vis the USSR. In response to Soviet allegations in July 1987 that Turkey was allowing the United States to build up its military presence in Turkey, the Foreign Ministry hastened to point out that Turkey was only participating in defensive maneuvers as any member of NATO would.[34] And when the United States requested that it be allowed to base "tanker aircraft" (which are used to refuel in-flight airplanes) in Turkey, Ankara refused. The Turkish newspaper *Hurriyet* suggested two possible reasons for the refusal: that Turkey was using the request as an opportunity to express its displeasure with the United States and that Turkey was afraid that the Soviet Union would view this as an offensive move. The tanker planes could be used to refuel the F-16s stationed at the Incirlik air base so that they could then fly deep into Soviet territory. The Turkish commentator specifically remarked that: "it is common knowledge that the basic principle of Turkey's nuclear policy is to have only defensive nuclear systems in the country. This principle is related to Turkey's wish to have good relations with its neighbors and to the effort it has been making to refrain from scaring the Soviet Union.[35]

Turkey and the United States: Some Disputes Between Allies

The Turkish denial of the U.S. request and the thaw in relations that some analysts see taking place between Ankara and Moscow are indications that there are tensions in relations between Turkey and the United States. The Turks have become more cautious about being perceived to be at the beck and call of the United States, and at the same time they have been stung by what they see as Washington's stinginess with aid. Nonetheless, the Turkish political and military leaders perceive that their overall interests are best served by remaining a close ally of the United States.

In U.S. foreign military sales credits, loans, and Military Assistance Program grants, Turkey is third in line after Israel and Egypt. Overall U.S. security assistance for Turkey peaked in 1984 at $715 million and dropped to $594 million in fiscal year 1987 and $526 million in 1988, although a higher percentage has been in grants lately. In addition, Turkey's foreign military sales credits have increasingly been provided at a concessional 5 percent rate, instead of the higher treasury rate.[36] Nevertheless, Turkish officials have expressed their frustration at the failure of their NATO allies to appreciate the heavy burden upon Turkey of maintaining the second largest standing army in NATO. During a visit to Washington in July 1988, President Evren commented on reports that Congress might cut aid further to help trim the U.S. deficit by issuing a warning: "Either there will be adequate security assistance to Turkey or we may have to consider the option of reducing the number of our armed forces."[37]

Turkey also received U.S. military aid in the form of the International Military Education and Training Program, which has provided $3 million annually since 1984 for the training of defense personnel. Under the Defense and Economic Cooperative Agreement (DECA) signed in 1980, seven Defense Industrial Cooperation projects have been established to manufacture and upgrade Turkey's military equipment. According to the agreement, the United States has provided low-cost leases of important equipment and technical information.[38] In the fall of 1987 the first F-16 comanufactured by a Turkish and an American company under the DECA made its first official flight, accompanied by speeches by both President Evren and Prime Minister Ozal.[39]

The coproduction of F-16s is an important achievement for the Turks. There is wide agreement, at least among the NATO countries, if not the Soviet Union, that the Turkish armed forces use equipment that is hopelessly out-of-date.[40] The Turks feel that the United States and other NATO members have not done enough to help them update their equipment, and in the wake of the INF treaty their anxiety about the weakness of their conventional forces has grown. The United States passed legislation in 1986 that permitted the transfer of unneeded military material to three NATO southern flank nations—Turkey, Portugal, and Greece. In October 1987, however, a Turkish correspondent in Washington wrote that the U.S. commitment to deliver arms to Turkey under this legislation would not be implemented as a result of unfavorable developments in Congress.[41]

Congressional opposition to aid to Turkey has often impeded administration efforts to raise aid levels. The comments of the correspondent mentioned above are illuminating. He (incorrectly) attributed the U.S. reversal to the influence of the "Jewish lobby," which he claimed was able to increase the share of arms going to Israel and Egypt, allegedly at the expense of Turkey. He also blamed aid restrictions on the continuing application of a ratio of ten to seven between Turkey and Greece on American military aid, which was inserted by Congress at the insistence of the Greek lobby. Congress has repeatedly linked U.S. aid to Turkey with progress on negotiations concerning Cyprus and periodically considers a resolution for the establishment of a day of memorial for the "Armenian Genocide." The Turkish government recognizes that it faces strong opposition from some members of Congress and has responded both by trying to woo Congress and by putting pressure on the administration to persuade Congress to be more sensitive to Turkish concerns.[42] During the visit of Michael Armacost, U.S. undersecretary of state for political affairs in 1987, a Turkish Foreign Ministry official blamed Congress for the recent deterioration in U.S.-Turkish relations and called on the Reagan administration to see that these negative developments did not persist. Both Turks and Americans attributed the congressional defeat of a bill to commemorate the "Armenian massacre" during World War I to strenuous administration efforts.[43]

In general, the Turks have responded indignantly to congressional meddling or administration insensitivity—as when Vice-President Bush remarked that the world should recognize Armenian claims of genocide—with actions that are the diplomatic equivalent of shots across the bow.[44] In October 1987, Foreign Minister Vahit Halefoglu refused a U.S. request to close Turkish airspace to Libyan and Iranian airplanes suspected of carrying chemical weapons from Libya in exchange for acoustic mines from Iran. Off the record, Foreign Ministry sources commented that in light of reports that the United States may have used Turkey's airspace to ship weapons to Iran in 1985, the U.S. request presented a "conflicting" situation.[45] Considering how embarrassing Turkish involvement in the Iran-Contra scandal could be for Turkey, Ankara's reaction was fairly restrained.

Probably the most serious step Turkey has taken to show its displeasure with the United States involves the implementation of the DECA, the agreement that controls U.S. use of NATO bases on Turkish soil. When the 1980 agreement expired in 1985, the Turks bargained for stronger aid guarantees and agreed to sign only when they had received a letter from Secretary of State Shultz stating that the "Administration would lobby Congress with 'vigor and determination' to help Turkey meet its NATO responsibilities."[46]

In April 1987, after Congress had lowered the administration's aid request by 36 percent, Prime Minister Ozal announced that Turkey was suspending the ratification of the Side Letter to the DECA. Shortly thereafter, President Evren postponed his scheduled visit to the United States. As Foreign Minister Halefoglu implicitly acknowledged in an interview in August, the suspension of the agreement was intended as a signal (as was the decision to postpone Evren's visit) but had little immediate effect on practical relations. In the fall, Ankara began to limit U.S. air force access to Incirlik, to reduce the number of aircraft permitted to participate in NATO exercises in Turkey, and to restrict U.S. aircraft flights in Turkish airspace.[47] These measures did not reflect a switch in political orientation; Turkey is clearly committed to cooperate with NATO. They were reminders that the relationship between Turkey and the United States is not only that of client to patron—Ankara was telling Washington that NATO needs Turkey too.

A high-level Senate delegation chaired by then Majority Leader Robert C. Byrd (D.-W.Va.) held two days of meetings with Turkish officials and parliamentarians in Ankara in mid-February 1988, focusing on bilateral relations and the Intermediate Nuclear Forces (INF) treaty. On February 28 the Turkish Council of Ministers formally ratified the Side Letter. Senator Byrd congratulated the Turkish government, noting that it followed other "statesmanlike actions" by Ozal, notably the meeting in Davos, Switzerland, with Greek Prime Minister Andreas Papandreou, and "signals a new era of forward-looking diplomacy in the region." Byrd emphasized Turkey's importance as an ally, its "vital strategic position for the NATO alliance," bordering not only the Soviet Union and Bulgaria but also Iran and Iraq. He characterized Turkey as a "staunch and loyal supporter" of NATO, "making a maximum effort within its limited financial resources" to modernize its forces and "play a full role in our common defense." Pointedly, Senator Byrd declared that "the Congress should recognize these positive developments and act in ways that will encourage rather than retard diplomatic progress." He pledged to work in the coming months to put together an aid package that "responds positively to these recent actions of Turkey."[48]

The INF Treaty: Turkish Vulnerability

The INF negotiations brought Turkish concerns about NATO and the Soviet Union to the fore. On balance, the Turks were cautiously favorable toward the negotiations, seeing elimination of intermediate range missiles as a first step in the disarmament process. But as soon as the negotiations got under way, Ankara began to worry out loud about how vulnerable Turkey would become as a result of the treaty because of Warsaw Pact superiority in conventional arms.

In a December interview, Prime Minister Ozal expressed Turkey's view of the INF treaty and the balance of forces in NATO's southern flank. "Naturally, this agreement comprises only a very small portion of all nuclear weapons. . . . I hope that this will lead to wider-ranging agreements. This, of course, is not the end; in addition to nuclear weapons, there is also chemical, biological, as well as conventional warfare. The Eastern bloc in general, has significant superiority over the West in conventional armaments. From this viewpoint, Turkey is located in a very critical region. I think that Turkey's role in the defense of Europe will gain greater importance in the coming period. The importance of conventional weapons will increase with the reduction of nuclear weapons.[49] Turkey's sensitivity to its increased vulnerability was evident in the strong Turkish reaction to Gorbachev's remark during the Washington summit. The Turks feel very strongly that the conventional arms talks in Vienna should include Soviet troops in the Caucasus but not Turkish forces. Gorbachev's comments about the superiority of NATO's southern wing forces over Warsaw Pact forces in the region were seen as an indication of Moscow's intent to put cutbacks in Turkish forces on the agenda.[50]

The Turkish press ran several articles commenting on Gorbachev's remark and the diplomatic activity of the Turks and the Soviets trying to explain it. Turkish anxiety about the Soviet Union was heightened by Ankara's nervousness about the reliability of its NATO allies. In late October, General Bernard Rogers, the former NATO commander in chief, reportedly said that if Turkey were attacked from the north he did not know whether other NATO countries would rush to its defense.[51] This is exactly what the Turks fear—that NATO takes Turkey for granted and does not consider her a full-fledged member of the alliance.

In the fall of 1987, the Turkish government rejected the idea of accepting additional nuclear missiles as part of a NATO plan to modernize its nuclear forces.[52] The Turks resisted for two reasons: they feel that they have been carrying more than their share of the burden for the defense of the southern flank, and they do not wish to antagonize the USSR by adding new nuclear weapons in an area so close to the Soviet border. In an interview in late December 1987, NATO Secretary General Lord Carrington attempted to allay Turkish suspicions. He reassured Ankara that Turkey would not have to accept new nuclear weapons as a result of the INF agreement, that the allies would stand by Turkey if she were attacked, and that NATO should take steps to help Turkey modernize its army.[53]

Improving Relations with Greece

One development that may ease tensions within the alliance is the rapprochement between Prime Minister Ozal and Greek Prime Minister Papandreou. Over the past several years repeated friction between Greece and Turkey over issues such as the exploitation of resources in the Aegean, air rights in the region, the remilitarization of the island of Limnos, and the continuing dispute over Cyprus has complicated relations with NATO.

After a near confrontation in March 1987 over drilling rights in the Aegean, apparently staged by Greece for domestic political reasons, Greece and Turkey began talks that culminated in the meeting of the two prime ministers late in January 1988. The prime ministers did not set out to resolve all the outstanding issues. Instead, they agreed to try to settle current and future disputes peacefully, and they discussed mechanisms for doing so.[54] In addition, the Greek Cypriots recently elected a president who has promised to work for reunification talks with the Turkish inhabitants of Cyprus. Since being elected, President George Vassiliou has backed away from his earlier conciliatory stance but has maintained that he is still committed to ending the hostility between Greek and Turkish Cypriots (the Turkish Cypriots established the Independent Turkish Republic of Northern Cyprus in 1983. Thus far only Turkey has recognized the new state).[55] Political expediency explains some of the interest in rapprochement; Prime Minister Papandreou is facing an election soon and would benefit from a foreign relations success, and Prime Minister Ozal is eager to remove any excuse for U.S. congressional opposition to aid to Turkey.[56] Nonetheless, the thaw seems to hold promise for long-term improvement in relations between these two old enemies and consequently for relations in the alliance as a whole.

Turkey and the Iran-Iraq War: The Value of Neutrality

In the context of superpower rivalries, Ankara has made its preference for the West known, although it maintains correct relations with the Soviets. In the regional context of the Middle East, the Turks have been extraordinarily scrupulous about preserving their neutrality in most political battles. The most impressive example of Turkish neutrality is Ankara's behavior with regard to Iran and Iraq.

Ankara's policy of neutrality has reaped profits for Turkey since the Iran-Iraq war broke out. Both Iran and Iraq have become significant trading partners for Turkey, and both are major oil suppliers. Although the OECD countries as a group remain Turkey's chief trading partners, exports to Iran and Iraq accounted for nearly 14 percent of the total in 1987. Turkey has also benefited from the transit fees the country has gained because of the disruption of shipping in the Persian Gulf resulting from the war. In addition to increased trucking and harbor traffic, Turkey has also profited from the opening of a second Turkish-Iraqi pipeline; the two together are expected to bring in revenues of about $500 million a year, and the two countries have been discussing the possibility of building a third.[57] Turkey and Iran have also been discussing building an oil and gas pipeline through Turkey to the Mediterranean.

Turkey's relationship with Iran has been instrumental in ensuring that the Turkish-Iraqi pipeline has not become a target of Iranian bombs or terrorist actions.[58] Following reports by the Turkish National Intelligence Organization that Iran was planning to send urban guerrillas into Turkey to attack American bases in retaliation for the U.S. attacks on Iranian oil platforms in October 1987, an Iranian Foreign Ministry official assured a Turkish journalist that this "is out of the question." An Iranian Majlis member added that Iran appreciated the importance of its relations with Turkey, stressing that "Iran has not harmed Turkey in the past, and it will not do so in the future." Ankara's response to incidents such as the Iraqi bombing of a Turkish border village or broadcasts from Iran attacking Turkey's secularism has been to complain through diplomatic channels but not to disrupt relations. A measure of how well Turkey has succeeded in gaining the confidence of both Baghdad and Tehran is that the two countries asked Turkey to represent their interests vis-à-vis each other after their embassies closed in the fall of 1987.[59]

Turkey has upheld its position of neutrality in international diplomatic circles as well. The Turks are concerned about the spread of the Gulf war, but they have refused to join the international community in blaming Iran for dragging out the war. When the International Democratic Union, an organization Turkey has just joined, issued a communique calling "on Iran to comply with a cease-fire agreement" and calling for an arms embargo against Iran if it refused, the Turkish delegation declared that "Turkey [would] comply with this provision to the extent its policy on the Iran-Iraq war allows it do so."[60]

The Turks have preferred the approach taken by the United Nations, as expressed by Security Council Resolution 598, which calls on both countries to cease hostilities and expresses the intention of the Security Council to begin an investigation of which country is responsible for starting the war. Ankara has repeatedly offered to facilitate efforts at dialogue between the warring parties, and reportedly acted as a go-between for the United States and Iran in late August 1987 in an unsuccessful attempt to defuse the growing tension in the Gulf. But Turkish authorities have stressed that Ankara would undertake a formal mediating role only if *both* sides explicitly requested it to do so. After Iran and Iraq accepted a U.N.-sponsored cease-fire in July 1988, Turkey contributed a fifteen-man delegation to the U.N. Iran-Iraq Military Observer Group.[61]

Both regional and global considerations have played a part in Ankara's decision to espouse neutrality in this conflict. Iran and Iraq have large Kurdish populations, including militant separatists who have increasingly bedeviled Turkey in recent years. Turkey has its own Islamic revivalists, and they receive encouragement from Iran via anti-Turkish broadcasts and pamphlets.[62] Although Turkey's relations with Iran and Iraq have not put an end to these problems, they have provided Ankara with official channels through which it can complain with some hope of redress. Iraq has gone so far as to permit Turkey to pursue Iraq-based Kurdish guerrillas over the border.[63] There is also a large ethnic Turkish population in the Mosul-Kirkuk area of Iraq, and there are persistent rumors—despite official denials—that Ankara would move into this area if Iran were to occupy southern Iraq. In the global context, the Turks are mindful of the Soviet and U.S. roles in the region. Ankara has consistently refused to allow the United States to use its bases in Turkey to support its military maneuvers in the Gulf.[64] The Turks did not want the superpowers to become embroiled in the war and were not happy that Kuwait invited the United States into the Gulf. They have very pragmatically decided that all these complicated factors are best balanced by a carefully reasoned neutrality.

Turkish-Syrian and Turkish-Bulgarian Relations: Long-Simmering Disputes

Turkey has had a troubled relationship with its neighbor to the south, Syria. The Syrians and the Turks share an 835-mile-long border, which is the subject of a long-standing dispute. In the early 1920s the Turks began to lobby the French, who then held the mandate over Syria, for a greater Turkish role in the administration of the province of Hatay, a short strip of land adjacent to Turkey on the eastern coast of the Mediterranean with a mixed Turkish-Arab population. In 1939, the French, who were eager to win Turkey's goodwill on the eve of World War II, agreed to cede Hatay to the Turkish republic.[65]

As superpower rivalry over the Middle East intensified and inter-Arab relations grew more contentious, tensions between Turkey and

Syria flared up again. Turkey openly allied itself with the United States after World War II, but the Arab states, eager to assert their independence from the Western colonial powers and to confront the Israeli challenge, were reluctant to form close strategic ties with the United States. They showed little interest in joining the U.S.- and British-sponsored Baghdad Pact, and by the mid-1950s, several Arab states were leaning toward the Soviet Union rather than the United States. Acting as an ally of the United States, Ankara hinted that the Turks would not stand idly by if the Syrian government became a communist or Soviet-oriented regime. Turkey also warned the Syrians that the Turks would respond to any Syrian attempt to support the radical Jordanian opposition to King Hussein. In October 1955 and April and August 1957, Turkey staged conspicuous troop maneuvers along its border with Syria to underscore the seriousness of its intentions.[66]

Since then relations with Syria have improved, in part because of the easing of the Cold War and in part because of Ankara's desire to improve its position within the Middle East. The two major issues that currently stand between Turkey and Syria are Syrian support for Kurdish guerrillas and Turkish construction of a major dam on the Euphrates River, which could endanger Syria's water supply. In July 1987, Prime Minister Ozal visited Syria for three days, during which he met with President Hafiz Assad and Prime Minister Dr. 'Abd al-Ra'uf al-Kasm. The talks produced a set of protocols, including a joint statement by the two countries that each would prevent hostile activities directed at the other from occurring on its territory and that there would be mutual extradition rights for the two countries.[67]

At a press conference during the visit, Ozal said that until the Ataturk dam began to store water, which was expected to occur in 1989, Turkey pledged to supply Syria with water at a minimum rate of five hundred cubic meters per second. After the dam begins to store water, Syria, Turkey, and Iraq would come to an agreement about the allocation of water. He also stated that Syria had agreed to provide technical assistance for a study of the economic feasibility of the Peace Pipeline project, a plan to tap vast quantities of unused water from the Seyhan and Ceyhan rivers and to convey it to Turkey's Arab neighbors. Originally, Israel was supposed to participate in the ambitious, $21 billion water project, but in response to Arab pressure, Ankara said that Israel would not participate without Arab approval.[68]

Shortly before Ozal's visit, Syria's ambassador to Ankara, 'Abd al-Aziz al-Rifa'i said that "as a Syrian national, I should clearly state that Syria neither shelters nor allows activities of separatist terrorists," adding that his government took all measures to prevent infiltration into Turkey.[69] Nevertheless, captured Kurdish militants have repeatedly claimed that they have been allowed to train in Syrian-controlled areas of Lebanon and that they have also benefited from Syrian intelligence. Reports about Kurdish guerrilla training camps persisted after the protocols were signed. For example, Yasar Parlak, a *Gunaydin* correspondent, who interviewed separatist Kudish Workers party leaders in northern Iraq, quoted them as saying that the Armenian Secret Army for the Liberation of Armenia (ASALA) provided funds and that "Syria also gives us moral and material support."[70] In November 1987, *Milliyet* published an article citing information from the Turkish National Intelligence Organization that Syria had intensified its espionage in Anatolia and that Syrian agents had taken part in Kurdish attacks in southeastern Turkey over the past four years.[71] It is unclear whether the extent of Syrian involvement has decreased as a result of the agreements. Some observers suggest that Turkish control of the major source of Syrian water will give the Turks leverage to compel the Syrians to crack down on Kurdish guerrillas and other anti-Turkish militants.

Relations between Turkey and Bulgaria have long been tense because of Bulgaria's mistreatment of its ethnic Turkish minority, including recent attempts by Sofia to force them to adopt non-Turkish names. In October 1987 the two governments resumed talks about their common border that had been broken off for two years.[72] In February 1988, at the urging of the Yugoslav government, the foreign ministers of the Balkan countries met for the first time since World War II. Ministers from Bulgaria, Turkey, Greece, Romania, Albania, and Yugoslavia discussed issues relating to economic cooperation, treatment of ethnic minorities, and the lowering of regional tensions.[73] Turkey and Bulgaria also agreed to initiate periodic ministerial visits, starting with a visit to Sofia by Turkish Foreign Minister Mesut Yilmaz in July 1988. Dissatisfaction over Bulgaria's failure in bilateral talks to take "the steps expected from her in humanitarian issues," Yilmaz said at a press conference in Ankara in August, prompted him to postpone his visit.[74] In general, Ankara hopes that improved relations with its neighbors will also facilitate Turkey's entrance to the EEC because the Europeans will not be able to use the excuse that they do not want to accept a member that could be embroiled in a European war in the near future.[75]

Turkey and the Arab-Israeli Conflict

Ankara has refused to be drawn militarily into the Arab-Israeli conflict. Turkey has established a working relationship with Israel, at the same time satisfying its Arab neighbors by taking an acceptable public position on the Israeli-Palestinian conflict.

Turkey was the first Muslim state to recognize Israel (and, as the Turks pointed out when the Arabs challenged them on this, the last European state to do so). Ankara feels some affinity with Israel because both are basically democratic, secular, pro-Western states, and Ankara admires Israel's military strength. Ankara also believes that good relations with Israel are helpful in building support for Turkey in the United States. Not only can it argue that the United States should look favorably on Turkey because, with the recent exception of Egypt, it is the only Middle Eastern state that has relations with Israel, but Ankara also can use its relations with Israel as a lever both with Israel and with the "Jewish lobby" (both of which Turkey perceives as being very influential in the United States) to enlist their help in obtaining support for Turkey.

The Turks, however, are a Muslim people on the edge of the Arab Middle East. Turkey's trade with the Muslim world continues to be lucrative; exports to Islamic countries rose 11.5 percent in 1987 to a total value of $2.3 billion for the first eleven months of the year. Imports were valued at $2.8 billion. By comparison, exports to Israel for 1987 were worth a mere $22 million and purchases from Israel totaled $40 million. Although the volume of trade with Israel was running about 50 percent higher in the first half of 1988, it was still only a small fraction of Turkey's trade with the Arab world. Turkey depends on Iran and Iraq for almost two-thirds of its oil imports. In 1980, Iraq and Saudi Arabia put pressure on Turkey to fall into line with the Arab position on Israel after the Knesset had passed the Jerusalem law. As a result, the Turkish Foreign Ministry announced that "Turkey has decided to limit its relations with Israel and to mutually reduce the level of representation. This decision was made after it became evident that Israel will not retreat from its intransigent policy concerning the Middle East conflict. . . . In accordance with this decision, all diplomatic personnel, with the exception of a second secretary who will have the title of temporary chargé d'affaires, will be called back within three months."[76] The Israelis complained that this hampered the conduct of relations. The United States had also made repeated diplomatic interventions with Ankara on behalf of Israel and sixty-eight senators sent a joint letter protesting the downgrading of relations.[77] Finally, in the fall of 1986, Turkey assigned Ekrem Guvendiren, an experienced diplomat with the personal rank of ambassador, to Tel Aviv as chargé d'affaires. In 1987 the size of the staffs of the legations in Tel Aviv and Ankara was significantly increased. But the formal level of relations has not returned to that of minister, which it was until the Sinai-Suez crisis of 1956. Ankara, under pressure from Iraq, had at the time pledged not to restore relations until the Palestine question was solved "in a just and lasting manner in accordance with the resolutions of the United Nations."[78]

In the U.N. vote on Israel's credentials, the Turks in 1987 and 1988 took their usual path and abstained. But they did not sign the letter from the Arab and Eastern bloc countries to the secretary general denouncing Israel. Turkish diplomats explained this decision by pointing out that the Arab countries wrote a separate letter and that therefore the letter was less important politically.[79]

The meeting between the foreign ministers of Turkey and Israel in New York in the fall of 1987 was the highest level official diplomatic contact the two countries have had in many years. The Turkish government tailored its comments on the meeting between Foreign Minister Halefoglu and Israeli Foreign Minister Shimon Peres to suit different audiences. The official Turkish radio broadcast a very brief account of the meeting. Although it noted that this was the first such meeting in twenty years, the radio quoted Foreign Ministry spokesman Inal Batu as telling journalists that "there is no change in Turkey's Middle East policy" and that there had been diplomatic relations between Turkey and Israel "since the establishment of Israel." In a special interview with the Jewish Telegraphic Agency, however, Ambassador Batu said: "The meeting between Peres and Halefoglu constitutes by itself an improvement in relations between the two countries. In addition, we demonstrated to the whole Moslem world that Israel is no longer taboo."[80] Some observers noted that the increase in warmth in relations came at a time when some African and Middle Eastern states—notably Egypt, Morocco, and Jordan—had been increasing their own contacts with Israel so that Turkey would not have to stand alone. In addition, oil prices were down, and Iraq and other Arab Gulf states were preoccupied with Iran, making Turkey less susceptible to Arab pressure.[81] Turkey's maintenance of ties with Israel was also given further justification when the Arab League summit conference in Amman in November 1987 in effect ended the ostracism of Egypt for its peace treaty with Israel and permitted Arab states to restore normal relations with Cairo.

Ankara's views on the Arab-Israel conflict are more or less in line with those of the mainstream Arab states and other Europeans, as, for example, in the Venice Declaration of June 1980. Turkey stands by the PLO as the "sole, legitimate representative of the Palestinian people," supports the concept of an international peace conference and "all initiatives which might help achieve a just and lasting peace," and calls on Israel to withdraw from all territories occupied in 1967, "including Jerusalem." The PLO has had an official representative in Turkey since 1979. He has full diplomatic immunity, and his status as "resident representative" is equivalent to that of a chargé.[82]

While acknowledging the PLO's preeminent role in the Palestinian movement, Turkey has also traditionally maintained good relations with the Hashemite Kingdom of Jordan, whose policy, until July 1988, had been to subsume the Palestinians in the West Bank within a joint Jordanian-Palestinian negotiating team and to create a Jordanian-Palestinian federation following Israeli withdrawal. Turkish relations with the PLO have also been strained by hostile actions undertaken within Turkey by various armed Palestinian factions, including attacks on the Egyptian embassy in Ankara, Israeli diplomats, and El Al offices and suspected involvement in the terrorist massacre of Jews in an Istanbul synagogue in September 1986. Moreover, when the Israeli Defense Forces overran PLO bases in southern Lebanon and Beirut in 1982 they reportedly captured twenty-six Turkish terrorists among the Palestinians and also provided Ankara with documentary evidence that not only Turkish extremists but also members of ASALA, the Armenian group assassinating Turkish diplomats around the world, had been receiving training and military equipment in PLO bases. The Turkish and Israeli secret services continue to exchange information in the joint battle against terrorism.[83]

On November 15, 1988, when the Palestine National Council in Algiers proclaimed the independence of a Palestinian state in the occupied territories, with its capital in Jerusalem, Turkey was one of the first thirteen states immediately to recognize the new PLO-led entity. The others were either Arab states or states with significant Muslim populations. The United States reiterated the position enunciated by Secretary of State George Shultz, on September 16, opposing "unilateral determination of the outcome of negotiations." Therefore, the United States opposed either Israeli annexation of the territories or a unilateral declaration of independence by the Palestinians. Britain's Foreign Office called the Palestinian declaration "premature." Norway termed the PNC political statement calling for an international conference a step forward in the peace process but added that under international law, a "state" that did not have a government in effective control of a territory could not be recognized.[84]

In Jerusalem, the Israeli government summoned the Turkish chargé d'affaires to the Foreign Ministry, where he was told of Israel's "disappointment, regret and dissatisfaction in the clearest words possible." At the same time, Ministry spokesman Dani Shak expressed the government's hope "that this will not mean that relations between Israel and Turkey will be hurt." Ekrem Guvendiren, the Turkish chargé, said he had reminded Israeli officials that Turkey was "the first country in Asia to recognize the independent state of Israel." After his meeting at the Foreign Ministry, Guvendiren said that "Turkey recognized the PLO as the legitimate representative of the Palestinian people and respects the decisions taken at the Palestine National Council meeting in Algiers." He added that Ankara "considers those decisions as realistic and constructive."[85]

Following the fall 1987 Peres-Halefoglu meeting, Israeli and Turkish sources confirmed that the Turkish foreign minister had accepted an invitation to visit Israel. The two had also discussed the possibility of increased commercial ties and joint industrial ventures, including Israeli cooperation in the upgrading of Turkish defense equipment. But the planned visit and most other public displays of friendship were put in the deep freeze by Ankara in reaction to the Palestinian uprising that broke out in the occupied territories in December and media reports of the harsh measures adopted by Israel in its attempts to quell the violent demonstrations.[86]

At a meeting of ambassadors from Arab states in Ankara on December 26, 1987, Ozal commented that the Turkish government had "been closely following the recent incidents in the Occupied Palestinian Territories and in Gaza. . . . I declared our strong condemnation of these incidents. . . . It is wrong to fail to condemn, or to support or remain silent in the face of these actions."[87]

As in other countries of Western Europe, the Israeli policies were widely condemned in Turkey across the political spectrum. For example, Social Democratic–Populist party leader Erdal Inonu on March 16 issued a declaration of his party asking the Turkish government to review all relations with Israel and to consider the application of sanctions against "this country committing a crime against humanity." On March 18 the Turkish Grand National Assembly unanimously adopted a communique, which had been prepared by the parliamentary deputy group chairmen of all three major parties, stating: "We denounce the violent actions of the Israelis against the Palestinians living in the occupied territories and the inhuman violation of Palestinians' human rights." Stressing their determination to follow events closely, the parliamentarians concluded with an expression of hope that the Turkish government would continue its efforts to convince Israel to stop its current actions in the occupied territories.[88] The conservative Islamic-oriented Welfare party of Necmettin Erbakan organized major anti-Israeli demonstrations. One in Istanbul on March 20 drew an estimated ten to twenty-five thousand participants, including Iranian, Saudi, and PLO officials. Israeli flags were burned and anti-Jewish as well as anti-Israeli slogans were chanted by the conservative Islamic crowd. The use of the Palestinian cause by Islamic elements drew criticism from secular elements in Turkey. Thus Ilnur Cevik wrote a column in the *Turkish Daily News* on March 22 stating that brutal Israeli actions should be denounced in the strongest terms, "yet we feel uneasy about the way anti-Israeli demonstrations are taking shape in Turkey." The Palestinian movement was being used for ulterior motives, he wrote, "by people who have nothing to do with the Palestinian movement or who have never lifted a finger for Palestinian rights." He noted that there were extremist groups prominent among the people who organized and attended the anti-Israeli protests in Istanbul and Diyarbekir. "These are the very people who would love to demonstrate for the creation of Islamic rule in Turkey but would not dare do this today. So they choose the second best method and exploit the current anti-Israel sentiment in Turkey to demonstrate for the Palestinians while rehearsing for something quite different." Cevik urged the Turkish people not to be misled about the motives of these people and called on the authorities also to realize these facts.

The Turkish authorities kept a watchful eye and acted against those exceeding the bounds of the law. For example, forty-eight persons charged with staging an illegal march denouncing Israel in Cagaloglu, Istanbul, in February were brought to trial in the Istanbul State Security Court in mid-March. The prosecutor demanded prison terms ranging from six months to one year.[89] In April the Iranian ambassador to Turkey, Manucher Mottaki, participated in other anti-Israeli demonstrations at which anti-Semitic and pro-Islamic sentiments were voiced in the traditional Islamic stronghold of Konya. This prompted the new Turkish foreign minister, Mesut Yilmaz, to declare that the Iranian's actions were contrary to diplomatic practice and protocol.[90]

Despite the Intifada, however, normal diplomatic contacts have been maintained with Israel. During his visit to the U.N. General Assembly in September 1988, Foreign Minister Mesur Yilmaz met with Israeli Foreign Minister Peres. But as a sign of Turkey's even-handed policies, he met with Farouk Kaddumi, the head of the PLO's political department, on the same day.

Thus, though there continued to be disturbing signs of pro-Islamic ferment among certain elements of the population, the Turkish authorities appeared to be well aware of the dangers and prepared to intervene when matters got out of hand. The relatively small percentage of the national vote which the Welfare party has thus far obtained indicates that for the present at least, Islamic fundamentalism remains restricted to the right-wing fringe of the Turkish polity.

If the United States and its other NATO allies respond with generos-

ity and openness to Turkey's efforts to become a full member of the
European Community, the reactionary Islamic elements will be further
marginalized. But if Europe rejects the Turkish overtures and the
United States fails to provide the necessary help for Turkey to modernize, the voices calling for Turkey to reject the "alien" West and return
to its Middle Eastern Islamic heritage will fall on increasingly receptive
ears.

Notes

1. Alan Cowell, *New York Times*, May 27, 1987.
2. Dankwart A. Rustow, *Turkey: America's Forgotten Ally* (New York: Council on Foreign Relations, 1987).
3. Organization for Economic Cooperation and Development, *OECD Economic Survey: Turkey, 1983* (Paris: OECD, 1983), p. 5; George E. Gruen, "Turkey after the Military Coup: Impact on the Jewish Community and on Turkish-Israeli Relations," background paper for the American Jewish Committee, New York City, Mar. 26, 1981, p. 3.
4. Alan Cowell, *New York Times*, Sept. 8, 1987.
5. Ankara Domestic Service, Dec. 9, 1987, (*FBIS:WE*, Dec. 9, 1987, p. 25).
6. Gruen, "Turkey after the Military Coup," pp. 3–4; Rustow, *Turkey*, pp. 77–79. The Welfare party is sometimes called the Prosperity party.
7. Ellenoff letter of Apr. 5, 1988, and Elekdag reply of Apr. 15, in American Jewish Committee Files, New York City.
8. PIAR poll published in *Sabah*, Mar. 25, 1988.
9. Rustow, *Turkey*, pp. 57–83.
10. *Anatolia*, English-language ed. (Turkey), Nov. 18, 1987 (*FBIS:WE*, Nov. 19, 1987, pp. 12–13).
11. AP report from Ankara, *New York Times*, June 19, 1988; Sam Cohen, *Christian Science Monitor*, June 20, 1988; *Washington Post*, June 28, 1988.
12. See, for example, the editorial in *Tercuman* (Istanbul), Nov. 14, 1987 (*FBIS:WE*, Nov. 18, 1987, p. 21).
13. Editorial, *Wall Street Journal*, June 23, 1988.
14. Helsinki Watch, *State of Flux: Human Rights in Turkey, December 1987 Update* (New York: Helsinki Watch, 1987). The report is a comprehensive review of the status of human rights in Turkey, published by a reliable human rights organization. See also the open letter to President Evren by Amnesty International on the occasion of his state visit to the United States, *Washington Post*, June 13, 1988.
15. Rustow, *Turkey*, p. 37.
16. Helsinki Watch, *State of Flux*, pp. 91–96.
17. Alan Cowell, *New York Times*, May 13, 1988, and Clyde Haberman, ibid., Sept. 22, 1988.
18. Jonathan C. Randal, *Washington Post*, Sept. 10, 1988.
19. *Ankara Domestic Service*, interview with Ozal, Sept. 1, 1988 (*FBIS:WE*, Sept. 1, 1988, p. 11). For a supportive statement by opposition party leader Erdal Inonu see *Wall Street Journal*, Sept. 19, 1988.
20. Interview in Ankara with Kathryn Christensen, *Wall Street Journal*, Sept.

15, 1988; Ankara Domestic Service, in Turkish, Sept. 16, 1988 (*FBIS:WE*, Sept. 16, 1988, p. 26).

21. *Tercuman*, Sept. 6, 1988 (*FBIS:WE*, Sept. 9, 1988, p. 29).

22. Alan Cowell, *New York Times*, Sept. 15, 1988.

23. The economic information in this section is drawn largely from the following sources: "Foreign Economic Trends and Their Implications for the United States: Turkey," prepared by the American Embassy in Ankara (Washington, D.C., U.S. Department of Commerce, 1987); *OECD Economic Survey, Turkey 1983; OECD Economic Survey: Turkey 1985/1986* (Paris: OECD, 1986).

24. Alan Cowell, *New York Times*, May 13, 1988; Kathryn Christensen, *Wall Street Journal*, May 25, Sept. 20, 1988.

25. See George E. Gruen, "Turkey's Relations with Israel and Its Arab Neighbors: The Impact of Basic Interests and Changing Circumstances," *Middle East Review* 17 (Spring 1985): 42; and *Milliyet*, Jan. 18, 1988.

26. The trade deficit figure for 1987 was provided by the Turkish embassy in Washington, D.C., in March 1988. See also the special section on Turkey, *Wall Street Journal*, Apr. 22, 1988, pp. 7–14.

27. James A. Phillips, "Turkey: An Increasingly Key Strategic Asset for the U.S." (Washington, D.C.: Heritage Foundation, Backgrounder, 1987), p. 3. For detailed discussions of Turkey's foreign policy in general and its Middle East relations in particular, see the articles in *Middle East, Turkey and the Atlantic Alliance*, ed. Ali L. Karaosmanoglu and Seyfi Tashan (Ankara: Foreign Policy Institute, 1987). See also Jed C. Snyder, *Defending the Fringe: NATO, the Mediterranean and the Persian Gulf*, SAIS Papers in International Affairs 11 (Washington, D.C.: Westview Press, Foreign Policy Institute, School of Advanced International Studies, Johns Hopkins University, 1987), pp. 45–62 and passim.

28. Rustow, *Turkey*, pp. 91–92.

29. George E. Gruen, "Ambivalence in the Alliance: U.S. Interests in the Middle East and the Evolution of Turkish Foreign Policy," *Orbis* 24 (Summer 1980):369–70.

30. *Hurriyet*, Nov. 14, 1987 (*FBIS:WE*, Nov. 18, 1987, p. 22).

31. *Hurriyet*, Aug. 9, 1987 (*FBIS:WE*, Aug. 12, 1987, p. Q1).

32. Ankara Domestic Service, in Turkish, Dec. 16, 1987 (*FBIS:WE*, Dec. 17, 1987, p. 20).

33. *Anatolia*, in Turkish, Dec. 15, 1987 (*FBIS:WE*, Dec. 16, 1987, p. 23).

34. Ankara Domestic Service, in Turkish, July 17, 1987 (*FBIS:WE*, July 20, 1987, p. Q2).

35. *Hurriyet*, Oct. 4, 1987 (*FBIS:WE*, Oct. 9, 1987, p. 12).

36. Richard N. Perle and Michael J. McNamara, "U.S. Security Assistance for Turkey and the Challenge of Aid for the Southern Flank," *NATO's Sixteen Nations*, Apr. 1987, pp. 95–96.

37. Interview with the *Wall Street Journal*, July 1, 1988.

38. Perle and McNamara, "U.S. Security Assistance," p. 97.

39. *Anatolia*, in English, Oct. 20, 1987 (*FBIS:WE*, Oct. 21, 1987, p. 25).

40. See NATO Secretary General Lord Carrington's remarks in an interview with a Turkish correspondent, *Hurriyet*, Dec. 18, 1987 (*FBIS:WE*, Dec. 23, 1987, pp. 11–13).

41. Sedat Ergin, *Hurriyet*, Oct. 10, 1987.

42. The Turks have concluded that one way to reach Congress is to use Turkey's relations with Israel as a source of influence with the "powerful" (as

the Turks see it) Jewish lobby in the United States; occasionally this intention is put in terms of a veiled threat concerning the damage that could be done to Turkish-Irraeli relations if Turkey does not get the right response from the United States. See *Milliyet*, Dec. 29, 1987 *(FBIS:WE*, Jan. 4, 1988, p. 13).

43. *Milliyet*, July 27, 1987 *(FBIS:WE*, July 29, 1987, p. Q1); *Milliyet*, July 30, 1987 *(FBIS:WE*, Aug. 6, 1987, p. Q1); *Hurriyet*, Aug. 9, 1987 *(FBIS:WE*, Aug. 12, 1987, p. Q1).

44. *Anatolia*, in English, Oct. 13, 1987 *(FBIS:WE*, Oct. 14, 1987, p. 10).

45. Loren Jenkins, *Washington Post*, Dec. 8, 1987; *Hurriyet*, Sept. 29, 1987 *(FBIS:WE*, Oct. 6, 1987, p. 11).

46. Phillips, "Turkey," p. 5.

47.Ibid., pp. 4–5; *Milliyet*, July 27, 1987 *(FBIS:WE*, July 29, 1987, p. Q1); *Milliyet*, Aug. 23, 1987 *(FBIS:WE*, Aug. 25, 1987, pp. Q2–Q3); *Hurriyet*, Sept. 23, 1987 *(FBIS:WE*, Sept. 29, 1987, p. 20).

48. *Congressional Record*, 100th Cong., 2d sess., vol. 134, no. 21, Feb. 29, 1988.

49. Ibid.

50. Ankara Domestic Service, in Turkish, Dec. 16, 1987 *(FBIS:WE*, Dec. 12, 1987, pp. 23–24).

51. Ankara Domestic Service, in Turkish, Oct. 27, 1987 *(FBIS:WE*, Oct. 28, 1987, p. 14); *Anatolia*, in English, Oct. 29, 1987 *(FBIS:WE*, Oct. 30, 1987, p. 19).

52. *Cumhuriyet*, Nov. 5, 1987 *(FBIS:WE*, Nov. 12, 1987, pp. 24–25); *Anatolia*, in English, Dec. 9, 1987 *(FBIS:WE*, Dec. 9, 1987, p. 24).

53. *Hurriyet*, Dec. 18, 1987 *(FBIS:WE*, Dec. 23, 1987, p. 11).

54. Steven Greenhouse, *New York Times*, Feb. 1, 1988; Sam Cohen, *Christian Science Monitor*, Jan. 1, 1988.

55. Associated Press report in the *New York Times*, Feb. 22, 1988; Alan Cowell, *New York Times*, Mar. 30, 1988.

56. The hypothesis explaining why Papandreou has become more receptive to talks with the Turks was put forward by officials at the Turkish embassy in Washington, D.C., in private conversations with the author.

57. Loren Jenkins, *Washington Post*, Aug. 3, 1987; Ankara Domestic Service, in Turkish, July 10, 1987 *(FBIS:WE*, July 13, 1987, p. Q4).

58. *Anatolia*, in English, Oct. 8, 1987 *(FBIS:WE*, Oct. 9, 1987, p. 13); *Milliyet*, Oct. 23, 1987 *(FBIS:WE*, Oct. 27, 1987, p. 12).

59. Ankara Domestic Service, in Turkish, Oct. 12, 1987 *(FBIS:WE*, Oct. 13, 1987, p. 28).

60. *Hurriyet*, Sept. 27, 1987 *(FBIS:WE*, Oct. 1, 1987, pp. 21–22).

61. Ankara Domestic Service, in Turkish, Aug. 16, 1988 *(FBIS:WE*, Aug. 17, 1988, p. 10).

62. The Turkish section of the Voice of the Islamic Republic of Iran is headed by Selahattin Es, a Turkish journalist who had supported the National Salvation party, criticized Ataturk's secularist policy, and called for the restoration of the *Shari'a* in Turkey. He fled to Iran when he was sought by the Turkish police for violating Article 163 of the penal code. Es reportedly joined the Shi'ite sect after Iranian Revolutionary Guard units had helped his family escape (Kadir Sabuncuoglu report in *Hurriyet*, Sept. 23, 1987 *(FBIS:WE*, Sept. 29, 1987, p. 22).

63. Loren Jenkins, *Washington Post*, Aug. 3, 1987.

64. Alan Cowell, *New York Times*, July 10, 1987.

65. A. L. Tibawi, *A Modern History of Syria* (London: Macmillan, 1969), pp. 352–54.

66. Patrick Seale, *The Struggle for Syria* (New York: Oxford Univ. Press, 1965), pp. 299–301. The underlying issues in Turkish-Syrian relations and a historical survey of Turkey's generally unsuccessful efforts to improve relations with its southern neighbor are provided by David Kushner in "Yahasei Turkiya-Suriya—Mabat MeAnkara" (Turkish-Syrian relations: View from Ankara) *Medina, Memshal veYahasim Beinleumi'im*, no. 26 (Jerusalem: Leonard Davis Institute, Hebrew University of Jerusalem, 1987), pp. 93–113. For a recent analysis of Turkish-Syrian-Soviet relations, see Adam Garfinkle, "Turkey Confronts the Syrian-Soviet Threat," *World and I* 2 (Aug. 1987):95–101.

67. *Anatolia*, in English, July 17, 1987 (*FBIS:WE*, July 17, 1987, p. 2). For extensive coverage of this meeting see *FBIS:NE/SA*, July 16, 17, 20, 1987.

68. Damascus television, in Arabic, July 17, 1987 (*FBIS:NE/SA*, July 20, 1987); and three-part series in *Tercuman*, Feb. 25–27, 1988. The pipeline is planned to extend as far as Oman, with the western branch passing through Syria, Jordan, and Saudi Arabia, while the Gulf branch will cover Saudi Arabia, Kuwait, Qatar, Bahrein, and the United Arab Emirates. For details see Cem Duna, "Turkey's Peace Pipeline," in *The Politics of Scarcity: Water in the Middle East*, ed. Joyce R. Starr and Daniel C. Stoll (Boulder, Colo.: Westview Press, 1988). pp. 119–24.

69. *Anatolia*, in English, July 7, 1987 (*FBIS:WE*, July 8, 1987, p. Q1).

70. *Milliyet*, Aug. 5, 1987, (*FBIS:WE*, Aug. 11, 1987, pp. Q1–Q2).

71. *Milliyet*, Nov. 15, 1987 (*FBIS:WE*, Nov. 18, 1987, p. 23).

72. *Anatolia*, in English, Oct. 20, 1987 (*FBIS:WE*, Oct. 21, 1987, p. 25).

73. *Turkey Today*, publication of the Turkish embassy, Washington, D.C., no. 100, Mar. 1988.

74. *Anatolia*, in English, Aug. 19, 1988 (*FBIS:WE*, Aug. 22, 1988, p. 13).

75. Kathryn Christensen, *Wall Street Journal*, May 25, 1988.

76. Gruen, "Turkey after the Military Coup," pp. 15–16.

77. James W. Spain, *American Diplomacy in Turkey* (New York: Praeger Special Studies, 1984), pp. 63–66.

78. See George Emanuel Gruen, "Turkey, Israel and the Palestine Question, 1948–1960: A Study in the Diplomacy of Ambivalence" (Ph.D. diss., Columbia Univ., 1970; (Ann Arbor: University Microfilms International, 1973), pp. 342–44.

79. Sebnem Atiyas, *Cumhuriyet*, Oct. 16, 1987.

80. Ankara Domestic Service, in Turkish, Sept. 30, 1987 (*FBIS:WE*, Oct. 1, 1987, p. 21). Yitzhak Rabi, dispatch from New York, Oct. 1, 1987, *JTA Daily News Bulletin*, Oct. 2, 1987.

81. Sam Cohen, *Christian Science Monitor*, Sept. 5, 1986.

82. Quotes from a Halefoglu speech to the U.N. General Assembly, Sept. 25, 1987. On the rank of the PLO representative, see Spain, *American Diplomacy in Turkey*, pp. 181–82.

83. *Christian Science Monitor*, July 8, 1982. For Turkish reaction see Gruen, "Turkey's Relations with Israel and Its Arab Neighbors," *Middle East Review* 17 (Spring 1985):33–35. Continuing antiterrorism cooperation reported by Yitzhak Rabi, Jewish Telegraphic Agency dispatch from New York, Oct. 1, 1987. The PLO implication in the attack on the Egyptian embassy in 1979 and the events leading to Turkey's decision to permit the opening of a PLO

office in Ankara are detailed in George E. Gruen, "Ambivalence in Ankara," *Jerusalem Post Magazine,* July 17, 1979.

84. Robert Pear, dispatch from Washington, D.C., and AP dispatch from Nicosia, *New York Times,* Nov. 16, 1988.

85. Dispatch from Jerusalem, *New York Times,* Nov. 17, 1988.

86. For example, a scheduled performance of "Fiddler on the Roof" by an Israeli troupe was suddenly canceled "for technical reasons."

87. *Anatolia,* in Turkish, Dec. 26, 1987 (*FBIS:WE,* Dec. 28, 1987, p. 13).

88. The Social Democratic–Populist party declaration and the statements by various deputies in the parliamentary debates received widespread coverage in the major papers, including *Cumhuriyet, Milliyet, Hurriyet, Tercuman,* and the *Turkish Daily News,* Mar. 15–19, 1988.

89. *Milliyet,* Mar. 19, 1988.

90. Sam Cohen, dispatch from Istanbul, *Jewish Chronicle* (London), Apr. 22, 1988.

Contributors
Bibliography
Index

Contributors

FREDERICK W. AXELGARD is a Fellow in Middle Eastern Studies at the Center for Strategic and International Studies. He received his undergraduate degree from Brigham Young University and his master's and Ph.D. degrees from Fletcher School of Diplomacy. Axelgard is the author of *A New Iraq: The Gulf War and Implications for U.S. Policy.*

PETER BECHTOLD is the Chairperson of the Near East–North African Area Studies program of the Foreign Service Institute of the Department of State and is also Professional Lecturer at George Washington University. His numerous publications include the book *Politics in the Sudan: Parliamentary and Military Rule in an Emerging African Nation.*

LOUIS J. CANTORI is Professor of Political Science at the University of Maryland, Baltimore County. He is the author of numerous books and articles on Egypt and the Middle East among which is *Local Politics and Development in the Middle East.* Cantori is also a consultant to the American Agency for International Development on its projects in Egypt.

HELENA COBBAN received her M.S. degree from Oxford University and worked for several years as a correspondent for the *Christian Science Monitor* in the Middle East. She is currently a guest scholar at the Brookings Institution and is the author of a book on the PLO, *The Palestinian Liberation Organization.*

MARIUS DEEB is a Senior Fellow at the Center for International Development and Conflict Management at the University of Maryland, College Park. He is the author of *The Lebanese Civil War* and with his wife, Mary Jane Deeb, is the coauthor of *Libya since the Revolution: Aspects of Social and Public Development.*

JOHN F. DEVLIN is a former Middle East analyst for the Central Intelligence Agency and is currently a consultant on Middle Eastern affairs. He is the author of *Syria: Modern State in an Ancient Land* and *The Ba'ath Party: A History from Its Origins to 1966.*

ROBERT O. FREEDMAN is Peggy Meyerhoff Pearlstone Professor of Political Science and Dean of the Graduate School of the Baltimore Hebrew University. He has written a number of books and articles on the Middle East, among them *Soviet Policy Toward the Middle East Since 1970* (now in its third edition) and is the editor of *The Middle East since Camp David, Israel in the Begin Era, World Politics and the Arab-Israeli Conflict,* and *The Middle East after the Israeli Invasion of Lebanon.*

ADAM M. GARFINKLE is Coordinator, Political Studies Program, and editor, *The Philadelphia Papers*, of the Foreign Policy Research Institute. Among his publications are "Negotiating by Proxy: Jordanian Foreign Policy and U.S. Options in the Middle East," *Orbis*, Winter 1981; "Jordan and Arab Polarization," *Current History*, January 1982; and "Jordanian Foreign Policy: Balancing the Perils," *Current History*, January 1984.

JERROLD D. GREEN is Director of the Center for Middle Eastern Studies at the University of Arizona, where he is also Professor of Political Science. He is the author of *Revolution in Iran*, as well as articles on various themes in Middle Eastern politics, among which are "Are Arab Politics Still Arab?" in *World Politics* and "Islam and Politics: Politics and Islam" in *Middle East Insight*.

GEORGE E. GRUEN is Director of Israel and Middle East Affairs of the American Jewish Committee. His articles relating to Turkey have included "Ambivalence in the Alliance: U.S. Interests in the Middle East and the Evolution of Turkish Foreign Policy," *Orbis*, Summer 1980; and "Turkey's Relations with Israel and Its Arab Neighbors," *Middle East Review*, Spring 1985.

ROBERT E. HUNTER is Director of European Studies and Senior Fellow in Middle Eastern Studies at the Center for Strategic and International Studies in Washington, D.C. During the Carter administration, Hunter served on the National Security Council staff, as Director of West European Affairs (1977–79) and then as Director of Middle East Affairs (1979–81). Among his many publications are *The Soviet Dilemma in the Middle East, Security in Europe* (third edition, 1988), *Presidential Control of Foreign Policy*, and *NATO: The Next Generation*.

SHIREEN T. HUNTER is Deputy Director of the Middle East project at the Center for Strategic and International Studies in Washington. From 1966 to 1978, she was a member of the Iranian Foreign Service. She is the author of *OPEC and the Third World: Politics of Aid* and editor of *The Politics of Islamic Revivalism*.

DAVID POLLOCK is Near East research analyst for the United States Information Agency and former visiting lecturer in government at Harvard University. Among his publications are *The Politics of Pressure: American Arms and Israeli Policy Since the Six-Day War* and *The Iranian Revolution: Implications for the Middle East*.

R. K. RAMAZANI is Harry Flood Byrd, Jr., Professor of Government and Foreign Affairs and former Chairman of the Woodrow Wilson Department of Government and Foreign Affairs at the University of Virginia. He is the author of numerous books on Iran and the Persian Gulf. Among his most recent publications are *The United States and Iran: The Patterns of Influence, Revolutionary Iran: Challenge and Response in the Middle East*, and *The Gulf Cooperation Council: Record and Analysis*.

BARRY RUBIN is a Fellow at the Johns Hopkins University School of Advanced International Studies. He is the author of a number of major books on the Middle East including *Paved with Good Intentions: The American Experience in Iran, Secrets of State*, and *Modern Dictators*.

Bibliography

Books

Abd-Allah, Umar F., *The Islamic Struggle in Syria*. Berkeley: Mizan Press, 1983.

Ajami, Fouad. *The Arab Predicament*. New York: Cambridge Univ. Press, 1981.

Arian, Asher. *Politics in Israel: The Second Generation*. Chatham, N.J.: Chatham House, 1985.

Axelgard, Frederick W. *A New Iraq? The Gulf War and Implications for U.S. Policy*. New York: Praeger for the Center for Strategic and International Studies, 1988.

―――. *U.S.–Arab Relations: The Iraq Dimension*. Washington, D.C.: National Council on U.S.-Arab Relations, 1985.

Bailey, Clinton. *Jordan's Palestinian Challenge, 1948 – 83*. Boulder, Colo.: Westview Press, 1984.

Bechtold, Peter. *Politics in the Sudan*. New York: Praeger, 1976.

Bill, James A. *The Eagle and the Lion: The Tragedy of American-Iranian Relations*. New Haven: Yale Univ. Press, 1988.

Carus, Seth. *NATO, Israel, and the Tactical Missile Challenge*. Washington, D.C.: Washington Institute for Near East Policy, Research Memorandum No. 4, May 1987.

Cobban, Helena. *The Palestinian Liberation Organization: People, Power and Politics*. New York: Cambridge Univ. Press, 1984.

Cordesman, Anthony. *The Gulf and the Search for Strategic Stability*. Boulder, Colo.: Westview Press, 1984.

Deeb, Marius. *Militant Islamic Movements in Lebanon: Orgins, Social Basis and Ideology*. Occasional Papers Series, Washington, D.C.: Center for Contemporary Arab Studies, Georgetown University, 1986.

Eizenstat, Stuart E. *Formalizing the Strategic Partnership: The Next Step in U.S.-Israeli Relations*. Washington, D.C.: Washington Institute for Near East Policy, Policy Paper 9, 1988.

Freedman, Robert O. *The Middle East after the Israeli Invasion of Lebanon*. Syracuse: Syracuse Univ. Press, 1986.

―――. *The Middle East since Camp David*. Boulder, Colo.: Westview Press, 1984.

―――. *Soviet Policy Toward the Middle East since 1970*. 3d ed. New York: Praeger, 1982.

Ghali, Boutros. *Achievements of Egyptian Diplomacy 1987*. Cairo: Ministry of Information, 1988.

Golan, Galia. *Yom Kippur and After: The Soviet Union and the Middle East Crisis*. London: Cambridge Univ. Press, 1977.

Greenville, J. A. S., and Bernard Wasserstein. *Major International Treaties since 1945: A History and Guide with Texts*. London: Methuen, 1987.

Harik, Iliya. *Politics and Change in a Traditional Society: Lebanon, 1711–1845*. Princeton: Princeton Univ. Press, 1968.

Hinnebusch, Raymond. *Egyptian Politics under Sadat*. Cambridge, Eng.: Cambridge Univ. Press, 1985.

Hunter, Robert E., and Geoffrey Kemp, rapporteurs. *Western Interests and U.S. Policy Options in the Middle East*. Washington, D.C.: Atlantic Council of the United States and the Middle East Institute, 1988.

Hussein, Saddam. *Economy and Management in Socialist Society*, translated by Naji al-Hadithi. Baghdad: Dar al-Ma'mun, 1988.

Huyser, Robert E. *Mission to Tehran*. New York: Harper & Row, 1986.

Inouye, Daniel K., and Lee H. Hamilton. *Report of the Congressional Committees Investigating the Iran-Contra Affair*, edited by Joel Brinkey and Steven Engelberg. New York: Times Books, 1988.

Joumblatt, Kamal. *I Speak for Lebanon*. London: Zed Press, 1982.

Karaosmanoglue, Ali L., and Seyfi Teashan, eds. *Middle East, Turkey and the Atlantic Alliance*. Ankara: Foreign Policy Institute, 1987.

Kepel, Giles. *The Prophet and the Pharaoh*. London: Saqi Books, 1985.

Klinghoffer, Arthur J. *Israel and the Soviet Union: Alienation or Reconciliation*. Boulder, Colo.: Westview Press, 1985.

Korany, Bahgat, Ali E. Hilal Kessouki, et al. *The Foreign Policies of Arab States*. Boulder, Colo.: Westview Press, 1984.

Ledeen, Michael, and William Lewis. *Debacle: The American Failure in Iran*. New York: Knopf, 1981.

Marr, Phebe. *The Modern History of Iraq*. Boulder, Colo.: Westview Press, 1985.

McNaugher, Thomas. *Arms and Oil: U.S. Military Strategy and the Persian Gulf*. Washington, D.C.: Brookings Institution, 1985.

Miller, Aaron David. *The Arab States and the Palestine Question: Between Ideology and Self-Interest*. Washington, D.C.: CSIS Books, 1986.

Mishal, Shaul. *The PLO under Arafat: Between Gun and Olive Branch*. New Haven: Yale Univ. Press, 1986.

———. *West Bank/East Bank*. New Haven: Yale Univ. Press, 1978.

National Security Archive. *The Chronology: The Documented Day-by-Day Account of the Secret Military Assistance to Iran and the Contras*. New York: Warner Books, 1987.

Parsons, Anthony. *The Pride and the Fall, Iran 1974–1979*. London: Jonathan Cape, 1984.

Plascov, Avi. *The Palestinian Refugees in Jordan, 1948–1957*. London: Frank Cass, 1981.

Posner, Steven. *Israel Undercover: Secret Warfare and Hidden Diplomacy in the Middle East*. Syracuse: Syracuse Univ. Press, 1987.

Quandt, William B., ed. *The Middle East Ten Years after Camp David*. Washington, D.C.: Brookings Institution, 1988.

Ramazani, Rouhollah K. *The Persian Gulf: Iran's Role*. Charlottesville: Univ. Press of Virginia, 1973.

———. *Revolutionary Iran: Challenges and Responses in the Middle East*. Baltimore: Johns Hopkins Univ. Press, 1986.

———. *The United States and Iran: Patterns of Influence*. New York: Praeger, 1982.

Rubin, Barry. *Paved with Good Intentions: The American Experience and Iran*. New York: Oxford Univ. Press, 1980.

———. *The PLO's Intractable Foreign Policy*. Washington, D.C.: Washington Institute for Near East Policy, 1986.

Rustow, Dankwart A. *Turkey: America's Forgotten Ally*. New York: Council on Foreign Relations, 1987.

Sachar, Howard. *A History of Israel: From the Rise of Zionism to Our Time*. New York: Knopf, 1982.

Satloff, Robert B. *Army and Politics in Mubarak's Egypt*. Washington, D.C.: Washington Institute for Near East Policy, 1988.

Schiff, Ze'ev and Ehud Ya'ari. *Israel's Lebanon War*. New York: Simon and Schuster, 1984.

Seale, Patrick. *The Struggle for Syria*. New York: Oxford Univ. Press, 1965.

Sick, Gary. *All Fall Down: America's Tragic Encounter with Iran*. New York: Random House, 1985.

Snyder, Jed. C. *Defending the Fringe: NATO, the Mediterranean and the Persian Gulf*. SAIS Papers in International Affairs, No. 11. Washington, D.C.: Westview Press, Foreign Policy Institute, School of Advanced International Studies, Johns Hopkins University, 1987.

Stempel, John. *Inside the Iranian Revolution*. Bloomington: Indiana Univ. Press, 1981.

Sullivan, William. *Mission to Iran*. New York: Norton, 1981.

Susser, Asher. *Double Jeopardy: PLO Strategy Toward Israel and Jordan*. Washington, D.C.: Washington Institute for Near East Policy, 1987.

Tower, John, Edmund Muskie, and Brent Scowcroft. *The Tower Commission Report*. New York: Times Books, 1987.

Van Dam, Nikolas. *The Struggle for Power in Syria: Sectarianism, Regionalism, and Tribalism in Politics, 1961–1980*. London: Croom Helm, 1981.

Waterbury, John. *The Egypt of Nasser and Sadat*. Princeton: Princeton Univ. Press, 1983.

Woodward, Bob. *Veil: The Secret Wars of the CIA, 1981–1987*. New York: Simon and Schuster, 1987.

Articles

Aly, Abdel Moneim Said. "Democratization in Egypt." *American Arab Affairs*, no. 22 (Fall 1987):11–27.

———. "Egypt: A Decade after Camp David." In William Quandt, ed., *The Middle East Ten Years after Camp David*. Washington, D.C.: Brookings Institution, 1988.

Axelgard, Fred. "Deception at Home and Abroad: Implications of the Iran Arms Scandal for U.S. Foreign Policy." *American Arab Affairs*, no. 20 (Spring 1987):5–12.

Bengio, Ofra. "Iraq." In *Middle East Contemporary Survey: Volume IX, 1984–85*, edited by Itamar Rabinovich and Haim Shaked. Boulder, Colo.: Westview Press for the Moshe Dayan Center for Middle Eastern and African Studies of Tel Aviv University, 1987.

Bochkaryov, V. "Exit Nimeri: What Happens Now?" *New Times* (Moscow), no. 17 (1985):10–11.

Breslauer, George. "Soviet Policy in the Middle East, 1967–1972: Unalterable Antagonism or Collaborative Competition?" In Alexander L. George, ed.,

Managing U.S.-Soviet Rivalry: Problems of Crisis Prevention. Boulder, Colo.: Westview Press, 1981.

Cantori, Louis J. "Egyptian Policy under Mubarak: The Politics of Continuity and Change." In Robert O. Freedman, ed., *The Middle East after the Israeli Invasion of Lebanon.* Syracuse: Syracuse Univ. Press, 1986.

————. "Religion and Politics in Egypt." In M. Curtis, ed., *Religion and Politics in the Middle East.* Boulder, Colo.: Westview Press, 1981.

Cigar, Norman. "South Yemen and the USSR: Prospects for the Relationship." *Middle East Journal* 39 (Autumn 1985):775–95.

Deeb, Marius. "Lebanon: Prospects for National Reconciliation in the Mid-1980s." *Middle East Journal* 38 (Spring 1984):267–83.

————. "Shia Movements in Lebanon: Their Formation, Ideology, Social Basis, and Their Links with Iran and Syria." *Third World Quarterly* 10 (Apr. 1988):694–96.

Devlin, John F. "Syria and Lebanon." *Current History* 87 (Feb. 1988):77–80, 90–96.

————. "Syrian Policy." In Robert O. Freedman, ed., *The Middle East after the Israeli Invasion of Lebanon.* Syracuse: Syracuse Univ. Press, 1986.

Duna, Cem. "Turkey's Peace Pipeline." In Joyce R. Starr and Daniel C. Stoll, eds., *The Politics of Scarcity: Water in the Middle East.* Boulder, Colo.: Westview Press, 1988.

Freedman, Robert O. "Religion, Politics, and the Israeli Elections of 1988." *Middle East Journal* 43 (Summer 1989):406–22.

————. "Soviet Jewry and Soviet-American Relations: A Historical Analysis." In Robert O. Freedman, ed., *Soviet Jewry in the Decisive Decade, 1971–1980.* Durham: Duke Univ. Press, 1984.

————. "Soviet Policy Toward the Persian Gulf from the Outbreak of the Iran-Iraq War to the Death of Konstantin Chernenko." In William J. Olson, ed., *U.S. Strategic Interests in the Gulf Region.* Boulder, Colo.: Westview Press, 1987.

————. "The Soviet Union, Syria and the Crisis in Lebanon." In David H. Partington, ed., *The Middle East Annual 1983.* Boston: G. K. Hall, 1984.

Garfinkle, Adam. "Sources of the al-Fatah Mutiny." *Orbis* 27 (Fall 1983):603–40.

Golan, Galia. "Gorbachev's Middle East Strategy." *Foreign Affairs* 66 (Fall 1987):41–57.

Green, Jerrold D. "Are Arab Politics Still Arab?" *World Politics* 37 (July 1986):611–25.

Gruen, George E. "Ambivalence in the Alliance: U.S. Interests in the Middle East and the Evolution of Turkish Foreign Policy." *Orbis* (Summer 1980):363–78.

————. "Turkey's Relations with Israel and Its Arab Neighbors: The Impact of Basic Interests and Changing Circumstances." *Middle East Review* 17 (Spring 1985):33–43.

Hoogland, Eric. "Factions Behind U.S. Policy in the Gulf." *Middle East Report* 18 (Mar.–Apr. 1988):29–31.

Hunter, Shireen T. "Beneath the Surface of Iran's Relations with the West." *World and I,* Nov. 1987, pp. 89–96.

————, and Robert E. "The Post-Camp David Arab World." In Robert O. Freedman, ed., *The Middle East since Camp David.* Syracuse: Syracuse Univ. Press, 1986.

Indyk, Martin. "Reagan and the Middle East: Learning the Art of the Possible." *SAIS Review* (Washington, D.C.) (Winter–Spring 1987):111–38.

Katz, Mark N. "Civil Conflict in South Yemen." *Middle East Review* 19 (Fall 1986):7–13.

Kramer, Martin. "Syria's Alawis and Shi'ism." In Martin Kramer, ed., *Shi'ism, Resistance, and Revolution*. Boulder, Colo.: Westview Press, 1987.

Kushner, David. "Yahasei Turkiya-Suriya—Mabat MeAnkara" (Turkish-Syrian relations: View from Ankara). *Medina, Memshal veYahasim Beinleumi'im*, no. 26 (1987):93–113.

Kutschera, Chris. "Inside Kurdistan." *Middle East*, Sept. 1986, pp. 10–12.

Miller, Aaron David. "Jordanian Policy: The Politics of Limitation and Constraint." In Robert O. Freedman, ed., *The Middle East after the Israeli Invasion of Lebanon*. Syracuse: Syracuse Univ. Press, 1986.

Mylroie, Laurie. "The Superpowers and the Iran-Iraq War." *American Arab Affairs*, no. 21 (Summer 1987):15–26.

Page, Stephen. "The USSR and the Gulf States." *American Arab Affairs*, no. 20, (Spring 1987):38–56.

Pererra, Judith. "Together Against the Red Peril: Iran and Saudi Arabia—Rivals for Superpower Role." *Middle East*, May 1978, pp. 16–27.

Peterson, J. E. "The GCC and Regional Security." *American Arab Affairs*, no. 20 (Spring 1987):62–69.

Pollock, David. "Israel since the Lebanon War." In Robert O. Freedman, ed., *The Middle East since the Israeli Invasion of Lebanon*. Syracuse: Syracuse Univ. Press, 1986.

———. "Moscow and Aden: Coping with a Coup." *Problems of Communism* 35 (May–June 1986):50–70.

Ramazani, R. K. "Iran: Burying the Hatchet." *Foreign Policy* no. 60 (Fall 1985):52–74.

———. "The Iran-Iraq War and the Persian Gulf Crisis." *Current History*, Feb. 1988, pp. 61–64, 86–88.

Roumani, Maurice M. "The Sephardi Factor in Israeli Politics." *Middle East Journal* (Washington, D.C.) 42 (Summer 1988):423–35.

Ross, Dennis. "The Soviet Union and the Persian Gulf." *Political Science Quarterly* 99 (Winter 1984–85):615 – 35.

Rubin, Barry. "Drowning in the Gulf." *Foreign Policy*, no. 69 (Winter 1987–88):120–34.

Sadowski, Yahya. "The Sphinx's New Riddle: Why Does Egypt Delay Economic Reform?" *American Arab Affairs*, no. 22 (Fall 1987):28–40.

Shadid, Mohammed, and Rick Seltzer. "Political Attitudes of Palestinians in the West Bank and Gaza Strip." *Middle East Journal* 42 (Winter 1988):16–32.

Spiegel, Steven L. "U.S. Relations with Israel: The Military Benefits." *Orbis* 30 (Fall 1986):475–98.

Volsky, Dmitry. "Behind the Prospective Israeli Pull-out from Southern Lebanon." *New Times*, no. 5 (1985):14–15.

Weinbaum, Marvin. "Politics and Development in Foreign Aid: U.S. Economic Assistance to Egypt, 1975–81." *Middle East Journal* 37 (1983):636–55.

Index

THE MIDDLE EAST FROM THE IRAN-CONTRA AFFAIR TO THE INTIFADA
was composed in 10 on 12 Baskerville on a Mergenthaler Linotron 202
by World Composition Services;
printed by sheet-fed offset on 50-pound, acid-free Glatfelter,
Smyth-sewn and bound over binder's boards in Holliston Roxite B,
and perfect bound with paper covers printed in 2 colors
by Thomson-Shore, Inc.;
designed by Kachergis Book Design
and published by
SYRACUSE UNIVERSITY PRESS
SYRACUSE, NEW YORK 13244-5160